American and French Culture, 1800–1900

American an

Interchang

French Culture, 1800-1900

in Art, Science, Literature, and Society

HENRY BLUMENTHAL

LOUISIANA STATE UNIVERSITY PRESS   *Baton Rouge*

ISBN 0–8071–0155–9
Library of Congress Catalog Card Number 74–27187
Copyright © 1975 by Louisiana State University Press
All rights reserved
Manufactured in the United States of America

This book was designed by Dwight Agner, and composed in Linotype and Intertype
Baskerville by Friedrich Typography, Santa Barbara, California. It was printed
and bound by Kingsport Press, Kingsport, Tennessee.

Acknowledgment is hereby made for permission to quote from the following works
and manuscript collections:
Jesse S. Myer, *Life and Letters of Dr. William Beaumont* (St. Louis: C. V. Mosby
Co., 1939); Albert Mordell (ed.), *Literary Reviews and Essays by Henry James on
American, English and French Literature* (New York: Twayne Publishers, Inc., 1957);
the Harvard College Library; and Yale University Archives, Yale University Library.

Culture is that complex whole which includes knowledge, belief, art, morals, law, custom, and any other
capabilities and habits acquired by man as a member
of society

Edward Tylor

Contents

Preface

As necessary as detailed studies of limited problems and periods are, it is also of vital importance to see long-term developments in historical perspective. I attempted to provide such a long view in my recent volume on the diplomatic relations between France and the United States from 1789 to 1914. The present study attempts the much more difficult task of studying French-American cultural relations in the nineteenth century. With the exception of Howard Mumford Jones's scholarly book, *America and French Culture,* 1750–1848, published about half a century ago, no major effort has been made to convey an overall picture of the social and cultural contacts and interactions of Americans and Frenchmen throughout the nineteenth century.

Since history is and must forever remain the study of evidence, I have over more than a decade amassed evidence in the hope that its analytical description and dispassionate synthesis would permit us to see French-American relations more completely than has heretofore been possible. In view of the chronological and substantive scope of this study I carried my research forward until it appeared that additional searches were not likely to substantially affect my already carefully collected data. Obviously, lines had to be drawn if this massive undertaking was ever to be published.

Using the term *culture* very broadly, I have focused sharply on the cultural interchanges between France and the United States and their citizens during the nineteenth century, fully realizing that multinational influences condition the complexity of cultural realities. Such sharp focus is an essential prerequisite to a better understanding of French-American relations; and arbitrary as its application to an entire century is, this is also a long enough period to provide a better perspective on the broader significance and evolution of cultural relations. In my judgment, the diplomatic, economic, and cultural relations between France and the United States have been so intertwined in the nineteenth century that one cannot really understand either of the three without relating them to the other two. Realistically, after the purchase of the Louisiana Territory and until 1914, the development of the United States and of France would not have been substantially different had these two countries had no diplomatic and economic relations. But, for better or for worse, their cultural relations were extensive and so mutually fruitful that both civilizations, were influenced.

Realizing that I have ventured into many areas in which a diplomatic historian needs professional guidance and criticism, I enlisted the assistance of several readers and gratefully acknowledge their helpful comments and suggestions: George Rosen, Professor of the History of Medicine and Epidemiology and Public Health (Yale); James Anderson, Professor of Zoology; David Cowen, Professor of History; Charles Pine, Professor of Physics; and George Weber, Professor of Art, all members of the Rutgers faculty. I am also indebted to the LSU Press readers for valuable suggestions and to Beverly Jarrett of the LSU Press for her superb editing of my manuscript.

In the pursuit of my research I have consulted the manuscript collections of many major universities and state historical societies throughout the United States. Though these institutions are too numerous to cite, I would nevertheless like to single out for special recognition the research libraries of Harvard, Yale, and Louisiana State University. In the United States, I am furthermore greatly indebted to the following libraries for having made their resources available to me: Academy of Natural Science of Philadelphia, American Philosophical Society, Archives of American Art, Bronx Botanical Garden, Huntington Library, Library of Congress, Lincoln Center Library for the Performing Arts, Metropolitan Museum of Art (New York), New York Academy of Medicine, New York Public Library, Smithsonian Institution, and the Walters Art Gallery in Baltimore. In France, I would like to express my special gratitude for privileges extended to me by: the Archives de France, Bibliothèque Nationale, Bibliothèque Victor Cousin, Bibliothèque pour le Protestantisme Français, Intitut de France, Musée d'Histoire Naturelle, and the Sorbonne. All I can sincerely say to the very sizable number of archivists and librarians who have been of assistance to me is that it is always a delight to acknowledge their professional competence and courteous cooperation.

My sincere thanks also go to two young ladies who cheerfully deciphered my longhand manuscript and handed me the competently typed copy: Mrs. Sallie Zeiss and Mrs. Elizabeth Nankivell. Finally, I wish to express my gratitude to the Rutgers Research Council for its financial support that facilitated the completion of this study.

Henry Blumenthal
South Orange, New Jersey

List of Abbreviations

AAA	Archives of American Art (New York)
AADS	American Academy of Dental Science
AFCU	American and Foreign Christian Union
AHR	*American Historical Review*
AJDS	*American Journal of Dental Science*
AJLDS	*American Journal and Library of Dental Science*
AJMS	*American Journal of Medical Science*
AJP	*American Journal of Pharmacy*
AMA	American Medical Association
AMAE	Archives, Ministère des Affaires Etrangères (Paris)
AMH	*Annals of Medical History*
ANF	Archives Nationales de France (Paris)
ANSP	Academy of Natural Sciences of Philadelphia
APS	American Philosophical Society (Philadelphia)
APSL	American Philosophical Society Library
AR	*Architectural Record*
BHM	*Bulletin of the History of Medicine*
BIHM	*Bulletin of the Institute of the History of Medicine*
BMJ	*Buffalo Medical Journal*
BMSJ	*Boston Medical and Surgical Journal*
BVC	Bibliothèque Victor Cousin (Paris)
CHR	*Catholic Historical Review*
CHSQ	*California Historical Society Quarterly*
CMJ	*Charleston Medical Journal*

CPEU	Correspondance Politique, Etats-Unis (AMAE)
DDFDS	Diplomatic dispatches from U.S. ministers in France to the Department of State
DJM	*Dwight's Journal of Music*
DS	Department of State
EMHL	Eleutherian Mills Historical Library (Greenville, Del.)
FIDS	Instructions from Department of State to U.S. ministers in France
FNTDS	Notes from the French Legation to the Department of State
GDBA	*Gazette des Beaux-Arts*
HCL	Harvard College Library
HNMM	*Harper's New Monthly Magazine*
JAAA	*Journal of Archives of American Art*
JDD	*Journal des Débats*
JHM	*Journal of History of Medicine*
JHMAS	*Journal of History of Medicine and Allied Sciences*
JMH	*Journal of Modern History*
LC	Library of Congress (Washington, D.C.)
LHQ	*Louisiana Historical Quarterly*
LSU	Louisiana State University (Baton Rouge)
MDJ	*Missouri Dental Journal*
MHS	Massachusetts Historical Society (Boston)
MoHS	Missouri Historical Society (St. Louis)
MVHR	*Mississippi Valley Historical Review*
NAR	*North American Review*
NEQ	*New England Quarterly*
NOMSJ	*New Orleans Medical and Surgical Journal*
NYAM	New York Academy of Medicine
NYDJ	*New York Dental Journal*
NYHS	New York Historical Society
NYJM	*New York Journal of Medicine*
NYMJ	*New York Medical Journal*
NYMMA	New York Metropolitan Museum of Art
NYPL	New York Public Library
NYT	New York *Times*
OSHS	Ohio State Historical Society (Columbus)
PHR	*Pacific Historical Review*
PHS	Pennsylvania Historical Society (Philadelphia)

PMHB	*Pennsylvania Magazine of History and Biography*
PMLA	*Publications of Modern Language Association*
PMSJ	*Philadelphia Medical and Surgical Journal*
PSQ	*Political Science Quarterly*
RDBA	*Revue des Beaux-Arts*
RDDM	*Revue des deux mondes*
RDLC	*Revue de littérature comparée*
RGMP	*Revue et gazette musicale de Paris*
SCHS	South Carolina Historical Society (Columbia)
SSSQ	*Southwestern Social Science Quarterly*
UC	University of California (Berkeley)
UNC	University of North Carolina (Southern Historical Collection, Chapel Hill)
USC	University of South Carolina
UV	University of Virginia (Charlottesville)
VHS	Virginia Historical Society (Richmond)
VMHB	*Virginia Magazine of History and Biography*

American and French Culture, 1800–1900

Introduction

The notion of particularly close ties between France and the United States was furthered by the sentiments of gratitude and camaraderie which remembrance of French assistance in the American Revolution seemed to evoke automatically. This affinity seemed deceptively genuine to nineteenth-century Frenchmen and Americans. Both evidently preferred to ignore the realities of their political relations, which did not justify perpetuation of the myth of a special, family-like relationship from Lafayette to the First World War. What, then, kept this image alive?

Searching for an answer to this question, we should recognize that French-American relations developed on three different levels—from government to government, from person to person, and, in a vague but equally meaningful way, from people to people. As we know, the Franco-American alliance of 1778 was sanctioned by a political expediency that saw French Catholics and monarchists join forces with American Protestants and republicans, both trying to accomplish their separate political ends at the expense of the British Empire. Taking advantage of the American struggle for independence, France fought to enhance its own power by helping to reduce that of Great Britain. And while French political philosophers envisioned the emergence of a rationally structured model society in the New World, a society in which their ideas could be applied in close cooperation with the Americans, the political leaders of France knew how to make naked political expediency more attractive by couching it in suave terms of friendly cooperation. As common experiences and enemies have often fostered the development of common political interests among allied countries, memories of them have a tendency to magnify their emotional impact beyond recognition. This was precisely what happened in the case of French-American relations, in which the notion of attachment between the two peoples continued to subsist long after divergent national interests had pulled their governments apart.

Sentimental references to this attachment conveniently softened the frequent tensions that marred, or jeopardized, "friendly" diplomatic relations. Although France and America never fought a full-fledged war against each other, the period up to the end of the nineteenth century was characterized by periodical controversies of substantial seriousness. Even a brief review of them establishes a sufficiently disturbing list of conflicts. Flagrant violations of American neutral rights during the era of the French Revolution produced undeclared naval war between France and the United States and led to the brink of actual war. So did the emotionally blown-up spoliation claims episode during President Jackson's administration, which ushered in a long period of critical exchanges between the evolving middle classes of the two countries. French apprehension of the long-range consequences of America's dynamic growth manifested itself at the enunciation of the Monroe Doctrine, accelerated during the period of American expansionism, and was heightened by intensified American propaganda spreading the liberating gospel of republicanism. When the establishment of the Second Empire frustrated these efforts and when Napoleon III pursued a policy during the American Civil War that exposed his unreliability, the United States felt let down by France. The emperor's clumsy attempt to exploit this calamity by pushing his imperial designs in Mexico created a much deeper rift than he had evidently anticipated. In subsequent years, economic warfare, particularly the prohibition of the import of pork into France in the century's final decades and the revival in 1898 of earlier suggestions for a European coalition against the "American danger," hardly reflected the spirit usually associated with close, though occasionally quarreling, partners.

Nevertheless, to interpret this record as objectively as possible, one must first realize that it contained more irritations and threats than harmful actions. In the perspective of history, moreover, these threats were made somewhat plausible by fear of the two clearly emerging superpowers, Russia and the United States, whose civilizations were related to but in many respects distinct from that of western Europe. Invariably, the risks of contemplated French actions against the United States were outweighed by the gains to be derived from trade and the friendly power-political potential of the sea power across the Atlantic. Under these circumstances, the lingering reservoir of goodwill—dating back to the glorious days when Generals Washington, Rochambeau, and Lafayette shaped the future course of world history—helped to prevent occasional animosities from developing into undesirable conflicts.

The image that French and American people formed about each other, based largely on inadequate information, is difficult to assess. Prejudiced descriptions and superficial observations by foreign visitors in either land hardly conveyed an accurate picture. And yet, this image affected not only their estimates of each other, but their relationship as well. Vague and distorted as the picture may have been, on balance it helped to perpetuate the notion that the courteous and culturally brilliant French and the easygoing and pragmatic Americans complemented each other.

Quite generally, the social life and cultural values of the two nations differed considerably. French emphasis on paternalism, security, and national glory and French appreciation of culture contrasted sharply with American advocacy of self-reliance, adventurous enterprise, and individual comfort. Frenchmen were inclined to philosophize, to change their government frequently, and to look back; Americans tended to be practical, to treasure political stability, and to look ahead. If appreciation of leisure, good manners, exquisite food, artistic creativity, and intellectual brilliance were characteristic of nineteenth-century French society, restlessness, simple food, relaxed manners, experimental curiosity, and a comfortable feeling with mediocrity distinguished contemporary American society. Americans generally criticized French immorality, superficiality, and snobbishness. Frenchmen, in turn, found Americans wanting in refinement and artistic and literary talent. They accused Americans, furthermore, of habitually failing to consider the social consequences of their actions and of disregarding their professed principles of liberty, equality, and law when they found it convenient.

Though they differed in these and many other respects, as the chapters on social contacts and religion will discuss in more specific detail, both nations also possessed many common features. Their similarities included an extraordinary industriousness and a capacity for facing challenges with a strong determination to overcome them. Both emphasized the dignity and equality of man and both believed in the capacity of humanity to advance to unprecedented heights. Both liked to enjoy life—in their particular ways—and both imagined themselves worthy examples for the rest of civilization. Somehow their similarities and dissimilarities contributed to the mutual feeling that each could benefit from the other.

Nothing substantiated this assumption more convincingly than direct personal contacts. The restrained amusement when socially informal Americans and etiquette-conscious Frenchmen first met really expressed a sudden awareness that a moderate blending of their two extremes of conduct might be socially desirable. As American Protestants took an active interest in their brethren in France, the Catholic Church in the United States became deeply indebted to French priests and teachers who devoted their professional and inspirational talents to its phenomenal growth. The close contacts that French and American scientists and medical doctors maintained throughout the century, particularly during the first half, produced invaluable professional cooperation, as well as mutual respect and, sometimes, personal friendships. And when the number of American artists who went to France, primarily though not exclusively to Paris, to study painting, sculpture, architecture, and music—when their number swelled by the end of the century to thousands, their talent, eagerness, and human qualities compelled French observers to revise their notion that Americans were too materialistic to appreciate, much less excel in, the performing and fine arts. Even selected illustrations of cooperation in each of these areas cannot fail to convey the impressive extent to which individual citizens contributed to the cultural cross-fertilization between France and the United States. This was a mutual, not a one-sided, process. No matter how much the policymakers in Paris and Washington became at times estranged, French and American citizens could not be strangers, knowing each other and working together as large numbers of them did throughout the nineteenth century. In fact, they derived a certain satisfaction from exaggerating their affinities.

As informative as the varied data presented in the following chapters may be alone, the total effect of Franco-American cultural contacts on the civilization of their societies involved more than the instructive contributions citizens of either country made to the other. Far-reaching in an overall respect were the cultural refinement and relaxed moral standards to which Frenchmen exposed Americans, who found these standards both stimulating and dangerously unwholesome. Similarly, Frenchmen looked upon American informality, pragmatism, and dynamism not only as a fascinating curiosity, but also as a disturbing threat to the survival of their own civilization. But French and American people found enough common cultural interests to overcome, if not overlook, mutual fears and criticisms. Bourgeois France and Puritan America sensed intuitively that their constructive cooperation would be infinitely more promising than a bitter confrontation.

CHAPTER I

Demographic and Social Aspects

Whatever the policies of their governments, Frenchmen and Americans studied, compared, and influenced each other throughout the nineteenth century. Many Frenchmen not already residing in former colonial possessions of France immigrated to the United States seeking either refuge or fortune. Visitors came to satisfy their curiosity about the life and institutions of the strangers three thousand miles away. France, "the country of Lafayette," seemed to Americans a paradise to which ever larger numbers were streaming in search of beauty, stimulation, and style, unless business or education attracted them. Since mid-century, quite a few members of the steadily growing American colony in Paris enjoyed the cosmopolitan atmosphere of the cultural capital of Europe, as well as the snob appeal that distinguished them from their Calvinistic countrymen back home. As much as the American and French life-styles differed, and as much as their historical backgrounds and outlooks seemed to set them apart, they developed a remarkable fascination for each other.

The expulsion of France from North America at the end of the Seven Years' War climaxed its long struggle for a colonial empire in the New World stretching from Canada through the Ohio and Mississippi valleys to the Gulf of Mexico. Such an ambitious design required more human, financial, and military resources than France, traditionally preoccupied with Europe, was willing to adventure so far from its own shores. The subsequent emigration of individual Frenchmen was usually stimulated by events in France and by the attractions America reputedly offered. During the era of the French Revolution and the mid-century revolutions, thousands of French refugees went to America to escape the dreaded consequences of their political actions. Even more Frenchmen were enticed to go to America by such economic opportunities as cheap land and high wages, the absence of peacetime conscription, and the vaunted freedom of its institutions.[1] Contrary to the original intention of the early revolutionary French exiles, many of them settled permanently in the United States, marrying into American families or becoming compatriots in order to escape the turbulent conditions in Europe. Although no large French colony ever developed in the United States, many individual Frenchmen made valuable contributions to the cultural diversity of their adopted country.[2]

French Immigrants in the United States

The number of native-born Frenchmen in the United States in 1850 was 54,069; it doubled and remained fairly constant thereafter, amounting to 104,197 in 1900. According to the United States Census Bureau figures of 1910, the majority lived in larger cities throughout the country.[3]

1. Carl Wittke, *We Who Built America* (New York, 1939), 316–17; Arnold Whitridge, *Men in Crisis: The Revolutions of* 1848 (New York, 1949), 297–98; and René Rémond, *Les Etats-Unis devant l'opinion française, 1815–1852* (2 vols.; Paris, 1962), I, 31–77.
2. Frances S. Childs, *French Refugee Life in the United States: An American Chapter of the French Revolution, 1790–1800* (Baltimore, 1940), 192–201; Edith Philips, "Les Réfugiés Bonapartistes en Amérique (1815–1830)" (Ph.D. dissertation, Université de Paris, 1923), 136–37.
3. U.S. Treasury Department, Bureau of Statistics, *Tables Showing Arrival of Alien Passengers and Immigrants in the United States from* 1820 to 1888 (Washington, D.C., 1889), 32–33; Bruno Wilson, *L'Evolution de la race française en Amérique* (Montreal, 1921), 11–12; Lawrence Guy Brown, *Immigration: Cultural Conflicts and Social Adjustments* (New York, 1933), 81; and M. L. Hansen, *Atlantic Migration, 1607–1860* (Cambridge, Mass., 1940), 280.

CHART I

French Population in the Principal Cities
of the United States (1910)

Cities	Canadian Origin	European Origin
Boston, Mass.	3,098	1,873
Cambridge, Mass.	1,145	152
Fall River, Mass.	15,281	160
Worcester, Mass.	4,988	143
Lowell, Mass.	12,269	274
Bridgeport, Conn.	499	179
New Haven, Conn.	454	269
Providence, R.I.	4,456	562
New York, N.Y.	2,844	20,519
Albany, N.Y.	286	127
Buffalo, N.Y.	566	729
Rochester, N.Y.	566	488
Philadelphia, Pa.	301	3,122
Pittsburgh, Pa.	86	990
Jersey City, N.J.	108	766
Newark, N.J.	194	888
Paterson, N.J.	155	1,541
Cincinnati, Ohio	73	789
Cleveland, Ohio	571	583
Toledo, Ohio	681	323
Chicago, Ill.	4,633	5,556
Detroit, Mich.	4,166	2,874
Milwaukee, Wisc.	218	458
Minneapolis, Minn.	1,637	390
St. Paul, Minn.	1,067	446
St. Louis, Mo.,	260	1,533
New Orleans, La.	101	3,727
Denver, Colo.	232	455
Seattle, Wash.	836	1,041
Portland, Ore.	442	729
San Francisco, Calif.	474	6,673
Los Angeles, Calif.	592	2,115
Oakland, Calif.	245	1,288

A convenient comparative chart confirms the reluctance of Frenchmen to live abroad, particularly in non-European countries. In view of its alarmingly stagnating population, the French government actually discouraged emigration or tried to channel it so as to strengthen its colonial empire.[4]

CHART II
Frenchmen Residing Abroad

Continent	In 1861	In 1886
Europe	127,000	200,000
Africa	15,000	30,000
Asia	3,000	15,000
North America	113,000	120,000
South America	58,000	40,000
Oceania		3,000

As one might expect, almost twice as many French men as women, the vast majority between fifteen and forty years old, immigrated into the United States. Quite a few were unskilled or semiskilled laborers; most were farmers and craftsmen. Americans welcomed the pleasant and industrious French immigrants and admired their reliability. Practically every profession was represented; chief among the professionals were teachers, priests, doctors, artists, and entertainers, who naturally tried to establish themselves in the cities. French jewelers, tailors, carpenters, hatters, glovemakers, confectioners, chefs, bakers, and gardeners enjoyed a superior reputation. French doctors, restaurateurs, hoteliers, merchants, and manufacturers usually found America to be the promised land. On the whole, French immigrants made out well, wherever they resided in the United States.[5]

The most solid center of French civilization in the United States

4. M. Turquan, "Les Etrangers en France," *Annales Economiques* (March 20, 1890), 392.

5. Edmond Bruwaert to Alexandre Ribot, March 31, 1892, in *Correspondance Commerciale,* Vol. 7, AMAE; see also Robert Ernst, *Immigrant Life in New York City* (New York, 1949), 70–89.

existed in Louisiana. When early in the nineteenth century Napoleon sold the Louisiana Territory, he expected France and the United States to cooperate for a long time to come in defense of maritime interests which Great Britain's control of the seas was capable of violating. Contemporary Frenchmen also believed that the population of this former colony would forever maintain its French character and stand by France should its loyalty be tested. Some of the nearly thirty thousand political exiles who had fled to America in the wake of the collapse of the Napoleonic Empire also displayed a disposition to think of America as a convenient base for the promotion of French interests. Many of them went to Philadelphia, seat of the French Agricultural and Manufacturing Society which had succeeded in obtaining land grants from Congress enabling these refugees to cultivate olives and vine, two areas of agriculture that needed development. French colonies sprang up in the southwestern part of the United States where the climate for this cultivation seemed most promising. Unfortunately, some of the Bonapartists, among them military officers and trained civilians who originally had sought merely a haven in America, soon began to scheme a Napoleonic confederation in the Southwest that might again place them in a commanding position. Such plots, however, were buried with the emperor's death in 1821.[6] Others, like the two future rulers of France, Louis Philippe and Napoleon III, resided in the United States merely temporarily and returned to France when the opportunity presented itself.[7]

Eventually, Frenchmen learned that in Louisiana, as elsewhere, a cultural and ethnic minority, however determined to preserve the culture of its ancestors, must strike roots in the land in which it lives.[8] In the course of a century, the process of Americanization had largely, though not entirely, succeeded, despite the valiant

6. Thomas W. Martin, *French Military Adventures in Alabama*, 1818–1828 (Princeton, N.J., 1937).

7. T. Wood Clarke, *Emigrés in the Wilderness* (New York, 1941), 125–30; Georges Bertin, *Joseph Bonaparte en Amérique* (Paris, 1893).

8. William A. Read, *Louisiana-French* (Baton Rouge, 1931), xvii; Selma Klein,

efforts of the older generation to preserve a lingering attachment to France. Their efforts were aided by the Creoles, descendants of French and Spanish people, and by the Acadians, who after their expulsion from Acadia (Nova Scotia) in 1755 drifted into Louisiana. As can still be seen in the Creole quarter of New Orleans, these people tenaciously resisted the pressures of Anglo-American civilization, holding on to their style of life, their appreciation of leisure and conviviality, their courtesy and cuisine, their fashions and language. Music lovers spending an evening at the French Opera in old New Orleans found the sight of the latest Parisian fashions displayed by Creole ladies a fascinating attraction.

The Acadians (Cajuns), who married freely into other elements of Louisiana's population, perpetuated the French language and traditions more persistently than any other group. The close family ties of the simple, rural people, whose Cajun folk songs tell a great deal about their sociable, though humble, life, evidently made them more immune to the influences undermining French tradition. The relative compactness of the French and Catholic population in South Louisiana undoubtedly facilitated the survival of cultural and recreational differences. The *joie de vivre* of the dancing, singing, community-oriented "French" Catholics set them clearly apart from the more restrained and less chattering, though usually more educated and better off, Protestant Americans. As the general nature of such differentiations somewhat oversimplifies these cultural distinctions, it should also be kept in mind that the French spoken in Louisiana is not universally the same. The Creole French, predominant in New Orleans and Baton Rouge, comes closest to the French of metropolitan France; Acadian French resembles the French prevalent in the provinces; and the *patois nègre* identifies the French spoken by blacks and whites in such

---

"Social Interaction of Creoles and Anglo-Americans in New Orleans, 1803–1860" (M.A. thesis, Tulane University, 1940), 73, 124, 148; Livingston DeLancey, "French Influence in New Orleans," *French Review*, XIII (May, 1940), 483–87.

southwestern localities of Louisiana as St. Martinville and Breaux Bridge.[9]

Many Frenchmen and Creoles took their civic responsibilities seriously; they distinguished themselves in the medical and literary professions. By gaining the recognition of their fellow citizens they placed themselves in the strongest position to command respect for French traditions. Proud of the fact that they had been trained in France, many surgeons and physicians in pre-Civil War Louisiana added the initials DMP (for Doctor of Medicine, Paris) to their names. Such publications as the *Journal de la société médicale de la Nouvelle Orléans and L'Union médicale de la Louisiane* reflected the dual desire of French doctors to raise the standards of their profession and to enhance the prestige of the French segment of the population.

In the pre-Civil War decades, many French-conscious families in New Orleans conversed at home only in French. Those who could afford it sent their sons to private schools with predominantly French teachers and entrusted the education of their daughters to the French nuns at the Convent of the Ursulines. Others, reared in France, acquired a thoroughly French mentality and an appreciation for French art and literature. Aided by French writers and journalists whom the revolutions of 1830 and 1848 had "encouraged" to rebuild their lives in the United States, these French-educated men and women could claim credit for the extraordinary flourishing of French literature and newspapers in Louisiana between 1820 and 1861. E. L. Tinker's excellent collection of Louisiana French literary activities leaves no doubt about the extent to which these writers were influenced by French romanticism.[10]

9. Louise Westfeldt, "A Study of the Persistence of the Culture of Early Rural France among Acadians of Rural Louisiana" (M.A. thesis, Tulane University, 1935), 63–78; Irene Therese Whitfield, *Acadian Folk Songs* (Baton Rouge, 1955), 1–6; Marie S. Dunn, "A Comparative Study: Louisiana's French and Anglo-Saxon Cultures," *Louisiana Studies*, X (1971), 131–69; Alvin L. Bertrand and Calvin L. Beale, *The French and Non-French in Rural Louisiana: A Study of the Relevance of Ethnic Factors to Rural Development,* Louisiana State University Bulletin No. 606 (December, 1965); Joseph LeSage Tisch, *French in Louisiana: A Study of the Historical Development of the French Language of Louisiana* (*New* Orleans, 1959), 50.

10. Edward Larocque Tinker, *Writings in the French Language in Louisiana*

Despite the culturally and economically disruptive effects of the Civil War and Reconstruction, the roots of French civilization in New Orleans and many smaller towns and parishes were so deeply embedded in the consciousness of the local population that they did not fade away entirely. In the last three decades of the century several new organizations made an enthusiastic effort to revive the French tradition. This was the objective of l'Union française, founded in 1872, l'Association Dramatique Orléanaise (1876), and the Société de la Fête du Quatorze Juillet (1890). Bookstores, libraries, and such a sophisticated summer resort as St. Martinville did their share to keep a French identity alive.[11]

Although most of the French newspapers in Louisiana enjoyed only an ephemeral existence, *L'Abeille* was read and supported for nearly one hundred years. It evidently satisfied the expectations of its French and American readers. Catering to an intellectual audience, a few French literary periodicals offered serials of the best French novels and musical and dramatic reviews. Ranking among the most distinguished and stimulating publications in French was the *L'Athénée louisianais,* which a group of Creoles launched in 1875 in the hope that it would encourage and perpetuate the use of the French language.

The assimilation of the younger generations, however, at best made the old French families genuinely bilingual. The Americanization process of the public schools indirectly discouraged French-speaking youngsters lest their classmates ridicule them by referring to them as the "Kis-Kee-Dees." The name was phonetically derived from *"Qu'est-ce qu'il dit?"* a question Creole chil-

---

in the 19th Century, trans. T. Rossi (Paris, 1932) ; Alcée Fortier, *Louisiana Studies: Literature, Customs and Dialects, History and Education* (New Orleans, 1894), 23–87.

11. Doris Landry Caffery, "French Literature in Louisiana Country Newspapers: *Le Meschacébé, Le Foyer Créole* and *L'Intérim* (1880–1899)" (M.A. thesis, Louisiana State University, 1944). See also Edward Larocque Tinker, *Creole City: Its Past and Its People* (New York, 1953), 164–83; Ruby Van Allen Caufeild, *The French Literature of Louisiana* (New York, 1929), 38–62; Elizabeth Avery, "The Influence of French Immigration on the Political History of the United States" (Ph.D. dissertation, University of Minnesota, 1895), 64.

dren asked when they were addressed in a language they did not understand.

When the Louisiana Constitution of 1868 discontinued the long-standing custom of issuing legislative proceedings in French as well as English, the French-speaking population was dismayed. This offensive provision seemed to signal the end of an era. Further contributing to the general weakening of French civilization in Louisiana was the steady, though sometimes imperceptible, loss of ground suffered in the field of law. Despite the survival of the civil-law system in Louisiana, with roots that could be traced to old Spanish codes and the Code Napoléon, common-law encroachments tended to modify the system by Americanizing it. Several gestures in the final quarter of the century offered little more than a ray of hope to practitioners of the French language. Until economic reasons put an end to it in 1916, notices of a juridical character were published in both languages. It was permissible to testify in French in a court of law, and the courts even provided interpreters for citizens who could not understand English.[12]

The post-Civil War activities of loyal American citizens who took pride in their French ancestry—whether Frenchmen, Creoles, Canadians, or Acadians—their attempts to infuse new blood into the body politic by encouraging the immigration of "Frenchmen from France" and by organizing stimulating social and cultural events produced some positive results. Historically, they prolonged the existence of a French consciousness among French Americans, and the customs and joyful outlook of these citizens left their imprint on the rest of the population. No matter how Americanized they became, New Orleans and many smaller communities in Louisiana continued to show traces of their French and Spanish

12. Tinker, *Writings in the French Language in Louisiana*, 5; Klein, "Social Interaction," 104; Lucy B. Foote, *American Imprints Inventory No.* 19: *Bibliography of the Official Publications of Louisiana*, 1803–1934 (Baton Rouge, 1942), 185. In 1968, the state legislature created the Council for the Development of French in Louisiana, an official state agency authorized to foster French as a second language in the state.

background. The architecture of the French Quarter, its decorative wrought-iron enclosures, its beautiful yard gardens, the names of many citizens and streets, the menus of better restaurants, and Mardi Gras remain living reminders of the French past. Even in modern elevators it is not unusual to overhear a conversation in French.[13]

Deeply embedded in American soil, the roots of French civilization showed promising signs of strength in the early nineteenth century and were carefully nurtured in the pre-Civil War period; but economic conditions and social pressures in the final decades of the century exacted a toll that proved to be too high for a vigorous survival. It was quite natural that the political differences which divided the French people in the Old World also manifested themselves in the New World. But while one might take this diversity of views for granted in France, it sapped the strength of struggling French communities in a foreign land.

Most of the French immigrants who settled down in scattered little communities in the South and Middle West were rather poor and uneducated.[14] Whether they lived in Ohio or Missouri, in Kentucky or Illinois, they liked their homes in the French pattern, surrounded by porches and a garden. As Catholics, they preferred French priests to guide them; and, to the shock of their Protestant fellow citizens, they enjoyed various kinds of entertainment on Sundays, particularly music and dancing. Even in a small town in Illinois, French ladies wore dresses at socials which have been described as "cut very décolleté, with short and narrow skirts, and only apologies for sleeves." Depending on their geographic location, these French settlers spoke a language that ranged from

13. M. de la Bretonne, "De L'Immigration française et des moyens de l'attirer en Louisiane" (Paper delivered at meeting of L'Athénée Louisianais, May 10, 1876) ; T. Lynn Smith and Homer L. Hitt, *The People of Louisiana* (Baton Rouge, 1952), 47–48 ; Albert Tissandier, *Six mois aux Etats-Unis* (Paris, 1886), 275.

14. Initially, many French immigrants earned less than Negro slaves. Félix Lelièvre, *De L'Emigration en Amérique depuis* 1815 *jusqu'en* 1843 (*Nantes,* 1843), 11. No French businessmen took the initiative in opening up French commercial houses in St. Louis, Chicago, or even in New Orleans. G. de Molinari, *Lettres sur les Etats-Unis et le Canada* (Paris, 1876), 281.

French-Canadian patois to a Creole dialect. The few "Americans" marrying into these small-town families tried their best to adopt the French style of life. Like many other "native" citizens, though, they conveniently Americanized the French language, pronouncing, for instance, *cinq hommes* as combs, and *vide poche* as wheat bush. New England fishermen corrupted the French language by transforming the fish stew Frenchmen call *chaudiére*, referring to the cauldron in which it was heated, into the Yankee version of chowder.[15]

Some Frenchmen experimented in the middle of the nineteenth century with communal settlements in Texas, Iowa, Illinois, and California.[16] Altogether, almost fifty phalanxes based on various types of associated living existed in the United States in the 1840s and 1850s. The North American Phalanx in New Jersey (1843–1854), the longest lasting and relatively successful American joint-stock farming community, set out to test Charles Fourier's notions of an enlightened cooperative society. Fourier (1772–1837) deplored the human and social consequences of the competitive production system resulting in class struggles and international rivalry. One of his most ardent followers, Victor Considerant (1808–1893), a French army engineer who chose to become a social apostle, advocated in his major work, *Destinée sociale,* and in the

15. For more detailed information on the French in Middle America, consult J. F. Snyder, "The Old French Towns of Illinois in 1839: A Reminiscence," *Journal of the Illinois State Historical Society,* XXXVI (December, 1943), 345–67; Harvey Wish, "The French of Old Missouri (1804–1821)," *Mid-America,* n.s., XII (1941), 1667–89; Francis P. Weisenburger, *The Passing of the Frontier, 1825–1850* (Columbus, Ohio, 1941), 51, 124–25, Vol. III of Carl Wittke (ed.), *The History of the State of Ohio;* William M. Miller, "A French Community in Ohio," *French Review,* XX (October, 1946), 8–13. For reference to the etymology of *chowder,* see Chevalier Jackson, *The Life of Chevalier Jackson: An Autobiography* (New York, 1938), 74.

16. On this topic, see Maurice Dommanget, *Victor Considerant: Sa vie, son oeuvre* (Paris, 1929); Jules Prudhommeaux, *Icarie et son fondateur: Etienne Cabet* (Paris, 1907); Félix Bonnaud, *Cabet et son oeuvre* (Paris, 1900); Harold Wilson, "The North American Phalanx: An Experiment in Communal Living," New Jersey Historical Society, *Proceedings,* LXX (1952), 188–209; Joseph G. Rosengarten, *French Colonists and Exiles in the United States* (Philadelphia, 1907), 152–58; Russell M. Jones, "The French Image of America, 1830 to 1848" (Ph.D. dissertation, University of Missouri, 1957), 245–51; Whitridge, *Men in Crisis,* 310–13, 358 ff.

Fourierist periodical *La Phalange*, the amelioration of working and living conditions through self-sustaining phalanxes of about one thousand persons each. Essentially thinking in terms of a social "revolution without a revolution," he constantly reappraised and adjusted his conceptions of a socialistic society in the light of changing exigencies. Inasmuch as Fourier had encompassed the whole universe in his scheme, Considerant decided to explore the feasibility of settlements in the United States, despite several known failures of communal experiments in the New World. Returning from an exploratory visit to America in 1853, he enthusiastically assured his followers that he had found the promised land and all that was necessary to improve there the quality of life was their resolute will. Contrary to what one might have expected from a socialist reformer, he founded the Colonization Society of Texas, with a capital of 5,400,000 francs ($1.08 million), an enterprise not conceived as a cooperative phalanx. To the dismay of Considerant and the slightly more than two hundred Europeans who composed the first two contingents of settlers, the settlements near Dallas, Texas, were not ready to receive them upon their arrival. This initial disappointment and disarray hastened the ultimate failure of the undertaking.

Though initially plagued by similar experiences, Etienne Cabet's Icarian communes in America at least demonstrated the potential as well as the pitfalls of such cooperatives. Cabet (1788–1856), trained in law and experienced in politics, was the idealistic son of a French cooper. Cabet was inspired to demonstrate that true Christianity meant the establishment of an order based on social equality. In his controversial and widely read *Le Voyage en Icarie* (1840) he depicted a communal society organized to promote universal happiness. To implement his ideas of a communist society he made arrangements for the acquisition of a million acres in the valley of the Red River in Texas. On February 3, 1848, without having inspected this land and its location, Cabet and his enthusiastic fellow-Icarians saw an advance group of sixty-nine "soldiers of humanity" off for Icaria. When they arrived in New Orleans on March 27, they were shocked to learn that their dreamland was barely accessible and that each settler could have only 320 acres, such half-sections not being contiguous, and provided he built a house on it by July 1. By that date, the determined immigrants had secured 10,000 acres spread over two townships.

By the end of the year, 485 Icarians had left France for Icaria. Faced with unexpected complications in America and in view of the promising prospects held out by the unexpected French Revolution of February, 1848, some Icarians on both sides of the Atlantic advocated the abandonment of the American settlement and the implementation of the society's ideals in France. Only Cabet's presence in America seemed to be capable of holding together the struggling and torn Icarian pioneers. Soon after his arrival in New Orleans in February, 1849, Cabet led 260 of his impoverished followers to Illinois where they found an answer to their prayers. In Nauvoo, Illinois, they ran into a community with huts and houses recently abandoned by the Mormons. Here, at last, they could settle down and translate their socialistic ideals into reality, demonstrating to their supporters and critics what kind of life they had in mind. Economically, they sustained themselves by raising their own foodstuffs; operating a sawmill, a flower mill, and a distillery; and being engaged in various crafts. Whatever resources they developed were shared by all members of their family-centered society. They took great pride in their musical and theatrical performances and in the development of their school, newspaper, and library. Indeed, much of the propaganda distributed by the Icarian Society in France had been shipped there from the print shop in Nauvoo. But despite these accomplishments and the renewed interest in them (following the collapse of the Second Republic) by Icarians in France, internal dissensions once again endangered this commune. Largely because of Cabet's dictatorial tendencies, he was expelled from the Nauvoo commune by a majority of its members. This forced Cabet and a few of his faithful followers to start anew in St. Louis, Missouri, where he was laid to rest in 1856. Overall, relatively few Frenchmen were willing to participate in these overseas experiments.

Lack of finances and facilities, extreme weather conditions, diseases, and factionalism contributed much to the ephemeral quality of their existence.

In comparison with Americans and Germans, Frenchmen frequently lacked the ambition needed in the highly competitive society of the United States. Perhaps overly harsh in his judgment, a metropolitan Frenchman who observed his compatriots in the United States in the late 1860s came to the conclusion that Frenchmen were on the whole rather helpless and frustrated once the government ceased to direct their lives.[17] Even if one makes allowance for exceptions to this all-too-general observation, the experience of the French in California in the second half of the nineteenth century did lend further support to it.

The news of the discovery of gold in California induced some 28,000 Frenchmen, of whom not more than 10,000 had come directly from France, to share in the "easy" acquisition of wealth.[18] The founding of numerous California societies in France was designed to accomplish the same goal. These societies made Paris the European headquarters for those small investors and rentiers who wanted to supplement their incomes without becoming directly involved in the fabulous activities on the Pacific Coast of America.[19] By 1870, the number of Frenchmen in California had declined to below 10,000. Some had by then succeeded in establishing themselves in finance and trade. But as far as French business enterprise abroad was concerned, one critical observer noted, with particular reference to California, that it simply did not compare with the aptitudes Frenchmen displayed in commerce at home. There seemed to be some psychological factors in their makeup that in certain practical respects reduced their effectiveness abroad. They

17. Edmond Leuba, *La Californie et les états du Pacifique: Souvenirs et impressions* (Paris, 1882), 46–54; Albert E. Portalis, *Les Etats-Unis: Le self-government et le césarisme* (Paris, 1869), 31.

18. Gilbert Chinard, "When the French Came to California," *CHSQ,* XXII (December, 1943), 313.

19. The failure of these societies affected the United States as well as French investors; see Henry Blumenthal, "The California Societies in France, 1849–1855," *PHR,* XXV (1956), 251–60.

found it very difficult to cope with the tough, and at times unscrupulous, competition from other European and American businessmen.[20]

A general analysis of the type of Frenchmen who emigrated to California compels at least a modification of the notion that in business they did not function effectively in a foreign environment. Most of the French emigrants were not businessmen in the first place. Nor could French workers who might have successfully exposed themselves to the arduous life of gold miners independently afford the expenses and risks the journey to California entailed. The majority of these French adventurers came from impoverished elements of the upper classes; often they were social outcasts whom the government of the Second Republic encouraged to depart. Among them were the younger sons of the French aristocracy—doctors, lawyers, bankers, intellectuals, and political nonconformists. These people discovered that they were more suited for life in San Francisco than for the hardships the mines exacted. They opened, therefore, hotels, restaurants, and gambling houses. They went into the banking and import business—all enterprises in which, by and large, they registered remarkable successes. Since many of the Frenchmen who had gone to the golden paradise on the West Coast intended to return to France with their fairly quickly acquired fortunes, they refused to become naturalized citizens. Consequently, the discriminatory taxes that local authorities had imposed on foreigners reduced their profits and their ability to be competitive.[21] Some of those French pioneers who had originally gone to the placer and hydraulic mines of the Coast Range and the Sierra Nevada pursued other activities once the gold rush had lost its attractiveness. They moved into the fertile California valleys, seeking

20. M. E. Wilbur (trans.), "A Frenchman in the Gold Rush," *CHSQ*, V (1926), 4, 346, based on the journal of Ernest de Massey.

21. See Rufus K. Wyllys, "The French of California and Sonora," *PHR*, I (1932), 337–43; H. Rouhaud, *Les Régions nouvelles: Histoire du commerce et de la civilisation au nord de l'Océan Pacifique* (Paris, 1868), 191–93; A. P. Nasatir, "A French Pessimist in California," *CHSQ*, XXXI (1952), 144; and Raoul H. Blanquie, "The Early Settlers Left an Indelible Mark on the State," San Francisco *Chronicle*, November, 16, 1950, p. 3.

new and more settled opportunities in viticulture, horticulture, and sheep raising.

French colonies developed, therefore, not only in San Francisco, but in many smaller California communities as well. Recognizing that many French residents did not speak English, the governors' annual messages were for several years translated into French and Spanish. The few thousand Frenchmen who remained in California felt the need for their own cultural, religious, and social organizations. San Francisco's fairly large colony lost little time in taking the initiative in these respects. *L'Echo du pacifique* was the first of the daily French newspapers, and from 1852 it kept the French population informed about local, national, and international affairs. By then, more immediate and urgent needs of the French-speaking population had already been attended to. On July 19, 1849, Father Anthony Langlois celebrated the first mass in a make-shift chapel; and in 1856 Father Dominique Blaive founded the French church, Notre Dame des Victoires. A French benevolent society looked after unfortunate compatriots who were ill and could not afford to pay medical bills. This society actually laid the foundation for the French Hospital in San Francisco, which was greatly aided by the presence of as many as eight French doctors whose inadequate knowledge of English greatly handicapped them in their private practices. The French population's appreciation of music and the theater encouraged interested groups to organize well-planned performances. Despite the quite understandable clannishness of this developing French colony, its contributions to the social, economic, and cultural life of the city of San Francisco were considerable.

The same held true, of course, for the leading cities in the East—Boston, New York, and Philadelphia—where French "colonies" managed to establish themselves very comfortably. Conscious of their origin and desirous of bringing their children up in a manner that would enable them to cope easily with this cultural duality, French residents in these cities took a keen interest in education. They supported private primary schools and patronized schools for "young ladies" as well as college preparatory institutions. For as long as it was possible they preferred to live the French way of life, modified only by the exigencies of their existence in America. They continued to delight as much in French conversations as in French cuisine, wines, and liqueurs. Their appreciation of artistic and intellectual stimulation diminished as little in their adopted land as did their sense of humor and gift for gossip.[22]

By far the greatest influx of Frenchmen came from Canada. The steady flow of French-Canadian farmers, workers, lumberjacks, and miners into the Great Lakes region and New England reached sizable proportions in the second half of the nineteenth century. The hardships of their existence and the lure of opportunities across the border finally defeated the efforts of their priests to persuade them to remain in their parishes. Traditionally close family ties, as well as language barriers and the guiding influence of French priests, delayed the assimilation of these religious, honest, and industrious people after they had finally settled down in the United States. The attempt to keep their French loyalties alive found effective expression in the slogan: *dénationaliser, c'est démoraliser.* When many small New England factory towns gradually assumed the appearance of French villages transported from Quebec, Yankee reaction deplored the socially undesirable tendency of French Canadians to maintain their foreign identity. In the late nineteenth century relatively few of them became United States citizens and those who did were suspected of rating their American citizenship so low as not to make a genuine effort to become fully assimilated. This state of affairs bred dissatisfaction both ways.[23]

Initially exposed to economic exploitation and social and religious prejudices, French Canadians from all parts of the United

---

22. Ernst, *Immigrant Life in New York City*, 141–42.
23. Alexandre Goulet, "Une Nouvelle France en Nouvelle Angleterre" (Ph.D. dissertation, Université de Paris, 1934); Emile Lauvrière, "Une Nouvelle France en Nouvelle Angleterre," *Revue de l'histoire des colonies françaises*, XXIII (1935), 89–106; Félix Gatineau, *Histoire des Franco-Américains de Southbridge, Massachusetts* (Framingham, Mass., 1919); Edward Billings Ham, "French National Societies in New England," *NEQ*, XII (1939), 315–32; M. L. Hansen, *The Immigrant in American History* (Cambridge, Mass., 1940), 170–89; "A Franco-American State," New York *Times*, August 13, 1889, p. 1.

States gathered frequently in conventions essentially designed to reinforce their ethnic traditions and to protect their common interests. People who were unprepared to cope with the demanding challenges of the new environment in which they had settled thus tried to overcome their second-class status by helping and encouraging each other. Once the local population accepted them as reliable workers and good customers, it turned around and actually encouraged the immigration of French Canadians. By the turn of the century these immigrants occupied a respectable and significant place in the New England economy.

Among families of French descent, the Du Ponts of Delaware have enriched American civilization notably. A long time before its industrial empire became a symbol of power, several generations of this remarkable family applied their extraordinary resourcefulness to the cultural, as well as economic, development of their adopted country. Pierre Samuel Du Pont de Nemours (1739–1817) and his family arrived in the United States on New Year's Day, 1800. He came to the land of liberty to escape the political harassments to which the French Revolution had subjected him and other public officials. Frankly, America's attractive economic opportunities also influenced his decision to emigrate. At his advanced age, however, he found the adjustment to the alien environment and language so uncomfortable that in 1802 he returned to France; and at the end of the Napoleonic era, he once again played a prominent official role until his return to Delaware in 1815. The advice this wise old man gave to his friend and fellow physiocrat, President Thomas Jefferson, to purchase New Orleans from France rather than go to a calamitous war over it enshrined his name in the annals of American history. His publication of several scientific papers in the *Transactions of the American Philosophical Society* and his report on *National Education in the United States,* prepared at Jefferson's request, merely illustrate the diversity of his interests.[24]

24. The Eleutherian Mills Historical Library (EMHL) in Greenville, Delaware, houses rich collections of the Du Pont Family Papers. For published references,

He obviously set an admirable example for his children. Among them, his son Eleuthère Irénée (1771–1834) helped lay the foundation on which the Du Pont industrial enterprise rested and contributed substantially to America's knowledge and development of horticulture and pomology. No less fascinating, moreover, was Irénée's espousal of quite progressive social experiments. Having been trained to manufacture gunpowder by Antoine Lavoisier, the famous French chemist, Irénée set out to exploit this knowledge in the United States. With capital, labor, and machinery for such an undertaking secured in Europe, he founded the company in Wilmington, Delaware, that throughout the nineteenth century supplied the United States with the gunpowder it needed in its wars. Gradually, he moved into the production of fertilizers and industrial chemicals, a field in which his eldest son, Alfred Victor, took a keen interest. A rather strange diversification resulted from Irénée's importation of Spanish merino sheep whose fine quality of wool, he ventured, would make the wool industry a profitable enterprise in the United States.

If the production of these and other goods furthered American industry and rendered vital services to the people, Irénée's enlightened concern for the welfare of his workers could not but create good feelings in the community.[25] To improve the education and citizenship of working children and workmen who could not attend school during the week, he helped organize the Brandywine Manufacturers' Sunday School, a nondenominational rural school. Perhaps even more illustrative of his humanitarian outlook was

see Ambrose Saricks, *Pierre Samuel Du Pont de Nemours* (Lawrence, Kansas, 1965), 284–90; Dumas Malone (ed.), *Correspondence Between Thomas Jefferson and Pierre Samuel Du Pont de Nemours*, 1798–1817 (New York, 1970), xiii–xix; Mack Thompson, "Causes and Circumstances of the Du Pont Family's Emigration," *French Historical Studies*, VI (1969), 59–77.

25. See William H. A. Carr, *The Du Ponts of Delaware: A Fantastic Dynasty* (New York, 1964); William S. Dutton, *Du Pont: One Hundred and Forty Years* (New York, 1942); Carroll Wish Pursell, "E. I. du Pont and the Merino Mania in Delaware, 1805–1815," *Agricultural History*, XXXVI (1962), 91–100; Raymond F. Betts, "Eleuthère Irénée du Pont and the Brandywine Sunday School," *Delaware History*, VIII (1959), 343–53; and Polly Jose Scafidi, "Doctor Pierre Didier and Early Industrial Medicine," *Delaware History*, XV (1972), 41–54.

his support of industrial medicine. Even during the early decades of its existence the Du Pont company retained a doctor and assumed financial responsibility for the treatment of injuries caused by explosions in the mills. In cases of fatal accidents, moreover, widows of company workers received pensions. The Du Ponts themselves had to learn to overcome the setbacks caused by the occasional explosions that shattered their proud achievements.

The delight Irénée took in botany, a field in which he had acquired considerable knowledge as a young student at the Jardin des plantes in Paris, provided him with much needed relaxation.[26] Regular exchanges of vegetable and flower seeds, as well as a great variety of fruit trees and woodland trees enriched his orchard at Eleutherian Mills and a good many French gardens and nurseries. When J. F. Nicholas Morel, a physician and botanist from Besançon, and Louis Lelieur, director of the gardens at St. Cloud, made these exchanges, they usually included instructions for proper planting and care. And when such naturalists as Constantine S. Rafinesque and Jean-Baptiste Theodore Leschenault spent a little time in the United States before returning to France with their collections of American and East Indian plants, Irénée made it a point to entertain them at the Eleutherian Mills. Although he was very much at home in the United States, naturally he liked to maintain close ties with the world in which he had grown up.

Neither Irénée's loyalty to the United States nor that of his descendants was ever in question. On the contrary, their decisions and actions, when the chips were down, invariably manifested a strong sense of American patriotism. Even though in 1846 the Du Pont company considered the American invasion of Mexico "shameful," it refused to sell powder to the enemy. Irénée's second son, Henry Du Pont (1812–1889), helped keep the strategically and industrially important state of Delaware within the Union. From the beginning, he warned against "the pestilential doctrines of

26. Norman B. Wilkinson, *E. I. du Pont, Botaniste: The Beginning of a Tradition* (Charlottesville, Va., 1972). See also J. F. N. Morel to E. I. du Pont (1802 ?), EMHL; and "Botanical Essays and Notes," in E. I. Du Pont, Special Papers, Group 3, Series B, Box 11, EMHL.

secession" and he insisted on absolute loyalty to the government and constitution of the United States. As the commanding general of Delaware's Home Guards, he rendered valuable service. Another member of the Du Pont family, Admiral Samuel Francis Du Pont (1816–1888), commanded the Southern Atlantic Blockading Squadron, also firmly believing that the dissolution of the Union would be a monumental and intolerable catastrophe.[27]

In private life, the earlier generations of the Du Ponts were obviously more conscious of their French descent than those who were entirely the product of their New World environment. Like other French immigrants, they loved to speak French, subscribe to a French newspaper, and educate their daughters in private schools providing an appreciation of French and American culture. The Du Pont family library contained French books on a variety of subjects and continued to be stocked with current French publications. As a prominent French family in America, they extended their hospitality to many French visitors, including Lafayette during his triumphal tour in 1824–1825. They entertained in French style and enjoyed French folk songs and music. Even their love of flowers and beautifully maintained gardens and orchards appeared to have a French touch.

American Visitors in France

Throughout the nineteenth century, Paris attracted thousands of American travelers. Most of them found it a fascinating place; only a few downgraded it. It would not be correct to ascribe these mixed feelings to the religious prejudices of Protestants and Catholics, though occasionally the religious backgrounds of the tourists influenced their reactions. The alleged immorality of Paris was a matter of major concern to many families, especially at the begin-

27. See Henry Francis du Pont to his son, January 12, 1861, in Group 7, Sons of E. I. du Pont, Box 6, Out File: 1861–67, EMHL; Dutton, *Du Pont*, 91–94; and John D. Hayes, *Samuel Francis Du Pont: A Selection from His Civil War Letters, 1860–1865* (3 vols.; Ithaca, N.Y., 1969), I, xlvi.

ning of the century. In 1818, for instance, an American traveler cautioned that "Paris is one of the last spots on earth to which a young man should come if he wishes to avoid being engulfed in the whirlpool of vicious and expensive dissipation, unless he has moral and religious principles on which he can rely as the anchor of his safety." In a city in which "vice is disguised under the specious name of venial indulgence," he thought, too many of his countrymen, released from the salutary restraint of their neighbors at home, might be tempted to drink from the poisoned cup. Though it may have been "the most wicked of all places on the face of the earth," the Reverend Dr. John McClintock, who attended to the spiritual needs of the American colony in Paris during the Civil War, also regarded it in 1850 as "the most desirable spot in the world to live in."[28] To him it was the capital of Europe, showy, absurd, and exciting. By the end of the century, it also enjoyed the reputation of possessing an unsurpassed system of public works and charities, as well as an excellent municipal administration and police.

In the 1820s and 1830s, though, American tourists in Paris and some of the smaller French towns complained frequently that walking in the streets was inconvenient because of the absence of sidewalks and hazardous because "the carriages and public cabriolets dash with a recklessness through filthy gutters, splashing the pedestrians." In those early years the streets of many small French towns had no sidewalks, gutters, or common sewers. It seemed that "the march of intellect" had not yet arrived at these luxuries. The high houses, moreover, were "mostly black of slate, and patched often till nothing is seen but the patches, and mushrooms and other vegetables grow through the cracks." To a contemporary American, villages at home had, by comparison, "an air of youth and freshness harmonising with their dimensions." Even in the late nineteenth century Americans visiting Paris or

28. John T. Bowdoin, "Travels in France," Diary entries for July 10 to December 14, 1818, pp. 140–42, VHS; George R. Crooks, *Life and Letters of the Rev. John McClintock, D.D.* (*New York*, 1876), 222.

provincial towns were continually surprised and inconvenienced by houses and hotels without proper plumbing.[29]

Nevertheless, Americans who revisited Paris after an interval of several years were usually much impressed by the external growth of the city and its improvements and embellishments during the Second Empire.[30] Some thought that Georges Haussmann, whom Napoleon III had charged with the beautification and modernization of the great metropolis, had opened magnificent vistas; others criticized him for having produced "a terribly monotonous looking city." Henry James deplored the Americanization of Paris that made the rue de la Paix "a perfect reproduction of Broadway."[31] Its broad avenues, exquisite fountains, and imposing monuments gave the city a studied appearance of grandeur. It was actually an impressive sight, suggesting to its beholders the power of the state and the wealth of the country that made it possible. The quaint and picturesque places Paris offered in great abundance delighted many visitors. James Russell Lowell, for example, had moved to the Latin Quarter, "away from the English and Americans who unfrenchify the Rue de Rivoli and its neighborhood," because he preferred its "queer chimneys and the delightful higgledy-piggledy of its streets."[32] Despite the luxurious gayness, vast pleasure grounds, brilliant gas lights, and dazzling spectacles of Paris, some American visitors were most impressed by the peculiar wit and good manners of all classes of Parisians. Somehow, however,

29. For such comments, see, among others, John Peter Geortuer Diary, May 26, 1828, MS 3487, UNC; Judith P. Rives Diary, July 12, 1831, MS in Duke University Library, Durham, N.C.; John W. Francis, November 8, 1818, MS in John W. Francis Papers, NYPL. For descriptions of the "antiquated city of Rouen, with its narrow, crooked and jagged streets and the ungracious image of Le Havre," see Thomas Sully, "Journal: Diary in France and England," July, 1838, p. 176, NYPL; Asher B. Durand, "Journal in France," August 2, 1840, p. 62, NYPL; and John Sanderson, *Sketches of Paris: In Familiar Letters to His Friends by an American Gentleman* (Philadelphia, 1838), 7.

30. See David H. Pinkney, *Napoleon III and the Rebuilding of Paris* (Princeton, N.J., 1958).

31. Henry James to William James, September 22, 1872, MS Am 1094, and William James to Alice James, October 29, 1873, MS Am 1092, both in HCL.

32. James Russell Lowell to Mabel (Lowell) Burnett, October 12, 1872, MS Am 1239.1, HCL.

there seemed to be too much emphasis on the external and superficial aspects of life. Paris appeared to be "the Elysium of the idler, and for barren minds a Paradise."[33] Such intellectuals as William and Henry James, though not typical of American travelers in France, preferred London to Paris. In 1877 Henry James commented: "For the practical conveniences of life, London is immeasurably inferior to Paris—no cafés, no restaurants, no kiosks, no theaters (that one can go to), no evening visits, etc. But it is more interesting."[34] Any evaluation of such comments must of course take into consideration the period when they were made. The tone of Parisian society during the Second Empire, reflecting its political prestige, was more cosmopolitan than provincial. In 1877, Henry James felt much more comfortable among the intellectuals and leaders of the powerful British Empire than in the French society of the struggling Third Republic. As a psychologist, his brother William probably offered the most honest explanation for the appraisal of many like-minded Americans when he observed: "These little French bourgeois live like mice in cheese—all right as long as they don't move outside."[35] In other words, satisfied with a style of life they considered comfortable, petit bourgeois Frenchmen showed little inclination to explore the progress of the larger world. When in the final decade of the century Henry Adams spent his summers in Paris, he did so merely because he sought there a "sense of the past" that he could not find in the United States. Otherwise, it struck him as at least as much "a dream of chaos" as New York.

Americans primarily concerned with the comforts and conveniences of life found New York by that time to be the world capital of luxury. Even some of the best French cooking and ice creams could be had in New York. Not only did well-to-do Americans engage the services of French cooks, the elegant ambiance of French restaurants in New York stimulated the appetite as much as the mind. As long as the trade of French cooks was "not to feed the

33. Henry Washington Wiley Diary, Paris, August 21, 1876, Box 212, LC.
34. Henry James to William James, Jan. 12, 1877, MS Am 1094, HCL.
35. William James to Henry James, July 22, 1893, MS Am 1092, HCL.

stomach, but the palate," they made the cuisine of many other lands look barbarous. The pride of French chefs in their tasty and beautiful art underwent severe tests with the quickening pace of modern life. In the final decades of the century many of the very particular French customers who in the past had encouraged the chefs of restaurants "to keep up the traditions of the dainty palates" began to frequent their private clubs in Paris. As a consequence, public cookery in France became increasingly more an industry than an art; some of the artists engaged in it were persuaded to practice it where it would be most appreciated, as for instance in some American mansions and expensive restaurants.[36]

The American Colony in Paris

An interesting phenomenon in French and American cultural relations in the nineteenth century was offered by the American colony in Paris. It counted no more than one hundred members during the Restoration; but, significantly, it was composed of as many as ten thousand by the end of the century.[37] By far the majority of them were southerners, hailing particularly from Louisiana and Virginia, though others had come from the North and the West. These transient and permanent residents, many of whom lived in the neighborhood of the Champs Elysées and the Arc de Triomphe,

36. Morris Phillip, *Abroad and At Home: Practical Hints for Tourists* (New York, 1893), 148; Samuel T. Chambers, "Observations and Opinions of French Travellers in the United States, 1790–1835" (M.A. thesis, Georgetown University, 1949), 13–14. See also Félix J. Deliée, *The Franco-American Cookery Book: Containing Over 2,000 Recipes* (New York, 1884); and "The City of Luxury," New York *Times,* May 21, 1877, p. 4.

37. Estimates of Americans who "visited" France between 1820 and 1848 range from three hundred to over two thousand annually; see Guillaume Bertier de Sauvigny, "American Travellers in France, 1814–1848," in Nancy Barker and Marvin Brown (eds.), *Diplomacy in the Age of Nationalism* (The Hague, 1971), 11–24. A "loose" unofficial estimate placed the number of Americans in Paris in the years 1868 and 1869 at five thousand; see *The Americans in Paris* (Paris, 1887), 59. In 1873, the editor of the Baltimore *American* referred to as many as thirty thousand permanent and ten thousand temporary American residents in Paris; see Charles C. Fulton, *Europe Viewed Through American Spectacles* (Philadelphia, 1874), 175. See also "Les Etrangers en France," *Le Journal de Paris,* April 8, 1890.

were by no means all old or affluent people. On the contrary, the younger and middle-aged groups predominated, and many persons of limited means simply found it cheaper to live quite comfortably in Paris than in an American city.[38] Also, quite a few well-to-do American families idled their time away in Paris, keeping up with the latest fashions and loving to display their diamonds at the opera and social occasions. Others were either sending their children to French schools or were engaged in business. In close cooperation with the British, the Anglo- American colony in Paris founded and financed, from 1832 on, English-speaking schools to make their children more comfortable and to be sure that upon their eventual return home they would not feel like aliens.[39]

The American colony grew rapidly during the two decades prior to the Civil War, declined sharply during the war, and experienced a noticeable increase again during the last two decades of the century, when Paris became the Mecca of thousands of American tourists and students. The temporary decline of the colony during the Civil War and its slow rise during Reconstruction must be traced primarily to the calamities and impoverishment of many southern families. Before the war many of them had crowded the best hotels and lived in the most sumptuous apartments in Paris. To the regret of those Frenchmen who had long been accustomed to profit from their dealings with wealthy American customers, these people practically disappeared during the first year of the war, unless reasons of health or urgent business compelled them to linger behind.[40] It was not until 1867 that large numbers of Americans from all parts of the United States visited Paris again, to see its magnificent Exposition. And Parisians welcomed the peaceful American invasion after 1872. They liked to rent rooms and apartments to generously paying and tipping Americans; many stores added English-speaking clerks to their staffs to cater to transatlantic

38. One American, for instance, claimed: "I can live better in Paris on $3,000 than in New York on $6,000. See "The American Colony," Paris *Continental Gazette*, August 22, 1878.
39. François Boucher, *American Footprints in Paris* (New York, 1921), 166.
40. See "Paris Correspondence," Washington, D.C., *National Intelligencer*, November 4, 1862.

customers who, rightly or wrongly, had the reputation of all being rich.[41]

Frenchmen liked the easygoing and ever-smiling Americans, even though their uncouth manners were at times exasperating. But the American colony as a whole, which was neither typically American nor typically Parisian, did not enjoy the unqualified respect of Frenchmen. Many members of this colony led idle, aimless, and frivolous lives. The worst among them, posing as high society, looked down on less well-to-do "low Americans" and addressed newcomers as "you Americans."[42] Titles intrigued these citizens of the American republic so much that quite a few of them married French nobility. Others derived pleasure from the ostentatious display of colorful decorations. A French proverb ridiculed this tendency by describing it as "décoré comme un dentiste américain." And in the "good old monarchial days," even the sturdiest of American democrats enjoyed being presented to the courts of Louis Philippe and Napoleon III. Monarchs belonging to other nations evidently impressed these republicans from the New World. The requests of American citizens in Paris for invitations to state balls and other entertaining spectacles usually outnumbered by far those from citizens of other foreign countries. Officials in the American legation in Paris were annoyed when too many of their visiting compatriots practically demanded to be introduced to their own French friends and acquaintances. This might be done in the United States, but it was not proper according to French customs. To gratify the curiosity of their compatriots, the staff of the legation invited them instead to large evening parties at which distinguished Frenchmen also made an appearance. [43]

Marriages between American heiresses and titled, but impoverished, Frenchmen, on the increase since the middle of the century, revealed certain sociological characteristics going far

41. Fulton, *Europe Viewed Through American Spectacles,* 153.

42. I. M., "The American Colony in France," *Nation,* XXVI (April 18, 1878), 257–59.

43. James A. Padgett (ed.), "Letters of James Brown to Henry Clay, 1804–1835," *LHQ,* XXIV (1941), 982–85.

beyond the private motivations of the individuals involved. The stereotypical French charge that Americans were excessively materialistic amazed and amused the Americans because it came from a people that loved money and acquired it at least as ingeniously as did the Yankees.[44] Similarly, while Americans were politically proud of their republican institutions, socially, quite a few of them were tuft-hunters and title-hungry. Just as many a French countess or noblewoman came from New York or Chicago, many an American "captain," "colonel," or "esquire" was merely a simple citizen. Ironically, such a "French countess" remained to her friends in the United States the same old Peggy or Pat she had always been and a nobody to her husband's aristocratic relatives. [45] But the notion that "if the society women of America had their own way, they would set up a monarchy to-morrow," [46] and that the principle of equality was not as generally accepted in America as Europeans had assumed, blurred the republican image of the United States abroad. Actually, the overwhelming majority of Americans opposed titles and aristocratic ideas, as well as a military caste and even an intellectual elite. [47] The relatively few eccentric exceptions in this regard did not justify the considerable publicity they received.

It was not at all surprising that, with very few exceptions, members of the American colony in Paris found the doors of French society closed to them. They really had very little in common. They organized therefore their own salons and dinner parties and socialized a great deal among themselves. Social cliques and gossip contributed some excitement to their otherwise usually uneventful

44. Contemporary American diaries and travel journals cited many specific illustrations in support of this contention. As one Frenchman correctly observed in 1876: "All worshippers of the golden calf are not in the United States." See de Molinari, *Lettres sur les Etats-Unis et le Canada,* 353.

45. See Elsie Porter Mende, *An American Soldier and Diplomat: Horace Porter* (New York, 1930), 226; Richard Harding Davis, *About Paris* (New York, 1895), 198–200.

46. Max O'Rell, *A Frenchman in America* (New York, 1891), 61.

47. Augustus J. Thébaud, *Three Quarters of a Century* (1807 *to* 1882), *A Retrospect: Forty Years in the United States of America* (New York, 1904) 105–106.

lives. [48] The ladies often took the lead in social snubs which kept the American colony seething. At times they would assume the air of the *grande dame,* offending former American acquaintances in a rude and uncivil manner. They would not invite to dinners and parties certain families whom they considered beneath them, or they would decline invitations because the drawing room of some American lady in Paris was allegedly not a proper place for well-bred ladies to be seen in. Feuds also arose when formerly friendly families suddenly and intentionally abstained from "sending their elegant carriage with the splendid pair of American horses to take an airing in the Champs Elysées or the Bois de Boulogne." Otherwise, the colony liked to make its presence known on public occasions, playing an ostentatious role at official celebrations and funerals. Among its constructive contributions was the opening, in the early 1840s, of an "American Athenaeum," at which books, magazines, and newspapers from back home were made available. Such cultural ambassadors in Paris as Consuls David Bailie Warden, Robert Walsh, and John Bigelow did their utmost, particularly through their connections with members of the prestigious Institut de France and Académie des Sciences, to disseminate information about literary and scientific progress in the United States. To enlighten Frenchmen about American culture, Eugene A. Vail published in 1841 his *De la Littérature et des hommes de lettres des Etats-Unis d'Amérique.* By being instrumental in introducing cultured American visitors to important French connections, American residents in Paris served as a very useful link in efforts to break down stereotyped Franco-American prejudices.

The whole mode of living of the large majority of the colony remained essentially American, including the preparation of food. Appreciating neither the intellectual nor the gastronomic sophistication of the French, they preferred ordinary American meals to the most exquisite French cuisine. Amusingly, though, they liked others to think of them as being wicked when at worst

48. Gabriel Edward Manigault, "Autobiography," 131–32, UNC. See also Davis, *About Paris,* 190–97.

they were not quite so puritan as their ancestors. In the post-Civil War period American girls danced cancans at the Jardin Mabille or the Château des Fleurs, an exhibition they would not have dared at home.[49] And while Frenchmen would not have hesitated openly to admit the existence of a mistress, Americans were customarily more discreet about their not-so-innocent love affairs. The reputation of Paris as a naughty city did not keep scores of Americans away from it.

Nevertheless, it was undoubtedly reassuring to many folks back home when a Presbyterian minister reported in 1896 that, in spite of invitations "to be immoral in order that they may have every sort of experience, and thus be able to thoroughly understand life," the resistance to great temptations by the more than three thousand American students in Paris compared favorably with that of students in any large city in America.[50] French students gave the Latin Quarter an unsavory reputation. This by no means justified categorizing American students, who had moved into the quarter to be closer to schools and to reduce living costs to a minimum, as similarly unconscionable bohemians. As another clergyman observed in 1902: "The sacrifices of many" of these serious and talented American students "are beyond anything imaginable or endurable in America. . . . It is a life of such privation and unselfish devotion to work that none but brave hearts could endure it."[51]

The great mass of the American people led simple and modest lives. Both their Calvinistic background and their democratic roots had taught them the virtues of simplicity. As the years went by, their pride in being Americans made them ever more ardently clamor for a truly American culture. But when it came to fashions, American society, led by its ladies, bowed to the capricious leadership of Paris. Quite a few American guardians of moral

49. Henry Morford, *Paris in '67* (New York, 1867), 62; Henry Armitt Brown, "Journal in Europe, 1866–1867," July 21, 1866, PHS.
50. Samuel P. Kelly, "The Truth Concerning American Students in Paris," *Quartier Latin,* I (July, 1896), 27–28.
51. Sylvester W. Beach, "The American Student in Paris," *Independent* (September 25, 1902), 2307–2308.

standards found it difficult to understand why virtuous women would want to follow the often bold and shameless leaders of French fashion.[52] The "scandalously low" dress at times worn at the imperial court of Napoleon III offended their good taste and their notion of wholesome standards. Ironically, American women did not seem to possess that sense for good taste that was so highly cultivated in France. French women understood instinctively that certain fashions were appropriate only for certain occasions and that it might be ludicrous and in bad taste to wear an elegant dress or a fancy hairdo in the wrong social setting. At any given time Parisians tolerated a variety of styles that gracefully avoided the stereotyped dominance of a new fashion.[53]

American tourists, both middle class and wealthy, found Paris a fascinating place for shopping. They spent their money lavishly on perfumes, jewelry, china, and furniture. French milliners and dressmakers occupied much of the time of well-to-do American ladies who crossed the ocean each year to keep up with the latest fashions.[54] Frenchmen were well aware of the fact that American men felt much more comfortable in London than in Paris. They went out of their way therefore to please the American ladies, who usually felt at home in Paris, speaking French, as many of them did, and altogether appreciating the refinement of French culture more than their husbands. Many of them left a little fortune in Paris for the purchases that they brought back home and that became for a long time a topic for conversation that added an air of sophistication to their lives. Even if they could afford very expensive jewelry, they were rather intrigued by the fact that the highest French society accepted it as perfectly legitimate to wear

52. H. A. Delille, "American Women and French Fashions," *Harper's Magazine,* XXXV (1867), 118–20; see also "Parisian Fashions and the Demi-Monde," *Atlanta Constitution,* August 25, 1870.

53. Henry P. Tappan, *A Step from the New World to the Old and Back Again* (2 vols.; New York, 1852), II, 261; Howard Mumford Jones, *America and French Culture,* 1750–1848 (Chapel Hill, 1927), 282–89.

54. Elizabeth Van R. De Peyster, diary of a trip to Europe in the latter part of the nineteenth century, NYHS; Denis William Brogan, *The Development of Modern France* (1870–1939) (London, 1953), 413–14.

imitation jewelry.[55] The best of it was practically indistinguishable from precious stones, and it appealed to the American sense of economy and beauty because it could be thrown away as fashions changed.[56]

Social and Sociological Comparisons

The private and public morals of a people are not only conditioned by its social traditions and political, economic, and religious institutions, but to some extent by a variety of foreign influences as well. The observations of travelers abroad and the images conveyed by foreign literature perhaps stimulated in the nineteenth century more comparison than emulation of habits and styles of life. As superficial as the general impressions thus gained undoubtedly were, they nevertheless helped shape the images in which Frenchmen and Americans saw each other. Curiosity about women and their world on both sides of the Atlantic led to many fascinating comments. The prevailing American view of French women accepted the sketches of Honoré de Balzac's and George Sand's heroines at face value. Reputedly, the women violated just about every moral decency. And as gallant and devoted as French men seemed to be to women, unlike Americans who treated their female companions with instinctive respect, French men appeared to treat them as attractive dolls.[57] Equally astonishing to Americans was the notion that in France love was an affair of married women, not of girls. French parents watched their daughters very carefully and guided them prudently before marriage. Customarily, the payment of a dowry provided the young couple with a desirable economic

55. Théodore-Justin Roustan to Eugène Spuller, May 31, 1889, CPEU, Vol. 165, AMAE; Catherine Brooks to her mother, March 19, 1868, NYHS.

56. For comments and references regarding French-American economic relations, see Chapter III herein.

57. Roving American, "French Morals and Manners," *Appleton's Journal of Popular Literature, Science, and Art* (April 24, 1869), 115; see also the editor's comments about French treatment of women in *Harper's Magazine*, VIII (1854), 268–69; and Emma Willard, *Journal and Letters from France and Great Britain* (Troy, N.Y., 1833), 62–63.

foundation on which to build a happy marriage. On occasion, some partners discovered that they were not really made for each other and sought satisfaction in escapades.

In the later part of the nineteenth century American tourists in France confessed bewilderment about this strange society which honored its ladies, but apparently closed its eyes when the integrity of the institution of marriage was violated. How else could Americans interpret the fact that in 1864, for example, nearly 28 percent of the births in Paris were illegitimate?[58] The imputed looseness with respect to conjugal faith in the higher and middle classes of French society may indeed have been exaggerated by French writers of fiction who chose to concentrate on the unwholesome aspects of Parisian life. And commercial interests may have deliberately exploited the reputation of Paris as "Sin City." Undoubtedly, however, the divorce laws in France were, in the words of the New York *Times*,[59] "simply barbarous." At best, they merely permitted a miserable pittance for the wife and, significantly, made it impossible for both partners to marry again. By the end of the century, the number of separated couples in France was rising at the relatively small rate of six thousand a year.[60] This state of affairs encouraged the higher classes even more than the bourgeoisie to forget virtue in search of personal happiness.

There was something about French women, particularly a Parisienne, that set them apart from all other women. Perhaps

58. Edward Gould Buffum, *Sights and Sensations in France, Germany, and Switzerland* (New York, 1869), 194. This high percentage of illegitimate births in Paris was somewhat misleading because many unwed mothers came from the provinces to Paris to escape embarrassment. Adna Ferrin Weber, *The Growth of Cities in the Nineteenth Century: A Study in Statistics* (Ithaca, N.Y., 1963), 405. See also "Journal of a Trip to England and France, 1864–65" (MS in William H. Brawley Papers, UV), 66–67; and Gerard Beckman to his father, December, 1864, NYHS. The sizable number of abandoned children, in one decade as many as 44,243, were cared for in a foundling home in Paris, the ancient Hospice des Enfants Trouvés. Thomas Hungerford Giddings, "Yankee Journalists in Europe, 1830–1848" (Ph.D. dissertation, Columbia University, 1956), 238.
59. New York *Times,* July 18, 1879, p. 4.
60. "Divorce in France," New York *Times,* June 12, 1884, p. 4.

not as beautiful as American women, according to many American comments, they were more feminine. Their graceful carriage, their elegant costumes, their dainty boots, and their perfectly gloved hands identified them. They enjoyed the reputation of being chic and having a pleasing air about them.[61] The New York *Times* ventured to assert that, as a rule, French women seemed "superior personally, morally, and mentally to French men . . . and to have more mind, industry, energy, and general capacity than the men have."[62] Instead of being narrowly confined to the family hearth and living in a romantic dreamland, French women were conspicuous in the business world long before the women's rights movement in Great Britain and the United States asked that the doors be opened to women in various fields of employment. They were often in charge of a business; many served as attendants and bookkeepers in shops and theaters.[63] Their business sense also enabled them occasionally to bring their influence to bear on the political life of their country. Permitted to earn higher degrees at the Sorbonne and the Collège de France, French society women displayed much more sophistication and a wider range of cultural interests than most American ladies. With the extraordinary capacity of the latter, however, to adapt themselves, at home and abroad, to changing circumstances, the Europeanization of American life was progressing rather rapidly by the turn of the century.[64]

Puritan traditions exercised a profoundly restraining influence on American society, and the people's deeply rooted democratic experience tended to encourage the pursuit of happiness and the

61. See James Jackson, Jr., to Elizabeth C. Jackson, February 2, 1832, MHS; George William Curtis to Christopher P. Cranch, January 10, 1849, MHS; Andrew D. Mellick, "Journal, Europe, 1880," pp. 28–29, MS at Rutgers University.

62. New York *Times*, August 5, 1878. About the complex status of French women, see Adeline Daumard, *La Bourgeoisie Parisienne de 1815 à 1848* (Paris, 1963), 357–76; and Frances Trollope, *Paris and the Parisians in 1835* (New York, 1836), 262–68.

63. Edith Wharton, *French Ways and Their Meaning* (New York, 1927), 111–12; Buffum, *Sights and Sensations*, 145.

64. Charles Victor de Varigny, *La Femme aux Etats-Unis* (Paris, 1893), 304–306; Henry Gaillard, "La Condition des femmes dans la législation des Etats-Unis" (Ph.D. dissertation, Université de Paris, 1899), 180–90.

freedom of the individual. These realities shaped the family life
of Americans in a manner very different from that of Frenchmen.
Divorce was relatively easily obtained in America, but it was
socially frowned upon. On the other hand, there was no country
in the world, as Alexis de Tocqueville wrote, "where the tie of
marriage is so much respected as in America."[65] What surprised
Frenchmen more than anything else was the freedom that girls
and women enjoyed in the United States. That American women
could travel alone without fear of being molested spoke well for
the progress of American civilization. Equally astonishing were
coeducational schools and the free association of American boys
and girls in their social lives. That American girls could choose
their own husbands caused considerable eyebrow-raising in France.
Frenchmen failed to understand that the innocent love affairs of
American youth prepared them for early marriage and helped to
develop an independence that French youth was customarily
denied.[66] One aspect of American family life which the French
found both amusing and objectionable was the special consideration shown to young girls. Their families often spoiled them in a
well-meaning but nevertheless questionable way.[67] American women appeared to start their social lives at the top, becoming bored
as the years went by rather monotonously. Americans conveyed the
impression that love was something for young people and that they
became prematurely old before they reached thirty.[68]

65. Alexis de Tocqueville, *Democracy in America* (2 vols.; London, 1835–40;
New York, 1900), II, 230; Alexis de Tocqueville, *Correspondance Inédite*, in *Œuvres
Complètes* (9 vols.; Paris, 1864–67), VII, 27, 66–67.

66. Young American girls were indignant at "the strict watch to which French
girls submit." Léodile de Champceix, *The American Colony in Paris in* 1867 (Boston,
1868), 8. See also Louis Wuarin, "La Femme et le féminisme aux Etats-Unis,"
Bibliothèque Universelle, LXIV (1894), 64–93.

67. At the end of the century, a critical American cautioned Frenchmen that
the vaunted freedom and independence of American girls and women produced
undesirable social consequences: "the rapidly diminishing importance of the family
as a social unit, the epidemic of divorce, the young girl's shrill and grating bump-
tiousness . . . domestic incapacity, extravagance, nervous invalidism, [and] morbid
sex consciousness." Alvan F. Sanborn, "French Open-mindedness," *Atlantic Monthly,*
LXXXIV (1899), 850.

68. See Genevieve Gregg Hubbard, "French Travellers in America, 1775–1840:
A Study of Their Observations" (Ph.D. dissertation, American University, 1936),

The "most stupid" development in the United States that alarmed the French was the women's rights movement. The notion that otherwise charming girls would want "to wear the pants" and enjoy equal rights in the social and political life of the nation threatened to blur the dividing line between the masculine and feminine members of society. This majority view was characteristically modified by the artist Rosa Bonheur who, when asked whether she had given any attention to the women's rights question, responded: "Women's rights! Women's nonsense! Women should seek to establish their rights by good and great works, and not by conventions. . . . I felt the power within me to paint. I cultivated it. . . . I have no patience with women who ask permission to think!"[69]

To the amazement of Frenchmen, married men in America did not possess the authority fathers and husbands exercised in Europe. They regarded it as a sign of weakness that American men could not defend themselves physically against a woman. And their heavy dependence on women for counsel and inspiration further indicated the extraordinary, if not superior, position women occupied in American life. From the point of view of perceptive French observers, however, what transcended these apparent weaknesses was the pride American men took in their ability to earn an honest living for themselves and their families. Whether they were poor or rich, young or old, the overwhelming majority of them liked to work and thus secure their independence rather than rely on dowries or some other form of degrading, unearned financial support. This independence underpinned their sense of freedom. There was also nothing artificial about them. Their lack of affectation clearly distinguished them from French men, reputedly even to the delight of French women.[70] The emphasis on

---

45; and John de Witt McBride, Jr., "America in the French Mind during the Bourbon Restoration" (Ph.D. dissertation, Syracuse University, 1954), 28.

69. "A Morning with Rosa Bonheur," DJM, XV (September 24, 1859), 205. See also Armand Parrot-Larivière, *Mes Pérégrinations aux Antilles françaises et aux Etats-Unis d'Amérique* (Paris, 1868), 23.

70. The affectation of American women, on the other hand, seemed to be more pronounced than that of French ladies. Willard, *Journal and Letters*, 170.

youth in America was another distinguishing feature. In France, men of age and experience usually occupied the important executive positions. In the United States, energetic and ambitious young men, capable of taking their chances with untried methods and programs, were entrusted with major responsibilities.[71]

To bring sociological complexities within the range of comprehension, Frenchmen and Americans considered it perfectly legitimate to single out dominant, even if not always universally observable, characteristics with respect to each other. Actually, throughout the nineteenth century Frenchmen knew less about the American people and the United States than Americans knew about France and its people. Frenchmen not only traveled abroad less than Americans, their controlled press often presented a distorted picture of the United States in order to reduce the favorable impact of its republican institutions on the monarchical system of France. In essence reiterating an attitude expressed throughout the nineteenth century, a French gentleman wrote in 1802 from Boston:

The admission of an infinite number of Foreigners to the Rights of Citizenship . . . has produced fatal Effects upon the National Character. From hence arises that heterogeneous Mixture of Manners, Habits, Morals, and Sentiments which are found among Pennsylvanians and the other Inhabitants of the Central States. They have no fixed Point, no solid Opinions, and are continually fluctuating between Right and Wrong, between Men and Principles. The possession of the social Virtues which everywhere form the Charm of Society have unfortunately but very little Influence when political Power is the Object of Pursuit. The citizens of Pennsylvania and New York are a proof of this Truth. They are generally humane and hospitable, and it is with Reason that they are reproached with a too great Cupidity in the Persuit [sic] of Money . . . a prevailing Stimulus which naturally arises in a Country where Riches alone establish Distinction among the Citizens.[72]

71. Marie de Grandfort, *The New World* (New Orleans, 1855), 128.
72. "Letters to l'Amérique du Nord," correspondence of a French gentleman who was a resident in the United States from 1795 to 1803, Misc. MS 1802, APS. Half a century later, Alexis de Tocqueville anticipated disturbing complications in America because of the great influx of foreign immigrants. The final test of democratic institutions, he suggested to Gustave Beaumont, might be adversely affected by it. Tocqueville, *Oeuvres Complètes*, VI, 266–68.

The American passion for money-making as a goal of life was not universally condemned by Frenchmen, because the Americans were not just savers or greedy hoarders; they made money to spend it in an effort to ameliorate man's earthly existence. While the Yankees' outlook was materialistic, as was that of many other nations, more than one observer suggested that the time would come when Americans would lend a hand to the aging civilizations of Europe and Asia because "generosity is like the essence of their race."[73] The prospect that the land of generosity and liberty would in the future carry the torch of civilization was as encouraging to French admirers of the model republic as it was frightening to those who held it in contempt.[74]

Whatever the shortcomings of Americans, they commanded great respect as a result of their restless search for a better life, their self-reliance, their youthful energy, their willingness to take risks and explore untried methods of doing things.[75] As essential as the Judeo-Christian and cooperative spirit of Americans was in the growth of their country, their determination to defy difficulties seemed an equally distinctive trait. Unlike Frenchmen, however, Americans had not cultivated a high degree of sensibility and delicate refinement. In their land of contradictions, a friendly French commentator contended in 1897, "far too much is done,

73. Emile Carrey, *Grandeur et avenir des Etats-Unis* (Paris, 1863), 6, 46–48; Isidore Loewnstern wrote in his *Les Etats-Unis et la Havanne: Souvenirs d'un voyageur* (Paris, 1842), 225: "I see in the future that this country will exercise a happy influence on the well-being of the world; but I would not like to live there."
74. See René Lefèbvre, *Paris in America*, trans. Mary L. Booth (New York, 1863), v; Mary S. Owen, "An Analysis of the Frontiersmen Based upon the Observations of Contemporary French Travellers" (Ph.D. dissertation, Indiana University, 1956), 522; Durand Echeverria, "Antoine Jay and the United States," *American Quarterly,* IV (Fall, 1952), 235–52; and Henry Blumenthal, *France and the United States: Their Diplomatic Relations, 1789–1914* (Chapel Hill, N.C., 1970).
75. Firmin Roz, *L'Energie américaine* (Paris, 1910), 33; Marie Dugard, *La Société américaine* (Paris, 1896). Ambassador Jules Cambon would have liked to see French university students spend some time in the United States to acquire "something of that spirit of initiative which is characteristic of American youth." Jules Cambon, *France and the United States: Essays and Addresses* (New York, 1903), 29.

far too little is thought out."[76] Long before that time, Frenchmen asserted that Americans were too busy to appreciate the aesthetic and intellectual aspects of life: they studied to apply their knowledge, not to enjoy it for its own sake; substance interested them more than form, accomplishment more than method.[77]

Whatever the merit of such broad observations, some Frenchmen knew enough about America to make regional distinctions. In their judgment, the society of Philadelphia, "the Athens of the New World," fared almost as well as that of Boston. In both cities culture seemed to be pursued for its own rewards rather than for lucrative ends. The ability to converse about intellectual subjects certainly set Bostonians apart from New Yorkers whose "commercial habits and financial spirit" rendered them "so vulgar."[78] The Old South, in general, and Virginians and Charlestonians, in particular, were usually singled out for special praise. The elegant manner of the old southern society—their ease, their grace, their hospitality, and, in contrast to the cultural centers in the Northeast, their notable freedom from pedantry in intellectual discussions— made Frenchmen feel at home.[79] By the same token, the relatively uncivilized life on the frontier of the West and Southwest, where "the very scum of society" sought "adventure and illicit gains," disgusted Frenchmen. Contrary to boastful American claims to moral, material, and institutional superiority over the rest of the human race, the severest French critics decried the bad faith of Americans who, one of them claimed, "with few exceptions are as dishonest as the Chinese."[80]

The nineteenth-century American image of the French people identified them as industrious and thrifty, ambitious and essentially

76. Price Collier, *America and the Americans: From a French Point of View* (New York, 1897), 274–75.

77. E. Regnault and J. Labaume, *Suite des Etats-Unis depuis 1812 jusqu'à nos jours* (Paris, 1849), 158.

78. Paul L. White, "American Manners in 1830," *Yale Review*, XII (1922), 124.

79. Achille Murat, *America and Americans* (New York, 1849), 246–47.

80. Jacques Benjamin Comte de Saint-Victor, *Lettres sur les Etats-Unis d'Amérique* (2 vols.; Paris, 1835), II, 201–205; see also Abbé Emmanuel Domenech, *Missionary Adventure in Texas and Mexico* (London, 1858), 228–31.

conservative—people with a keen sense for beauty and an unusual appreciation of the creative arts and literary skills. But, regrettably, Americans saw the French also as a people without morals or religion, superficial, vain, and parochial. In view of the French nation's love of glory and its aspirations for a leading role in international affairs, its complacent ignorance about foreign lands and peoples struck Americans as incredibly incongruous. Indeed, some attributed the relative decline of France as a world power to the conceit of its people. Believing that *la belle France* represented the most advanced stage of civilization, one that foreigners from all parts of the world came to study and admire, the large majority of Frenchmen simply concluded that it was not particularly worthwhile for them to leave France or to explore the non-European world.[81]

On the whole, informed Americans appreciated the refinement that typified the French style of life. But time and again they were repelled by French emphasis on external appearances, on beauty, grace, charm, elegance, and wit. Excelling in these respects, Frenchmen developed an air of superiority based on unrealistic appraisals of their true place in the family of nations. The appearance in the late nineteenth century of Germany, Italy, Japan, and the United States on the international chessboard of powers and the impact of the industrial revolution on modern civilization at best subordinated to an ornamental place the social values Frenchmen identified with a superior civilization. In the modern age, substantive material progress and the virtues most conducive to its promotion were increasingly considered the desirable goals of civilization. Because of their pragmatic nature, these goals were expected to serve socially moral ends by benefitting the masses rather than satisfying self-centered individuals. Throughout the century American critics of French society deplored its "colossal

---

81. W. C. Brownell, *French Traits: An Essay in Comparative Criticism* (New York, 1902), 283; see also an anonymous review of A. F. de Bacourt's memoirs in *Atlantic Monthly*, LI (1883), 272. Not even civil servants were looking forward to going abroad. "French and German Colonization," *Nation*, LXV (December 16, 1897), 471.

vanity."[82] The occasional brilliance of some of their compatriots hardly justified the condescension with which Frenchmen all too frequently treated foreigners—particularly Americans, whose boastfulness, informality, and materialism they found annoying and at times detestable. Such snobbishness naturally caused resentment and, occasionally, unfortunate insults. Mark Twain, for instance, reacted to Napoleon's alleged comment that Americans were frequently embarrassed to trace their grandfathers by responding that some Frenchmen might be embarrassed to identify their fathers.[83] Such a rebuttal not only flattered the national ego of Americans, it also reinforced their belief that the French were immoral. Protestant prejudices tended to sustain this persistently held notion with respect to the cultivated pagans of the nineteenth century.

This unflattering reputation was sometimes modified by Americans who could not reconcile it with other, deeply rooted, French traits. Whatever moral laxity may have been tolerated by the upper classes in Paris, the middle and working classes in the provinces and Paris generally valued domestic affections with more sincerity than they were given credit for. The delight of the French people in proprieties and politeness reflected an almost religious respect for the other person and constituted a manifestation of a high degree of morality. A society that assiduously cultivated civilized manners and good taste in human relations and fondness for pets offered no refuge to vulgarity and barbarism.[84] By themselves, the external graces may at times have looked grotesque

82. Alice James, *The Diary of Alice James* (Cambridge, Mass., 1894), 133; Ruth Putnam (ed.), *Life and Letters of Mary Putnam Jacobi* (New York, 1925), 112–13.

83. August Lynn Altenbernd, "The Influence of European Travel on the Political and Social Outlook of Henry Adams, William Dean Howells, and Mark Twain" (Ph.D. dissertation, Ohio State University, 1954), 229.

84. James Gordon Bennett, editor of the New York *Herald*, thought the French were "far more religious and moral than the English," because their morals resulted "from taste and propriety, not from the gloomy austerity of a creed." See New York *Herald*, September 18 and 27, 1838. See also, C. E. Norton (ed.), *Letters of James Russell Lowell* (2 vols.; New York, 1894), II, 198–99; and F. E. Thomas, "The French," *Musical Courier*, XXXVIII (1899), 12.

and artificial, but once one realized that they acknowledged automatically the dignity of all human beings and facilitated interpersonal relations, one had to admit that these courtesies were far more than superficial. In a real sense they helped to democratize life in France, even at times when political democracy was either taboo or weak. As Ralph Waldo Emerson remarked in the middle of the century: "It is quite easy for any young man of liberal tastes to enter . . . the best houses" of French society.[85] At about the same time the noted American landscape architect Frederick Law Olmsted thought that, in social life, the masses in France and Germany enjoyed "a far higher level" of culture than those in republican America.[86] The unrivaled external splendors in France enriched the life of all classes of people by making available to them, at public expense, art galleries, libraries, and parks. People of all conditions and ages found the boulevards attractive, especially in the evening and on Sundays. The gracious tone and gesture, so typical in the daily life of Frenchmen, nurtured the roots of social democracy and, consequently, those of respect for human existence as well.[87] Self-respect gave French citizens a sense of equality, regardless of their trade, profession, or class, that yielded nothing to the ideal of equality in America. Just as the great sense of humor and courtesy Frenchmen displayed in their daily contact reflected their natural capacity for sensitive human relationships, so their favorite forum of salons as an informal social means of exchanging ideas effectively strengthened the intellectual foundations of French society. So fashionable were these gatherings that Robert Walsh, the highly regarded American

85. Lestrois Parish, "Emerson's View of France and the French," *Franco-American Pamphlet Series*, V (1935), 8.

86. Frederick Law Olmsted, "A Talk about Public Parks and Gardens," *ca.* 1848, LC. Visiting France after thirty-five years of self-imposed exile, Elias Durand wrote to Asa Gray on July 27, 1860: "I see here more security, more justice, more honesty, more true happiness than I have of late seen in the United States" (MS in Gray Herbarium, Cambridge).

87.This respect was also extended to the deceased. Customarily, Frenchmen lifted their hats whenever a funeral procession happened to pass on the street.

consul-general in Paris from 1845 to 1851, successfully conducted the first American salon in the French metropolis.[88]

As far as one can compare and contrast foreign peoples, Frenchmen and Americans resembled each other in many *general* respects. As peoples, they were impetuous and progressive, courageous and aggressive, proud and sensitive. Both claimed superiority over other nations and civilizations; and both enjoyed the reputation of being "swift to resent, and swift to forgive."[89] Both possessed a vigorous capacity for surmounting crises, and both were guided by similar social principles and objectives. In the words of Philarète Chasles, one of the most distinguished mid-century French experts on the United States: "Both believe in the equality of man, which is dangerous; both believe in the essential goodness of man, as if neither passion nor interest existed, which is foolish; both believe that the production of goods offers an irresistible panacea, which is false." Chasles drew the conclusion that "popular tendencies cheapen life in both countries . . . for originality will never be on a par with equality."[90]

In a number of *specific* respects, however, their civilizations and outlooks differed characteristically. In one of his letters from America in 1835, Michel Chevalier, the prominent French economist, observed for instance that "the multitude in the United States is superior to the multitude in Europe, but the higher classes in the New World are inferior to those of the Old."[91] It may not be too farfetched to relate this generalization to the great fluctuations in France between the extremes of aristocratic conservatism and sporadic attempts at militant democracy. In the United States, on the other hand, where education and wealth were more widely

88. Albert Feuillerat, *French Life and Ideals*, trans. Vera Barbour (New Haven, 1925), 118. See also, Anne Marie Dolan, "The Literary Salon in New York, 1830–1860" (Ph.D. dissertation, Columbia University, 1957); and Mary F. Lochemes, *Robert Walsh: His Story* (New York, 1941), 181–84.

89. American Citizens, Paris, *Mr. Whitelaw Reid in France*, 1889–1892 (Paris, 1892), 52.

90. Philarète Chasles, "Les Américains en Europe et les Européens aux Etats-Unis," *RDDM* (February 1, 1843), 451–52.

91. Michel Chevalier, *Society, Manners and Politics in the United States* (Boston, 1839; New York, 1966), 438.

diffused and society equalized, democratic institutions contributed to an extraordinary political and social stability.[92] Unlike French citizens, who preferred literary and brilliant men in high public offices, American citizens generally preferred intellectually mediocre but practical-minded men in executive positions.[93] Quite consistently, Americans valued the application of education, while Frenchmen appreciated its higher intrinsic value. To the French, politeness was as meaningful as rendering a service was to Americans. Frenchmen enjoyed a good conversation; they loved to philosophize and to look backward.[94] Americans were more apt to be taciturn, to do things, to look ahead. Similarly, Frenchmen stressed national glory and individual vanity, whereas Americans emphasized the pursuit of happiness and pride in individual accomplishment. Magnificent castles and public gardens and a strong military establishment were as characteristic of France as comfortable private homes and opposition to an expensive war machine were of the United States.

The number of differences travelers detected in the life-styles of the two peoples seemed endless, and sociologically enlightening. Despite the general nature of most observations, the fascinating conclusion emerged from them that while the American people possessed freer institutions, the French people actually possessed more freedom as individual human beings and therefore led more civilized lives. In France, not just a few privileged people, but the great masses found the time for leisure, the value of which seemed to have escaped most Americans. Publicly supported places of recreation and the availability of a great variety of free or inexpensive entertainments made life enjoyable for these masses. On Sundays, entire families, old and young, rich and poor, participated in such simple pleasures as dancing, singing, and promenading. The common sense and courtesies of French society,

92. "Life in Paris," *Harper's Magazine,* VII (June, 1853), 38–39.
93. Collier, *America and Americans,* 290–92.
94. Exaggerating somewhat, an American tourist observed about Frenchmen: "Give one a half loaf of bread and a novel and he is perfectly happy as long as it lasts." Charles H. Parke, "Notes on Europe," October 28, 1856, p. 143 (MS in Huntington Library, San Marino, Calif.).

moreover, repressed artificial class distinctions by showing concern for the comfort and true happiness of the whole population. Customarily, the French dined elaborately and leisurely, to gratify their appetites; Americans ate fairly simple, though nourishing, meals, merely to appease their appetites, often wastefully leaving food on their plates. The French population never hesitated to show simple-hearted affections in public, unlike Americans who, as a rule, repressed any tender exhibitions, including kissing and weeping, in public.[95] On the other hand, Americans were almost embarrassingly open and outspoken, whereas the French instinctively tended to hide their innermost feelings. And with reference to institutions, it could not be denied that the pressure of public opinion could deprive an individual of his freedom almost as effectively as the repressive methods of a tyrant. A nineteenth-century American possessed the freedom of choice in regard to the many religious denominations flourishing in the United States; but if he did not belong to one of these denominations, his life could be made miserable by his "religious" neighbors.[96] In Paris, one could wear a hat of any form or a coat of any cut or color without attracting the disapproving curiosity of the members of a conforming society boasting of free institutions.

Contemporary Americans and Frenchmen who gave some thought to different conceptions of life found much that puzzled them. As a young nation, composed of a high percentage of young people, America was youth oriented. And yet, in France, where age and experience counted much, young men, especially university students, were more feared and respected, particularly in the first half of the nineteenth century, than in the United States. At the same time, youthful America was more disposed to sustain the respect it once had for a man in his prime years of eminence than was

95. Mary Lesley Ames (ed.), *Life and Letters of Peter and Susan Lesley* (New York, 1909), 65; Sanderson, *Sketches of Paris*, 60–75.

96. Michel Chevalier, *La Liberté aux Etats-Unis* (Paris, 1849), 29–31; see also Augustus Kinsley Gardner, *Old Wine in New Bottles: Or, Spare Hours of a Student in Paris* (New York, 1848), 101; and Ralph L. Rusk (ed.), *The Letters of Ralph Waldo Emerson* (6 vols.; New York, 1939), I, 389–91.

the case in France, where such a man was more readily exposed to the toll of time.[97] In another respect, the French outlook on life displayed not just a certain resignation, but a wholesome maturity. American observers found most striking the modesty and quiet absence of any appearance of ambition in such French intellectuals as the poet Claude André Theuriet and the historian Hippolyte Adolphe Taine. The tranquillity of these men and their willingness to live modestly, and in comparative obscurity, set them apart from most American men. Somehow the medieval pleasure of these Frenchmen "in doing one's work well and in tranquil ease, waiting for it to be appreciated" was quite un-American.[98]

In a significant address delivered near the end of the century before the Society of American Universities a prominent French speaker compared French and American culture.[99] In France, he pointed out, nature continued to be regarded as a magnificent mystery which mathematically oriented scientists simply loved to divine. In America, a determined effort was being made to bring nature under control, with the intent of making life and labor a little easier. As a result of the technological revolution led by America, the Old World, which used to set the tone in the world, was faced with the prospect of having to adopt the new life, a prospect that was anything but enchanting. The triumph of man over nature, the most ingenious application of science and technology to the problems of society, the conquest of distance and time itself, and all the practical comforts the machine age could produce did not impress this speaker as a worthwhile improvement of civilization. "Après tout," he philosophized, "la force n'est pas la gaité, le bienêtre n'est pas le bonheur, l'instruction n'est pas la poésie." Well-being did not necessarily bring happiness and artificially created comforts could deprive humanity of the simple joys of nature and life itself. A certain inner emptiness,

---

97. Samuel F. B. Morse, *His Letters and Journals,* edited and supplemented by his son, Edward Lind Morse (2 vols.; Boston, 1914), I, 89–90.

98. M. E. W. Sherwood, *Here & There & Everywhere: Reminiscences* (Chicago, 1898), 125.

99. Edouard Rod, *Reflets d'Amérique* (Paris, 1905), 111–19.

he feared, would be the end result of the growing mechanization and dehumanization of the modern world. Modern man was therefore likely to accomplish the opposite of what he intended and thought desirable. A sensitive and alert mind like Harriet Beecher Stowe's expressed this same concern a long time before the industrial and technological revolutions were far enough advanced to reveal their effects. Thoroughly captivated by the French people's appreciation of beauty, which led even poor families to "give cheerfully a part of their bread money to buy a flower" for their modest homes, Mrs. Stowe deplored the effect of New England's orientation toward practical efficiency. "There is a long withering of the soul's more ethereal part," she lamented, "a crushing of the beautiful, which is horrible."[100]

100. Harriet Beecher Stowe, *Sunny Memories of Foreign Lands* (2 vols.; Boston, 1853), II, 392.

CHAPTER II

Institutional Differences
and Influences

French Views of American Democracy

From the time of the American Revolution, the republican institutions of the United States aroused a great deal of curiosity. The restoration of monarchy made disappointed French citizens who continued to strive for the political emancipation of man look hopefully to the United States as the great laboratory of freedom. French travelers in the United States who were impressed by "the immensity of the forests, the extent of the waters . . . and the movement and colouring they spread over the landscape"[1] also found much to admire in the American way of life. In the early nineteenth century European visitors were amazed by the simplicity and unpretentiousness of Americans in private life and by their ready availability as public officials. The degree of self-government and the freedom of movement Americans enjoyed in thought, travel, and assembly demonstrated the workability of free institutions beyond the fondest hopes of those Europeans who advocated them. The passage of time merely seemed to confirm that this freedom constituted more a social safety valve than a danger to organized society. America's vast laboratory of social and political thought gave it a headstart worth watching. "While Europe discussed certain

1. Félix de Beaujour, *Aperçu des Etats-Unis depuis* 1800 *jusqu'en* 1810 (Paris, 1814), 38–39.

ideas," commented one French traveler in 1861,[2] "America knows already their faults and advantages from practical experience." Whether Frenchmen sympathized with the United States or regarded it as a growing social and international menace, in the second half of the nineteenth century they treated it as an institutional and technological proving ground.[3]

As was to be expected, French critics gradually began to find fault with the American system. Some became disenchanted with it; others rejected it as an example of maladministration. Unlike Alexis de Tocqueville, who thought that the conservative influence of lawyers in the American government served a beneficial purpose by restraining American democracy, Louis A. F. de Beaucourt, in his *Sketch of the United States*, suggested that lawyers lacked the capacity to govern others. Their legalistic approach to the problems of society, he feared, would be inadequate.[4] Equally serious criticisms were prompted by the political spoils system that invaded the efficient and honest operation of the governmental machine.

Criticisms became more outspoken and numerous after 1830. The rise of the middle class in republican America caused economic, diplomatic, and political differences of genuine concern to the middle class of monarchial France and later on to that of the Third Republic. President Jackson's offensive statements in the course of the Franco-American spoliation controversy in the mid-thirties and his display of personal power and vindictiveness in his controversy with the president of the United States Bank disturbed Frenchmen enough to precipitate realistic reappraisals of the much-too-fast-changing and on the whole ill-mannered American society. Honoré de Balzac, for instance, did not hesitate to react defiantly to President Jackson's threat of retaliation against the French government's failure to honor its spoliation treaty agreement. If, contrary to his expectations, this mismanaged episode should lead

2. Oscar Comettant, *Le Nouveau Monde: Scènes de la vie américaine* (Paris, 1861), 284; Hubbard, *French Travellers,* 407.
3. "Amérique," Paris *Messager Franco-Américain,* July 11, 1850.
4. Beaujour, *Aperçu,* 64–65.

to war, Balzac warned, "France could do much harm to the United States."[5] Leading among those who were lashing out against the national egoism of Americans was the poet and statesman Alphonse de Lamartine. In a chauvinistic article he published in November of 1865, he charged that Americans' "liberty, which is entirely personal, has always in it something hostile to someone else . . . the art of being disagreeable is their second nature. They love no one; no one loves them. . . . It is the expiation of selfishness."[6] Such an antagonistic comment perhaps brought out better than a moderate or friendly one the fact that many Frenchman had long judged the United States and its people from the point of view of Europe's interests. Their European image of America did not necessarily mirror America's realities. French travelers who spent a month or two in the United States and then wrote a book or article about it had acquired only a superficial view of America, and a view colored by their backgrounds and anticipations.[7]

Comparing the quality of American statesmanship in the era of Washington and Jefferson with that of the professional politicians of the late nineteenth century, informed Frenchmen were appalled by the deterioration that had taken place.[8] This impression was in part influenced by their fear of the power and competition of the United States, a continent-sized country with a rapidly growing population that was remarkably industrious and innovative. But there was also genuine concern for the declining moral fiber the French discerned among the industrial-empire builders and political leaders of America, as well as for the growing mediocrity in its administrative offices and decision-making councils. What could be the future of a country in which men of integrity and demon-

---

5. Rémond, *Les Etats-Unis devant l'opinion française*, II, 859–67; Anne Wharton Smith, "Criticism of American Life and Letters in the *Revue Encyclopédique*, 1819–35" (Ph.D. dissertation, Northwestern University, 1943), 93–96, 204–205; K. P. Wormeley, *The Personal Opinions of Honoré de Balzac* (Boston, 1899), 83.

6. Quoted in Beckles Willson, *American Ambassadors to France, 1777–1927* (London, 1928), 285–86.

7. Echeverria, "Antoine Jay and the United States," 235–36.

8. Claudio Jannet, *Les Etats-Unis contemporains ou les moeurs, les institutions et les idées depuis la guerre de sécession* (2 vols.; Paris, 1889), I, 121, 262.

strated ability no longer aspired to positions of leadership in public life?[9] In spite of a high degree of uniformity in the pattern of life in America, it appeared to French observers that somehow individualism was being permitted to ignore the limitations society must set on it. When individual Americans began to act as if the world around them could largely be ignored by them, they began to destroy individual freedom, which is relative rather than absolute and which can survive only within the moral and institutional framework of society.

On the whole, Frenchmen showed a sympathetic interest in the American experiment in self-government. Those who speculated about its evil consequences had to let time pass before their theoretical arguments could be subjected to the test of hard evidence. That time came in 1830 when the coincidence of the July Revolution in France and accelerated American democratization during the Jacksonian era foreshadowed apparently irresistible trends. One has to keep this in mind to understand Alexis de Tocqueville's speculative inquiry, *Democracy in America*. The noble French magistrate's perceptive analyses of American democracy were actually designed to serve as an analytical basis for his wider concern with political institutions in general and the compatibility of liberty and equality within the existing institutional framework of France and the United States. This interest in establishing general principles affecting modern society secured for his work a place in political literature hardly less significant or controversial than Jean Jacques Rousseau's *Contrat social*.[10]

In an exchange of ideas with Tocqueville, François Châteaubriand, the well-known statesman and author, interpreted the revolutionary turn of events in 1830: "The result of the July Revolution is democracy; the principle of the sovereignty of the

9. Emmett H. Anderson, "Appraisal of American Life by French Travellers, 1860–1914" (Ph.D. dissertation, University of Virginia, 1953), 364.

10. Will Mercer Cook, "French Travellers in the United States, 1840–1870" (Ph.D. dissertation, Brown University, 1936), 40; Halvdan Koht, *The American Spirit in Europe: A Survey of Transatlantic Influences* (Philadelphia, 1949), 34–36.

people replaces that of the sovereignty of kings."[11] Although this interpretation was rushing French history by several decades, Tocqueville confided to John Stuart Mill in later years that he went to America to study "democracy" in action, with a view toward possibly drawing lessons from it applicable to the institutional evolution in Europe.[12] Though not an advocate of democracy, Tocqueville helped weaken the prejudices associated with the word from the time of the French Revolution. His enlightening demonstration that democracy did not and could not function in a political vacuum and that it drew its vitality from the moral strength of the nation offered some reassurance to skeptical Europeans. Since the gradual elimination of privilege and inequality had been a long-term historical trend, Tocqueville saw in the early nineteenth-century evolution evidence of this trend progressing at a rather fast pace.[13] Periodical attempts made in Europe to break its momentum, he believed, were unlikely to succeed; for equality, rather than democracy per se, even though destined to bring about the triumph of mediocrity, was sought by an ever-widening circle of people in Europe and America.[14] Tocqueville realized that equality might well be acquired at the expense of individual freedom. With the focus on universal equality, the individual was likely to be lost in the mass; he would have to identify with it or lose his identity altogether. "In the democratic ages which are opening upon us," Tocqueville wrote, "individual independence and local liberties will ever be the produce of artificial contrivance;

11. Quoted in Mlle. Liégeois, *Tocqueville: La Démocratie en Amérique* (Paris, 1933), 5.
12. André Chevrillon, *Alexis de Tocqueville et les Etats-Unis* (Paris, 1936), 13; René Rémond, "Tocqueville et la démocratie en Amérique," in *Alexis de Tocqueville, Livre du centenaire, 1859–1959* (Paris; Centre national de la recherche scientifique, 1961), 188; George W. Pierson, *Tocqueville and Beaumont in America* (New York, 1938), 748.
13. Roger Soltau, *French Political Thought in the Nineteenth Century* (New Haven, 1931), 52–53; J. P. Mayer, *Prophet of the Mass Age: A Study of Alexis de Tocqueville* (London, 1939), 45–50; Charles A. Sainte-Beuve, *Premiers Lundis* (3 vols.; Paris, 1874–75), II, 288.
14. Pierson, *Tocqueville and Beaumont*, 746–47; "On the Centenary of Tocqueville's *Democracy in America*," Yale University *Library Gazette*, X (1935), 37.

centralization will be the natural form of government." In the end, he contended, it will depend upon man "whether the principle of equality is to lead them to servitude or freedom, to knowledge or barbarism, to prosperity or wretchedness."[15]

The historical background of America, a relatively young country with strong equalizing tendencies traditionally at work, held out a much greater hope for the preservation of freedom than the class-structured and historically rooted society of Europe. Not less significant in Tocqueville's judgment were the close links in America between religious faith and individual freedom. Without them, he thought, little hope would be warranted for the survival of American democracy. He was quite sure that the exercise of governmental power without moral restraints, regardless of whether this power was in the hands of the people themselves or used "in the name of the people," would degenerate into tyranny and the ultimate enslavement of the individual in a human rather than a political sense.[16] He also wondered whether a successful war would not destroy the roots of democracy. "There are two things which a democratic people will always find very difficult," he commented, "to begin a war and to end it."[17] The toxic experience of military victory, he suggested, could make both peace and democracy elusive.

For a long time Tocqueville's work stimulated many oral and written discussions of democracy in America and its chances in Europe. French believers in the virtue and efficacy of democratic institutions drew inspiration from his study.[18] They saw in America, as Victor Hugo phrased it, a "society which is itself the affirmation of civilization," free from imposed political guardianship and the

15. Tocqueville, *Democracy in America,* II, 348.

16. Henry Wasser, "Alexis de Tocqueville and America," *South Atlantic Quarterly* (July, 1948), 352–60; Edmond Scherer, *La Démocratie et la France* (Paris, 1883), 8–9; Helmut Göring, *Tocqueville und die Demokratie* (Munich, 1928), 24–25.

17. John Graham Brooks, "A Century of Foreign Criticism on the United States: A Study of Progress," *Chautauquan,* XLIX (1908), 206.

18. Simon J. Copans, "Tocqueville's Later Years: A Reaffirmation of Faith," *Romantic Review,* XXXVI (1945), 14–32; B. Dureau, *Les Etats-Unis en 1850* (Paris, 1891), 390.

plague of standing armies, the curse of Europe. The subordinate role of the military in the affairs of the American republic, as well as freedom of the press, perhaps the most effective restraint on ambitious political leaders, held out the highest hopes for all humanity. To Edgar Quinet, America represented "a safeguard of liberty in the world." This liberty was firmly anchored in the federal system that prevented "the simple and brutal domination of numbers." The American people, others believed, were politically disciplined and socially sophisticated enough to accept legitmate political and social distinctions in their egalitarian society. These qualifications were important, for if democracy should dominate the future, then, speaking for many reluctant liberal Catholics, Count Charles Forbes Montalembert naturally preferred the kind of enlightenment found in America to any servile democracy that would lead to a repressive system.[19]

This was precisely the fear the philosopher Auguste Comte expressed. To him, modern democracy with its universal suffrage was a prelude to anarchy.[20] In order to block the importation of American democracy into France, such an ardent supporter of the monarchical system as Jacques Saint Victor tried to scare people by describing American democracy as the rule of the worst rabble.[21] Many French critics took issue with Tocqueville's contention that the prosperity of the American people and the stability of their political system could be credited to their republican institutions. They contended instead that these virtues should be attributed to the sound moral foundations the British aristocracy had laid in America during the colonial period. If anything, America began to decline morally as its lower classes gained ascendancy.[22]

19. Evelyn M. Acomb and Marvin L. Brown, Jr., *French Society and Culture Since the Old Regime* (New York, 1966), 160.

20. J. P. Mayer, *Political Thought: The European Tradition* (London, 1939), 266.

21. Saint-Victor, *Lettres sur les Etats-Unis*, I, 123.

22. Jannet, *Les Etats-Unis contemporains*, xxi-xxii; A. de Pontmartin, *Nouveaux Samedis* (Paris, 1877), 11.

Different and realistically challenging arguments were those that questioned the very existence of democracy and equality in America. Frédéric Gaillardet, an immigrant lawyer who published the most widely read French newspaper in the United States, the *Courrier des Etats-Unis*, denied the existence of equality and democracy. In his provocatively entitled book, *Aristocracy in America*,[23] he described the United States as a thoroughly aristocratic land in which menial tasks were performed by Negroes and foreigners and in which individuals were free only to the extent that they lost themselves in the crowd. Woe unto him who did not move in the paths laid out by society—for in America, the "people" count, not the individual. Despite considerable political liberty, Gaillardet argued, social liberty was often intolerably restricted by such pressure groups as the Christian Temperance Union, churches, and civic organizations. Several French publications reiterated and expanded these arguments in the final decade of the century. By then, an intellectual elite and economic aristocracy set itself apart from the mass of the American people, only to discover that the "ancient aristocracy," the old patrician families of Boston, New York, Philadelphia, Baltimore, and the South were not opening their doors to the parvenus. Similarly, older generations of native-born citizens often treated the foreign-born with an air of condescension.[24] Talent, wealth, family background, race, nationality, and religion spawned unequal treatment in social, economic, and legal respects and cast serious doubt on the integrity of American democracy and the spirit of equality. The gulf between claims and realities with respect to American democracy seemed to widen embarrassingly as the century neared its end.

Even such an exceptionally well-informed authority on America as the mid-century critic and publicist Emile Montégut (1825–1895) envisioned the possibility of the ultimate displacement of

23. Frédéric Gaillardet, *L'Aristocratie en Amérique* (Paris, 1883), 188–90.
24. F. E. Johannet, *Autour du monde millionnaire américain* (Paris, 1898), 181–228; de Varigny, *La Femme aux Etats-Unis*, 133-36; Anderson, "French Travellers," 63–72.

American democracy by an aristocratic or monarchical system.[25] The heterogeneous ethnic composition of the American population, as well as the size of the country and the rapid growth of the population, seemed to justify this possibility. For that matter, Charles Maurice de Talleyrand, the astute French statesman who knew the young American republic firsthand, remarked once: "It is patent . . . that there is something of a 'republic' in the representative constitution of England and something of a 'monarchy' in the executive power controlling Americans." Presidential power in the United States could assume dominating proportions if a strong and skillful occupant of the White House wished to manipulate it, and a perceptive French parliamentarian who had visited the United States in 1892 for several months detected still another basically undemocratic source of power in its political system. The Constitution of the United States, he maintained, had in fact been replaced by permanent congressional committees. Paul Deschanel contended that these committees "have drawn to themselves all legislative power. The laws are the work of a committee; and in this democratic constitution the democracy has no share in the direction of affairs."[26]

An entirely different approach to the ideal of American democracy was taken by Ernest Renan. In his *Philosophical Dialogues* (1871), written before he became reconciled with democracy, he questioned the compatibility of the desires of the individual and the needs of society in a democratic system. He feared that ultimately "the degenerate masses will care for nothing but the ignoble pleasures of vulgarity." In his considered judgment, "The end of humanity is the production of great men; the great work will be accomplished by science, not by democracy."[27]

From the beginning of the American republic Frenchmen understood clearly, though at times apprehensively, that the outcome

25. Emile Montégut, *Libres opinions: Morales et historiques* (Paris, 1888), 318.
26. "Former French Visitors," New York *Times,* November 9, 1890, p. 12; "French Colonial Power," New York *Tribune,* May 6, 1894, p. 24.
27. "Renan's Latest Work," *Nation,* XXXIII (July 13, 1876), 23–24.

of the novel social and institutional experiment across the Atlantic would, for better or for worse, affect the destinies of Europe. Americans, on the other hand, were too self-assured and self-centered to worry about the impact of Europe's monarchical institutions upon their republic. And as far as France was concerned, even most of those Americans who were very sympathetic toward it had little doubt that it did not provide a fertile soil for republican institutions. Institutional revolutions and political instabiliy weakened nineteenth-century France so much that Americans deplored its evident inability to spearhead the movement toward political emancipation of the masses on the European continent.[28] From the American point of view, it mattered little whether one attributed this historic tragedy to the lack of common sense, to inadequately developed discipline and responsibility, or to excessive intellectualization of political processes.

It took some time before pragmatically oriented Americans and abstract-thinking Frenchmen discovered that the effect of even opposite institutional systems on the freedom of the individual is complex and relative, rather than obvious and absolute. Americans who enjoyed considerable political freedom often felt intellectually and socially restrained by powerful social customs. By the same token, politically restrained Frenchmen often enjoyed an intellectual and social freedom that permitted creative genius to find its natural limits. It must be remembered that the interests of the individual and those of society often differ fundamentally, and their respective interpretations of freedom differ correspondingly. Ultimately, self-realization is the individual's most meaningful test of freedom. For society, this test is the degree of cooperation and/or sacrifice the individual is voluntarily willing to render for the sake of the whole.

28. See de Tocqueville's speech in the Chamber of Deputies, delivered on January 27, 1848, in *Moniteur*, January 28, 1848; Pierre Marcel, *Essai politique sur Alexis de Tocqueville* (Paris, 1910), 374; "French Democracy," NAR (October, 1849), 279–81. Senator John Bell of Tennessee deplored "the arrogant pretensions of the European champions of liberty" because they proceeded upon abstractions instead of founding their theories upon experience. *Congressional Globe*, 32nd Cong., 1st Sess., 442.

Significant Legal and Constitutional Considerations

More light can be thrown on these institutional differences by comparing the legal systems of the two countries. The origins of French and American law differ historically in that one was essentially based on Roman law and the other on common law. The legal by-products of the era of the American and French revolutions, the United States Constitution and the Napoleonic Codes, provided the overall authority in the United States and France respectively. Both the Constitution and the Napoleonic Codes were designed to protect the life, liberty, and property of the individual and to support the principle of equality before the law. Both adhered to the principle of separation of state and church. But while the Napoleonic Codes established legal and judicial uniformity in France, the Constitution of the United States, though the supreme law of the land, had to recognize the supremacy of the states in their respective spheres. The resultant legal and judicial multiplicity in the United States was anything but reassuring to French students of the American legal system.[29]

The situation was further complicated by the unique legal system of Louisiana, a civil-law state in a common-law federation.[30] Even a brief review of its evolution impresses upon us the remarkable tenaciousness of the defenders of the civil-law tradition. Reliance on this "tradition" was prompted by the clarity and security provided by the familiar old Spanish and new French codes and

29. Frederick Longchamp, *Asmodée à New York: Revue critique des institutions politiques et civiles de l'Amérique* (Paris, 1868), 123.
30. See Louisiana Legislative Council, *The Government of Louisiana* (Baton Rouge, 1959), 129-31; Joseph Dainow (ed.), *Civil Code of Louisiana: Revision of 1870, with Amendments to 1960* (St. Paul, Minn., 1961), xv–xxxiii; Lawrence M. Friedman, *A History of American Law* (New York, 1973), 151–55; William W. Howe, "Roman and Civil Law in America," *Harvard Law Review*, XVI (1903), 342–58; George A. Pope, "How Real is the Difference Today Between the Law of Louisiana and That of the Other Forty-Seven States?" *George Washington Law Review*, XVII (1949), 186–98; Sidney L. Harold, "The French Language and the Louisiana Lawyer," *Tulane Law Review*, V (1931), 169–77; and S. B. Groner, "Louisiana Law: Its Development in the First Quarter Century of American Rule," *Louisiana Law Review*, VIII (1948), 380–82.

by the hope that they would protect the Creole population against the social and economic pressures of the Anglo-Americans. But as Jefferson's and later administrations had to resign themselves to toleration of legal pluralism in the United States, Louisiana legislatures and courts repeatedly saw the wisdom of making compromises that amounted to common-law infiltrations into the civil law. Legal precedents and principles established by the courts in previous cases play a decisive role in common law; under civil law, however, codes established by the legislature govern the civil relations of citizens, and judges are not bound by legal precedents. As early as 1805, though, the territorial legislature of Louisiana agreed to be guided by common-law procedures in criminal cases. And while Louisiana had not adopted codes of commerce or of evidence, its common-law rules of evidence have been applied within the framework of civil-law concepts. Instead of the admissibility of evidence so important in common law, for instance, Louisiana courts have been more concerned with its relative significance. It was to be expected, of course, that the steadily increasing number of Louisiana lawyers and judges who did not master the French language sufficiently to understand French codes and legal treatises would object to the perpetuation of these traditions.

In the conflict between the two legal systems and in the competition between French and American civilization, Louisianians sought above all to protect their own identity. Hence, early in the century, their lawyers liked to interpret the term *common law* as meaning the "common law of Louisiana," reflecting the Spanish-French cultural heritage on which it was based. Similarly, and indeed significantly, the incorporation of earlier French provisions into the Civil Code of 1825 divested them of their French identity and made them emphatically part of the Louisiana civil law. In the course of the century Louisiana's legal system tried to cope realistically with the challenges presented by the prevailing law of the land. In this process, Louisiana made concessions and adjustments without abandoning its essentially civil-law base.[31] Its

31. See Elizabeth G. Brown, "Legal Systems in Conflict: Orleans Territory,

special status, however, added an extraordinary and to some degree bewildering diversity to the legal system of the United States. In a larger sense, as Roscoe Pound has pointed out, French law has had little influence on American law. At best, French treatises on law stimulated the reasoning processes of nineteenth-century American judges and courts.

Institutional stability in the United States contrasted so strongly with the repeated upheavals Frenchmen had experienced since the Great Revolution that in 1848 the National Assembly looked to the American Constitution for guidance. Along with several provisions in the French Constitution of 1848 guaranteeing civil liberties and rights, universal manhood suffrage was adopted as a safeguard for popular sovereignty. The Assembly drafting the constitution had no difficulty following the American example by recognizing the principle of separation of powers as fundamental to a free government. The form in which it should be implemented, however, was the subject of a highly controversial debate. The extent of the president's power and the respective merits of a unicameral or bicameral legislature were the central issues in this debate.

Edouard Laboulaye argued eloquently that "a unicameral assembly, erroneously believing itself to be sovereign, constitutes the most dangerous and perfidious political power." He asked the Assembly to be inspired by the prudent American system of two chambers. Its checks and balances, others suggested, were even more essential in France because of her centralized government. But the liberal and radical politicians feared that a second chamber would impair their own power, and they finally voted for a unicameral system. With respect to the presidency, the federal system of the United States justified a strong president with sufficient authority to preserve national unity. The centralized

1804–1812," *American Journal of Legal History*, XXXV (1957), 35–38; Athanassios N. Yiannopoulos (ed.), *Civil Law in the Modern World* (Baton Rouge, 1965), 12–13, 192; Gordon Ireland, "Louisiana's Legal System Reappraised," *Tulane Law Review*, XI (1937), 585–98; Roscoe Pound, "The Influence of French Law in America," *Illinois Law Review*, III (1909), 354–63.

system of France, some deputies argued, needed a head of state with limited powers to prevent executive usurpation of power. But despite these differences, believers in a strong executive adopted the American type of president—one to be popularly elected for four years, or elected by the legislature in case candidates failed to receive an absolute majority. Historically, the extent to which French leaders actually followed American precedents in 1848 seems less significant than the fact that they considered them probingly.[32] Workable political institutions, after all, must essentially be a homegrown product; they cannot be copies of alien experiences which, theoretically, appear to be promising. Central features of the Constitution of 1875 resembled the English form of parliamentary government much more than the American model. That constitution provided for a bicameral legislature and a weak president, one who could neither rule nor reign; the 1875 constitution seemed designed to head off a repetition of the experiences following the election of Louis Napoleon Bonaparte to the presidency of the Second Republic. With the disaster of the Franco-Prussian War in mind, the Constitution of 1875 did incorporate the important provision contained in the United States Constitution: "The President cannot declare war except by the previous assent of the two chambers."

Regarding a number of everyday individual liberties, France was in the nineteenth century far behind England and the United States. Unlike Americans and Englishmen, Frenchmen were not protected in their personal freedom by a *habeas corpus* mandate. And the unavailability of a jury trial in political offenses opened the door to politically controlled court decisions. Michel Chevalier noted in the middle of the century that American law protected the sanctity of the home, as well as the liberty of the individual. To his dismay, he lamented, French policemen could very un-

32. For the debate in the Assemblée Nationale, see *Le Moniteur Universel,* September 6, 8, 27, 1848, pp. 2332–33, 2350, 2605–2606; Eugene Newton Curtis, *The French Assembly of 1848 and American Constitutional Doctrines* (New York, 1918), 164–215, 266, 324–28; Edouard Laboulaye, *Lettres politiques: Esquisse d'une constitution républicaine* (Paris, 1872), 11, 66, 74–75, 88, 91; Frank Maloy Anderson, *The Constitutions and Other Select Documents Illustrative of the History*

ceremoniously invade the home of a citizen and by turning it up-side down violate the rights of a citizen.[33]

Frenchmen were not consoled by the fact that the theory and the practice of law in the United States in regard to protection of life and liberty showed some shocking contradictions. That law-abiding citizens tolerated occasional mob trials climaxing in public hangings and even took the law into their own hands cast much doubt on the existing system of justice and on the moral integrity of the citizens who for too long a time failed to ban effectively such acts of unlawful violence. Although the assertion that the American government was one of law rather than men opened itself to realistic challenges, it was a clearly understood ad-ministrative principle in America that every public officer owed his allegiance to the law rather than to any official. By contrast, the administration of law in France called for the minister to direct the prefect to implement a law. Under the French system, "the prefect's duty of obedience is first to the minister and only in-directly to the law." As far as court cases were concerned, the law's delays were not known in France. Cases were usually tried and decided in one sitting; experts were paid by the courts, questioned only by the judge, and their "expert testimony" was so judiciously handled that even the experts did not know in whose behalf they testified.[34]

One of the more annoying differences of opinion between the French and American governments involved questions of natu-ralization and dual nationality. Throughout the nineteenth century the French government adhered strictly to the principle laid down in Article I of the Napoleonic Decree of 1811 that no Frenchman could be naturalized in a foreign country without the

---

of France (New York, 1967), 522–37, 633–40. On efforts to influence the drafting of the French Constitution of 1848, see Henry Blumenthal, *A Reappraisal of Franco-American Relations, 1830–1871* (Chapel Hill, 1959), 8–13.

33. Chevalier, *La Liberté aux Etats-Unis*, 4.

34. Ernest Freund, "The Law of the Administration in America," *PSQ*, IX (1894), 409; S. Pollak, *The Autobiography and Reminiscences of S. Pollak, M.D.* (St. Louis, 1904), 230–31.

consent of the French government.[35] In practice, the French Courts of Justice generally held that foreign citizenship legally acquired abroad was valid. It was Article X of the Decree of 1811 that caused extended controversies and complications. According to it, any child born of a Frenchman in a foreign country was French in the eyes of the French law as long as a competent tribunal did not decide otherwise. In this respect the French law applied the principle prevailing among the Latin races that citizenship is determined by the nationality of parents and not, as was the case in the United States and Great Britain, by the place of birth. Consequently, the child of a Frenchman born abroad was French, and the child of a foreigner born in France was not French. This meant, time and again, that the American-born sons of naturalized American citizens of French descent were expected to serve in the French army.[36] After years of seemingly endless correspondence, Secretary of State Thomas F. Bayard let the French government know "that the Government of the United States holds that a decree of naturalization granted by it to a French citizen is not open to impeachment by the French government, either in its executive or its judicial branch."[37] He also insisted, with reference to specific instances, "that citizens of the United States whose parents happened to be naturalized American citizens of French descent must be immediately released from forced military service and be compensated for the losses they suffered as a result of such detention." Aside from the extremely important human problems of these cases, there was an irreconcilable legal conflict between the Constitution of the United States and the statutes of France that made American citizens of French descent into French citizens against their will. Secretary of State Elihu Root regretted as late as 1907 that no conventional agreement defined the status of United States citizens of French origin who even temporarily returned to France. Many of the French-Americans who desired to visit France were reluctant to do so because they were

35. Levi P. Morton to Frederick Frelinghuysen, February 5, 1884, DDFDS.
36. Morton to Frelinghuysen, May 6, 1884, *ibid.*
37. Thomas F. Bayard to Robert M. McLane, February 15, 1888, *FIDS.*

afraid of being caught in the web of French conscription laws. The United States welcomed French immigrants, who compared favorably with those from other countries. They were known to be responsible, industrious, congenial, and loyal to the United States while continuing "to cherish a lively affection for the land of their birth." American authorities wished to protect native-born and naturalized American citizens of French descent against the inconveniences in which the French bureaucracy ensnarled them.[38] It was not until the French government enacted the Nationality Code of October, 1945, that this annoying situation was realistically settled.

The American government also made a determined effort to gain for American corporations in France nondiscriminatory treatment, a privilege all foreign corporations enjoyed in the United States. The French law of 1857 subjected branch offices in France to discriminatory legal restrictions which the French government finally lifted by its decree of August 6, 1882. Until then, American corporations were greatly handicapped because they could not bring a suit in a French court of competent jurisdiction. Even after 1882, foreign corporations encountered many discouraging bureaucratic hurdles that in effect resulted in intended advantages for French firms. Whatever the theoretical differences in their legal systems, in both countries practice subjected juridical law to interpretation and legislative law to implementation, with both capable of modifying either law.[39]

Similar frustrations were experienced in regard to extradition. Characteristically, several years passed before France and the United States agreed upon a new extradition treaty to supersede the old Convention of 1843. The new draft Washington submitted to Paris in 1890, trying not only to reconcile different definitions of crime under the French civil code and American criminal law, but also

38. Elihu Root to Robert S. McCormick, January 26, 1907, Numerical File, 1906–1910, DS, Vol. 385, Case 4306. See also, F. H. Lawson, A. E. Anton, and L. Neville Brown (eds.), *Amos' and Walton's Introduction to French Law* (3rd ed.; Oxford, 1967), 34–35.
39. Charles Gerson Loeb, *Legal Status of American Corporations in France* (Paris, 1921), 30, 61, 70, 88.

to specify crimes subject to extradition as exactly as possible, was not ratified until 1911.[40]

In the law-related area of prisons, Alexis de Tocqueville and Gustave Beaumont pointed out that the reformation-oriented American penitentiary system merited study, even if its application in France was not quite feasible.[41] In several respects, such as neatness, ventilation, and food, the American prison system was superior to the French. The American objective of reforming criminals in humanely directed and secure prisons appealed to the French sense of humanity. In regard to the severity of penalties for juvenile offenders, France actually proceeded more intelligently by reforming them through discipline and instruction over a long period of time. In the United States, the young offender served a short sentence; but he was imprisoned with hardened criminals, and thus the punishment frequently turned out to be self-defeating.[42] Beaumont's skepticism concerning prison reform in France grew from two general observations that he thought summed up significant differences between France and the United States. "There is in France," he wrote, "in the spirit of the mass, an unhappy tendency to violate the law." In the United States, "there is a spirit of obedience to the law" that is widely diffused. In France, moreover, religion was identified with authority, and Beaumont could not see how it could assist prison reformers to the extent that it did in America.

Education: Schools, Books, and the Press

Somebody totally ignorant about the relative state of public education in France and the United States in the nineteenth century would most likely take it for granted that in this field the United

40. U.S. Department of State, *Treaty Series, No.* 561 (Washington, D.C.,1911), 1–12.
41. Gustave de Beaumont and Alexis de Tocqueville, *On the Penitentiary System in the United States and Its Application in France* (Carbondale, Ill., 1964), 115–35; Charles Lucas, *Du système pénitentiaire en Europe et aux Etats-Unis* (3 vols.; Paris, 1828–30).
42. "Relation of Education to Prevention of Crime," *De Bow's Review,* XVIII (1855), 416–17.

States lagged far behind France, the leading cultural center. In fact, however, the reverse was true. During the early period of the Restoration a young American student who later became a prominent historian and statesman, George Bancroft, recorded in his diary that several speakers at the French Chamber of Deputies argued in support of public instruction because "the ignorance of the peasantry of France is frightful." In 1844 the Philadelphia *Public Ledger*[43] reported that two-thirds of the French population—peasants, workers, and women—could neither read nor write. Only the remaining third was properly educated, and among these were the brilliant few who actually advanced the frontiers of civilization and gave France the outstanding reputation it enjoyed as a cultural center. Although the Second Empire made a great stride in the fight against illiteracy, obligatory school attendance continued to be postponed. In a letter to an American correspondent, dated December 20, 1873, Hippolyte Taine frankly worried about the future of France under a democratic republic, because "our populace is far more ignorant than yours, there is more class jealousy and far less common sense."[44]

Nevertheless, structurally, American education profited from experiments made in France.[45] The South, in particular, was open to French influences. Impressed by his observation of the schools in Paris, Jefferson implanted "the idea of distinct schools of arts and science" in the structure of the University of Virginia. In the first two decades of the nineteenth century, several American

43. Philadelphia *Public Ledger,* August 23, 1844. According to French sources, one child out of every four in the United States was educated; in Prussia, one out of six; in England, one out of eleven; and in France, one out of twenty. Douglas Johnson, *Guizot: Aspects of French History,* 1787–1874 (London, 1963), 123. In 1839, 57 percent of French conscripts were completely illiterate. Philip Spencer, "The French Reading Public about 1850," *Modern Language Review,* XLV (1950), 473. See also, George Bancroft Diary, June 12, 1821, MHS.

44. Célestin Hippeau, *L'Instruction publique aux Etats-Unis* (Paris, 1878), 204–205; E. Sparvel-Bayly, *Life and Letters of Hippolyte Taine,* 1870–1892 (London, 1908), 129–31.

45. See B. A. Hinsdale, "Notes on the History of Foreign Influence upon Education in the United States," in U.S. Bureau of Education, *Report of the Commissioner of Education for* 1897–98 (Washington, D.C., 1899), 598–603; Elwood P. Cubberly, *Public Education in the United States: A Study of Interpretation of American Educational History* (Boston, 1919), 258–59, 272–73.

colleges carefully studied Napoleon's 1802 law organizing instruction throughout France. Particularly the University of Michigan adopted the French system of public instruction in which the state extended its control from the elementary school to the university.

The French practice of frequently reviewing and revising the school system commended itself to American educators and officials. As the French government studied the German educational system for possible reform in its own, as evidenced by Victor Cousin's *Report on German Education* (1831) , Americans paid close attention to their Gallic friends. The French law of 1833, which François Guizot, then Minister of Public Instruction, helped to adopt, eventually exercised great influence on the development of American schools, initially especially in Michigan and Massachusetts. Cousin's *Report,* in part implemented in the law of 1833, stressed the merits of some form of centralized direction and the necessity for teacher training to maintain uniformly high standards. Believing that "the schoolmaster makes the school," Guizot contended that quality education could not be achieved without state training and certification of all primary teachers.

As Tocqueville had correctly perceived, public education in the United States was designed to help students apply their knowledge to their diverse occupations and to make better citizens of them. The leaders of American society understood perfectly well that its republican institutions would have to be sustained by an enlightened citizenry. Universal suffrage called for universal education. The public schools that developed in America became a great laboratory of democracy in which students from all social classes were imbued with the spirit of equality and individual initiative.[46] In the United States control over education was exercised by the states, not by the federal government. Unlike the French system of centralized control, the decentralized American approach left room for considerable flexibility. Young teachers, many of them women,

46. S. E. Frost, Jr., *Historical and Philosophical Foundations of Western Education* (Columbus, Ohio, 1966), 420–24; Anderson, "French Travellers," 310, 314, 324.

helped to develop the capacities of the future citizens as fully as possible. Much more than in France, local public libraries and inexpensive newspapers also stimulated the reading habits of the well informed American people. In the 1830s Tocqueville could with considerable justification assert that no country in the world possessed so few ignorant and so few learned people as the United States. Later in the century, French professionals were tremendously impressed by the high academic attainments of numerous Americans. What turned out to be of the greatest historical significance was the extraordinary ability of Americans to transform into action and energy what they had learned.[47] French emphasis on intellectual discipline, the value of tradition, and a humanistic orientation in secondary and higher education did not strike Americans as appropriate for their democratic and innovative society. Their pragmatic orientation called for the development of competent, open-minded, and resourceful citizens, not bookwormish intellectuals preoccupied with the past.

In regard to higher education, too, the superiority of French institutions was by no means a foregone conclusion. At given times and in certain fields, such as art, medicine, and music, American students profited from instruction in France.[48] But in the post–Civil War period, American colleges were modeled more after German and English than French universities. Educational considerations determined this course. French professors had long had the reputation of not overexerting themselves. A holiday was a holiday under the Second Empire as much as under the Third Republic:

---

47. Francis Wayland, *A Memoir of the Life and Labors of Francis Wayland* (2 vols.; New York, 1867), II, 24–25. Specialized private schools, such as the Lycée Français in Philadelphia, founded in 1841, afforded French families additional opportunities. In 1845 the French Church of St. Vincent de Paul established a primary school in New York where the French Benevolent Society had already in 1834 opened a free school for French boys and girls to keep them out of mischief. Peter Sheridan, "The Immigrant in Philadelphia, 1827–1860" (Ph.D. dissertation, Georgetown University, 1957), 264; Ernst, *Immigrant Life in New York City*, 141–42.

48. In the pre–Civil War period, many well-to-do French and American families sent their sons to colleges in France. G. W. McGinty, *A History of Louisiana* (New York, 1951), 172.

classes were frequently canceled.[49] An American student who spent three years in France was "frankly bewildered" when the university opened as late as November, and he was shocked by the "carelessness of earnest thought" in lectures on literature.[50]

One of the major differences in the mode of instruction involved the lecture system which prevailed in France and enabled students to listen to eloquent, and often vain, professors. When literary polish took the place of competent scholarship, professors were frequently more concerned with the entertaining effect of the moment than with the thorough training of their students. In the United States, students and professors worked much more closely actively engaging each other in factual and analytical exchanges.[51] In defense of French professors, it must of course be noted that their institutions did not receive the financial support American universities enjoyed. The instruments and facilities available to American scholars in their science laboratories had since the Civil War increasingly attracted the attention of their French colleagues. The accomplishments of higher education in America astonished French visitors. Contrary to their preconceived assumptions about conditions in the business-oriented United States, they found American students intensely interested in science and literature. Equally impressive was the fact that these young American students were so uninhibited that they could address a large audience with perfect ease and good sense. French visitors were amazed to discover that the American educational system produced more scholars and gentlemen than they had expected.[52]

American interest in the French language fluctuated consider-

49. Joseph Blyth Allston to his aunt, November 15, 1855, in Joseph Blyth Allston Collection, SCHS. "Whereas in 1850 a French professor's salary was about 5,000 francs per annum, a well-known professor in America could command as much as 500 francs for one lecture." Philarète Chasles, "Les Américains et l'avenir de l'Amérique," RDDM (May 15, 1850), 662.

50. Henry W. Steed, Through Thirty Years, 1892–1922 (New York, 1924), 37.

51. J. H. Kirkland, "The Influence of German Universities on the Thought of the World," Methodist Review, 2nd ser., VIII (July, 1890), 313.

52. J. H. Grandpierre, Parisian Pastor's Glance at America (Boston, 1854), 34–38; Delaye Gager, French Comment on American Education, 1889–1914 (New York, 1925), 64.

ably during the nineteenth century. The importance of French as an international language was initially reinforced by French refugees to the United States and by the close attachment between the French and American peoples. Strained political relations between the two countries in the middle third of the century and the large scale immigration of North Europeans, however, resulted in a declining interest in the French language. Actually, as far back as 1735, Harvard College had authorized the teaching of the French language. However, when the French instructor who had been engaged for this purpose disseminated "in the college dangerous errors of religion," Harvard promptly terminated his contract and did not resume instruction in French until 1780. At that time the college once again authorized study of the French language—"to such students as their parents or guardians should permit." Realizing that it would be advantageous for the citizens of the commercial seapower into which the United States was developing to know modern languages, George Ticknor shifted the emphasis during his years at Harvard (1819–1835) from classical writers and languages to "living" authors and languages. During the next eighteen years, Henry Wadsworth Longfellow built on this foundation of the Harvard language department, even though his enthusiasm had been somewhat dampened by the fact that his "poetic dreams were shaded by French irregular verbs." Under President Charles F. Eliot, modern languages continued to be encouraged at Harvard. The founding of the Cercle français by its 1874 and 1875 classes attested to the vigorous pursuit of French studies.[53] Columbia, Johns Hopkins, the University of Michigan, and other institutions of higher learning also provided their students with opportunities for studying the language, literature, and history of France. And although post–Civil War high schools also offered modern languages, it was noteworthy on all levels of instruction that about twice as many students preferred German to French

53. Charles Hart Handshin, *The Teaching of Foreign Languages in the United States* (Washington, D.C., 1913), 9–30; Bernard Fay, "La Langue française à Harvard, 1636–1936," in *Harvard et la France* (Paris, 1936), 154–212; Gabriel Compayré, *Enseignement supérieur* (Paris, 1896), 212–19.

and that by about the same ratio girls preferred French and boys German.

To counteract these tendencies, a determined effort was made at the end of the century to boost the study of French culture. But this largely politically motivated appeal did not produce spectacular results. The intent of the boosters was on the whole not matched by techniques designed to stimulate enthusiasm. Students were better prepared to read and write French than to carry on a fluent conversation in it. Contemporaries also criticized many American and other non-French teachers for failing to arouse a genuine interest in the aesthetic and psychological aspects of French culture.

This uneven state of affairs would probably not have arisen had the project of the American Academy of Arts and Sciences in Richmond, Virginia, sponsored by the Royal Academy of France, become a reality, as Thomas Jefferson and the French nobleman Quesnay de Beaurepaire had hoped it would. The aim of this project, which the outbreak of the French Revolution prevented from being realized, was to multiply the cultural and economic ties between the two peoples and, as a welcome by-product, to solidify the political bonds between the two countries.[54] Had French teachers and ideas been afforded the opportunity to decisively influence the shaping of America's educational institutions, the growing desire for complete independence from foreign influences would, nevertheless, have gradually lessened the French hold on American education. The limited area in which this hold actually existed and survived until the end of the century was in Roman Catholic parochial schools.

It appears to be even more significant that until the end of the Second Empire French students were by and large kept in ignorance about the history and institutions of the United States.

54. Le Chevalier Quesnay de Beaurepaire, *Mémoire, statuts et prospectus concernant l'Académie des Sciences et Beaux-Arts des Etats-Unis de l'Amérique, établie à Richmond* (Paris, 1788). See also, Raphaël Georges Lévy, "Les Etudiants américains en France," *Revue internationale de l'enseignement*, XXXIII (1897), 109.

When the French *idéologues* realized that the young American republic did not live up to their preconceived notions of Western civilization, they expressed their disappointment in either harsh criticism or growing disinterest. With the exception of Tocqueville's two volumes on *American Democracy* and the revival in 1830 of the Lafayette legend of Franco-American friendship, relatively little was done in monarchical France to familiarize its people with the growth of the American republic. In the 1860s French professors began to take a renewed interest in English and American culture. Occasionally, they offered a course in American literature; but for another generation no American literary work appeared on their examination lists. As in most other European countries, the French government discouraged courses in American history. Two distinguished French academicians, Edouard Laboulaye and Jules Michelet, who taught American history and frequently drew pointed inferences from it with reference to contemporary conditions in the Second Empire, suddenly found the doors of the Sorbonne and the Collège de France closed.

A great change came after the battle at Sedan, which shocked Frenchmen into the realization that the recent Franco-American estrangement had been unwise and that their educational system needed modernization. President Adolphe Thiers signed a decree on August 12, 1872, making the teaching of United States history obligatory in lyceums.[55] The colleges in Paris and in the provinces henceforth saw to it that future generations of Frenchmen would be better informed about America. More was at stake in this change of attitude than the cultural and political relations with the United States. The traditional orientation toward the Greeks and Romans tended to isolate France intellectually. In rather strong words, Raoul Frary, a noted journalist and social critic, warned his countrymen in 1885: "We have meditated enough on the ruins of classical antiquity; let us open our eyes at last to the

---

55. "America at the Continental Universities," *Appleton's Journal of Literature, Science, and Art,* IX (1873), 494–95; Sigmund Skard, *American Studies in Europe* (2 vols.; Philadelphia, 1958), I, 133–50.

light of the modern world." Gradually overcoming its petit bourgeois conservatism, late nineteenth century France provided its university students with more American studies than other continental countries. The exchange, furthermore, of such prominent professors as Charles Cestre and André Siegfried who lectured in the United States and Barrett Wendell, George Santayana, and Bliss Perry who enlightened students at the Sorbonne before the First World War manifested the new awareness of mutual interest.[56]

Having belatedly become concerned about the fact that American students were in the final decades of the century flocking to German universities, French statesmen and scholars attempted to reverse this trend that was so fraught with political and cultural ramifications. Students were attracted to Germany not only because of the great reputation of its universities, but also because the Germans made it infinitely less cumbersome to earn higher degrees in two or three years than did France. And although American students usually found it more difficult to write German, it was a widely experienced phenomenon that they learned to speak German more readily than French. In 1895, American friends of France—prominent among them the astronomer Simon Newcomb and the Chicago lawyer Harry J. Furber—took the initiative in recommending certain changes that would facilitate the opening up of French universities to American students. This objective was sympathetically furthered by a newly created Franco-American committee that many of the leading French educators supported. By the middle of 1896 this committee could proudly point to a decree issued by the Council of Higher Instruction admitting American men and women to French universities under very liberal conditions.[57] At the same time, the American Chamber of

56. Sigmund Skard, *The American Myth and the European Mind: American Studies in Europe,* 1776–1960 (Philadelphia, 1961), 33–45.

57. Simon Newcomb to Harry J. Furber, September 4, and November 5, 1895, and Harry J. Furber to Simon Newcomb, September 7, 1895, and November 26, 1896, both in Simon Newcomb Papers, container 6, container 22, LC; A. T. Smith, "Education in France," in *Annual Report of the U.S. Commissioner of Education,* 1897–98 (Washington, D.C., 1899), 749–50.

Commerce in France helped to establish the Benjamin Franklin Library in Paris, which constituted an invaluable source of readily accessible information about America.

Before long, the number of Americans pursuing literary and scientific studies in Paris began to increase. In addition to the various doctoral degrees, a certificate of competence in the French language, the Certificat d'études françaises, could be earned by those planning to teach French upon their return home.[58] This new exchange enriched the American nation and the students who had gone abroad, for as those who had studied in Germany had been exposed to German thoroughness and attention to detail, those trained in France received a taste of precise analysis, brilliance, originality, and what is meant by *savoir vivre*. Distinguished French professors were invited to lecture at American universities, particularly Harvard and Johns Hopkins. By the beginning of the twentieth century, privately funded arrangements were made for American exchange professors to lecture in French universities, both in Paris and in the provinces.[59] Besides being mutually stimulating and helpful in the promotion of better understanding, these exchanges afforded educated Frenchmen an opportunity to acquaint themselves with the excellence of American universities and to see the extraordinary progress the United States had made in the arts, sciences, and literature.

Ambassador Jules Cambon (1845–1935), who was intimately familiar with the entire American scene, approached these cultural questions from a political point of view.[60] His analysis led him to the realistic conclusion that for the last 150 years France had been relatively disinterested in America. France's energies had been devoted instead to extending its intellectual and political influence in the Orient. Cambon believed that the changing con-

58. "Americans at the University of Paris," *Nation,* LXVIII (May, 1899), 352–53. See also, Henri Merou to Théophile Delcassé, March 30, and April 12, 1899, in *Questions culturelles et scientifiques, 1897–1907,* AMAE.

59. "American Lectures in Paris Popular," New York *Times,* December 4, 1904.

60. Jules Cambon to Théophile Delcassé, April 14, 1899, in *Questions culturelles et scientifiques, 1897–1907,* AMAE.

stellation of power in the world made it imperative that France cease to neglect America. But what steps could be taken toward closer alliance with a country that counted some thirty million people of German and Irish descent and only about two million of French descent? In Cambon's judgment, these two million Americans merited top priority, for they constituted the nucleus for any effective cultural-revival efforts France might undertake. And these efforts, he further recommended, should be concentrated on regions in which people of French descent were living together in a fairly compact fashion—as in New Orleans, many Mississippi Valley villages, and in New England where nearly one million French Canadians had settled. Cambon expected cultural-revival efforts to pay political dividends as well. He realized that French-Americans could be politically effective only in communities in which they predominated, or if, as a cultural unit, they developed sufficient strength to influence their state legislatures and perhaps even the federal government, as German- and Irish-Americans had done all along.

Economically, France could not compete with the Germans in the United States. The negative reaction in the "pharisaic" United States to avant-garde French literature and the competitive outlook of even those American artists who had attended French schools discouraged reliance on popular support. Therefore, in 1902, Cambon suggested to Théophile Delcassé, the minister heading the Quai d'Orsay, that another way for France to enhance its influence in the United States was to enlist the cooperation of American society women.[61] In his judgment, these women exercised an immense influence in the United States, and many of them still admired French culture so much that they continued to regard the knowledge of French as a socially desirable asset. And Cambon repeatedly reiterated that the region in which France would find the greatest sympathies was the Midwest, the region that promised to hold the key to America's future.

61. Cambon to Delcassé, April 8, 1899, *ibid.*

The Transatlantic Press

A few individuals truly interested in acquainting the French and American people with each other recognized early in the nineteenth century the importance of exchanging books and articles. Making one country's publications available to the other country obviously meant more when distance constituted a far greater barrier than in the jet age. Government officials and the learned professions in both countries were eager for vitally needed information. They wholeheartedly supported the international exchange of printed materials that was originally systematically pursued by David Bailie Warden (1772–1845), the Irish-born American consul who after 1814 spent his retirement in Paris. In the middle of the century, the exchange was further pursued by Alexandre Vattemare, the United States agent of the International Exchange System.[62] In France, the *Revue encyclopédique* went to great lengths to collect and disseminate literary, scientific, and technical writings that kept Europe abreast of developments in the United States.[63]

François Guizot, the noted French historian and statesman, reported in 1855 that "by way of the international exchanges more than 70,000 American volumes have already been brought to France, and over 100,000 French volumes taken to America."[64] Guizot did not limit himself to this quantitative statement; he *interpreted* these formal exchanges as abundant proof that the notion of American civilization being exclusively devoted to the pursuit of material values "is one of the vulgar slanders which

62. Hippolyte Vattemare, "Notes of the Life of Alexandre Vattemare: Founder of the System of International Exchange," *Historical Magazine*, 2nd ser., IV (December, 1868), 297–300; William Crawford Winlock, "The International Exchange System," in George B. Goode (ed.), *The Smithsonian Institution*, 1846–1896 (Washington, D.C., 1897), 398–99. Vattemare has been credited with having added 300,000 volumes to American libraries.

63. McBride, "America in the French Mind," 40–46. The *Revue encyclopédique* tried to enlist the cooperation of many Americans interested in its enterprise.

64. François Guizot, *Report upon the International Exchanges Undertaken by Alexandre Vattemare and upon the Actual State of Letters and Especially of Historical Investigations in the United States of America* (Paris, 1855).

may prejudice kindly relations." Next to Britain, the United States had published by 1900 the largest number of books of the respectable quality that French publicists acknowledged without hesitation. That Americans liked to read books, magazines, and newspapers was evidenced by the fact that near the end of the century the United States annually imported an average of $2 million worth of books. Only 10 percent of this amount went to France, largely for fiction of every variety; 75 percent went to Great Britain and Germany, for Bibles and books on science, medicine, and philosophy.[65] To put an end to literary piracy and to safeguard the works of authors and artists, the United States Congress passed on March 3, 1891, the copyright bill which was promptly signed into law. This gesture of good faith was a step in the right direction, which the more generous French copyright law of March 11, 1902, demonstrated was subject to future improvements.[66]

The freedom of the American press was not only a vital safeguard of the people's liberties, it also performed a major educational function. Near the end of the nineteenth century 17,140 newspapers were published in the United States, about 2,000 more than in England, Germany, and France combined.[67] Historically, a number of differences distinguished the French and American press. French journalism was dominated by a variety of editorial leaders whose personal interpretations helped form public opinion, especially in political questions. The American press reflected public opinion more than it tried to shape it; in its emphasis on social questions, it respected the privacy of individuals as little as it regarded the

65. Gaston Choisy, "Les Lettres françaises aux Etats-Unis," *Revue bleue* (September 1, 1900), 283–84.

66. Charles de Varigny, "La Protection littéraire et le 'Copyright Bill' aux Etats-Unis," *Revue bleue*, XLVIII (1891), 303–307. Intellectual contacts between the two countries were also encouraged by membership of selected individuals in their respective cultural and scientific organizations. For the sizable number of French members in the American Philosophical Society, see APS, *Yearbook,* 1964 (Philadelphia, 1965), 94–106.

67. S. C. de Soissons, *A Parisian in America* (Boston, 1896), 108–109. Although the number of American newspapers in 1870 was about one-third that of a generation later, the proportion between American and European papers remained stable. Charles de Varigny, *Les Etats-Unis: Esquisses historiques* (Paris, 1898), 61.

consequences of public ridicule or exposure. A French newspaper was usually a well-planned and well-executed literary production in clear and graceful language. "The average American newspaper," it appeared to French readers, "flounders about in crime, gossip, accidents, sensations, personalities, fiction, pictures, and news, apparently unable to decide just what it wants to do."[68] This chaos of news, sometimes scattered over more than twenty pages, offered a variety of useful and amusing items, even if its art form left something to be desired. The great mass of the American people liked to read newspapers and magazines on a much larger scale than Europeans customarily did. Americans preferred to have their papers inform and educate, hopefully accurately, rather than entertain or propagandize. And they expected them to serve as public watchdogs.[69]

French newspapers exercised a great influence. They were launched as money-making enterprises, and they often prepared French editors' careers as parliamentarians. As far as news about the United States was concerned, France depended even late in the century on news agencies; none of its papers had a correspondent regularly assigned to the United States.

There were a few exceptions, notably during very "newsworthy" times.[70] The *Journal des débats*, for instance, had a correspondent in California to report on the drama of the gold rush. Young Duvergier de Hauranne's comments on the Civil War and

68. Oliver Carlson, *The Man Who Made News: James Gordon Bennett* (New York, 1942), 222; O'Rell, *A Frenchman in America,* 116–17; "French Journalism," Richmond *Daily Dispatch,* June 25, 1861.

69. Paul de Rousiers, *La Vie américaine* (Paris, 1892), 623–24; Cucheval Clarigny, "La Presse américaine depuis l'indépendance," *RDDM* (May 15, 1857), 300–301.

70. See A. P. Nasatir (ed.), "A French Journalist in the California Gold Rush: The Letters of Etienne Derbec," *AHR,* LXX (1965), 1242–43; Ernest Duvergier de Hauranne, *Les Etats-Unis pendant la Guerre de Sécession: Vu par un journaliste français* (Paris, 1966), 8–10; Albert Krebs, "L'Expérience américaine de Clemenceau," *Rapports France–Etats-Unis* (October, 1952), 52–60; L. Gabriel-Robinet, *Journaux et journalistes: Hier et aujourd'hui* (Paris, 1962), 77–78; John Hohenberg, *Foreign Correspondence: The Great Reporters and Their Times* (New York, 1964), 69; W. Reed West, *Contemporary French Opinion on the American Civil War* (Baltimore, 1924).

life in America, gathered during his stay in the United States from June, 1864, to February, 1865, were published after the war in the *Revue des deux mondes*. And Georges Clemenceau, later known as "the Tiger," wrote his *Lettres des Etats-Unis* for *Le Temps*. During his residence in the United States from 1866 to 1870, Clemenceau was fascinated by Reconstruction activities, particularly the impeachment trial of President Andrew Johnson, and explained them to his countrymen in a lively way.

The economics of transatlantic news-gathering justified only occasional foreign correspondents in either country until the relative significance of news called for more effective permanent arrangements. Early in the century it took six weeks and as late as in 1858 it took twelve days for boats to carry reports and newspapers across the ocean. Obviously, this news was always stale. The telegraph and the transatlantic cable, effectively in operation after 1865, naturally accelerated the dissemination of and interest in world news. However, it initially cost five dollars to transmit a word; thus the pooling of overseas journalistic resources seemed a reasonable way to reduce costs. From the middle of the century, Agence Havas,[71] already practically monopolizing th distribution of foreign news in France, tried to include the United States in its Atlantic news empire. By 1870 it had concluded an agreement with the Associated Press for exchange of information in Paris and New York. An international cartel established in 1870 by the four major news agencies then in existence—Havas, Reuters, Wolff, and Associated Press—further reduced costs by dividing the world into four "spheres of influence." Ultimately Reuters became the main channel for the distribution of American news in Europe and European news in America, thereby giving England substantial political leverage in the processing of this news.

71. Robert W. Jones, *Journalism in the United States* (New York, 1947), 398; Clifford F. Weigle, "The Rise and Fall of the Havas News Agency," *Journalism Quarterly*, XIX (September, 1942), 277–86; Graham Storey, *Reuters: The Story of a Century of Newsgathering* (New York, 1951), 115–17; Al Laney, Paris Herald: *The Incredible Newspaper* (New York, 1947), 13, 18.

Under these circumstances, it was enterprising and refreshing for a successful New York newspaperman, James Gordon Bennett, to launch in 1877 an independent paper, the Paris *Herald. Le New York*, as Parisians referred to it, offered them more personal views about America, views that, if nothing else, differed from those of the empire services.

The French press had shown a more lively concern with developments in the United States during the Restoration and the reign of Louis Philippe than during the Second Empire. During the Restoration, French papers argued the merits and demerits of the republican institutions in the United States. The *Revue encyclopédique* alone published almost three thousand articles about the United States, hoping to influence public opinion in favor of the adoption of democratic institutions in France. The *Minerve française,* founded and edited by Benjamin Constant, enthusiastically acclaimed the social utilitarianism and political liberalism with which European liberals identified the American republic. *Le Constitutionnel,* courting the favor of the petit bourgeoisie, leaned toward the American system; but, like others until the end of the Second Empire, it often used conditions in the United States as an indirect and safe means of criticizing conditions in France. The influential conservative *Journal des débats,* representing the richer classes who desired political stability that would protect their property interests, leaned toward a vigorous monarchy and was therefore critical of the transatlantic experiment and the unsettling social and political changes it was endeavoring to bring about. And the ultraconservatives, who did not even bother to analyze the life and government of a country whose revolution had helped to trigger the bloody French Revolution, could always find anti-American diatribes in *L'Etoile.*[72]

72. For a more elaborate description of these papers, see McBride, "America in the French Mind," 81–84; and Sanderson, *Sketches of Paris,* 85–86. While *Le Figaro*'s pages found little good in the United States, William James described this "most hideous little sheet . . . and its bawdry anecdotes, spun out with that infernal grinning flippancy and galvanized gaiety" as the work "of minds lost and putrefying." William James to Henry James, December 26, 1867, HCL.

French papers continued the debate about the model republic in the years following the July Revolution.[73] *Le Constitutionnel* supported the newly established constitutional monarchy, but it expressed neither fear nor envy of the American republic. Similarly, *Le Temps* and the *Journal des débats* expressed the view that the United States was a territorial giant whose institutions were not likely to work equally well in Europe. They were not even sure of its vaunted efficacy. Also the Catholic *Correspondant,* a partisan of civil and religious liberty in the constitutional monarchy, rejected the notion of the universal republic. *Le National* ranked among the few French papers that placed the model republic at the head of modern civilization. Its chief, Armant Carrel, in the issue of May 29, 1832, raised the question: "Could it be that the Americans, inferior to us in civilization, possessed a political genius superior to ours? No," he replied, "American democracy is the outgrowth of the French Enlightenment."

News of English affairs was given more space in American papers than was news of France.[74] And France certainly received less attention in American papers than American affairs enjoyed in French papers. The mid-century revolutions and the growing political tensions between Napoleon III and the United States changed this state of affairs. During these years, polemics and vituperations characterized many of the comments about French policies and society in the American press. In the final decades of the century, the French minister to the United States, Théodore-Justin Roustan, complained about the unfriendly attitude of the American press toward France, whose imperialistic diplomacy it labeled "perverse" and "unscrupulous" and whose contemporary literature it often condemned as obscene. These comments found

73. Robert G. Mahieu, "Les Enquêteurs français aux Etats-Unis de 1830 à 1837: L'Influence américaine sur l'évolution démocratique en France" (Ph.D. dissertation, Université de Paris, 1934).

74. See the comments of the prominent French journalist Charles Chambrun in his *Impressions of Lincoln and the Civil War: A Foreigner's Account* (New York, 1952), 56–57. Such mid-century papers as *Le Messager Franco-Américain* and *Europe et Amérique* did not survive for more than one year. Hugh Awtrey, *La Presse anglo-américaine de Paris* (Paris, 1932), 31–32.

their counterpart in recurring French criticism of the Monroe Doctrine and in a sensational focus on American eccentricities. Neither performance did anything to promote mutual understanding. Unfortunately, these negative emphases overshadowed the many descriptive and newsworthy articles that informed readers about current actualities.

Whatever the orientation, the French and American presses served as a forum of mutual enlightenment from an international point of view. Of course, the French-American press that drew on both aimed primarily at keeping the cultural identity of French families alive. Wherever even small French communities existed in a cluster, from New England to California, and from Michigan to Louisiana, French newspapers appeared. *Le Courrier des États-Unis de New York, L'Abeille de la Nouvelle Orléans, La Revue de l'Ouest de St. Louis,* and the *Franco-Californien* were among the few of these publications that enjoyed more than an ephemeral existence. Many papers disappeared as suddenly, particularly in the 1840s and 1850s, as they had come into existence. The early demise of these often enthusiastically and ably directed literary productions was usually caused by financial difficulties, which in turn reflected the declining identification with French cultural institutions in America.[75]

Social Prejudices: The Race Question
and the Dreyfus Affair

Americans were so proud of their institutions, which, they were convinced, assured their steady material and cultural progress, that they almost thoughtlessly overlooked the unsteadying consequences of their "peculiar institution." This human and institutional tragedy raised serious doubts about Americans' often

75. See Alexandre Belisle, *Histoire de la presse franco-américaine* (Worcester, Mass., 1911); John S. Kendall, "The Foreign Language Press of New Orleans," *LHQ,* XII (1929), 363–80; Douglas C. McMurtrie, "The French Press of Louisiana," *LHQ,* XVIII (1935), 947–65; E. B. Ham, "Journalism and the French Survival in New England," *NEQ,* XI (1938), 89–107; Georges J. Joyaux, "French Press in Michigan: A Bibliography," *Michigan History,* XXXVI (1952), 260–78.

immodestly expressed pride. Even though the Baron de Montlezun's prejudices against the United States weakened his credentials
as a judge, public records substantiated the accuracy of his assertion
in 1818 that Americans arrogantly boasted "of their superiority
over the English, over the French, their creator, over the entire
world, in war, on land and on sea."[76] This air of superiority
manifested itself even more tragically and far-reachingly in the
relations between white and black Americans.

With few exceptions, Frenchmen looked upon the institution
of slavery as the most outstanding contradiction in the social and
institutional structure of the United States. In France, people did
not feel the repugnance toward Negroes that was customary in
the United States.[77] On the contrary, experience had taught the
French that educated blacks could be just as polished and sophisticated as whites. Frenchmen thought, therefore, that the United
States was the loser when after the Civil War northern society
discriminated against even highly educated Negroes. And for
uneducated poor whites in the North and South to display an
arrogant attitude in their daily contacts with black people revealed
narrow-minded prejudices that simply could not be reconciled with
the notion of a model republic boasting of freedom, equality, and
recognition of the dignity of man. The fact that white Americans,
northerners and southerners, democrats and "aristocrats," rejected
Negroes as social equals led many Frenchmen to question the
sincerity of the professed political principles of these transatlantic
republicans. The French also questioned the sincerity of abolition-
ists who, they thought, advocated abolition as an appealing and
self-satisfying abstract idea.[78]

Before the Civil War French detractors of the American system
of government reproached it on account of its tolerance of slavery,

<hr />

76. Baron Barthélemi de Montlezun, *Voyage de New York fait dans les années*
1816 et 1817 à la Nouvelle-Orléans (2 vols.; Paris, 1818), I, 164–66.
77. Franklin J. Didier, *Letters from Paris* (New York, 1821), 24–25; de Molinari, *Lettres sur les Etats-Unis et le Canada,* 197–98.
78. John Lemoinne, "De La Question de l'esclavage," *JDD,* December 4, 1852.

whereas other French commentators attempted to offer some qualifying explanations. The latter pointed out that it was neither fair nor accurate to condemn the political system of the whole country when slavery existed as an institution only in a part of the country and, even there, was most likely only a temporary institution. Such knowledgeable writers as Prince Achille Murat and Alexis de Tocqueville speculated that slavery would disappear from the American scene, because it was not only undesirable, but unprofitable as well. It may very well have "cultivated" the leading southern families, as Murat suggested, by making a more leisurely social life possible. But, as Tocqueville saw it, this leisure largely explained the lack of drive and enterprising spirit that prevented the South from keeping pace with the economic development of the North. These students of American life felt confident that once the slavocrats realized that free labor was more productive and cheaper than slave labor the "peculiar institution" would be on its way out.[79] With remarkable insight, Tocqueville anticipated that abolition of slavery, once accomplished, would not put an end to race antagonism. On the contrary, he expected the social troubles to increase when freed slaves demanded political rights. He based this opinion on his observation that "the prejudice of race appears to be stronger in the States which have abolished slavery than in those where it still exists; and nowhere is it so intolerant as in those States where servitude has never been known."[80]

Critical Frenchmen were very displeased when the formal abolition of slavery was not accompanied by land grants that would have meaningfully underpinned the newly acquired freedom of the former slaves. They were also disappointed that the abolition of slavery did not mean the end of social prejudice and economic exploitation. Such discriminatory treatment of freed Negroes as their ejection from public conveyances caused Frenchmen to be severely critical of American society; and the refusal of churches

79. Chambers, "Observations and Opinions of French Travellers," 215–26.
80. Tocqueville, *Democracy in America,* I, 364.

to admit Negroes to religious services seemed to French critics counter to all professions of Christian charity.[81]

The French also noted other racial prejudices of Americans, e.g., their discriminatory treatment in the post–Civil War period of Mexican-Americans, Creoles, Indians, and Orientals. Perhaps more than with any other group French critics sympathized with the Indians, whose fate had taught them to be disdainful of the white man who, apparently, lacked "all respect for honor and good faith."[82] The dualistic trends in the development of American democracy exposed the United States to charges of hypocrisy. The existence of this hypocrisy foreshadowed future social troubles, evoking sentiments of doubt about a political system that presumably dispensed equal justice under law to the members of its classless society, but that actually applied different standards to certain citizens who, for all practical purposes, were arbitrarily treated as second-class citizens. The double standards of American society were, according to some French critics, further accentuated by its oligarchic rather than truly democratic tendencies. The detachment of well-informed foreigners enabled them to see serious flaws more honestly and perceptively than most American citizens, who tolerated admission of minor imperfections in their institutions, but self-righteously rejected the existence of fundamental weaknesses and contradictions.

Those Americans who believed in the inequality of races were of course greatly encouraged by the publications of Count Arthur de Gobineau. They saw to it that the English translation of this race theorist's work, *Essai sur l'inégalité des races humaines* (1853-1855), became as widely known as possible. Two American ethnologists, George K. Gliddon and Joseph C. Nott, among others, acknowledged their appreciation of Gobineau's "historical truths."[83] In order to popularize Gobineau's theories concerning

81. Ernest Duvergier de Hauranne, *Huit mois en Amérique* (2 vols.; Paris, 1866), I, 24; Jannet, *Les Etats-Unis contemporains*, II, 119.

82. Oscar Comettant, *Voyage pittoresque et anecdotique dans le nord et le sud des Etats-Unis d'Amérique* (Paris, 1866), 195.

83. Ludwig Schemann, *Gobineaus Rassenwerk* (Stuttgart, 1910), 189–200.

the superiority of the white race and the rejection of the wholesome influence of democratic ideas on the human race, the English version of his work omitted references that would have been offensive to Protestants, especially Presbyterians. Any intimation of original diversity of races, for instance, would have been contrary to the Calvinistic dogma of hereditary sin. In a predominantly Protestant country like the United States, in which the pulpit exercised a more potent influence than was usually assumed, many potential readers would have been frightened away by theories suspected of religious infidelity. Gobineau's thesis of the gradual degeneracy of the human race and its ultimate extinction was originally also left out of the translated essay for fear of an unfavorable reception in America. This Frenchman's view of the "opulent" United States as an evil and corrupting influence rather than a "temple of virtue and happiness" naturally limited his American influence.[84]

Except in Germany, Gobineau did not succeed in arousing widespread interest in his work. However, some of his general notions were echoed by others, including the physician Alfred Mercier, author of a pamphlet on pan-Latinism.[85] Mercier condemned the fusion of races in Latin America as an agent of decadence and a threat to the area's vigorous existence; he traced the vitality of Anglo-Saxon America at least in part to its practice of not mingling the white and black races. Speaking as a European and motivated by imperialistic considerations, Mercier decried the fusion of races in Mexico and Central and South America as an evil that must be stopped "by reconstituting the ancient aristocracy of the white race, by restoring the direction of affairs to the population of pure European origin, and by classifying the descendants of Indians and Africans according to their aptitudes." Failure to do this, he prophesied, would bring Latin America under the control of the United States, a development he thought

---

84. *Ibid.*, 282–93, 376–77, 434-35.
85. Alfred Mercier, *Du Panlatinisme: Nécessité d'une alliance entre la France et la Confédération du Sud* (Paris, 1863).

France was duty bound to prevent by helping its Latin American friends regenerate themselves.

The absence of homogeneity in this country of immigrants and different races cast doubts in the minds of serious French students as to the possibility of the eventual emergence of an American nation.[86] The geographic distance between areas and the contrasts between sparsity and density of population in different areas of the continental United States, as well as conflicting interests between rural and urban communities, foreshadowed political complications and challenges that, these skeptics thought, even the federal system and a growing economic interdependence might be unable to overcome.

If deep-rooted racial prejudices challenged the integrity of the American social and political system, a dramatic episode convinced the world that France was not exactly the paragon of institutional integrity either. The Dreyfus affair, which shook France to its foundations in the final years of the nineteenth century, raised many legal, political, and religious questions that ultimately produced a profound impact on the American people. When Emile Zola challenged the sentencing of Captain Alfred Dreyfus to life imprisonment on the mosquito-infested tropical island of Cayenne for allegedly being engaged in treasonable espionage, the American public was as much stirred by the circumstances surrounding the trial as was the rest of the civilized world. Many Americans wondered what had happened to France, once the leader of enlightenment and civilization? Senator James B. Eustis from Louisiana, former ambassador to France, tried to explain French circumstances in an informative and dispassionate article he published in 1899 in the *Conservative Review*.[87] He frankly admitted that antisemitism had deep roots in Catholic France

---

86. E. Boutmy, "La Formation de la nationalité aux Etats-Unis," *Annales de l'Ecole Libre des Sciences Politiques*, VI (1891), 603. Tocqueville expressed a similar reservation; see Alexis de Tocqueville to Gustav Beaumont, August 6, 1854, in Tocqueville, *Oeuvres Complètes*, VI, 266–68.

87. James B. Eustis, "Dreyfus and the Jewish Question in France: French and American Democracy," *Conservative Review*, II (August, 1899), 7–21.

and that the case of Captain Dreyfus, a Jew, could not very well be understood without keeping in mind the apprehension of many prejudiced Frenchmen that Jews tried "to dominate and control the Government of France to the detriment of the State" and that they were responsible for the corruption prevailing in high places. Clerical and army circles, aided by Edouard Drumont's viciously antisemitic publication, *La France juive,*[88] had carefully cultivated this malicious propaganda.

According to Eustis, the Dreyfus case could never have occurred in the United States where the system of criminal procedure was very different from that in France. French criminal law did not distinguish between legal and illegal evidence, nor did it provide for direct cross-examination of witnesses. As Eustis summed it up: "The right of bail, the writ of habeas corpus, and all those other guarantees to secure the rights and safeguard the personal liberty of the citizen against the arbitrary acts of the Government, which are provided for in our Constitution, are not to be found in the French Constitution." One of the more important safeguards in the United States, furthermore, was the jury system, providing for the participation of ordinary citizens in the administration of justice.

As interesting as these comparative legal explanations were, it was the drama of the case, in which the principle of justice and the integrity of France were as much on trial as was the obscure Jewish army officer, that held the breathless attention of the American public. Zola's charge that Dreyfus had been caught in the web of sinister intrigues, engineered by high French army circles and evidently accepted by the court that sentenced him unjustly, touched many Americans profoundly. The public and the press admired Zola's courage when, unafraid of the consequences to him personally, he accused French authorities of a travesty of justice in his memorable charge: "We witness the infamous spectacle of men weighted down with debts and crimes

88. Robert F. Byrnes, *Antisemitism in Modern France: The Prologue to the Dreyfus Affair* (New York, 1969), 150–55; Adrien Dansette, *Histoire religieuse de la France contemporaine* (Paris, 1965), 545.

being proclaimed to all the world as innocent and virtuous, while the very soul of honor, a man without a stain, is dragged in the mire! When a country, when a civilization has come to this, it must fall apart in decay!"[89]

Americans praised Zola for his defiance of cowards and hypocrites. It was noteworthy, however, that the reaction of American Catholics, Protestants, and Jews differed sufficiently to reveal distinct shades of sentiment. Perhaps out of a false sense of solidarity with the clerical hierarchy in France, American Catholics maintained at best a reserved attitude when the rest of the public was seething with indignation.[90] For instance, the *Globe*, a Catholic publication, had little use for Zola, who had been "depicting social filth and ridiculing Christ and His People."[91] This attempt to downgrade the French novelist was obviously irrelevant and diverted attention from the central issues of the Dreyfus case. The Catholic Church, acting through its head, Pope Leo XIII, remained aloof and evidently tried not to offend France or to upset the hierarchy of the Church in France. But as the devout Catholic scientist St. George Mivart commented with respect to "the Pope's amazing and appalling silence" in a letter published by the London *Times*: "To keep silence may often be to participate in the evil left undenounced."[92]

American and French Protestants clearly sided with the cause Zola was fighting for. The *Congregationalist* summed up their judgment by finding "the French judicial system, the French

---

89. Nicholas Halasz, *Captain Dreyfus: The Story of Mass Hysteria* (New York, 1955), 133–36; Frederick W. Whitridge, "Zola, Dreyfus, and the Republic," *PSQ*, XIII (1898), 259–72.

90. One of the tangible consequences of the Dreyfus affair was the temporary boycott of French goods in some large American cities. New York *Times*, May 23, 1898. French officials were very much concerned about the threatened boycott of the Paris Exposition in 1900. R. D. Mandell, "The Affair and the Fair: Some Observations on the Closing Stages of the Dreyfus Case," *JMH*, XXXIX (September, 1967), 257–58.

91. Rose A. Halpern "The American Reaction to the Dreyfus Case" (M.A. thesis, Columbia University, 1941), 46–47. John Durand, an eccentric American expatriate artist who held Zola in contempt, was amused to see "the sympathy and applause awarded to this arrogant, conceited, literary fungus called Zola, whose mind is a cesspool of nastiness, and whose works are a disgrace to French literature." John Durand to C. H. Hart, March 16, 1898, NYPL.

92. "A Significant Silence," *Outlook*, November 11, 1899, pp. 624–25.

army, the French press, and the French public" guilty in this case at the bar of the world's public opinion.[93] To them, the collapse of military honor and integrity was contemptible beyond belief. The Jews expressed their gratitude to Emile Zola for his eloquent and valiant attempt to exonerate a Jew whom he believed to be innocent.[94] And as far as France was concerned, the *American Hebrew* managed after the second court-martial at Rennes to put into words the heavy-hearted sigh: "O, France, how art thou fallen low!" From the point of view of American Jewry, however, more was at stake than the fate of one Jew. If antisemitism could flourish in a civilized country like France, what hope was there for an enlightened attitude towards Jews in the rest of the world, including the United States?[95] A New York lawyer, Jocelyn Johnstone, was inspired by the Dreyfus case to express the broader concern of Christians in this verse:[96]

RENNES 1899

A white souled Jew before the judgment seat
Of Pilate stood for trial; his offence
Treason against the State; his innocence
Clear as His own high gospel; yet defeat,
Born on the venal voices of the street
And barbed by frenzied faith's intolerance,
Awaited him, the condemnation meet
For crime's red hand, the cross and winding sheet.
Swift time reversed that judgment: with white lips
Millions, who love the Galilean, cry
In wrath against the criminal eclipse
Of justice, when the mob shrieked, "Crucify!"
Now, by Thine agony and bloody sweat
O Christ, can all thy worshippers forget?

93. Halpern, "The American Reaction," 48.
94. *Ibid.*, 63–72.
95. Z. Szajkowski, "The *Alliance Israélite Universelle* in the United States, 1860–1949," *American Jewish Historical Society Publications*, XXXIX (June, 1950), 416–17.
96. New York *Tribune*, September 10, 1899, p. 3. Leona Queyrouze, Louisiana's "petite Mme. de Staël," sent to Zola American newspapers and journals reacting to the "affaire" and reassured him of the American people's unbounded respect for his moral courage. Leona Queyrouze to Emile Zola, June 27, 1899, LSU Archives.

The emotional impact of the Dreyfus affair prompted American public opinion to condemn the "medieval" system of justice in France and to praise God for the superior system of justice in the United States. The legal systems of the two countries were indeed different, but it took the expert knowledge of a professional man to show that, quite aside from the Dreyfus case per se, courts-martial in France compared in many important respects very favorably with those in the United States.[97] Captain Dreyfus was originally sentenced by a military court whose judgment was, under the French criminal code, subject to reversal by a civil tribunal upon demonstration of new evidence claiming to establish the innocence of the condemned party. Even the good name of an unjustly executed "convict" could thus be cleared, to the satisfaction of his surviving family. French law also provided for material redress and the official publication of the reversal decision once the innocence of the party had been established.

By comparison, a court-martial in the United States was the only court authorized to decide cases of military offense. It was "altogether beyond the jurisdiction or inquiry of any civil tribunal whatever." Even if new evidence could establish the innocence of a person sentenced by a court-martial, the civil authorities were in no position to redress the wrong the "convicted" party had suffered. The reviewing authority was vested in the commander who originally convened the court-martial. But all he could do was approve or disapprove its proceedings. At best, American procedure was permitted "to right a wrong by pardoning it" and "to forgive a crime which never was committed." Even in these circumstances, no provision was allowed for material compensation. As far as the procedural system of French justice was concerned, the American press, in its discussion of the Dreyfus case, beheld "the mote in thy brother's eye, but did not perceive the beam in thy own eye."

97. Arthur Ameisen, "The Effect of Judgments of Courts-Martial in France and in America: A Comparative Study of the Dreyfus Case," *American Law Review,* XXXIII (1899), 75–83.

The functional processes of institutions are subject to different interpretations and impressions even when they are well known; they are obviously subject to misunderstandings and embarrassments when judged by people too involved in them or inadequately informed about them. That Alexis de Tocqueville's analyses regarding the United States have stood the test of time and that Frenchmen and Americans were capable of revising their opinions about each other's educational, legal, and other institutional developments is certainly to their credit. And that each investigated whether it could improve its own institutions by more effective processes and conditions found in the other country held out hope for a more progressive future. But nothing seems as instructive as the fact that well-informed foreign observers possess the kind of independence potentially best suited for truly objective evaluations. National pride and prejudices, if not consciously kept in check, are less likely to see and admit the existence of potentially disastrous shortcomings.

CHAPTER III

Socioeconomic Aspects

Society values the application of knowledge more than its mere acquisition. The benefits that France and the United States derived from their exchange of ideas were further enlarged by cross-fertilization in the area of inventions and the development of labor-saving devices. Europeans watched with amazement, admiration, and some apprehension the technological ingenuity Americans displayed. The social problems growing out of the Industrial Revolution demanded the fulfillment of economic promises if political democracy was to survive. Impatiently, therefore, Americans spearheaded a modern age in which man's life would be made easier through mechanical-labor devices and a production system that would benefit the masses and provide undreamed of comforts for the more prosperous classes. That the Yankees' vision of a more comfortable life made the European intellectual and business world uneasy, because of economic competition and because the Europeans did not share these optimistic expectations, in no way deterred Americans from going ahead with their exploratory experiments.

Their approach was so pragmatic that applied science fascinated them infinitely more than the basic science in which Europeans distinguished themselves. This disposition to think in practical rather than theoretical terms led Americans to defy general formulae and often to engage in astonishing intellectual gymnastics in their search for workable solutions.[1] As Napoleon III once correctly remarked, Americans did not permit themselves "to be bound hand and foot by the usages and customs of centuries." A new invention could titillate them as much as an antique could Frenchmen. The vastness of their continent and natural resources of course facilitated the Americans' restless search for new methods and gadgets.

Economist Michel Chevalier (1806–1879) and engineer Guillaume Tell Poussin (1794–1876) possessed sufficient firsthand knowledge to attribute divergent economic developments in France and the United States to significant differences in social habits and physical conditions rather than to different political institutions.[2] They were aware that institutions could facilitate or stifle private initiative likely to promote a nation's prosperity. In two important respects, Chevalier and Poussin observed in the 1830s, the United States jumped ahead of France: it developed a network of railroads and canals that tied the nation together politically and provided the foundation for national economic growth; and it provided a credit and banking system in which metal currency did not assume a value infinitely superior to that of paper money, a risk cautious Frenchmen continued to frown upon. Similar developments in Europe, Chevalier speculated, would have "completely blended together in interests, feelings, and opinions" all the peoples of Europe and created a united continent instead of a Europe exhausting itself in divisive wars.

These two French observers also noted other advantages that contributed to the amazing economic achievements of the American people. Americans loved to work, whereas Frenchmen worked from necessity. The Calvinistic work ethic induced Yankees to produce, to make the most of their time, and to create wealth

1. E. Malezieux, *Souvenirs d'une mission aux Etats-Unis d'Amérique* (Paris, 1874), 165–71.
2. Chevalier, *Society, Manners and Politics*, 204, 270–75, 345–50; Guillaume Tell Poussin, *Chemins de fer américains: Histoire de leur construction* (Paris, 1836), xiiii–xvi.

rather than to live on their incomes as proprietors or to be satisfied with a less ambitious but more leisurely life. Americans took it for granted that their contributions to the material well-being of society through their own usefulness improved the quality of life for everybody. If this meant, as it did for countless young farmers and their families, pursuing one's productive goals in the relative loneliness of the frontier, the Americans did not mind. But the much more socially inclined Frenchmen would have found frontier life unbearable. Prophetically, though, Chevalier referred in a letter, dated January 4, 1835, to Charles Fourier's characterization of the spirit of the nineteenth century as "industrial feudalism" in which the new masters, "the princes of manufactures, banks, and commerce . . . will increase the body's pittance, but diminish the soul's." And, in the end, he wondered whether this industrial feudalism would not be "creeping beneath the democratic institutions, like the snake under the grass."

In the application of science and technology, Frenchmen and Americans differed considerably. Perceptive Frenchmen marveled at the speed with which America put inventions into use—unlike France, where drawn-out deliberations frequently delayed the exploitation of inventions. Usually Frenchmen were much more reluctant than their inventive friends across the ocean to put up necessary risk capital; thus many French inventors sought and found financial support abroad for the development of their inventions.[3] The dexterity with which Americans could practically from the start operate the sewing machine, a French invention perfected by Americans, amazed initially less-skillful Frenchmen. In addition to these conditions and the already cited differences with respect to transportation and the credit system, the lack of metallurgical coke handicapped the speedy industrial development of France.[4] In the last analysis, however, different mentalities

3. Henri Sée, *Histoire économique de la France* (2 vols.; Paris, 1942), II, 299–300; D. S. Landes, "French Entrepreneurship and Industrial Growth in the Nineteenth Century," *Journal of Economic History,* IX (1949), 51.

4. Robert J. Forbes, *Man, the Maker: A History of Technology and Engineering* (New York, 1950), 273.

helped create different conditions and affected the pace at which France and the United States moved into the technological age. The impressive number of ingenious inventors France produced demonstrated its potential technological capacities. The country was merely slow in taking advantage of them. François Appert's process of preserving food, J. Dubosc's portable stereoscope, Pierre Foucault's writing machine, Philippe Henri de Girard's spinning machine, Jean Laurent Palmer's special type of micrometer, Pierre Louis Sauvage's screw propeller, and Charles Tellier's refrigerator —these were only a few examples of French inventiveness in the last century.[5]

The display of American machines and gadgets at the famous international expositions in Paris between 1855 and 1900 aroused considerable interest. Even in the first half of the century Americans gained a reputation for technical resourcefulness that facilitated the demonstration of their inventions in Europe. Whenever possible, they patented their inventions in France, as elsewhere, often to find out, however, that Frenchmen tended to show a greater intellectual curiosity about them than disposition to capitalize on them. For example, the demonstration by Robert Fulton and Samuel Morse of the workability of the steamboat and the telegraph elicited such enthusiastic comments as *"extraordinaire"* and *"magnifique,"* but there were no immediate business orders.[6] Interestingly, when Morse struck up a friendship with Louis Jacques Daguerre, inventor of the photographic process, the people in the United States were at first skeptical about Daguerre's mysterious, though exquisite, reproduction of true images that Morse brought back home. Only gradually did exhibitions of

5. Charles Singer (ed.), *A History of Technology* (5 vols.; Oxford, 1954–58), V, 26–52; David A. Wells (ed.), *Annual of Scientific Discovery for* 1858 (Boston, 1859), 27–29; Georges Iles, *Leading American Inventors* (New York, 1912), 326; Herkimer County Historical Society, *The Story of the Typewriter,* 1873–1923 (Herkimer, N.Y., 1923), 20–21.

6. Morse, *His Letters and Journals,* II, 104; Charleton Mabee, *The American Leonardo: A Life of Samuel F. B. Morse* (New York, 1943), 218–24; M. Amyot, "Note sur le télégraphe électrique," *Journal des Sciences Physiques* (1838), 257–61.

daguerreotypes convince Americans of the potentialities of this new art, and then they very skillfully perfected it.[7]

As the mid-century witnessed social and political revolutions, it also turned out to be a period of remarkable technological innovation. The rotary press, embodying patents taken out by Richard M. Hoe, created a revolution in the newspaper world.[8] In 1848, *La Patrie* was the first paper to adopt it in France. Practically all of Europe availed itself of the useful patent for making horseshoes by machine. People living in an age of live horsepower appreciated its benefits in peace and war. As much as Napoleon III disliked the republican gospel of the United States, he took advantage of the Yankees' technological genius whenever possible. The development of his ironclad fleet owed much to the inventive ideas of the Swedish-American engineer John Ericsson.[9] Economically most beneficial was, or course, the introduction of Charles Goodyear's hard rubber goods and Cyrus Hall McCormick's reapers.

Goodyear's perseverance in his search for a workable process by which vulcanized rubber could be produced perhaps evokes more sympathy than admiration for the man whose neighbors thought him aimed toward an insane asylum.[10] They would have been more prophetic had they expected him to become the inmate of a poorhouse, for this was precisely his temporary address when the French government honored him for his incidental discovery of vulcanizing rubber. In the pursuit of his obsession he had gone so deeply into debt that he had several times been locked up in the debtors' prison at Clichy. This might never have occurred had he not been too honest to decline an offer of several thousand dollars which a French manufacturing company had made to him

7. Morse, *His Letters and Journals*, II, 128–41; Robert Taft, *Photography and the American Scene: A Social History*, 1839–1889 (New York, 1938), 40–42, 54.

8. Robert Hoe, *A Short History of the Printing Press* (New York, 1902), 31–33.

9. William Conant Church, *The Life of John Ericsson* (2 vols.; New York, 1890), 240–44; W. B. Edwards, *The Story of Colt's Revolver* (Harrisburg, Pa., 1953), 42–44; Baron Treuille de Beaulieu, *Armes de guerre—portatives: Exposition Universelle de 1867* (Paris, 1867), 27–28. The excellent quality of French weapons secured French firms a good market in the United States.

10. Adolph C. Regli, *Rubber's Goodyear* (New York, 1941), 84–87, 181; P. W. Barker, *Charles Goodyear: A Biography* (Boston, 1940), 81–96.

in 1839 for exclusive rights to his acid-gas process. At that time, however, he knew that should he succeed in discovering the vulcanization of rubber the acid-gas process would be rendered obsolete. The French emperor's personal attention to Goodyear, once the potential uses of rubber merely challenged the imagination of man, was a source of great gratification to him. The dogged inventor was showered with honors in the few remaining years of his life. He had the satisfaction of seeing the beginning of the industrial exploitation of his rubber process in many foreign lands, including France.

The demonstrated performance of the McCormick reaper at the Paris Exposition of 1855 brought international fame to the inventor and much credit to his native country. McCormick's reaper so outdistanced foreign machines, collecting harvests in one-third of their time and at a very low cost, that its adoption by economy-minded French farmers would have seemed to be a logical investment. However, most French farms may not have been large enough to draw optimum benefits from the American reaper, and the traditional ways of French farmers defied the logic of calculable profits resulting from the use of the reaper. The French firm licensed to manufacture McCormick reapers for France could hardly sell a dozen of them. Always on the lookout for improved methods of production, Napoleon III was so impressed with the 1867 demonstration performance of this harvesting machine that he honored the American inventor at a ceremony in the Tuileries as "a benefactor of mankind." The publicity attending such ceremonies evidently helped to convince some old-fashioned farmers of the merits of this agricultural machine. However profitable modern farming methods might be, French peasants adopted them only slowly and reluctantly. They remained skeptical about the economic and social consequences of a break with tested traditions.[11]

11. William T. Hutchinson, *Cyrus Hall McCormick: Harvest,* 1856–1884 (New York, 1935), 409–35; Emile Thomas, "Exposition Universelle de 1855: Les Machines," *Journal des Economistes,* 2nd ser., VII (September 15, 1855), 445. The productivity of farm labor in France was judged to be one-fourth to one-third less than that of American farmers.

American inventiveness was conspicuously recognized at the Paris Expositions of 1878, 1889, and 1900. The device by which bottles could be sealed hermetically, the safe process of preserving meats, and improved American methods in the production of agricultural produce were destined to benefit mankind.[12] But the French masses and their leaders had mixed feelings about these benefits. They appreciated the wholesome contributions Americans made, but at the same time they feared their ruinous impact on the economy of France. So great was this concern that the French government adopted defensive economic policies that tended more to mar friendly relations between the two nations than to protect the future interests of France. The mentality that later produced the Maginot Line was merely an adaptation of earlier defensive designs against undesirable economic competitors. In the 1890s Frenchmen became particularly concerned about American competition in the decorative arts, an industry in which French exports to the United States had long reaped handsome profits. Now, ingenious processes enabled Americans to supply their own woodwork, furniture, stained glass, and jewelry of high artistic quality, thus reducing outlets for such French products. Indeed, the "barbarian Yankees," instructed in these decorative arts by Frenchmen, dared invade the French market as well.[13]

To protect its agriculture, France did not hesitate to go to extremes, even at the expense of its people. The import prohibition on American pork in the 1880s was a case in point. One has only to study French-American trade treaty negotiations in the nineteenth century to realize that French procrastinations for over a quarter of a century at a time and leading to no results revealed

12. Dwight W. Morrow, Jr., "The Impact of American Agricultural Machinery on France, 1851–1914, with Some Consideration of the General Agricultural Impact Until 1880" (Ph.D. dissertation, Harvard University, 1957), 300–21, 640–45. American progress in this field was accelerated by contributions of French chemists and agronomists, *ibid.*, 441.

13. L. de Fourcaud, "L'Art en Amérique," *L'Art dans les deux mondes,* November 22, 1890, p. 3; see also, Samuel E. Morss to Josiah Quincy, November 10, 1893, in Consular Dispatches, Paris, T 1-27, DS.

a defensive mentality in economic affairs that contrasted sharply with the imaginative boldness of French artists and writers. If any further indication of France's overly cautious approaches in business and finance were needed, most glaring would be their failure to establish large business houses in the United States or to cash in on American profits by investing in its market opportunities. Instead, French leaders sounded the alarm warning against America's capacity to overwhelm Europe economically. By contrast, Great Britain and Germany were much more enterprising in the United States.

Although during most of the century the tariff policies of both countries moved in opposite directions, each figured prominently in the international trade of the other.[14] The United States supplied France with raw materials, especially cotton and tobacco, while France shipped its fashionable products to the United States, with the trade balance usually in favor of France. Entire French communities and certain producers depended heavily on the American market. Prominent among them were the silk plants of Lyons, the lace producers of Mirecourt, the hat makers of Bordeaux, and the China manufacturers of Limoges. Furthermore, the Alsation cotton mills depended on the steady flow of the long fiber cotton from the southern plantations. And Le Havre and Cherbourg, more so than Marseilles, benefited greatly as shipping centers to America, the country of European immigrants. In America the view prevailed that Americans could much better get along without French luxury goods than France could without American staples. French leaders generally felt uncomfortable with an excessive dependence on American supplies, a dependence their colonial policies tried to head off.

A close look at trade relations reveals that America's trade with France did not grow in comparison to her trade with Great Britain and Germany. France was falling behind in the industrial

14. For details on broader economic questions, see Blumenthal, *A Reappraisal of Franco-American Relations,* 86–118, 153–56; and Blumenthal, *France and the United States,* 167–80, 233–39.

competition. Bureaucratic red tape and obstructions created barriers that French officials usually removed only when poor crops and other calamities persuaded them to make exceptions. Likewise, American business and industry stepped up efforts in France only during periods of economic decline. To complicate matters, differences in taste regarding meat and wine, psychological differences in the taking of financial risks, discriminatory treatment against American merchantmen, and even fear of drawn-out legal ensnarlments in either alien country tended to hold down the full potential of Franco-American relations in trade, commerce, and finance. Contrary to expectations by republicans in both countries, the form of government in France had no bearing on this state of affairs.

Instinctively, the French were not anxious to race into the twentieth century, whereas the optimistic Americans were excited about it. But the usefulness of the rapidly growing number of important inventions, such as the typewriter, the telephone, the electric light bulb and others, which Americans produced in mass quantity, was too obvious to be withheld from people with an appreciation for the comforts of life. In the final two decades of the century, twenty-eight American-owned industrial enterprises in Europe helped to modernize life for many Europeans.[15] Before long, "the Yanks were coming" to Europe by the thousands to study all manifestations of its civilization. And they brought to Europe the productive know-how of American civilization which, without setting out to do so, gradually transformed the pace and shape of life in the Old World.

In a country like the United States in which in the last century the labor supply had been short and cheap land plentiful, workingmen naturally developed certain attitudes that distinguished them from their French counterparts. When in 1802 Eleuthère Irénée du Pont de Nemours founded a gunpowder company in the United

15. Eric Fischer, *The Passing of the European Age: A Study of the Transfer of Western Civilization and Its Renewal in Other Continents* (Cambridge, Mass., 1948), 82–83.

States, having been taught by the famous French chemist Antoine Lavoisier how to manufacture powder, he requested some workmen from the Commissioner of Powders at Essone, France. Du Pont had judged Americans very perceptively. He found them to be generally good workers, but because they were in demand they asked for high wages; they were, moreover, very independent, and inclined to change jobs whenever they felt like it. To reduce the financial risks involved in the investment he was making, Du Pont wanted steady workers who were attached to their employer. With the lure of high wages and a steady job, he tried to bring to America some Frenchmen who "would form a nucleus of which I could always be sure."[16] It is noteworthy that near the end of the century Frenchmen would still single out as a major characteristic the mobility of American workers who were always prepared "to take their chances." American laborers were clearly better off than their European counterparts whose modest life-styles they would have been unwilling to accept. They were better paid, housed, fed, clad, and educated than French workers.[17] Rich in resources and practically doubling its population about every twenty years, America was in a strong position to provide better living conditions for its industrious and spirited people. Even so, it would be a mistake to assume that labor in America did not have to fight its way up every inch of the road.

The basically different material conditions in France and the United States undoubtedly resulted in different psychological attitudes. The fear of unemployment and the sense of a secure position, even at small pay, exercised a great influence on French labor. French employees looked upon their employers in a different light.[18] The prestige and authority of a great company, such as the French railroads, that concerned itself with many details of their daily lives meant something positive to French workers,

16. Bessie Gardner du Pont, *Life of Eleuthère Irénée du Pont: From Contemporary Correspondence* (12 vols.; Newark, Del., 1923–26), V, 359–62.
17. Emile Levasseur, *The American Workman*, trans. Thomas S. Adams (Baltimore, 1900), 144, 228, 329, 365–67.
18. "American Railways and the French System," New York *Times*, September 21, 1877, p. 4; André and Jules Siegfried, "The American Workman and the French," *International Quarterly*, VI (1902–1903), 353–65.

but left American employees quite cool. Unless such intangibles enhanced the chances of advancement and provided better working conditions, American labor was disposed to discount them. Less class-conscious than European workers, American workingmen actually longed for the good life of middle-class families, a goal that was by no means utopian in the land of plenty. But while genuine opportunities existed in the United States for moving from one class to another, its industrial managers were concerned that such movement might interfere with their labor needs.

In the final decades of the nineteenth century quite a few delegations of French workers visited the United States to study the methods of American industry and the progress of the American labor movement.[19] In the summer of 1887 Samuel Gompers welcomed a member of the municipal council of Paris who visited thirty of the largest organized trade unions and about one hundred of the largest factories in America. The French visitor was taken aback by the depth of antagonism between American capital and organized labor. The United States was then clearly far behind French and other European trade unions in social legislation. The one advantage American labor organizations enjoyed over European was the official compilation and publication of statistics, the availability of which held out the hope of materially facilitating the solution to many economic questions.

French labor delegates who had come to visit the Chicago Exposition (1893) were above all else impressed by the highly specialized and costly industrial machines that could produce great quantities of low-priced products.[20] The disposition of the larger American manufacturers to invest great amounts of capital in the most up-to-date machines, even though this meant a high obsolescence rate, disturbed these French visitors because its consequences were likely to be far-reaching to trade and civilization. They realized that the specialization of American machinery was

19. See L. Carissand to foreign minister, December 11, 1883, in Correspondance Commerciale, Boston, Vol. 9, AMAE; and "A French Visitor's Views," New York Times, July 4, 1887, p. 5.
20. Levasseur, The American Workman, 61–89.

in part the by-product of competition between giant concerns, a competition that was much fiercer in America than in France where no market for mass production existed. They were also bothered by a related issue. The age of mass production called for advertising techniques that fascinated Americans, but often disgusted their Gallic friends. The large and loud advertisements at which Americans excelled offended the taste of Frenchmen. Exaggerated claims and pressure tactics also offended them, because they threatened to deprive them of complete freedom of decision in making purchases.[21]

Most disturbing to Frenchmen was the declining role of the individual worker and the small producer in this mechanized mass-production system. Pride in one's work meant a great deal to them. Was the machine destined to replace and perhaps enslave man? Was it destined to speed up the pace of life? Would the material comforts put in the reach of great masses of people enrich or impoverish society? Frenchmen were much more inclined to ponder over the social and human consequences of the machine age than were their "go-ahead" American friends. Too much was at stake to rush into the industrialization and mechanization without carefully considering perhaps irreversible social effects. It appeared to the French that the all-too-optimistic Americans assumed awful responsibilities without thinking through their potential effect on Western civilization.

Inasmuch as the British and Germans were also deeply engaged in this process of industrialization, France was confronted with alternative choices it did not care to make. Instead, it compromised by moving into the modern age at its own more deliberate pace. From a human and psychological point of view, this attempt to prolong the life span of a creative and manageable civilization appeared reasonable enough. But the leading industrial powers permitted the emerging world order to move into the unknown future at its own dynamic speed. Nostalgic France alone could neither direct nor control it.

21. Léo Claretie, "La Réclame aux Etats-Unis," *Revue bleue,* LII (1893) 397–401.

CHAPTER IV

The Impact of Catholic and Protestant Influences

French and American Protestantism

Although religion played a subordinate role in diplomatic relations between France and the United States, religious interactions significantly deepened cultural relations of the two countries. The contributions of French Catholics to the development of Catholicism in the United States, particularly in the first half of the century, and the influence of some American Catholics on the Church in France, particularly in the final quarter of the century, were quite extraordinary. These influences clearly overshadowed the impact of American Protestants on the revitalization of Protestantism in France.

In many social and cultural respects Frenchmen and Americans cooperated in the nineteenth century, showing respect and sometimes admiration for each other, in spite of many cultural differences. The fact, however, that the French population was predominantly Catholic and the American predominantly Protestant affected many personal attitudes and occasionally even influenced policies. Generally speaking, though, the declining role of religion in the nineteenth century and the rising power of the United States tended to minimize the significance of these religious differences.

The usually critical observations Americans made about religion in France reflected their Protestant backgrounds and prejudices. In an illustrative letter from an articulate American traveler in France to the editors of the *Episcopal Recorder* (1841) , we read:

By far the greater portion of the people of France are *infidels*. They have no bibles, attend no place of worship and are grossly ignorant even of the theory of Christianity. . . . The observance rendered even to forms of religion is chiefly confined to females & to the poor & to the illiterate. . . . Romanism in France has lost its hold on the national mind and seems not likely to be the instrument of reforming a licentious people. . . . To keep up the interest of the people reliance seems to be placed mainly upon appeals to the senses. Among these are georgeous decorations of the churches, the gay attire of priests, processions, music. . . . The result of this system is that the educated and intelligent portion of the community have abandoned the churches. The consequence is that a spirit of scepticism and a torrent of immorality has overspread the country. The Sabbath is profaned not only by the prosecution of all kinds of worldly business but by being made a special day for sports and amusements. . . . Gambling is on that day carried to a greater excess, the theatres are unusually crowded.

Two weeks later, writing from Naples, the same observer drew the conclusion: "If the people of France are ever turned from their infidelity & their idols it will be by the application of the doctrines of the word of God to their consciences. And until this shall take place the sight of high altars and the emblems of spiritual power will be of small benefit."[1]

Only a few years later, the president of Dickinson College, John P. Durbin, reiterated the substance of these comments, but in a significantly qualifying version. Quite appropriately he distinguished between Paris and the provinces. With reference to politics and science, he noted that "Paris is France"; but this did not hold true in regard to morals and religion. In spite of the Revolution, which attempted to break down "all sense of religious obligation in the common mind," Durbin argued, "the religious sentiment was never extinguished in the provinces as it was in

---

1. Charles Wesley Andrews to the editors of the *Episcopal Recorder,* October 12 and 25, 1841, in Charles Wesley Andrews Letters, Duke University Library, Durham, N.C.

the capital."[2] Although the bulk of the French people professed the Catholic religion, large numbers of professional men, literati, and politicians evidently prided themselves on being "enlightened" enough to live without it. "The great men of France," commented Mrs. Harriet Beecher Stowe, "have always seemed to be in confusion as to whether they made God or he made them." But the infidelity of prominent French intellectuals and political leaders to Catholicism had undergone a noticeable change since the French Revolution. "It has lost its positive aggressive character and become indifferent," wrote Durbin in 1844. "It does not denounce religion, but pities it. It does not write books against Christianity, for it knows nothing about it."

Other Americans visiting France in the middle period of the nineteenth century frequently deplored the emphasis on splendid churches and superstitious forms rather than on contemplation and conscience, on stimulation of the senses rather than on the deepening of faith. They interpreted the burning of candles before "doll-baby images" as a pitiful exercise of ignorant people who had no conception of the spiritual meaning of religion. Nathaniel Hawthorne was not alone in his judgment that Mass at the Madeleine was "a great stage show." After attending "a splendid service" at the crowded Madeleine, Leslie Ames went to a little undecorated room in which sixty Protestants worshiped God "in spirit and in truth." This contrast demonstrated how "the wealth of the (French) nation is devoted to the Papal idolatry" and made Ames "wonder at the strange perversion of the intellect."[3]

It is interesting that such influential public-opinion media in the United States as the *Nation* and the New York *Tribune* were more objective in their discussion of Catholicism in France than were individual American citizens. The *Nation*, for instance, ex-

2. John P. Durbin, *Observations in Europe* (2 vols.; New York, 1844), I, 110–13, 135.

3. Ames (ed.), *Life and Letters of Peter and Susan Lesley*, I, 56–59; B. M. Palmer, *The Life and Letters of James Henly Thornwell* (Richmond, Va., 1875), 177–79, 233–34; and Rev. John W. M. Williams, "Diary of a European Trip, June 29–October 18, 1867," X, 255–56, John W. M. Williams Papers, UNC.

pressed the view in 1869 that there was a larger amount of genuine religious feeling in France than in any other Catholic country. In its judgment, there was also more Christian faith in France than its atheists were willing to admit.[4] And the New York *Tribune* detected in the final decade of the century "a marked revival of religious feeling" in France, following "the marked decline of materialism and skepticism." Even traditionally atheistic students at the University of Paris apparently manifested "a desire to believe in something—a sort of craving for spiritual sustenance."[5] Believing that atheism and materialism undermined the social fabric and imperiled state authority, the government of the Third Republic fostered freedom of worship for all creeds. The quite frequent return of nonbelievers to the folds of either the Catholic or Protestant religions confirmed the widely held conviction that most human beings longed for some kind of spiritual satisfaction.

Although critical of French Catholicism because of its alleged spiritual emptiness and its political conservatism, American Protestants manifested considerable interest in and sympathy for their French coreligionists. Realizing that the use of religion as an instrument of national and international policy was a historical fact of life, they nevertheless found it extraordinary that France's leading Protestant statesman, Francois Guizot, saw no reason in 1843 "why France should not become . . . the protectress of the Catholic religion in the world: this belongs to her history, her tradition, her situation."[6] The grandeur of France as a world power was thus to be furthered by virtue of the fact that it was a Catholic country. If a Protestant leader viewed the role of France in such

4. "The Church in France," *Nation*, IX (1869), 288–89.
5. "A French Revival," New York *Tribune*, January 24, 1890, p. 6.
6. Durbin, *Observations*, I, 130. Athanase Coquerel, the eminent liberal Protestant preacher in Paris, rejected Guizot's half-hearted estimate that "France will not become Protestant" and "Protestantism will not perish in France." Coquerel confidently predicted that France "will acquire religion as she has her liberties," through a conversion brought about by herself rather than by outsiders. A. Coquerel, "Catholicism and Protestantism in France," *Christian Examiner*, XLV (1848), 363–89.

expedient terms, what possible chance did French Protestantism have in the future? This question was of uppermost concern to Protestants in America and elsewhere.

Although American Protestants endeavored in the first instance to spread the true spiritual gospel in Europe and other continents, they too related religion to politics when they condemned Catholic France as being incapable of leading the Western world to new heights of individual freedom and social morality. Because they sincerely believed that the future of France and its people, as well as that of the world, would look brighter if France were Protestant,[7] American Protestants extended a helping hand to their French coreligionists. They cooperated with them in every possible way through personal contacts, missionary work, and generous financial contributions.

Only profound faith and perseverance enabled French Protestants to survive at all the persecutions and discriminations to which the laws and society of their homeland had subjected them for long periods of time. The Edict of Nantes, promulgated by Henry IV in 1598, granted the Huguenots considerable civil and religious liberties. They were grateful for these concessions, even though several restrictions deprived them of complete equality with Catholics. They could live quite tolerably with this second-class citizenship, looking toward the future for full emancipation. These hopes, however, were badly shattered by the revocation of the Edict of Nantes in 1685, an act of intolerance from which French Protestants never really recovered. For that matter, France and its system of self-government sustained a loss of incalculable consequence following the decline of the wholesome influence of the Huguenot provincial nobility. A ray of new hope for French Protestants appeared on the horizon when Napoleon Bonaparte concluded his Concordat of 1801. Despite the fact that this agreement with the Pope recognized Catholicism as the religion of "the great majority of Frenchmen," Napoleon had no intention of strengthening the notion of an established church. So as to leave

7. For a more detailed discussion of this viewpoint, see *American Eclectic* (November, 1841), 440–54.

no doubt about this determination, he decided to pay the salaries of the Protestant as well as those of the Catholic clergy out of the state treasury. Napoleon's political expediency thus provided French Protestants with vitally needed resources for meeting the religious needs of their congregations.

By the middle of the nineteenth century approximately 500 pastors ministered to about 750,000 French Protestants.[8] Even if one assumes, as contemporaries have suggested, that fear of discrimination induced an equal number of Protestants not to state their religious affiliation accurately in the census of 1851, the number still obviously represented a very small minority (about 2 percent) of the total French population. In certain departments, though, they constituted 10 percent of the population; and in certain rural regions, Protestants constituted as much as 30 percent. The small aggregate percentage of Protestants in France, therefore, did not truly reflect their real power and influence in French society. They wielded an influence far beyond their numerical strength, particularly in government, diplomacy, banking, and education.[9] An explanation for this influence may be found in André Siegfried's observation that "far more than their Catholic countrymen French Protestants appeared to be members of the international community." They moved with great ease in the business and financial circles of leading Protestant countries and acquired skills of great value in the modern world.

If geographic concentration and family tradition aided French

8. By comparison, the number of actively officiating Catholic priests in France was then about 50,000. J. J. Clamageran, *De L'Etat actuel du protestantisme en France* (Paris, 1857), 3; Henry M. Baird, *The Life of the Reverend Robert Baird, D.D.* (New York, 1866), 96.

9. For detailed statistical information, see Pierre Poujol, *Notes pour une histoire du protestantisme dans la France moderne,* 1870–1931 (2 vols.; Paris, 1960–61), I, 2; see also, G. de Bertier de Sauvigny, "Le Protestantisme français sous la monarchie constitutionelle vu par les voyageurs américains," *Société de l'histoire du protestantisme français, Bulletin* (January–March, 1970), 85–101; Charles J. Miller, "British and American Influences on the Religious Revival in French Europe, 1816–48" (Ph.D. dissertation, Northwestern University, 1947); and André Siegfried, "Le Protestantisme," in André Latreille, *Les Forces religieuses et la vie politique: Le Catholicisme et le protestantisme* (Paris, 1951), 206–16.

Protestants in their struggle for survival, the reawakening of a more fervent faith after the Restoration, though fostered by similar developments abroad, gained its own momentum. That it combined Martin Luther's notion of faith with John Calvin's idea of social action evidently strengthened the appeal of Protestantism at a time when the emerging industrial age created social problems of an unprecedented nature. But the frequent organizational and theological controversies between liberal and conservative Protestants sapped their strength and created doubts about Protestantism's capacity to be an effective spiritual guide.

As fate would have it, the mildly successful Protestant revival efforts, especially after the 1830s, suffered a serious blow at the end of the Franco-Prussian War, when nearly 200,000 Protestants of Alsace and Lorraine came under German control. Soon after the War of 1870–1871, the *Nation* described the remaining Protestant churches in Paris and a few provincial cities as "ruins of the old Huguenot Church. There is no life in them; . . . no real desire to make proselytes."[10] The Reformed Church of the old Huguenots had suffered irreparable damage from the long-range effects of the revocation of the Edict of Nantes. Persecution drove large numbers of self-reliant Huguenots into exile, many to the United States. War took its toll, and liberalism in the final decades of the century further weakened the already unsteady foundation of French Protestantism. Even in a theological sense Protestantism was so divided that in some important respects it retained "little of Protestantism except the name." Some French Protestants practically ignored the Bible as an inspired book and observed the Sabbath as little as French Catholics. Others, on the contrary, abounded in all the Christian graces and humbly professed the spiritual nature of the Protestant faith.[11]

As long as liberal and orthodox Protestants in France continued to believe in the divinity of Jesus Christ, their organizational

10. "French Protestantism," *Nation,* XIV (1872), 117–18.

11. "The Division of a Historic Church," New York *Times,* January 4, 1874, p. 4; Grace King, *Memories of a Southern Woman of Letters* (New York, 1932), 130–31.

differences in the liberal-dominated consistories could be overcome. But when the progress of science and the social problems growing out of the Industrial Revolution led some radical thinkers to declare Christianity dead, when in 1863 Ernest Renan described Jesus in his *Vie de Jésus* as "an incomparable man," and when Ferdinand Buisson two years later brought Jesus Christ down to earth in his *Le Christianisme libéral*—orthodox Protestants reacted sharply against what they considered blasphemies.[12] As one of the most prominent among them, François Guizot convinced many moderate members of the Reformed Church of the necessity for checking the ungodly modern voices in its midst. As far back as 1836 he had pleaded in his famous paper on "Roman Catholicism, Protestantism, and Philosophy in France" for these three modes of religion and thought to contribute to the morality and stability of organized society. As a conservative statesman and orthodox elder of his church, Guizot preferred risking internal dissension over silently accepting the dangers inherent in the new religious interpretations.[13] More than anyone else, Auguste Sabatier, the eminent Protestant theologian, succeeded in the 1870s in reconciling the divergent views in French Protestantism by emphasizing the transcendent importance of implementing the ideals personified by Jesus Christ. Faced, by the end of the nineteenth century, with strong anti-Protestant attacks by Ultramontane Catholics, liberal and orthodox Protestants deemed it wise to close their ranks again in order to meet this powerful and dangerous onslaught. In a real sense, their reconciliation at the fraternal conference in Lyons (1899) merely climaxed a century-old struggle for existence. Unlike the splendid and fascinating attractions of the strongly organized Roman church, the Protestant churches had little to offer their adherents besides deeply satisfying spiritual values. If these

12. Georges Weill, "Le Protestantisme français au 19e siècle," *Revue de synthèse historique,* XXIII (1911), 214–19; Dansette, *Histoire religieuse,* 327–28. For American reaction to Renan, see Ralph H. Brown, "American Opinion on Ernest Renan, 1863–1892" (M.A. thesis, Columbia University, 1938).

13. Weill, "Le Protestantisme français," 223–24; Dansette, *Histoire religieuse,* 397–400; "Protestantism in France," New York *Times,* November 27, 1874, p. 1; Louis Chaigne and Jean Balédent, *Guide religieux de la France* (Paris, 1967), 62.

values alone did not sufficiently attract the masses, internal dissension among the Protestants and the social disadvantages that resulted from belonging to a religious minority went far toward explaining the uphill fight of Protestantism in nineteenth-century France.[14]

Although the main credit for the survival of French Protestantism belongs to its devoted believers and inspiring leaders, much of its energy in the nineteenth century was infused into it from England, Holland, Switzerland, and the United States. A new era began in 1818, with the founding of the Bible Society in Paris.[15] At about the same time, American Baptists, Methodists, and Presbyterians established their separate missions in France, and the American Tract Society began to distribute millions of religious leaflets printed in the French language. The endless appeals for funds that French Protestants sent to America following the Revolution of 1830 brought a great variety of positive responses and organizations, aiming at both supporting the activities of French Protestants and at converting European Catholics. By 1846, the Protestant churches had begun to realize that their many separate efforts should be better integrated. The formation of the Evangelical Alliance in London (1846) and its subsequent ecumenical assemblies in Europe and America served that purpose.

Among the multitude of Protestant organizations, at least one more holds our special interest. Though designed to provide for the religious needs of American Protestants in Europe, the American and Foreign Christian Union, founded in 1849, rendered through the American Chapel in Paris greatly appreciated assistance to all Protestants.[16] Early in the nineteenth century,

14. N. A. F. Puaux, *Histoire populaire du protestantisme français* (Paris, 1894), 381.

15. In the same year appeared *Les Archives du christianisme* through which the learned Protestant theologian Frédéric Monod appealed for a religious revival. Chaigne and Balédent, *Guide,* 61–62.

16. See Louise Seymour Houghton, *Handbook of French and Belgian Protestantism* (New York, 1919), 35–38; Jean Bianquis, *Les Origines de la société des missions évangéliques de Paris,* 1822–1830 (3 vols.; Paris, 1930–35); O. Doen, *Histoire de la société biblique protestante de Paris,* 1818–1868 (Paris, 1868); and Ray Allen Billington, *The Protestant Crusade,* 1800–1860 (New York, 1938), 281.

English Protestants had made arrangements for religious services in Paris for interested American residents and travelers. As the number of these Americans increased, an American chapel in Paris became feasible. This was a prospect to which French Protestants looked forward with great anticipation. In 1835 the Reverend Dr. Robert Baird arrived in Paris to assume his functions as secretary of the Foreign Evangelical Society. Although this organization concerned itself primarily with the religious welfare and work of French Protestant churches, Baird also looked after the religious needs of his American compatriots.[17] In 1837 he invited the Reverend Edward N. Kirk, then on a study tour for the American Board of Commissioners for Foreign Missions, to initiate a Sabbath service in a little chapel in the rue St. Anne. This chapel became an American institution. It attempted, in addition to holding the customary religious services, to prevent American youth temporarily residing in Paris "from being swept away from the morality of their fathers and the love of their country." The little chapel attracted much attention every Sunday; the long line of coaches that brought its worshipers reflected their prosperity as much as their devotion.

It must be kept in mind that American Protestants in France always pursued several objectives simultaneously. They helped to sustain the spiritual well-being of their American and French coreligionists; they entertained ambitious missionary goals; and they hoped to collect political dividends as a by-product of their religious propagation efforts. In the judgment of the Reverend Baird, silent examples of pure Christianity rather than sarcastic polemics would succeed in convincing quite a few French Roman Catholics of the virtue of conversion to Protestantism. And a Protestant France, he believed, would be a powerful instrument in evangelizing the rest of the world and depriving the papacy of a strong pillar in its worldwide missionary operations. A Protestant France, many Americans contended, would also be best

17. David O. Mears, *Life of Edward Norris Kirk, D.D.* (Boston, 1877), 114–16; Edward G. Thurber, *Historical Sermon* (Paris, 1907), 5.

able to assume leadership in the movement for political emancipation of the masses. The Reverend Kirk, pastor of Mount Vernon Congregational Church of Boston, whom the American Board of Commissioners for Foreign Missions appointed in 1857 as head of the American Chapel in Paris, shared these larger policy views.

The pastorate of this church, then located near the Champs Elysées, was a demanding one. At that time, nearly three thousand Americans from all parts of the United States resided in Paris, including some two hundred medical and other college students who depended largely on English-speaking clergymen for their religious instruction.[18] A very broadminded attitude was required to satisfy Christian people of all denominations, of various social backgrounds, and of different political outlooks. In a spirit of generous concession, though, Episcopalians, Presbyterians, Baptists, and Methodists united in an extraordinarily mature fashion. The chapel indeed symbolized "the essential unity of American Evangelical Christians in all points of the common faith."[19]

The Catholic church obviously did not look with favor upon these expanding Protestant activities. Since American missionaries set out to propagate not only religious equality and freedom, but universal political freedom as well, and since they identified popery with political authoritarianism and Christian impurity, they ran into considerable opposition.[20] Attempts to prejudice Napoleon III, who regarded himself as the worldly defender of Catholi-

18. "American Chapel in Paris," *AFCU* (January, 1856), 197–98. To accommodate American students in Paris, special services were held in the Latin Quarter. In accordance with the students' express wish for privacy, these services were not publicly advertised. Beach, "The American Student in Paris," 2307–2308.

19. Crooks, *Life and Letters of McClintock,* 344–45. Rev. McClintock regretted the sectarian efforts "of a few extreme Episcopalians." John McClintock to C. C. North, October 29, 1863, John McClintock Letters, Emory University, Atlanta. See also, "The American Church in Paris," New York *Times,* December 20, 1888, p. 4.

20. Ray Allen Billington, "The Anti-Catholic Propaganda and the Home Missionary Movement, 1800–1860," *MVHR,* XXII (1935), 370–71. In the 1850s, John Taylor, an elder of the Mormon church, attempted to establish a Mormon mission at Boulogne. Vehemently opposed by French authorities, the Mormon movement made no headway in France and maintained no French-speaking missionaries. Furthermore the French were very skeptical about the mystic dreams of Joseph Smith, the Mormon leader. Prosper Mérimée, *Etudes anglo-américaines* (Paris, 1930), 40–57.

cism, against the building of the new American church, resulted in the restriction "that there should be no services in the French language in the chapel." The emperor found American propaganda in support of republicanism alarming enough. He and his devoutly Catholic wife, Empress Eugénie, certainly did not wish to facilitate Protestant propaganda among the French people. Nevertheless, in various parts of France evangelists made impressive progress during the Second Empire. About twelve hundred places of Protestant worship in France owed their existence largely to the untiring efforts of these evangelists. Lyons and St. Etienne, among other communities, furnished irrefutable proof that the conversion of Roman Catholics was possible. This was further substantiated by the June, 1861, issue of *Le Monde chrétien,* the organ of the French branch of the Evangelical Alliance. It reported on the evangelistic work that had been going on for some years in l'Aisne. Through the perseverance of Baptist ministers, hundreds of Roman Catholics there passed "from the darkness of Popery into the light of the Gospel."[21]

If French monarchists objected to what they regarded as a dangerous ideological challenge by American republicans, French Protestants and Catholics alike expressed their reservations when Americans presented themselves as the champions of social equality and political freedom. American missionaries were frequently embarrassed by criticism of the tolerance of slavery and race prejudice in the United States. The tolerance of these injustices handicapped all efforts at persuading Frenchmen to emulate the political and religious examples of the model republic. In February of 1857 French Protestants sent an appeal to the United States; it had been signed by more that 5,700 Protestants, including pastors and elders of 579 churches of all denominations.[22] This appeal, as they explained, was prompted by their individual consciences and their concern for the honor of Protestantism.

21. See "Appeal" *AFCU,* IX (1858), 242–43; "Jubilee Year of the Evangelical Society of France," *Christian World,* XXXV (1883), 52–53.
22. See *Archives du Christianisme au 19e Siècle,* August 8, and December 12, 1857, pp. 129–30, 196–97.

"Slavery", it declared, "is a scandal in the nineteenth century." They explained why they could no longer be silent if they wanted to be true to their faith, and they deplored the fact that they themselves were "being accused of tolerating slavery because otherwise they would have denounced its acceptance by Christians in Protestant America." Later in the same year other Protestants in Europe were asked to join in this fight against human bondage and racial prejudice. There can be no doubt that honest conviction guided these Frenchmen in their denunciation of human indignities. But they were also sufficiently practical to fear the consequences of a civil war in America, in terms of both the loss of human lives and the loss of financial aid.[23] They felt the impact of the American Civil War very seriously and prayed for its early end.

This war and the Franco-Prussian War hurt French Protestantism badly and almost brought its upward momentum to an abrupt halt. The peace terms that Protestant leaders of Prussia-Germany imposed upon Catholic France, for political and strategic rather than religious reasons, did not exactly reflect a charitable spirit on the part of German Protestants. Even more direct was the impact on French Protestantism caused by the loss of sizable Protestant populations in Alsace and Lorraine.

The religious interpretation of America's neutrality during the Franco-Prussian War also tended to freeze traditional French sympathies for the United States. This neutrality could realistically be traced to America's usual nonentanglement in strictly European affairs, its resentful reaction to Napoleon's meddling policies in the western hemisphere, and the recent tragedy of the Civil War. Unfortunately, however, some Germans and Americans chose to interpret the Franco-Prussian War as a conflict between Protestantism and Catholicism. It helped neither Franco-American relations nor the religious cause of French Protestants when the Reverend Charles B. Boynton of the Presbyterian church in Washington, D.C., expressing the view of many anti-Catholics,

23. Edouard Borel, *Statistique des associations protestantes, religieuses et charitables de France* (Paris, 1864), 10–11.

saw in this war "an attempt on a giant scale to arrest the progress of civil and religious freedom and to bring first Europe and then the world under the control of the Romish Church by the military power of France."[24] This prejudiced interpretation of a primarily politico-military conflict could only widen the gulf between Protestants and Catholics everywhere. From the point of view of many French patriots, who happened to be Catholics, the American government and Protestant clergy did nothing to relieve France because it was a Catholic country. This erroneous conclusion was quickly refuted by the United States' prompt recognition of the Third Republic soon after the hated Second Empire had completely collapsed. But first impressions and disappointments have a way of lingering on.

Despite the growing religious freedom French Protestants enjoyed under the Third Republic, during the last decades of the century they failed to register noticeable accomplishments in their opposition to Catholicism and atheism. On the contrary, schisms in their own ranks, declining contributions from their own members and from abroad, as well as budgetary cuts by the French government gradually forced such strongholds of French Protestantism as Normandy and the Gironde district to close down many churches.[25] Throughout the nineteenth century Americans contributed generously to the evangelical societies in France.[26] It is difficult, and perhaps impossible, to determine from the available fragmentary evidence the total amount of their financial assistance in the nineteenth century. A conservative estimate would put it at about $1.5 million for the cause of French Protestantism. Yet, in the end, when the evangelistic effort in France, once regarded as the foremost mission field of the world, did not produce the

24. Charles B. Boynton, *The War in Europe: Its Religious and Political Significance* (Washington, D.C., 1870), 3.
25. New York *Tribune*, November 26, 1893, p. 6.
26. See *Christian World*, XXXIV (February, 1883), 52–53; "Evangelization of France," New York *Times*, February 27, 1893, p. 8; Thurber, *Historical Sermon*, 22–23; Henry Tuckley, *In Sunny France: Present-Day Life in the French Republic* (Cincinnati, 1894), 93.

desired results, American Protestants were accused of contributing little more than a pittance to the needs of their French coreligionists. Quite literally trying to cash in on the prejudiced religious and political sentiments some Americans harbored against France, one desperate appeal for funds emphasized the political significance of evangelizing France: "Make France Protestant, Christian, and Europe will be Christ's."[27] Was it not, after all, the historic mission of the United States to spread the gospel of Protestantism throughout the world?

Many Americans gave more than money. Evangelical workers provided convincing evidence of their sincere desire not just to preach the gospel of Christ, but to practice it. For nearly two years (1881–1883) a medical mission at Grenelle opened its doors free of charge to sick people in Paris. In addition to a visiting evangelist and volunteer workers, the medical doctor in charge of this mission took care of from three to four hundred cases monthly, treating them in his dispensary or in home visits.[28] Previously, the medical mission of the American Chapel in Paris had for some years rendered benevolent services to thousands of sick people. After singing a hymn or reading from the Bible, the many persons who came to the mission daily, except Sundays, were admitted to the dispensary in the order in which they had arrived.[29]

Among the remarkably successful evangelizing operations in France ranked the McAll Mission, named after a minister who cared for the poor in Paris and some of the other larger towns in France. In time, he extended his charitable activities to the poor in the villages and hamlets of France, reaching them by means of the mission boat, *Bon Messager*. His efforts to carry the gospel along the "silent highway" of the inland waters of France proved to be very worthwhile. An English pastor, Robert W. McAll visited

27. L. T. Chamberlain, "France and the American and Foreign Christian Union," *Christian World*, XXXV (April, 1884), 139–41.
28. Joseph Wilson Cochran, *Friendly Adventures: A Chronicle of the American Church in Paris*, 1857–1931 (Paris, 1931), 110–11.
29. "Annual Report of the Missionary and Benevolent Work of the American Chapel in Paris," *Christian World*, XXVI (April, 1875), 103–10.

Paris with his wife in August, 1871.[30] In the proletarian section of this city a workingman started a chance conversation with McAll in the course of which he contended that "throughout this whole district . . . we cannot accept an imposed religion. But if anyone would come to teach us religion of another kind, a religion of freedom and reality, many of us are ready for it." In response to this challenging suggestion, McAll opened in 1872 a mission in Belleville, the communistic quarter of Paris; three years later the average weekly attendance in various mission halls had swelled to over 2,500 people to whom McAll meant renewed hope for a more tolerable life. The American McAll Mission Association, founded in 1883, contributed more than one-third of the funds that kept the mission going. McAll's purely evangelistic teachings moved a good many freethinking Frenchmen, some of whom had in the past turned their backs on Roman Catholicism to accept what they considered the *living* gospel of Christ. McAll's religious meetings, lending libraries, and counseling services moved one prefect of a department to declare: "Wherever the McAll missionaries go, fewer police are needed."

One of the most constructive American social and religious enterprises in Paris, supplementing McAll's work, was the "Children's Mission."[31] Attached to the American Chapel, an industrial school for very poor children in the six-to-twelve-year-old age group provided an education and an atmosphere the youngsters learned to appreciate. At first the parents were skeptical that anyone would take an interest in their children merely out of goodness of heart. The school opened its doors in December, 1876, with twenty-six children; by the end of the winter the number of these noisy and undisciplined youngsters had risen to eighty. In subsequent years between two and three hundred of these defiant and disadvantaged children, to whom the distinction between right and wrong was at first incomprehensible, responded to kind-

30. H. O. Dwight, H. A. Tupper, and E. M. Bliss (eds.), *The Encyclopedia of Missions* (New York and London, 1904), 443–44.
31. Cordelia E. LeGay, "Work of the American Chapel: Poor Children in Paris," *Christian World*, XXXV (February, 1884), 48–51.

ness and care. Gradually the mothers of these children acknowledged the astonishing accomplishments of the teachers in the "Children's Mission," and as an expression of simple gratitude they welcomed the missionaries to their modest homes. The beneficial effects of the school on their children convinced many parents of the truly meaningful value of the Protestant gospel. This tendency led late nineteenth-century evangelists to pay special attention to the welfare of French youth. Following the American example, Christian endeavor societies concentrated on saving the souls of the younger generation of France. Substantial financial assistance from America facilitated such endeavors. A philanthropic American, for instance, offered a large sum of money for a French YMCA to be located adjacent to one of the great boulevards, provided a like sum be raised in Paris.[32] Since some of the leading bankers in Paris were Protestants, this condition posed no problem.

Unlike American Protestants in France, French Protestants in America exercised more cultural and spiritual than political and missionary influence. Since colonial times, Huguenots had been coming to America, leaving French notions of government behind in the old country. Strong believers in the political institutions of the United States, they became thoroughly Americanized and took pride in being loyal citizens of their adopted country.[33] Like other French immigrants, however, many French Protestant families remained bilingual at home and in their social life, so long as the younger generation did not object to this lingering attachment to the language of their ancestors.

Founded in the seventeenth century, the French Protestant Church in Charleston, South Carolina, still followed in the late nineteenth century the beautiful liturgy that Huguenots had brought "from the vine clad hills and fertile valleys of France."

---

32. Raoul Stephan, *Histoire du protestantisme français* (Paris, 1961), 282; Tuckley, *In Sunny France,* 89–90.
33. Avery, "The Influence of French Immigration," 63–65. R. P. Duclos, *Histoire du protestantisme français au Canada et aux Etats-Unis* (2 *vols.;* Paris, 1913), II, 209.

But even though the prayer book of this congregation was a translation of Calvin's Geneva Liturgy of 1542, the use of the French language in the services had to be abandoned in 1828 because too many members of the congregation had ceased to speak or understand it.[34] From its founding in 1830, on the other hand, the French Evangelical Church in New Orleans, also known as l'Eglise protestante française, continued to serve as a place of prayer for all French-speaking Protestants.[35] And as late as 1860 a relatively small group of French and Swiss Protestants in Philadelphia invited a French pastor to attend to the spiritual needs of the congregation gathered in l'Eglise française de Philadelphie.[36]

These churches not only satisfied their own congregations, they tried to extend their functions to the missionary field as well, preaching the gospel in the wilderness and "among the Romanists" in neighboring communities. To many members of the congregations, these churches also offered convenient and welcome opportunities for a pleasant social life. Not to be underestimated, moreover, was the satisfaction members derived from practicing Christianity by providing desperately needed help to newly arrived foreigners from France and French Switzerland. The Young Women's Home Society, under the auspices of the French Evangelical Church in the City of New York, for instance, offered temporary shelter at moderate cost and in a wholesome environment to French-speaking young women who had just arrived in the United States or who might be temporarily unemployed.[37] In many other American communities French benevolent societies offered help to needy transient compatriots. Common bonds of

34. See French Protestant Church, Charleston, S.C., *The French Protestant (Huguenot) Church in the City of Charleston, S.C.* (Charleston, 1898), 1–8; and Huguenot Society of America, *Publications,* I (1886), 65–68.

35. Georgia Fairbanks Taylor, "The Establishment of the Episcopal Church in New Orleans, 1805–1840" (M.A. thesis, Tulane University, 1938), 49–52.

36. See *Annuaire protestant* (Paris, 1861), 198, 203; and Sheridan, "The Immigrant in Philadelphia, 1827–1860," 269.

37. French Evangelical Home, New York, *Annual Reports of the Young Women's Home Society of the French Evangelical Church of the City of New York,* 1891–1899 (New York, 1892–1900).

nationality and religion evidently assumed a more vital significance abroad than they customarily did back home.

French reactions to religious life in the United States did not differ much from American reactions to religion in France; they ranged from sympathetic comments to severely critical observations. French travelers were bewildered by the multitude of religious sects in the United States and amazed at the relative tolerance with which they treated each other. Alexis de Tocqueville and other Frenchmen attributed this tolerance to the spirit of religious freedom and the principle of separation of state and church that the American people guarded very jealously. Not everybody accepted this rather superficial explanation. Some French critics noted that although no official church existed and none of the Protestant denominations was in a position to control religious life in the United States, people were expected to be practicing Christians. It was expected that one at least profess some religious belief.[38] Even the Unitarian church, which denied the Trinity and Incarnation, came to be regarded as respectable in spite of its deistic doctrines. Rather unsubtle social pressures made life difficult for those who did not attend a church. The majority of Americans, though, exhibited freely and devotedly their allegiance to the ideals and tenets of the Christian denomination to which they belonged. It was perhaps the greatest tribute that Frenchmen could pay to Americans when they praised their Christianity as a living, earthly kind.[39]

Nevertheless, particularly up to the end of the Second Empire, French monarchists and devout Catholics challenged the vaunted merits of religious freedom in America. To them, Protestantism weakened society at large and carried the seeds of its own destruction because it rested on the principle of the sovereignty of individual reason.[40] As they saw it, the ease with which individuals

38. Chambers, "Observations and Opinions of French Travellers," 89–99; Eugène Véron, "Des Progrès de la liberté dans la théologie protestante," *Revue nationale et étrangère* (September–October, 1861), 321–55.
39. Agenor de Gasparin, *L'Egalité* (Paris, 1876), 335.
40. Philadelphia *Public Ledger*, August 30, and September 4, 1844.

could establish a new religious sect and recruit zealous disciples who interpreted the Bible in their personal way amounted to an abuse of liberty of conscience. If it were true, as Voltaire had once quipped, that "every Protestant is a pope," then Protestantism as a religion failed to fill the heart of man and give him faith in the future.[41] Listening to some nineteenth-century Protestant preachers, hell seemed to be the only certainty in the next world. And after the economic panic of 1857, Americans, exhorted by their pastors, manifested a national penitence, asking forgiveness for their sins that had precipitated the panic. Puritanism and the ability to inflict punishment upon oneself had evidently not yet completely disappeared. One of the more extreme French critics asserted that Christianity was embodied in the laws of the land, but that divinity enjoyed no recognized right. "The United States are above all the land of apostacy," he asserted. "Millions of Americans have not been baptized. This becomes of Christianity when it is only a form of deism." What kind of a Christian people is this anyway, he asked in his condemning analysis, that sanctions slavery and tolerates divorce?[42] Another French critic went even further, charging that where "there is . . . no pride, no devotion, no spirit of justice, there can be no future." Gradually abandoning the traditional civilizing influences of religion and family, America, he thought, seemed headed toward an era of shameless arrogance and cynicism.[43] Reversing the political pronouncement American Protestants used to make with respect to Catholic France, Eugene Veuillot contended that "if anything can elevate them [the United States] to the rank of a nation, it will be the return among them to the only true faith: Catholicism."

41. B. H. Revoil, "Souvenirs des Etats-Unis: Religions bizarres professées dans l'union américaine," *L'Illustration*, XV (1850), 212–14; de Grandfort, *The New World*, 122; Emile Jonveaux, "Eccentricités sociales et religieuses de la Nouvelle-Amérique," *Le Correspondant*, LXXI (1867), 77–121.

42. Eugène Veuillot, "Etudes sur les Etats-Unis," *Revue du monde catholique*, XVII (1867), 75–101. Some French Catholics condemned divorce as a system of "legalized concubinage." See Cook, "French Travellers in the United States," 100.

43. Jannet, *Les Etats-Unis contemporains*, I, xx–xxi.

French travelers in the United States[44] noted with astonishment that in the land of equality, liberty, and religious tolerance there was so much class consciousness and racial and religious prejudice. On the whole, they noticed, the rich upper class, particularly in the South and East, belonged to the Episcopalian church; the fairly educated middle classes were largely in the fold of the doctrinaire and socially strict Presbyterian church; and the "fanatic" Baptists and Methodists recruited their following from the lower classes and, in the South, from Negroes. French visitors found the odious system of separation of races in churches both shocking and un-Christian. They understood perfectly well that the election of the Protestant pastors by their congregations made the ministers the victims of popular passions and prejudices and prevented them, as the Catholic church could do, from applying essential Christian principles without bowing to intolerable customs of the land.

Equally offensive to French visitors was the realization that ever since the American Revolution Catholics were subjected to discriminations and persecutions, for religious reasons as well as to stem the influx of Catholic immigrants. In New York, for instance, foreign-born Catholics could not, up to 1821, become citizens unless they abjured their allegiance to the Pope. In Massachusetts, up to 1833, Catholics had to contribute to the support of Protestant churches; and the constitutions of New Jersey and New Hampshire contained anti-Catholic provisions up to 1844 and 1877 respectively. And although the Catholic population of New Orleans literally enjoyed their Sundays singing and dancing and playing, their coreligionists in New York or Boston would not have dared to defy their Protestant neighbors by disrespecting the Sabbath in such "Sodomic" activities.

French travelers were as struck by the large number of churches they found all over the United States as by the modest architecture and simple interiors of the churches. The majestic impression conveyed by the external structure, precious sculptures,

44. See Elisabeth M. Rodrigue, "Les Voyageurs français aux Etats-Unis pendant la première moitié du 19e siècle" (Ph.D. dissertation, Radcliffe College, 1945), 134–68.

and colorful stained windows of the churches and cathedrals in France seemed to symbolize wealth and power, as well as an appeal to the sense of beauty. In Protestant America, the simplicity of political institutions and daily life graced religion as well. The interdependence of democratic and religious institutions indeed became characteristic of American life, even to the paradoxical extent of the immodest claim that republican America was God's own country.[45] The substantial voluntary financial support American Protestants gave to their numerous churches was in part prompted by the belief that the social fabric of the country was benefited as much by religion as by the individual. This pragmatic approach to religion actually led Henry Bargy to discern by the turn of the twentieth century the existence of an American religion, a religion of humanity that cared more for the welfare of society than for that of the individual and that took a greater interest in human existence than in supernatural ideas. Although this oversimplified generalization contained a grain of truth, it also sounded very much like the superficial Protestant charge that French Catholicism impiously appealed more to the pleasures of man than to the contemplative life and reverence for God.

French and American Catholicism

Paralleling the aid and encouragement American Protestants extended to their French brethren, French Catholics took an active interest in the growth and development of the Catholic church in the United States. French priests and French money, particularly in the first half of the nineteenth century, helped to establish and maintain Catholic churches and schools in the United States. Historically, French Catholics had good reason to claim proudly that "the Church of France is the mother of the Church in America."[46] In the second half of the century, however, the large num-

---

45. Henry Bargy, *La Religion dans la société aux Etats-Unis* (Paris, 1902), vii, 295; Michel Chevalier, "Etude sur la Constitution des Etats-Unis," *JDD* (May 25, 1848).
46. C. N. Moreau, *Les Prêtres français émigrés aux Etats-Unis* (Paris, 1856), 5.

ber of Irish and German Catholics who migrated to America successfully challenged the influence of the French priests. Actually, the Catholic church in America went its own way, and by the end of the century the social direction of Catholicism in the United States caused a major controversy in the Catholic world, in France no less than in Rome.

A dramatic scene in 1783 set the stage for the kind of religious tolerance that, in spite of subsequent decades of discrimination against Catholics, enabled them by the turn of the twentieth century to count their numerous blessings. At the end of the Revolutionary War in America, the French minister to the United States had made arrangements for the singing of the Te Deum in St. Joseph's Chapel in Philadelphia. It was an historic occasion attended by George Washington and General Lafayette.[47] The example set by the father of the American republic established a precedent that made it easier for future Protestant presidents of the United States to attend Catholic services. The refugee priests and many other French exiles of the Revolution who came to America in the 1790s did much to lay the foundation for the future of the Roman Catholic church in the United States. Between 1791 and 1815 nearly one hundred French émigré priests came to this country and scattered out in all directions. The learned and tactful priests of Saint Sulpice and many French Sisters and Brothers provided seminary and school education of high quality and inspiration.[48] The Society for the Propagation of the Faith, founded in Lyons in 1823, contributed a major portion of the financial resources for Catholic missions in the United States. Year after year, sizable amounts of money were sent from Europe to the Roman Catholic church in America. During the first hundred years of its existence, this society channeled over seven million dollars to the United States. The Catholic Councils of Baltimore periodi-

47. Ibid., 93.

48. Childs, French Refugee Life in the United States, 99; Thomas T. McAvoy, The Great Crisis in American Catholic History, 1895–1900 (Chicago, 1957), 95; Leo F. Ruskowski, "French Emigré Priests in the United States, 1791–1815" (Ph.D. dissertation, Catholic University of America, 1940).

cally requested more aid from it. For the millions of poor Catholic immigrants from Europe, priests, teachers, churches, and some temporary material assistance were needed.[49]

Despite frequent acts of discrimination against Catholics and attacks against "un-American" French priests, the representatives of a "foreign aristocracy," the Roman church seemed to appeal more to the soul and sentiments of many Americans than did the various Protestant denominations that tried to reach the minds of people in a rather abstract and not always inspiring manner. Wherever Frenchmen settled down, along the frontier in the West, in New Orleans, or even in Boston, the Catholic church struck roots, and the preservation of French culture was assured for some time. Bishop Jean Louis Cheverus, who became Archbishop of Bordeaux in 1826 and ten years later was elevated to the rank of cardinal, arrived in Boston in 1796; from that time he furthered the interests of the Church directly, as well as indirectly by befriending many leading Protestants. Among his many friends he counted John Adams, the first subscriber to the new Catholic church built in Boston. Somehow Bishop Cheverus' charity, integrity, and refinement convinced dubious New England Protestants that "a priest could be a good man."[50]

The Enlightenment had brought French Catholics and American Protestants closer together than either seemed to be willing consciously to admit. The assistance France had rendered the struggling American republic during its War of Independence, regardless of its political motivations, narrowed the gulf of mistrust that had previously existed between Frenchmen and Americans. If a less dogmatic and more cosmopolitan religious outlook, moreover, facilitated Franco-American cooperation in the late

49. Edward John Hickey, "The Society for the Propagation of the Faith: Its Foundation, Organization and Success" (Ph.D. dissertation, Catholic University of America, 1922), 75–93, 116, 188–89; Raymond Corrigan, *The Church and the Nineteenth Century* (Milwaukee, 1948), 88; Robert Baird, *De La Religion aux Etats-Unis* (2 vols.; Paris, 1844), II, 287.

50. Ruskowski, "French Emigré Priests," 15; Allan Forbes and Paul F. Cadman, *Boston and Some Noted Emigrés* (Boston, 1938), 38–42; André Jean Marie Hamon, *The Life of Cardinal Cheverus* (Boston, 1839), 50–51.

eighteenth century, it was also noteworthy that Catholic belief in the equality of man before God gave substantial meaning to American belief in the equality of man before the law. The attack by deists, skeptics, atheists, and materialists against orthodox theology, both Catholic and Protestant, in late eighteenth-century Europe and the religious revival of the 1830s were movements that did not leave the United States untouched.[51] Political declarations of independence from Europe, whether issued in 1776 or 1823, could not becloud the fact that in the main currents of civilization the United States clearly remained a part of the Western world. The predominance of the French clergy in the early history of the young republic suggested political motivation, with the French aiming at control of America. But at the end of the Napoleonic Wars, France was too exhausted for such an ambitious undertaking; and the confused state of its religious affairs during the French Revolution and the years following it simply encouraged quite a few Catholic clergy to propagate their faith abroad, even in the lonely and raw regions of the American frontier.[52]

The sizable number of French-Canadians who arrived in Chicago in the 1840s and 1850s replaced the Frenchmen who had decided to migrate westward. As was frequently the case in such circumstances, a priest came along from Canada to Chicago to care for these French-Canadian families.[53] He tried to help the settlers overcome their initial hardships, enlisting their Catholic faith as a vital means of survival. He also saw to it that their attachment to French culture be kept alive in the face of many pressures and temptations to adapt as quickly as possible to the American environment. Similar conditions prevailed

51. Howard Mumford Jones, *America and French Culture*, 365–77.
52. Theodore Maynard, *The Story of American Catholicism* (New York, 1941), 220–22; Willard L. Sperry, *Religion in America* (New York, 1946), 210–11.
53. In the words of Alexis de Tocqueville, a French-Canadian priest was "in every true sense the pastor of the flock," not an "entrepreneur of religious industry." White, "American Manners in 1830," 129; see also, Gilbert Joseph Garraghan, *The Catholic Church in Chicago, 1673–1871* (Chicago, 1921), 149–50; and Thomas T. McAvoy, *The Catholic Church in Indiana, 1789–1834* (New York, 1940), 32–51.

then and for some decades to come in New England, the ancient citadel of Puritanism to which many impoverished French-Canadians migrated. Enlisting the aid of French newspapers,[54] the priests tried to preserve the French background of these immigrants in the belief that by resisting Americanization they could also resist the inroads of Protestantism. The uncompromising attitude of these foreigners caused serious antagonism between Irish and French Catholics, because the Irish were anxious to adapt themselves as quickly as possible to American living conditions without abandoning their Catholic faith. Naturally, Protestant New Englanders resented the stubborn resistance the French clergy encouraged against American civilization. In the ensuing social conflicts French-Canadians received some moral support from Montreal and Quebec, but little sympathy and even less aid from France, which was not particularly interested in the French-Canadians and their fate.

Sometimes such charitable actions as those of the Sisters of Charity who cared for the victims of cholera outbreaks, from which Protestant ministers allegedly fled with their families, helped the cause of Catholicism. And Protestant ministers who failed to keep in touch with frontiersmen in the no-man's-land of the West unwittingly helped secure converts to the Catholic church.[55] By 1855, the Catholic church in the United States embraced 41 dioceses, 1,712 parishes, 34 seminaries, 20 colleges, and 112 religious community centers for the education of girls.[56] Eleven French bishops and more than one hundred French priests contributed to the amazing vitality of the Roman church in America, in spite of the strongly anti-Catholic Know-Nothing movement of the 1850s. The Know-Nothings harassed Catholics in an often frightening manner,

---

54. Maximilienne Tétrault, "Le Rôle de la presse dans l'évolution du peuple franco-américain de la Nouvelle-Angleterre" (Ph.D. dissertation, Université de Paris, 1935), 121; Mason Wade, "The French Parish and Survivance in Nineteenth Century New England," *CHR*, XXXVI (1950), 163–89.

55. Maxime de Montrond, *Missions d'Amérique, d'Océanie et d'Afrique: Lettres, récits et fragments divers* (Lille, 1861), 23–26.

56. Moreau, *Les Prêtres français émigrés*, 8, 115.

but they failed to break the spirit of American Catholics and inadvertently evoked the sympathies and support of French and other European Catholics for their persecuted brethren in America.

During the Civil War in America and the years following it Frenchmen took an ever keener interest in the political and religious affairs of the Protestant republic across the Atlantic. In his wisdom, President Lincoln sent the able New York clergyman, Archbishop John Hughes, to France and charged him with the mission of convincing the French clergy and the political leaders of the Second Empire that the future and progress of Catholicism in the United States looked far more assuring in the North than in the South. Although the monarchical hierarchy of the Church in France entertained serious reservations about the republican institutions in the United States and the unorthodox tendencies of American Catholics, it did not push Napoleon III into a policy of intervention in the Civil War. Liberal French Catholics of the Montalembert orientation, moreover, who opposed the monarchy's firm hold on the Church and education, responded sympathetically to the cause of the Union, for the sake of French political and economic interests as well as because of enlightened institutions. The ill-conceived attempt to block the advance of Protestantism and republicanism by erecting a barrier to the south of the United States by establishing a Catholic monarchy in Mexico evidently satisfied the French emperor and his clerical supporters sufficiently to prevent them from decisively aiding the Confederacy.

The tragedies of the Civil War—its massive destruction of lives and properties, its disruptive and ruinous economic effects, and the anguish it caused to millions of citizens of the "model republic"—also demonstrated a strange human paradox. The hatred and miseries engendered by this war taught a good many citizens, northerners and southerners, Protestants and Catholics, the virtues of compassion and tolerance. The zeal of Catholic chaplains and the devotion of Catholic nurses, among them many French Sisters who cared for those wounded in body and soul, helped to break down prejudices on an unaccustomed scale. Furthermore, the abolition of slavery opened up a huge, previously unavailable Catholic missionary field among poor Negroes. In a communication to the journal published by the Society of Jesus, one observer criticized French missionary circles for extending their apostolic activities to India, China, and Madagascar while ignoring the vast possibilities of making converts in America.[57] Millions of Negroes and several hundred thousand Indians in America led wretched lives, and evidently few missionaries showed genuine concern for them. The relatively small number of priests (2,600) in the giant United States confined Catholic missionaries in the 1860s to entirely inadequate attempts at counterbalancing the zealous missionary efforts of Protestants.

Foreigners were not the only ones to swell the ranks of the Catholic church in America after the Civil War. Quite a few were converted Protestants or, particularly in New Orleans, people who had long been imbued with Voltairian notions of deism and anticlericalism. Whatever attitudes separated American Protestants and Catholics, Protestants were usually much more conciliatory toward Catholicism—and even more so toward Catholics as human beings—than were their European coreligionists. Without the slightest reservation they frequently enjoyed attending Catholic services. It is no wonder that instead of referring to Protestants as irreconcilable enemies, Cardinal James Gibbons of Baltimore invariably spoke of them as "our dissident brethren." The prelate of a western diocese traced this reciprocal tolerance to the observation that Americans "are true Christians who are not preoccupied with theological doctrines."[58]

Writing from New York in May, 1831, Alexis de Tocqueville predicted confidently that the essentially Christian United States offered a favorable climate for the future of the Catholic church. The vigorous progress of Catholicism in a predominantly Protes-

57. "Varia," *Etudes religieuses, historiques et littéraires,* X (1866), 387–95, and XII (1867), 299–300.
58. Marie C. A. Meaux, *L'Eglise catholique et la liberté aux Etats-Unis* (Paris, 1893), 333; *Louis Eugène Louvet, Les Missions catholiques au 19e siècle* (Paris, 1895), 262–303; William W. Sweet, *Religion in the Development of American Culture* (New York, 1952), 48–49.

tant society seemed to prove irrefutably that the Catholic church had nothing to fear from liberal institutions. In a series of articles published by the *Correspondant* between 1867 and 1869, Emile Jonveaux, among other contributors writing about religious questions in the United States, went so far as to express the view that the Catholic church in America held out genuine promise of becoming "the most powerful auxiliary to the cause of progress and civilization."[59] As early as 1868 Jonveaux enthusiastically defended the views of Father Isaac T. Hecker, who tried to reconcile the traditionally orthodox structural and ecclesiastical ways of the Church with the more independent political, social, and religious ways of Americans. This great difference in approach and outlook, almost revolutionary in nature and involving the survival of the Catholic church in the age of the Industrial Revolution, climaxed a generation later in an internal Church controversy of major scope.

As far as the future of American Catholicism was concerned, enlightened American Catholics realized in the final decades of the nineteenth century, that certain essential requisites had to be met in order to create the atmosphere conducive to the Church's steady upward movement. These essentials included continued loyalty to the American government and its democratic institutions, acceptance of the principle of separation of state and church, a friendly relationship with other religious groups in the United States, and concern for the social, economic, and religious welfare of the people. Regardless of religious affiliation, American laymen and clergy did not like to divorce religion from the activities of daily life. Helpful concern for millions of poor European immigrants made the Church a friend rather than an enemy of the people.

Those Frenchmen who would have liked to see Catholicism in France liberalize itself after the successful pattern of the Church

59. Emile Jonveaux, "Les Catholiques du nouveau-monde jugés par les protestants," *Le Correspondant,* LXXVI (1868), 826–64; John J. Meng, "A Century of American Catholicism as Seen Through French Eyes," *CHR,* XXVII (1941), 40–50.

in America were not unaware of the historical differences in French and American Catholics. In Europe, advocates of the principle of separation of state and church usually wanted to express an anti-Christian viewpoint. In the United States, however, the principle of separation was intended to protect all faiths from interference by the state. The strong ties of the Church in France with the supporters of monarchical institutions did anything but strengthen the precarious situation in which the Third Republic found itself in the difficult years after Sedan. Even Pope Leo XIII's appeal to the Catholics of France in the final decade of the century, urging them to abandon their resistance to republican institutions, failed to bring about immediately the kind of loyalty to the existing institutions that American Catholics had traditionally supported. In the Old World, moreover, the Catholic church possessed deep historical roots of a political and ecclesiastical nature; in the United States where, realistically, these roots did not exist, the church was free to grow with the rest of the young and modern society.[60] And, as we have already mentioned, Catholics and Protestants in Europe were much more distant from each other than were their counterparts in the United States. In the conflict between liberty and authority, in political and religious respects, different backgrounds and traditions made it difficult for the most influential leaders of the Church in France and the United States to maintain harmony.

Though a Catholic country, Catholicism in France has not always favored the supreme authority of the Pope. The conflict between supporters of the Gallican church and defenders of the Roman Catholic church clearly showed a strong desire in France for independence from Rome.[61] The attitudes of its monarchical rulers and the social and political problems accompanying the Industrial Revolution confronted the Roman church with serious problems. The rather cynical treatment of the Pope by Napoleon I

60. McAvoy, *The Great Crisis*, 96–97.
61. P. L. Péchenard, "The End of Americanism in France," *N*AR, CLXX (1900), 420–32.

was followed by the great hypocrisy in religious matters during the reign of Charles X and the low ebb of religion during the kingship of Louis Philippe. The volatility of the religious situation in France was perhaps most dramatically demonstrated in 1848 by the pulpits that blessed the February Revolution and by workers who, having plundered the Tuileries, reverently carried the crucifix from its chapel to the famous Church of St. Roch.[62] But the close ties between the clergy and Napoleon III revitalized the anticlerical forces on the left who looked upon the clergy and capital both as enemies of the people and the teachings of Christ.[63]

Too preoccupied with their own parochial interests, French royalists and Ultramontanes tried one scheme after another to entrench themselves in power. Blindly ignoring the fact that the times did not favor the restoration of dynasties, they never ceased undermining the foundations of the Third Republic. Their ambitions gave Pope Leo XIII serious concern, for he realized that the future of the Church in France would be endangered without the support of the masses. Historically, French governments have been accused of having supported Catholicism for the glory of France rather than for the glory of God. From the time of the French Revolution, religion in France was regarded with persistent skepticism by intellectuals and growing numbers of workers. The first Empire had de-Christianized France; and the Revolution, which Joseph de Maistre, the eloquent and unyielding advocate of the restoration of papal authority, described as *satanique par essence,* had left in its wake a division that weakened society as well as the Church.[64] Surprisingly, the situation changed after determined attacks against the socially insensitive Church and the hated regime of Charles X in 1830, despite the fact that Louis Philippe's religious indifference held out little hope for the fortunes of the

62. C. S. P. Phillip, *The Church in France,* 1848–1907 (London, 1936), 24.

63. Dansette, *Histoire religieuse,* 295–326; Jean Maurain, *La Politique ecclésiastique du Second Empire* de 1852 à 1869 (Paris, 1930), 958; Henri Guillemin, *Histoire des catholiques français au 19e siècle,* 1815–1905 (Paris, 1947,) 247–50.

64. M. D. R. Leys, *Between Two Empires* (London, 1955), 214–16; Orestes A. Brownson, *The Works of Orestes A. Brownson* (20 vols.; New York, 1966), X, 506, and XI, 295–98.

Church. Spearheaded by French Protestants, a religious renaissance seemed also to be a popular Catholic reaction to decades of disgust with unbelieving devils of all kinds.[65] Such Catholic leaders as Félicité Robert de Lamennais, Charles de Montalembert, and Jean Baptiste Lacordaire, who chose "God and Liberty" as the motto of their journal *L'Avenir,* made efforts to reform the Church so as to avoid its traditional identification with reactionary monarchy and the privileged classes. The "liberal Catholics" understood perfectly that the future of Catholicism in France was tied to political liberalism and social reform.

Realizing that the strong anticlerical movement could only diminish the popular support and loyalty the Church needed, Pope Leo XIII tried his best to convince all French Catholics that they should accept the Third Republic in good faith. His encyclical *Rerum novarum* (1891), designed to bring people seeking social justice back to the folds of the Church, was soon followed by his attempt to identify the interests of the Church in France with those of the Third Republic. He chose Archbishop John Ireland of St. Paul, Minnesota, who happened to be in Rome in 1891, as his ideal unofficial representative in France. Archbishop Ireland had gained reputation as the spokesman of the American, rather than the Roman, Catholic clergy. The son of Irish immigrants, John Ireland (1838–1918) had for eight years attended seminary at Belly, France. His flawless French and his keen interest in French politics and church affairs ultimately involved him deeply in both areas.[66]

Though invited to speak in Paris as an American prelate about "Conditions in America," Archbishop Ireland addressed the audience of some twelve hundred distinguished French citizens of all political and religious shades with the blessings of the Holy Father. In this address, enthusiastically received and widely disseminated in the French press, Archbishop Ireland stressed the loyalty of

65. John E. C. Bodley, *The Church in France* (London, 1906), 46; Michel Darbon, *Le Conflit entre la droite et la gauche dans le catholicisme français, 1830–1953* (Toulouse, 1953), 37–38; Alec Mellor, *Histoire de l'anticléricalisme français* (Tours, 1966), 276–87.
66. James H. Moynihan, *The Life of Archbishop John Ireland* (New York, 1953), 136–47.

American Catholics to the republican form of government and their appreciation of the blessings of liberty that made it possible for Catholicism to flourish in the predominantly Protestant United States. The intended contrast with conditions in France was too obvious to be missed. There, conflicts between church and state and Ultramontanes and liberals inevitably accelerated the people's drifting away from the Church. A few days later, the Archbishop addressed the students of the Catholic Circle, urging them to stand behind the Third Republic and to participate in the search for improved material conditions while at the same time satisfying their needs for spiritual sustenance. Talking frankly to the priests of Paris, Archbishop Ireland criticized them for neither knowing the people in their care nor adequately promoting their welfare. He reminded them that the workingmen were far more interested in happiness in this world than in the next. It was indeed extra-ordinary for an American citizen, even though a dignitary of the Church, to tell French citizens what to do and to expound views which were anathema to the orthodox clergy. He obviously felt free to do so for the sake of the Church; the fact that he was an American was in this context merely incidental. The experience of American Catholicism, on the other hand, inspired him to help implement Leo XIII's social encyclical. Addressing a group of priests, the gray-haired and forceful Archbishop Ireland elaborated his thoughts plainly and logically: "Today, the people is a force. If the Church wants to triumph, it must triumph with the help of the people. The time is gone when the Church could count on the people by counting on those who governed them. In an age of universal suffrage the poorest workingman is judge in his land. Tell the people that they have not only duties, but also rights. . . . Priests, it is up to you to win over the giant of modern democracy. Let us develop a Christian democracy, and Christ will win and reign."[67] He was even more outspoken in a private letter to a French writer: "Your priests," he charged, "live in the past; they are the prisoners of theology and they have no

67. Albert Houtin, *L'Américanisme* (Paris, 1904), 204–12.

contact with modern life or vision of the future . . . the Church in Europe, and particularly in France, is asleep; it does not progress."[68] Its beautiful cathedrals and priests in gold-embroidered vestments burying themselves in theology, he warned, could not hope to secure the loyalty and devotion of the flock. Similarly, Monsignor John Lancaster Spalding, Bishop of Peoria, Illinois, reminded orthodox theologian doctrinaires: "Jesus Christ did not teach philosophy; he founded a church, not an academy."[69] Cardinal James Gibbons of Baltimore (1834–1921), another leading figure in the American hierarchy who had been educated by Sulpicians, also let no opportunity pass without confirming the compatibility of the Catholic church with republican institutions and reiterating the obligation of the Church to help promote the welfare of the masses. Material progress, he maintained, was after all a manifestation of divine goodness.

Immigration and natural reproduction rather than mass conversions accounted for the growth of the Catholic population in the United States from three million in 1860 to six million in 1880, and to twelve million in 1900. By the turn of the century American Catholics could proudly point to more than 10,000 churches and chapels, more than 10,000 priests and seminary students, some 100 colleges, and 4,000 parochial schools and academies. Cardinal Gibbons explained the ability of the Church in America to cope with the tremendous problems raised by such rapid growth as having been due to its organization and devotion no less than to the institutions of the land.[70] Through his adviser Abbé Magnien,

68. Max Leclerc, *Choses d'Amérique: Les Crises économique et religieuse aux Etats-Unis en* 1890 (Paris, 1891), 245–51. Archbishop Ireland played a significant diplomatic role prior to the outbreak of the Spanish-American War. In 1900, President McKinley commissioned him to deliver the address on the occasion of the presentation to France of a statue of General Lafayette. It disappointed President Theodore Roosevelt that his behind-the-scene efforts to elevate Archbishop Ireland to the rank of cardinal were not successful. Moynihan, *The Life of Archbishop Ireland,* 151–55.

69. Dansette, *Histoire religieuse,* 520.

70. Leclerc, *Choses d'Amérique,* 215–56; Jules A. Baisnée, "L'Influence religieuse française aux Etats-Unis," *Les Etudes américaines,* V (1947), 21–31; James Cardinal Gibbons, *A Retrospect of Fifty Years* (2 vols.; Baltimore, 1916).

sixth president of the Baltimore Seminary, Cardinal Gibbons kept in touch with many distinguished liberal Catholics in France. Perhaps the most authoritative theoretician of progressive Catholicism in the United States was the Sulpician Abbé Hogan, for thirty-two years professor at the Seminary of Saint Sulpice at Issy, founder of the Seminary at Boston, and president of the Divinity College of the Catholic University of America in Washington, D.C. Frenchmen identified Abbé Hogan and Father Isaac T. Hecker as the exponents of what they called religious "Americanism."[71] Father Hecker (1819–1888), a former transcendentalist and member of the Brook Farm community, converted to Catholicism at the persuasive appeals of his good friend Orestes Brownson, himself a well-known convert to Catholicism. Founder of the Paulist Fathers, a religious community organized to improve the living conditions of poverty-stricken Irish immigrants and to Americanize all Catholic immigrants, Father Hecker selflessly devoted his life to these tasks. His approach, he was convinced, would not only strengthen the Church, it would also preserve its unity and head off potentially explosive demands for separate churches, schools, and priests for each immigrant nationality group in the United States. In time, Father Hecker came to symbolize a modern kind of Catholicism that emphasized individual conscience and social concern for the poor and de-emphasized the religious rituals and rules of the Roman Catholic church.

When Father Hecker died in 1888, a fellow Paulist, Father William Elliott, wrote *The Life of Father Hecker* to which Archbishop Ireland contributed an introduction. When this eulogy of Hecker was published in French, a storm broke loose. Liberal French Catholics who deplored the growing unpopularity of the Church in France found Hecker's social-gospel type of Catholicism appealing. It was likely to appeal also to the people, the poor, the workers, and the intellectuals. Conservative clericals, however,

71. Houtin, *L'Américanisme*, 80–81; Howard Mumford Jones, *America and French Culture*, 444–45.

opposed it bitterly. They saw in religious "Americanism" a threat to the authority of the Pope and the doctrines of the Church. A flood of usually polemic articles in 1898 attacked the attempt to sacrifice Catholic dogma on the altar of simple morality. "Americanism," French opponents charged, was just another attempt to force Catholicism into a Protestant mold; it was a barbarous assault against established society.[72] Religious laissez-faire notions disturbed those Frenchmen who wanted the authority of the Church to be upheld and who did not believe that "all liberty is equally acceptable to God." "Americanism's" emphasis on material welfare offended their concept of the spiritual nature of the Church; and the essentially deist tenets of the new religion appeared to place humanity above Christ. These opponents of "Americanism" specifically challenged the validity of the claim that the Catholic Church in America was a remarkably successful organization. Aside from the fact that its rapid growth could not be traced to mass conversions, these critics noted that the Church in America had failed to grow in the South or to attract followers from the Negro and white populations of that region. Inasmuch as for all practical purposes separation of church and state meant Protestant education in "Godless" schools, it did not surprise orthodox French Catholics that American statistics indicated a higher rate of crimes and poverty among those students not attending parochial schools. And could there be any doubt, they asked, that in the "land of liberty" Catholics ran into social and job discriminations, no matter how cultured and competent they were? Would it be possible, they inquired knowledgeably, for the most highly qualified Catholic to become President of the United States?[73]

No matter how justified, these specific criticisms could hardly detract from the genuine accomplishments of the Catholic church in America. From a realistic point of view, they did not even ad-

---

72. Guillemin, *Histoire des catholiques français*, 363.
73. Meng, "A Century of American Catholicism," 49–61; McAvoy, *The Great Crisis*, 239–49.

dress themselves to the central issues raised by religious "Americanism," which advanced neither a new theology nor a scientific system. Beset by internal stresses that the success of the rapidly growing Church brought with it, "Americanism" answered in a peculiarly American way the needs of the country of immigrants. It manifested no pretensions of imposing upon Catholics from other countries new religious ideals or principles, though it ventured to hope that its example might contribute to an internal reform of the Church.[74] All the Americanists set out to do, within the framework of the constitution of the United States, was to advance "the kingdom of the Father who is in Heaven." The French translation of *The Life of Father Hecker* was in many respects inaccurate; and despite the fact that shortly after its publication there were seven French editions, Abbé Klein tried to put an end to the furor by withdrawing it from circulation.[75] When Leo XIII wrote to Cardinal Gibbons on January 3, 1899, that he took no exception to the word *Americanism* as far as it applied to the laws and customs of the American people, he took the only position really open to him, even though he had previously warned against the separation of church and state, a system that would subject the Church to the common law governing the life of all citizens. However, the Pope took a firm stand against *Americanism,* if it meant "a series of doctrines prejudicial to the integrity and maintenance of dogma and to the obedience due to the authority of the Church."[76]

Questioning the exact meaning of the Pope's statement, the talented editor of *La Quinzaine,* George Fonsegrive, tried to reason that Americans were not guilty of the errors Leo XIII condemned. In defense of the Americanists, Fonsegrive argued that American bishops did not lack sincerity "when they disavowed beliefs they never held." The whole controversy over "Ameri-

74. Maynard, *The Story of American Catholicism,* 516–17; Jules Tardivel, *La Situation religieuse aux Etats-Unis: Illusions et réalité* (Paris, 1900), vi.
75. Thomas T. McAvoy, "Americanism: Fact and Fiction," *CHR,* XXXI (1945), 141–46; Vincent F. Holden, "A Myth in *L'Américanisme,*" *CHR,* XXXI (1945), 154–70.
76. Péchenard, "The End of Americanism in France," 420–32.

canism," he thought, had been blown out of proportion.[77] As he saw it, "American mentality is essentially practical and concrete, that of the French is primarily theoretical and abstract. Americans think pragmatically, the French with words." He furthermore believed that certain of the American practices might well be adaptable to French needs and the national genius of the French people. But such explanations were unacceptable to the supporters of clericalism in France. Their part in the Dreyfus affair embarrassed these clericals profoundly and lowered their standing with many conscience-stricken French citizens. To lose power and authority, as well as prestige, by yielding to the democratic and social-minded notions of certain American Catholics, they felt, was truly too much to accept.

Preoccupation with political considerations in essentially religious questions manifested itself in other contexts as well. The prominent place Cardinal Gibbons and Archbishop Ireland occupied in the Catholic world encouraged some Catholics in the United States to dream of an American pope. Evidently not dismissing the possibility that "Rome ne sera plus dans Rome, mais dans Baltimore," the French minister in Washington, Théodore-Justin Roustan, warned the Quai d'Orsay of the undesirable political ramifications that France should keep in mind should Cardinal Gibbons ever be considered for elevation to the throne of St. Peter, since Gibbons "unjustly believed that German Catholic priests were superior to the French clergy."[78] Three years later, Jules Patenôtre, Roustan's successor, at length explained to his foreign minister why the French clergy had been steadily losing ground in the United States, clearly a matter of political consequence to France.[79] Patenôtre sent the following significant chart to Paris showing that in 1892 as many as 56 percent of the Catholic bishops

---

77. Georges Fonsegrive, "Américanisme et Américains," *La Quinzaine,* XXVII (1899), 306–18.
    78. Théodore-Justin Roustan to Eugène Spuller, May 17, 1889, CPEU, Vol. 165, AMAE.
    79. Jules Patenôtre to Alexandre Ribot, June 23, 1892, CPEU, Vol. 169, AMAE.

and archbishops in the United States were of foreign origin, but only slightly over 7 percent of the total number were French.

Present Number of Archbishops
and Bishops in the United States
1892

Origin	*Number*
American	37
Irish	16
Belgian	10
German	9
French	6
Austrian	2
Swiss	2
Spanish	1
Alsation	1
Total	84

The justification for the relatively large number of Beligan bishops may be found in contemporary American history. In religion, as in the arts and literature, Americans were striving to develop their own national identity. To become a more homogeneous nation, they increasingly emphasized the need for Americanization of all aspects of life. Leading American Catholics fully understood this trend, and they tried to implement it by putting an early end to conflicts arising from competition among priests of various foreign nationalities in the United States. The choice of Belgian bishops was to be a transitory appeasement, since Belgian origin was practically synonymous with neutral origin. French ecclesiastics were usually entrusted with the very difficult task of establishing new Catholic centers; and when the dioceses originally organized by them became vacant, Belgian and Swiss priests were appointed to them, to be succeeded eventually by Americans. The declining influence of the French clergy in the United States was also reflected by the fact that French bishops were assigned, with the exception of Burlington, Vermont, to such minor episcopal sees as Tuscon, Arizona; Helena, Montana; Natchitoches, Louisiana; San Antonio, Texas; and Santa Fe, New Mexico.

Anxious to restore their standing in American society, Monsignor A. Léon Bouland, parish priest of Notre Dame des Victoires in Boston, suggested in 1883 the establishment of a French-directed Catholic university.[80] With the exception of the Jesuit College at Worcester, no Catholic college existed in the United States; the founding of a Franco-American Sorbonne, he thought, would hold out great promise for all connected with it. Politically even more revealing were the comments Ambassador Jules Cambon submitted in June of 1901 to French Foreign Minister Théophile Delcassé.[81] Cambon, by far the most distinguished diplomat France had sent to the United States, regretted that the great contributions Frenchmen had been making in America were not being taught in France. French schools paid much attention to missionary work in the Orient, but they were not sufficiently alert to the growing significance of the United States as a major factor in modern civilization. They ignored the influential role French priests and religious orders of women played in America. According to Cambon, these people occupied a strategic position enabling them to exercise moral influence very effectively upon Catholic masses. Their network embraced the entire country; and, as in the case of the Petites Soeurs des Pauvres who hailed from St. Servan in Brittany, they enjoyed universal respect.

The overall strength of religious orders in the United States encouraged Cambon, because he judged the orders to be of considerable significance to the cultural and political interest of France. French Sisters instructed nearly half of the half-million students in parochial schools. In spite of the sizable number of German immigrants, neither the Germans nor the Italians nor

80. See enclosure in Théodore-Justin Roustan to Clément Armand Fallières, February 16, 1883, CPEU, Vol. 159, AMAE.

81. Jules Cambon to Théophile Delcassé, June 12, 1901, "Les Congrégations françaises aux Etats-Unis," in Papers of René Waldeck-Rousseau, Institut de France, MS 4607. Although the "Little Sisters of the Poor" were joined by a few Irish women, the use of the French language continued to be obligatory in their homes.

any other foreigners came even close to duplicating the hold of French educators on the religious and educational institutions in the United States. In addition to the cultural contributions made by these Sisters, Sulpicians contributed to the fine reputations of the seminaries at Baltimore, Boston, New York, and San Francisco by directing them so well. Because French influence on American culture was actually and potentially greater than was generally assumed, Cambon deplored the fact that France did not politically exploit this strong position. By thus belittling French contributions to American life, he believed his compatriots "confirmed the Anglo-Saxons in the arrogant opinion they have of themselves and the disdain with which they regard French mores."

In the overall development of American Catholicism, the considerable influence of the French clergy in the early nineteenth century gradually declined during the rest of the century, though Catholic French teachers managed to hold an important place in American parochial schools. In their endeavors to strengthen the foundations of Catholicism in America, many French diplomats and priests were so concerned with their own cultural and political objectives that they alienated many Americans of all faiths in the process. If French Catholics were looking for some consolation for the rise and fall of their clergy in the United States, they could easily find it in the failure of American Protestants to accomplish little more than to help keep Protestantism in France alive. French Catholics had at least the satisfaction of witnessing a truly impressive growth of the Catholic church in the United States. Its progressive social and moral example constituted a greater challenge to French Catholicism than French Protestants had ever been capable of mounting.

In the nineteenth century, Protestant America overtook Catholic France as a commercial sea power. As far as the material well-being of the masses contributed to the dignity of man, the Calvinistic doctrines that so greatly influenced the economic life of the American people also sustained its spiritual existence. In terms of institutionalized religion, by the end of the nineteenth century American Catholicism had caught up with the less cohesively organized Protestant denominations. This phenomenal development perhaps overshadowed the far-reaching impact of the progressive type of American Catholicism on the younger generation of French Catholics. Within the span of a century the earlier missionary work of French Catholics in the United States had laid the foundation for a Church that beyond all expectations turned out to be so strong and viable as to suggest to Catholics in France the direction that would safely lead them into the twentieth century.

American Catholics also did not hesitate to intervene in the religious affairs of France, at least indirectly. Following the Law of Associations, which withdrew state recognition and subsidization of religion, American archbishops asked Cardinal Gibbons in 1906 to assure François Cardinal Richard, Archbishop of Paris, of their concern for the Church of France. In his letter Cardinal Gibbons protested that American Catholics found it difficult "to understand how a civilized government can, in the name of liberty, subject an entire Christian people to the yoke of official atheism."[82]

Catholic and Protestant citizens of both countries, who would have disclaimed any desire to interfere in the political affairs of the other country, obviously took it for granted that they not only had the right, but the obligation, to participate in its religious affairs. Nineteenth-century French and American civilization believed in the concept of humanity as a magnificent ideal and saw no conflict in treating coreligionists anywhere as brothers and sisters, as long as they did not interfere with national interests. In violation of this ideal, however, humans of a different religious denomination did not always experience the same unprejudiced treatment.

82. Allen S. Will, *Life of James Cardinal Gibbons* (Baltimore, 1911), 335–38.

CHAPTER V

Interchanges in Philosophy

The scientific revolution of the seventeenth century set an evolution in motion that challenged and secularized traditional notions concerning God and society. The convictions that nature was governed by certain discoverable laws and that scientific observation, experimentation, and analysis were superior to metaphysical speculation gained further ascendency in the eighteenth and nineteenth centuries. During the age of Enlightenment the view spread from Europe to America that mankind was capable of improving its conditions and thereafter experiencing steady existential progress. Intellectual leaders nevertheless perpetuated philosophical doubts and controversies with their shifting arguments regarding the relative significance of reason, feeling, and morality in the interpretation of nature and man. To complicate matters, the cosmopolitan nature of philosophical development in the seventeenth and eighteenth centuries manifested itself in the cross-fertilization of ideas, so that in the nineteenth century philosophers of different nations tended to treat their subjects in such a variety of ways that no integrated direction developed.

French thinkers of the late eighteenth century exercised considerable influence on American thought, particularly through such prominent Americans as Benjamin Franklin and Thomas Jefferson. The materialistic and pragmatic orientation of the

French *idéologues* appealed to these practical philosophers of the New World and helped to nourish deism in their country. The writings of the naturalist George Louis Leclerc de Buffon and of the "ideologists" Pierre Jean Georges Cabanis and Antoine Louis Claude Destutt de Tracy fascinated American intellectuals almost as much as Jean de Crèvecoeur's embellished description of America as "the most perfect society now existing in the world."[1]

Jefferson's election to the presidency delighted the *idéologues* who saw in it further justification for the intellectual *entente cordiale* between themselves and the United States. Aside from their imagined notions of what America represented, the *idéologues*, like the *philosophes* before them, used the United States as a political example to justify the practicability of their philosophical concepts of modern society. Harassed by Napoleon, they applauded Jefferson's inaugural defense of the liberties of the press, religion, and person, as well as equality before the law and majority rule. The *Décade*, the *idéologues'* publication, found it heartening to see "the first magistrate of a great people . . . proclaim them as the only ones proper to raise a nation to its highest prosperity and felicity"— and this at a time when in Europe notions of government founded on liberal and philosophical ideas were relegated to the land of fantasy. Better yet, despite the abusive press attacks against him, Thomas Jefferson set an example, gratefully noted by the *idéologues*, when his second inaugural address reiterated his faith in truth and reason: "The press, confined to truth," he contended, "needs no other legal restraint; the public judgment will correct false reasonings and opinions on a full hearing of all parties."[2]

Whether in France or the United States, believers in orthodox

1. Isaac Woodbridge Riley, *American .Thought: From Puritanism to Pragmatism and Beyond* (New York, 1941), 96–99; Isaac Woodbridge Riley, "La Philosophie française en Amérique, *Revue philosophique,* LXXXIV (1917), 393–97; Durand Echeverria, *Mirage in the West: A History of the French Image of American Society to* 1815 (Princeton, N.J., 1957), 206–207, 271–73; Lawrence S. Kaplan, *Jefferson and France* (New Haven, 1967), 29, 92.

2. Gilbert Chinard, *Jefferson et les idéologues: D'Après sa correspondance inédite avec Destutt de Tracy, Cabanis, J.-B. Say et Auguste Comte* (Baltimore, 1925), 29–30.

religion were outraged by the heresies of eighteenth-century French intellectuals. Voltaire's rejection of supernatural revelation, his sociological explanation of religion, and Jean Jacques Rousseau's infidel belief in a loving God outside the framework of an established church were in both countries subjected to severe criticism. And the evil influences of the French Revolution, in the course of which millions "prostrated themselves, with religious reverence, before the word of Reason," prompted the "Pope of Connecticut," Yale President Timothy Dwight (1752–1817), to deplore the atheistic and agnostic views of many of the French disciples of Voltaire, Rousseau, Jean le Rond d'Alembert, and Denis Diderot who had accompanied Lafayette to America. "The whole mass of [antireligious] pollution," Dwight recorded, "was emptied on this country."[3] His fear of the consequences likely to result from this poisonous pollution was shared by many devout Christians.

Between 1820 and 1850 philosophy in France and the United States turned from the skeptical and sensual theories of the eighteenth century to a new awareness of spirituality. But instead of relying on the authority of the Bible, philosphers in both countries recognized the divine moral conscience of man as the most hopeful guide toward the evolution of a truly enlightened society. Believing in the perfectibility of man, American transcendentalists and French eclectics envisioned a universal order furthered by the harmonious application of scientific and religious ideas.[4] Since Victor Cousin (1792–1867) and Theodore Jouffroy (1796–1842), two of the most prominent French philosophers of this period, found many admirers among American men of letters, their influence on American thought merits a more detailed inquiry.

The fact that eclecticism constituted more a synthesis of the "truths" of different philosophical systems than a philosophy it-

3. Timothy Dwight, *Travels in New England and New York* (4 vols.; London, 1823), IV, 366–73.
4. Riley, "La Philosophie française en Amérique," 398–412; William Girard, "Du Transcendentalisme considéré sous son aspect social," *University of California Publications in Modern Philology*, VIII (1918), 220; "Transcendentalism," *Princeton Review*, n.s., XI (1839), 37–101.

self reveals its limitations as well as its cosmopolitan roots. By the same token, New England transcendentalists did not introduce new philosophical principles; they based their idealistic doctrines on modified versions of philosophical views expounded by German, French, and English philosophers. Kantian idealism, for instance, reached the United States via England and France. Samuel Taylor Coleridge's *Aids to Reflection* and George Ripley's translation of Victor Cousin's *Philosophical Fragments* led an American critic to declare as early as 1832 that Cousin rather than Immanuel Kant was the leading spirit in the new philosophical movement. In his introduction to *Specimens of Foreign Standard Literature,* Ripley elaborated: "The objects at which Mr. Coleridge aims, it seems to me, are in a great measure accomplished by the philosophy of Cousin. This philosopher demolishes . . . the system of sensation, against which Mr. Coleridge utters such eloquent and pathetic denunciations. It establishes on a rock the truth of the everlasting sentiments of the human heart. It exhibits to the speculative inquirer, in the rigorous form of science, the reality of instinctive faith in God, in virtue, in the human soul . . . and the immortality of man."[5] Influenced by Thomas Reid, Kant, Friedrich Wilhelm von Schelling, and the philosophical works of their countrymen François Pierre Maine de Biran and Pierre Laromiguière, Cousin and Jouffroy emphasized the key importance of human consciousness and the vital roles of common sense and impersonal reason. Believing that psychology was the basis of philosophy, they tried to harmonize "emotional impulse and rational reflection" as a means of elevating man. So strong was this social goal that under the impact of the developing industrial civilization of France the philosophical idealism of the eclectics gradually inclined toward the utilitarian philosophy implemented by the socialistic experiments of Charles Fourier.[6]

5. Octavius Brooks Frothingham, *Transcendentalism in New England: A History* (New York, 1876), 66, 73–75; Walter L. Leighton, *French Philosophers and New England Transcendentalism* (New York, 1968), 27–43, 54–56, 93.

6. Henry A. Pochman, *German Culture in America: Philosophical and Literary Influences,* 1600–1900 (Madison, Wisc., 1957), 85.

Victor Cousin's popularity in America during this period of social and intellectual ferment is well illustrated by the circulation of his works in several translated editions, by the large number of favorable and critical references to him in periodical publications, and by the extraordinary correspondence he carried on with a number of American intellectuals.[7] Interest in Cousin evidently persuaded Henning G. Linberg in 1832 to publish an English version of Cousin's *Introduction à l'histoire de la philosophie*. Two years later, Caleb S. Henry introduced his translation, with notes and appendices, of Cousin's *Elements of Psychology: Included in a Critical Examination of Locke's Essay on the Human Understanding*. The popular reception of this rendition was evidenced by its fourth edition in 1856. George Ripley's *Philosophical Miscellanies from the French of Cousin, Jouffroy, and Benjamin Constant* in 1838 and William H. Channing's translation of Jouffroy's *Introduction to Ethics* in 1840 both added to the better understanding of the French eclectics in America.[8] The study of these texts at several American colleges, not only in New England, but as far west as Michigan, where Henry Tappan (1805–1881) delivered several lectures on "Cousin and Eclecticism,"[9] expressed the intellectual appeal of their optimistic, tolerance-promoting, and essentially religious teachings. That in the decades from 1828 to 1848 alone American periodicals discussing French philosophy referred to Cousin fifty-one out of sixty-six times offers additional external evidence of American interest in the French eclectics, sometimes also referred to as transcendentalists.

In a remarkable letter to Cousin, dated March 28, 1837, George Ripley justified this interest substantively: "I am anxious," he wrote, "to explain and to recommend the Eclectic Philosophy

7. See Georges J. Joyaux, "French Thought in American Magazines: 1800–1848" (Ph.D. dissertation, Michigan State College, 1951), 58–66.
8. Riley, *American Thought*, 392–95; Pochman, *German Culture in America*, 102–103.
9. Adrian Jaffe, "Letters of Henry Tappan to Victor Cousin," *Michigan History*, XXXVI (1952), 301.

in our country. I see clearly that it is destined to exert a mighty influence on the progress of the American nation. It gives us a source of strength which we have all long wanted and which hereafter will fill our high places of learning and government with sages instead of pedants, and statesmen instead of politicians." In an overly enthusiastic vein he continued to assure Cousin: "You are clearly marked out in the Providency of God as the philosopher of our western world and to preside over that branch of the intellectual development of our people. Enlightened minds from the Atlantic cities to the villages of the Mississippi pronounce your name with gratitude. We want a philosophy, a more spiritual faith, a more enlightened religion. We want Schleiermacher and yourself." Some seven months later, he reiterated that "according to present appearances, French eclecticism is to be the guiding light of American democracy. We need it more than anything else to purify and elevate our policies, and to give a firm basis to our rapidly advancing civilization."[10] In his correspondence with George Ripley and Caleb Henry, Cousin encouraged the active development of philosophy in the United States, and he related it to political goals in the sense that he questioned the feasibility of liberty in a society that would not believe in the dignity and rights of man, or in the grandeur of his destiny.[11]

It naturally pleased Henry Tappan that Cousin praised his *Elements of Logic* as a work equal to any European work on this subject. When Tappan visited his "dear friend and master" in mid-century, the sight of "quite a full collection of American authors on philosophical subjects" in the French philosopher's library reinforced the cordiality with which Cousin received him and his daughter. His admiration for the French eclectic who proposed "to bring together all truth, wherever found, into one harmonious system," never waned. In contrast to the infidel doctrines

---

10. George Ripley to Victor Cousin, March 28 and November 6, 1837, Correspondance de Victor Cousin, BVC.

11. J. Barthélmy-Saint Hilaire, *Victor Cousin: Sa vie et sa correspondance* (3 vols.; Paris, 1895), II, 461–65.

of Voltaire, Cousin, after all, "has arrayed himself on the side of Christianity and morality."[12]

Inasmuch as this religious, but nonsectarian, philosophy aimed more at stimulating thought than at seeking disciples, it was relatively easy for soul-searching individuals like Orestes A. Brownson to switch from enthusiastic acceptance to critical evaluation of it after his conversion to Catholicism. In a letter written in 1832 Brownson acknowledged the inspiring effect of Cousin's philosophical works; they had convinced him "that metaphysics may aspire to the rank and certainty of a science" and enabled him "to find a scientific basis for my belief in nature, in God, and immortality."[13] Writing in 1837 in the *Christian Examiner*, he once again expressed his satisfaction over the French eclectics' "strictly scientific" method of solving philosophical problems. "It is the experimental method," he elaborated, "that of observation and induction."[14] In later years, Brownson treated eclecticism only as a method, not a philosophy, and, in accordance with Cousin's view, "a method of verification rather than of construction."[15] He also rejected Cousin's assumption that philosophy had its beginning in psychology. To him, philosophy sought "to explain the origin, principle, and genesis of things," whereas psychology sought "to explain the origin, conditions, and validity of our cognitions."[16] Despite additional differences with respect to God and causality, Brownson nonetheless believed that his philosophical differences with Cousin were less "than might at first sight be thought."[17]

12. Charles M. Perry, *Henry Philip Tappan: Philosopher and University President* (Ann Arbor, Mich., 1933), 137–39; Tappan, *A Step from the New World to the Old*, II, 294–96. On Cousin's recommendation, Tappan was elected to membership in the Institut de France.

13. Orestes A. Brownson to Victor Cousin, November 13, 1832, Correspondance de Victor Cousin, BVC.

14. Orestes A. Brownson, "Jouffroy's Contributions to Philosophy," *Christian Examiner*, XXII (1837), 190; Pochman, *German Culture in America*, 104–105.

15. Brownson, *The Works of Orestes A. Brownson*, II, 310.

16. *Ibid.*, I, 134–35.

17. Orestes A. Brownson to Victor Cousin, December 22, 1958, Correspondance de Victor Cousin, BVC.

Not the least contribution for which Brownson thanked Cousin was his eloquent articulation of the rather involved works of such German philosophers as Kant, Hegel, and Schelling. "We like Germany all the better," he confessed, "for being filtered through the brain of France."[18] This Franco-German infusion of thought promised to check, if not overcome, the powerful influence English and Scotch philosophers had long exercised in America. Even so, he suggested that the transcendentalist movement in America had been merely influenced, not caused, by "the attachment of its prominent actors to the literature of France and Germany."[19]

Despite individual enthusiasts and a popular vogue for a little more than a decade, French eclecticism really never assumed the significance that British, German, and Greek philosophy had more lastingly attained in the United States. Charles Fourier's socialistic schemes, furthermore, fared no better in the United States than in France. The visionary experiments at Brook Farm and Fruitlands, by-products of the transcendentalist movement in the United States, made still less of an impact on American society than the philosophy of the French eclectics. Even Ralph Waldo Emerson and Margaret Fuller, two of the leading spirits of American transcendentalism, expressed some reservations with respect to the oversimplifications and practical soundness of the French eclectics.[20] Others, led by such orthodox religious journals as the *Christian Review* and the *Princeton Review*, actually launched determined attacks against what they described as the French eclectics' poisonous blend of long-discredited theories. The *Princeton Review* rejected Cousin's psychology as a "seductive and destructive form of error."[21] As pious Christians saw danger in the eclectics' attempts to liberalize religious teachings, the

18. Orestes A. Brownson to Victor Cousin, November 13, 1832, *ibid.*

19. Clarence L. F. Gohdes, *The Periodicals of American Transcendentalism* (Durham, N.C., 1931), 53, 64, 80; Vincent Y. Bowditch, *Life and Correspondence of Henry Ingersoll Bowditch* (2 vols.; Boston, 1902), I, 45–46.

20. Gohdes, *Periodicals of American Transcendentalism*, 111–25; Girard, "Du Transcendentalisme," 470–92.

21. Riley, "La Philosophie française en Amérique," 404–405; Pochman, *German Culture in America*, 104–105.

large mass of believers in political nationalism also found Jouffroy's concern for the priority of "the future of humanity" quite disturbing.[22]

Traditionalists faced a much more serious challenge to their thoughts and beliefs from the philosophical and sociological system of Auguste Comte (1798–1857) . As if Darwinism did not provoke enough theological controversy, Auguste Comte's "social science" and "religion of humanity" also put orthodox religion in jeopardy. Although Comte had published his *Cours de philosophie positive* between 1830 and 1842, it was not until late in 1853 that Harriet Martineau's translated condensation of this work set the stage for a wider discussion of it in the United States. The article the *United States Magazine and Democratic Review* published on Comte's philosophy in 1847 did not reach a sizable audience; and the Reverend Joseph Henry Allen's discussion of it in the March, 1851, issue of the *Christian Examiner* dismissed this "ultimate form of religious unbelief" as an attempt to give "the whole world . . . over to the reign of charlatanism and mediocrity."[23]

The central core of Comte's *Positive Philosophy* was his law of the three stages—theological, metaphysical, and positive— according to which the human mind explains phenomena in this successive order. The objective of this philosophy was to free humans from the limiting restrictions of theological and metaphysical conceptions and to apply to the study of society scientific processes and laws, in the manner of the natural sciences. Instead of trying to explain social and political conditions by reference to divinity and metaphysics, the positivist would limit himself to a factual analysis of their interrelated existence. To Comte, "society" did not only embrace the whole human race. The "scientific spirit," he contended, "does not permit us to look

22. George Boas, *French Philosophies of the Romantic Period* (Baltimore, 1925), 243.

23. Richard Laurin Hawkins, *Auguste Comte and the United States,* 1816–53 (Cambridge, Mass., 1936), 19–25; J. H. Allen, "Comte's Positive Philosophy," *Christian Examiner,* L (1851), 174–202.

upon society as being really composed of individuals."[24] He identified the family as the element that held the societal structure together. It was the family that instinctively civilized individuals, rather than the external laws imposed by institutional authorities. Though basically utilitarian and scientific, Comte was convinced that there could be no progress of society unless the individual's moral development culminated in altruistic beliefs sustaining the "religion of humanity." The elaborate role he assigned for the direction of this religion to an appropriately qualified priesthood elicited the criticism that Comte's system amounted to Catholicism without Christianity. Even the questionable defense that it constituted a combination of Catholicism and science at best hinted at the relative closeness of Comtism to Catholicism. Comte's association of Protestantism with social anarchy obviously irked American Protestants. He charged that the Protestants' emphasis on individual conscience and their approval of divorce interfered with the implementation of his social order that rested on the pillar of the family.[25] His contention, moreover, that theology and metaphysics were dying a natural death in the age of science, presented a danger neither Protestants nor Catholics could responsibly ignore. By comparison, atheism, deism, pantheism, and transcendentalism appeared to be more concrete challenges to orthodox religion; at least their triumph was anything but "inevitable."[26]

In his *Positive Philosophy* and *Positive Polity*, Comte revealed himself to be a brilliant child of the post-Revolution era, earnestly searching for intelligent ways in which society could be systematically reconstructed. Convinced that "from science comes prevision: from prevision comes action," he naturally advocated scientific approaches to the problems of society and its institutions.

24. George H. Mead, *Movements of Thought in the Nineteenth Century* (Chicago, 1936), 461–62.
25. Hawkins, *Comte and the United States,* 10–14.
26. Richard Laurin Hawkins, *Positivism in the United States,* 1853–1861 (Cambridge, Mass., 1938), 20–26; Ralph H. Gabriel, *The Course of American Democratic Thought* (New York, 1940), 260–61.

His unworthy denials notwithstanding, Comte's early association with Saint-Simon had conditioned his mind to think about society in broad and dynamic terms. In one significant respect he was prophetically, but hopelessly, ahead of his time. His vision of the future led him to the conclusion that excessive loyalty to national ties was so harmful that he pleaded for the unification of Europe as a preliminary step to the union of humanity. Quite consistent in his thinking that moved from the general to the specific, he did not believe that any part of society could long maintain its well-being without that of humanity as a whole.[27]

Considering that the United States presented a fertile soil for schemes designed to improve the lot of mankind, it was disheartening for Comte that, contrary to his expectations, his positive philosophy did not strike roots in the transatlanic republic. For a time he hoped that Henry Edger and John Metcalf, the American apostles of positivism, would be able to win adherents among the working masses of the eastern cities and, subsequently, convert the Western hemisphere.[28] But the "self-chosen Pontiff of the human race" had evidently failed to grasp that Americans cherished their personal liberty too much to permit the positive priesthood to interfere with it and that they would be unwilling to substitute the "religion of humanity" for the deeply satisfying mystic notion of an unknown God. Moreover, as in 1846 a French critic had denounced Comte's positive philosophy as an epicurean scheme destined to enslave the human spirit rather than liberate it,[29] in the 1850s the Protestant clergy in the United States launched a devastating attack against it. The arguments advanced in an issue of the *Methodist Review* (1852) were echoed by Presbyterians, Unitarians, and others until the danger of positivism had passed:

27. Ronald Fletcher, *Auguste Comte and the Making of Sociology* (London, 1966), 8–18; David Shillan, *The Order of Mankind as Seen by Auguste Comte* (Richmond Hill, England, 1963), 3; Frank E. Manuel, *The New World of Henri Saint-Simon* (Notre Dame, Ind., 1963), 136.
28. Hawkins, *Positivism in the United States*, 209–218.
29. Emile Saisset, "La Philosophie positive," *RDDM* (July 15, 1846), 185–220.

Comte's Positive Philosophy is the last word of modern infidelity. . . .
It is the most undiluted development of the material, money-seeking,
selfish and self-sufficient tendencies of the late centuries. A disposition to
reject all restraint . . . to bow to no sovereign but human reason, and to
adore human intellect with a base and beggarly worship, as corrupting as
it is blind, has become the main characteristic of this nineteenth century,
and has matured in anarchy, revolution, and social distress, its fatal fruits.
These tendencies have at length crystallized into a brilliant system in the
Positive Philosophy; but its brilliance is death.[30]

Not all American critics of Auguste Comte were as negative
or uncompromising. Although he had no large following in the
United States, he exercised direct and indirect influence on several Americans. In his editorial notes for *Putnam's Monthly
Magazine*,[31] Parke Godwin, for instance, defended Comte against
the charge that his Godless religion was amoral; to him, Comte's
unconventional religion did provide for spiritual morality. Godwin could not accept, however, Comte's notion that science superseded the infantile conceptions of the ideas of God and causality.
Instead, Godwin suggested, it was the function of science to substantiate these ideas.[32] Others saw a possible compromise in the
argument that in the customary manner of scientific assumptions
religious truth could be accepted as an hypothesis. Reverend
Charles Woodruff Shields, since 1865 a professor of the harmony
of science and religion in the College of New Jersey at Princeton,
even went so far as to deny any conflict between theology and
positive science by simply accepting God as the "Sublime Mecha-
nician" of the universe.[33]

Among the Americans who thought that Comte advanced man's
search for a deeper understanding of society, the Philadelphia
lawyer and doctor Horace B. Wallace believed that Comte had not
ruled out coexistence of the three methods of philosophizing.[34]

30. "Faith and Science," *Methodist Review*, XXXIV (1852), 199.
31. *Putnam's Monthly Magazine* (December, 1853), 683.
32. Hawkins, *Positivism in the United States,* 27–32.
33. *Ibid.,* 50.
34. Hawkins, *Comte and the United States,* 72. At Harvard, Chauncey Wright
shared this view, but as a mathematical physicist he considered only scientific
inquiry worthwhile.

Others, including the scientist John William Draper, applauded the desirability of moving from speculative to positive science and of trying to bring about a unity of knowledge.[35] Though influenced by Comte, the economist Henry Charles Carey, whose *Principles of Social Science* appeared in Paris in 1861, did not accept Comte's hierarchy of the sciences, each with its own laws. Unlike Comte, Carey believed in the feasibility and necessity of studying the social sciences by moving from the part to the whole.[36] And although Lester Frank Ward, author of *Dynamic Sociology,* appreciated Comte's treatment of society as an organism that could be scientifically studied, unlike Comte, he maintained that sociology depended more on psychology than biology.[37]

As this discussion of Cousin and Comte has already noted peripherally, such prominent French utopian socialists as Claude Henri Saint-Simon (1760–1825) and Charles Fourier (1772–1837) left their imprint on the social and philosophical thought in Europe and America. Saint-Simon, who had accompanied Lafayette at the time of the American Revolution and who followed the social experiment in America with much satisfaction, dedicated his life to the improvement of the deplorable condition of society's poor. This concern prompted him to write *The New Christianity,* a work in which he emphasized society's obligation to raise the moral and material standards of the poor.[38] Toward that end, he advocated an industrial state in which the most capable men of science would be in charge of producing the essentials of life for all members of society. His scheme of things was to be ac-

35. Donald Fleming, *John William Draper and the Religion of Science* (Philadelphia, 1950), 49, 58, 108–109.

36. Arnold W. Green, *Henry Charles Carey: Nineteenth Century Sociologist* (Philadelphia, 1951), 54–56.

37. Gabriel, *The Course of American Thought,* 206–207; Max I. Baym, *The French Education of Henry Adams* (New York, 1951), 94.

38. Herbert N. Casson, "Saint-Simon, the First American," *Arena* (1904), 513–19. The Saint-Simonians traced the all-too-extensive influence of lawyers in the United States to old English feudal customs. They saw, moreover, in American generals' all-too-easily obtained importance in the government "a stepping stone toward reconstruction of feudalism." A. S. Tillett, "Some Saint-Simonian Criticism of the United States Before 1835," *Romanic Review,* LII (1961), 3–16.

complished through productive work, cooperation, and universal love; it opposed idleness, competition, and war. In theory, his system expected each individual to produce to the best of his ability and promised to reward him in accordance with his contribution. In the end, however, Saint-Simon's followers, Auguste Comte among them until 1828, failed to sustain their early enthusiasm. But the conviction persisted that a social and economic order based upon competition among individuals was not likely to create morally defensible living conditions.

Foremost among the utopian reformers holding this view was Charles Fourier whose proposed reconstruction of society based on agriculture and the joint-stock principle differed not only from that of the Saint-Simonians, but also from the plan of Robert Owen (1771-1858), who advocated the acceptance of industrialism and communistic principles. Both Fourier and Owen opposed class antagonisms and believed in the essential goodness of human nature. Fourier, however, claimed to be "the only reformer who has rallied around human nature by accepting it as it is and devising the means of utilizing it with all the defects which are inseparable from man." In a letter of October 3, 1831, to Victor Considerant, the disciple who later assumed the leadership of the Fourierist movement, Fourier continued to explain his philosophy: "All the sophists who pretend to change it [human nature] are working *in denial of man,* and what is more, in denial of God since they want to change or stifle the passions which God has bestowed on us as our fundamental drives."[39]

The timing of the first publication of the Fourierist pamphlet in the United States in 1838, a period of religious and intellectual ferment, and the traditional disposition of Americans to engage in social experiment and to respect the settlements of a great variety of religious sects probably accounted for the spectacular, though relatively short-lived, success of Fourierism in America.

39. Quoted in Frank E. Manuel, *The Prophets of Paris* (Cambridge, Mass., 1962), 203–209; see also Arthur Eugene Bestor, "American Phalanxes: A Study of Fourierist Socialism in the United States" (Ph.D. dissertation, Yale University, 1938), 1–15.

Several thousand Americans, exhorted by such influential reformers and journalists as Albert Brisbane (1809–1890) and Horace
Greeley (1811–1872), joined the community units or phalanxes.
Impressed with this initial response to the movement in the United
States, Considerant decided, following a visit to America in 1853,
to found a colonization company in Texas for the benefit of
European immigrants. To his great disappointment, it was much
easier to conceive such a plan than to guide it through a multitude
of practical obstacles. Eventually, communal settlements in the
United States failed, not so much because the American public
at large began to denounce the phalanxists as fools, criminals,
and atheists, but because of disorganization, discomfort, disil-
lusionment, and misfortunes. Although the American version
of the attempted implementation of Fourier's social philosophy
may not have done justice to the master's principles, his alien
philosophy was held responsible for tantalizing the world with
a utopian paradise.

The experience of Etienne Cabet (1788–1856), an enthusiastic
follower of Robert Owen and author of *True Christianity*, also
demonstrated the practical limitations of his community-property
oriented Icarian colonies.[40] At best, the Icarian settlements in
Texas, Illinois, and Iowa showed that Christian concepts of broth-
erly love did not necessarily fare better in an idealistically structured social organization than in a competitively organized social
order. That Saint-Simon, Fourier, Considerant, and Cabet were
able to convince thousands of social-minded Americans of the
attractiveness of life in a utopian community reflected a certain
disenchantment with the emerging social order in Western civilization, including the United States. The influence of these Frenchmen on American thought illustrated a preoccupation in America
with the practical implementation of religious and philosophical
ideas that was not limited merely to the utopians.

As far as philosophy was concerned, the relatively small num-

40. Martha Browning Smith, "The Story of Icaria," *Annals of Iowa*, 3rd ser.,
XXXVIII (1965), 36–64.

ber of Americans who occupied themselves with systematized analytical inquiries about the truths and principles of the manifold manifestations of life constituted such an isolated intellectual minority that their discussions had little impact on the masses. Rationalism, skepticism, the religion of humanity, and the religion of science did not, in the nineteenth century, fundamentally change the traditional role of religion in American life. Historically, it is noteworthy that in different ages philosophy was expected to serve different, indeed contradictory, functions, aside from its intellectual exercise per se. The medievals expected philosophy to confirm theology as convincingly as moderns have attempted to negate it. In somewhat modified versions, some modern philosophical thinkers have tried to identify religion with philosophy, while many scientists of the late nineteenth century expected philosophy to uphold science. That rationalists, transscendentalists, positivists, and pragmatists developed themes in conflict with religious orthodoxy established a common denominator among these otherwise distinct philosophies, and this tended to provoke in the United States a more than usual interest in them.

To the surprise of many Frenchmen, late nineteenth-century Americans made contributions in philosophy, as in the arts and sciences, that attracted French attention, if not always admiration. By way of a condescending compliment, J. Bourdeau described pragmatism as a typically Yankee philosophy, a philosophy stressing experience, action, and results rather than reason as the vital considerations in man's progress.[41] Once again, pragmatism was less a philosophy than a method of analyzing the meanings of intellectual concepts. Less concerned with abstract ideas than with their practical applicability, this "philosophy" nevertheless appeared to some Frenchmen to be "an excellent antidote to an aristocratic intellectualism disdainful of consequences."[42] In fact, the works of Charles S. Peirce (1839–1914),

41. Isaac Woodbridge Riley, "Continental Critics of Pragmatism," *Journal of Philosophy, Psychology and Scientific Methods,* VIII (1911), 225–32; J. Bourdeau, *Pragmatisme et modernisme* (Paris, 1909), 45, 60–62.
42. Riley, *American Thought,* 332–36.

who had coined the term *pragmatism,* and of William James (1842–1910) received a very respectful hearing in France. Superficially, there seemed to be a certain resemblance between positivism and pragmatism; both emphasized science, nature, and the needs of humanity. But while positivism dogmatized idea, pragmatism dogmatized action. Pragmatism granted meaning to conceptions only if they could be applied. In William James's words, "the whole meaning of a conception expresses itself in practical consequences, either in the shape of conduct to be recommended or in that of experience to be expected if the conception is true." As a corollary, John Dewey's (1859–1952) distrust of formal logic made the study of concepts meaningful only in the contexts in which they were used.

James acknowledged that particularly two French philosophers had exercised a great influence on him, Charles Bernard Renouvier (1815–1903) and Henri Bergson (1859–1941). As a young student in Germany he began reading Renouvier's *Essais de criticisme générale,* which produced a lasting effect on his life. In 1868 he had by chance read a little book, *L'Année 1867 philosophique,* to which a French philosopher, heretofore unknown to him, had written an introductory review of the state of philosophy in France. In an enthusiastic letter to his father he praised this author, Charles B. Renouvier, "who, for vigor of style and compression, going to the core of half a dozen things in a single sentence, so different from the namby-pamby diffusiveness of most Frenchmen, is unequalled by anyone."[43] Renouvier's belief in personal experience and in liberty as man's fundamental characteristic appealed to James at that time as much as his belief in human immortality and a finite God. Renouvier's definition of free will as "the sustaining of a thought *because I choose to* when I might have other thoughts" did not appear to James to be an illusion.[44] James's own emphasis on free will and his consequent aban-

43. William James, *The Letters of William James* (2 vols.; Boston, 1920), I, 137–38.
44. Paul R. Anderson and Max H. Fisch, *Philosophy in America: From the Puritans to James* (New York, 1939), 521; Hunter Guthrie, "American Philosophical Past and Present," in Jesuit Philosophical Association of the Eastern States, *Phases of American Culture* (Worcester, Mass., 1942), 46–47.

donment of all deterministic approaches governed his thinking fundamentally. In a letter to Renouvier in November, 1872, James acknowledged his appreciation for the *Essais* which, he confessed, gave him for the first time a reasonable conception of liberty. In subsequent letters and lectures at Harvard, as well as in his article "Bain and Renouvier," published in the *Nation* on June 8, 1876, he extolled the virtues of Renouvier's pluralism without which, he speculated, "I might never have got free from the monistic superstition under which I had grown up."[45] Eventually, the two philosophers met near Grenoble and discussed philosophical differences regarding the infinity of space and time, as well as other questions that had been the subject matter of an elaborate correspondence between them. As James disseminatd Renouvier's ideas in the United States, the French philosopher introduced James to the readers of the *Critique philosophique,* which carried translations of several of James's essays.

Even closer was James's friendship with Henri Bergson, whose greatness and originality he explained in a chapter of his *Pluralistic Universe.* Living at a time when awe of science threatened the possibility of making it the foundation of social morality, Bergson probed deeply into the so-called "truths of science." By the end of the century, other French intellectuals, notably Ferdinand Brunetière, the editor of the *Revue des deux mondes,* and the mathematician Jules Henri Poincaré had also challenged some of the general assumptions of science. Brunetière demonstrated the need for adjusting opinions to constantly evolving experiences. Poincaré argued brilliantly that nature was too complex for scientists to think about it in fixed general terms. Since scientific formulae were at best approximations of reality, he thought it would be more accurate for scientists to operate with awareness of the relativity of hypotheses.[46]

45. James, *Letters,* I, 163–64; see also, Gay Wilson Allen, *William James: A Biography* (London, 1967), 168, 202.
46. Riley, *American Thought,* 325, 333–35; Jean Wahl, "William James d'après sa correspondance," *Revue philosophique,* XCIII (1922), 381–416, and XCIV (1922), 298–347; Ralph B. Perry, "Correspondance de Charles Renouvier et de William James," *Revue de métaphysique et de morale,* XXXVI (1929), 1–35, 193–222.

James and Bergson expounded similar opinions about the alogical nature of reality. While their views were not identical in all respects, these two pragmatists who respected each other had much in common. Both were believers in biological evolution, James leaning toward the Darwinian interpretation and Bergson inclined more toward Lamarck. Both philosophers perceived reality as a flux and not as a system. They treated reality as a varying experience constantly calling for new adaptations.[47] Bergson elaborated this notion when he wrote: "Reality flows; we flow with it; and we call true any affirmation which, in guiding us through moving reality, gives us a grip upon it and places us under more favorable conditions for acting." Contrary to traditional definitions, James defined truth "by its relation to what does not yet exist. The true, according to William James, does not copy something which has been or which is: . . . it prepares our action upon what is going to be."[48] James and Bergson drew a sharp dividing line between doctrines considering a new truth a discovery and pragmatism treating it as an invention. In Bergson's words: "We invent truth to utilize reality, as we create mechanical devices to utilize the forces of nature."[49] It followed, of course, that scientific truths, existing in the plural only, were instruments rather than valuable ends in themselves and that all determinisms with respect to scientific, theological, and metaphysical questions were out of order.

James and Bergson were humanists who regarded "religious experience" and "religious sentiment" as belonging to the inward nature of man, whereas ideas in religion were something external. They differed, however, in regard to God. For Bergson, God was the eternal source of both matter and life, the *élan vital* revealed to man in intuition. Rejecting the notion of a superhuman *élan vital*, James expected the gods, if gods there be, to reveal them-

47. Ralph B. Perry, *The Thought and Character of William James* (New York, 1954), 339–40; Horace M. Kallen, *William James and Henri Bergson: A Study in Contrasting Theories of Life* (Chicago, 1914), 37–42.

48. Henri Bergson, *The Creative Mind: A Study in Metaphysics* (New York, 1946), 215.

49. *Ibid.*

selves "as a datum of immediate experience." His main concern was mankind that moved forward only through the initiative of creative men. Unlike Bergson, who assumed that the world was the home into which man was born, James contended that man had to make a home of it. Man's efforts determined the quality of his life.[50]

Bergson and James, who realized in the 1890s that they had independently arrived at similar conclusions in their studies of the mind and rationality, developed a mutually stimulating relationship. In one of his letters, dated December 14, 1902, James expressed a thought that appealed to Bergson as well: "How good it is sometimes simply to *break away* from all categories, deny old worn-out beliefs, and restate things *ab initio.*" Immensely impressed by Bergson's *L'Evolution créatrice* (1907), which to his mind "inflicts an irrevocable death-wound upon Intellectualism," James found his own recently published book on pragmatism so congruent with parts of Bergson's system that he was pleased to see they were both at bottom fighting the same fight. "The position we are rescuing," he wrote to Bergson on June 13, 1907, "is 'Tychism' and a really growing world. . . . I . . . by affirming its spontaneous addition of *discrete* elements of being . . . you set things straight at a single stroke by your fundamental conception of the continuously creative nature of reality."[51]

Greatly indebted to Claude Bernard's theory of the experimental method, these two philosophers applied it to their study of psychology. When James, originally a medical doctor, taught psychology at Harvard, he concentrated on physiological psychology rather than on the traditional "mental science." It was no surprise therefore that his pragmatic inclinations found expression in his emphasis on functional aspects in his *Principles of Psychology* (1891). In France, experimental psychology was advanced by the philosopher and historian Hippolyte Taine,

50. Kallen, *William James and Henri Bergson*, 185–204, 232–41.
51. James, *Letters*, II, 178–80, 290–94; André Chaumeix, "William James," *RDDM* (October 15, 1910), 849–63.

whose philosophy has been defined as "Spinozism superimposed upon positivism," but unlike Comte's positivism, since Taine's gave due respect to psychology. As a matter of fact, Taine's interest in abnormal subjects set the stage for the more penetrating inquiries into pathological conditions by the so-called Paris school of psychologists and neurologists, prominently including Théodule Armand Ribot (1839–1916), Jean Martin Charcot (1825–1893), Pierre Janet (1859–1947), and Charles Robert Richet (1850–1935).[52] William James worked very closely with these distinguished Frenchmen. Personally, he corresponded with them and attended their lectures when he visited Paris. In the winter of 1898 he accepted Professor Richet's gracious offer of making himself comfortable at his chateau on the Mediterranean. In the same spirit, he extended his hospitality to Dr. Janet and his wife when they visited Cambridge in 1904. Professionally, they not only read and quoted each others' works, they used them in their own analyses.[53]

One of James's major concerns involved the effect of time and space on the senses. He contended that they are directly felt and that "the present" plays an extremely important role in our consciousness. Fully agreeing, Ribot went so far as to contend that "the present is the only psychological element which, consciously or unconsciously, gives a content and a reality to duration."[54] According to James, man's effective consciousness is measured by his after-consciousness. For that reason, "without memory there is no consciousness known 'outside of itself.'"[55] In their search for a better understanding of personality changes and hysteria, the Paris school scientists experimented with therapeutic

52. Alfred Fouillée, "The Philosophy of Taine and Renan," *International Quarterly*, VI (1902–1903), 266; J. Alexander Gunn, "Ribot and His Contribution to Psychology," *Monist*, XXXIV (1924), 1–14.

53. Charles Richet to William James, letter dated 1891, MS Am 1092 (800), HCL; Allen, *William James*, 408.

54. Théodule Ribot, *The Evolution of General Ideas* (Chicago, 1899), 162; Raymond Lenoir, "The Psychology of Ribot and Contemporary Thought," *Monist*, XXX (1920), 375.

55. William James, *Principles of Psychology* (2 vols.; London, 1890), I, 644.

measures of great fascination to James. Charcot, the greatest neurologist of his day, studied hysteria in relation to hypnotism. Extending these studies, Pierre Janet pointed out in his *L'Automatisme psychologique* (1889) that during the period of anaesthesia *sensibility to the anaesthetic parts is also there in the form of a secondary consciousness.*[56] James felt that these researches were infinitely more constructive than obscure metaphysical speculations. Interestingly, James's books, *Varieties of Religious Experience* and *Energies of Men,* reminded Janet of the uplifting nature of stirring religious experiences.[57] The therapeutic appeal of religion in cases of psychological depressions was of course no novel discovery; but its reassertion in the context of modern neurology invested it with a degree of scientific usefulness.

Although Ernest Renan (1823–1892) intended to save "religion" by freeing it from theological dogmas, he expressed his Comtian belief in the merits of science and his ideas about religion and philosophy in such vague terms that his star never rose in America. Perhaps nobody was as annoyed with him as William James. In a review of "Renan's Dialogues" he dismissed them as "simply priggishness rampant." Despite Renan's literary genius, which he acknowledged, James objected to his "pretension and deep ignorance . . . where the subject is the history of philosophical thought."[58] A more recent evaluation concluded that, despite his many contradictions and ambiguities, Renan eminently epitomized "the characteristic intellectual developments of the century." The evolution of his thought from Catholic Christianity to modern skepticism, via positivism and a religion

56. Fred H. Mackay and Emile Legrand, "Jean Martin Charcot, 1825–1893," *Archives of Neurology and Psychiatry,* XXXIV (1935), 394–96; W. Osler, "Jean Martin Charcot," *Johns Hopkins Hospital Bulletin,* IV (1893), 87–89; James, *Principles of Psychology,* I, 203.

57. Pierre Janet, *Principles of Psychotherapy* (New York, 1924), 68–70, 222.

58. Herman G. A. Brauer, "The Philosophy of Ernest Renan," *Bulletin of the University of Wisconsin,* Philology and Literature Series, II (1902), 323–29; Fouillée, "The Philosophy of Taine and Renan," 261; William James, *Collected Essays and Reviews* (London, 1920), 36–37.

of humanity and science, reflected philosophical currents that profoundly stirred society.[59]

The various philosophical "isms" of the nineteenth century, like those just preceding them, shook orthodox theology to its very foundations. The survival of institutionalized Christian religion in the Western world depended much on its capacity to develop sufficient flexibility to meet the onslaughts of "practical substitute religions" in the guise of philosophy. In a strict sense, philosophy is a logically structured system of thought rationally investigating fundamental principles of being. The French and American philosophers discussed in this chapter represented a much broader category of thinkers trying to rationalize needed social adjustments in accordance with the changing orientation of each generation. Their emphasis on methodology and applicability of philosophical thought apparently evoked a wider response in America than philosophical abstractions normally did.

59. See D. G. Charlton, *Positivist Thought in France During the Second Empire,* 1852–1870 (Oxford, 1959), 125–26.

CHAPTER VI

Literature

Throughout the nineteenth century, French literature caused much controversy in the United States. Only once before in modern history, in the seventeenth century, had France produced plays that clearly excelled those of other countries. Although the harvest of plays from 1830 to 1880 might in quality not be comparable to the works of Corneille, Molière, and Racine, mid-nineteenth-century French authors once again demonstrated that their mastery of wit, exquisite prose, and showmanship found its most natural expression in drama. But since Anglo-Americans, accustomed to using Shakespeare as a yardstick of dramatic perfection, have been critical of Molière's lack of poetic soul and of Corneille's and Racine's failure to reanimate rather than merely take stock of the tragic subjects of antiquity, it should not be surprising that they have been much more critical of nineteenth-century writers who presented French civilization in a light exaggerating the existence of a shabby morality.[1]

1. See J. Brander Matthews, *French Dramatists of the Nineteenth Century* (New York, 1901), Preface; Albert L. Rabinowitz, "Criticism of French Novels in Boston Magazines, 1830–60," *NEQ*, XIV (1941), 488–504; Claude C. Spiker, "The North American Revolution and French Morals" *West Virginia University Philological Studies* (September, 1943), 3–14; and Gilbert Chinard, "La Littérature française dans le sud des Etats-Unis, d'après le *Southern Literary Messenger* (1834–1864)," *RDLC*, VIII (1928), 87–99. Neither Voltaire, the "great

From the 1830s, such periodicals as the *North American Review,* the *Atlantic Monthly,* and the *Southern Literary Messenger* devoted many pages to European, and particularly French, literature. On the whole, they reiterated the notion that decadent France produced a decadent literature that foreshadowed the ultimate doom of its rotten civilization. Only the most dispassionate American critics did not go to such an extreme. They acknowledged that many French citizens did not condone the indecent characters in the works of their compatriots, and that Boston and New York had their share of "cheap" literature. More broadmindedness was called for on the part of the *New Englander* [VI (1848), 595], a Methodist magazine, to tell its readers: "We do not believe her [France] so atheistic and godless as she is sometimes presented," than was required for Francis Bowen, professor of philosophy at Harvard, to suggest that a people judges its own morality and writings in a way that differs substantially from that of foreigners.

Of all critical charges, Frenchmen found it most difficult to understand that Americans attributed to their mid-nineteenth-century literature a want of vitality. Borrowing Dr. Johnson's phrase, one American critic described French literature as coming "from reservoirs, not springs." Perhaps even more astonishing was the repeated comment that the romantic dramas of Hugo and others were "empty of poetry." James Russell Lowell argued that the nature of the language made all French poetry purely artificial and that "the length of their dramatic verse forces the French into much tautology . . . the stuffing out a thought with words till it fills the line." Emerson, too, believed that French poetry "is always . . . *prose ornée,* but never poesy."[2]

If the puritan and middle-class mentality of Americans hurt

---

demolisher," nor the "occasionally brilliant," but on the whole superficial and factually unreliable François René de Chateaubriand were favorites in early America. This distinction was held by Madame de Staël. Howard Mumford Jones, *The Theory of American Literature* (Ithaca, N.Y., 1966), 67; see also Gilbert Chinard, "Chateaubriand en Amérique," *Modern Philology,* IX (1911–12), 129–49.

2. Edward Waldo Emerson and Waldo Emerson Forbes (eds.), *Journals of Ralph Waldo Emerson* (10 vols.; Boston, 1909–1914), VII, 451; James Russell Lowell, *Writings of James Russell Lowell* (12 vols.; Cambridge, Mass., 1890–92), III, 158; and Firmin Roz, *L'Evolution des idées et des moeurs américaines* (Paris, 1931), 50–51.

French influence in America, no matter how innovative French poets tried to be, the growing appeal of German literature in America could not thus be overcome. Searching for an explanation of this state of affairs, William James came up with the persuasive contention that German literature was "really classical and cosmopolitan . . . compared to which French and English both seem in very important respects provincial."[3]

Americans had read so much about the Epicurean and debauched life-style of French society that their reactions to it became as monotonous as the themes of the books they read. Occasionally, an author with a superior mind and writing ability would write about personal love affairs, probing deeply into the psyche of human beings and the environment that caused them joy and pain. When this happened, as in the case of George Sand (1804–1876), American condemnation of immorality would be softened by touches of pity and rationalization. In its issue of June 15, 1876, for instance, the *Nation* found "her method of telling a story . . . beyond all praise," but it deplored the fact that "she was always at odds with society, and often with those rudimentary principles which distinguish civilization from barbarism, and indeed from the mode of life of the beasts that perish." The *North American Review* mourned in her case "the prostitution of genius that appears in the corrupt and pernicious products of a diseased literary style."[4] That such productions could poison the minds of American youth concerned easterners and southerners alike. Their magazines and reviews tried therefore to discourage dissemination of this literature.

What was much more astounding in American reactions to George Sand was the discovery of social significance in her work. When Margaret Fuller (1810–1850), the remarkable high priestess

3. See William James letters, April 23, 1869, HCL; and A. Schalck de la Faverie, *Les Premiers interprètes de la pensée américaine: Essai d'histoire et littérature sur l'évolution du puritanisme aux Etats-Unis* (Paris, 1909), 352–53.

4. Howard Mumford Jones, "American Comments on George Sand, 1837–1848," *American Literature*, III (1932), 389–407; see also the essay by Marie Reynes, "Les Femmes dans la littérature française," *ca.* 1899, in J. Reynes Family Papers, LSU Archives, Baton Rouge.

of transcendentalism, met George Sand in 1846, she came away with the awareness of having been in the presence of an essentially good and noble woman whose soul was pure, despite her licentiousness. Margaret Fuller, Orestes Brownson, and other contemporaries recognized her as the champion of women's rights and as an advocate of the cause of humbler members of society. The manifold experiences of her own life helped her to understand the struggles and emotions of the hurt and oppressed and led her to oppose social, religious, and political institutions that exploited people and perpetuated their misery.[5] She saw no virtue in chastity and marriage, and she found no solace in the Church. As a nonconformist, she wished to stir the conscience of society into more enlightened standards. It was one thing for learned American critics to charge her with immorality, emotionalism, and exaggeration; it was another to appease the public conscience in a truly honest and responsible manner. George Sand, whom Emerson described in his journal [VII (1848) , 501] as "quite conversant with all the ideas which occupy us here in America," exposed herself to especially severe criticism in the United States because she attacked all social institutions. This controversial lady, who smoked cigars and dressed eccentrically, benefited sufficiently, however, from the more relaxed trend of American literary criticism in the 1840s to see her writings described as being "of greater aesthetics and moral merits" than those of Victor Hugo.[6]

Among the great literary figures, Victor Hugo (1802–1885) occupies a special place in France and the United States. Controversial on both sides of the Atlantic, he lived long enough to experience the triumphs and failures of a poet who wore the hat of revolutionary, prophet, and martyr. Self-confident and yet cautious, intellectually imaginative and yet limited, prophetic and yet trivial, he obviously established his reputation with his decisive moves and brilliant works. And there were enough of them to overshadow his weaknesses.

5. Rabinowitz, "Criticism of French Novels," 493–96; Henry James, *French Poets and Novelists* (London, 1878), 220–21.
6. Joyaux, "French Thought in American Magazines: 1800–1848, 39–44."

If rigid neoclassic rules stifled the originality of French poets in the eighteenth century, the restrictions imposed upon French theaters during the era of the French Revolution compounded the deadening effects of these official checks. When in 1827 some of England's most accomplished actors excited Parisian audiences with their performances of Shakespeare, the contrast between "the decorous declamation of French classic tragedy" and "the tumultuous action of Shakespeare" finally spurred the younger generation of restless French romanticists on to declare their independence from outmoded rules and rigidities. It was at this moment that Victor Hugo assumed the leadership of the romantic movement, backed by his young friends Théophile Gautier, Alexandre Dumas, George Sand, Alfred de Vigny, and others, including Châteaubriand and Lamartine. In the preface to his historical drama *Cromwell* (1827), Hugo eloquently protested that "the object of modern art is not beauty, but life," life in a constant flux calling for evolutionary adjustments. The eventful occasion that symbolized the breakaway of the romanticists from the classical tradition was the lively performance of *Hernani* at the Théâtre français on the evening of February 25, 1830. This tumultuous evening heralded the liberation of the French stage and the acclaim of Hugo as "the rising sun" among its writers.[7] If to Frenchmen the beauty and strength of his masterful poetry merited more lasting recognition than many of his dramas and novels, altogether his literary influence extended over the whole span of his adult life. According to Zola, though, the celebrated writer of "poems in prose" exercised no influence on the naturalistic literature of the late nineteenth century.

Less attuned to the rhythm and strength of the French language, Americans judged Hugo more by his dramas and novels than by his poetry, if they were at all familiar with him. Strangely, with the exception of Edgar Allan Poe, American authors seemed to ignore him while his reputation grew in France.[8] The American

7. Matthews, *French Dramatists*, 23, 42–43.
8. Albert C. George, "Early American Criticism of Victor Hugo," *French Review,* XI (1938), 293.

public's introduction to the author of *Notre dame de Paris, Le Dernier jour d'un condamné,* and *Les Misérables* was circumscribed by the usual prejudices of its middle-class critics. If in their opinion *Notre dame de Paris* deserved to be proscribed in America because it was tainted with the "deepest, most comprehensive libertinism," *Le Roi s'amuse* was found to be such "an absurd, immoral, and indecent composition" that it was "unfit to be exhibited or read."[9] Firmly convinced that free institutions could flourish only in a moral environment, Americans would have been more receptive to a Hugo whose prominence among the satanic writers and "horror-daubers" rested on a sober respect for moral principles and self-control. Even those who in time recognized the genius of this "able maker of phrases" deplored the arrogance with which he used his intellectual freedom.

As one of the few intellectuals in monarchical France who courageously professed his admiration for America's republican institutions, Victor Hugo appeared to be closer to Americans politically than he was as a poet. His assertion of independence and his self-imposed exile during the reign of "Napoleon the Little," in addition to his strong antislavery views, commanded a respect that only the pre–Civil War South abjured. He who loved "America as a Fatherland, the great republic of Washington and John Brown—a glory to civilization," and who for the sake of a more enlightened civilization pleaded repeatedly for the union of the states of Europe with those of America considered his concern for humanity a vital aspect of his life. American response to these flattering professions showed itself in private gestures of appreciation and, after the Civil War, in more frequent discussions and presentations of his work. Apparently few Americans were as aware as Walt Whitman that Hugo's sincerity vis-à-vis the United States could not be taken for granted. Although Whitman's regret that Hugo was "not truer and less bom-

9. Thomas Hungerford Giddings, "Yankee Journalists in Europe, 1830–1848" (Ph.D. dissertation, Columbia University, 1956), 82, 217; "Writings of Victor Hugo," *NAR,* XLIII (1836), 133–63.

bastic" merely expressed his personal reservation, existing evidence justified his doubt.[10] Depending on changing political situations, Hugo in fact oscillated between the Church and America as the instruments for establishing "the universal republic." Before 1842, the model republic was a country "without a soul"; during the Second Empire, he referred to the United States as "the great example," only "to weep for America" when its "redskins" kept silent during the "Terrible Year." Actually, his personal contacts with Americans were limited and his knowledge of the United States was quite superficial.

If, greatly influenced by unfavorable British commentaries, New England and Philadelphia originally tried to ignore this prolific writer, the New York *Tribune* took the lead in later years to extol the variety of his themes and the virtuosity of his imagination. Eventually, the author of *"Lee's Miserables"* (as some Americans facetiously called it) was widely known and read in the United States. But no amount of "Hugolatria" could suppress the serious reservations summed up in the *Atlantic Monthly's* review (July, 1862) of *Les Misérables:* "Its tendency is to weaken that abhorrence of crime which is the great shield of most of the virtues which society possesses, and it does this by attempting to prove that society itself is responsible for crimes it cannot prevent, but can only punish."[11]

Some of Hugo's contemporaries fared better in the United States than he did—the critics disapproving them and the public devouring their works. Gilbert Chinard charitably attributed Paul de Kock's popularity in the United States to "mysterious reasons." That the novels of this "literary prince of nastiness," which rendered "virtue ridiculous and vice attractive, spread like wildfire"

10. Maurice O. Johnson, *Walt Whitman as a Critic of Literature* (Lincoln, Nebr., 1938), 21; Monique LeBreton-Savigny, *Victor Hugo et les Américains 1825–1885* (Paris, 1971), 304; Albert Schinz, "Victor Hugo: Le Grand poète humanitaire," *French Review*, IX (November, 1935), 17.

11. Pierre de Lacretelle, *Vie politique de Victor Hugo* (Paris, 1928), 198, 220; see also George McLean Harper, *Masters of French Literature* (Freeport, N.Y., 1968), 194–214.

in the presumably puritan United States obviously indicated that many Americans were quenching their thirst "at the muddy and polluted streams of German mysticism or French licentiousness."[12] The fabulous success of Eugene Sue's socially and religiously reprehensible *The Wandering Jew* and the money-making works of Alexandre Dumas, *pére* and *fils,* from The Count of Monte Cristo and *The Three Musketeers* to *La Dame aux camélias* and *Le Demi-monde,* entertained an American public that evidently cared more for enjoyment than literary value. With respect to the French romanticists, the noted scholar Brander Matthews observed that they cleared away "the rubbish of classicism, and that was all."[13] Then, they proceeded, by and large, to produce their own rubbish, often insulting Americans in the process by either ridiculing American society or shipping their villains across the ocean to become part of this society.[14]

One of the truly towering literary figures of the century was Honoré de Balzac (1799-1850). When Henry James referred to him as the philosophic novelist *par excellence,* he paid tribute to Balzac's sagacious imagination rather than to his capacity for deep philosophical thought. An incredibly prolific writer and extraordinarily astute observer of human society, Balzac possessed the unsurpassed gift of describing things and people minutely, vividly, and powerfully. He set out to depict contemporary French civilization with such forceful realism that he excelled in painting the seamy side of life. Indeed, the author of *The Human Comedy* caught the fancy of Americans as a master anatomist of human corruption. His creative impulses were undoubtedly stimulated by the fact that, as Henry James phrased it, "he believed in his own magnificent rubbish."[15] As much, however, as the "Dante of the bourgeoisie" fascinated his readers with his pictures of a vain, hypocritical, materialistic, and at times depraved society,

12. Chinard, "La Littérature française dans le sud des Etats-Unis," 93–94.
13. Matthews, *French Dramatists,* 136–48; Rabinowitz, "Criticism of French Novels," 498–501.
14. Hjlamar Hjorth Boyesen, *Literary and Social Silhouettes* (New York, 1894), 28–30.
15. James, *French Poets and Novelists,* 84–150.

his essentially skeptical outlook seemed to hold out precious little hope for a better world.

The large number of translations of Balzac's novels and short stories, as well as excerpts from them, that circulated in the United States between 1836 and 1845 attested to his temporary popularity in America. Although the public renewed its lost interest in him again after unabridged translations of *The Human Comedy* were made available in the final years of the century, American writers and critics never ceased to occupy themselves with this author who, according to Emerson, had two merits: "talent and Paris."[16] Emerson, of course, liked Balzac's concept of "unity in nature's variety" and incorporated it in his own philosophy of nature. While Orestes A. Brownson appreciated Balzac's literary genius, despite the apparent absence of "a genuine love of humanity," Margaret Fuller expressed the reaction of those who were shocked by this "heartless surgeon, probing the wounds and describing the delirium of suffering men for the amusement of his students." Theodore Tuckerman, writing in the *Southern Literary Messenger* in 1859, discovered in Balzac a masterful social historian who probed more deeply and skillfully into the totality of the human condition and its environment than others had done before him. Those of his American readers who took exception to his objective fiction on moral and humanitarian grounds might well have considered the advice of a wealthy New York banker who asked them to remember: "We do not apply our standard of morality or taste to the writers of antiquity, nor ought we any more to judge the French, the Italian and the German, by the codes of England and America."[17]

Whether Balzac's realism and technique in spinning his elaborate settings and intriguing characters influenced such American poets as James Fenimore Cooper, Edgar Allan Poe, and John De Forest is difficult to document, despite striking similarities. His su-

16. Rubin Cohen, "Balzac in the United States During the Nineteenth Century" (Ph.D. dissertation, Columbia University, 1950), 37–39, 67–93, 132, 450.

17. John Stafford, "Samuel Ward's Defense of Balzac's 'Objective' Fiction," *American Literature,* XXIV (1952), 167–76; Bernard Weinberg, *French Realism: The Critical Reaction,* 1830–1870 (New York, 1937), 33–90.

perb craftsmanship no doubt invited close study. Contemporaries recognized in his prose narrative and characterization a perfection that revealed an artist as well as an artisan. Henry James summed it up well when he wrote that with all of Balzac's "faults of pedantry, ponderosity, pretentiousness, bad taste and charmless form," he displayed a Shakespearean knowledge and insight with respect to the complexities of human existence.[18] Without intending to be moral or immoral in his writings, Balzac sincerely believed: "When the insight is deep, the analysis thorough, the description true to nature, then inevitably the impression is profoundly moral." Great artist that he was, he painted his characters in such a lively and detailed fashion as to enable his readers to put themselves in their place. Only belatedly did Americans understand that his realism was designed to arouse a moral sense. At the end of the century American readers were made aware that the success of his vicious characters "only renders them more odious. In no case is it so represented as to be seductive." The subtlety and skill of this masterful spinner of intrigues and plots accomplished still another result. Despite possibly justified criticism of one or the other of his novels, all his novels taken together constituted an impressive achievement. Nevertheless, none other than the renowned historian-philosopher Taine deplored Balzac's unbalanced concentration on vices and passions and his failure to evaluate contemporary conditions in the light of their historical evolution. As dominant as evil and egotism are in society, according to Taine, progress had been made in checking them, as was evidenced by the peace and prosperity of the United States.[19]

18. Cohen, "Balzac in the United States," 95, 102–104, 166–67; Henry James, *The Lessons of Balzac* (New York, 1905), 94.

19. See Ray P. Bowen, "A Comparison of the Methods of Composition in Cooper and Balzac," *French American Review*, III (1950), 297–313; Eliot G. Fay, "Balzac and Henry James," *French Review*, XXIV (1951), 325–30; Benjamin Griffith, *Balzac aux Etats-Unis* (Paris, 1931), 161–63; and H. T. Tuckerman, "Balzac," *Southern Literary Messenger* (February, 1859), 81–99. See also, Malcolm B. Jones, "French Literature and American Criticism, 1870–1900" (Ph.D. dissertation, Harvard University, 1936), 156, 215–16; and Hippolyte Taine, *Nouveaux essais de critique et d'histoire* (Paris, 1880), 128–33.

The image of France and its nineteenth-century writers being hopelessly immoral was also contradicted by Charles Augustin Sainte-Beuve (1804–1869) and his work. Impressed by the early statesmen of the American republic, the eminent French critic studied its institutions and inquired about them in conversations and correspondence with such well-informed Americans as John Bigelow, George Ticknor, professor Theodore Tuckerman of Harvard, and Judge Henri Harrisse of the supreme court of the state of New York. Yet he did not feel strongly enough about the American experiment to study it firsthand, as an 1848 offer to teach at Harvard would have afforded him. Evidently convinced that France needed and preferred strong political leaders, Sainte-Beuve was too busy writing his famous *Causeries du lundi* to acquire more than a superficial knowledge about the life and literature of the United States.[20]

His own literary merits, on the other hand, were recognized in the United States where several of his works were translated and discussed. Stressing intellectual integrity, logic, taste, and judicious judgment, he enjoyed a reputation as one of the century's genuine humanists. Not accustomed to finding French writers overly concerned with questions of morality, it was refreshing to discover that Sainte-Beuve's high standards as a critic expected truly great art to have an elevating effect on society. Always sensitive to literary excellence in others, he strove to attain it himself. To cite only one example in which he accomplished this objective, according to a critic in the *North American Review* (July, 1860, p. 13), Sainte-Beuve's *Port-Royal* merited reading by all who were interested in a thorough and impartial picture of French society in the seventeenth century. His enthusiasm for this century coincided with his lack of enthusiasm for the nineteenth century, a sentiment often echoed in the *North American Review*. It was remarkable how many American men

20. Lander MacClintock, "Sainte-Beuve's Critical Theory and Practice After 1849" (Ph.D. dissertation, University of Chicago, 1920), 427–36; Robert G. Mahieu, *Sainte-Beuve aux Etats-Unis* (Princeton, N.J., 1945), 8–9, 112; Henry James, "Sainte-Beuve," *NAR*, CXXX (1880), 51–68; Harper, *Masters of French Literature*, 251–59.

of letters acknowledged Sainte-Beuve's salutary influence on them. Quite a few of them, however, regretted that, unlike Taine who went too far in his deterministic interpretations of history and literature, Sainte-Beuve exercised too much discretion in his "chatty" comments.

In more than one respect, Gustave Flaubert (1821–1880) stands by himself. Often compared with Balzac and Zola, his relatively few works have survived the test of time with greater appreciation in America than those of other nineteenth-century writers. Greatly admired for his beautiful and truthful description of life, the author of *Madame Bovary* was also severely condemned by contemporaries for his choice of wicked themes. Accused by some critics of a lack of creative genius, Flaubert also stirred up considerable controversy on account of his literary philosophy. The creator of the modern realistic novel most likely found himself the subject of so many critical comments because it was his fate to bridge a period that witnessed the movement from romanticism to realism and from metaphysical speculative philosophy to scientific dogma. In his lifetime, moreover, he saw traditional methods, standards, and styles in the arts and literature being supplemented, if not overtaken, by impressionism and symbolism. Undoubtedly complicating his fate, the rise and fall of French regimes from the Restoration past the collapse of the Second Empire and the rise of the common man disillusioned him so much that he saw no link between creative genius and the crowd, between the reality of life and the world of the writer. Essentially, he was a loner with an independent mind.

Strangely, Flaubert, who described the real, actually despised reality. And believing in the consoling priority of art, he contended that "art is not reality." He saw his function as a novelist to create beauty with the help of scientific objectivity. It was in this respect that he was so painfully misunderstood, both in the United States and in France.[21] He maintained that "the novelist hasn't the right

21. See Ernest Jackson, *The Critical Reception of Gustave Flaubert in the United States, 1860–1960* (The Hague, 1966), 33–35, 105; Willard H. Wright, "Flaubert: A Re-evaluation," *NAR*, CCVI (1907), 455–63; Enid Starkie, *Flaubert:*

to express his opinion on anything." He deemed it essential that his characters' identity be kept intact and not be intruded upon by the author's personal prejudices. His characters' actions, he believed, must speak for them. All the author had to aim for was perfection in detail, style, and choice of words. One of the more severe criticisms of this viewpoint, expressed in 1917 in the *North American Review,* took exception to this emphasis on stylistic perfection at the expense of the inner structure of art and "a complete vision of life brought to a small focus." The author of this article on Flaubert protested that "because no number of accurate trivialities can create an aesthetic unity unless they are related to the causes which produced them, he failed in the highest requirements of his art." Henry James, on the other hand, was so taken in by the elegance of Flaubert's style that he tried to emulate it. And the critic James Huneker fell so in love with "the verbal music" of Flaubert's *Salammbo* that he regarded it an artistic masterpiece. "If he fails to strike chords of pity of Dostoievsky, Turgenev, and Tolstoy; if he lacks the teeming variety of Balzac," Huneker observed, "he is superior to them all as an artist." Similarly, Will Durant praised Flaubert's *Salammbo* for its sheer beauty and freedom from trite phrases or metaphors. He found in it "nothing nervous as in Taine, nothing crude or abrupt as in Balzac, nothing excitedly rhetoric as in Hugo."

As soon as *Madame Bovary* was published in English, in 1881, and *Salammbo* in 1886, the American reading audience made them best sellers. Despite the fact that a French court had cleared the author and his publisher of the original charge of immorality in *Madame Bovary,* the anticipation of reading an exciting French love story no doubt contributed to its popularity. But later generations of Americans, who probably had never heard of the original court case, continued to enjoy reading this work and Flaubert's other novels. His later *L'Education sentimentale,* in

---

The Making of the Master (New York, 1967), 335–41; James Huneker, *Egoists: A Book of Supermen* (New York, 1909), 106; and Louise Bogan, *Selected Criticism: Prose, Poetry* (New York, 1955), 8.

which he skillfully conveyed the spirit of his time and its effect on man's spirit, attracted considerable interest. Stratton Buck explained Flaubert's lasting appeal to modern man on grounds of relevancy: "We need his feeling of his own strength . . . his awareness of the disparity between the life of the imagination and the life of reality. . . . We need the magnificent anger . . . excoriating in splendid anathemas whatever is mean, vulgar, phony, pretentious, or self-seeking." Whatever credit Flaubert could claim for his technical perfection, he obviously had something to say. As Louise Bogan has pointed out, Flaubert and Baudelaire must be credited with having "charted the direction of modern prose and poetry toward 'innerness,' poetic naturalism, [and] the direct examination of the contemporary scene."

In the final decades of the nineteenth century, French literature bore the imprint of recent scientific and industrial developments. Known under the identifying label of naturalism, the literature marked the beginning of a new age. Outwardly, the fall of the Second Empire had shaken France to its foundations. As Darwin's theories challenged ancient theological contentions, Claude Bernard's "experimental medicine" undermined the traditional scientific authority. And as Karl Marx developed his provocative theories of economic determinism, Hippolyte Taine applied scientific methods to literary criticism. Altogether, the search for political and economic security and greater intellectual certainty seemed to create new uncertainties. Before long, however, at least some writers saw sufficient merit in these new approaches and interpretations to apply them to their works. As the leader of naturalism in modern literature, Emile Zola (1840–1902), for instance, began to think in terms of biological, economic, and sociological determinism. Less concerned with ethical standards than with amoral realities, Zola advocated that "we naturalists, we men of science, must admit of nothing occult; men are but phenomena and the conditions of phenomena." His scientific and deterministic orientation in literature led him to explain the individual's social and psychological problems in terms of conditions created by a mass and class society. In this process, Zola believed he was merely extending the tradition of realism in literature to a degree not heretofore practiced. Rousseau's *Confessions,* Balzac's phenomenally detailed sketches of places and people, and Flaubert's naturalism, among other examples, had already suggested to Zola the potential force of unembellished pictures of life. But unlike earlier writers, Zola's ruthless realism did not concern itself with "that higher life for which the human soul forever pants," in part at least because he was not sure the soul really existed.[22] The function of art, he believed, was to study and paint life as it was, not as people imagined it to be. As a corollary, the theater's role was to depict life realistically and not to merely amuse the intellect in a superficially established manner.

At this point, reference to the distinction between literary realism and naturalism might help clarify contemporary differences of opinion. "The realist," argued Albion W. Tourgee in the March, 1889, issue of the *North American Review,* "depicts suffering and cowardice, duplicity and despair, but omits hope, aspiration and triumph. He says that the heroic is exceptional, abnormal, and therefore unreal; but weakness, self-distrust and self-consciousness, these are universal, normal, real. The naturalist, on the other hand, says truth does not lie mid-way between extremes, but embraces the antipodes. The absence of vice or virtue is not life, but the union and contrast of them." Another literary critic defined naturalism as "an impersonal encyclopedia of materiality and its only merit is in its spirit of minute analysis." With respect to "Emile Zola, robust and gloomy genius," he charged, he has by no means followed his theories of scientific observation; he allows his temperament continually

22. Vernon Louis Parrington, *Main Currents in American Thought* (3 vols.; New York, 1930), III, 180–81, 323; Albert J. Salvan, *Zola aux Etats-Unis* (Providence, R.I., 1943), 66; Mayo Williamson Hazeltine, *Chats About Books, Poets, and Novelists* (New York, 1883), 188–89.

to transform and color reality; his pretended observation is often nothing but imagination and vision."[23]

More specifically, Zola's novels initially shocked Americans. Despite some critical reservations, they could enjoy Flaubert and Maupassant. But as the translated versions of Zola's novels appeared on the American scene, *L'Assommoir, Nana, Pot-bouille,* the outrage of American critics seemed to know no bounds. *Harper's Magazine*[24] issued the warning about *L'Assommoir:* "We would as soon introduce smallpox into our homes as permit this unclean volume to come into contact with the pure-minded maidens and ingenious youth who form their chiefest ornament." Summarizing its disgust, the *North American Review*[25] introduced *Nana* to its readers with the comment: "These foreign purveyors of infection turn the gutters into our wholesome gardens and cast the uncleanliness of the divorce court about our hearthstones." Characteristically, the novel *Pot-bouille* became promptly known as Zola's "Stink Pot," full of "filthy, immoral garbage."[26] In contrast to the purifying effects of Victorian English novels, which deemed it proper to keep silent about many sensual aspects of human nature, Zola's unprecedentedly shameless novels repulsed Americans because they contained such a complete "assortment of indecencies."

Although even at this time, between 1879 and 1885, some American readers referred in their private diaries to Zola's "very striking work" and "wonderfully realistic picture of the vice of intemperance," gradually even public reviews of his novels began to change their tone. In view of the earlier moralistic reactions, it required courage and a more mature understanding to come around celebrating Zola as a supremely moral voice of modern society. Henry James and William Dean Howells took the lead

23. For similar critical comments, see George Chatelain, "M. Emile Zola," *Comptes Rendus de l'Athénée Louisianais* (March, 1880), 335–42; and Theodore Child, "Literary Paris," *Harper's Magazine* (August, 1892), 489–506.

24. *Harper's Magazine,* LIX (1879), 309.

25. *NAR,* CXXXI (1880), 79–89.

26. Herbert Edwards, "Zola and the American Critics," *American Literature,* IV (1932), 115–17.

in this public reappraisal of Zola's accomplishments. James, who had met Zola at Flaubert's home in 1876, and thereafter regularly exchanged ideas with members of the Flaubert circle, including Daudet, Goncourt, Maupassant, Zola, and Turgenev, frankly confessed in a letter to Howells, dated February 21, 1884, that this infernally intelligent little group of writers was the only contemporary one that commanded his respect. "In spite of their ferocious pessimism and their handling of unclean things," he maintained, "they are at least serious and honest."[27] Whatever his misgivings with respect to Zola's uncomfortably naked facts, Howells too could not help but see in their truth infinitely greater morality than in the works of other French novelists. James and Howells eventually rationalized that "art and morality are too perfectly different things" and they agreed that Zola supremely met the test of treating even the vulgar with literary perfection. Their view was substantially reinforced by the lecture about "The Irony of Plato," delivered by a prominent professor before the "Concord School" in the summer of 1886. In it, he stunned his listeners by including Zola in his identification of the men who shared common characteristics of irony, such as Socrates, Aristotle, Jesus, and Goethe. "In the whole range of literature," Professor Davidson noted with great conviction, "I know of no more cool, calm, terrible irony than that of Zola. It is the very irony of truth itself." In his judgment, moreover, the press reported merely disagreeable facts, whereas Zola's novels explained their causes and effects and suggested possible remedies.[28] It took Mark Twain some time before he changed his mind about the author of *La Terre;* but once he did, he admitted that life in some American communities could be just as atrocious as that depicted in *La Terre.* Zola's realism, honesty, and courage impressed him.[29] Mark Twain's change of attitude reflected that of American readers generally. Once they understood that Zola

27. Henry James, "Emile Zola," *Atlantic Monthly,* XCII (August, 1903), 201–208; Salvan, *Zola aux Etats-Unis,* 42–54.
28. William C. Frierson and Herbert Edwards, "Impact of French Naturalism on American Critical Opinion, 1877–1892," *PMLA,* LXIII (1948), 1013–14.
29. Sydney J. Krause, *Mark Twain as Critic* (Baltimore, 1967), 276–82.

did not write for the amusement of the vile-minded, that he
strenuously objected to the past romanticization of vice, and that
his fiction was to represent life in its truest, though often painfully
coarse, nature, he became enormously popular in the United
States.[30] His courageous role in the Dreyfus affair merely helped
to accentuate this trend so well justified by Edwin Arlington
Robinson's poem "Zola":

> Because he puts the compromising chart
> Of hell before your eyes, you are afraid;
> Because he counts the price that you have paid
> For innocence, and counts it from the start,
> You loathe him. But he sees the human heart
> Of God meanwhile, and in His hand was weighed
> Your squeamish and emasculate crusade
> Against the grim dominion of his art.
>
> Never until we conquer the uncouth
> Connivings of our shamed indifference
> (We call it Christian faith) are we to scan
> The racked and shrieking hideousness of Truth
> To find, in hate's polluted self-defence
> Throbbing, the pulse, the divine heart of man.

If any further persuasion was needed to convince Americans
of Zola's essentially humanitarian outlook, the New York *World*[31]
interview with him sufficed. Published on the threshold of the
twentieth century, the interview revealed Zola pleading for a
better world. Despite many material comforts gained in the course
of the nineteenth century, Zola cautioned, the world would not
be truly civilized until stupid prejudices and oppressive, obsolete
laws serving a small group of privileged people ceased to make
the life of the great mass of humanity miserable.

    30. William Dean Howells, "Emile Zola," *NAR*, CLXXV (1902), 587–90; Edwards, "Zola and the American Critics," 121–27. Between 1878 and 1900, thirty-one American publishers offered to the American public some 180 Zola books, including duplications and new editions. Malcolm B. Jones, "Translations of Zola in the United States Prior to 1900," *Modern Language Notes*, LV (November, 1940), 520.
    31. New York *World,* December, 30, 1900.

Less concerned with the real world at large, but also seeking the essence of truth, were the so-called decadent poets. As symbolists and impressionists, such leading representatives of this school as Verlaine, Mallarmé, and Joris Karl Huysmans interpreted poetry as something "vague, intangible, evanescent, a winged soul in flight." Looking more inward than outward, they wrote poetry full of music and subtle shades of color.[32]

Among the young Americans in Paris by the turn of the twentieth century were the symbolists Stuart Fitz-Randolph Merrill (1963–1915), a New York lawyer, and Francis Viélé-Griffin (1863–1937) from Norfolk, Virginia. Their familiarity with American literature and civilization and their close identification with French culture made them cultural ambassadors *par excellence*. In his *Pastels in Prose* (1890), Merrill acquainted Americans with the French decadents and symbolists, succeeding beautifully in transposing into English the music and exotic fantasies of these poets.[33] But even this ideal exposure resulted in anything but an enthusiastic reaction.

The appeal of Guy de Maupassant's (1850–1893) naturalistic novels and short stories realistically dealing with the frustrations of life, on the other hand, made him one of the favorites in America. Some of the credit for this popularity must be attributed to H. C. Bunner who introduced Maupassant to the American public—not by translating him, but rather by using some of his "ethical situations" and inspirations in a volume of his own, properly entitled *Made in France: French Tales with a United States Twist* (1893).[34]

Special attention must finally be called to those nineteenth-

---

32. Arthur Symons, "The Decadent Movement in Literature," *Harper's Magazine* (November, 1893), 858–67.

33. Gustave Leopold van Roosbroeck, "An American Poet: Stuart Merrill, 1863–1915," *Columbia University Quarterly*, XXVI (1934), 23–34; see also René Taupin, "L'Influence du symbolisme français sur la poésie américaine (1910 à 1920)," *Bibliothèque de la revue de littérature comparée*, LXII (1929), 63.

34. Gerard E. Jensen, *The Life and Letters of Henry Cuyler Bunner* (Durham, N.C., 1939), 148–49.

century French writers who chose the natural scenery, customs, and people of America as a theme in their literary works.[35] With few exceptions, Tocqueville and Laboulaye prominently among them, they drew a very unreal and often ridiculous picture of American life. In the long run, this tendency hurt the interests of the French people more than the sensitivities of Americans, because it created a totally distorted image of the dynamic society across the Atlantic. Starting with Châteaubriand's romanticization of the American wilderness, up to 1830 America was portrayed as a land in which noble savages, well-to-do property owners, upright Quakers, virtuous women, and on the whole satisfied slaves lived a life free from governmental and priestly regulation. Strangely, even Balzac, following the disillusioning comments of bourgeois French travelers, depicted in his *Le Curé de village* (1839) an immigrant family in Ohio that left the United States again because it found "in this coldly materialistic and soulless land neither hope, nor faith, nor charity."

During the next half-century French writers frequently resorted to biting satire and crude cynicism in their descriptions of American society. *Les Femmes d'Amérique* (1853) by A. Bellegarrique, *L'Autre monde* (1855) by M. de Grandfort, and *Flânerie parisienne aux Etats-Unis* (1856) by Alfred d'Almbert, for instance, described Americans as bandits, imposters, and whores. Other writers exaggerated American taste for speculation, publicity, and frequent occupational changes. Victorien Sardou's (1831–1908) *L'Oncle Sam* (1872–1873) helped to perpetuate the notion that Americans were rascals bent on amassing fortunes, by hook or by crook, and knowing neither respect, nor friendship, nor love. Quite a few French observers maintained that the logic

---

35. For an excellent discussion of this theme, see Simon Jeune, *De F. T. Graindorge à A. O. Barnabooth: Les Types américains dans le roman et le théâtre français* (1861–1917) (Paris, 1963), 11–19, 73–77, 123–25, 152–81. See also, Maurice Baudin, "L'Américain dans le théâtre français," *Philological Quarterly*, IV (1925), 75–90; René Rémond, *Les Etats-Unis devant l'opinion française*, 1815–1852 (2 vols.; Paris, 1962), I, 398–411; and Carl Wittke, "The American Theme in Continental European Literatures," *Mississippi Valley Historical Review*, XXVIII (1941), 3–26.

and morality of this race of determined, bad-mannered, and generally naive and unprincipled people clearly differed from that of Europeans. By the end of the century, Villiers de l'Isle-Adam typically chose Thomas Edison, the wizard of Menlo Park, as the central theme in his scientific fantasy *L'Eve future* (1886). With telling irony he attacked in it the exploitation of technological advances likely to end up destroying the dignity of the human kind.

As Simon Jeune has pointed out in his excellent study, only occasionally did the extremely grotesque presentation of Americans yield to some more moderate and favorable portrayals. Alfred Assolant's *Un Quaker à Paris* (1886), Maurice Sand's *Miss Mary* (1867), and Alexandre Dumas' *L'Étrangère* (1876), for example, extolled the virtues of American women, the independent queens in American society, and the good sense and industriousness of the men. And contrary to Villiers de l'Isle-Adam, Jules Verne (1828–1905) enthusiastically observed American energy and science and the willingness to take great risks in amazing experiments. "Because Americans care more for humanity in general than for the individual in particular" and because of their technological exploits, he judged them best suited for the peaceful conquest of the universe.

A brief survey of the development of American literature and French reaction to it shows that the educated Frenchmen followed it closely and that principally James Fenimore Cooper and Edgar Allan Poe were widely appreciated in France. Such truly creative and in time influential writers as Walt Whitman and Mark Twain seemed to be beyond the comprehension of the contemporary French public. Let us trace this development historically.

Moses Coit Tyler's literary history of colonial America, first published in 1878, dealt with authors little known in Europe. St. Jean de Crèvecoeur presented in his *Letters from an American Farmer* (1770–1781) the idealized notion of America as a country "where nature guides and virtue rules," and he also confidently asserted that its inhabitants would "entertain new ideas and form new opinions." Actually, it took about another half-century before Frenchmen began to take an interest in American literature, and only in the second half of the nineteenth century did American literary contributions attract more than an exotic curiosity in France Several journals, notably the *Mercure du 19ᵉ siècle* (1824), the *Revue encyclopédique,* and the *Revue des deux mondes,* took cognizance of American literature when it was still disappointingly patterned after that of England.[36]

The growing clamor in America for independence from Europe's literary genius and the strong desire in France to see American artists and writers paint American scenes in an American style turned out to be easier to express than to implement. Culturally, Americans were not as independent as these desires suggested. Aside from the international cross-fertilization of ideas, the Protestant churches in the United States exercised as controlling an influence on American culture as the Roman Catholic church customarily did in Catholic countries.[37] The cultural predilections of the American middle-class and its enterprising economic leaders also placed limits on the range of imaginative minds. Specifically: in France the artistic ideal aimed at aesthetic enjoyment; in the United States it was expected to support the prevailing morality and to uphold the faith in God, country, family, and business.

Alexis de Tocqueville wrote his *Democracy in America* at a time when he could observe that, "properly speaking," the United States had no literature. Americans read a great deal, but besides Bibles, pamphlets, and magazines, they drew primarily on the treasures of English literature, exposing themselves therefore to the literary fashions of an aristocratic nation. In his general discussion of literature in America, Tocqueville mused about different attitudes affecting the literature of aristocratic and

36. Schalck de la Faverie, *Les Premiers interprètes de la pensée américaine,* 169; James L. Shepherd, "L'Amérique du Nord dans la littérature française, 1830–1840" (Ph.D. dissertation, Université de Paris, 1953).

37. See the thought-provoking essay by Howard Mumford Jones, "The European Background," in Norman Foerster (ed.), *The Reinterpretation of American Literature* (New York, 1928), 76–80.

democratic peoples. He noted, for instance, that the aristocratic mind was inclined to contemplate about the past, whereas in a democracy people were preoccupied with the present and the future. As he saw it, the clash of the principles of privilege and equality—the great contrasts between eminent personage and ordinary crowd and between the potential self-control of cultivated persons and the strong emotions of the masses—was destined to be reflected in America's literature. Sure that eventually it would develop, however limited in scope and depth, he predicted that it would, in all probability, tend to accommodate democratic proclivities toward broad generalizations and unabashed bombast.[38]

Until about the end of the Second Empire, many Frenchmen approached the question of compatibility between American democracy and literature in a prejudiced way. Instead of realizing that a young nation required time to produce its own literature and to foster high standards, they expected the materialistically inclined democratic masses to suffocate literary productivity. When Irving, Cooper, Longfellow, Hawthorne, and Emerson appeared on the scene, if Frenchmen paid attention to them at all, they usually downgraded them as being either "mediocre" or "too English." At first astonished that the "model republic" produced any poets, they then deplored the absence of peculiarly American eccentricities in their writings.[39]

From the early 1830s on, Philarète Chasles (1798–1873) displayed an intimate familiarity with American literature in the pages of the *Revue des deux mondes*. Unfortunately, his strong aristocratic and Catholic inclinations tended to color his opinions. In his judgment, the Protestant American republic was culturally

38. Alexis de Tocqueville, *Democracy in America* (2 vols.; London, 1835–40), II, 58–59, 76–77; Harold Mantz, *French Criticism of American Literature Before 1850* (New York, 1917), 99–116; K. Harrison, "A French Forecast of American Literature," *South Atlantic Quarterly,* XXV (1926), 350–53.

39. Sidney Lauront McGee, "La Littérature américaine dans la *Revue des deux mondes,* 1831–1900" (Ph.D. dissertation, Université de Montpellier, 1927), 13, 28–30; Léon Lemonnier, "Quelques vieux judgments français sur la littérature américaine," *La Revue européenne* (July–December, 1927), 175–80.

too closely tied to England and neither historically rooted nor socially homogeneous enough to produce its own first-rate literature. It was not until the 1850s that he changed his mind about this possibility,[40] encouraged in his views by J. J. Ampère's optimistic impression about the progress of American literature. Admitting that American poets did not write for the broad masses, Ampère also contended that a literature could be democratic in spirit without being so in form.[41] Next to Chasles, the most knowledgeable French critic of American literature, Emile Montégut (1826–1895), studied it for its possible lessons for France, as well as for his personal interests. Sometimes discouraged by developments in Europe, where the middle-classes seemed, in their own fashion, to follow the footsteps of American materialism, Montégut drew encouragement from the remarkable literary activities going on in New England. In some thirty articles published in the *Revue des deux mondes* and the *Moniteur universel* he elaborated upon his sympathetic views regarding American literature and philosophy. Careful studies of and about them convinced him that ideals, charm, and artistic talent were not necessarily a monopoly of aristocratic societies. The wisdom contained in Emerson's moral philosophy held out the hope for which Montégut was vainly searching in France. In a world dominated by men relentlessly following the path of industrial conquest, humanitarian writers like Margaret Fuller, moreover, suggested to him the vision of women as the most wholesome civilizing agents in the industrial age. In the light of these sentiments, his detailed criticisms of American "imitators of European literature" assumed a subordinate significance.[42] Before long, however, Montégut deplored the ephemeral existence of the transcendentalists and the cultural drought that followed when their moral and intellectual examples were displaced by shameful compromises of noble principles. When Montégut wrote about

40. Eva M. Phillips, *Philarète Chasles* (Paris, 1933), 209–15.
41. McGee, "La Littérature américaine," 43–46.
42. *Ibid*, 53–54; see also Ruth E. Brown, "A French Interpretation of New England's Literature, 1846–1865," *NEQ*, XIII (1940), 305–16.

this "American conversion" in 1858, his reputation carried more weight in France than one would surmise from Henry James's later comment (1876) that this "unhumorous type" of Frenchman was "spinning about his shallow ingeniosities with a complacency to make the angels howl."[43]

The *Revue des deux mondes* continued to publish a steady flow of information about American literature. In the final decades of the century, Thérèse Bentzon and Théodor de Wyzewa followed its evolution very closely, discussing general literary developments as well as commenting on individual works. Here, after all, was not only a more or less independent literature coming into existence, but a new society. Paradoxically, as Henri Peyre has more recently pointed out,[44] this society displayed an extraordinary degree of morbidity in its literature, despite the optimism it liked to profess rather demonstratively.

Early in the nineteenth century, a group of young Americans known as the Knickerbockers, prominent among them Washington Irving (1783-1859) and James Fenimore Cooper (1789-1851), began to disprove the taunting European refrain that America was neither interested in nor capable of developing its own literature. Eventually, both Irving and Cooper made names for themselves in the literary world, particularly in France where they spent several years. Irving, essentially an entertaining writer of historical and biographical sketches, as well as of life scenes in American and European settings, was greatly influenced by English literature. He prepared his manuscripts carefully and in the refined style that set his generation apart from the more stirring romantic period that followed it. In essence, the rather left-handed compliment the *Revue encyclopédique* (1831) bestowed upon the genial author of the *Sketch-Book* and *Rip van Winkle*—that he was a poet who "made the most of a little mind and a little talent"—did not seem to be off the mark. Irving did not

43. Henry James to Alice James, February 22, 1876, MS 1094 (1572), HCL.

44. Henri Peyre, "American Literature Seen Through French Eyes," *Virginia Quarterly Review*, XXIII (1947), 421-38.

set out to teach, to preach, or to innovate, but to provide the public with clean and, hopefully, delightful reading material.[45] The French became so fond of this cultivated American writer that their high society lionized him and, from 1822 on, publishing firms circulated many translations of his work. In fact, by 1842 at least thirty-eight separate editions of one or the other of his books were available in the French market. Many reviews and articles also featured the works of this "American from England" and, from 1876 on he appeared on the reading lists in French schools. Nonetheless, his writings were not outstanding enough to make an impact on literary France. If anything, his enthusiasm for British literature might have spilled over to some Frenchmen.

The other Knickerbocker, James Fenimore Cooper, enjoyed an extraordinary popularity in France. Admired for his action-packed Leatherstocking tales, "the Walter Scott of America" attracted many translators who actually improved the stylistic quality of his picturesque and exciting stories. The famous translator A. J. B. Defauconpret not only condensed the text occasionally, he also omitted from *The Last of the Mohicans* comments that might have been offensive to the citizens of France. Cooper's popularity in France reached its height during the first two years of his stay there, from 1826 to 1828, and began to show signs of decline after his return from a two-year visit to other European countries.[46] In the meantime, the Revolution of 1830 had not only brought about a change of rulers, to both of whom General Lafayette had introduced him, but also a change of political attitude on the part of the French bourgeoisie. It became irritated with Cooper's frequent assertion of the superiority of American institutions, about which most Europeans seemed to

45. Francis P. Smith, "Washington Irving and France" (Ph.D. dissertation, Harvard University, 1938), 226–36; George D. Morris, "Washington Irving's Fiction in the Light of French Criticism," *Indiana University Studies*, III (1916), 5–26; and George S. Hellman, *Washington Irving, Esquire: Ambassador at Large from the New World to the Old* (New York, 1925), 263.

46. Fernand Baldensperger, *James Fenimore Cooper in France*. Franco-American Pamphlets, Second Series, No. 12 (New York, 1940); New York State Historical Association, *James Fenimore Cooper: A Reappraisal* (Coopertown, N.Y., 1954), 522–39.

him to be as ignorant as Americans generally were about the finer aspects of European culture. Despite this irritation, though, he found much more acclaim abroad than at home.

Cooper's reputation in France rested on such "descriptive masterpieces" as *The Spy, The Pilot,* and *The Last of the Mohicans.* Châteaubriand, Sainte-Beuve, Balzac, George Sand, Dumas, and many others praised the originality of his magnificent American and naval scenes. Despite some occasional faulty constructions, his vigor and imagination were much admired. His descriptions of the customs and costumes of American Indians and his intimate familiarity with life on the sea stimulated an unusual interest in Cooper's novels.[47] Some French critics, to be sure, found his lengthy digressions and inadequate character sketches to be shortcomings that called for correction. Ultimately, though, his waning fortune in France in the late 1830s coincided with his declining originality.

By then, however, Cooper was so well known in France that, whatever the critics had to say, the reading public continued to enjoy his "typically American" stories. Indeed, French readers assumed that Cooper acquainted them with the realities of life in America generally. Favorable reviews of his earlier works had laid the foundation for his reputation as a significant writer whom French society began to lionize. The excitement created by the publication of *The Last of the Mohicans* (1826) helped to identify him as a genius, capable of excelling Walter Scott in some respects. Reviewing this novel, the *Globe* (June 19, 1827) praised "the noble type of American republican" who had sketched these fascinatingly original American scenes. In his discussion of this novel, Louis de Loménie[48] reaffirmed in 1894 that "the vigor of the description of the characters and the dramatic interest evoked by their actions" propelled the Cooper vogue in Europe, particularly in France.

47. Marcel Clavel, *Fenimore Cooper and His Critics* (Aix-en-Provence, 1938), 246, 369–70, 381–83; Eric Partridge, "Fenimore Cooper's Influence on the French Romantics," *Modern Language Review,* XX (1925), 174–78.
48. See *Galleries des Contemporains Illustres,* VIII (1844), 13–18.

Balzac was less impressed by those of Cooper's characters who, he felt, were overshadowed by the scenery than by his vivid descriptions of the landscape and the Indians' life-style. Inspired by *The Pathfinder*, Balzac wrote in the *Revue parisienne* for July 25, 1840: "Leatherstocking is a statue, a magnificent moral hermaphrodite, born half-savage, half-civilized. I do not know if the extraordinary work of Walter Scott has given us any creation as magnificent as this hero of the savannahs and forests." What Balzac admired most in Cooper's novels was his superb ability to fuse characters and landscape. To him, Cooper's topographical descriptions were comparable to the paintings of a great master. Similarly, Sainte-Beuve appreciated Cooper's unique understanding of the sea and the special attachment of seamen to their ships. When Cooper died in 1851, Hector Berlioz paid tribute to him by naming one of his overtures, then performed in London, *Le Corsaire rouge (Red Rover)*.

Cooper's enduring popularity in France was attested by four collective editions of his works in 1855 and by forty-five pages of references in the catalog of the Bibliothèque Nationale, listing French versions and adaptations of his work up to the end of the century. His influence on French writers in the middle of the century was remarkable. He inspired two new genres of French fiction, the *roman d'aventure* and the *roman maritime*. While it has been argued that Cooper's influence on Balzac was minimal and that both responded to the public taste of their contemporaries for "thrillers," a stronger case for his influence has also been made. Philippe Van Tieghem has more recently expressed the opinion that Balzac's *Les Chouans* (1829) was in a sense modeled after *The Last of the Mohicans*.[49] As Cooper's American Indians fought the invader, Balzac's Vendeans fought for the preservation

49. Margaret M. Gibb, *Le Roman de Bas-de-Cuir*: *Etude sur Fenimore Cooper et son influence en France* (Paris, 1927), 176. See also, André LeBreton, "Origines du roman balzacien," *Revue de Paris*, V (1903), 781–826; Bowen, "A Comparison of the Methods of Composition in Cooper and Balzac," 297–313; Thomas R. Palfrey, "Cooper and Balzac: The Headsman," *Modern Philology*, XXIX (1932), 335–41; and Philippe Van Tieghem, *Les Influences étrangères sur la littérature française* (1550–1880) (Paris, 1961), 125–27.

of their traditions; and, as Balzac emphasized, both peoples displayed the same tenacity, loyalty, cunningness, and naive superstitions. The enormous popularity of Gabriel Ferry's *Le Coureur des bois* (1853), dealing with the life and struggles of French-Canadian frontiersmen, may also be attributed to the appetite Cooper had created for this type of story. Dumas *père* acknowledged that in his *Le Capitaine Paul* he wished to go beyond the experiences Cooper had so fascinatingly sketched in *The Pilot*. It was furthermore no coincidence that, in imitation of Cooper's work, he published *Les Mohicans de Paris* (1854–1858), a description of the Paris underworld. Gustave Aimard (1818–1883), who went to the United States to gather material for his Indian and western stories, admittedly aspired to be known as "the French Fenimore Cooper." But his tales, full of violence and sensationalism, fell short of the literary accomplishments of his model.[50] Neither did other French writers who tried it equal Cooper's mastery of Indian portraits.

Eugene Sue did not hesitate to admit in his preface to *Plik et Plok* (1831) that the development of the maritime novel in France owed much to Cooper's inspiration. Indeed, Cooper's brilliantly developed theme of the struggles of man against the sea attracted not only Sue but the perhaps even more prominent Edouard Corbière. It apparently was also no coincidence that such French maritime periodicals as *Le Navigateur* and *La France maritime* made their appearance in the 1830s.

The 1830s attempt of the younger generation of French artists and writers to free themselves from the overly confining tradition of the arts found its counterpart in the desire of young American minds to shake off those intellectual influences from abroad that had long delayed the development of a literature soundly rooted in America. As each period seemed to produce its own eloquent spokesmen of ideas and changes for which the time was ripe, Ralph Waldo Emerson (1803–1882) assumed this role for his generation. Essayist, lecturer, preacher, and philosopher, this

50. Virgil L. Jones, "Gustave Aimard," *Southern Review*, XV (1930), 452–65; Wittke, "The American Theme," 3–26.

New Englander possessed the eloquence, sagacity, and independence of spirit to command a respectful hearing at home and abroad. Whatever he may have lacked in intellectual precision and depth, he captivated his audience with his serenity and self-reliance.[51]

Emerson's broad interests reflected his universal education and extensive travels. Next to England and Germany, his personal acquaintance with France and its culture helped him to formulate some of his thoughts about life. In a lecture he first delivered at Concord in 1848, after his second visit of Paris, he spoke about "France, or Urbanity" in a vein that revealed certain critical reservations. In his estimate, Frenchmen excelled more in the exact sciences and the popularization of ideas and the arts than in original thought. "In literature," he contended, "they are lucid and agreeable; but they have only a few examples of a profounder class; no single examination of imagination; and never a poet."[52] Still critical in 1859, and with a touch of annoyance, he recorded in his journal: "The French all write alike . . . you would think all the novels and all the criticism were written by one and the same man." This criticism did not apply to Michel de Montaigne (1533–1592), whom Emerson studied and revered the most and who taught him the wisdom of constructive skepticism. Emerson counted Montaigne's *Essays* among the most valuable books in world literature. Like this great French rational moralist, Emerson, an intuitive moralist, believed that the laws of conscience were subject to changing circumstances and, more particularly, that morality itself was not the creation of and did not need the sanctions of state or church. Emerson's faith in the essential divinity of human nature, though, spawned the transcendental optimism that distinguished him from the thorough skeptic Montaigne.[53]

51. Firmin Roz, "L'Idéalisme américain: Ralph Waldo Emerson," *RDDM* (February, 1902), 661–75.

52. James E. Cabot, *A Memoir of Ralph Waldo Emerson* (Boston, 1887), 755–57.

53. See Régis Michaud, "Emerson et Montaigne," *Revue germanique*, X (1914), 425–37; Charles L. Young, *Emerson's Montaigne* (New York, 1941), 197–213; and Ralph Waldo Emerson, "Montaigne: Or, the Skeptic," in his *Representative Men: Seven Lectures* (Boston, 1856), 149–86.

To French men and women of letters Emerson represented a most welcome cultural phenomenon. Unknown in France until Philarète Chasles introduced him in 1844 as "the most original mind the United States has produced," Emerson was thereafter called frequently to the public's favorable attention. In a lecture Edgar Quinet delivered in 1845 at the Collège de France, he singled out Emerson as an example of a moral seeker who impressed him as a more original thinker than many of the more involved German philosophers. In the following year, the Comtesse d'Agoult (Marie de Flavigny), also known by the pen name of Daniel Stern, published an important article on Emerson in the *Revue indépendante* (July 25, 1846). In it she alerted her compatriots to the necessity of revising their completely erroneous opinions about the intellectual potential of America. With keen insight, she asserted that the young American giant still needed "noise and confusion more than rhythm and harmony," but then she prophesied that this giant was on the threshold of cultural breakthrough. In her estimate, Washington Irving, William Cullen Bryant, and Henry Wadsworth Longfellow were forerunners of a more substantial national literature likely to emerge in the near future. Emerson's high-mindedness impressed her immensely. His lofty independence, his courageous nonconformity, and his religious respect for the individual epitomized to her the American genius. His opposition to religious dogmatism, which fostered the secularization of puritanism, and the importance he attached to living in the present were wholesome signs of vigor and flexibility. Comtesse d'Agoult interpreted the mixture of Emerson's Protestant individualism with his vague pantheism and mystic conception of nature as a combination of views other American writers might in the future accept as typifying American thought.[54] As if to substantiate this speculation, Walt Whitman indeed later shared Emerson's belief that the soul was God in man.

Gradually, Emerson's *Essays* became a frequent topic of conversation in French intellectual circles. This development was

54. Besse D. Howard, "The First French Estimate of Emerson," *NEQ*, X (1937), 447–63; Hans Keller, *Emerson in Frankreich: Wirkungen und Parallelen* (Giessen, 1932), 77–79.

accelerated by Emile Montégut's favorable exposition of Emerson's thoughts in the *Revue des deux mondes* (August, 1847). Delighted by the absence of dogmatism in the writings of this modern sage, Montégut, a critic of considerable weight, lavished unusual praise on the "new Plato" from Concord. This democratic aristocrat renewed Montégut's hope for the survival of individualism despite the threatening pressures of the masses. As aware as Montégut that the leveling tendencies of the egalitarian masses were capable of destroying the aristocracy of character and creative geniuses, Emerson pleaded vigorously for the rights of the individual and against oppression by the multitudes. As pleased as Montégut was with Emerson's moral and religious framework of individual existence, it saddened him to see the virtues of American democracy gradually decline. What Montégut apparently did not realize was that his and Emerson's concern with the individual was not at all identical. Whereas Montégut was primarily interested in the political and external ramifications of Emerson's thought, the New England philosopher, a believer in instinct and spontaneity as the divine faculties connecting God and man, was primarily concerned with the inner world of the individual and his potential greatness.[55]

Emerson's elevating essays and charming poetry made him a towering figure in America's literary elite. The Académie des Sciences Morales et Politiques belatedly acknowledged this standing in 1877 when it elected him one of its foreign correspondents. Such renowned personalities as Renan and Taine had already accorded him the recognition and courtesies due such a noble intellect when he visited Europe after the fall of the Second Empire.[56] A generation later, social and world conditions had changed so much that retrospective thoughts about Emerson reduced his standing. Following Victor Basch's earnest reappraisal of Emerson at the beginning of the twentieth century, in which he pointed

55. Emile Montégut, "Un Penseur et poéte américain: Ralph Waldo Emerson," *RDDM* (August, 1847), 462–93; Olive S. Parish, "The French View of Emerson" (M.A. thesis, Yale University, 1929), 17–33; and Reine Virtanen, "Emile Montégut as a Critic of American Literature," *PMLA*, LXIII (1948), 1265–75.

56. Parish, "The French View of Emerson," 40–57.

out the contradictions between Emerson "the mystic transcendental idealist" and Emerson "the energetic pragmatic leader of a people that took pride in its concepts of self-government and self-reliance," Marie Dugard analyzed this paradoxical life and work in penetrating depth. Even as a human being she found this outspoken advocate of robust individualism to be impersonal and unapproachable, a lofty loner who combined the "simplicity of a child" with "a sort of patrician pride." As a thinker, she found him too vague and elusive to guide people in their search for workable answers to the questions of life.[57]

None of America's nineteenth-century poets was as highly regarded in France as Henry Wadsworth Longfellow (1807–1882). Intimately familiar with Europe and several of its languages, the Harvard professor of literature, poet, and translator possessed a fine collection of French books in his private library. But as familiar as he was with classic and modern French literature, he cared little for the contemporary literature and, in fact, expressed a special preference for French literature of the Middle Ages.[58]

Early in 1849 the French Minister to the United States, Guillaume Tell Poussin, notified Longfellow of the desire of the influential *Revue des deux mondes* henceforth to include discussions of American literary productions, and he invited him to send his works to the editor of the *Revue* so as to be able "to give a full account of them." Soon thereafter, Poussin commented on Longfellow's "beautiful tale of Acadia" and his "rapid, glowing, and impressive rhymes," which, he was sure, would be appreciatively greeted in France.[59] Only a few months later, Philarète Chasles complimented Longfellow on the unsurpassed "originality, energy and purity" of his poetry. Emile Montégut

57. Marie Dugard, *Ralph Waldo Emerson: Sa vie, son oeuvre* (Paris, 1907); Victor Basch, "Individualistes modernes: Ralph Waldo Emerson," *La Grande revue* (April, 1903), 73–102.

58. Edward Estève, "Longfellow et la France," *Bowdoin College Bulletin,* No. 146 (October, 1925), 4–10.

59. Guillaume Tell Poussin to Henry Wadsworth Longfellow, February 21, and March 7, 1849, MS Am 1340.2 (4488), HCL.

also thought that Longfellow's talent and culture placed him well above other American poets. Among other famous Frenchmen, Victor Hugo assured his American confrère that his poetry honored his country.[60] Longfellow carried on a more extensive correspondence with Louis Dépret whose lecture about him before the Société des Sciences de Lille was published in 1876. As Dépret indicated in his correspondence with the *"cher et illustre poète"* in America, such honored French men of letters as Xavier Marmier and Auguste Baribier, whom Longfellow knew personally, shared the public's appreciation of his poetry.[61] They all admired his *Song of Hiawatha, Evangeline,* and his important description of the life of the Indian race.

Since Longfellow was neither a courageous crusader nor a profound thinker, his popularity abroad, evidenced by the many translations of his works, must be traced to the same source that caused it at home: his lyricism, purity, and human understanding.[62] Not the least appealing was his inspiring optimism and the frequent reminder "There is no Death! What seems so is transition." This belief, of course, found its unforgettable expression in the rhythmic verse:

> Life is real! Life is earnest!
> And the grave is not its goal;
> Dust thou art, to dust returnest,
> Was not spoken of the soul.

Whatever the reaction to Nathaniel Hawthorne (1804–1864) in the United States, his puritan and parochial New England background was hardly suited to evoke a lively interest in his short stories and novels in France. When rather late in his life

60. Philarète Chasles to Longfellow, July 15, 1849, MS Am 1340.2 (1080), HCL; Victor Hugo to Longfellow, April 22, 1867, MS Am 1340.2 (2900), HCL.
61. Louis Dépret to Longfellow, February 7, 1877, MS Am 1340.2 (1543), HCL; see also Louis Dépret, "La Poésie en Amérique: Henry Wadsworth Longfellow," *Mémoires de la Société de Lille,* 4th ser., II (1876), 306, 340.
62. A. Schalck de la Faverie, "Henry Wadsworth Longfellow," *Revue britannique* (1901), 247–68. Baudelaire frankly admitted that two passages of *Les Fleurs du Mal* had been "borrowed" from Longfellow. Van Wyck Brooks also noted a passage of *Hiawatha* in Baudelaire's poem "Calumet de Paix." Van Wyck Brooks, *New England: Indian Summer, 1865–1915* (New York, 1940), 30.

his old college friend, President Franklin Pierce, appointed him to the consulates at Liverpool and Manchester, Hawthorne was finally afforded the opportunity to visit the Old World, the great showcase of Western civilization. The splendor of Paris, which he saw for the first time in January, 1858, admittedly took him by surprise. His reaction to the paintings and sculptures in the Louvre was, as one might have expected in his case, generally less enthusiastic than that to "the vast and beautiful edifice" in which they were exhibited.[63] The great personal sacrifices he had made for the sake of his freely chosen literary career were perhaps also reflected in the limited range of influences to which he exposed himself. In any case, the contemporary literary currents of French romanticism and German idealism appealed to him much less than those prevailing in England. Quite in character, his skeptical Calvinistic notions of life also kept him at a distance from transcendental thought and social-reform activities in the United States, despite the fact that for a time he had resided at Brook Farm.[64]

What, then, led prominent French critics to the conclusion that Hawthorne belonged to the most remarkable writers of the period? Why did Emile Montégut take special interest in this "man of genius," in "somber Hawthorne," America's most accomplished writer? For one thing, he found *The Scarlet Letter, The House of Seven Gables, Mosses from an Old Manse*, and *Twice Told Tales* delightful reading. On the occasion of Hawthorne's death Montégut eulogized his superb gift for describing solitude, superstition, and fear, sentiments that fitted him better for short stories than for long novels requiring great vitality. To Montégut's satisfaction, Hawthorne's style possessed so much charm, precision, and polish that it compensated satisfactorily for his lack of humor. But, above all, he had made the important psychological discovery that sensibility was the dominant function

63. Louis Emile Chrétien, "La Pensée morale de Nathaniel Hawthorne, 1804–64, symboliste néo-puritain: Esquisse d'une interprétation" (Ph.D. dissertation, Université de Paris, 1932). See also Nathaniel Hawthorne, *Passages from the French and Italian Notebooks* (Boston, 1874), 11–13.

64. Parrington, *Main Currents in American Thought*, II, 443.

of the soul. Through skillful repetition and bits of detail he gradually introduced his most subtle conceptions.[65] As L. Dhaleine has pointed out in his biography of Hawthorne (1905), he successfully led his readers to his dreamland, "a land in which it seemed always afternoon," as well as to the most hidden spots of the human soul. Unfortunately though, his almost morbid preoccupation with death, suffering, and hidden crime overshadowed his genuine talents as a writer. Neither capable nor consciously willing to escape from the puritan heritage that had taught him to believe that evil was everywhere in the world, Hawthorne applied himself primarily to an analysis of the conscience.[66] This was hardly a theme to endear him to other than like-minded people, no matter how great his genius.

Several other American poets, well known at home, remained little more than names in France. Frenchmen practically ignored, for instance, Herman Melville (1819–1891), James Russell Lowell (1819–1891), and Henry David Thoreau (1817–1862).[67] *Uncle Tom's Cabin* (1852), on the other hand, became such a sensation that in one year alone eleven translations were devoured by the public. Frenchmen were touched by Harriet Beecher Stowe's sincerity, courage, and literary integrity; and they were ashamed that in any land, but particularly in "the land of the free," the degrading institution of slavery was still tolerated. John Lemoinne's articles about *Uncle Tom's Cabin* in the *Journal des débats*, October 20, and November 15, 1852, emphasized once again that women seemed to possess irresistible gifts as publicists because "they know how to make people weep." George Sand did not miss this opportunity to lend her support to the cause of human justice.

65. Emile Montégut, "Nathaniel Hawthorne," *Moniteur universel*, June 27, July 11, and August 27, 1864; L. Dhaleine, *N. Hawthorne: Sa vie et son oeuvre* (Paris, 1905), 398.
66. Emile Lauvrière, "La Morbidité en Hawthorne," *Revue germanique* (January-February, 1906), 130–35; Dhaleine, *Hawthorne*, 454–58.
67. See Cyrille Arnavon, *Les Lettres américaines devant la critique française, 1887–1917* (Paris, 1951), 27–36; Charles O. Stewart, *Lowell and France* (Nashville, Tenn., 1951); Christof Wegelin, *The Concept of Europe in American Fiction from Irving to Hawthorne* (Baltimore, 1947), 130–31; and Eugene F. Timpe (ed.), *Thoreau Abroad: Twelve Bibliographical Essays* (Hamden, Conn., 1971), 33–34.

The little woman who wrote this classic set a social revolution in motion not only in the United States; the French vogue of anti-slavery literature could also be attributed to her great success.[68]

In this discussion of Franco-American literary relations, the significance of four American writers clearly merits special emphasis: they are Poe, Whitman, Mark Twain, and Henry James. The duality of Edgar Allan Poe's life (1809–1849) and the controversies surrounding his reputation as a poet cannot deny the fact that, thanks to Charles Pierre Baudelaire's (1821–1867) superb translations of Poe's work, his popularity in France made him one of the few "naturalized citizens of the French republic of letters." By extraordinary coincidence, Baudelaire and Poe found not only their literary antennas attuned to each other, but in their short lives they also experienced similar hurdles and miseries. Poe tried to forget them by consuming excessive amounts of liquor; they induced Baudelaire to experiment with wine and opium as means of stimulating as well as numbing his senses. Though he struggled against poverty and human disappointments and was a friendless man who in his final years suffered "intervals of horrible sanity," Poe managed to be a creative writer and critic. Indeed, his mysteries and poems revealed a touch of genius peculiarly his own. They also revealed a duality in him ranging from the beautiful visions of an idealist to the frightening fantasies of a mind abnormally obsessed with the empire of death or the ingenious plots of a carefully calculating realist.

The French public read Poe before it knew that it was reading Poe; for from 1844 on, imitations, adaptations, and translations of his work appeared in French publications without reference to the original author. A lawsuit about this type of plagiarism attracted some attention to him. But Poe's eventual popularity in France rested, of course, on a much more solid foundation. More significant than Alphonse Borgher's translation of Poe's

68. E. Lucas, *La Littérature anti-esclavagiste au 19ᵉ siècle: Etude sur Madame Beecher Stowe et son influence en France* (Paris, 1930).

"The Gold Bug," published in the November, 1845, issue of the *Revue britannique*, E. D. Forgues' favorable review of Poe's *Tales* in the *Revue des deux mondes* (October, 1846) had the effect of arousing considerable curiosity about this evidently major American author whom Forgues described as a "logician, a pursuer of abstract truths, a lover of the most eccentric hypotheses."[69]

Baudelaire became so fascinated with Poe that he wanted to share his experience with as many people as he could reach. In articles published in 1852 in the *Revue de Paris*, he conveyed the impression that his profound admiration for Poe was based on intimate familiarity with his works. To let French readers judge for themselves, he set out to translate Poe's poems and tales. But this was more than an ordinary undertaking.[70] About ten years after he had been introduced to Poe's work, Baudelaire wrote to Armand Fraisse about an almost unbelievable occurrence: "In 1846 or 1847 I read some fragments of Poe's writings. Since his collected works were published posthumously, I patiently inquired of Americans living in Paris whether they knew Poe and I collected all the journals with which Poe had once been associated. To my surprise, I found among them . . . poems and novels which had existed in my mind in a vague, confused, and unfinished form, but which Poe had already perfectly completed." In a letter to Théophile Thoré, Baudelaire elaborated in 1864: "The first time I opened one of Poe's books, I saw with horror and delight not only subjects about which I had dreamed, but also sentences I had formulated in my mind, sentences which he had already written twenty years before!" Carried away by this amazing resemblance of thought, Baudelaire went ahead to translate Poe's work as conscientiously as if it were his own.[71]

69. Célestin Pierre Cambiaire, *The Influence of Edgar Allan Poe in France* (New York, 1927), 305; Arthur Hobson Quinn, *Edgar Allan Poe: A Critical Biography* (New York, 1941), 516–17.
70. W. T. Bandy, "New Light on Baudelaire and Poe," *Yale French Studies*, No. 10 (1952), 65–69.
71. Walter Mönch, *Das Gastmahl: Begegnungen abendländischer Dichter und Philosophen* (Hamburg, 1947), 362–66.

Typical of many French intellectuals of his time, who showed little understanding for a democratic society that developed a life-style and institutions in conflict with their own prejudiced notions, Baudelaire blamed the anti-intellectual climate in America for his idol's mental anguish and premature demise. In his introduction to the translations of Poe's work, in the *Histoires extraordinaires* (1856), and in *Nouvelles histoires extraordinaires* (1857), Baudelaire emotionally charged America, this "great gaslighted barbarity," with having driven Poe into desperation. "All his inner and spiritual life, whether drunkard's or poet's, was one constant effort to escape from this antipathetic atmosphere," in which, Baudelaire continued, "the impious love of liberty has given birth to a new tyranny." In America's "seething mass of mediocrity and commonplace" a brilliant artist like Poe was lost, the more so because he believed in art for art's sake and not for practical ends.[72] In a similar vein, among many other French writers and critics, Barbey d'Aurevilly asserted that Poe had been "trampled to death by the elephantine feet of American materialism."

The fact that Poe was familiar with many French authors and that some of his own characters may have originated when he read Balzac and other French writers, did not necessarily make him a "gallicized" poet. Why, then, did he become so popular in France? The logic, order, and clarity of his stories seemed to appeal to French readers as much as his treatment of perversity and the grotesque. The "rigor of his analysis" and his science fiction proved to be very attractive features in his writing. French symbolists were intrigued, moreover, by his power to suggest more than met the eye. And some Frenchmen recognized in him a very intellectual artist who possessed the rare ability to paint the darker sides of life both realistically and with consoling beauty.[73]

72. Marcel Françon, "Poe et Baudelaire," *PMLA*, LX (1945), 852; Curtis Hidden Page, "Poe in France," *Nation*, LXXXVIII (January 14, 1909), 32–34.
73. Léon Lemonnier, *Edgar Poe et la critique française de 1845 à 1875* (Paris, 1928), 103, 133, 150, 199; John Matthew, "Poe's Indebtedness to French Literature," *French Review* (February, 1936), 217–23.

The numerous translations and discussions of Poe in France tacitly acknowledged the existence of an American writer in whose mysteries, fantasies, and poems Europeans could find as much stimulation and entertainment as in the books of their own poets. French opinion regarding him, however, was by no means unanimous. Some Frenchmen, including his two most prominent translators, Baudelaire and Stephane Mallarmé, saw in Poe a leading literary genius of the nineteenth century. Others evaluated him in a severely critical fashion. D'Aurevilly, for instance, deplored that Poe applied his descriptive gifts to rather superficial fads of the moment and that he wrote fiction that practically ignored the heart and the soul. Louis Etienne, writing in 1857 in the *Revue contemporaine,* did not like Poe's frequent exploitation of the horrible, evil, and perverse. He took particular exception to Poe's theory of evil, according to which "it comes not from man's weakness, but from a primordial element of perversity in his nature." The noted writer Arthur Arnould and Madame Charles Vincens discovered neither creative imagination nor an impressive conception of life in Poe's stories. And Emile Lauvrière, in his study of Poe, mercilessly argued: "Everywhere in this monstrous temple of madness we witness, enthralled by the irresistible charm of a dangerous art, the fascinating but exhausting spectacle of the human faculties, sensibility, energy, intelligence, imagination, reason and taste outrageously overtaxed in paroxysms of pain. If the frightful superiority of this extraordinary being comes from genius, then genius is nothing but frenzied excess."[74] Twentieth-century critics in England and America have found it somewhat mysterious that this "mediocre and vulgar talent" could have been hailed in France as a literary genius. T. S. Eliot's intelligent suggestion that the French saw in Poe something that English-speaking readers missed undoubtedly played a part in this mystery. Jules Verne has offered a more specific explanation. As a Frenchman, he liked the positive

74. George D. Morris, "French Criticism of Poe," *South Atlantic Quarterly* (October, 1915), 324–29; Emile Lauvrière, *Le Génie morbide d'Edgar Poe* (Paris, 1935), 319–20; Cambiaire, *Influence of Poe in France,* 45–46.

approach of Poe, an American writer who succeeded, for him, in convincing his readers of the credibility of impossible situations. He admired, moreover, Poe's "discussion of little known facts . . . the always strange personality of his heroes, their abnormal and nervous temperament, and the bizarre manner in which they expressed themselves."[75]

The split of opinion with respect to Poe's merit and influence has not been eliminated in modern times. As we have seen, his most extreme critics discovered little in his work that seemed worth emulating. Twentieth-century students of Poe's work have concluded that his own countrymen misunderstood him because his theory of aesthetic and moral values was far ahead of his time. Baudelaire and Verlaine specifically acknowledged their indebtedness to Poe. Baudelaire and Poe shared the view that the main principle of poetry involves "the rhythmical creation of beauty." But despite the fact that some of Baudelaire's writings clearly evidence Poe's inspiration, the extent of his influence on Baudelaire's poetry and prose is likely to remain an open question. The contention of Poe's influence on the symbolist poets of France —Mallarmé, Rimbaud, Verlaine, and others—is usually based on the observation that they, like Poe, emphasized the importance of melodic music and suggestive allusions to some "superior reality" in poetry.[76]

According to Célestin Pierre Cambiaire, who has written a book about Poe's influence, "Poe is one of the greatest leaders in the moulding of French literature."[77] Charles Morice, one

75. See T. S. Eliot, "From Poe to Valéry," *Hudson Review*, II (1949), 327–42; Patrick F. Quinn, *The French Face of Edgar Poe* (Carbondale, Ill., 1957), 4–8; Yvor Winters, "Edgar Allan Poe: A Crisis in the History of American Obscurantism," *American Literature*, VIII (1937), 379–401; and Laura Riding, *Contemporaries and Snobs* (New York, 1928), 222, 253. See also Jules Verne, "Edgar Poe et ses oeuvres," *Musée des familles*, XXXI (1864), 193–208. A comparison of Jules Verne's *Around the World in Eighty Days* with Poe's *Three Sundays in a Week* shows striking similarities.

76. Charles Cestre, "Poe et Baudelaire," *Revue anglo-américaine*, XI (1934), 322–29; Charles Navarre, *Les Grands ecrivains étrangers et leur influence sur la littérature française* (Paris, 1930), 701.

77. Célestin Pierre Cambiaire to George E. Woodberry, March 29, 1925, MS Am 790.5, HCL.

of the leading symbolist critics, included Poe in his *Littérature de tout à l'heure* as one among many outstanding creative minds who directly or indirectly contributed to the evolution of modern French literature. He admired Poe as "the poet of Love in Fear, of Love in Madness, of Love in Death . . . the poet who in his divine works first inaugurates the poetic conscience . . . who painted the grotesque not like Victor Hugo, to our eyes, but to our souls." In the same vein, the brothers Edmond Louis Antoine and Jules Alfred de Goncourt predicted that in the future, thanks to Poe, French writers "will have to deal more with the mind than with the heart of humanity."[78] Captivated by Poe's works, Marcel Schwob copied some of his techniques. And Villiers de l'Isle-Adam, who could recite by heart entire pages of Poe, came as close to "dignifying the horrible" as Poe, whose methods and themes were very evident in his own tales.[79] Whether Poe was "perhaps the intellectual god of this century," as the symbolist Stephane Mallarmé suggested, or enthusiasm for Poe was "the mark of a decidedly primitive stage of reflection," as the realistic novelist Henry James suggested,[80] no other nineteenth-century American poet matched his accomplishments in France.

Unlike Poe in France, Baudelaire remained a relatively obscure figure in the contemporary United States. Also, unlike Poe, the poet of *Les Fleurs du mal* possessed a genius for the delicate treatment of sensuous matter. Despite his lasting contributions to the evolution of modern poetry, his inclination "to seek beauty in evil" made him a controversial writer on both sides of the Atlantic. In an article Eugene Benson published in the February, 1869, issue of the *Atlantic Monthly*, entitled "Charles Baudelaire, Poet of the Malign," he condemned French society more than Baudelaire's poetry: *"Les Fleurs du mal,"* he suggested, "grew not out of the poet's mind alone. They were fed and nourished

78. C. H. Page, "Poe in France," 32–39.
79. Louis Seylaz, *Edgar Poe et les premiers symbolistes français* (Lausanne, 1923), 175–76; Camille Faust, *Le Génie d'Edgar Poe* (Paris, 1925), 285–86; and Robert du Pontavice de Heussy, *Villiers de l'Isle-Adam* (New York, 1894).
80. James, *French Poets and Novelists*, 76.

by the moral soil of French life. . . . You dare not reproach the poet for it, but the civilization which made his experience and emotions possible." As irony would have it, William James, who liked *The Flowers of Evil*, recommended it in 1876 to his brother Henry. He lauded its originality and, yes, its spirituality, and he was amused that this volume was originally considered scandalous. How attitudes had changed within one generation! In his review in the *Nation*, Henry James first acknowledged Baudelaire's "extraordinary verbal instinct" and "exquisite felicity of epithet," but then he dismissed him as a serious poet because he had really nothing to say. In probably his most devastating review, he landed Baudelaire on the literary dung heap: "Scattered flowers," he snarled, "incontestably do bloom in the quaking swamps of evil. . . . But Baudelaire has not plucked flowers—he has plucked weeds."[81] This unduly severe judgment seemed to have been directed at the concept of "art for art's sake," as well as at Baudelaire. It evidently annoyed Henry James that *Les Fleurs du mal* did not contain a substantial discussion of social, political, or philosophical questions and, instead, was all "charm, music, powerful, abstract sensuality," as a recent analyst aptly put it.[82] It is noteworthy that in this instance history has by and large sustained the judgment of the philosopher-psychologist of the two James brothers. The reaction of the literary critic and novelist has gone down as a classic example of intemperate misjudgment. The rhythm and sound of Baudelaire's lines unmistakably distinguished his work as pure poetry, a poetry that continued to make waves long into the future.

With Walt Whitman (1819–1892), Frenchmen finally came face to face with the poet of American democracy. Whitman loved America; and of all foreign nations, France was closest to him.

81. George Markow, "Henry James et la France, 1843–1876" (Ph.D. dissertation, Université de Paris, 1952), 91–92; Eliot G. Fay, "Henry James as a Critic of French Literature," *French American Review*, II (1949), 190.
82. Henri Peyre (ed.), *Baudelaire: A Collection of Essays* (Englewood Cliffs, N. J., 1962), 16–17.

Typically, he did not hesitate to proclaim his feelings publicly by dedicating a hymn to France at the end of the disastrous Franco-Prussian War:

O STAR OF FRANCE

The brightness of thy hope and strength and fame,
Like some proud ship that led the fleet so long,
Beseems to-day a wreck driven by the gale, a mastless hulk,
And 'mid its teeming madden'd half-drowned crowds,
Nor helm nor helmsman.

Star crucified. O Star! O ship of France!
O mitten orb! O ship continue on!
When lo! reborn, high o'er the European world,
Again thy star, O France, fair lustrous star,
In heavenly peace, clear, more bright than ever,
Shall beam immortal.

These innermost sentiments completely disregarded the previously uncomplimentary reception of Whitman's poetry in France. Perhaps misunderstanding or not at all understanding its unorthodox form and philosophy, French literary circles had called him a wild and vulgar vagabond, an egalitarian madman, pantheist, mystic, a dangerous democrat. Before he died, Whitman had the inner satisfaction of knowing that in France, as elsewhere, the pendulum of judgment had already begun to swing in the other direction, proclaiming him to be a Brahman, a genius, the poet of the future.[83]

If the author of *Leaves of Grass* (1855) puzzled democratic America, how much more difficult must it have been for foreigners to grasp the meaning of his strange and provocative poetry. Apparently incredibly egotistical and all encompassing, Walt Whitman proclaimed: "I am the poet of the body . . . and of the soul.

---

83. Martin Kanes, "La Fortune de Walt Whitman" (Ph.D. dissertation, Université de Paris, 1953), 54, 519. Whatever the merit of the thesis that William Cullen Bryant "was far more than Whitman the poet of the people," the originality of Whitman's poetry as an art form expressing the ideals of democracy made him stand out in French literary circles. Charles I. Glicksberg, "William Cullen Bryant: A Reinterpretation," *Revue anglo-américaine*, XI (1934), 496.

I am the poet of the woman the same as the man." These lines from his *Song of Myself* could easily be misinterpreted unless studied in the context of his revealing religious declaration: "I see something of God each hour of the twenty-four. . . . In the faces of men and women I see God."[84] Whitman's extreme realism and lack of restraint as found in such thoughts as, "I love everything and I condemn nothing. The good and the evil *exist*," disturbed Thérèse Bentzon sufficiently to warn the readers of the *Revue des deux mondes* (1872) against such "bizarre" philosophy and religion. She accused Whitman's realism of "confounding muscles with genius" and of "pushing the naturalism in his poetry up to pantheism."[85]

Other early French critics might in retrospect feel embarrassed that they had described *Leaves of Grass* as a work written in "an often incomprehensible barbaric jargon." Henri Cochin described it in 1877: "Democracy run wild, a form of insanity and megalomania." If Whitman's so-called "theories" seemed to Cochin to be hidden in a chaotic stream of incoherent words, Whitman's belief that the happiness of the individual superseded the importance of the nation and the family shocked the critic so profoundly that he felt impelled to warn: "Woe unto those who refuse to acknowledge the continuity of social existence!"[86] Even more recently, in 1930, Professor Charles Cestre criticized Whitman's lack of balance and taste and the tendency of this prophetic poet of the masses to glorify the display of energy for its own sake.

The reappraisal of Whitman in France extended well into the twentieth century. The Parnassian poet Emile Blémont (1839–1927) belonged to the few who from the start understood Whitman's synthesis of body and soul, the "ensemble" of matter and

---

84. S. A. Rhodes, "The Influence of Walt Whitman on André Gide," *Romantic Review*, XXXI (1940), 161–62.

85. Thérèse Bentzon, "Un Poète américain: Walt Whitman," *RDDM*, XLII (1872), 565–82.

86. Kanes, "La Fortune de Walt Whitman," 21–29; Frances E. Oakes, "The Whitman Controversy in France" (Ph.D. dissertation, Florida State University, 1955), 17; Henri Cochin, "Un Poète américain: Walt Whitman," *Le Correspondant*, CIX (Nov., 1877), 634–60.

spirit. Instead of being afraid of the appearance of an authentic American poet, Blémont defended this eccentric and original champion of individualism and democracy. In several articles for *La Renaissance artistique et littéraire* (June–July, 1872) Blémont commented on "Poetry in England and the United States."[87] Despite Whitman's defects of style, he admired his power, breadth, and universality. He was perfectly willing to overlook Whitman's many faults, because in his judgment the American poet was a giant: "S'il n'est pas art, il est bien plus, il est la vie." To him, Whitman filled the place in literature that Richard Wagner occupied in music. Perhaps, like Wagner, there was something contrary to French genius in Whitman, since for many years he continued to be little known, much less accepted, in France. The ice was finally broken by a long essay Gabriel Sarrazin published in 1888 on "The Poetry of Walt Whitman," in which he evidently succeeded in explaining to Frenchmen the American poet's ingenious way of building a philosophical bridge between spirit and matter. As future developments demonstrated, this essay constituted a turning point to be superseded in significance only by Léon Bazalgette's enthusiastic biography of Whitman in 1908 and his complete translation of *Leaves of Grass* a year later.[88]

These publications clarified Whitman's philosophy and concept of poetry and finally made him intelligible to French readers. The age in which he lived witnessed a scientific revolution that so transformed social relationships as to require, in his judgment and in Emerson's, new philosophical solutions to man's quest for freedom. To Whitman, the old Christian theology had outlived its usefulness. The world needed specialists of the soul, poets

87. Kanes, "La Fortune de Walt Whitman," 30–34; Emile Blémont, "La Poésie en Angleterre et aux Etats-Unis: Walt Whitman," *La Renaissance littéraire et artistique* (June and July, 1872), 53–55, 86–87, 90-91; Léo Quesnel, "Poètes américains: Walt Whitman," *Revue politique et littéraire*, XXXIII (1884), 212–17; P. M. Jones, "Whitman in France," *Modern Language Review*, X (1915), 1–27.

88. Gabriel Sarrazin, "Poètes modernes de l'Amérique," *La Nouvelle revue*, LII (May 1, 1888), 164–84; Oakes, "The Whitman Controversy," 7–15; Oreste F. Pucciani, "The Literary Reputation of Walt Whitman in France" (Ph.D. dissertation, Harvard University, 1943). Although it was almost impossible to translate Whitman, Léon Bazalgette's version was the most accomplished.

rather than clergymen, people capable of satisfying the spiritual and worldly needs of man. Whitman saw the answer in his concept of the human divine, shifting the authority once vested in God to man himself, limited only by nature. He believed that the universe was "God visible" and that one's body was one's "visible soul." But the soul itself was the hidden inner reality of man, not subject to external recognition. Consequently, the message of his poetry centered around the notions of man's obedience to the laws of nature and his identification with the universe. He was convinced that within this framework the most effective way for a nation to become strong was for individuals to develop confidence in themselves and to permit the "God within themselves" to shape their destinies.[89]

Whitman's optimistic faith in the individual and the masses went much too far for French taste, and the lack of form in his poetry bewildered French readers. Many of them found his disregard for the conventional rules of versification upsetting until Sarrazin explained to them why they could not judge Whitman's form by traditional standards: "He creates a rhythm of his own, less rigid than verse, more broken than prose,—a rhythm adapted to the movement of his emotion, hastened as it hastens, precipitated, abated, and let down to repose."[90] As Whitman himself explained: "Poetic style, when address'd to the soul, is less definite form . . . and becomes vista, music, half-tints." He did not feel the need for style and rules; what mattered to him was what he had to say, not how he said it. Even in this respect he prophesied that the poetry of the future would "aim at the free expression of emotion . . . and [attempt] to arouse and initiate, more than to define and finish."[91] To him, "the greatest poet is he who suggests the most" and excites the reader "the most himself to poetize."

89. Pucciani, "The Literary Reputation of Walt Whitman in France," 5–10, 24, 49; Charles Cestre, "American Literature Through French Eyes," *Yale Review,* X (1920), 96–97.

90. Fernand Baldensperger, "Walt Whitman and France," *Columbia University Quarterly,* XXI (1919), 303.

91. Gay Wilson Allen (ed.), *Walt Whitman Abroad* (Syracuse, N.Y., 1955), 57.

For this reason the symbolists felt sufficiently attracted to Whitman to recognize a literary kinship with him. Their translations and sympathetic discussions of his poetry were instrumental in his growing popularity. Such noted literary figures as Jules Laforgue (1860–1887), Marcel Schwob (1867–1905), André Gide (1869–1951), and the American-born poets Francis Viélé-Griffin and Stuart Merrill contributed much to this developing trend. To some of them, especially Gide, Whitman's poetic message offered relief from those "pent-up aching rivers." Gide felt immensely close and indebted to Whitman for having helped him overcome his spiritual dilemmas and break down the bars that had imprisoned his mind. When he read *Calamus*, the group of poems in which Whitman celebrated "the manly love of comrades," Gide experienced a liberating sense of relief, convinced that, after all, "la perversion de [son] instinct était naturelle."[92] He also admired Whitman's lighthearted disregard of traditional conventions and restrictions, which, it seemed to him, set an example of individual freedom worthy of emulation. Others simply appreciated his lyricism, idealism, and mysticism and easily identified with his vast concept of life: "life immense in passion, pulse, and power,/cheerful, for freest action form'd under the laws divine."

Despite certain resemblances between his forms and ideas and those of the French symbolists, scholarly inquiries have rejected the suggestion that Whitman exercised a significant influence on the symbolists and the *vers libre*. At best, he supplied additional evidence to support the views of Rimbaud and Mallarmé.[93] Actually, contrary to the evolution of French symbolism, which moved in the direction of growing acceptance of realism, Whitman ended up in an ever more mystic vein. He had a general impact, however, on the mentality of the younger

92. Rhodes, "The Influence of Whitman on Gide," 156–71.
93. Théodor de Wyzewa, "Notes sur les littératures étrangères: Walt Whitman (1819–1892)," *Revue bleue*, XLIX (1892), 513–19; Kanes, "La Fortune de Walt Whitman," 178–81; Pierrre de Lanux, *Young France and New America* (New York, 1917), 116; see also P. M. Jones, "Influence of Walt Whitman on the Origin of the 'Vers Libre,'" *Modern Language Review*, XI (1916), 186–94.

generation of poets who entered the twentieth century with a
new awareness of the challenges of modern life. Probably read
by relatively few Frenchmen, Walt Whitman nevertheless
possessed the genial capacity of "speaking to the whole world."[94]

In a class all by himself, Mark Twain (1835–1910) insulted and
mystified Frenchmen more than any other American writer.
Having traveled extensively in Europe, the author of *The Inno-
cents Abroad* made no secret of his prejudices regarding France.
Only in his later years did he somewhat modify them. His notebooks of 1896 and 1897 contained such typical comments as: "The
Race consists of human beings and French. . . . There is a Moral
Sense and many nations have it. Also there is an Immoral Sense.
The French have it." Despite several visits to France, Mark Twain
really possessed few qualifications for judging the French or,
for that matter, for setting himself up as a critic of European
civilization, as he was fond of doing.[95] He evidently did not regard
his limited knowledge of the French language and his merely
superficial impressions of French life as serious critical drawbacks.
Neither did his anything but warm reception in France, both
as a visitor and as an author, oblige him to resist the natural
temptation of applying his American and Victorian attitudes to
French society. The Protestant Missourian, who loved the simple
life along the Mississippi and in the American West, detested
the "gigantic vanity," the "skin-deep politeness," and "rabbit-
docility" of the "partly-civilized" French people.[96] As one who
could neither forget nor forgive the "monumental" massacre
of St. Bartholomew, he attributed to the French people a special
capacity for "burning and slaughtering each other." At a time

94. Leon Bazalgette, *Walt Whitman: The Man and His Work* (Garden City,
N.Y., 1920), Preface. According to Henri Ghéon, "Les Poèmes," *Nouvelle revue
française* (June 1, 1912), 1053–71, "le whitmanisme" had more influence on
French poetry than has generally been assumed.
95. Arthur Lincoln Scott, "Mark Twain as a Critic of Europe" (Ph.D. dissertation, University of Michigan, 1947); Robert Gilkey, "Mark Twain: Voyageur et
son image de l'Europe" (Ph.D. dissertation, Université de Paris, 1951).
96. Consult Mark Twain Papers, University of California at Berkeley, DV
no. 67, MTP no. 97, pp. 35, 43, 50, 59–61.

when France thought of itself as the shining example of modern civilization, he suggested quite seriously that the only way France might be morally and intellectually elevated was through "the employment of a trained corps of lay American missionaries."

Taking issue with Paul Bourget's observation that Americans took "pell-mell all the best and the worst of our [French] civilization," Mark Twain disputed the implied claim that France possessed the most advanced civilization.[97] To him, what did modern civilization mean but certain "features which make man's life easier and freer and pleasanter than it was before and less mean and bitter and hampered?" Did not the honor of advancing these features historically belong to the United States? Who, he asked, led the way toward more humane principles of law and equality before the law, toward women's rights, and in technological advancements freeing man from the drudgery of labor? Did not these pioneering trends benefit European civilization, admittedly, through the help of "our pupil, the French Revolution?" In other words, he wanted to leave no doubt that Americans had reason to be proud of their enlightened progress and to be resentful of the condescending arrogance with which in many respects backward and pretentious Frenchmen treated the United States. He would not deny that by the end of the nineteenth century American civilization showed signs of the French malaise, but that was another sad story.

Mark Twain's sense of justice for the unfairly treated members of society also emerged from his commentaries on domestic situations. Unless one understood that he put little stock in the fundamental goodness of the human race and the purposefulness of life one would be even more hard put to appreciate his strange mixture of seriousness and humor. His extravagant, provocative, and uniquely folksy way of writing required not only a mastery of the American language and its regional nuances, but also of American humor, something very few, if any, Frenchmen could claim. No wonder, then, that for a long time the author of such

97. *Ibid*, DV no. 317, MTP, 1894.

classics as *Tom Sawyer, Huckleberry Finn,* and *A Connecticut Yankee in King Arthur's Court* was little read, translated, or valued in France. Initially, the professional French critics were not prepared to dignify Mark Twain's frivolous commentaries, grotesque situations, and often coarse humor as legitimate literature. He appeared to be an uncouth western American, without a sense of tradition and so overwhelmed by the *Weltschmerz* that he wanted "to make others laugh in order to laugh himself."[98] In the process, he hoped to make people more socially conscious and responsible than they had been.

As Mark Twain became famous and was probably overrated in his own country, he saw his fortunes in France improve as well. By the turn of the century, his tales had been readably translated by François de Gail and Michel Epuy and were more available, particularly to French youngsters who liked *Tom Sawyer* and *Huckleberry Finn,* than were the intellectually more challenging works of Walt Whitman. In view of the icy reception Mark Twain had originally received in France, Gabriel Syveton's article in the *Revue bleue* (February 13, 1897) amounted to a complete reversal of attitude. Syveton protested that it did not do to read merely excerpts from Mark Twain's stories. To enjoy the incomparable mastery of this social critic, he insisted, one had to read the full text. Only then could one understand that Mark Twain was a humorist who epitomized humor. There was nothing studied in his spontaneous humor. Admitting that, ordinarily, savage Anglo-Saxon humor did not appeal to Latin taste, Michel Epuy pleaded that in the cases of such exceptional and rare masters of burlesque literature as Jonathan Swift and Mark Twain, Latins would do well to show them special consideration.[99] As time passed and translations improved, Mark Twain's deadly

98. Roger Assellineau, *The Literary Reputation of Mark Twain: From* 1910 *to* 1950 (Paris, 1954), 16; Simon Hornstein, *Mark Twain: La Faillite d'un idéal* (Paris, 1950), 150–77; Léon Lemonnier, *Mark Twain* (Paris, 1946), 155–59, 255-59; and Maurice LeBreton, "Un Centenaire: Mark Twain," *Revue anglo-américaine,* XII (1935), 401.

99. Michel Epuy, *Anthologie des humoristes anglais et américains, du* 17e *siècle à nos jours* (Paris, 1910), Preface.

earnest humor, though often offending the vanity of Europeans, delighted even a growing number of French readers. In fact, such prominent late nineteenth-century French humorists as Pierre Veber, Alphonse Allais, Alfred Capus, and Tristan Bernard incorporated traces of Mark Twain's art in their "new humor."[100] More recently, Simon Hornstein's analysis placed the self-educated midwestern humorist among the great writers of world literature. This distinction, Hornstein reasoned, must be accorded to Mark Twain because "he liberated his country from England's intellectual guardianship. His purely indigenous prose had absolutely nothing more in common with that of London, even as far as the language itself was concerned." Significantly, Hornstein added, "this revolution in prose is in every respect comparable with that of Walt Whitman in poetry."[101]

Following an entirely different literary road, William Dean Howells (1837–1920) and his friend Henry James (1843–1916) ranked among the most prolific and influential American writers in the second half of the nineteenth-century. They shared certain significant characteristics. For one thing, they looked upon writing as an art requiring constant attention to polish, in form and content. What distinguished them from continental writers was their version of realism, which Howells defined as "fidelity to experience," but the ordinary experience, not the exceptional; focus on the typical, not the unusual. Howells saw enough beauty and grandeur in this world for artists to paint and write about so as to elevate humanity, not to depress it. This philosophical outlook on life, rather than puritanism and prudishness, guided him

100. See Régis Michaud, *Mystiques et réalistes anglo-saxons* (Paris, 1918), 136–37; René Doumic, "Nos Humoristes," *RDDM* (October 15, 1899), 932; and R. Bosc, "Mark Twain et l'humeur américain," in *Publications de la Revue de Synthèse Historique: Psychologie des Etats-Unis* (Paris, 1920), 149–55. In the late nineteenth century, French translations of Mark Twain's works included: *Tom Sawyer* (1884), *Huckleberry Finn* (1886), *The Prince and the Pauper* (1883–94, eight editions). In the twentieth century, French publishers offered translated versions of: *Tom Sawyer*, up to 1958, eight editions; *Huckleberry Finn*, up to 1951, five editions; *The American Claimant* (1906), three editions; *The Prince and the Pauper* (1909–59), twelve editions; *A Connecticut Yankee in King Arthur's Court* (1950–59), two editions.
101. Hornstein, *Mark Twain*, 9.

in his determination not to copy the French version of realism which exploited sex, perversity, and ugliness in society. To qualify this observation, one must hasten to add that he regarded Zola so highly that he was willing to expose himself to vitriolic attacks from outraged American critics of Zola. All charges to the contrary notwithstanding, Zola was a writer whom Howells found "always most terribly and most pitilessly moral." In defense of this view, he went straight to the heart of his justification, arguing that "not Tolstoy, not Ibsen himself, has more profoundly and indignantly felt the injustice of civilization, or more insistently shown the fatality of its fundamental pretensions."[102] Although Henry James and others eloquently supported Howells' battle for literary realism, James actually took a more balanced position by justifying the coexistence of literary realism and romance, or any other mode of writing.

Henry James's intimate familiarity with life in England, France, and the United States and his acquaintance with other European societies and their literatures placed him in a unique position. Essentially, an expatriate writer, the accomplished artist of the international novel always remained very conscious of his American roots. He addressed himself to the important question of morality and discussed in his voluminous novels and tales sociological contrasts between America and Europe. His analyses of the different concepts of morality in France and the United States developed the paradoxical complexities of different national standards of morality. French authors, for instance, titillated their readers unhesitatingly with detailed descriptions of "rash infatuations," which American authors and readers considered improper and at times degenerate. Certainly, as a realist Henry James did not wish to shy away from any aspect of life; but in his own stories he preferred to treat "delicate" situations in a delicate manner.[103]

102. Van Wyck Brooks, *Howells: His Life and World* (New York, 1939), 178; Edwin H. Cady, *The Realist at War: The Mature Years, 1885–1920, of William Dean Howells* (Syracuse, N.Y., 1958), 39–43.

103. Christof Wegelin, *The Image of Europe in Henry James* (Dallas, 1958), 11, 38–43.

In the context of Franco-American cultural relations in the nineteenth century, Henry James rendered an unmatched service as a superbly qualified American critic of contemporary French literature.[104] His mastery of literature and languages, as well as his analytical insights and elegance of style distinguished his critical reviews in such magazines as the *Nation*, the *North American Review*, *Atlantic Monthly*, and *Galaxy*. His personal acquaintance with many French authors lent additional weight to his comments. The picture of this Yankee intellectual being a member of the famous Flaubert circle was alone fascinating to behold. By chance, Ivan Turgenev, the Russian expatriate with whom James developed a very friendly relationship, introduced him late in 1875 to Gustave Flaubert. In a letter to his parents James observed that he "took a mighty fancy to Flaubert." The following year he wrote to Howells that this simple, kindly, elderly man was "the most interesting and influential artist of his circle." Anxious to be accepted by Flaubert, James cherished "the whole hour" Flaubert spent with him alone when on one occasion he paid him a courtesy visit. The exchange of ideas with the members of the Flaubert circle naturally deepened James's understanding of French writers as only personal contacts could have done. Although he was at times saddened by the awareness that he was looked upon as an outsider in this circle, he felt, particularly in retrospect, that he had gained much from this association. His own novels resembled those of French realists in two significant respects: the playing down of elaborate plots and the attempt to hold the author's personal opinions to a minimum.[105]

James was of course fully aware of the enormous influence Balzac continued to exercise on French literature. In one brief

104. Altogether, Henry James published more than ninety essays on French literature.

105. See Henry James to his parents, December 20, 1875, MS Am 1094 (1831), Henry James to William James, February 8, 1876, MS Am 1094 (1963), both in HCL; Marie Reine Garnier, *Henry James et la France* (Paris, 1927), 8–9; and Lyall H. Powers, "Henry James and French Naturalism" (Ph.D. dissertation, Indiana University, 1955), 300–305.

sentence he pertinently described the chain of literary inter-relationships: "Gustave Flaubert is of the school of Balzac; the brothers de Goncourt and Emile Zola are of the school of Flaubert."[106] As much as James felt indebted to Balzac for having taught him "more of the lessons of the engaging mastery of fiction than anyone else," he could not help faulting Balzac, Flaubert, and indeed most of the popular nineteenth-century French poets and novelists for being "morally and intellectually so superficial" that they practically ignored the soul of man. It disturbed him that French writers evidently did not know how to penetrate the depth of man's conscience in the manner of George Eliot and Ivan Turgenev. He did not object to the tendency of the naturalistic French writers to stress hereditary and environmental factors and to treat natural phenomena in an objective, amoral way. But he did deplore the one-sided emphasis on the vulgarities and frustrations of life without so much as a suggestion of a more hopeful existence.[107] In a severely critical review of Flaubert's *Temptation of St. Anthony*, Henry James regretfully noted that the author's own deficiencies really mirrored the dilemma of contemporary French literature. "M. Flaubert and his contemporaries," he charged, "have pushed so far the education of the senses and the cultivation of the grotesque in literature and the arts that it has left them morally stranded and helpless." Courageously asserting the integrity of his own views, he further elaborated: "In the perception of the materially curious, in fantastic refinement of taste and marked ingenuity of expression, they seem to us now to have reached the limits of the possible. Behind M. Flaubert stands a whole society of aesthetic *raffinés*, demanding stronger and stronger spices in its intellectual diet."[108]

106. Henry James, "The Minor French Novelists," *Galaxy*, XXI (1876), 224.

107. Markow, "Henry James et la France," 247; Powers, "Henry James and French Naturalism," 24–28; and W. C. D. Pacey, "Henry James and His Contemporaries," *American Literature*, XIII (1941), 240–44.

108. Weinberg, *French Realism*, 173; Albert Mordell (ed.), *Literary Reviews and Essays by Henry James on American, English, and French Literature* (New York, 1957), 150; and Leon Edel, *Henry James* (5 vols.; Philadelphia, 1962–1972), III, 100–102.

Who but a disappointed admirer of French literature could have made such a perceptive observation?

The longer Henry James stayed in France, the more disenchanted he became with it and its literature. French writers were so tortured by the "torments of style," to borrow the phrase of his good friend Alphonse Daudet, that their preoccupation with style exhausted them intellectually. James realized quickly that French writers had much to offer to him in regard to style and that such French critics as E. Schérer and Sainte-Beuve were worth studying for their analytical and technical qualities. But somehow he merely absorbed their techniques without copying any particular one. The same applied of course to the influence of English writers on him. Determined to establish his own identity as a novelist, James invested literary realism with greater depth than was customary in France by going more deeply into psychological analyses of his characters.[109] Considering his brilliant imagination and literary gifts, Henry James's probing into conscience and motives and the restraining effects of his puritan instincts in the treatment of passions probably accounted for the fact that basically he remained a stranger to the French reading public. As fate would have it, this American expatriate conveyed too much the impression of a European aristocrat and intellectual elitist to be popular at home.[110]

One interesting sidelight ought to be brought out. In both countries the public by and large ignored the views of its professional literary critics. Condemnations of socially undesirable French books did not keep large numbers of Americans from reading

109. Markow, "Henry James et la France," 245–50. Henry James also noted that French writers, while trying to be simple, were "all tormented and all self-conscious." Richard L. Shoemaker, "The France of Henry James," *French Review,* XXI (1948), 294.

110. Marie-Anne de Bovet, "Un Ecrivain cosmopolite: Henry James," *La Nouvelle revue* (February, 1891), 532–56. Edith Wharton, Frank Norris, and Theodore Dreiser, who preferred the trend of literary realism in the fashion of the twentieth century, continued to look abroad for inspiration. See Francis O. Matthiessen, *Theodore Dreiser* (New York, 1951), 67–73; and Marius Biencourt, *Une Influence du naturalisme français en Amérique: Frank Norris* (Paris, 1933).

them. Similarly, even favorable reviews of the works of the most outstanding American poets did not induce large numbers of Frenchmen to acquaint themselves with nineteenth-century American authors. The late nineteenth-century requirement in French universities to be prepared for examination questions on American literature failed to promote widespread interest in a foreign literature that apparently appealed neither to the taste nor to the temperament of French readers. Inasmuch as the currents of nineteenth-century American fiction had been influenced by trends in French literature, French readers obviously preferred their own to American imitations of it. "Fearful of international criticism," American authors showed less independence and more modesty than was characteristic of their countrymen in other respects.[111]

Whatever the extent of French ignorance and indifference about American literature prior to World War I, the fact that of all nineteenth-century American writers James Fenimore Cooper, Walt Whitman, and Mark Twain stood the test of time in twentieth-century France makes more sense to Americans than does the strange adoration and emulation of Edgar Allan Poe. Aside from the fact that the growing material prosperity of France weakened the traditional argument against American materialism, it is noteworthy that the enduring popularity of these three pronounced "American" authors coincided with the expanding acceptance of the democratic ideal in France.

If the writing and reading of literature reflects prevailing social conditions and reactions to them, the history of nineteenth-century literature relating to France and the United States presents us with many unreal realities. The rebellion against the artificial and rationalistic tendencies of classicism resulted in the superficial humanity and artificial features of the romantic period, only to be overtaken by naturalistic and realistic writers who exaggerated their concern with the signs of degeneracy in their surroundings.

111. Maurice Thompson, "Foreign Influence on American Fiction," *NAR*, CXLIX (July, 1889), 118–20.

Though appealing to a much more limited audience at the end
of the century, the symbolist poets did not concern themselves
with the realistic aspects of life; recording subtle moods in
pleasing cadences, they preferred to *suggest* its infinite beauty.[112]
As this search for novel literary ways of dealing with contemporary observations of society paralleled the social and
political changes observable in society, their dividing lines were
apt to overlap. Flaubert, for instance, was both a realist and
a symbolist, just as Zola was both a realist and a romantic.

Next to English, French literature enjoyed the widest circulation in the United States. In the final decades of the nineteenth century alone, American publishers brought out English
translations of the works of some 260 different French authors.[113]
Balzac, Zola, and Daudet headed the list of best sellers in the
United States. Americans secretly devoured French novels they
publicly censured for their immorality. And finally, to add another
touch of puzzling unreality, Americans, who usually were inclined
to think of life in ideal and optimistic terms, enjoyed reading
French authors who excelled in describing life's ugliest realities.

112. A. E. Carter, *The Idea of Decadence in French Literature,* 1830–1900
(Toronto, 1958), vii–viii; T. S. Perry, "The Latest Literary Fashion in France,"
Cosmopolitan, XIII (1892), 359–65.
113. Malcolm B. Jones, "French Literature and American Criticism," 1–3, 55.

CHAPTER VII

Theater

The eminence of the French theater prior to the Great Revolution has been traced as much to the genius and wit of accomplished poets as to the taste of the sophisticated aristocratic audiences who appreciated entertaining performances.[1] If the popular theater that developed in the aftermath of the Revolution seemed, by comparison, vulgar and inferior, it reflected not only the political trends of the time, but also the changing tastes of the emancipated masses. Conscious of the satisfaction people derived from shows, monarchical and republican governments alike deemed it worthwhile to extend their financial support to the theaters and other forms of entertainment in France.[2]

Even the most serious Frenchmen considered the theater one of the necessities of life, one that enabled them to recognize themselves more vividly than they did in any other setting. The government-subsidized Théâtre français, one of the "institutions of France," occupied the central place among the theaters of

1. Echeverria, "Antoine Jay and the United States," 242.
2. Theodore Parker acknowledged the wisdom of such subsidies, "for if the 'surplus revenue' of spirit in the effervescent population of France is not expended in frolic," he wrote in 1843, "there will be revolutions and mobs and all sorts of trouble, so the Government finds it more politic to pay dancers and musicians . . . who make people laugh for their fun . . . than to pay soldiers who make them sour with powder and cannon shot." John Weiss, *Life and Correspondence of Theodore Parker* (2 vols.; New York, 1864), I, 323–25.

different variety and merit. There, works of Jean Baptiste Molière and other old and new classics entertained the people in the purest French and with breathtaking stage settings and gorgeous contemporary costumes. On the left side of the Seine and in a less fashionable environment, the Odéon theater performed largely for student audiences whose enthusiasm could at times be as lively as their noisy disapproval of plays offensive to them. Occasionally, they would simply hiss a play off the stage. The Palais Royal was known for its sparkling wit, amusing slang, and a good deal of vulgarity. The Théâtre italien prided itself on engaging the finest artists of the world; and other theaters were primarily devoted to spectacular pieces and vaudeville shows. Paris naturally led in the entertainment world; but the larger provincial towns in France took great pride in their own theaters, even though they were unable to compete with Paris.[3]

An American physician, who in the mid-century attended a theater performance in Strasbourg, described certain technical aspects and the conduct of the audience at this presentation quite minutely:

The theatre is large and dark. . . . The stage was perfectly well lighted. There was no orchestra. Scenes were changed and curtain raised, by strokes of a hammer on the floor of the stage. The manner of the audience attracted my attention at once. From the beginning to the end, there was perfect and entire silence, and fixed attention. There was no music, still the intervals between the acts were not disturbed by impatience or noisy demands of any kind. . . . Even applause was subdued to the occasion, and had its depth in its delicacy. . . . In regard to the prevailing character of the audience towards the actors, a like respectful attention was paid to all.[4]

Quite a few Americans who visited Paris in the nineteenth century took a keen interest in the French theater. During the

3. "Journal of a Trip to England and France, 1864–65" (MS in William H. Brawley Papers, UV), 80–84. See also, "The Parisian Stage," Nation, XVI (January 9, 1873), 23–24; and J. Brander Matthews, The Theatres of Paris (London, 1880), 156.
4. Walter Channing, A Physician's Vacation: Or, A Summer in Europe (Boston, 1856), 427.

Restoration they raved about some of the most outstanding performers of that period, "the courtly graceful Fleury and his exquisite style," Talma's "language of the soul, with a voice that weakens all the sympathies of the heart," and Mlle. Duchesnois, "magnificent beyond description." Young George Bancroft who saw Duchesnois in the Théâtre français in Racine's *Phèdre* lauded her and "the great power of the poet." One of the greatest French actresses of all time, Mlle. Mars, excited Americans no less than Frenchmen. Bancroft admired her graceful and natural moves "without the perpetual gestures other actresses use." Edwin Forrest, the great American tragedian, also found that "her quiet, yet effective style of acting is the most enchanting and delicate triumph of the mimic art." Her bewitching smile and sparkling dark eyes blended beautifully with her perfectly clear and pure voice. When Bancroft saw her in Alexandre Duval's *Fille d'honneur* he was so deeply moved by her expression of innocence and purity that he, who thought he could not be touched by acting, "was ready to weep with delight."[5] A decade later, Mlle. Mars, then fifty-eight years old, was still the model of classic French and deportment on the stage. In 1833, Oliver Wendell Holmes went to see her twice in Molière's *Tartuffe,* so much was he impressed by her dignity and perfection.[6]

George Ticknor, another American intellectual, cared little for French tragedy which, he felt, lacked force and passion, even though it had "all the beauties of inimitable diction." He delighted, instead, in French comedies and comedians. "Their light and flexible and equivocal language," he commented, "lends itself superbly to express comical shades and inflexions."[7] On another visit to Paris twenty years later, in 1838, Ticknor noted that the

5. George Bancroft Diary, May 11, and June 29, 1821, MHS; New York *Post,* February 23, 1835.

6. John T. Morse, Jr., *Life and Letters of Oliver Wendell Holmes* (2 vols.; Boston, 1896), I, 117–20. The theater experience Kenyon Cox related to his mother on March 30, 1878, was unusual: "I never saw worse strutting, bellowing, howling and generally tasteless acting in my life than in the Théâtre Français, the other night." (MS in Kenyon Cox Correspondence, Columbia University).

7. George S. Hillard (ed.), *Life, Letters, and Journals of George Ticknor* (2 vols.; Boston, 1876), I, 149–50.

tone of the French theater had changed decidedly. Although the old French drama, especially the comedy, often contained indelicate phrases and allusions, it nevertheless maintained a respectable tone. Ticknor deplored the recent theater and popular literature of Dumas *père*, Victor Hugo, Honoré de Balzac, George Sand, Paul de Kock, and others, which he thought adopted a shockingly immoral tone.[8] In this respect, civilization seemed to regress and become more vulgar with the passage of time.

The invasion of the French romantic drama indeed prompted a great deal of literary criticism in America, precisely because it leveled "the distinction between vice and virtue." In the *American Quarterly Review* of 1836, Elizabeth Fries Ellet deplored the "corruption in the public taste of France" that permitted such writers as Hugo and Dumas to give full sway to their licentious characters. Leading American literary journals repeatedly alerted their readers to the disgraceful moral recklessness of the French romantic theater. The success the French romantics continued to enjoy on the American stage despite such critical comments, in St. Louis as well as in New York and Philadelphia, obviously pleased theater managers economically. But more important were the historical and professional factors that explained this great success in France and the United States.[9]

The time had evidently come to make a sharp break with the conventional and no longer vital elements of the neoclassic theater so long dominant in France.[10] When in 1827 young Victor Hugo proclaimed the complete freedom of the theater, in substance and in form, he signaled the end of the strict rules that for ages had barred adventurous experimentation on the stage. The "theatrical revolution," significantly, preceded the July Revolution by at least several months. Dressed in a crimson waistcoat,

8. *Ibid.*, II, 140–41.
9. C. M. Lombard, "French Romanticism on the American Stage," *RDLC*, XLIII (1969), 161–72.
10. Carl Mantzius, *A History of Theatrical Art in Ancient and Modern Times* (6 vols.; New York, 1937), VI, 210–11.

Théophile Gautier, a gifted young poet, headed the colorfully dressed, long haired, and bearded young admirers of Victor Hugo who, on the evening of February 25, 1830, stood their ground against the neoclassics' noisy attempts to remove *Hernani* from the program of the Théâtre français. Henceforth, the realities of contemporary life, including its growing tendencies toward emotionalism, escapism, and restlessness, found ever more unrestrained expression on the stage. Somehow the notion prevailed that the theater's function was to entertain rather than to educate, to portray the beauty and ugliness of life rather than to teach lessons in morality. But while the deceptive "realism" of such entertaining playwrights as Eugene Scribe and Victorien Sardou perfected the "well-made play," the French drama degenerated into cleverly conceived plots and attractively executed journalistic productions. Gradually, Frenchmen became tired of this superficiality, and Americans became increasingly disgusted with the themes.[11] It seemed that new ideas were scarce and that many new plays simply rearranged old situations with desperate ingenuity. Many Americans found it most annoying that novels and dramas betrayed "an incredibly superficial perception of the moral side of life. It is not only that adultery is their only theme, but that the treatment of it is so monstrously vicious and avid." In the Victorian age Americans were not yet prepared to accept without blushing the morality depicted in modern French literature. In the spring of 1874 editorials in the New York *Times* singled out Sardou and Octave Feuillet as writers who misdirected their talents by inclining too much toward plots that fearlessly violated the Seventh Commandment. Some French journals and the recently formed Association for the Improvement of the French Stage in Paris echoed the same criticism. In an exchange of views between the New York-based *Courrier* des *Etats-Unis* and the New York *Times,* the *Courrier* defended these

11. Sheldon Cheney, *The Theatre: Three Thousand Years of Drama, Acting and Stagecraft* (New York, 1963), 430–54; John Gassner, *Directions in Modern Theatre and Drama* (New York, 1966), 7–9; Paul H. Lang, *Music in Western Civilization* (New York, 1941), 924–25.

French authors on the ground that they portrayed "life as it exists in contemporary society" and that they and the stage should be at liberty to deal with the realities of society. In its rebuttal, the *Times*[12] insisted that because French plays exercised a great influence on English and American audiences, they had an obligation to respect the moral concepts of American society. It questioned, furthermore, whether the immoral works of French dramatists could be satisfactorily translated and asserted that they may be more meaningful to Parisian than to American society. The Philadelphia *Evening Bulletin* condemned in even stronger language the foulness that saturated French literature of the lighter class. "A nation," it commented, "which upon its stage in its fiction expresses itself in the exaltation of unhallowed passion and manifests an insatiable appetite for gross impurity, must have some rottenness at its core."[13] By contemptuously casting aside all respect for purity and decency, the *Bulletin* concluded, such a nation was destroying the Christian roots of Western civilization.

The "realistic" reaction to "Scribisme" in the final decades of the century, though nourished by such "realists" as Balzac, Flaubert, the Goncourts, and Zola, owed much to the originality and resourcefulness of André Antoine (1857–1943), the founder of the Théâtre-libre. To challenge the disgustingly commercialized and sterile bourgeois theaters of France, Antoine started in 1887 his experimental theater in Paris. He possessed more courage, energy, and ideas than capital when he launched his avant-garde theatrical enterprise to liberate the theater from the stifling reign of certain authors, critics, and managers. In a manifesto he published in May, 1890, Antoine deplored the unsafe and uncomfortable theater facilities in Paris, opposed the "star" system, which in his mind blocked the development of homogeneous theater groups, and protested against the tendency to sacrifice literary content to eye-catching, sumptuous decorations. Firmly

12. New York *Times*, May 27, 28, 30, and September 28, 1874.
13. Quoted in *DJM*, XXXVII (December 8, 1877), 140.

believing in the illusion of reality on the stage, Antoine provided stage settings reflecting contemporary surroundings and giving "the impression of solidity and weight." Instead of sharply focused footlights, he preferred lighting that approximated natural conditions. And as far as the style of acting was concerned, he preferred that performers act in a natural way, without artificial poses and gestures, and that they make effective use of silence.[14] Above all, however, his experimental theater opened up opportunities that normally would not have been available to the public, potential performers, and playwrights.[15] His introduction of Henrik Ibsen, Leo Tolstoi, August Strindberg, Björnstjerne Björnson, and other writers foreign to the French public, in addition to the works of sometimes unknown compatriots, gave his theater a vitality Paris had not seen for a long time.[16] Antoine's enthusiasm for theatrical art heightened his stubborn refusal to be unduly concerned about the financial difficulties with which he had to struggle. Though his Théâtre-libre had to close down by the mid-nineties, Antoine's creative and competitive spirit produced lasting and beneficial effects.

The extent to which the growing power of the press affected the theater in the Western world by the close of the century disturbed professional observers. The manipulation of public opinion by the press may have contributed, as the noted Irish-American actor and playwright Dion Boucicault contended, to the encouragement of "a trivial kind of drama."[17] But if "the press has practically displaced the public in the exercise of judgment"— and, in Boucicault's view, to the detriment of the stage—it was by no means a foregone conclusion that the public's judgment would

14. Francis Pruner, *Les Luttes d'Antoine au théâtre-libre* (2 vols.; Paris, 1964), I, 415–18; S. M. Waxman, *Antoine and the théâtre-libre* (Paris, 1926), 58–59, 75, 128–29; Gassner, *Directions*, 18–21.

15. Whereas the Comédie française, Odéon, Gymnase, and Vaudeville together presented 154 plays between 1887 and 1890, the Théâtre-libre alone presented 125. André Antoine, *Memories of the Théâtre-libre* (Coral Gables, Fla., 1964), 163.

16. Francis Pruner, *Le Théâtre-libre d' Antoine: Le Repertoire étranger* (Paris, 1958).

17. Dion Boucicault to William Winter, January 1, 1889, in Folger Shakespeare Library, Washington, D.C.

have been much different without the influence that some journalists exerted. The quality of theater, after all, was related to the quality of life the public found desirable. If burlesque and society melodrama monopolized the stage, they mirrored the state of society. Ironically, Boucicault's personal belief that the play was more important than the actor may have contributed to the decline of the early drama.

The young American nation was too preoccupied with its practical pioneer tasks and too much restrained by its religious upbringing to be concerned with more than simple entertainment. The bare necessities of life, after all, came before prose and poetry. To Calvinistic Americans, leisure was a luxury, and possibly a sin. However, theatrical exposure to the sophisticated pleasures of life enjoyed by the British and French, introduced by European immigrants and visiting foreign performers, gradually developed in America a taste for the more refined aspects of life. The theater actually became one of the few "civilized distractions" in an otherwise rather drab life.[18]

European influence on the American theater abated only late in the nineteenth century. With the exception of minstrel shows, which alluded to contemporary conditions in America, no national theater existed in the United States before the twentieth century. Even such successful American playwrights as William Dunlap (1766–1839) and John Howard Payne (1791–1852) relied heavily on the trends of the European theater world. To circumvent possible popular objections to translations of French plays, theatrical entrepreneurs resorted to the apparently more original technique of advertising plays as "adaptations."[19] Adaptations

18. Barnard Hewitt, *Theatre U.S.A.*, 1665 *to* 1957 (New York, 1959), 164–65.
19. See Ralph Hartman Ware, *American Adaptations of French Plays on the New York and Philadelphia Stages from* 1834 *to the Civil War* (Philadelphia, 1930) ; Alexander Hamilton Mason IV, *French Theatre in New York: A List of Plays, 1899–1939* (New York, 1940), 3–5; and Louis Laurent Simonin, *Le Monde américain: Souvenirs de mes voyages aux Etats-Unis* (Paris, 1877), 20–21. As American adaptations of French plays at times mutilated the original work, some French adaptations of *Uncle Tom's Cabin* distorted it. Victorien Sardou's *Uncle Sam*, a

of French romantic tragedies and popular comedies continued to be in vogue, particularly in the pre–Civil War period. Actually, the romantic influence on melodrama lasted longer in the United States than in France. Although Americans built magnificent theaters in most of their larger communities, an outward indication of cultural growth and refinement, during most of the century they continued to depend largely on Europeans for inspiration, guidance, and performances. In communities with sizable numbers of French residents, visiting entertainers from France also helped, as a by-product, to perpetuate French culture in America.

As early as 1791, a Parisian company offered performances to the French-speaking inhabitants of New Orleans. By 1809, this city sustained three theaters that offered classic French plays, operas, dances, and light spectacles. People from all over the Southwest came to see these French shows and, incidentally, the Parisian fashions that some of the theater-patronizing ladies liked to display at these events. In 1793, a French theater also opened in Charleston. The sizable French-speaking population of this city, augmented by many refugees from Santo Domingo, was joined by the general public, people who could follow the shows because they emphasized music, dances, and pantomime more than conversations in French. The success of this theater prompted within another decade the extension of its circuit to Savannah and Richmond. Presidents Jackson, Van Buren, and Taylor lent their moral support to the French theater in New Orleans by attending performances whenever they were in town. It was not until the end of 1817 that an American theater company managed to sustain itself in this culturally French-dominated town.[20]

collection of prejudiced clichés about unscrupulous American merchants, scoundrels, and flirts, actually demeaned the author more than the United States. *New York Times*, December 4, 1873, and March 15, 1875. See also Glenn Hughes, *A History of the American Theatre*, 1700–1950 (New York, 1951), 303.

20. J. G. de Baroncelli, *Le Théâtre français à la Nouvelle Orléans* (New Orleans, 1906), 54; Lewis W. Newton, "Creoles and Anglo-Americans in Old Louisiana: A Study in Cultural Conflicts," *SSSQ*, XIV (1933), 44–46; and G. Hughes, *History of American Theatre*, 71, 123.

The New Orleans *Weekly Picayune* of January 7, 1839, contained the comment of an elderly French gentleman regarding American theater audiences. His remarks delightfully reflected significant contemporary differences in attitudes. The old man complained: "I 'ave nevaire see one people like des Americaines. . . . When de grand overture is play superb, magnifique, he no make de applause . . . he chew away on apple and chestnut . . . like pig, and make such disturbance dat he keep every one from de enjoyment. . . . When dat gal come on de stage, and begin for sing 'one petite baby catch some sleep', aha! dat is de music for him—den he clap his hand and make de grand encore all for noting. . . . Oh, mon Dieu! mon Dieu! dis is too much for one man to carry."

Also in San Francisco, where the French theater dominated by 1853 and survived until the 1880s, even though some of its citizens advocated greater support for the American theater, different social customs reflecting profound cultural differences set foreign and American theatergoers apart. The San Francisco *Wide West* of February 11, 1855, for instance, published the following interesting observation with respect to these audiences:

The scene in the lobby during the intervals between acts was a curious one, evidencing the individuality of nationalities, even in California, where all nationalities might be expected to blend into one. Accustomed to "long waits" between curtains, any foreign friends had lighted cigars and were collected in groups discussing the merits of the opera. The difference between this and the American style of rushing out for a drink and speedily returning to the theater to pass an impatient five minutes prior to the raising of the curtain, was quite manifest and amusing. The intervals between acts being so much shorter than they anticipated, the chatting and smoking of the foreign gentlemen was summarily interrupted, greatly to their chagrin and disappointment.[21]

The culturally refined audiences of the Boston Theater showed equal interest in American and French attractions. Often they attended not only classic French tragedies, but also charming

21. See San Francisco *Chronicle*, November 16, 1950; and George R. Mac-Minn, *The Theater of the Golden Era in California* (Caldwell, Idaho, 1941).

comedies and wonderfully relaxing vaudevilles, played by first-rate French actors displaying elegant costumes, jewelry, and equipment imported from the French and other European stages.[22] As far as variety went, New York's many theaters—including the Théâtre français, the Booth Theater, the Bowery, the Olympic, the Union League Theater, Niblo's, Wallack's—presented every type of ancient and modern, light and serious entertainment. Newspaper advertisements announced the days on which "French artists of acknowledged talent," often entire groups of actors from Lyons, Strasbourg, and Paris, would perform in the French classics and in the works of such modern playwrights as Scribe, Hugo, Dumas *fils*, Sardou, de Musset, Feuillet, and many others.[23] The theatrical world in New York did not lack incentive and originality. In 1862, for instance, Paul Juignet offered a series of very successful Soirées dramatiques. Typically, the New York *Herald* reported on January 20, 1862, that the vaudeville trifle, *Il ne faut pas jouer avec l'amour,* "was given with all that care of gesture and colloquial elegance which are the distinctive characteristics of the French stage." Such entertainment with a French accent offered the audiences welcome amusement and relaxation; but usually it also paid French artists more generously than they were accustomed to being paid in France. Even lesser-known French performers found opportunities in the United States that simply did not exist for them in their native country.

One of the most memorable theatrical events took place in the 1855 season when Rachel, the brilliant French tragedienne, appeared in New York, Boston, Philadelphia, and Charleston. Her fabulous reputation had preceded her arrival in America. Quite a few Americans had already admired her in Paris. As one of them described her in 1846: "Her features have a masked yet flexible outline, which conveys the minutest shades of expression. Her voice is clear, deep and thrilling, and like some grand strain

22. See "Boston Theatre, 1854–1889: A Full and Complete List of All Plays and Star Performers" (Boston, 1889), MS in MHS.
23. See George C. D. Odell, *Annals of the New York Stage* (15 vols.; New York, 1927–49), VI, 121–22, 157, 302, 321, and VII, 163–65, 264–67, 418–19.

of music, there are power and meaning in its slightest modulations."[24] Her stunning performances had been enthusiastically appreciated in England and Russia, where audiences familiar with the great French classics were accustomed to judging performers quite critically. Rachel hoped to duplicate this feat in America; and, encouraged by Jenny Lind's, "the Swedish Nightingale's," total purse of $335,409 for thirty-seven performances, Rachel hoped to earn an unprecedented fortune in the process. She expected the reputation of her dramatic perfection to silence those American moralists who might decry the fact that she was the unmarried mother of two sons.[25] Her debut in the packed Metropolitan Theater in New York indeed turned into a personal triumph. A distinguished audience paid such tribute to her genius that *Harper's Monthly* commented: "Rachel has come, and seen, and conquered." One critic was so carried away by Rachel's performance in Corneille's *Horace* that he reported: "So deep, vibrant and magnetic were the first tones of that voice that they sent a thrill through the vast assembly."[26] The gifted slender actress clearly fascinated the audience far more than the work in which she played. In *Phèdre,* the same critic described her as "almost intolerably exciting"; she summed up "a vision of the polychromatic statues of Greece . . . a goddess chiselled by Phidias in ivory and gold." In this play she portrayed the suffering "woman of the older Grecian mould, the victim of Fate, and of a passion which loses her soul. . . . And because it is the silence, not the sound of passion," an American artist who saw her perform was convinced that "there can never be a suspicion of rant."[27] On balance, though, her American tour fell short of expectations. During her three-month stay her reception varied

24. Bayard Taylor, *Views A-Foot: Or, Europe Seen with Knapsack and Staff* (New York, 1902), 367–68. Some Americans thought that Rachel mastered pathos better than tenderness; see Giddings, "Yankee Journalists in Europe," 92–93.

25. Bernard Falk, *Rachel the Immortal* (London, 1935), 273–75; Gustave Naquet, "Rachel et la tragédie," *RDBA*, I (1860), 261–62.

26. Odell, *New York Stage*, VI, 447–49; Henry Knepler, *The Gilded Stage: The Years of the Great International Actresses* (New York, 1968), 100–102.

27. Leonora Cranch Scott, *The Life and Letters of Christopher Pearse Cranch* (Boston, 1917), 167.

from enthusiastic to lukewarm. She netted the relatively disappointing total of $119,758 and contracted a cold that bothered her during her tour and signaled her premature death upon her return to France.[28]

What had happened to Rachel in America? Steeped in the tradition of Shakespearean drama, American audiences on the whole lacked the cultivated sense of appreciation of the great French classics. If they understood French at all, they found Corneille too stiff and formal and Racine artificial and effeminate. Reflecting a typical American reaction, the New York *Times* described the Alexandrine verse in which French tragedy was written as "a kind of barrel organ music that grows very wearisome."[29] Rachel's refined art evidently escaped so many of her listeners that one of her French admirers asked in exasperation: "Why exhibit to Americans Monime prostrate at the knees of Mithridates, expiring? . . . Why relate to them all those charming and famous love passages, which brought tears into the sweetest eyes at the Court of Augustus and Louis XIV?"[30] With few exceptions, Americans of the romantic era evidently had little taste for the all too serious and cold French tragedies. When they went to a theater, they preferred gay and entertaining spectacles that they could enjoy rather than complex and challenging themes that might disturb them. When the audience initially demanded impiously that Rachel sing the Marseillaise, she reluctantly did so; but outraged reaction in France suggested that this greatest of all French tragedians should have replied: "I bring you Corneille and Racine, and you call for . . . Danton! Leave me! You are unworthy of such a great fortune; you are incapable of understanding so much sacred sorrow, so much brilliant majesty!" French monarchists used this experience

28. Madame de B——, *Memoirs of Rachel* (New York, 1858), 327; Charles Sedgwick, "Unpublished Letters of French Actresses, 1798–1861" (Ph.D. dissertation, Harvard University, 1950), 241.
29. Otis Fellows, "Rachel and America: A Re-appraisal," *Romanic Review*, XXX (1939), 402–13.
30. Leon Beauvallet, *Rachel and the New World* (New York, 1856), 243; Mantzius, *History of Theatrical Art*, VI, 203.

to belittle democracy, which evidently "comprehended only the tumultuous drama of the mob yelling at the crossroads." Jules Janin, drama critic of the *Journal des débats,* infuriated the American public with his article, "Rachel et la tragedie aux Etats-Unis," in which he attacked America's ignorance regarding ancient works written with great harmony and taste. It seemed to him that "nothing annoys such a people more than the importance and the majesty of certain great men in the destinies of the world and in the admiration of poetry."[31] It was Rachel's misfortune that she became the victim of mid-nineteenth-century America's aversion to the classical writers of France. Though not fully appreciated in America, her superb art did leave lasting memories.

A generation later Sarah Bernhardt, the "divine," toured America with her entire company and twenty-eight trunks. Henry James, who had seen the star of the Comédie française perform in Paris, lauded her unsurpassed understanding of the art of motion and attitude and her extraordinary personal grace. When her beautiful voice, which Victor Hugo described as "a voice of gold," was heard in the United States in 1880, she received tumultuous applause wherever she went. Her repertoire, which included *Adrienne Lecouvreur, Frou Frou, Hermani, Phèdre, Le Passant,* and *La Dame aux camélias,* pleased her American audiences, and she in turn flattered them for their ability "to note the smallest effects and shades of diction." Her appearances in the completely packed Grand Opera House in New Orleans evoked high praise. Of the famous death scene in Octave Feuillet's *Le Sphinx,* for example, in which the unfaithful wife poisons herself, a critic wrote: "Her eye betrayed the poison's action; her breathing grew stentorious. . . . The voice became almost sepulchral. Mlle. Bernhardt's art was no longer art—it was nature."[32] In 1891 she toured America again and regarded it as her proudest achievement that she "planted French language in the heart of foreign literature." So well established was her

31. Beauvallet, *Rachel,* 238.
32. Jules Huret, *Sarah Bernhardt* (London, 1899), 86–88; John Smith Kendall, "Sarah Bernhardt in New Orleans," *LHQ,* XXVI (1943), 770–82.

reputation in America that when a monopolistic theater war in 1905–1906 kept her out of most legitimate theater houses in the United States, she defiantly filled the huge tents erected for her performances.[33] Many citizens of the New World admired the superb talents of this great actress; women activists also appreciated her contributions to the emancipation of women.

Naturally, Sarah Bernhardt had her detractors too, among them Henry Adams' wife Marian, who detested the voice and posing of the noted actress who, on outings, walked around in pants. Mrs. Adams hoped that Boston would "snub her off the stage."[34] As in the case of Rachel, it was whispered about the Jewish-born but baptized Sarah that she had perfected her art more successfully than her morals. One day she entered by chance a Protestant church in America and was taken aback hearing the minister denoune her as an "imp of darkness, a female demon sent from the modern Babylon to corrupt the New World." She promptly sent the pastor a little note: "My dear colleague: Why attack me so violently? Actors ought not to be hard on one another. Sarah Bernhardt."[35] As her purse and correspondence indicated, her American admirers by far outnumbered her critics.

America continued to be a major attraction to the best French actors. Benoit Constant Coquelin, the late nineteenth-century star of the Comédie française, brought his company to New York in the fall of 1888, presenting, among other plays, Moliére's *Les Précieuses ridicules*. In 1900 he returned with Sarah Bernhardt, featuring Edmond Rostand's *Cyrano de Bergerac* and *L'Aiglon.*

---

33. Knepler, *The Gilded Stage,* 266.
34. Baym, *French Education of Henry Adams,* 181.
35. Huret, *Sarah Bernhardt,* 88. Although Mildred Aldrich was convinced that Sarah Bernhardt "could never play a good woman convincingly," she "loved to see *how* she did things." Miss Bernhardt was, after all, "past-mistress of every trick of her métier." Mildred Aldrich, "Confessions of a Breadwinner" (4 vols.), I (1926), 300 (MS at Radcliffe College, Cambridge). In her memoirs, Miss Bernhardt recorded the letter her manager had sent to the Bishop of Chicago who had publicly criticized the "corrupting influence" of her art. The Bishop's denunciation had unintentionally advertised her performances, and she sent him a check of $200 "for your poor," half the amount she usually spent on advertising. Sarah Bernhardt, *Memories of My Life* (New York, 1968), 419.

Coquelin, who by then was no stranger to America and had quite
a few American friends, enjoyed the reputation of being a versatile
and spontaneous artist who impressed his audience with the
message that "acting is an art and that art is style."[36] People
who saw him perform confirmed, as did one of his admirers from
Louisiana, that in every minute detail he lived his role on the
stage, never permitting wit and humor to degenerate into
vulgarity. Also Gabrielle Réjane (1857–1920), a leading comic
actress whose "pulse of living beat with painful intensity," successfully entertained American audiences. In addition to contributing delightful memories, exposure to French stars was a
stimulating educational experience for Americans. François
Delsarte's experiments with "natural acting" and André Antoine's
Théâtre-libre, providing in little experimental theaters an ideal
artistic stage for contemporary productions of merit, encouraged
similar dramatic experimentation in the New World.[37] As a
developing country, the United States needed encouraging in-
centives for dramatic talents, tastes, and productions more
urgently than exquisite treats by star performers. France, of
course, provided not only stars, but plays, ideas, and example
as its invaluable contribution to the evolution of the American
theater in general, and the French-American theater in particular.

36. Marie Reynes, "Coquelin et son repertoire," in J. Reynes Family Papers,
LSU Archives, Baton Rouge; G. Hughes, *History of American Theatre*, 256; James,
French Poets and Novelists, 429–30. At a dinner honoring Edwin Booth, Coquelin
praised Booth as "the first, the greatest tragic artist of America." Coquelin Address,
New York, 1889 (MS in Folger Shakespeare Library, Washington, D.C.)

37. G. Hughes, *History of American Theatre*, 235, 368–69; see also Joseph
Blyth Allston to his aunt, July 15, 1855, in Allston Collection, SCHS.

CHAPTER VIII
Music and Dance

The nineteenth century produced many musically creative minds, thus from generation to generation giving new expression, both in style and in substance, to the unchanging ideal of this art form. The individual and national roots of music notwithstanding, its international character and language helped build cultural bridges that contributed to the pleasure of people in many lands. In the nineteenth century, French, German, Italian and Russian composers directed the evolution of music and enriched this art with a great variety of symphonies, concertos, organ music, operas, operettas, and lieder.

America was not yet ready to make its distinct contribution to this evolution. The attempts of a few American artists to go beyond folksongs and short compositions and to write operas and symphonies were not significant enough to be considered part of the mainstream of nineteenth-century music. The incorporation of Indian dances and Negro spirituals in some of the late romantic compositions expressed the growing desire for music with an American flavor. But a petition to Congress asking it to support a national conservatory with an appropriation of $200,000 evoked, as late as 1888, newspaper comments that clearly separated the minority of music lovers from the large majority who believed that music was "a luxury for the wealthy." To spend that much public money "to teach young people how to execute vocal gymnastics or play on the fiddle" seemed extravagant. After all, commented an Indianapolis journal in characteristic fashion, "we are not so esthetic as that."[1]

Even though German and Italian music dominated the American musical scene in the nineteenth century, French composers enjoyed a wide welcome. In the context of this study, we must obviously focus on them. If the perfection of instrumental forms by Haydn, Mozart, and Beethoven enhanced the beauty of music and the sublime heights that Beethoven's genius reached elevated the soul of man, nineteenth-century French composers, mostly using opera as their favorite medium, endeavored to add a little pleasure to man's existence. Their willingness to defy classical orthodoxy and to pioneer original ideas was from a broader cultural point of view as revealing as the popular search for political freedom. In music no less than in politics the French bourgeoisie tried by 1830 to break with the absolutism and abstractions of the past and to substitute for them the new freedom and sentiment of the romantic era, reflecting its anticlerical and antiaristocratic notions. The decline of instrumental music and the rise of the grand opera in France, from the time of the constitutional monarchy of Louis Philippe on, outwardly symbolized this shift of interests.[2] It is not surprising that this process of experimentation with new styles and forms and the impact of foreign concepts on French music revealed uncertainties regarding the future direction of this art.

The knowledge that even the music of the ancient civilization of modern France was greatly influenced by foreigners made it a little easier for Americans to swallow their pride as citizens of a pioneer nation that was as yet underdeveloped in the field of music and consequently leaned heavily on foreign artists. In the nineteenth century alone, a number of foreigners figured

1. Paul Henry Lang (ed.), *One Hundred Years of Music in America* (New York, 1961), 114.
2. Lang, *Music in Western Civilization*, 825–53; William L. Crosten, *French Grand Opera: An Art and a Business* (New York, 1948), 50–51, 73–75.

prominently in the evolution of French music. The strict disciplinarian Luigi Cherubini (1760–1842), eminent director of the Conservatoire in Paris and pioneer of French opera, and Gioacchino Antonio Rossini (1782–1868), the popular Italian operatic composer in Paris, both helped develop French talent and taste. Rossini's *Barber of Seville* and *William Tell* introduced wit and modernity to operatic performances, very much to the liking of audiences that found the themes of the past dull and boring.[3] Giacome Meyerbeer (1791–1864) and Jacques Offenbach (1819–1880), two German-born artists who lived and died in Paris, ranked among the outstanding composers of nineteenth-century French opera and operetta. Meyerbeer, best remembered for his operas *Les Huguenots* and *Le Prophète*, succeeded brilliantly in amalgamating such different musical currents as Rossinian strains, the emerging romantic school, and the unorthodox orchestral explorations of Hector Berlioz—adding to them his own emphasis on dramatic effects.[4] The levity of Offenbach's operettas delighted the public looking for pleasant entertainment, and it infuriated the self-appointed guardians of classic art. Even his serious work, *The Tales of Hoffmann*, did not satisfy these critics' standards. Interestingly, though, almost a century after its premiere, listeners still found this opera pleasant entertainment. Frederic Chopin (1810–1849), the Polish patriot of partly French parentage who made France his home, wrote in the less than four decades of his brief life an amazingly large number of beautifully harmonious compositions for the piano. Chopin's piano pieces were unsurpassed in style and sentiment. Disregarding classical forms, his romantic and melodic music displayed an extraordinary degree of independence and originality.[5] And César Franck

3. Arthur Hervey, *French Music in the Nineteenth Century* (London and New York, 1903), 16, 29–31, 48.

4. Many critics, nevertheless, denounced the unevenness and shallowness of Meyerbeer's music. Edward Dickinson, *The Study of the History of Music* (New York, 1923), 303–304. For Meyerbeer's interest in America, see *DJM*, XIX (August 17, 1861), 157–58.

5. Dickinson, *History of Music*, 243–50; Lang, *Music in Western Civilization*, 814.

(1822–1890), the naturalized Frenchman of Belgian birth and German descent, whose saintly modesty and quiet dedication kept him out of the limelight, also made a unique contribution to French music. Of his oratorio, *Les Béatitudes*, "a musical paraphrase of the Sermon on the Mount," his pupil Ernest Chausson said: "The fourth *Béatitude* certainly surpasses all other French music in sublimity. One would have to go back to the very first classical masters to find so powerful an expression of the soul's despair, its appeal to Divine justice, its striving after the ideal, after holiness."[6] A romanticist by nature, César Franck's musical inspiration led him to combine the polyphonic methods of old masters with the most modern modulations. His symphonic music constituted a major challenge to the dominance of grand opera.[7]

Still another, and perhaps the greatest, influence brought to bear on French music originated with the German musical genius Richard Wagner (1813–1883). When Nietzsche prophesied that France would have to "Wagnerize" itself if it wished "to adapt itself to the actual needs of the *âme moderne*," he asked for more than many Frenchmen were willing to do. On his first visit to Paris in 1839, the young Wagner experienced many disappointments and hardships. When he visited it again in 1860, now as a famous, though controversial, composer, his works encountered little understanding and were in fact subjected to uncivilized reception. A performance of *Tannhäuser* at the Grand Opera was disrupted by disapproving whistlers. Parisians laughed at Wagner's "burlesque orchestration." Even Berlioz wrote: "Nothing can be made of this *Tannhäuser* music."[8] A decade later, the famous death march from *Götterdämmerung* was received with noisy hisses by those who suffered from Wagnerphobia or who rejected "the music of the future." For nothing less was Wagner's objective and accomplishment than a synthesis

6. Jules Van Ackere, *L'Âge d'or de la musique française* (1870–1950) (Bruxelles, 1966), 23–40; Hervey, *French Music*, 220–21.

7. W. Wright Roberts, "César Franck," *Music and Letters*, III (1922), 318; Hervey, *French Music*, 132–50.

8. H. Sutherland Edwards, *Famous First Representations* (London, 1886), 233, 237.

of music, text, drama, scenery, and acting. To bring about this unification of the various arts in his music, he introduced the *leitmotif*, blended a continuous flow of melody with the needs of the drama, and enriched the orchestration very forcefully. So great became his influence in time and so slow and reluctant were the French to acknowledge it, that modern French composers suspect of imitating the German master had to deny such taint. The legacy of bitterness engendered by the Franco-Prussian War and unwisely accentuated by Wagner's victory compositions of the *Kaisermarsch* and the satirical comedy *A Capitulation* embroiled artistic controversy in anti-Teutonic antics.

Of the French composers, Hector Berlioz (1803–1869) took the lead in unconventional music that disregarded traditional rules of the classical school without violating such fundamentals as truth and beauty. In defense of his emancipation, he argued: "In its union with the drama, music must always be connected with the sentiments expressed by the words, the accent and vocal inflection. Operas should not be written for singers; singers, on the contrary, should be found for operas . . . it is for him [the master] to command. Sound and sonority rank below the musical idea. The musical idea ranks below sentiment and passion. Runs, vocal ornaments, trills and rhythm cannot express a serious and profound sentiment."[9] Berlioz was only twenty-five when he declared his musical independence with the *Symphonie Fantastique,* a work of "the thousand alternatives of sadness and joy . . . of silence and of tumult, of the grotesque and the sublime." In his music he combined a keen and reassuring sense for power and rhythm with the soul of an artist puzzled by the infinite mystery of life and death. He reached the height in his musical odyssey in his "Requiem." His dramatic inclinations were characteristically reflected in masterful orchestrations, which he referred to as "instrumental dramas." Berlioz, the first representative of the romantic movement, was also a realist in the sense that he made it a point to select contemporary themes. In France, Berlioz remained a controversial voice in the wilder-

9. Hervey, *French Music,* 89, 101–102; Dickinson, *History of Music,* 260–70.

ness, long compelled to supplement his income as a music critic, which, he confessed, "is my shame and my despair." The bourgeois French public preferred the lighter music of composers like Daniel-François Auber so much that Berlioz reacted to his dilemma with contempt for a public that regarded "any music which deviates from the little path where the makers of comic operas trot back and forth . . . the music of a lunatic." Somehow, novelty in music seemed to encounter more resistance than it did in literature and painting.[10]

Berlioz' reception in the United States was more favorable, even in his early career, than in his own country. Americans respected the fact that Berlioz persevered in his peculiar style in spite of the opposition to him. And he was glad that they remained faithful to his symphonies at a time when some of his compatriots rejected them as "youthful mistakes." Contrary to French critics who greeted his music with contempt and sarcasm, American commentators appreciated his originality and powerful individualistic compositions. "Music is the language of the soul, not of logic," wrote the Philadelphia *Sunday Transcript*. "Hector Berlioz has comprehended this mission."[11] Although he eventually gained worldwide recognition, the poor state of his health allowed him little comfort and peace in his final years. In a response he wrote in 1863 to a disillusioned composer in Vermont, he aired his innermost feelings: "You doubtless have formed a very mistaken idea of the life that artists worthy of the name lead in Paris. If to you New York is the Purgatory of musicians, then to me, who knows it well, Paris is their Hell. Therefore do not be too downhearted."[12] And as a testament of one who

10. Jacques Barzun, *Berlioz and the Romantic Century* (2 vols.; New York, 1969), II, 45–46, 131; J. Chantavoine and J. Gaudefroy-Demombyrnes, *Le Romantisme dans la musique européenne* (Paris, 1955), 131; Crosten, *French Grand Opera*, 50–51.

11. For comments on Berlioz, see *DJM*, XIX (1861), 178–79, and XXXVIII (1878), 225–26; Barzun, *Berlioz*, II, 310–11. By the end of the century, the favorable comments of the 1870s gave way to the opinion that Berlioz had really nothing to say, but said it beautifully.

12. Jacques Barzun (trans.), *New Letters of Berlioz, 1830–1868* (New York, 1954), 229–31.

passionately loved and respected music as the greatest of the arts, he added this comment and advice: "One must scorn the crowd and its prejudices, put no value on success that is bought by weak concessions, and protect oneself carefully from contact with fools and with fanatics and with sophists who know how to give folly the semblance of reason."

Though different in his methods, Charles Gounod (1818–1893) was also an individualist to whom music was a religion. Unlike Berlioz, the composer of the operas *Faust* and *Romeo and Juliette* preferred simplicity and dignity to dramatic emphasis. A master at expressing tenderness, Gounod chose love as the central theme of his compositions; and he expressed that theme in accordance with his deep conviction that any form of musical creation must reveal itself in the language that God had given the artist.[13] In one way or another, Meyerbeer, Berlioz, Gounod, and Wagner influenced some of the other French composers who in their otherwise independent work added further luster to the high esteem in which the arts of France were held. They included, of course, Georges Bizet (1838–1875), the musical painter of color, passion, and rhythm; Jules Massenet (1842–1912), the popular romantic whose refined music portrayed tenderness very appealingly;[14] and Camille Saint-Saëns (1835–1921), the versatile master of many techniques, who combined elegance with precision and harmony in a manner that pleased Parisians.

Recognizing their novel character, Americans were also fascinated by the tone painter Félicien David (1810–1876) and the rebel Claude Debussy (1862–1918). David's masterwork, the cantata *Le Désert,* contained oriental rhythms and exotic songs and dances of genuine charm. In his impressionistic compositions he revealed himself as an exceptionally imaginative and refined artist. Young Debussy, the recipient of the coveted

13. Hervey, *French Music,* 108–29; Dickinson, *History of Music,* 349–65.
14. Lang, *Music in Western Civilization,* 923. When an American visitor told Massenet in 1882 that his works were immensely popular in America, he expressed surprise that his music was "already played over there." Rudolph Aronson, *Theatrical and Musical Memoirs* (New York, 1913), 40.

Prix de Rome, found any academic restrictions imposed upon him unbearable; nothing but complete artistic freedom would satisfy him. He returned to Paris to write his *own* music, in a fashion his teachers at the conservatory condemned as heresy. He did indeed write music of great originality, developing his avant-garde concepts of harmony, tonality, and form. And yet, he would have been the first to admit that the new tendencies in poetry and painting, symbolism and impressionism, inspired him in his search for new musical expression. Nor would he have denied that he also borrowed ideas from German, Italian, and, significantly, Russian composers. But the final work was his own, with a typical French accent.[15] Since Debussy helped to lead modern music into the twentieth century, Berlioz stood out as the most influential French composer in the nineteenth cenury. Compared wih the contributions other European countries made to the development of music in this century, that of France was not overly impressive. But compared with that of the United States, it loomed large.[16]

In the summer of 1835 an American admirer of the French Opera and its *corps de ballet* confessed downheartedly: "Mercy! how deficient we are in our country in these elegant accomplishments. In many things we are not yet born."[17] Others, before and after him, learned in France—"the very nursery of the graces"—to appreciate music in its various forms. Unforgettable grand opera and ballet performances prompted enthusiastic responses, in part at least because Frenchmen and Americans possessed a common love of spectacles. French opera was characteristically staged in a fashion that would "give equal pleasure to the eyes and to the ears." According to Americans who traveled extensively in Europe, its fabulous *mise-en-scène* clearly distinguished Parisian

15. Ackere, *L'Âge d'or*, 53–108.
16. Martin Cooper, *French Music: From the Death of Berlioz to the Death of Fauré* (London, 1951), 1–6. The Société Nationale de Musique, founded in 1871, was instrumental in seeing to it that the public became familiar with the music of the younger generation of French composers.
17. Sanderson, *Sketches of Paris*, 30.

opera from that in Italy. An orchestra of at least one hundred instruments and a chorus of one hundred voices, supporting forty or more ballet dancers on the stage, all performing perfectly, individually and in harmony with each other, created fascinating effects.[18] Since Italy was too poor to pay its most talented artists handsomely, France and England attracted an unequaled galaxy of Italian singers and dancers whose performances added charm to splendor.[19] And the colorful dresses of the artists delighted the audiences and further enlivened the already picturesque stage. But what Paris accepted as a "perfectly proper" dress on stage could cause more than the raising of eyebrows in the United States. When in 1827 Madame Francisque Hutin of the Paris Opera introduced French ballet to an audience in New York, her flimsy attire so outraged American ladies that they left the theater in protest.[20] Except for people in frontier regions, however, Americans gradually ceased to be scandalized by the short dresses of French dancers.

Americans always availed themselves of opportunities to listen to French music and musicians. Before and after the Great Revolution, French musicians who had sought a haven in the United States tried to earn a living by teaching Americans to play the violin, flute, or piano. Others offered singing and dancing lessons, advertising instruction in minuets, gavottes, and, to the shock of contemporary society, the latest waltzes.[21] In many communities French émigrés took the initiative in organizing

18. For more detailed American comments on Paris opera and ballet performances before 1860, see J. Francis Fischer, "Journal of a European Visit, 1831–33," November 7, 1831, in Cadwalader Collection, PHS; see also J. A. Young to Mary L. Young, July 28, 1836, in Young Family Papers, USC; Diary of George Endicott, September 27, 1847, NYPL; and Thomas Ryan, *Recollections of an Old Musician* (New York, 1899), 31–32.

19. Hezekiah H. Wright, *Desultory Reminiscences of a Tour through Germany, Switzerland, and France* (Boston, 1838), 251–58.

20. Julius Mattfeld, *Variety: Music Cavalcade, 1620–1950* (New York, 1952), 38; Harold E. and Ernestine Bennett Briggs, "The Early Theater on the Northern Plains," *MVHR*, XXXVI (1950), 260.

21. Henry A. Kmen, *Music in New Orleans: The Formative Years, 1791–1841* (Baton Rouge, 1966), 21; Constance Rourke, *The Roots of American Culture and Other Essays* (New York, 1942), 164–66; and Harold D. Eberlein and Cortlandt Van Dyke Hubbard, "Music in the Early Federal Era," *PMHB*, LXIX (1945), 117.

orchestras that promoted a local interest in French music. Before long, French operas and ballets introduced an unaccustomed elegance and enjoyment. Such strongholds of French culture as New Orleans and Charleston took the lead in these endeavors. Although New Orleans' regular opera seasons, featuring many French composers, had been a local event since 1809, they became a popular national attraction in 1837 with the appearance of Mlle. Julia Calvé, the famous soprano of the *Théâtre d'Orléans*.[22] Under Calvé's leadership the New Orleans company also traveled to New York, presenting there in the summer of 1845 Gaetano Donizetti's opera *La Favorite* and Halévy's masterpiece *La Juive*. The successful reception of these presentations by what the New York *Herald* called a "remarkable ensemble" was also extended to many visiting opera and ballet companies from France.[23] A steady stream of brilliant violinists and pianists crossed the ocean hoping to enhance their fame and fortune in the New World. Some of them decided to stay in the United States. Eugene Prévost (1809–1872), for instance, trained at the Paris Conservatory and honored by the Institut de France for his compositions *Cléopatre* and *Bianca Capello*, assumed in 1840 the leadership of the French Opera in New Orleans, a post in which he served with distinction for twenty-seven years.[24] Often playing before packed houses, these artists could judge for themselves the great strides America

22. In 1859 this theater was replaced by the Opera House of New Orleans. Lorelle Causey Bender, "The French Opera House of New Orleans, 1859–1890" (M.A. thesis, Louisiana State University, 1940), 2; Kmen, *Music in New Orleans*, 62–63, 99, 103–104. The opera began at 5:30 P.M. and usually lasted until 11 P.M. "At its close it was the custom for the beaux and belles, well chaperoned by mothers, cousins and aunts," to have a cup of coffee in the nearby French Market. Catherine Cole, *The Story of the Old French Market* (New Orleans, 1916), 9.

23. Frederick L. Ritter, *Music in America* (New York, 1883), 303; Odell, *New York Stage*, V, 103–105.

24. In 1869 the French consul in Philadelphia asked his government to help protect those French artists in the United States who occasionally were paid less than their contracts called for or who were the first victims of financially failing enterprises. *Correspondance Consulaire et Commerciale*, Philadelphia, March 23, 1869, AMAE. See also J. de Filippi, "Des Conditions économiques de la musique et du théâtre en France," *La Chronique musicale*, III (1874), 14–15; and Grace H. Yerbury, "Concert Music in Early New Orleans," *LHQ*, XL (April, 1957), 106.

was making in transforming itself from an artistic desert into a culturally fertile land.

Evidently inadequately informed, Jean Jacques Ampère, a member of the French Academy and professor of history and literature at the Collège de France, visited the United States in 1851 and expressed the typical opinion that, with the exception of black people, Americans lacked natural musical instinct and ability.[25] Up to this time, they had indeed not composed much music. Evidence attests the fact, however, that even in the pre–Civil War era interest in music had been growing steadily. In addition to New Orleans, New York, Boston, Philadelphia, Cincinnati, and St. Louis, many other cities had organized choral societies, philharmonic orchestras, and concerts.[26] As has already been noted, sufficient interest and patronage evidently warranted tours by foreign companies and virtuosos who presented classical and contemporary works of every musical genre. The repertoire of the French artists emphasized French and Italian pieces, familiarizing American audiences with Auber, Berlioz, Cherubini, André Ernest Grétry, Halévy, Rossini, and Henri François Joseph Vieuxtemps.[27] Frenchmen residing in American cities also made music stores centers of education where people could meet to discuss music and to purchase scores and instruments often imported from France and Germany.

In at least one instance, a well-reputed Frenchman added such flavor of showmanship to his musical presentations that he caused quite a sensation in the United States. Louis Antoine Jullien, an exciting conductor of dance music, visited the United States in 1853. Setting out to popularize good music, he brought a first-rate

25. Berthe Ruth Leaman, "A Frenchman Visits Philadelphia in 1851," *Pennsylvania History*, VIII (1941), 267.

26. M. D. Tajan-Rogé, *Les Beaux-Arts aux Etats-Unis d'Amérique* (Paris, 1857), 33–37; Ferdinand H. Walthers, "Music and Musicians in St. Louis," in *Music Papers, 1830–1937,* MoHS. Such encouragement of music appreciation ran parallel with similar efforts in France. "Editorial Corrrespondence," August 10, 1860, *DJM*, XVII (September 22, 1860), 205–206.

27. Julius Mattfeld, *A Hundred Years of Grand Opera in New York, 1825–1925: A Record of Performances* (New York, 1927), 23–35.

orchestra along, including Antoine Joseph Lavigne, the most outstanding oboist of his time, and Giovanni Bottesini, the most highly reputed contrabass player. Starting with forty musicians, his success soon justified an orchestra of ninety-seven players, the largest Americans had ever heard. Anticipating the custom of modern jazz bands, he arranged certain airs so that the musicians could sing them as they played them. Jullien demonstrated how bold and showy he could be one night at the Crystal Palace in New York. While the orchestra was playing the music of *The Firemen's Quadrille,* he dramatized the piece so realistically with firebells, flames, and firemen actually using water hoses that, in spite of the reassurance by ushers that there was no real fire, women fainted and the audience became frightened momentarily. Nevertheless, his spectacular showmanship pleased Americans; and so did the fact that he also played the works of American composers.[28]

The devastating economic effects of the Civil War and the declining influence of Creoles and French civilization in postwar America made the major eastern cities rather than New Orleans the Mecca of many accomplished French artists.[29] Despite the widespread appeal of German music in America, leading contemporary French composers, including those specializing in modern organ music, were accorded a warm reception. For a generation following the Civil War, French comic opera, or *opéra bouffe,* appealed especially to those Americans who preferred light entertainment to legitimate opera.[30] It must nevertheless

28. See John T. Howard and George K. Bellows, *A Short History of Music in America* (New York, 1957), 120; Louis C. Elson, *American Music* (New York, 1904), 69; Irving Lowens, *Music and Musicians in Early America* (New York, 1964), 221; and "Jullien's Concerts," *DJM*, IV (October 29, 1853), 29–30.

29. John Cornelius Griggs, *Studien über die Musik in Amerika* (Leipzig, 1894), 78. When in 1893 the young French violinist Henri Marteau performed at symphony concerts in Boston, the enthusiasm of the audience assured his early return. Other French musicians experienced similar gratification. Henry C. Lahee, *Famous Violinists of Today and Yesterday* (Boston, 1916), 293–95.

30. George P. Upton, *Musical Memoirs: My Recollections of Celebrities of the Half Century,* 1850–1890 (Chicago, 1908), 152–54; Henry C. Lahee, *Annals of Music in America* (Boston, 1922), 78–116. See also, *L'Art musical,* XXV (1886), 84–86, XXVII (1888), 173, XXXII (1893), 46; and *RGMP* (1880), pp. 48, 143, 375.

be kept in mind that, as the vitality of German community influences was greatly strengthened by the steady influx of German people, the cultural influences of the much smaller French population in America declined noticeably. Although German music did not displace French music, enthusiastic interest in this German art was clearly on the ascent and it was naturally encouraged by the German immigrants.[31]

In any case, not all Americans found French music inspiring, or even pleasing to their ears. An American youth, for instance, invited to the home of a French family, wrote to his mother in 1846 that he played several pieces together with his host's sister-in-law, a superb pianist and guitarist. And then he mentioned rather proudly that "I astonished the natives with Lucey Long and Lucey Neal" and a few other specimens of American music. . . . They liked our style of music very much here, and I don't wonder at it, for most of *their* songs are miserable affairs in my opinion."[32] A few years later, another American visitor recorded in his diary: "I have as yet heard of nothing above mediocrity in Paris—no concert to compare with those I heard in Boston!"[33] The most frequent criticism of French music was that, though it excelled in form, it distinctly lacked melody and depth. No matter how well received by the American public at large, most nineteenth-century French composers did not fare as well in professional evaluations in the United States. Offenbach, a master of melody and harmony, for instance, was accused of having "made them subservient to the spirit of grotesque humor."[34] Much in Meyerbeer's *Huguenots* was found to be "very flat" and "transparently factitious"; little in it struck the reviewer as "convincingly spontaneous and great."[35] According to one contemporary American critic, the charmingly beautiful melodies in Bizet's *Carmen* became rather "tiresome" because it contained too many

31. Lang, *Music in Western Civilization*, 933.
32. Charles Michael Clerc to his mother, November 19, 1846, in NYHS.
33. "Diary Abroad," *DJM*, VI (1854), 100.
34. "Offenbach," *DJM*, XXVII (1867), 132.
35. "Music," *Atlantic Monthly*, XXXIII (1874), 511.

"very cloying" Spanish dance tunes.[36] It was hardly a compliment to describe a composer as being "less tormented than some of his contemporaries," or to charge that many French composers merely wished to please "a grossly ignorant French public." Specifically, in his *Story of Music* (1897) William James Henderson criticized Gounod's *Faust*: "It seems to me that the work fails to reach real greatness and a permanent influence on operatic art only because of Gounod's concessions to the tawdry sentimentality and uneducated musical demands of the masses."[37] In a lengthy review of Gounod's *Faust*, William Fry, who praised the composer as "a master of orchestration," regretted that in an opera of five acts and embracing nineteen pieces" we look in vain for a first-class memorable melody, the prime requisite of an opera."[38] Another American critic commented similarly, with respect to Halévy's *La Juive*: To listen to an opera in five acts and not to hear even one pleasant melody or a couple of "morceaux" of a superior order was pathetic.[39] Even the sympathetic *Daily Picayune*, which in its issue of November 20, 1853, defended the French against British contentions that the French language was unfit for musical expression and that France could not claim any great musicians, admitted that serious operas were not "as suited to the genius and character of the French nation as . . . to that of the Germans and Italians." It hastened to add, however, that in its opinion France excelled in comic opera, orchestral music, and music criticism.[40] Time obviously had to pass before the modern school of French music could be judged without contemporary prejudices. By the beginning of the twentieth century, French music was on the whole judged to possess originality, richness, and even intellectual quality.

The early history of music in America was greatly influenced

36. "Carmen," *DJM*, XXXIX (1879), 13–14.
37. Elizabeth B. White, *American Opinion of France from Lafayette to Poincaré* (New York, 1927), 242.
38. New York *Daily Tribune*, December 23, 1863, p. 3.
39. *DJM*, I (1852), 63.
40. "French School of Music," New Orleans *Daily Picayune*, November 20, 1853.

by the view of the Puritan fathers that such "popish" exercises as singing by note would cause disturbances and disorderly conduct in churches and probably encourage the introduction of instruments of questionable social value. Though later generations discounted the "evil" social side effects of music, music education in the United States had a slow beginning in the early nineteenth century.[41] The establishment of five conservatories and musical colleges in the years immediately following the Civil War gave it a remarkable lift, and it developed rapidly, also qualitatively, in the first quarter of the twentieth century.[42] In the meantime, American youth interested in perfecting their knowledge of music and seeking special instrumental and voice training availed themselves primarily of the excellent schools in France and Germany. In the final decades of the century thousands of American students of music tried to further their education in Europe. Considering that it was extremely difficult to pass the entrance examinations of the Conservatoire de Musique,[43] it was astonishing how many American teenagers met the requirements. And considering the talented competition these youngsters faced, it was extraordinary that quite a few of them won first prizes in the yearly contests the Conservatoire conducted, and even more collected second and third prizes. Although the strict methods and somewhat stuffy atmosphere of the Paris Conservatory were rather hard to take for American students accustomed to more relaxed environments, the fact that it treated foreign students objectively in these contests and awarded prizes strictly on merit attested to its high professional standards.[44]

41. Rupert Hughes, *Famous American Composers* (Boston, 1906), 14–15.

42. The general democratization of American life also extended to music. James H. Stone, "Mid-Nineteenth Century American Beliefs in the Social Values of Music," *Musical Quarterly*, XLIII (1957), 38–49.

43. During the Second Empire it changed its name to Conservatoire Impérial de Musique. With the usual exception of students from New Orleans, most Americans had to acquire mastery of the French language as a prerequisite to their musical studies in French schools.

44. For the yearly lists of prize winners, see Constant Pierre, *Le Conservatoire national de musique et de déclamation* (Paris, 1900), 684–872; Harold Bauer, "The Paris Conservatoire: Some Reminiscences," *Musical Quarterly*, XXXIII (1947), 533–42; and Gilbert Chase, *America's Music: From the Pilgrims to the Present* (New York, 1955), 348.

Toward the turn of the twentieth century some Americans began to argue that their schools and colleges had reached an academic level that put them at least on a par with European schools. They questioned the value of foreign diplomas in the field of music. Indeed, one observer claimed that Americans in touch with "graduates" from European schools of music knew "the full extent of the glittering sham . . . [and] deception about this matter of 'studying abroad.'"[45] Others, however, continued to believe that French schooling in music was indispensable to the well rounded student, not merely for the sake of technical perfection, but much more importantly because "Paris has art conviction which . . . leans towards the spiritual rather than the material side of life."[46] To artists inclined toward self-glorification, Paris offered balance and perspective of the most sobering nature. For that very reason it seemed most beneficial for American artists to work with a European master after they had completed their basic training at home and reached a certain level of independence and maturity.

While posterity focuses more on the relatively few outstanding artists than on the multitude of mediocrities and failures who studied abroad, historical perspective also requires awareness that changing economic and cultural conditions justify different opinions with respect to the advisability and timing of instruction abroad, as do the extent of the knowledge, talent, maturity, and circumstances of each individual at any given time. Marguerite Samuel, Paris-born resident of New Orleans, was only ten or eleven years old when the Conservatoire Impérial de Musique in Paris took her under its wings. In time, she became the most celebrated interpreter of Chopin in her adopted country. To be sure, she studied intensively and for many years under the direction of Auber, Rossini, her cousin Halévy, Victor Massé,

45. A. J. Goodrich, "Several Reasons Why Americans Should Remain at Home," *Musical Courier*, XXXVII (July 4, 1898).
46. Fannie Edgar Thomas, "American Interests in Paris: Musical Relations Between France and America," *Musical Courier*, XXXVII (July 4, and December 7, 1898), and XXXVIII (May 10, 17, 1899).

Bizet, and many others, and she also circulated in the most talented and prominent musical circles of her time.[47] Similarly Camilla Urso, who in 1852 had moved from Nantes to the United States and whom the Conservatoire in Paris had accepted as a student, was only ten years old when her violin concerts created a sensation in the United States. She turned into one of the most accomplished violinists and evidently inspired many American girls to take up violin studies.[48]

That musical talents from France earned the gratitude and esteem of American music lovers came to be taken for granted. But the fact that from the middle of the nineteenth century on, quite a few American singers brought Parisians to their feet applauding the thrilling voices of American ladies has been less widely known.[49] A few specific examples will best illustrate this artistic reciprocity. Dolores Nau, a New York girl who distinguished herself at the Conservatoire, owed her success as a star of the Paris Grand Opera to an unexpected break. She performed beautifully when she was suddenly asked to sing the part of the page in Meyerbeer's *The Huguenots,* substituting for the featured singer who had suddenly taken ill. Once the audience listened to her voice she was on her way of becoming an American prima donna in Paris. An enthusiastic French music critic described her voice as "a high soprano . . . which warbles and lets fall the notes in pearls fine and delicately moulded. Its tone . . . shunning the false éclat . . . has a certain sonorous and silvery sound and . . . is of incomparable purity and celestial sweetness." The exquisite taste Miss Nau displayed in her off-stage wardrobe also endeared the artist to the fashion-conscious society of Paris.[50] Mrs. Bouligny Nott, the granddaughter of Governor Bouligny of Louisiana, possessed a natural trill "as perfect as that of a

47. May W. Mount, *Some Notables of New Orleans* (New Orleans, 1896), 146–47.
48. Elson, *American Music,* 309; Lahee, *Famous Violinists,* 319.
49. "Coals to Newcastle: American Singers in Europe," *DJM,* XXXIII (1874), 156; Griggs, *Musik in Amerika,* 73–74.
50. "An American Prima Donna," *DJM,* IV (1854), 170–71.

bird." There was not a vacant seat in the Paris Opera when this exceptionally gifted and beautiful lady appeared on the stage. Her vocal education at the Conservatoire and later under the guidance of Mme. Niolan Carvalho, the leading singing star in Paris, merely helped to perfect her natural talent.[51] Another American favorite, the dramatic soprano Minnie Hauk, had for some time been directed by a French singing master in New Orleans. Mademoiselle Miauk, as Parisians endearingly called her, made her debut at seventeen, in 1869, as Amina in Bellini's *Sonnambula*. Her manager, Moritz Strakosch, the influential impressario of the famous Adelina Patti, recorded that Napoleon III and Empress Eugenie headed the high society at Mlle. Hauk's first appearance in the completely filled opera house. "The little American girl," he said, "sang herself into the heart of the French." Old Daniel-François Auber, the king of the *opéra comique*, sent her his card with the penciled congratulation: "Bravo, ma chère enfant! . . . I am enchanted."[52] In time, audiences in every European capital overwhelmed her with applause. In later years, two California opera singers, Emma Nevada and Sybil Sanderson, were enthusiastically acclaimed in Paris. Miss Nevada's beautiful altissimo and staccato effects made her a brilliant star. Massenet described Sybil Sanderson as an "ideal Manon." He found her voice, with its range of three octaves, and her gift as an accomplished actress so impressive that he wrote for her the role of Esclarmonde in which she starred in 1889, under Massenet's guidance, at the Opéra Comique. Her performance in *Thais*, which he also created for her, elated him so much that he called it unforgettable.

It seems unlikely that such enthusiastic receptions could be surpassed. But this did happen the moment Emma Thursby sang Mozart's "Mia speranza adorata" in the Théâtre du Châtelet. And when on Sunday, March 23, 1879, she next rendered Proch's

51. Mount, *Some Notables of New Orleans*, 122–23.
52. Minnie Hauk, *Memories of a Singer* (London, 1925), 23, 43–46. When the neophyte starling sang several arias at a party given by Théophile Gautier, the young man who accompanied her at the piano was George Bizet. Mina Stein Curtiss, *Bizet and His World* (New York, 1958), 428.

"Variation," the audience and the press took this accomplished singer into their hearts. Miss Thursby, who declined all offers to sing in operas and who was the first American to be honored with the Commemorative Medal of the Société des Concerts of the Paris Conservatory, was as successful in Marseilles as in Paris. As one French critic commented after a concert: "The unpretending woman sang like a bird . . . pouring forth the full strain of unpremeditated art."[53]

A final example of famous American singers in Europe illustrates the capriciousness of public reactions that can swing from wild applause to pitiless condemnation. Marie Van Zandt's success as Mignon at the Opéra Comique in 1880 gained her a good contract and the social status of a celebrity. Parisian society went wild over her. Alas, four years later, when her voice betrayed her nervousness in a performance of Rossini's *Barber of Seville*, the public and the press treated the Texas-born star in a devastatingly cruel manner.[54] She regained her confidence and poise on other continental stages, and, upon her return to Paris in 1885, she was able to resume her successful career, but not without initially braving a mob of one thousand protesters in front of the opera building. It was open to question whether this large demonstration was organized to express resentment against foreign artists generally or disapproval of Marie Van Zandt personally. As Emma Eames, the Australian star who only after a wait of two years and with the help of her friend Charles Gounod was finally granted the privilege of performing at the Grand Opera in 1889, observed: "In opera, as in many other lines of human endeavor, there is a political background that is often black with intrigue and machinations."[55]

53. Henry C. Lahee, *Famous Singers of Today and Yesterday* (Boston, 1936), 230–55; see also Richard M. Gipson, *The Life of Emma Thursby* (New York, 1940), 203–10.

54. Lahee, *Famous Singers*, 215–17.

55. Emma Eames, "Personal Recollections of Charles Gounod," *The Etude*, XXXII (1914), 247. Occasionally, brilliant private gatherings listened to musical treats by American singers; see "American Singers in Paris," *DJM*, XVI (1859), 307; and Laura McProud, *American Students' Census* (Paris, 1903), 107–108.

Contrary to their overconfident notion that the United States could not compete wih Europeans in the field of the arts, experience gradually compelled Frenchmen to revise this opinion not only in regard to mastery of the performing arts, but regarding the manufacture of musical instruments as well. No American would have questioned the high quality of the carefully constructed and finished Pleyel pianos. Those Americans who could afford to spend between $200 and $500 were proud to own this famous French instrument, because of its sound and quality rather than as a piece of furniture as European cynics sneeringly suggested. It was a major accomplishment, though, that at the Universal Exposition in Paris in 1867 two American firms, Steinway and Chickering, won two of the four gold medals for pianos. The resonance, response to touch, and control of vibration of these pianos earned them these awards and a lasting reputation.[56] Many eminent violinists also acknowledged the great merits of American-made violins. Expecting that there would be no future for violin makers in America, Jean Baptiste Vuillaume, the renowned French master of this art, tried to dissuade his German pupil Georg Gemunder from going to the New World. Judging the market for musical instruments in America more confidently than his master, Gemunder followed his own judgment and, in the process, won a bronze award for America at the Exposition.[57] The remarkable vocal talent and vocational skill in instrument making that Americans demonstrated from mid-century amazed particularly those foreigners who entertained entirely erroneous notions about America's art potential.

In the nineteenth century the United States could indeed boast of few composers of any standing, as many Frenchmen loved

56. A. de Pontécoulant, *La Musique à l'Exposition de* 1867 (Paris, 1868), 37–40, 71–73, 229–31; E. Mathieu de Monter, "Exposition Universelle de 1867," *RGMP,* December 8, 1867. Acknowledging these great merits, Hector Berlioz sent a gracious note to Henry E. Steinway congratulating him for his outstanding contributions in the manufacturing of pianos. Berlioz Correspondence, Box 3, September 25, 1867, Columbia University.

57. W. S. B. Mathews (ed.), *A Hundred Years of Music in America* (Chicago, 1889), 347–48.

to point out repeatedly. Frenchmen took a particular liking to Louis Moreau Gottschalk (1829–1869), the son of a Creole mother and an English doctor in New Orleans. At the age of thirteen, he studied piano and harmony under the direction of such distinguished Parisian teachers as Karl Halle, Camille-Marie Stamaty, P. Maleden, and Berlioz. He had the good fortune, moreover, that a grandaunt from his mother's side, the Comtesse de Lagrange, introduced him to the highest social and artistic circles of French society. This helped him to mature both personally and intellectually, aside from providing valuable connections for him. But Gottschalk appeared to possess natural gifts that were destined to be recognized on their own merit: he had rhythm, imagination, and enthusiasm; and he combined a flare for individualistic expression in music with professional discipline. Some of his most successful pieces, *La Bamboula*, *Le Bananier*, and the two ballades, *Ossian* and *Danse des Ombres*, he composed at the age of fifteen. His themes embodied the Creole tunes that had become part of him and enabled him to introduce Europeans to American folk music and its Afro-Caribbean strains.[58]

His first concert in the Salle Pleyel, in April, 1845, was a great triumph for him. The artists, aristocrats, and connoisseurs in the audience felt, as Chopin phrased it, that they were in the presence of the future "king of the pianists." In the next season Gottschalk was featured with Hector Berlioz at the Théâtre italien and became the idol of Parisian concertgoers. Berlioz said of him that he "is one of the very small number who possess all the different elements of a consummate pianist"—a certain fancy, exquisite grace, boldness, and originality of playing that "at once dazzles and astonishes."[59] When Gottschalk played in 1851 in the provinces, he universally charmed his listeners. Newspapers in Bordeaux and Toulouse went overboard praising the rare combination of qualities this artist displayed: "talent, modesty, bounty, and gallantry." In him they discovered "the audacity

58. John T. Howard, *Our American Music* (New York, 1948), 205–10.
59. Chase, *America's Music*, 315–16.

and thunder of Liszt . . . tempered with the melodious sentiments of the German masters."[60] Théophile Gautier, the eminent critic of the *Feuilleton de la Presse*, flattered Gottschalk by crediting him with "an originality marked by good taste and a little eccentricity devoid of charlatanism . . . the two chief qualities in an artist of the true talent."[61]

Upon his return home in 1853, the composer and pianist who had been hailed by the European elite toured the United States and continued to be creative—composing, among others, his *The Banjo, La Marche de nuit, Le Chant du soldat, La Valse poétique,* and *Fantasy of the Troubadour*. Wherever he went, in New York, Boston, California, or Louisiana, crowds came to listen to him. Nevertheless, he knew and sensed that his essentially French taste conflicted with American predilections for German music.[62] It was revealing that he once told his friend, the piano teacher and composer William Mason, upon hearing him play Schumann: "I do not understand why you spend so much of your time over music like that; it is stiff and labored, lacks melody, spontaneity, and naiveté."[63] Identifying Gottschalk as a virtuoso lacking the one essential of a true artist, soul, his American critics seriously doubted that "his trivial though graceful fantasies were enough to place him in the rank of finely original piano-forte composers."[64] But many of Gottschalk's French friends begged him to return to France. The Comtesse de Flavigny even mentioned the possibility of his appointment as pianist to the imperial court. He declined all these suggestions, perhaps assessing reaction to him at home in an unduly pessimistic fashion. "It was painful to me," he explained, "to return to Paris, first theater of my great success, and confess that I had not succeeded in my own

60. Louis Gottschalk, *Notes of a Pianist*, ed. Jeanne Behrend (New York, 1964), 40–42, 55–56.
61. *Ibid.*, 53.
62. See notices concerning Gottschalk in *L'Art Musical,* IV (May 19, 1864), V (August 10, and September 2, 1865).
63. William Mason, *Memories of a Musical Life* (New York, 1901), 206.
64. *DJM,* XXI (July 12, 1862), 119–20; *DJM,* XXII (October 11, 18, 1862), 222–23, 230–31.

country."[65] Besides continuing to play his compositions, Frenchmen also honored Gottschalk's younger brother Gaston, a talented singer who had been educated in Paris.

Ernest Guiraud (1837–1892) also rose to professional heights that caused his birthplace, New Orleans, to be proud of him, even though he decided to spend his life in France. The composer of an opera at fifteen, the age at which he entered the Conservatory in Paris, he became in 1880 a professor of composition in this famous institution. Guiraud counted Bizet and Saint-Saëns among his friends and led a happy and musically prodigious life. The recipient of the Prix de Rome in 1859, he saw his life as composer and teacher crowned in 1891 by being made a member of the Académie des Beaux-Arts. Another native of New Orleans, Edmond Dédé, had even more reason than Guiraud to become an expatriate. A black man of Creole descent, he found the artistic atmosphere in Paris so stimulating and cosmopolitan when he was admitted to the Conservatory as an auditor that New Orleans did not compare with it. More influential, of course, in his decision to stay in France were the social limitations the racially prejudiced society of the United States set on his professional aspirations as a violinist. His talent and perseverance opened up opportunities for him in France that would have been unthinkable in the contemporary United States. In 1893, at the age of sixty-four, the honored composer and long-time conductor of the Bordeaux theater orchestra gave several concerts in his "hometown."[66] Practically a foreign guest then, the public and the press paid him the tribute for his outstanding accomplishments that would have been out of reach for United States citizen Dédé! To the credit of the editor of *L'Abeille,* he did not hesitate to praise Dédé in the most glowing terms, thus indirectly demon-

---

65. Gottschalk, *Notes of a Pianist*, 48.
66. John Smith Kendall, "The Friend of Chopin and Some Other New Orleans Musical Celebrities," *LHQ*, XXXI (1948), 873–74. For other French-educated American composers, see R. Hughes, *Famous American Composers*, 36–38, 357–58; Rodolphe Lucien Desdunes, *Nos Hommes et notre histoire* (Montreal, 1919), 117–18; see also the version translated and edited by Sister Dorothea Olga McCants, *Our People and Our History* (Baton Rouge, 1973).

strating the fallacies of race prejudices that would have denied this Creole a truly dignified and productive life had he lived in the country of his birth.

Generally considered to have been America's most accomplished composer in the nineteenth century, young Edward MacDowell (1861–1908) left the French Conservatory after a couple of years in the hope that the school in Stuttgart would permit him to develop his talents without the inhibiting restraints he experienced in Paris. His admiration of Richard Wagner and Edward Grieg allowed precious little appreciation for the music of such modern French composers as his former fellow-student Claude Debussy, or for Ravel and Vincent d'Indy.[67]

A composer by preference and a journalist by profession, William Henry Fry (1815–1864) spent the years from 1846 to 1852 as representative of the New York *Tribune* in Paris and London.[68] He was more in love with Paris, "that center of beauty, art, and bold thinking," than with the musical productions of contemporary French composers. In music, as in literature and the theater, he was convinced that there could be no great creations without great situations and plots. Since he was primarily interested in opera, he was rather disappointed that, as he believed, no truly outstanding opera had been written since Meyerbeer's *Huguenots.* Many of the musical celebrities in Paris with whom he was in contact, including Berlioz, disputed this contention. In France, Fry was often compared with Berlioz, another newspaper critic and composer who wrote music that was difficult to execute. Just before he left for Paris, Fry had completed his opera "Leonore" in the style of French and Italian grand opera. But when he tried to have it produced in Paris, the director of the Paris Opera turned him down, presumably because he feared that the French public

67. Elizabeth F. Page, *Edward MacDowell: His Work and Ideals* (New York, 1910), 24; Lawrence Gilman, *Edward MacDowell: A Study* (New York, 1938), 4–6, 73–75.

68. William Treat Upton, *William Henry Fry: American Journalist and Composer Critic* (New York, 1954) ; see also *RGMP*, June 17, August 12, 1855.

"would think me crazy to produce an opera by an American."[69] In those days the great cosmopolitan metropolis could in some respects be quite parochial. This attitude contrasted sharply with the keen French interest in native American compositions, folksongs, and descriptive music at the time of the Universal Exposition of 1900. John Philip Sousa's American Band then elicited universally the highest praise from leading musical experts in France. How much times and attitudes had changed was best evidenced by the comment of one member of the band of the Garde républicaine:

This is exactly the sort of music our countrymen want. . . . We are likely to perform music far too abstract, away above the heads of 99 out of 100 listeners. We get polite recognition, but we fail to stir the masses of the people to enthusiasm, as the American band does. Besides American descriptive music, the American band plays a classical repertory Chopin, Liszt, Beethoven—fully as well as we do. I feel certain that the example given by this American band will be followed by the majority of French military orchestras on account of the immense hold it obtains over the ordinary listener's emotions.[70]

Even the favorable impression made by Sousa's marches hardly justified the prophecy that America would in the twentieth century play a major role in the evolution of music. In part encouraged and assisted by French example, America made in the nineteenth century relatively slight progress in the field of music. In fact, it took this puritanistic and materialistic people a whole century to lay the foundation for its unexpected productivity in music.

The romantic period, which liberated every medium of artistic expression from the impersonal and formalistic aspects of classical culture, coincided with the golden age of ballet in the nineteenth century. The introduction of gas light in theaters in the 1820s and the desire of the rising middle-class to be entertained in novel fashion provided unprecedented opportunities for the populariza-

69. Chase, *America's Music*, 331.
70. "Sousa's Triumph in Paris," *Musical Courier*, XL (May 23, 1900), 14.

tion of the ballet. In the fantasy world of the bourgeoisie the ballet and the opera made life seem more delightful than its daily realities warranted. Defined by Théophile Gautier as an art that "is sensual refinement and delights the spirit," the ballet gave rise in the nineteenth century to the dominance of the ballerina, thus historically reducing the male dancer to an unaccustomed supporting role. The leading artistic center, Paris lived up to its reputation as the stage of magnificent dance spectacles. But in regard to originality and technique of ballets, it relied heavily on Italy and, in the second half of the century, on Russia, where the dancing genius of Marius Petipa was encouraged to the fullest extent.[71]

The famous ballet that became an exciting classic, *La Sylphide,* had been composed by Phillippe Taglioni. When his daughter Marie, dressed in a specially designed white skirt, appeared in Paris in 1832, her dancing delighted the viewers beyond all expectations. In about another decade Jean Coralli's *Giselle* permitted Carlotta Grisi, the ballerina who excelled in her graceful and stunning performance, to demonstrate the multidimensional potentialities of this exacting art form.[72]

Perhaps nothing could have illustrated these dimensions more dramatically than did the factional split between the Taglionis and the Elsslerites.[73] Taglioni's admirers were carried away by the serious, almost mystical and spiritual, nature of her movements. Fanny Elssler, the charming Austrian dancer, was literally more down-to-earth when she incorporated in her ballets lively national folk dances. The two ballerina rivals obviously symbolized different tastes in dance. Even if Marie Taglioni had come to America, it stands to reason that Fanny Elssler, who took a two-month leave of absence from the Paris Opera to tour

71. Walter Sorell, *The Dance Through the Ages* (New York, 1967), 137, 143–44; John Martin, *Book of the Dance* (New York, 1963), 32–34, 37.
72. Sorell, *Dance Through the Ages,* 138–40; J. Martin, *Book of the Dance,* 35–36.
73. Olga Maynard, *The American Ballet* (Philadephia, 1959), 18–19.

the United States in 1838, would have been the darling of American audiences. Her Italian, Polish, Spanish, and other national dances and her dynamic and somewhat coquettish personality won her such acclaim in the United States that, to the annoyance of the Paris Opera, she extended her stay in America for two years. Her success there may well have been more a personal triumph than an appreciation and acceptance of ballet *per se*. But that a foreign ballet dancer could arouse so much public enthusiasm that her young American admirers drank champagne out of her slippers or occasionally took the place of horses drawing her carriage made Europeans wonder how emotionally restrained and self-controlled Americans really were.

Since the 1820s public interest had been stimulated in the United States to make it worthwhile for primarily French ballet dancers to entertain Americans with their pirouettes and *danses sur les pointes*. The technical difficulties encountered by these artists, compelled to fall back on many stage improvisations and untrained support personnel, did not dampen their spirits or discourage others from traveling through the United States. In view of the fact that the classic ballet nevertheless remained a rather outlandish art in America, it was astonishing that even a few native Americans distinguished themselves in it. By coincidence, the most notable of them, Augusta Maywood, Mary Ann Lee, and George Washington Smith, hailed from Philadelphia and all three entered the limelight during Van Buren's presidency.[74] Smith, the first American choreographer and *premier danseur*, gained in his time a great reputation as a ballet dancer and teacher.[75] Miss Maywood, a child prodigy, received formal training at the ballet school of the Paris Opera and amazed Paris with "her little legs of a wild doe" capable of making "steps as long as those of Mlle. Taglioni." Her private life, however, interfered with her professional career, at least insofar as her

74. All three had been students of Paul Hazard, who had been associated with the Paris Opera before he settled down in Philadelphia in 1830.
75. Lillian Moore, "George Washington Smith," *Dance Index*, IV (1945), 88.

elopement with the dancer Charles Mabille terminated her association with the Paris Opera.[76] After several years of public performances Mary Ann Lee decided in 1844 to perfect her techniques at the ballet school of the Paris Opera, where Jean Coralli, the famous choreographer of *Giselle,* polished her style.[77] When she returned to the United States the following year, she produced in the leading cities in the East marvelous authentic versions of *Giselle,* Taglioni's ballet *La Fille du Danube,* and Carlotta Grisi's *La Jolie fille du gand.*

In the second half of the nineteenth century, ballet lost its attractiveness in America even more so than in Europe, where Petipa, and later Michel Fokine and Anna Pavlova, gave it a new lease on life.[78] At the end of the century, though, two American dancers gained a rather sensational international reputation. Loïe Fuller and Isadora Duncan introduced simple techniques that suddenly revived a catching interest in dancing. Miss Fuller's career as a dancer started accidentally; she did not prepare herself for it and, strictly speaking, she created more a fabulous illusion of dancing than bodily dance itself. When a friend of the young actress sent her a long scarf of thin Indian silk, she was fascinated by its floating power. Her artistic imagination was lively enough to conceive the idea of using this fluttering silk to convey dance motions. Her *Serpentine Dance,* as it came to be known, evoked an astonishingly favorable reaction in America. When the Folies-Bergère billed "la belle Américaine" in the fall of 1892, she took Paris by storm with her *Fire Dance,* another accidental discovery of the beautiful effect of lights on the colorful yards of whirling silk.[79] Henry de Toulouse-Lautrec

76. Lillian Moore, "Some Early American Dancers," *Dancing Times* (August, 1950), 668.

77. Lillian Moore, "Mary Ann Lee: First American Giselle," *Dance Index,* II (1943), 60–67; Maynard, *American Ballet,* 19–20.

78. Lillian Moore, "The Petipa Family in Europe and America," *Dance Index,* I (1942), 71–84.

79. Loïe Fuller, *Fifteen Years of a Dancer's Life: With Some Account of Her Distinguished Friends,* with an introduction by Anatole France (Boston, 1913), viii, 56–58, 126–27. See also Troy and Margaret Kinney, *The Dance: Its Place in Art*

captured the picture of "dancing flames" enveloped by silky "smoke" in his unforgettable lithograph of the "fire dancer." Anatole France admired Loïe Fuller's ability to depict, "with keen and brilliant stroke, the humble folk in whom she finds some ennobling and magnifying beauty"; and for the famous sculptor Auguste Rodin she "reawakened the spirit of antiquity showing the Tanagra figurines in action."

Through her deliberately natural movements Isadora Duncan tried to renew the art and beauty of dance and to make it more than merely a choreographic exercise. "The great fault of modern dance," she wrote, "is that it tries to invent instead of being satisfied with discovery," discovery of the rhythmic flow and soul of all living things and then translation of them into completely relaxed movement.[80] Her theories regarding aesthetic expression in dance were related to those of François Delsarte.[81] Both emphasized that the true form of expression was to be found in nature. Isadora Duncan was only twenty-two years old when she and her mother went to Europe in 1900, first to London and from there to Paris. Not knowing how and how long they could manage to stay in Paris, the serious and studious young dancer invited guests to a soireé in this charming way: "Miss Duncan will dance to the sound of Harp and flute in her Studio next Thursday Evening and if you feel that seeing this small person dance against the waves of an overpowering destiny is of ten francs benefit to you—Why Come along!"[82] An ever-widening circle of French society gradually began to take genuine interest in this phenomenal girl from San Francisco. Madame de St.

---

and Life (New York, 1935), 235–36. Emile Gallé, the outstanding glass-worker in France, applied Miss Fuller's light effects in his glass colorings. Claude Anet, "Loïe Fuller in French Sculpture," *AR*, XIII (1903), 278.

80. Isadora Duncan, *Ecrits sur la danse* (Paris, 1927), 27–29.

81. See Ted Shawn, *Every Little Movement: A Book About François Delsarte* (Pittsfield, Mass., 1954), 10–11, 82–84; and Virginia Elizabeth Morris, "The Influence of Delsarte in America as Revealed through the Lectures of Steele Mackaye" (M.A. thesis, Louisiana State University, 1941).

82. Irma Duncan, *Isadora Duncan: Pioneer in the Art of Dance* (New York, 1958), 3–6; Isadora Duncan, *My Life* (New York, 1933), 69–82.

Marcedu, wife of the distinguished sculptor, arranged an evening at her chic salon at which Isadora's dances propted the dramatist Victorien Sardou to express the pleasure of the company, exclaiming: *"Bravo, bravo, comme elle est exquise!"* Other such evenings at which she danced the music of *Orphée* or the waltzes and mazurkas of Chopin gave her the confidence and recognition needed to shape her future. One of her most successful dance concerts, she relates in her autobiography, was sponsored by the Princess de Polignac. On that occasion, the Prince, who deeply sympathized with her desire to bring about the renaissance of the dance as an art, accompanied her "delightfully on a charming old harpsichord." These innocently struggling years, preceding her international fame and final tragedy, were undoubtedly the happiest of her personal life. In the history of interpretative dance, she made her mark at a time when it was needed.

CHAPTER IX

Painting

Although in art, as in politics, the beginning and the
end of the nineteenth century reflected entirely different conditions in France and the United States, in both countries certain
prejudices about the state of the arts persisted throughout the
century. The joyless Puritan background of America seemed to
Frenchmen to be in sharp contrast to the encouragement the
Catholic church extended to the fine arts and music.[1] The lack of
a proud historical tradition in the arts and the overly materialistic
orientation of America's pioneer society, moreover, seemed to
hold out little hope for the development of the arts in the United
States, a few exceptions to these basic reservations notwithstanding.
Even indications of genuine talent and interest in the arts in the
United States did not hold such Frenchmen as Alfred d'Almbert
back from expressing stereotypical sneers about America's accomplishments in the fine arts. In his *Flânerie parisienne* (1856)
d'Almbert dramatized his offensive attitude with three blank
pages in his chapter on Beaux-arts en Amérique,[2] as if Americans

1. Louis Cons, *Les Etats-Unis de* 1789 à 1912 (Paris, 1912), 219.
2. Washington Allston recalled in the 1820s how annoyed he was when some
French artists, evidently unfamiliar with glazing, watched him copy a Rubens,
using the glazing process. These "French gazers derived great amusement from
my picture at my expense," he said, and told Vanderlyn that he "was in a sad mess."
Edgar Preston Richardson, *Washington Allston: A Study of the Romantic Artist
in America* (Chicago, 1948), 57.

neither produced nor cared for art. Certainly, as long as the rather ungracious and uninspiring American women failed to play a more active civilizing role, wrote another French art critic in 1855, "art will not take roots in the United States."[3]

American enthusiasm about European art collections revealed an appreciation that ran counter to these prejudiced notions. When the widely acclaimed preacher Henry Ward Beecher, for instance, visited the Louvre and the Luxembourg in the summer of 1850, he was so overwhelmed by the beauty of their holdings that he found himself "trembling, and laughing and weeping."[4] According to most personal travel diaries, a visit to the Louvre was indeed a delightful experience for American tourists. The humorous verse describing a legendary American sightseer in Paris caught the American spirit quite realistically:

> Mrs. Dick is very sick
> And nothing can improve her;
> Until she sees the Tooleries
> And gallops through the Louvre

Actually, such accomplished portrait and landscape artists as John Singleton Copley (1738–1815), Benjamin West (1738–1820), John Vanderlyn (1776–1852), Gilbert Stuart (1755–1828), and Washington Allston (1779–1843) justified an optimistic outlook on the future of American art. These Americans, who during the late colonial and early national period resided in England or France, had already achieved international recognition.[5] French refugee and immigrant artists around the turn of the nineteenth century contributed their share to the steadily growing ap-

3. Antoine Etex, "De L'Etat des beaux-arts aux Etats-Unis d'Amérique en 1855," *RDDM*, VIII (1857), 61–63.

4. Henry Ward Beecher, *Star Papers: Or, Experiences of Art and Nature* (New York, 1855), 56–75.

5. Yvon Bizardel, *American Painters in Paris* (New York, 1960), 81–86. A century later, a noted American artist described them as "second-rate painters of the English School." Kenyon Cox, *Old Masters and New Essays in Art Criticism* (New York, 1905), 144. On the influence of French art in America in the late eighteenth and early nineteenth century, consult Howard Mumford Jones, *America and French Culture*, 315–26. See also M. L. Welch, "Some Americans in Napoleon's Paris," *American Society Legion of Honor Magazine*, XXIV (1953), 25–41.

preciation of aesthetic values in America.[6] The realization of the ever-rising number of American tourists in France that their great republic fell far behind France in the cultural enjoyments provided by the arts also served as a stimulus in the United States.[7] From the middle of the nineteenth century on, a shift took place in America from the longstanding English influence toward a clearly French orientation in the arts. Henceforth, literally thousands of serious American students and artists were exposed to the changing techniques and styles of French artists.[8] From this time on, art schools, galleries, and artists' organizations, as well as special art exhibitions and a noticeable increase in private art collections, evidenced at least a heightened interest in, if not yet a flourishing of, the arts in the United States.[9] By the end of the century, a knowledgeable Parisian art dealer in New York cautioned one of his traditionally prejudiced country-men: *"Détrompez-vous, il y a ici autant d'individus que chez nous capables de connaître un bon tableau."*[10] To the regret of many struggling American artists, European art was then more widely known in America than were their own works.

In a modified form, American art had until the end of the nineteenth century been guided by European examples. American artists usually caught up with the major European changes in style, technique, and conception. As far as French influence was concerned, the succession of neoclassicism, romanticism, realism, and impressionism developed at least in a parallel fashion in the United States. It is also of historical interest that some Americans prominently contributed to this evolution, instead

6. Anna Wells Rutledge, "Artists in the Life of Charleston: Through Colony and State, from Restoration to Reconstruction," APS *Transactions*, n.s., XXXIX (1949), Pt. 2, p. 126.

7. Neil Harris, *The Artist in American Society: The Formative Years*, 1790–1860 (New York, 1966), 158; Durbin, *Observations*, 92.

8. Léonce Bénédite, "La Peinture française et les Etats-Unis," in E. Boutroux *et al., Les Etats-Unis et la France* (Paris, 1914), 73–88.

9. George W. Sheldon, *Hours with Art and Artists* (New York, 1882), 15.

10. "Make no mistake, there are as many individuals in the United States capable of recognizing a good painting as in France." de Rousiers, *La Vie américaine*, 644.

of merely passively adopting it. Unlike Jacques Louis David's neoclassical style in France, for instance, Benjamin West modified his neoclassicism in regard to color and conception by neither entirely abandoning the coloristic techniques of the eighteenth century nor concentrating merely on Greek and Roman antiquity. Paintings by West and Allston anticipated the coloristic style and dramatic themes of Eugène Delacroix, the distinguished leader of the romantic movement in France. Asher B. Durand's natural realism and his use of local color preceded rather than followed Gustave Courbet's realistic naturalism. And the imaginative attention to light and shadow in Allston's *Italian Landscape* and, above all, Winslow Homer's use of luminous colors occupy a significant place in the evolution of French impressionism.[11] The United States, appearing to strangers provincial and culturally underdeveloped, was in fact in step with the cultural currents of the century. The rationalism of the Enlightenment, the transcendental idealism of the romantic period, and the realism of the age of science manifested themselves in the United States as much as the unfettered individualism that in the arts of the Western world tended to break down the tradition of the unifying sense of society.

It was obvious, however, that the art of a country without strong artistic traditions would not evolve along the same lines and for the same reasons as would art in such an ancient civilization as France. American interest in the ideal of Greek democracy was far removed from French admiration of Greek and Roman notions of ideal beauty. While French romanticism was largely a critical reaction to the stifling effects of the neoclassical school, in expanding America, romanticism expressed primarily an optimistic affirmation of life and nature. The desire of French impressionists to use pure color and broken lines to

11. See Edgar Preston Richardson, *Painting in America: The Story of 450 Years* (New York, 1956), 88–89, 129–30, 142, 169–70, 312–13; Barbara Novak, *American Painting in the Nineteenth Century: Realism, Idealism, and the American Experience* (New York, 1969), 59, 88–89, 171–72; and John I. H. Baur, *American Painting in the Nineteenth Century: Main Trends and Movements* (New York, 1953), 24–25.

render their images went much too far for American tastes accustomed to linear visions. These different approaches and emphases reflected deep underlying differences between people inclining toward abstractions or facts respectively. In this context, the photographic camera enabled European artists to study the deeper reality of the picture, whereas for the American artist like Theodore Robinson, "the camera helps to retain the picture in your mind."[12]

Unfortunately, many American painters whose income depended primarily on portraiture were put out of business by the advent of the camera. Their difficulties were further aggravated by a public that preferred European over American painting. This preference did not seem to be affected by the steady flow of American criticism of nineteenth-century French art or by the great strides American artists had made in the second half of the century. The paradox of underwriting the development of native talent while snubbing its canvases apparently reflected the artistic pretensions of the rising American middle class.[13]

Nothing in modern history gave as much impetus to the public exhibition of art works as the opening in 1793 of the Palace of the Louvre. The thrill experienced by the view of its masterful paintings suggested aesthetic and artistic possibilities of universal interest. In the United States, Charleston, Baltimore, Washington, Philadelphia, New York, Boston and Chicago, the Massachusetts and New York Historical Societies, and such colleges as Harvard and Yale tried at the beginning of the nineteenth century to acquire facilities and art objects for public display. It was not until after the Civil War, however, that substantial progress toward the establishment of major American museums was made. The Corcoran Gallery in Washington, the Metropolitan Museum of Art in New York, the Boston Museum of Fine Arts, the Art In-

---

12. Novak, *American Painting*, 199.
13. French Strother, "Frederick MacMonnies, Sculptor," *World's Work*, XI (1905), 6968.

stitute of Chicago, and the Cincinnati Art Museum began to open their doors between 1869 and 1880. Primarily the creations of private enterprise and civic pride, these major art galleries owed their growth and many of their treasures to the generosity and good taste of an ever-growing number of private collectors. Many of them eventually donated their art treasures to public museums. In Boston, for instance, Quincy Adams Shaw bequeathed, in addition to some old masters and Corots, some 110 paintings and pastels by Jean François Millet to the Boston Museum. In 1893, Henry Field gave a rich collection of Barbizon and some Salon painters to the Art Institute of Chicago. And the Havemeyers of Philadelphia, whose acquisitions in the late nineteenth and early twentieth centuries were usually recommended by their good friend Mary Cassatt, enriched the New York Metropolitan Museum with a large collection of the best-known French impressionists and some paintings by Courbet and Paul Cézanne.[14]

Art collecting itself developed into an art in the sense that one had to become an expert connoisseur of paintings, as well as of painters. Familiarity with living artists and dealers on either side of the Atlantic was as essential in the art business as was an operating knowledge of the most fashionable auction rooms. By the 1840s a few American art collectors already made it a habit to attend such high-class sales rooms in Paris as those in the Rue Druot where occasionally owners or heirs of magnificent paintings were compelled to auction them off. This was one way Americans built up their collections. Such prominent nineteenth-century American art dealers and collectors as George S. Lucas, William T. and Henry Walters, and Thomas J. Bryan maintained extensive and very personal contacts with artists and dealers in France, either acquiring "old masters" or negotiating sales

14. See W. G. Constable, *Art Collecting in the United States of America* (London, 1964), 12–20, 31–42, 69.78; L. V. Coleman, *The Museum in America* (3 vols.; Washington, D.C., 1939), I, 6–15; and Walter Pach, *The Art Museum in America: Its History and Achievement* (New York, 1948), 40–42, 98–99. Upon inquiry, the archivist of the Metropolitan Museum of Art in New York has advised me that the Metropolitan "did not begin any correspondence with the Louvre until 1906."

on contemporary canvases.[15] Alexander Turney Stewart, an art-loving American businessman in Paris, built up a first-rate private collection of modern art. By the middle of the century, Goupil–Vibert and Company of Paris opened a gallery for the sale of prints and paintings in New York; the French firm of Georges Petit opened a branch in the United States; and a Belgian dealer operated in Boston a flourishing business in French and other European art.

In the final decades of the century, rich Americans, following the lead of the old European upper classes, invested heavily in the paintings and sculptures of famous European artists. Bostonians more than New Yorkers preferred European to American works, and at prices that simply amazed the French.[16] Dealers naturally took advantage of the profitable market, and at times they did not hesitate to pressure the artist to deliver paintings without the final finishing touches that normally improved their quality. In some instances, well-known French painters even signed contracts with their personal sales agents, paying them a commission of about 20 percent for every picture they sold.[17] Some enterprising dealers, anticipating a great future for the French impressionists, bought up their work.[18]

15. See "Gabriel Manigault's Notes on Art," in Manigault Papers, SCHS; George Lucas to S. P. Avery, October 16, 1865, in NYMMA; Charles Gabriel Gleyre to George Lucas, September 12, 1867, MS in Walters Art Gallery, Baltimore; R. B. Gruelle, *Notes: Critical Biographical Collection of W. T. Walters* (Indianapolis, 1895). Americans were indebted to France also for the development of lithograph techniques and daguerreotype. The resulting availability of fairly inexpensive prints helped to popularize works of art. John Thomas Carey, "The American Lithograph: From Its Inception to 1865" (Ph.D. dissertation, Ohio State University, 1954), 29, 45–46, 56, 223–24.

16. See Constable, *Art Collecting*, 40–43; Samuel Isham, *The History of American Painting* (New York, 1905), 208; Lois Marie Fink, "The Role of France in American Art, 1850–1870" (Ph.D. dissertation, University of Chicago, 1970), 178–248, 422; and William S. Mount to Goupil, Vibert & Co., December 13, 1848, in William S. Mount Papers, NYHS.

17. Francis C. Sessions, *On the Wing Through Europe* (New York, 1889), 266; Percy Mackaye, *Epoch: The Life of Steele Mackaye* (2 vols.; New York, 1927), I, 120–22.

18. Theodore Robinson to Kenyon Cox, July 3, 1886, in Kenyon Cox Correspondence, Box 3, Columbia University.

Significantly, American collectors who could not afford to purchase the works of the most renowned old masters built up French collections of newcomers whose artistic creations pleased them enough to justify their patronage and encouragement long before Frenchmen appreciated the talents of so many of their own nineteenth-century artists. At a time when Frenchmen still ignored or laughed at Antoine Louis Barye (1795–1875), Camille Corot (1796–1875), Thomas Couture (1815–1879), Edgar Degas (1834–1917), Edouard Manet (1832–1883), Jean François Millet (1814–1875), Claude Monet (1840–1926), Camille Pissarro (1830–1903), Pierre Auguste Renoir (1841–1919), Théodore Rousseau (1812–1867), Constant Troyon (1813–1865), and others, art-appreciating Americans extended to them their moral and financial support.[19] Acknowledging that "we [impressionists] perhaps owe it to the Americans that we did not die of hunger," Renoir attributed American broadmindedness with respect to the arts to greater tolerance rather than to better understanding.[20]

In later years, Frenchmen regretted that "the museums of the future" would be in America and that their modern collections would contain many French canvases that should have remained in France or at least have come back to be exhibited, instead of permanently being "buried" in America. When in the course of this "legal pillage" some American owners refused to loan paintings for exhibitions in Paris, French artists thereafter made it a point to insist on this right as a condition of sale.[21] A related though more fundamental question was raised by the action of an American lady who had paid Jean-Louis-Ernest Meissonier $16,000 for her portrait and then destroyed it because she did not like it. Did she have the right to do this just because she "owned" this picture? Whatever the property right, contended outraged Europeans, the art of a painter of Meissonier's standing

19. American Federation of Art, "Report of the Committee on Painting," *Art and Progress*, III (1912), 659; Albert Ludovici, *An Artist's Life in London and Paris, 1870–1925* (London, 1926), 45–46.
20. Jean Renoir, *Renoir: My Father* (Boston, 1962), 252–53.
21. Robert H. Sherard, "American Artists in Paris," *Magazine of Art*, XVIII (1895), 225.

"belongs to all humanity."[22] A delightful story, told by Renoir, raised still another issue. The art dealer Paul Durand-Ruel feared that American customs officials might object to the entry of Renoir nudes on the ground that in their judgment these paintings were pornography rather than art. Searching for a way to head off undesirable delays and complications, Durand-Ruel thought of a simple scheme that worked beautifully. One Sunday he accompanied the chief customs official to church and contributed generously and ostentatiously to the collection plate. Without a deal or a word exchanged about them, Renoir's paintings satisfied the customs' concept of art.[23] It is of course conceivable that the precaution the art dealer took in this instance was unnecessary, as well as slightly dishonest.

Perhaps the most embarrassing controversy was one involving the American tariff on French art, a by-product of the tariff war between France and the United States in the 1880s. After decades of the most generous treatment of American artists in France as students and competitors in French salons, French artists were hurt to see "their exports" to the United States sharply decline and also be treated as if they were "sardines in oil" or "smoked ham."[24] Alhough the tariff on French art in retaliation for French prohibition of American imports was eventually removed, it prompted more legitimate reproaches than an elightened government should have given cause to justify. This discrimination was of course aggravated by the fact that it did not apply to the works of American artists residing in France, thus giving these Americans, already aided by the prestige of their identification with Parisian art, a decisive competitive

22. de Soissons, *A Parisian in America*, 123–24. Having worked on his canvas *1807* for a decade, Meissonier "could bear the sadness of parting with it only because of his knowledge that the purchaser would take good care of it." J. L. E. Meissonier to A. T. Stewart, January 27, 1876, in NYMMA. Meissonier was indebted to Governor Leland Stanford of California for unsurpassed photographic studies of horses in motion. Vallery C. O. Gréard, *Meissonier: His Life and His Art* (New York, 1897), 77.

23. Renoir, *Renoir*, 254–55.

24. George W. Sheldon, *Recent Ideals of American Art* (New York, 1888), 32–35.

advantage. On the other hand, even as late as the final quarter of the century, Frenchmen would normally regard it as rather absurd to buy the paintings of American artists in Paris, regardless of their quality. As one American artist wrote in 1860, they "must sit and abide their time like the hungry spiders."[25] Still, French discrimination in art, no matter how snobbish, could not possibly be compared with America's temporary economic discrimination against French works of art.

Exhibition at the yearly Salon in Paris had throughout the century been an incentive for artists anxious to submit their paintings for critical appraisal and sale. In the second half of the century France organized each decade a universal exhibition that afforded artists of all lands the opportuniy to compete for recognition of excellence and originality and provided potential buyers with comparative choices on a grand scale. That the leaders of the Second Empire and the Third Republic lent their enthusiastic support to these exhibitions to promote the glory of France as the artistic center of the world disturbed at least a few members of Congress enough to make them oppose the underwriting of the American pavilion at these exhibitions.[26] Obviously France always dominated at these shows (of 1855, 1867, 1878, 1889, and 1900) numerically, if not in all respects qualitatively. By the same token, American artists in France and the rest of Europe were usually better represented than those who had to ship their canvases across the Atlantic.

A review of the American exhibitions substantiates the remarkable improvement from the pitiful showing in 1855 to the astonishing accomplishments by 1900. Still, throughout this period French critics regretted American dependence on European theories and practices, particularly English, German, Italian, and after the 1870s French schools. Time and again they deplored the absence of originality in American art. Even though Frederic

25. Christopher P. Cranch to Mrs. Sterns, April 19, 1860, in C. P. Cranch Papers, MHS.
26. For Senator Benjamin F. Wade's comment, see *Congressional Globe*, 39th Cong., 1st Sess., June 14, 1866, p. 3156.

A. Bridgman, Edwin Church, George P. A. Healy, John Singer-Sargent, James Mc Neill Whistler, and many others were awarded medals for the virtuosity, beauty, and eloquence of their works, all too many American artists exhibiting in a European show would have been identified more readily as of European rather than American origin.[27] Those who would have preferred to see American scenes relayed to the Old World in a bold and vigorous American style never doubted the Americans' ability to escape from their "voluntary imprisonment" in the arts. Their emancipation was merely a question of time. In the meantime, the international exhibitions at Philadelphia (1876) and even more so at Chicago (1893) confirmed the promise of American art and the continuing massive infusions of French taste. Earlier exhibitions in New York, of paintings by contemporary French artists, had already demonstrated the public's great appreciation of them.[28] Historically, nations developing new art schools have learned primarily from those already masters of art; the Romans learned it in Greece, the English in Flanders, the Americans in France and other continental countries. If in the case of the Americans there was anything strange about this natural development, it was their rather curious tendency to rely on the English for guidance in literature, but not in art.

The collection and display of works of French art in the United States probably influenced American taste in the second half of the nineteenth century more effectively than did the exposure of American students of art to their teachers in France. The presence of French artists in America during the formative years

27. For comments on these expositions, see E. J. Delécluze, *Les Beaux-Arts dans les deux mondes en* 1855 (Paris, 1856), 65–67; Paul Mantz, "Les Beaux-Arts a l'Exposition Universelle: Etats-Unis," *GDBA*, XXIII (1867), 229–30; Henry Morford, *Paris, and Half-Europe in '78: The Paris Exposition of* 1878 (New York, 1879), 318–43; Maurice Hamel, "L'Exposition Universelle: Les Ecoles étrangères," *GDBA*, XXXI (1889), 382–84; and Philip Gilbert Hamerton, *Art Essays: Modern Schools of Art—American and European* (New York, 1889), 3–4, 29–30.

28. For the exhibitions in New York in 1857 and 1859, see American Art Archives, microfilm P 41, pp. 199–216; see also *L'Illustration* (June 17, 1876).

of the young republic, and occasionally in later years, must be credited with vitally stimulating interest in the arts. Among the thousands of refugees from France and Santo Domingo who, during the era of the French Revolution, came to the United States were quite a few who earned their living and reputation as accomplished artists. Charles Fevret de Saint-Mémin, for instance, a painter and engraver who worked in the larger cities of the United States until his return to France in 1815, left a legacy of nearly eight hundred portraits of some of the most prominent Americans of his time. In Richmond, Virginia, Philippe Abraham Peticolas (1760–1843), a refugee from Santo Domingo, established himself as a popular miniature painter; and in St. Louis, François Guyol gained in the first quarter of the century a regional reputation as a portraitist. Lavigne, a well-reputed engraver in Boston; Anthony Imbert, the first lithographer in New York; Jules Marchais des Gentils, teacher of drawing and painting in Charleston, South Carolina, a city that attracted numerous French painters; and the collection of Jacques Milbert's picturesque drawings during his visit to North America in the first quarter of the nineteenth century set examples worthy of emulation.[29] For decades to come French artists in America benefited from the reputation French art enjoyed in America, knowingly or by hearsay. Among the better-known French artists who lived in the United States in the mid-century were the silhouettist Augustin Edouart; Hippolyte Sebron, who became known for his numerous pastel portraits and his *View of the Niagara;* Régis Gignoux and Adolphe Yvon, students of the historical painter Paul Delaroche; and Constant Mayer of Besançon, whose inspiring canvas of *Washington Crossing the Delaware* appealed to the patriotic sentiments of the American people.[30] Out on the Pacific coast, Jules Tarvernier's studio in Monterey, California, attracted in the 1870s and

29. See Fillmore Norflett, *Saint-Mémin in Virginia: Portraits and Biographies* (Richmond, Va., 1942), 55–64; John Hill Morgan, "The Work of M. Fevret de Saint-Mémin," *Brooklyn Museum Quarterly,* V (1918), 5–26; and Paul L. Grigaut, *The French in America,* 1520–1880 (Detroit, 1951), 23–24, 179–82.

30. L. Dussieux, *Les Artistes français à l'étranger* (Paris, 1876), 252–53; Louis Réau, *L'Art français aux Etats-Unis* (Paris, 1926), 103–105.

1880s many fellow artists, most of them born in France or of French descent, such as Jules Pages, Amédée Joullin, Ernest Narjot, and Sidonie Petetin, the then-noted woman painter. Their pictures of mining camps, Amerind life, and western landscapes decorated many contemporary homes.[31] On the southwestern frontier, Eugène Etionnette Lavender, née Auband (1817–1898), a first cousin of Guizot and a most promising student of Paul Delaroche and Ary Scheffer, gained a reputation in Texas. Once she and her family had settled at Waco, even the unavailability of paints did not prevent her from pursuing the art she loved so much. Preparing her own paints out of herbs and clay, she painted to the delight of many families to whom she gave her pictures. She was particularly happy to see her large painting of a saint decorate the cathedral at Corpus Christi.[32] Another artist born and trained in France, Théodore Gentilz (1820–1906), became a well-known painter in San Antonio, though isolated from the main currents of the art world. Louis Mathieu Didier Guillaume, a friend of Robert E. Lee's family, painted portraits of the leaders of the Confederacy. As Guillaume's portraits often deliberately flattered his subjects, Jacques Amans, an able French immigrant portraitist, sometimes improved the appearance of the ladies he painted by slightly elongating their torsos.

Amans (1801–1888), a student and exhibitor in Paris in the 1830s, belonged to the sizable group of portraitists and genre painters who found New Orleans a hospitable place to practice their art.[33] The simplicity of Amans' likenesses and his "delicate rainbow halftones in the skin shading" evidently pleased his

31. J. Biétry-Salinger, "The French in California: One Hundred Years of Achievement, 1850–1950," San Francisco *Chronicle*, November 16, 1950.
32. Virgil Barker, *American Painting: History and Interpretation* (New York, 1950), 400, 455.
33. Henry Woodhouse to Mrs. A. R. Troubetzkoy, May 14, 1930, MSS 2 R 5246, in VHS. On Louisiana painters, see Cara Lu Salam, "French Portraitists Who Worked in New Orleans During the Period 1830–1860" (M.A. thesis, Louisiana State University, 1967); Isaac Monroe Cline, *Art and Artists in New Orleans During the Last Century* (New Orleans, 1922); and Martin and Margaret Wiesendanger, *Nineteenth Century Louisiana Painters and Paintings from the Collection of W. E. Groves* (Gretna, La., 1971).

contemporaries. Although Alfred Boisseau (1823–1901), a student of Paul Delaroche, traveled to his clients wherever they resided in the United States, he spent several years in New Orleans. His *Marche d'Indiens de la Louisiane,* painted in the 1840s, is as much a historical document as an artistic treasure. Similarly, George D. Coulon (1822–1904), who came from his native France to New Orleans at the age of eleven, depicted nature, animals, and humans in such a variety of styles that his work also assumes historical as well as artistic significance. E. B. D. Fabrino Julio (1843–1879), is remembered for his painting *The Last Meeting of General Lee and Stonewall Jackson* and the shadow patterns in his Louisiana landscapes; and Paul Poincy (1833–1909), a student of the Beaux-Arts in Paris, who gained distinction as a painter of street scenes in his native New Orleans, did much to further local art. By arousing curiosity in daguerreotypes as early as 1840, Jules Lion (1816–1866), a French portrait and miniature painter of "superior merit," also helped Louisianians appreciate the arts.

On his visit to New Orleans in 1872–1873, Edgar Degas was so reminded of Jean Auguste Dominque Ingres' art when he saw the pictures of Jean Joseph Vaudechamp (1790–1866), that he took one of his well-drawn paintings back to Paris.[34] This highly reputed neoclassical portraitist found it in every sense rewarding in the 1830s and probably the early 1840s to paint members of New Orleans' leading families. The elegant style of this French artist and the accomplished works of other French-trained painters contributed significantly to New Orleans' reputation as one of the major art centers in the United States.

Among the most outstanding contributions to French painting in America rank Pierre Puvis de Chavannes' murals in the Boston

---

34. *La Peinture française*: *Collections américaines,* Catalog of the Exposition Bordeaux (Bordeaux, 1966), 56. See also Albert Krebs, "Degas à la Nouvelle-Orléans," *Rapports France–Etats-Unis* (August, 1952), 63–72. While visiting the New Orleans office of the cotton business of his mother's family, Degas painted a memorable canvas entitled *Marchands de Coton.*

Public Library, decorative masterpieces expressing "the Muses of Inspiration." Reluctant, in the autumn of his life, to undertake this challenging assignment, despite the for him unprecedented remuneration of $40,000, Puvis de Chavannes (1824–1898), parted with these panels with a heavy heart. "Never again," he reportedly confessed, "shall I accept such a task. I am like a father whose daughters are leaving him for a convent."[35]

If paintings reveal the personal feelings of an artist and his environment, then even the international roots of art can only cumulatively and in a strictly technical sense "influence" native artists. Even though American artists yearned for freedom from inhibiting foreign influences, as long as practically all facilities for thorough training in the fine arts were inadequate in the United States, the temptation to study abroad was irresistible. The long period during which English example and guidance dominated art in America came to an end in the 1820s. During the rest of the century most American painters preferred to go to the continent for instruction, particularly to France, Germany, and Italy.

Paris, the permanently fermenting art capital of Europe, attracted most of them. For one thing, unlike their English colleagues, French artists taught students without compensation. But far more important was the fact that in Paris were the best Venetian, Flemish, and Dutch paintings essential for the study of color. The regeneration of French art by such masters as Delacroix, Rousseau, Corot, Millet, Charles François Daubigny, and Troyon was a major attraction. Nor should one underestimate the challenge and value of the Parisian Salons to the individual American artist. Only temporarily, between 1870 and 1890, it became fashionable for Americans to be exposed to the training offered at the Royal Academy and ateliers in Munich. With the exception of Charles Carolus-Duran, the teachers in Munich paid more attention to effective brush-work than did those in Paris,

35. Ruth Clark, "Puvis de Chavannes," Boston *Transcript*, October 11, 1924; "Centenary of Puvis de Chavannes," MS in Boston Public Library.

who emphasized accurate drawing from nude models.[36] But the excitement caused by the French impressionists made Paris once again the undisputed Mecca of the art world.

The adventurous urge to go abroad and learn from past and present masters confronted American students with difficult financial and psychological challenges. Often unable to speak French well enough to get around, students suddenly finding themselves in the strange environment of the Latin Quarter were stunned. The practically uniform dress of painters—black silk cravats and velvet capes covering their shabby clothes—and the sight of sculptors in blue blouses and with long flowing locks were less arresting than was the air of superiority these people displayed. Somehow this attitude seemed to be irreconcilable with casual appearance and easy virtue that gave the colorful Quarter its spicy reputation.[37] But what surprised American art students and often made them most uncomfortable was "the outrageous behavior of native students toward American nouveaux." Americans were helplessly shrugging off the traditional treatment to which older French students subjected all incoming "freshmen"; but they resented being treated in a humiliating way. Several contemporary American observers themselves found French students "brutal and disgusting to a degree that would lead one to consider them convicts of the galleys." Trist Wood wrote in 1893, "The contemptible cowards attack the nouveau in a body whenever he shows the slightest resistance to their tyranny." Sometimes they set upon American students at the Ecole des Beaux-Arts for refusing to submit to their demands for money or to personal indignities. Erroneously

36. See Albert D. Smith, *European Influence on American Painting of the Nineteenth Century* (Huntington, N.Y., 1947), 27–29; S. Bing, *La Culture artistique en Amérique* (Paris, 1896), 16–19; and John Vanderlyn to Alexander Day, September 7, 1810, in John Vanderlyn Correspondence, NYHS. The diversity of French painters who did things "different from each other" delighted the accomplished landscapist William Keith, who had studied in Düsseldorf, so much that he decided to free himself from his "German style." Brother Cornelius, *Keith: Old Master of California* (2 vols.; New York, 1942), I, 42–43, 212.

37. George W. Norris Diary, September, 1898, PHS; Royal Cortissoz, *American Artists* (New York, 1923), 69–70.

assuming that all Americans were rich, they probably thought it was funny when the easel and stool of a newly arrived American "disappeared permanently" from the studio. J. Alden Weir, whose portfolio had been taken twice, accused these honorless students of stealing "anything they can lay their hands on." These tactics were designed to discourage foreigners altogether. For unlike their institutions and professors, French students would occasionally go so far as to suggest: "Let us turn out all Americans and foreigners."[38] They evidently felt threatened by them. The innate talent and earnest motivation of American art students earned them so much praise and recognition from their French teachers that resident students began to resent this competition from foreigners. Not only did examinations at the Ecole des Beaux-Arts become ever more demanding toward the end of the nineteenth century, Americans usually ranked among the top students in their classes. The more these Americans enhanced their prestige, the more frustrated felt their French classmates. In a speech that Whitelaw Reid, minister of the United States to France, delivered in May of 1890 at the inaugural meeting of the American Art Association in Paris, he referred to the presence of 1,500 American art students in Paris, nearly one-third of them women, despite the fact that French authorities frowned upon their presence in art schools.[39] Providing a homelike non-Bohemian meeting place, this Association strengthened the morale and esprit de corps of these young artists in a wholesome way. While the overwhelming majority of American art students were hard-working aspirants, occasionally a "wise guy" thought he could avoid the tedious discipline of drawing day after day from antiques or of copying the old masters by simply "pur-

38. Trist Wood to his mother, December 12, 1893, UNC, MS No. 800; Dorothy Weir Young, *The Life and Letters of J. Alden Weir* (New Haven, 1960), 22; Lloyd Goodrich, *Thomas Eakins: His Life and Work* (New York, 1933), 12–13. It spoke for itself that some American art students in Paris before the Civil War founded the "Out of Money Club" (OMC).

39. Edmund Henry Wuerpel, *American Art Association of Paris* (Philadelphia, 1894), 25–26; Lucy H. Hooper, "Art Schools of Paris," *Cosmopolitan*, XIV (1892), 59–62; and Ione Perry to Leona Queyrouze, March 20, 1890, LSU.

chasing" the secrets of the art. Paul Bartlett, for instance, knew such an "instant artist" who thought he could approach Adolphe William Bouguereau and tell him: "Old chap, I want to paint. Here is the tin. Show me the trick." This French painter, instead, showed him the door. Neither personal integrity nor mastery of the arts, as Bouguereau (1825–1905) understood them, tolerated such shortcuts.[40]

By the turn of the century, Americans had gained enough confidence to envision a future in which their training would no longer depend on rather costly and not always rewarding residence abroad. This aspiration, of course, did not preclude keeping in constant touch with the international art communities. For the large majority the experience of foreign training turned out to be a mixed blessing, because the acquisition of technical skills was merely a means toward a substantive end—a painting conveying a sentiment, an idea, a theme deeply rooted in oneself. Many American art students who returned from Brittany, Normandy, or Paris to the United States discovered differences in light, color, and picturesque scenes that even from a technical point of view did not admit reliance mainly on styles they had studied abroad.[41]

Despite French instruction and stimulation, American artists wanted to be neither simple copyists nor mere imitators of French painters. So-called "Paris Americans," as distinguished from "American Americans," displayed remarkable freshness and originality. As in medicine, so in painting, American students were flocking to certain French teachers because, in addition to their skill, style, and reputation, they respected the individuality of their students. Charles Carolus-Duran (1838–1917), Thomas Couture (1815–1904), and above all Jean Léon Gérôme (1824–1904) were known as teachers of Americans. Gérôme, "old growls and spitfire," exemplified the demanding and critical teacher

40. Consult Truman H. Bartlett's handwritten draft of his speech, "Sculpture in the United States and the French Influence," MS in container 24, Paul Bartlett Papers, LC.
41. Richardson, *Painting in America*, 279.

who did not permit his own views and methods to destroy the individualistic approach of his students. They valued his critical comments on the details and ensemble of their work.[42] It meant a great deal to J. Alden Weir, for instance, when Gérôme once commented on a portrait he had painted: "Ce n'est pas mal du tout, du tout!"[43] In time, students left Carolus-Duran's studio aware that the education of the eyes was ultimately more significant than the skillful application of the brushes. Kenyon Cox, who found Carolus-Duran to be "rather a snob," wearing tight pantaloons and an "elaborately curley" beard and mustache, nevertheless picked this fashionable portrait painter as a teacher because he felt he could learn much from him.[44]

The accessibility of most French masters to American students and artists, their willingness to be consulted and to criticize work freely and constructively often led to close friendships and to the genuine advancement of American art. Doubts regarding their artistic futures or vanishing confidence in their talent created psychological problems in American students that a word of encouragement from their French teachers could quickly dissipate. The personal closeness between many French and American artists went far beyond the bonds of professional fraternity. The friendship that developed between William Morris Hunt (1824–1879) and François Millet (1814–1875) is of course legendary. William James Stillman, who in the 1850s studied under Adolphe Yvon, the director of the Ecole des Beaux-Arts, cherished his friendly visits with Theodore Rousseau, whom he admired as "the greatest of the French landscape painters."[45] Daniel R. Knight (1840–

42. Kenyon Cox, *Artist and Public: And Other Essays on Art Subjects* (New York, 1914), 151–53; Will H. Low, *A Painter's Progress* (New York, 1910), 165–66; Trist Wood to his mother, December 8, 1893, and March 15, 1894, UNC, MS No. 800.

43. Young, *J. Alden Weir*, 33.

44. Kenyon Cox to his mother, December 18, 1877, and April 2, 1879; and George Becker to Kenyon Cox, May 15, 1883, both in Cox Correspondence, Columbia University. See also Charles Merrill Mount, *John Singer Sargent: A Biography* (New York, 1955), 32.

45. William James Stillman, *The Autobiography of a Journalist* (2 vols.; Boston, 1901), I, 163–78; Helen L. Earle, *Biographical Sketches of American Artists* (Lansing, Mich., 1924), 178.

1924) of Philadelphia, who in 1873 settled down in Poissy, had the good fortune of counting Meissonier his close friend and master. Julian Alden Weir (1852–1919), who studied for four years under Gérôme's direction, told a story that in essence hundreds of American artists experienced: One evening he met Jules Bastien-Lepage (1848–1884) at a restaurant where certain painters dined every night; subsequent contacts with this "earnest and sincere" painter of portraits and peasant scenes culminated in a lifelong friendship. Theodore Robinson's and John Singer Sargent's informal visits with Claude Monet and Mary Cassatt's genuine friendship with Degas also illustrate the numerous cordial and relaxed associations among artists of the United States and France.

Landscape painting in nineteenth-century France owed much to the inspiration of the two most splendid landscape painters of England, John Constable (1776–1837) and Joseph Mallord William Turner (1775–1851), imaginative masters in the art of using color to produce complex illusions and impressions of nature. When Constable's *The Hay Wain* was shown in the Paris Salon of 1824 and won a gold medal, it stirred its French admirers to greater naturalness and challenged classical traditions vigorously.[46] The Barbizon School, often associated with the romantic movement's opposition to classical conventions, was at best merely a branch of it. In a strict sense, the group of painters who in the 1840s had settled down in a small village near the forest of Fontainebleau did not constitute a school; nor were they merely ordinary landscape painters. Their closeness to the soil and the people who tilled it and the animals who lived on it inspired them to paint the majesty and dignity of life, regardless of its humble circumstances. Starting their paintings in the open air, they usually finished them in their private studios, relying on memory and impression of what they had "seen." Millet, Rousseau, Daubigny, Narcisse-Virgile Diaz, Jules Dupré, Charles-Emile

46. David Croal Thomson, *The Barbizon School of Painters* (London, 1890), xi–xii.

Jacque, Constant Troyon, Rosa Bonheur, and others who composed the Barbizon colony were more interested in nature than in form, in color than in perfection, in the message of their paintings than in the picture. Perhaps nobody symbolized the difference between the romantic naturalists and the neoclassicists better than Jean Auguste Ingres (1780–1867), who said "form is everything, colour nothing."[47] By placing art above nature, he denied the merit of the Barbizon painters' premise that one must learn from nature, not improve upon it. Nature, they believed, was too much attuned to the soul of man to be treated as a subordinate matter. Equally striking was the contrast between Ingres and the Barbizon artists in the choice of their subjects, the sumptous and immodest wealthy members of society as against the humble and God-fearing working classes. By comparison, the grandeur of the natural scenery surrounding them inspired the landscapists of the Hudson River School to concentrate on painting its colorful poetry.[48]

Though sometimes included in this Barbizon group, Camille Corot (1796–1875), whose landscapes combined a poetic naturalness with minute accuracy, was more akin to the Barbizon painters than actually one of them.[49] Simple in dress and cheerful in disposition, Père Corot loved to sing *mélodies champêtres,* the kind of song French peasants often sang on their way home from the field at the end of the day. In the middle period of his evolution, roughly from the late 1840s until 1860, the twilights of dusk and dawn fascinated him. The blackish green tones of his trees and the gray of his sky brought back memories of Claude Lorraine, the famous seventeenth-century landscape painter. Without intending to disparage Corot's genuine accomplishments and his "truly and thoroughly spontaneous representations of nature," some knowledgeable Americans detected weaknesses in

47. John J. Conway, *Footprints of Famous Americans in Paris* (New York, 1912), 126.
48. Baur, *American Painting,* 5–8; N. Ponente, *Les Structures du monde moderne* (Geneva, 1965), 86.
49. Regina Shoolman and Charles Slatkin, *The Story of Art: The Lives and Times of the Great Masters* (New York, 1940), 260.

Corot's use of color. Comparing him with Rousseau (1812–1867), they also noted his rather limited range of conception and treatment.[50]

As in politics, chance and coincidence have historically played a role in the world of art. The impact on the arts of the totally unexpected February Revolution (1848) suddenly challenged the powerful French Academy of Arts by establishing a broadly representative jury of artists for the annual Salons.[51] But while this change offered the Barbizon painters a better chance, it did not immediately gain recognition for them. This they accomplished ultimately with the help of Americans, particularly William Morris Hunt, the devoted friend of Jean François Millet. Hunt who in 1844 began to study in the atelier of Antoine Louis Barye, the renowned French sculptor of animals, also spent five instructive years under the direction of Thomas Couture. The very length of this association attested to its mutual satisfaction. In fact, for a time the two occupied a studio together and occasionally painted on each other's canvases so skillfully as to confuse even connoisseurs of Couture's work in their attempts to identify the authorship of these paintings. Gradually, however, Hunt developed doubts about Couture's methods and, though grateful for what he had learned, sought his further development elsewhere, very much to the displeasure of Couture.[52]

Going through the Salon one day Hunt noticed Millet's painting *The Sower*. He liked it so much that he went to Barbizon to purchase it from the obscure and struggling artist who had painted it. Thus began a friendship of genuine significance to both artists. "Millet's pictures," Hunt commented once, "have infinity beyond them. Couture's have a limit. . . . When I came to know Millet, I took broader views of humanity, of the world, of life. He took

50. George Inness, Jr., *Life, Art, and Letters of George Inness* (New York, 1917), 33; Wallace Thompson, "Richard Miller: A Parisian American Artist," *Fine Arts Journal*, XXVII (1912), 709–714.

51. Thomson, *Barbizon School*, 34.

52. Sheldon, *Hours with Art and Artists*, 101–104; Rose V. S. Berry, "William Morris Hunt," *Art & Archaeology*, XV (1923), 203–10.

his subjects from the real people, the people who have work to do."[53] In his paintings even a haystack suggested life. Of peasant stock, Millet was himself a man of the fields, honestly sharing the rugged and impoverished conditions of these rural people to whose labor and self-respect he dedicated his art. His tribute to *the* sower, *the* reaper, *the* gleaner brought out the humble nobility of these men and women, all living souls striving to exist with dignity. Aside from the artistic merits of Millet's paintings, many of his contemporaries in France erroneously saw in them a social protest; and Americans, enthusiastically introduced to Millet's works by Hunt and his friend William Babcock, appreciated their essentially democratic and religious spirit.[54] At a time when, with few exceptions, his compatriots looked upon his pictures as *"des tristes affaires,"* only a handful of his French and American admirers encouraged his work morally and materially. Hunt, "the mad American" who spread the word about "the greatest man in Europe," watched the master working in a cellar and worried about the deterioration of his work and health likely to result from the dampness. A friendly but basically lonely human being living in his own small universe, Millet was touched by the understanding and concern of this friend from America.

Although Millet did not formally take on students, he usually agreed to criticize the work of young American artists who came to visit him in Barbizon. Edward Wheelwright, for instance, took his chance in the fall of 1855, hoping that his drawings and studies in oil would persuade Millet to make an exception and accept him as a student, as indeed Millet reluctantly did for the next eight months. Since Millet was not in the habit of carrying on a conversation unless his visitor really had

53. William Morris Hunt, *Talks on Art*, comp. Helen M. Knowlton (2nd ser.; Boston, 1898), 87.
54. Helen M. Knowlton, *Art-Life of William Morris Hunt* (Boston, 1899); John LaFarge, "The Barbizon School," *McClure's Magazine*, XXI (1903), 595–97. Hunt and Babcock were witnesses at Millet's official wedding at Chailly. Etienne Moreau-Nélaton, *Millet raconté par lui-même* (3 vols.; Paris, 1921), I, 117.

something to say, he agreed to visit Wheelwright in the room
he had been fortunate enough to rent in Barbizon whenever he
had sufficient work done to comment upon. In time, however,
he asked the young American to drop in whenever he felt like
it. Kind, but keeping his distance, Millet criticized and corrected
Wheelwright's drawings, emphasizing time and again that "to
see things as they are is to draw." But to Millet "see things"·
meant more than mere visual perception; it meant to perceive
the beauty, unity, and genuineness of nature and to express a
sincere feeling for humanity.[55] As one of Millet's American admirers described his poetic picture *The Sheepfold:* "Into this
little picture there is painted such a great sense of vastness that
you lose all thought of dimensions and feel the real depth and
breadth of nature."[56] Wyatt Eaton, who came to the United States
from Canada when he was eighteen, was another American who
profited from Millet's example and conversations. In the summer
of 1873 and the autumn of the following year, Eaton managed
to become more familiar with the great master, spending many
an evening drinking coffee with the family or playing dominoes
with Millet when his declining eyesight no longer permitted him
to work by the dim light of a lamp. Millet taught Eaton that art
involved more than technique and color; without "a governing
thought eloquently expressed," he believed, art did not amount
to much. And as a distinguished Italian historian once defined
culture as "what remains after the facts have been forgotten,"
so Millet defined the evolution of a master painter: he must learn
and forget much before he can acquire perspective and command
of his own powers.[57]

Of the other Barbizon painters, Americans showed particular
respect for Millet's close friend Theodore Rousseau. When James
Russell Lowell saw some of Rousseau's paintings during his trip

55. Edward Wheelwright, "Personal Recollections of Jean François Millet,"
Atlantic Monthly, XXXVIII (1876), 257–76; Julia Cartwright, *Jean François Millet: His Life and Letters* (London, 1896), 156–61.
56. Gruelle, *Collection of W. T. Walters,* 3.
57. Wyatt Eaton, "Jean François Millet," in John C. Van Dyke (ed.), *Modern
French Masters* (New York, 1896), 181–89.

to Europe in 1855, he recognized the artist's "true love of nature and confidence in her." He admired Rousseau's ability to "make a landscape out of a little pool of water and a few reeds, just as she does."[58] Even though he may have concentrated too much on little details, he possessed the ability to render the grand harmony of nature in its own magnificent way. His oaks were "living monarchs of the forest that have withstood the storms of centuries." Americans who knew Rousseau and his accomplishments well looked upon him as the greatest French landscape painter. Displeased with the reception of his art in France where, he wrote, "an ignorant public and merchants dominate the scene," he was grateful to Americans who evidently shared with him the real joy of nature, "which consoles us for the misery and vanities of the world we live in."[59]

The popularity of French landscapists in the United States was as undeniable in the last century as their influence on quite a few American artists. The extent of this influence, however, could neither be specifically traced nor accurately determined. George Inness (1825–1894), for instance, who established a lasting reputation in France and the United States, remained an individualistic American painter despite the fact that he had carefully studied the works of French landscape artists with whom he had established personal contact during his stay in France in the mid-1850s. Though he admired the robust themes of Rousseau, the pastoral softness of Daubigny, and the inspiring sentiments in Millet's paintings, and though French commentators discovered in Inness' masterpieces the influence of Corot and to a degree even of Poussin and Claude, Inness' son expressed it well when he attributed the genius in his father's pictures to having come from within.[60] Various French masters widened

58. Norton (ed.), *Letters of Lowell,* I, 236.
59. Alfred Sensier, *Souvenirs sur Th. Rousseau* (Paris, 1872), 307–308; Ira Moskowitz, *French Impressionists* (New York, 1962), 17.
60. Inness, Jr., *George Inness,* 27–29; Réau, *L'Art français,* 112; Eugene Neuhaus, *The History and Ideals of American Art* (Palo Alto, Calif., 1931), 101–13.

his horizon, and he culled from their diverse techniques what he considered worthwhile. But Inness, who interpreted art as "the expression of the inner life of the spirit," an expression of one's "feelings," and who considered its function to be not edification but arousal of emotion, liked to convey in his landscapes the poetic spirit of nature. Benjamin Constant (1845–1902), the eminent French portrait painter, who met Inness on his visit to the United States in 1890, described him as a sensitive artist who "especially liked the evenings of autumn, the autumn of his native country. He brought out of it powerful works, full of emotion and painted in rutilant colors. He was always careful, however, to retain for all painting its special qualities of material and enamel, and never tried to put the essential qualities of either pastel or coater colors into oil-painting. Thus he was proceeding from Millet, Jules Dupré, and Rousseau, while preserving his original work."[61] Constant's appraisal of the *"magnifique"* work of Inness prompted him upon his return to Paris to recommend to Bouissart-Vallidon and Company "to buy all the Innesses they could get." A notable indication of changing times and attitudes, a Frenchman acknowledging the greatness of a nineteenth-century American artist! Less known in France than Inness, William M. Hunt strove to express rather solemn moods in his landscapes, in accordance with his observation: "When you paint what you see, you paint an object. When you paint what you feel, you paint a poem." Ever on the lookout for originality in American landscapes, Frenchmen reacted favorably to the paintings of the German-trained Albert Bierstadt (1830–1902). His conception and colorful execution of brilliant mountain summits and rather dark valleys appealed to them.[62]

So did the accomplishments of various other American painters. George Healy (1813–1894), one of the early American artists who made a name for himself as a portrait painter, went to France in 1834 when he was about twenty-one years old. His original

61. Inness, Jr., *George Inness*, 179–80.
62. Henri Kowalski, *À Travers l'Amérique: Impression d'un musicien* (Paris, 1872), 45.

vague intention of taking advantage for a year or two of the many opportunities available to artists in France ultimately developed into a pleasant and productive residence that essentially lasted as long as the reign of his patron, King Louis Philippe. Ignorant of the French language and customs when he arrived in Paris, he adapted himself so well to his new environment that he gradually felt completely at home in it. The very fact that he initially worked in Baron Antoine Jean Gros's atelier threw him into the midst of the quarrel then raging between the classical and romantic painters—a challenge between schools of thought that caught the greatly admired Gros in the tragic personal fate of loyally standing by the classical teachings of his late master, Jacques Louis David, and his personal proclivities for painting lively contemporary scenes.[63] As chance would have it, young Thomas Couture spent a short while in Gros's studio. One day, Healy later recorded, this fellow student "unceremoniously pushed me aside . . . turned over my sheet of gray paper and sketched the model. . . . The outline drawing was so strong, so full of life, so easily done, that I never received a better lesson." Couture, who remained aloof from the contemporary controversies about art, was admired by Healy and many others for his vigorous portraits and historical paintings. The close and lasting personal friendship between Healy and Couture was solidified by their respect for each other as artists and as human beings with a great sense of humor.[64] The depth and sincerity of Healy's friendship with the miniature painter Savinien Edmé Dubourjal further attested to human relationships seldom brought out in contemporary literature about French society. The somewhat older Dubourjal, able, joyful, and unselfish, possessed the admirable ability to applaud the success of others even when he did not find for himself the recognition he deserved. Totally impoverished in his advanced years, he was deeply touched by the

63. George P. A. Healy, *The Reminiscences of a Portrait Painter* (Chicago, 1894), 35–37.
64. Marie Healy Bigot, *Life of George P. A. Healy* (Chicago, 1913); George P. A. Healy, "Thomas Couture," in Van Dyke (ed.), *Modern French Masters*, 5–10.

assistance Healy extended to him as a matter of course.[65] Fortunately, Healy had been chosen by Louis Philippe to paint for the Versailles Gallery portraits of leading American statesmen. The king himself and such prominent French leaders as Guizot, Léon Gambetta, and Thiers sat for their portraits by him, and a gold medal was awarded to him at the Universal Exhibition of 1855 for his large picture *Franklin Before Louis XVI*; these experiences obviously added fortune to his fame. Temporarily, though, the revolution that swept Louis Philippe's constitutional monarchy into the rubbish heap of history and brought the short-lived Second Republic into existence, ended his fortune in France. Soon, however, he satisfied the middle-class tastes of well-to-do Chicagoans who had invited him to work in their flourishing community.[66]

As we have already noted in William M. Hunt's case, Couture's experience with Americans was not always as gratifying as was his relationship with Healy. Couture's influence on John LaFarge (1835–1910), a promising New York art student of French parentage, made itself felt in two ways. Couture encouraged LaFarge to study on his own and for a long time to copy the drawings of the old masters in the Louvre before practicing the art of painting. "Your place," advised the master in 1856, "is not among these students in my atelier. They have no ideas. They imitate me. They are all trying to be little Coutures." And Couture's methods quickly dissatisfied LaFarge, who objected particularly to Couture's use of color "merely as a manner of decorating . . . [the] painted drawing."[67] Already immensely interested in the question of the effect of complementary colors, young LaFarge wished to see "some scheme of colour-light that should allow oppositions and gradations representing the effects of the different directions and intensities of light in nature." His oil paintings and water colors attested to his keen interest in color-

65. Bigot, *Life of Healy*, 15–18.

66. George Catlin, the noted painter of American Indians, also found his profitable stay in Paris suddenly upset by the February Revolution.

67. Cecilia Waern, *John LaFarge, Artist and Writer* (London, 1896), 10–11.

light and minute detail. Historically, however, his incomparable reputation rested on his masterful creation of "transparent mosaics," colorful windows that decorated many churches in the United States. As the jury of the French Exhibition of 1889 acknowledged: "He is the great innovator, the inventor of opaline glass. He has created in all its details an art unknown before."[68]

As much as Thomas Eakins (1844–1916) enjoyed the benefit of the guidance of Gérôme and Léon Joseph Bonnat when he studied in France in the late 1860s, like so many other American artists abroad, he maintained his independent approach. He owed much to the discipline in precise observation and drawing that Gérôme fostered. And he respected this teacher who in later years was pleased to watch his former student progress far beyond his expectations. Eakins was indifferent to the controversies over painting techniques that excited the French art community; he concentrated instead on his own perfection by studying anatomy and sculpture, as well as the Spanish realists Diego Rodriquez Velazquez and José Ribera. With such a background, Eakins naturally shied away from the scintillating colors and broken lines of the impressionists. The theme and execution of his most famous painting, *The Gross Clinic,* revealed him as a master of shadow and light in interior surroundings in an age emphasizing science.[69] When the Pennsylvania Academy of Fine Arts, at which he had received his original training, honored him with a teaching appointment by virtue of his balanced and extensive qualifications, it hardly expected him to cause the stir he did with his insistence on drawing from life in the French fashion. In a strictly professional sense, he felt that nothing tested the skill of an artist more severely than the study of the nude, an opinion the directors of the academy left no doubt they did not share.

In the final quarter of the nineteenth century thousands of American artists and students were busily engaged in Paris and the French provinces, not to mention those who had gone to

68. *Ibid.,* 52.
69. Goodrich, *Thomas Eakins,* 48–49, 154–55; Charles H. Caffin, *The Story of American Painting* (New York, 1907), 230–31.

Germany and Italy. An article published in 1895 noted that more than three hundred Americans had exhibited in the Paris Salons,[70] and many of them had been singled out for honors ranging from "honorable mention" to gold medals and knighthood in the Legion of Honor. Not all of them remained in Paris or could for long stand the stifling discipline of the Beaux-Arts. Nor did all of them follow the mainstream of fashionable French styles. Daniel Ridgeway Knight, a student of Charles Gabriel Gleyre and Meissonier, for instance, and Charles Sprague Pearce (1851–1914), a student of Bonnat, successfully painted the peasant women of Brittany. Thomas Alexander Harrison (1853–1930), for a time a student of Gérôme and Jules Bastien-Lepage, chose to spend several years in Brittany devoting himself largely to marine paintings. Both he and his brother Birge, a student of Carolus-Duran and Alexandre Cabanel, were members of the artist colony at Port-Aven, Brittany. The French government recognized their talents by purchasing their paintings *Arcadia* and *November*.

Homer Dodge Martin (1836–1897), who between 1879 and 1887 spent several happy years at Villerville, Normandy, and in Brittany, was originally drawn to the art of the Barbizon painters, only to shift in later years toward the more colorful and sophisticated techniques of the impressionists. According to Mrs. Martin's explanation, the natural scenery of Normandy moved her husband as much in this direction as the ideas of the avant-garde artists: "All this external loveliness which helps to endear their native soil to men," she wrote, "is here in full perfection—the blue sea stretching to the horizon or limited by the rosy gray of headlands and the purple of distant shores—the spread of flowery meadows—the shadow of graceful trees."[71] French critics ranked Martin's Normandy landscape *The Old Church of Criqueboeuf* among the truly outstanding landscapes painted by an American. Americans and French alike admired his

70. Sherard, "American Artists in Paris," 226–27.

71. Frank Jewett Mather, Jr., *Homer Martin: Poet in Landscape* (New York, 1912), 47; Louis Gillet, "L'Art aux Etats-Unis," in André Michel (ed.), *Histoire de l'art* (8 vols.; Paris, 1905–29), VIII, 1144.

masterpiece, the delightful view of the Seine caught in *The Harp of the Winds* (1895).

To cite only a few more, Paris readily saluted such gifted Americans as Frederic A. Bridgman (1847-1927), another of Gérôme's students, who gradually shifted from painting Breton subjects to Algerian scenes and whose distinguished works eventually placed him "hors concours"; the portraitist John W. Alexander (1856-1915), whose "originality both in conception and execution" offered a refreshingly charming sight; Walter Gay (1856-1937), an officially honored painter of French peasant life; and Childe Hassam (1859-1935), the American impressionist who gained distinction at the Paris Exhibitions of 1889 and 1900.

Some ingenious and talented American women resented the French academies' closed doors for members of their sex. Determined to receive the art education she desired, Elizabeth Gardner, of Exeter, New Hampshire, disguised herself as a man in order to be admitted to the Julien Academy in Paris. Eventually, she confided her secret to one of her teachers, who not only helped her win the battle for equal treatment of women by the academy, but also became her husband.[72] Madame Elizabeth Gardner Bouguereau (1851-1922), whose painting *Impudence* earned her a gold medal in 1889—admitting her paintings to future Salons "hors concours"—blazed a trail for French and American women that was soon used by another American girl, Elizabeth Nourse (1860-1938), a descendent of a Huguenot family, who hailed from Cincinnati, Ohio. Soon after she entered the atelier of Julien in 1888 her teachers recognized her extraordinary drawing ability and recommended that she chart her own course. When Puvis de Chavannes, one of the founders of the Société Nationale des Beaux-Arts, congratulated her in 1895 on

72. Earle, *Biographical Sketches,* 54. In one highly regarded atelier in Paris several women worked side by side with men. One of them, an American woman, expressed the matter-of-fact attitude: "If a woman wants to paint strong and well like a man, she must go through the same training. . . . There is no sex here: the students, men and women, are simply painters." Albert Rhodes, *The French at Home* (New York, 1875), 173-76.

the occasion of her appointment as an associate of this new Salon, of which she ultimately became a full member, Miss Nourse was the first American to receive such an honor. Her paintings *Good Friday* and *The Family Meal*, executed in beautiful color and with firm strokes, revealed the spiritual quality of her art.[73]

Interestingly, another contemporary American artist in Paris, Henry Ossawa Tanner (1859–1937), also emphasized spirituality in his magnificent work. "There is breadth, a generosity, an absolute cosmopolitanism about her [France's] recognition of the fine arts which bars no nationality, no race, no school or variation of artistic method."[74] Thus spoke the American artist who was invited twice to the Elysée to dine with the president of the French Republic; who was honored as chevalier of the Legion of Honor; and whose paintings *The Resurrection of Lazarus* and *Christ and the Disciples at Emmaus* were purchased by the French government to be exhibited at the Luxembourg Museum. Depressed by the racial affronts his father, "an exceedingly sensitive" Methodist minister, had to endure in the United States, Henry O. Tanner escaped a similar fate by going in 1891 to France where he entered the Julien Academy.[75] There, learning and working, he struggled for many years. His great talents and serious search for expressing his somewhat mystical thoughts in a highly individualistic art form were vitally encouraged by the "honorable mention" the Salon of 1896 awarded his painting *Daniel in the Lion's Den*.[76] His tireless courage, sense of perfection, and abiding faith carried him to the position of distinction he achieved during his lifetime. Even the critics in the United States, who had ignored

73. Anna Seaton Schmidt, "The Paintings of Elisabeth Nourse," *International Studio*, XXVII (1906), 247–54; Keyzer, "American Artists in Paris," 251. Following her successful exhibition of six paintings at the Salon of the Champ de Mars (1896), Cecilia Beaux, a Philadelphian of French descent and former student of the Académie Julien, was elected to an associate membership in the Société Nationale des Beaux-Arts; Earle, *Biographical Sketches*, 37–38.

74. "Afro-American Painter Who Has Become Famous in Paris," *Current Literature*, XLV (1908), 405–408.

75. See Henry O. Tanner Papers, Microfilm No. D 306, AAA.

76. H. O. Tanner, "The Story of an Artist's Life," *World's Work*, XVIII (1909), 11,772.

this Negro painter for a long time, praised him highly after France had honored his remarkable achievements. The subtle half-tones of this master of religious paintings, his beautifully poetic and deep reverence led a French critic to observe: "I find in his talent something of the genius of Rembrandt. . . . The compositon of his pictures is veiled, being indicated less by distinct and precise drawing than by the play of lights and shadows."[77]

What French critics of American culture had long been missing, a native talent painting American scenes in a refreshingly Yankee manner, they finally discovered in Winslow Homer (1836–1910). From the moment that this authentic Yankee exhibited in Paris in 1867, he attracted attention. And the fulfillment of his promise in later years came like a welcome breeze from the Maine coast. If Homer won merely praise, but no medals in 1867, it must be understood that he was at that time less known than Frederic E. Church (1826–1900), whose landscapes the Goupils had been making available to the French public. Formal French recognition of Homer's greatness came late in his life. Of the four oil paintings he exhibited at the Paris Exposition of 1900, *A Summer Night* earned him a gold medal and the honor of its purchase for the Luxembourg.[78] Homer's hunting and fishing paintings vividly depicted the struggle between man and nature, and his fascinating marine canvases demonstrated his masterful treatment of water. Like many other great artists, he led a relatively withdrawn life. There was no trace of eccentricity in his private life or in his paintings. Nor could any master or school claim him as evidence of their influence.

These characteristics, however, did not halt controversy about the foreign influences in his art. Three schools of thought have advanced different interpretations with respect to it. William Howe Downes (1911) found no evidence of French influence in Homer's works, despite the fact that in 1867 he had made mental

77. "Afro-American Painter," 406–407.
78. William Howe Downes, *The Life and Works of Winslow Homer* (Boston, 1911), 57, 207; Novak, *American Painting*, 166–77.

notes in the Louvre and had visited many French art exhibitions. Half a century later, Albert T. E. Gardner (1961) challenged this oversimplification with a much more sophisticated argument.[79] Gardner would not accept the unflattering notion that as perceptive an observer as Homer could for a whole year be exposed to a great many artists with different styles and techniques without being affected by them. Gardner's theory was further supported by the fact that in Paris Homer ran into his old friend Joseph Foxcroft Cole, whose familiarity with the leading personalities and developments in the French art world made him an exceptionally well-informed guide. Gardner noted, moreover, a difference in Homer's style of painting following his stay in France. Even the landscapes the rugged American individualist had painted in France, *A French Farm* and *Girl with Pitchfork,* suggested a slight influence, not of the recognized contemporary French elite, but of the avant-garde led by Manet. The paintings Manet and the Japanese had exhibited at the Universal Exposition in 1867 broke so much with Western traditions that no one taking an interest in the arts could have been left untouched by them. Finally, the large exhibition of modern British watercolors afforded Homer a splendid opportunity to bring himself up-to-date in a medium in which he wished to perfect himself. Lloyd Goodrich (1944) and Edgar Preston Richardson (1956) [80] have presented the quite realistic third possibility that Homer, though familiar with various foreign painting practices, as well as with Michel Eugène Chevreul's color theory and the new brilliant

79. Albert Ten Eyck Gardner, *Winslow Homer, American Artist*: *His World and His Work* (New York, 1961), 89–93, 102, 112, 116. It is noteworthy that in 1908 John LaFarge called to public attention "the inevitable teachings" Winslow Homer had received from the lithographs of a few Millets available in the United States in the 1850s; John LaFarge, *The Higher Life in Art*: *A Series of Lectures on the Barbizon School in France* (New York, 1908), 172–73.

80. Lloyd Goodrich, *Winslow Homer* (New York, 1944), 37–42. Charles S. Sawyer noted in his essay, "Naturalism in America," that Homer's illustrations for *Harper's* and *Every Saturday* in the 1860s suggest his familiarity with the work of contemporary French painters. Sawyer singled out Eakins and Homer as the two American painters who "present the closest parallel to the French naturalists of their time." George Boas (ed.), *Courbet and the Naturalist Movement* (Baltimore, 1938), 118–21.

chemical paints, developed his own style independently and merely chanced to parallel certain impressionistic developments in Europe. His close observation of nature, his robust vision of man and nature, and his imaginative exploration of *plein-airisme* shaped his vigorous, realistic, and colorful style. Trying to capture the vibrations and colors of the sea and the varying shades of light, he studied them searchingly. Significantly, he wrote to his brother in 1895: "The sun will not rise, or set, without my notice, and thanks." His solidly realistic art had matured as the result of his study of nature and his exposure to the latest subtleties and techniques of French and British artists and Japanese prints. He followed none of them specifically, but absorbed and integrated a trace of each of them.

One could hardly imagine a greater contrast than that between Winslow Homer and James Abbott McNeill Whistler (1834–1903). Contemporaries in a changing art world, Homer, the robust Yankee to whom affectation was alien, differed sharply from Whistler, the refined color symphonist and elegant bohemian. But they had also certain characteristics in common. Both were motivated by a burning desire for originality and independence. Whistler, whose paintings were appropriately identified by a tiny butterfly, was, as an artist, as much a loner as Homer, only in a different style. And as a human being, he was probably more lonely than Homer, in spite of his outwardly fascinating social life. At least Homer had struck deep psychological and geographic roots in his homeland. Whistler, born in New England, spent part of his boyhood in Russia, studied and frequently painted in France, established his adult living base in London, and traveled back and forth between England and the continent. An American artist by birth only, this cosmopolitan artist lived his adult life abroad. In Europe he maintained a close relationship with certain French literati who applauded him, and he kept in touch with the art world in Paris, which received his unorthodox paintings with more mixed feelings than the English. On balance, he was engaged in a lifelong search for the most satisfying expression of beauty, a search that taught him to rely principally on himself and more on Velazquez and Japanese art than on the avant-garde painters of France.[81]

Officially discharged from the Military Academy at West Point for "deficiency in chemistry," Whistler spent a year as a navy cartographer in Washington, D.C., acquiring skills in etching and engraving that later proved very useful. When barely of age in 1855, he went to Paris where, two years later, he entered the studio of Charles Gabriel Gleyre (1808–1874), one of the most influential art figures in the French capital. Known in the Latin Quarter as a swinger, young Whistler enjoyed his early student years in a carefree fashion. He liked to live it up lavishly when he had money, and he smiled at poverty which seemed to put him in an ingeniously creative mood. Despite his merely occasional class attendance, Whistler had mastered the fundamentals of painting by the time he left Gleyre's studio. If nothing else, he had been thoroughly indoctrinated to remember that the tonality of a canvas should be determined at the very outset.[82] Many other lessons he learned in the Louvre whose collections of the great masters made it an artist's paradise as well as the most convenient place for meeting fellow artists. It was there that he became acquainted with the engravers Felix Joseph Auguste Bracquemond and Alphonse Legros and many other French painters, sculptors, and engravers who engaged him in stimulating discussions about the best approaches to art. While at first he shied away from controversies, he and his friends Degas and Henri Fantin-Latour gradually drifted toward the new realism in painting that Courbet was advocating in defiance of the classical and romantic traditions. Manet also belonged to this group of young rebels whose ever-widening circle included some of the best-known future impressionists. These associations constituted only passing phases in Whistler's evolution. Initially, though, they

81. Never reluctant to be outspoken, Whistler told Degas in 1883 that "there wasn't an artist in Paris." Wayne Andrews and Garnett McCoy, "Realists and Mystics, 1860–1900," *Art in America* (August-September, 1965), LIII, 63.

82. Eugene Matthew Becker, "Whistler and the Aesthetic Movement" (Ph.D. dissertation, Princeton University, 1959), 11–23; E. R. and J. Pennell, *The Life of James McNeill Whistler* (2 vols.; London, 1908), I, 48–58.

were important and helpful. Fantin-Latour's contribution to his technical perfection and the moral support Courbet rendered the "petit Américain" when the jury of the 1859 Salon rejected his picture *At the Piano* attest to the early influences on Whistler's career. If his formal instruction in art taught Whistler the much-needed lesson of balancing imagination and discipline, Courbet's brush stroke and realistic effects originally impressed him considerably. By 1860, however, he had already begun to reject Courbet's "damned realism" and to be influenced by others only to the extent that his personal concepts of art found tolerable.[83] Art, he became convinced, involved interpretation, not a photocopy of nature. Foreshadowing the direction in which he intended to move, he contended that "a painting in which the subject dominates is the antithesis of art. A painter is attraced by the colored harmony of the ensemble."[84] But if to find this harmony meant to disregard the rules of painting, Whistler was perfectly willing to accept Courbet's defiant opinion as realistic advice.

In the early 1860s Whistler and some of his friends hiked through many provinces of *la belle France* and while on the road he painted typical French scenes and characters. When he decided to engrave his *French Set,* his friend Carolus-Duran introduced him to Delâtre's shop in the rue St. Jacques in Paris, in which Bracquemond had by chance come across the album of Katsushika Hokusai, the renowned master of Japanese color prints.[85] Whistler's enchantment with Japanese art subsequently became one of the important elements in the evolution of his own style. Eventually, it overshadowed the reputation he was beginning to gain in Paris as an accomplished etcher and engraver. The appearance, moreover, in the Salon des Refusés (1863) of his strangely charming *Girl or Symphony in White No. 1,* which, together with Manet's *Déjeuner sur l'herbe,* caused a sensational

83. Elisabeth L. Cary, "French Influences in Whistler's Art," *The Scrip,* I (1906), 312–26; Theodore Duret, *Whistler* (Philadelphia, 1917), 21; Léonce Bénédite, "Whistler," *GDBA,* XXXIII (1905), 403–10; and Horace Gregory, *The World of James McNeill Whistler* (Freeport, N.Y., 1969), 66, 85–86.

84. F. Cabot, L. M. Michon, and C. Charrier, *L'Art et les artistes* (Paris, 1937), 304–305.

85. Bizardel, *American Painters in Paris,* 142.

stir in Parisian art circles, focused attention on this promising heretic.[86] It was perhaps heightened by Whistler's decision not to send paintings to the Paris Salon until its jury system had been liberalized in 1881 by the new rules inaugurated by the Société des Artistes Français. The Salon of 1883 to which he submitted a painting already in his possession for a decade, the portrait of his mother, awarded him a medal for it. The combination of the surface harmony of this painting and its tonality in the manner of Velazquez made it a masterpiece. Reviewing this painting in the prestigious *Gazette des Beaux-Arts,* Charles Bigot found its peaceful dignity most impressive. Though previously not an admirer of Whistler, Bigot then felt impelled to acknowledge "his sincerity, will power, patient observation, and artistic conscience." Theodore Duret attributed the lasting success of Whistler's *Mother* to the immense appeal evoked by its simplicity and artistic mastery.[87] Finally officially recognized in Paris, he also began to be recognized in England where his work had been exhibited throughout the 1870s.

Although Whistler ignored the Paris Salon during this decade, Durand-Ruel exhibited the American's works in the rue Lafitte. How anxiously Whistler awaited French reaction to his canvases is evidenced by a letter he sent in 1873 from London to his friend George Lucas, an American art collector in Paris. These paintings, he wrote, "are intended to indicate slightly to 'those to whom it may concern' something of my theory in art—the *science* of color and *picture pattern* as I have worked it out for myself during these years." He asked Lucas to "fight any battles for me about them with the painter fellows you may find opposed to them—of whom by the way there will doubtless be many." He was also concerned about the total unity of his paintings, the canvas, the

86. Paul Mantz, "Le Salon de 1863: Peinture et sculpture," *GDBA,* XV (1863), 60–61; Jerome Mellquist, *The Emergence of American Art* (New York, 1942), 9.

87. Duret, *Whistler,* 100–105; Charles Bigot, "Le Salon de 1883," *GDBA,* XXVIII (1883), 10–11. By 1891, the year in which the French government bought this portrait, he had already been made a chevalier of the Legion of Honor. The highest French honor, however, membership in the Academy of Fine Arts, was not bestowed upon him.

name given it alluding to his theory of painting, and even the carefully designed frames "carrying on the particular harmony throughout." He wished it to be known in Paris that he was "the inventor of all this kind of decoration in color in the frames" so that not "a lot of clever little Frenchmen" would trespass on his ground.[88] When his *Arrangement in Black No. 5* was about to be displayed by the House of Goupil in Paris, Whistler, apparently concerned in London, asked the critic Theodore Duret to check whether the varnish had "bloomed" and covered the picture "with a sort of nasty thick blue veil." In that case, he wanted it to be gently rubbed "with a soft silk handkerchief and afterwards when it is hung in the Salon, just before opening . . . to be varnished again." And once again, with all his outward reassurance betraying an inner insecurity, he begged Duret to write him a long letter "and tell me if you are still pleased with your Godchild—for after all you know it is you who have fathered this black 'harmony!'"[89]

One of the remarkable aspects in Whistler's career, his friendship with Stephane Mallarmé and his enthusiastic acceptance by Baudelaire and Verlaine, had significant bearing on his place in the art world.[90] The painter who was not moving along the mainstream of contemporary French art discovered a mutual affinity with the symbolist poets of France who invited him to their weekly Tuesday meetings at Verlaine's home. Whistler and these poets loved the misty twilight, "the suggestion of mystery," and the dreamy sentiment of the soul. It also was no coincidence that Debussy, a participant in this group of "mardistes," admired the American whose search for beautiful tones and perfect harmonies in his color symphonies, arrangements, and nocturnes touched familiar chords.[91]

88. James McNeill Whistler to George Lucas, January 18, 1873, in Walters Art Gallery, Baltimore.

89. James Abbott McNeill Whistler to Theodore Duret, undated, in NYMMA.

90. Mallarmé published Whistler's "Ten O'Clock" lecture in French.

91. James Laver, *Whistler* (New York, 1930), 260–65; Simone Olivier Wormser, "Whistler: Peintre protée" (Ph.D. dissertation, Université de Paris, 1955), 70–72, 82–90.

Despite these ties, French symbolists ultimately found Vincent Van Gogh, Cézanne, and Paul Gauguin more genuinely expressive of their ideas than Whistler. Similarly, his naturalist background made him less an impressionist than superficially he appeared to be. On balance, his influence on French art was minimal, as was its influence on his mature works. His solid English base and his intimate familiarity with developments in France, however, made him an ideal link between the cross-Channel art cultures. Whistler had been too individualistic and curious about art everywhere to be classified simply. As Degas aptly put it, Whistler "has really found a personal note," perhaps "excessively subtle, but of a quality."[92] There was more than ironic conceit in the arrogant response Whistler reportedly made to an admirer who told him that there were only two painters, Whistler and Velazquez: "Why drag in Velazquez?"[93] He formed no school, nor was he the product or apostle of any particular one. Nevertheless, he secured a permanent place for himself in the history of art.

The last in the periodically changing painting styles in nineteenth-century France, impressionism, must be attributed to a genuine urge to be original. Applying the latest optical research in France and the United States with respect to colors and light and exploring the unprecedented availability of chemically produced paints in a variety of bright colors, a few imaginative French artists literally opened up new vistas. It is conceivable, as Hassam has contended, that Turner and Constable also inspired Monet and Pissaro during their temporary residence in England at the time of the War of 1870/71 to carry on their impressionistic explorations.[94] By the time Monet, Pissarro, Degas, and Renoir organized L'Exposition des Impressionistes (1874), Edouard Manet, the avant-garde impressionist, had already developed the technique of reproducing tone values through the skillful use of

92. Edgar Germain Hilaire Degas, *Letters* (Oxford, 1948), 17, 65.
93. William James to Theodore Flourney, July 23, 1902, MS Am 1505, HCL.
94. Adeline Adams, *Childe Hassam* (New York, 1938), 46–48.

light and shadow and of presenting "unfinished" impressions. The publication in Paris (1881) of a Columbia University physicist's theory suggesting that broken colors result in color vibrations greatly enhancing the effects of light, gave the impressionist avant-garde the scientific respectability that encouraged their boldness.[95] The moderate success in 1886 of the American exhibition of about three hundred paintings by the leading French impressionists amounted to another boost from America at a time when Frenchmen were still skeptical about the latest fad. Even under these circumstances, Monet and Renoir would have preferred to see Durand-Ruel more vigorously exploring European outlets for their works, quite aside from the risks involved in shipping the canvases across the ocean.[96]

The positive effects of this exhibition notwithstanding, some American reactions were anything but flattering. Expressing their own prejudices, superficially and all too hastily, these contemporary critics accused the impressionists of preoccupation with light at the neglect of composition, drawing, and color *per se*. Perhaps the most charitable of them identified impressionists as interesting experimentalists and poets, but not painters.[97] An outraged Inness reserved his greatest condemnation for Claude Monet (1840–1926), the most forceful of the French impressionists, charging him with "stupidity" and calling him a "humbug" for suggesting, in the words of the accomplished American landscapist, that "the painter sees nature in the way the Impressionists paint it." Inness continued, "It appears as though the Im-

95. Albert D. Smith, *European Influences*, 33–36; Richardson, *Painting in America*, 218–19.

96. Frederick A. Sweet, *Miss Mary Cassatt: Impressionist from Pennsylvania* (Norman, Okla., 1966), 104–106; Lawrence Hanson, *Renoir: The Man, the Painter, and His World* (New York, 1968), 222, 231–32. C. Bergeron made the same arguments in letters to Courbet in which he advised him to exhibit his paintings in London rather than at the Exposition in Philadelphia. In London, he felt, "Jemmie" Whistler could be helpful in promoting their sale and the hazards of transatlantic shipping would be avoided. C. Bergeron to Gustave Courbet, April 27, 1876, and February 17, 1877, in Papiers Courbet, *Correspondance Manuscrits*, II, Bibliothèque Nationale, Paris.

97. Cornelius, *Keith*, I, 589.

pressionists were imbued with the idea to divest painting of all mental attributes and, overleaping the traveled road which art has created by hard labor, by plastering over and presenting us with the original pancake of visual imbecility, the childlike naiveté of unexpressed vision."[98] To think that neat workmanship and compositional theme were no longer relevant in painting struck him as ridiculously irrational. Another well-known American artist, Jervis McEntee, could not believe that sane men would exhibit such works that shocked all his "ideas of art or even common sense." In his judgment, it was the work of lunatics. Unfortunately, the intolerance displayed by the rising middle classes toward unconventional art was also manifested by many contemporary critics in France and the United States. They treated Manet, a "grotesque painter," as an outcast; and his paintings looked to them "like childish scribbles." Failing to recognize the unusual merits of the new techniques and contemporary themes used by the impressionists, these critics simply concluded that they "could not paint."[99]

Among the American impressionists, Mary Cassatt (1845–1926) occupies a prominent place. Born in Pittsburgh and trained at the Pennsylvania Academy of the Fine Arts, she grew up in Paris, the city she loved so much that in 1874 she decided to settle in it permanently. A serious artist, this cosmopolitan expatriate shunned the time-wasting fashionable society of Paris. In her private life, she was charitable toward the needy, enthusiastic about horses, and sentimental about flowers. In her professional activities, she maintained a firmness, an integrity and independence that commanded the respect of friends and critics alike. Her "individual vision" and "spontaneous spirit" manifested themselves in many ways.[100] She cherished her independence as an artist so much that she did not send her paintings to the official Salon, thus symbolically refusing to submit to what she considered to be the tyranny of a jury. "What we want,"

98. Inness, Jr., George Inness, 168–74.
99. Andrews and McCoy, "Realists and Mystics," 65; George H. Hamilton, Manet and His Critics (New Haven, 1954), 1–5.
100. Edith Valerio, Mary Cassatt (Paris, 1930), 1–4; Sweet, Mary Cassatt, 32–33.

she explained later, "is the certainty that the one spark of original genius shall not be extinguished.—Most of the artists of original talent . . . would never have had a chance in the official Salons. Ours is an enslaved profession."[101] It outraged her that Gérôme, serving on the jury of practically every official exhibition, said shortly before he died that "if Millet were then alive, he would refuse his pictures; that the world consecrated Millet's genius made no difference to him."[102]

An observant student of old masters, particularly of Corregio and Rubens, keenly interested in Japanese prints, and closely following the contemporary art scene, Mary Cassatt was wise enough to learn from all and determined enough to be her own master. This did not prevent her from openly admitting her great admiration for the works of Manet, Courbet, and Degas. Recognizing her promise and predilections, Degas, who became one of her closest friends, liked to encourage and guide her gently. But he sensed that, although Miss Cassatt respected his judgment very much, she was somewhat afraid to consult him lest "he would demolish me so completely that I could never pick myself up in time to finish for the exposition."[103] She gladly accepted his invitation in 1877 to participate in an exhibition of the emerging group of impressionists, although neither she nor Degas painted in the manner of Monet. Indeed, Mary Cassatt and Degas were specifically excluded from the scathing criticism the *Revue des deux mondes* directed at the Fourth Impressionist Exhibition (1879), "this pretentious show of window dressing and infantile daubing."[104] Miss Cassatt's famous picture at this exhibition, *La Loge,* a lively study of contrast between dimness and colorfulness, has indeed remained one of the beautifully executed examples of her impressionistic period. Typical of her humanity,

101. Garnett McCoy, "Artists and Juries: The Tenth Annual Carnegie Institute International Exhibition," *JAAA,* VII (1967), 24. Will H. Low deplored the "politics of art in Europe," organized and controlled by a cunning oligarchy, in his *A Chronicle of Friendships, 1783–1900* (New York, 1908), 116–17.
102. Mary Cassatt to Harrison Morris, March 2, 1904, in Pennsylvania Academy of Fine Arts, Correspondence, P. 73, AAA.
103. Degas, Letters, 62–63.
104. Sweet, *Mary Cassatt,* 40–43; Cortissoz, *American Artists,* 185–88; James Gibbons Huneker, *Promenades of an Impressionist* (New York, 1910), 77–78, 232.

which endeared her so much to the French people, was an episode connected with this exhibition. When it turned out that not a single picture had been sold at this very well-attended show, after it was over she purchased a Degas and a Monet for herself. She felt completely "at home" in her French environment, counting not only these two impressionists, but also Renoir, Pissarro, Manet, Bracquemond, and Mallarmé among her many stimulating friends. Pierre Renoir (1844–1919), the painter of women who did not particularly like women painters, gladly made an exception in Cassatt's case. One evening, when the two discussed art over a glass of cider, she warned him in her forthright manner that the public was not likely to react favorably to his simple technique. Rather flattered, Renoir responded to Miss Cassatt's amused surprise: "complicated theories can always be thought up afterwards."[105] Cassatt's own oils and pastels required the observer's eye to fuse her "pure, delicately modulated color."[106] But if she became identified as an artist whose favorite theme was mother and child, her style was much too individualistic to be "typical" of a school.

Quite a few of the most talented American painters who in the last quarter of the century went to France to perfect their art did not "adopt" the methods of the leading French impressionists, no matter how much impressionist art attracted and fascinated them. Perhaps indicatively, closer study establishes that American artists leaning toward impressionism chose French teachers who stressed academic traditions. Mary Cassatt had studied for a while under the conservative Charles J. Chaplin; J. Alden Weir and Theodore Robinson under Gérôme; John H. Twachtman and Childe Hassam under Gustave Boulanger and Jules Joseph Lefèbre; John Singer Sargent under Carolus-Duran.[107] They had furthermore been trained in drawing before

105. Renoir, *Renoir*, 253–54.
106. John Palmer Leeper, "Mary Cassatt and Her Parisian Friends," *Bulletin of the Pasadena Art Institute* (October, 1951), 3–10; Achille Segard, *Un Peintre des enfants et des mères* (Paris, 1913).
107. John I. H. Baur, *Theodore Robinson* (New York, 1946), 15.

they attended the classes of these prominent French teachers. Even as free and independent "postgraduates" these American artists stopped short of the luminous colors and broken lines they admired so much in the French impressionists. Their background in linear and thematic realism tended to modify their "American impressionism." The all important education of their eyes evidently differed from that of their French colleagues. Even Martin Heade, John Twachtman, and Childe Hassam, who liked to experiment with Monet's palette, did not violate their conceptual integrity. "American impressionism" was at best an adaptation of French impressionism to the different cultural conditions prevailing in the United States.[108]

Theodore Robinson (1852–1896), one of the American impressionists, felt somewhat more reassured when to his surprise his good friend Claude Monet denied the French impressionists' desire to ignore such fundamentals as drawing, form, and values. These two artists spent many enjoyable hours in the relaxed atmosphere of Monet's home at Giverny, a small beautiful village on the Seine.[109] Whether at dinner or in the garden, they talked shop, enlightening each other about Robinson's sometimes "curious" paintings and Monet's "vibrant" canvases which at "a little distance give the impression of broad tranquil masses." True to the impressionists' credo, Monet and Robinson did not interpret their association in terms of a student-teacher relationship. They regarded each other as fellow artists, each seeing nature "through individual temperament."

In the spring of 1876, when Monet's avant-garde paintings still caused as much eyebrow-lifting as stir, John Singer Sargent (1856–1925), then a young American student in France, visited Jules Joseph Lefèbvre; John Singer Sargent under Carolus-one day the gallery of Durand-Ruel. When incidentally he noted

108. Richardson, *Painting in America*, 221, 304–306; Novak, *American Painting*, 129–33, 244–45; Robert G. McIntyre, *Martin Johnson Heade*, 1819–1904 (New York, 1948), 43–47.
109. Baur, *Theodore Robinson*, 23–32; Pierre Toulgouat, "Peintres américains à Giverny," *Rapports France–Etats-Unis* (May, 1952), 65–73.

Monet's presence in the gallery, he did not for a second hesitate to introduce himself to the artist whose paintings made an overwhelming impression on him. Nor did he lose any time arranging a rendezvous at the Café de la Paix for that very evening. Because Sargent had proudly brought along a few of his fellow students from Carolus-Duran's atelier, Monet suggested transferring the "meeting" to another café where they could talk and eat more leisurely. To Monet's embarrassment, the Café Helder to which they had moved displayed quite a few of his paintings on its walls, either in payment or as pawns for meals he had previously eaten there. Sargent and Monet solidified their friendship as the years went by, despite the fact that their personalities, temperaments, and painting styles differed considerably.[110] Sargent looked forward to his visits to Giverny where, on one occasion, the two artists painted each other; Monet, sitting down and painting leisurely, while Sargent was moving forth and back rather strenuously. Though to a degree inspired by Monet's techniques, Sargent did not adopt the *petit point* of his impressionist friend. These intimate contacts between French and American artists established cultural bridges linking not only France and the United States, but frequently also making Americans welcome middlemen between the French and the British. Vanderlyn and Allston were as much cases in point early in the century as Whistler and Sargent were in later years.

Once America could claim its own reputable artists, educated amateurs, and first-rate galleries, American criticism of nineteenth-century French art was to be expected. But that Americans of the precentennial period did not hesitate to criticize French art severely, as well as admire it, seems quite remarkable. Generally, one finds the often-repeated charge that French art, as far as it existed at all as a school of art, emphasized external effects and lacked depth, soul, and morality.

The pioneer art collector and critic James Jackson Jarves

110. Mount, *John Singer Sargent*, 43, 153, 215.

reiterated the long-held view that French artists "display all that vivid glare of coloring, which may for a while arrest the eye; but you look in vain for the sublime beauty of expression." By comparison with the great Italian masters of the sixteenth century who excelled in making color a vital accessory to motive, in the judgment of American critics modern French artists lacked the skill of using color to express moods and ideas in their compositions. Again, comparing the purity of the Greek and Italian masters in the presentation of nude figures with the at-best counterfeit virtue French painters displayed, these critics deplored that either by intent or because of artistic inferiority French artists painted nude bodies without laying bare their souls as a concealment of their flesh. These comments were not prompted by prudishness. The chastity of the *Venus de Milo,* these critics maintained, was so complete as not even to arouse the awareness of nudity. And nobody took exception to Michelangelo's figures. Not only French artists of the classical school who adopted the coarse Roman emphasis on physical rather than the more refined Grecian spirit of beauty, but also later nineteenth-century French artists offended American taste with their overly sensual works.[111]

When Harriet Beecher Stowe visited the Louvre in the summer of 1853, she reacted negatively to the French use of classic antiquity. Unlike the beautiful art of ancient Greece, modern French imitations of it struck her as "stale, wearisome, and repetitious." As far as she was concerned, Louis David "had neither heart nor soul." With the exception of Théodore Géricault's *Le Radeau de la Méduse,* a painting in which the artist had clearly "felt in the very depths of his soul the suffering and mysteries of human existence," Mrs. Stowe characterized French art as "the work of a race whose senses and perceptions of the outward have been cultivated more than the deep inward emotions."[112] Later American critics, who attributed the generally "depraving

111. James Jackson Jarves, *Art Thoughts* (New York, 1869), 250–60; John Neagle, "Concerning Artists and Works of Art" (1826?), B–N 125, No. 4, APSL.
112. Stowe, *Sunny Memories,* II, 165–67.

character of French art" to the demoralizing influences of Napoleon III's regime, nevertheless acknowledged its technical distinction. But they expressed their displeasure with the huge canvases flaunting surface color and "constantly growing sensationalism of subject" that ultimately resulted "in all sorts of fads and technical extremes." The rivalry among French artists became so great that qualified American judges interpreted their feverish and diseased art as "a mercantile development" designed to "surprise, bewilder, or stun."[113]

More specifically, when in the spring of 1831 Thomas Cole, the leading representative of the Hudson River School, visited the Louvre and the Luxembourg he was "painfully disappointed" on finding "wretched French productions" of modern painters instead of the old masters on the walls of these galleries. He did not expect the modern artists, with few exceptions, to be "so totally devoid of merit." It disgusted him that "battle, murder and death, Venuses and Psyches, the bloody and the voluptuous, are the things in which they seem to delight; and they are portrayed in a cold, hard, and often tawdry style with an almost universal deficiency of chiaroscuro."[114] On another visit, a decade later, Cole praised Nicolas Poussin for the "expression, compositon, fine design, and admirable propriety" of his historical works. These qualities clearly outweighed in his judgment such shortcomings as incorrect costumes and "a statuesque appearance in his figures." Viewing historical pictures of modern French artists in the Luxembourg, Asher B. Durand, the realistic representative of the Hudson River School, concluded that their grandeur of composition and their superb drawing and anatomical correctness entitled them to high recognition, despite the fact that "their figures are too often academick [sic] . . . theatrical, with exaggeration action and expression."[115] Horatio Greenough,

113. S. G. W. Benjamin, *Contemporary Art in Europe* (New York, 1877), 58–76.
114. Louis Legrand Noble, *The Life and Works of Thomas Cole* (Cambridge, Mass., 1964), 125–26, 226–31. George Ticknor shared Cole's view on contemporary French art. George Ticknor to Richard H. Dana, Sr., February 22, 1833, MHS.
115. Asher B. Durand, "Journal in France," August 8, 1840, p. 76 (MS in NYPL).

the neoclassical American sculptor, thought in 1831 that he had probably grown too callous to be as disgusted with the modern French pictures as he might have been before he went to Paris. Nevertheless, while allowing David "great cleverness," he too found the French-Greek physiognomy of David's ideal figures "nauseous" and, in general, French art "at a pretty low ebb."[116]

As a picture reflects the artistic skill and personal taste and state of mind of the painter, all of which are to some degree reflections of the age, so do the reactions and evaluations of the viewer offer a bewildering multiplicity of contemporary and retrospective opinions. In many instances Americans would therefore hold opposite opinions with respect to the same artist. William M. Hunt, for example, referred to Géricault, Delacroix, Millet, and Corot as "great painters," not to be confounded with Gérôme, Bouguereau, and the like.[117] Agreeing with Hunt regarding Bouguereau, Winslow Homer described Bouguereau's pictures as "false," "waxy and artificial," failing to reproduce outdoor light and the truth of his subject. According to Homer, "they are extremely near being frauds."[118] John G. Brown, on the other hand, admired Bouguereau; Brown and another Anglo-American artist, Thomas Moran, also admired Gérôme "for his conception of subject, and for his extreme refinement and beauty of drawing." Robert W. Weir, professor of drawing at the United States Military Academy, contrarily, accused Gérôme of lacking "refinement of feeling" while acknowledging his "immense technical power."[119] And with respect to Delacroix, Martin Brimmer was a little surprised to find that "his color seems rather hot & somewhat monotonous & his magnificent vigor is sometimes dearly bought."[120] Similarly, Courbet was accused of the "coarsest

116. Horatio Greenough to Washington Allston, October, 1831, in Edward Everett Papers, MHS.

117. Hunt, *Talks on Art*, 79.

118. Albert Gardner, *Winslow Homer*, 140.

119. George W. Sheldon, *American Painters*, (New York, 1881), 126–27, 162–63.

120. Martin Brimmer to Mrs. Sarah Wyman Whitman, June 22, 1883, in Martin Brimmer letters for the years 1880–1895, Microfilm D-32, AAA.

realism," most likely inspired by "the lowest depths of society," only to be enthusiastically applauded by another critic for his vigorous and harmonious interpretation of nature. "He is the strongest, the truest, and the most satisfying of realists" wrote James J. Jarves.[121] Although as respected an artist as George Inness praised Meissonier's clarity of thought and careful reproduction of details, he nonetheless believed that this "very wonderful painter" was too technically oriented "to awaken our emotion." Confirming this judgment in more severe terms, Thomas Moran held that Gérôme was "intellectually, emotionally, [and] poetically . . . infinitely the superior of Meissonier." Disapproval of Couture's method of putting on thin color conflicted with the comment that his orgy picture *The Romans of the Decadence* "was rich in its coloring."[122] In the same vein, the reverence with which many Americans regarded the artistic angel, Millet, "whose aim was to present pure and holy human sentiments," found its counterpart in the minority view that his pictures were "coarse and vulgar in character" and because they suggested "nothing noble," Millet, of all things, libeled French peasantry![123]

One of the sharpest differences of opinion with Hunt concerned Narcisse-Virgile Diaz, who "paints forever the forest of Fontainebleau," and Corot, the artist "of small conceptions and large surfaces," whose works the Hudson River School artist Jervis McEntee found to be "incomplete and slovenly." "His landscapes," McEntee aserted, "are ghosts of landscapes." Writing in the *Crayon*, Christopher Pearse Cranch labeled Corot's landscapes "cold, colorless, and without vitality." Rather severe in his criticism of Corot's works, he observed: "Leaden, cheerless skies, misty grey distances, formless unfinished furry-looking trees, water looking as if the chill of winter's ice were hardly off it, they suggest to me little of the poetry and romance of nature. . . . Neither the glow of Claude nor the solemn gloom of Rembrandt are here." Mary Knight Potter, on the contrary, praised

121. Mellick Journal, May 24, 1880, pp. 32–33; Jarves, *Art Thoughts*, 274.
122. Hunt, *Talks on Art*, 75.
123. Sheldon, *American Painters*, 126–27.

Corot's works in 1912 as true color-harmonies: "No one else has ever expressed more perfect concord between sky and foliage, foliage and trunk, trunk and lake or stream."[124]

Such differences of opinion could be almost endlessly multiplied. After all, sharply disagreeing with thousands of his fellow Americans, a writer in the *American Monthly Magazine* arrogantly contended in 1838 that only 50 of 1,850 paintings in the Louvre merited any attention at all.[125] When a generation later a Harvard professor of art contemptuously downgraded a collection of French paintings exhibited at the Boston Athenaeum and in the process referred to Millet as a trifler, William Morris Hunt, the devoted friend and admirer of Millet, was so infuriated that he published a stinging letter in the Boston *Daily Advertiser*. In it he cited the honored works of well-known nineteenth-century French artists whose unforgettable contributions professors of art could hardly sweep into oblivion "with the whisk of a quill. The unpardonable conceit of such stuff," he confessed, "makes one's blood tingle for shame. . . . It would hardly be mortifying if a Millet or a Delacroix should be developed in Boston."[126]

In the context of these sweeping criticisms, Kenyon Cox's letter to his mother, dated November 11, 1877, contained arguments that commanded thoughtful attention. After several visits to the Louvre he concluded that "the bulk of modern French work, Delacroix, Delaroche, Ingres, and many more, *is* far below the old standard." Even with respect to the best of the old masters in the museum he felt that there was "nothing before which I could say, 'this is the height of art. There is no use hoping anything will approach this again.' " The technical advances "by one or two modern men," he indicated, were not matched by the intellectual and psychological depth of which the old masters were capable.[127]

124. Christopher P. Cranch, "French Landscapes," *Crayon,* III (1856), 183–84; Mary Knight Potter, *The Art Galleries of Europe: The Louvre* (Boston, 1912), 341.

125. Howard Mumford Jones, *America and French Culture,* 326.

126. Quoted in Knowlton, *Art-Life of William Morris Hunt,* 68–69.

127. Kenyon Cox Correspondence, Columbia University.

Anyone following the art scene at the end of the century was of course familiar with the mixed feelings with which each successive style in the evolution of nineteenth-century painting had been received. The enthusiasm of avant-gardists was usually matched by the derision of traditionalists who conveniently forgot that at one time in history their style too had been unorthodox, heretical. French impressionism, as exemplified by Claude Monet's paintings, made its debut in New York and Boston respectively, in 1886 and 1892. The reactions ranged from one extreme to another, from the "the worst" to "fantastic," from "ridiculous" to "sublime." If Monet has not "discovered the art of painting," wrote one critic, "he has certainly painted moving waters, skies, air, and sunlight with a vividness and truth before unknown." But others condemned the "willful exaggeration of color." Manet, "the painter-in-chief of Ugliness," was described as "one of the eccentricities of modern art as Whistler is another, but better, variety induced by the popular love of the sensational and the extravagant."[128] With reference to a Manet exhibition in the mid-eighties, an American observer seriously questioned whether Manet or the viewer was insane. "Converting trees into rainbows and painting the sky arsenic green and the grass permanent blue" seemed "peculiar," to say the least.[129] Somewhat paradoxically, Americans, who were always ready to hail a new technological experiment, were inclined to be rather conservative in aesthetic areas. With respect to the latest French art, they were outright concerned about "flinging paint-pots in the sacred features of tradition."

In a class by himself, Paul Cézanne (1839–1906) was so little known in the United States that hardly any attention was paid to him when he died in 1906. Associated with the impressionists, Cézanne emerged as a leading postimpressionist who used the pure colors of impressionism to create the illusion of massive volume. Americans took favorable notice of his paintings, which

128. Theodore Robinson, "Claude Monnet," *Century Magazine*, XLIV (September, 1892), 696.
129. Cornelius, *Keith*, I, 142.

to them conveyed an appealing degree of realism. In the judgment of one contemporary critic, Cézanne's landscapes and still lifes displayed "brute strength, a tang of the soil that is bitter and also invigorating, after the false, perfumed boudoir art of so many of his contemporaries. . . . When Paul Cézanne paints an onion you smell it."[130] That American collectors accorded these refreshing qualities full recognition before they were appreciated in France meant much to Cézanne.

Generally speaking, there can be no doubt that the thousands of American painters who took advantage of the many instructional opportunities available in nineteenth-century France were exposed to sobering criticism and stimulating experiences of great value. But in the end, they tried very consciously to maintain their artistic independence, not only in their own themes and styles, but also in their critical evaluation of French art. Just because Paris was the world capital of art, especially in the second half of the nineteenth century, did not mean that American artists and laymen accepted the frequently changing art movements with unqualified enthusiasm. Significantly, though, the various schools of French painters who introduced new styles and techniques found more understanding and vital support in America than they initially enjoyed in their own country. Although Frenchmen had long been misled to believe that Americans totally lacked an appreciation of the arts, not to mention talents for them, American art collectors and the steadily increasing number of amateur and professional artists demonstrated that art could flourish very well in a democratic and materialistically oriented society. Indeed, the remarkable degree of originality that such talented American painters as Vanderlyn, Durand, Homer, and Whistler displayed, substantiated the contention that, in whatever relatively small measure, Americans imaginatively contributed to the evolution of nineteenth-century painting. But while taking pride in the creative accomplishments of its native artists, the art collecting

130. Arnold T. Schwab, *James Gibbons Huneker: Critic of the Arts* (Stanford, Calif., 1963), 177–78.

American public also revealed its prejudice by attaching greater value and prestige to the works of European artists. American art was making progress in the nineteenth century, but the inspirational center of the artistic revolution continued to be located in Europe, led by France.

CHAPTER X

Sculpture

As in other civilizations, art developed in America more rapidly with the growing acquisition of wealth. In the ancient three-dimensional art of sculpture, Americans were deeply indebted to such nineteenth-century French masters as Jean Antoine Houdon, Pierre Jean David d'Angers, François Rude, Antoine Louis Barye, Jean Baptiste Carpeaux, Paul Dubois, Jean Alexandre Falguière, Emmanuel Frémiet, François Jouffroy, Marius Jean Antonin Mercié, and Auguste Rodin. Houdon, a leading portrait sculptor of his time, who had come to America to make his life-sized marble statue of George Washington, and David d'Angers, the renowned sculptor of the famous marble bust of Lafayette and of a bronze statue of Jefferson, taught the people of the young American republic the pleasures to be derived from sculptures.[1] Although French sculptors changed their styles in the course of the century, these changes were not as pronounced as their parallels in painting. It did make a great deal of difference, however, whether sculptured surfaces were smooth or rough, whether forms were pictorial or powerful, and expressions studied or casual, static or dynamic.

1. See Gilbert Chinard (ed.), *Houdon in America* (Baltimore, 1930); Dussieux, *Les Artistes français*, 249–52; Henry Jouin, *David d'Angers et ses relations littéraires* (Paris, 1890), 368–69; Réau, *L'Art français;* and Homer Saint-Gaudens (ed.), *The Reminiscences of August Saint-Gaudens* (2 vols.; New York, 1913), II, 49.

In sculpture, Americans followed the lead of different countries at different times. Young sculptors who formerly might have turned to England for guidance went after the 1820s to Rome and Florence, following the lead of many French artists. By the 1870s they preferred to go to Paris, where teachers who had much to offer were willing to train them thoroughly in the great tradition and where their work found public recognition more readily than anywhere else. To be sure, Americans occasionally found fault with the French emphasis on sculptural style over theme, thought, and individuality. If, moreover, sculpture was the means by which the artist wished to express his feelings and ideas in plastic form, it would have been desirable to enjoy more freedom than the ever-present shadow of powerful conservative influences tolerated.[2]

In the first half of the nineteenth century relatively few Americans chose sculpturing as a profession, and merely a few of them truly stood out. Among those who did were Horatio Greenough, Thomas Crawford, Hiram Powers, and Randolph Rogers—all primarily products of the neoclassical Italian environment.[3] Their accomplishments encouraged other young Americans to follow their example, even though they realized that the American public still had a long way to go before it could fully appreciate art in all its nakedness. So shocked were the people back home when they saw Greenough's *Chanting Cherubs* that the innocent nude infants of this beautiful sculpture had for a time to be dressed up a little so as not to offend the prevailing sense of public morality. Such "indecent exhibitions" might be tolerated in the Louvre, but not in God's own country. Hiram Powers' internationally admired nude masterpiece in marble,

2. Paul Bartlett, "American Sculptors and France," lecture, January 22, 1913, in Paul Bartlett Papers, container 24, LC; George Henry Calvert to Hiram Powers, April 4, 1843, in Special Collections, Columbia University; and Richardson, *Painting in America*, 183.

3. Wayne Craven, *Sculpture in America* (New York, 1968), 95, 104–111; Cox, *Old Masters*, 267–69; M. Courtois, "Sculpture américaine," *RDBA* (1853), 329–30; and William C. Brownell, "French Sculptors," *Century Magazine*, XXXIII (1887), 336.

the *Greek Slave*,[4] had in some communities to pass the inspection of pastors before it could be publicly exhibited in the United States. The clergymen concluded that this statue was anything but profane and voluptuous—indeed, that it portrayed chastity and propriety, evoking not just an appreciation of beauty but sentiments of awe and reverence. This kind of intolerable censorship based on irrelevant misconceptions of the nature of art had to be disregarded and, hopefully, removed if American sculptors were to enjoy the relative freedom of unrestricted creativeness.

Not only humans, but nature itself imposed certain limitations upon American sculptors. Although white plaster, stone, and clay were available in the United States, the quality and variety of the marble found in Italy was clearly superior to that in America. The American climate, furthermore, did not treat marble very kindly. Statues and monuments survived open exposure so much better in bronze that in the second half of the nineteenth century American sculptors developed considerable skill and ingenuity in bronze casting. Lacking skill and facilities for casting, they depended initially on France and Germany for the technical execution of their projects. But thanks to Henry Kirke Brown (1814–1886), who had imported a corps of Frenchmen skilled in making bronze castings, the process was studiously observed and ultimately perfected in the United States.[5]

Particularly after the 1870s American sculptors shifted from emphasis on neoclassical forms to a simple naturalism. Even those who had gone to Italy tried to keep up with the trends of the time. One of the early examples of the more impressionistic French style, Anne Whitney's *Le Modèle*, a bronze bust of an elderly peasant woman, expressed the kind of simple earthiness in theme and form that suited the simple tastes of the American people. George Edwin Bissell (1839–1920), who had been trained in France and who maintained studios in Poughkeepsie as well

4. William C. Clark, *Great American Sculptors* (Philadelphia, 1878); Craven, *Sculpture in America*, 117–18.
5. Adeline Adams, *John Quincy Adams Ward: An Appreciation* (New York, 1912), 20–21.

as in Paris, produced naturalistic portrait sculpture for which he borrowed some ideas from the masters of the Italian Renaissance or his French teachers, but his works essentially reflected his own conceptions of art.[6] This tendency was also displayed by John Quincy Adams Ward (1830–1910) who, contrary to his father's wishes, dreamed of following an artistic career rather than becoming a farmer or physician. Ward summed up well the views of his contemporaries who refused to follow the lead of the neoclassicists but were still groping for the right kind of naturalism: "There is a cursed atmosphere about that place [Rome] which somehow kills every artist who goes there. . . . A modern man has modern themes to deal with; and if art is a living thing . . . fresh from a man's soul, he must live in that of which he treats. . . . The true significance of art lies in its improving upon nature." Believing as he did that an American sculptor would serve himself and his age best by working at home, he nevertheless credited the modern French school with having "the best draughtsmen in the world" and with excellence in teaching "the movement of figures and accuracy of representation."[7] Eventually, some of his well-known statues and portraits, including his *Lafayette*, *Garfield Monument*, and *Roscoe Conkling*, showed traces of French influence in learning, design, dress, and surface execution, without denying their authentic American character.

As late as the third quarter of the century many American sculptors continued to make Rome their Mecca. But at the end of this period, copying antiquity and drawing inspiration from classical mythology satisfied them little, and those who explored the art of sculpturing at home felt, around the era of the Civil War, that their rather prosaic works were neither contemporary enough in theme nor exciting in style. Once in a while an artist would relate themes to the burning issues of the age. Edmonia Lewis (1845–1890), the orphaned daughter of an Indian mother

6. Craven, *Sculpture in America*, 243–45.
7. Adams, *John Quincy Adams Ward*, 22.

and a Negro father, for instance, modeled at the end of the Civil War her statue of *The Freedwoman*. John Rogers (1829-1904), whose experiences in Paris and Rome had convinced him that copying from old statues in the old country actually inhibited American creativeness,[8] won much acclaim for the human tragedy he related in *The Slave Auction* and *The Fugitive Story*. William Rimmer's (1816-1879) statue *Despair*, a teenager's attempt to express anatomically and emotionally the tragedy of his French father's life had, as far back as 1830, shown possibilities that Auguste Rodin advanced several decades later with greater scientific accuracy and polish. Even a superficial glance at Rodin's masterpiece *The Thinker* immediately brings to mind Rimmer's *Despair*. And finally, Meta Vaux Warrick Fuller of Philadelphia (1877-1967), the great great granddaughter of an enslaved African princess, expressed pride in her ancestry in such superb works of sculpture that she became the most distinguishd woman sculptor in the United States. Instructed by demanding teachers at the Ecole des Beaux-Arts in Paris, she gained official professional standing at the age of twenty. After careful examination of her figure *Silent Sorrow*, Rodin acknowledged her great gifts: "My child, you are a sculptor; you have the sense of form."[9] To Rodin's delight, her subsequent work confirmed this original impression.

Following the centennial of 1876 a great change came about in American sculpture. It was dominated by professionals trained in France, but artistically attuned to the innovative spirit of phenomenally energetic Americans in the realms of business, industry, and technology. A towering figure among them, Augustus Saint-Gaudens (1848-1907) spent his creative years in Paris, Rome, New York, and at his country home in the relaxing atmosphere of Cornish, New Hampshire. The son of a Gascon shoemaker

---

8. See John Rogers, Jr., to Sarah Ellen Derby Rogers, November 19, 1858, in NYHS; and David H. Wallace, *John Rogers: The People's Sculptor* (Middletown, Conn., 1967).

9. Earle, *Biographical Sketches*, 127–28; see also William F. O'Donnell, "Meta Vaux Warrick, Sculptor of Horrors," *World To-Day*, XIII (1907), 1139–45. In her work she stressed "the soul rather than the figure."

and his Irish wife who in 1848 immigrated to the United States and proudly opened the best shop in New York for "French Ladies' Boots and Shoes," Augustus grew up in a home where French was spoken. His early desire to become an artist received sympathetic understanding.[10] At thirteen, his father secured him an apprenticeship with a cutter of cameo stones, a skill that enabled him to earn a living when he arrived in Paris in 1867. By that time he had withstood the unbearably strict discipline of his first master in New York, he had experienced the gentle direction of the shell-cameo carver Jules LeBrethon and of the drawing instructors at Cooper Union, and he had completed his practical studies at the National Academy of Design. In view of the severe demands made on him by one of the professors at the overcrowded little preparatory school he attended in Paris, it was not surprising that he developed the habit in later years of consantly groping for perfection and revising his work until he was satisfied with it.[11]

Saint-Gaudens was naturally elated when the Ecole des Beaux-Arts accepted him. At first the only American student in Jouffroy's atelier, he felt more comfortable when six months later Olin Warner joined him in the atelier of the favorite sculpture teacher of American students. Jouffroy's frequent encouragement and constructive criticism, which respected Saint-Gaudens' individuality and originality, sustained the young artist's morale in the sometimes unfriendly environment in which his fellow French students compelled him repeatedly to sing the Marseillaise in English.[12] Once he had passed his initiation at the Beaux-Arts, he befriended such fine classmates as Alfred Garnier and Paul Binon and enjoyed life in the carefree fashion of art students in the Latin Quarter. Gradually, his circle of friends widened to include such brilliant artists as Bastien-Lepage, Mercié, Rodin,

10. Louise Hall Tharp, *Saint-Gaudens and the Gilded Era* (Boston, 1969), 7–10.
11. A. de Chambrun, "Un Sculpteur américain né français: Saint-Gaudens," *RDDM* (February 1, 1932), 669.
12. Saint-Gaudens (ed.), *Reminiscences*, I, 77–78; Truman H. Bartlett, "Saint-Gaudens: As I Knew Him," in Paul Bartlett Papers, container 77, LC.

and Whistler.[13] So spontaneous was his identification with France and so deep his sense of gratitude for the privilege it had extended to him that upon the outbreak of hostilities in 1870 he seriously considered serving in the French army. Dissuaded, however, by his mother whom he adored, he went instead to Rome. There he studied the Italian masters of the Renaissance when he was not cutting cameos to maintain himself. In Rome he shared a little studio with his Portuguese friend and former classmate in the Beaux-Arts, Soares dos Reis, who had no choice but to adjust to Augustus' lifelong habit of singing while he worked.[14]

Between 1867 and 1897, Saint-Gaudens crossed the Atlantic several times, acquiring in the process a cosmopolitan outlook. Hiking trips with fellow students familiarized him with Paris and its suburbs, as well as with the South of France, which left unforgettable impressions on his mind. And when in 1899 he first visited Aspet, the little French village his father had come from, he attributed the fact that he felt at home here to "inherited memory."[15] Considering his family background, there was nothing extraordinary about these sentiments. They neither affected nor contradicted his innermost conviction: "I belong in America, that is my home." Ultimately, the restlessly and rapidly growing United States was the vital source of his artistic life. And what a rich legacy of monumental art this ingenious sculptor has left behind! His monuments—*General Sherman, Admiral Farragut, The Puritan*, the standing *Abraham Lincoln*, the *Shaw Memorial*, the *Adams Memorial*, and the figure *Silence*, to cite merely a few of his outstanding creations—differed in conception and execution from the neoclassical and mid-century naturalistic sculpture enough to give them a new and distinctly American touch.

13. A. de Chambrun, "Saint-Gaudens," 668; J. Walker McSpadden, *Famous American Sculptors* (New York, 1924), 39–40; and Lorado Taft, *The History of American Sculpture* (New York, 1925), 282–83.

14. Hamilton Bell, "Un Sculpteur américain de descendance française: Auguste Saint-Gaudens (1848–1907)," *GDBA*, 5e période, I (1920), 368–69.

15. Homer Saint-Gaudens (ed.), "Intimate Letters of Stanford White," *AR*, XXX (1911), 108; Rose Standish Nichols (ed.), "Family Letters of Augustus Saint-Gaudens," *McClure's Magazine*, XXXII (1908), 1–16.

His delicately executed low reliefs, his use of the base as an integral part of the statue, the contrasting effects created by his decorative linear inscriptions, his "more" natural and vigorous surfaces, the timelessness of his many abstract figures belonging to no particular age or country, the inscrutable, distant look conveyed in the *Adams Memorial,* and the living messages expressed in the faces, postures, and themes of his sculpture ranked Saint-Gaudens among the truly creative masters. The choice of so many national figures in his sculpture and his belief at the end of the century that American art could at last stand on its own legs gave his contributions a significant national flavor. Art connoisseurs respected the beautiful integrity of this man who would not dream of using clever tricks to promote his art. The genuine charm, grace, and simplicity of his quantitatively and qualitatively impressive works earned him an international standing that he treasured very dearly.[16] His professional pride, for instance, made him insist that when the Luxembourg acquired his *Angel with the Tablet* or *Amor Caritas,* it was "clearly understood that it was *solicited* and *bought.* . . . I do not wish to have it thought in France that I offered my work to museums."[17]

While he was enthusiastic about Mercié's, Falguière's, and Rodin's early productions, Rodin's statue of Balzac reminded him in 1898 "too much of a guttering candle." Saint-Gaudens reserved great admiration for Paul Dubois' "high standards and thorough discipline." In his judgment, Dubois' *Joan of Arc* ranked among the most beautiful masterpieces in the world.[18] Photo copies of Dubois' versions of *Joan of Arc* graced Saint-Gaudens' living room and studio in New York. He never tired of this French sculptor's masterful technique and dignity. He naturally felt flattered when Dubois invited him between 1898 and 1900 to dine

16. Royal Cortissoz, *Augustus Saint-Gaudens* (Boston, 1907), 23–24; Buckner Hollingsworth, *Augustus Saint-Gaudens,* American Sculptor Series, VIII (New York, 1948), 3; and Gaston Migeon, "Le Sculpteur Augustin Saint-Gaudens," *Art et Décoration,* V (1899), 43–49.
17. Nichols (ed.), "Family Letters," 6.
18. Saint-Gaudens (ed.), *Reminiscences,* II, 49–50, 183–84.

with him and once asked him "if I would really tell him what I thought of his sculpture." When he left Dubois' studio on March 10, 1899, Saint-Gaudens recorded, the French artist's assistant remarked: "Dubois must like [you] a great deal to talk to [you] in the open way he did and as volubly because he is silent and reserved with almost everyone. He must also have great confidence in you to show you as he did all his sketches."[19] By the end of the century this confidence was officially acknowledged when Saint-Gauden's equestrian statue *General Sherman* was awarded the highest honors at the Paris Exposition of 1900 and he was made an officer of the Legion of Honor and a corresponding member of the Société des Beaux-Arts. He had indeed arrived when French art critics praised his "grasp of composition," his ability to express "depth of sentiment . . . without any splurge or noise" and his "dignity without parade." The highest compliments were paid to him in *Art et Décoration* by Paul Liprieur: "While presenting prodigies of skill," Liprieur wrote, Saint-Gaudens "modeled with a great freedom and understanding of how to arrange the various groups of lines in perspective," and in the process he kept everything "subordinate to the ensemble and to the predetermined unity of motion."[20]

Saint-Gaudens did not care to delve into the complex intricacies of the philosophy of art. And yet, deeply embedded religious roots seem to have nurtured his indefatigable creative drives. Taking pride in his work, but being personally humble and modest, he was disturbed by the degree of "misery and unhappiness in this world" and by "the preoccupation of the people with sex." In view of these "terribly sad" conditions, he despaired at times that "all this struggle for beauty seems so vain and hopeless." Nevertheless, the moral imperative, as he interpreted it, was "to try and do good."[21]

Several other American sculptors had the benefit of at least

19. Nichols (ed.), "Family Letters," 9–10.
20. Saint-Gaudens (ed.), *Reminiscences,* II, 187–88.
21. *Ibid.,* 204–205.

some experience in France. Olin Levi Warner's (1844–1896) early life was characterized by unusual promise and poverty. His clergyman father could not afford to send his son abroad to study the fine art of sculpture which seemed to be Olin's natural calling. Young Warner worked six years as a telegrapher before he had saved enough money to reach the destination of his ambition: the Ecole des Beaux-Arts in Paris. By good fortune, Saint-Gaudens took an interest in him after his arrival in the French capital. Olin Warner's admission to Jouffroy's atelier and the extraordinary opportunity afforded him as assistant of the renowned decorative sculptor Jean Baptiste Carpeaux acquainted him with the most advanced stages of sculpture. Had it not been for the Franco-Prussian War, for the duration of which he enlisted in the French Foreign Legion, he might have continued to work as assistant in Carpeaux's studio, an honor of considerable prestige in contemporary France.[22] Another professionally valuable experience, his association with Falguière and Mercié, two of the promising young sculptors of France, also attested to the esteem in which French artists held Warner.[23] He was disillusioned upon his return to the United States in 1872 in part because of the realization of his own relative obscurity in his native country and also because of the indifference and lack of understanding the American public displayed, particularly in regard to sculpture. After several lean years, this master of delicate low reliefs and of such simple, sensitive, and beautiful creations as *Cupid and Psyche, Diana,* and the portrait bust of *J. Alden Weir* belatedly found the recognition he had hoped for.[24] Tragically, though, a fatal accident deprived him prematurely of the fruits of his labor.

Fate was much kinder to Daniel Chester French (1850–1931),

22. Ripley Hitchcock, "Notes on an American Sculptor," *Art Review,* I (1887), 1–5; Chandler R. Post, *A History of European and American Sculpture* (2 vols.; Cambridge, Mass., 1921), II, 238.

23. Charles H. Caffin, *American Masters of Sculpture* (New York, 1903), 133–35.

24. William C. Brownell, "The Sculpture of Olin Warner," *Scribner's Magazine,* XX (1896), 429–41; Craven, *Sculpture in America,* 406–409.

another contemporary American sculptor modeling in the new Paris-oriented fashion. Without special training in sculpturing, he demonstrated in his youth so much innate talent that the people of Concord, Massachusetts, were not surprised when their confidence in the relatively inexperienced artist in their midst was confirmed at the unveiling of his *Minute Man,* a bronze statue honoring patriots who had died at Concord Bridge a century before. A distinctly American sculptor, he regretted in later years that in 1875 he had gone to Italy rather than France where new art styles were in the making. In 1886 he went to Paris and made the most of a couple of years there to perfect his mastery of modeling. He worked in Paris on his marble statue of *General Cass,* which now graces the rotunda of the Capitol in Washington, and he studied the best sculpture exhibited in the Louvre and other galleries. French also attended sculpture classes under the direction of Mercié. The customary camaraderie among American artists abroad enlivened his stay in Paris and since French, the celebrated sculptor of the *Ralph Waldo Emerson* and other busts, was in a position to extend his hospitality to young compatriots in Paris, he helped perpetuate that stimulating intimacy among American artists that benefited American art as well as its artists. George P. A. Healy, who happened to be in Paris at this time and who had once painted a portrait of General Lewis Cass, lent D. Chester French a welcome hand in bringing out the solid features of this prominent statesman-soldier. French's Parisian experience improved his sculptural techniques.[25] The crispness of the surface, the liveliness of the form and expression, and the unity of the composition in his masterful human-interest group *Gallaudet and his First Deaf-Mute Pupil,* on which he went to work soon after his return from Paris, clearly reflected the beneficial impact of his recent exposure to French art.

25. Margaret French Cresson, *The Life of Daniel Chester French: Journey into Fame* (Cambridge, Mass., 1947), 144–47; Lorado Taft, "Daniel Chester French: Sculptor," *Brush and Pencil,* V (1900), 149; and Daniel Chester French to Charles Moore, July 2, 1887, in Charles Moore Papers, Box 5, LC.

The phenomenal rise of American architecture in the final decades of the century boosted the related art of sculpture beyond all expectations. A contemporary sculptor, Frederick William McMonnies (1863–1937), was deeply involved in this relationship, and even combined architecture and sculpture with painting as well. Originally, poverty prevented him from pursuing his artistic inclinations. When, after working as a clerk in a jewelry store, he finally found himself at the age of eighteen in Saint-Gaudens' studio, he felt for a while terribly frustrated because he was assigned various menial jobs in the studio, instead of being put on projects that offered creative opportunities. But as chance would have it, when Augustus Saint-Gaudens' irritable frame of mind required that he take a rest, the two assistants in his studio, his brother Louis and René de Quélin, permitted young McMonnies to copy, among other works, one of Donatello's low reliefs.[26] Upon his return, Saint-Gaudens inquired about the authorship of the superbly modeled statuettes he saw in his studio. At first, he thought that his assistants were deceiving him when they identified the young handyman as the talented artist. Thereafter, Saint-Gaudens gave McMonnies the kind of artistic training that rapidly advanced his potential. By the time he was admitted to the Ecole des Beaux-Arts in Paris he was so far advanced that Alexandre Falguière, whose atelier he entered, soon made him an assistant in his private studio to help guide other students' work.[27] His brilliance won McMonnies early recognition in France, and in 1887 and 1889 he was the recipient of the Prix d'Atelier, the highest award open to foreign students. On Falguière's advice, he opened his own studio in Paris, traveling, as Saint-Gaudens did, forth and back between France and the United States. Also as restlessly productive as Saint-Gaudens, but not as disciplined a perfectionist as his first master, McMonnies created works in the fashionable French style of his day.

26. René de Quélin, "Early Days with MacMonnies in St. Gaudens' Studio," *Arts and Decoration,* XVI (1922), 424–25, 479.
27. French Strother, "Frederick MacMonnies, Sculptor," *World's Work,* XI (1905), 6966; McSpadden, *Famous Sculptors,* 76–95.

Like other sculptors before him, early in his career he ran into difficulties with such organizations as the American Purity League in New York and the Women's Christian Temperance Union. He shocked Bostonians who objected strenuously to his masterfully executed figure *Bacchante with an Infant Faun.* The dancing, laughing, beautifully shaped nude woman, symbolically dangling grapes from one hand and holding a playful child on her other arm, struck these Victorians as too vulgar and suggestive to be displayed publicly. Too upsetting to the friends of the Boston Public Library, the original destination of the *Bacchante,* it was finally acquired by the Metropolitan Museum of Art in New York. Typically, French art circles were enchanted with the *Bacchante*—its grace, illusion of motion, and love of life. The Luxembourg acquired a replica of this beautiful figure and, in the same year, 1896, McMonnies was also honored by being made a chevalier of the Legion of Honor.[28]

The sincere realism of his patriotic statue *Nathan Hale,* the lively characterization of his *Stranahan,* his reflective *Shakespeare,* his fantastically spirited *Horse Tamers,* the delicacy of his *Diana,* and his marvelous fountains and beautiful allegorical figures, among many other works, had by the turn of the century established his reputation as an American sculptor of distinction. Nevertheless, in a review of the works of American artists exhibited at the Salon in 1898, an American critic felt that Saint-Gaudens and McMonnies, "admirable as they are, are not the superiors, nor even yet the rivals of Rodin."[29]

Another American critic, the well-known James Gibbons Huneker, referred to Rodin as the "one genius of whom France can boast today." Perhaps best known for such masterpieces as *The Thinker, The Kiss,* and *St. John the Baptist Preaching,* Auguste Rodin (1840–1917) became the most celebrated sculptor of the French romantic school. Widely experienced and hard

28. Strother, "MacMonnies," 6972–74; H. H. Greer, "Frederick MacMonnies, Sculptor," *Brush and Pencil,* X (1902), 10.

29. Rowland Strong, "The Salon: Work by American Artists," New York *Times,* May 14, 1898; Craven, *Sculpture in America,* 420–28.

working, he was also, as he desired to be, original and self-expressive. According to his own statement, the sight of Michelangelo's works freed him from "academism" and inspired him to express in his bronze and marble works emotions and character with his own accents. Rough surfaces and profiles in depth distinguished his technique. Appropriately, Huneker mentioned another characteristic of this influential and controversial artist: "He is the most rhythmic sculptor of them all. And rhythm is the codification of beauty."[30]

But while France continued to be the imaginative leader in this art form, the United States also continued to produce sculptors of amazing gifts. George Grey Barnard's (1863–1938) determined uphill struggle from poverty to fame illustrated his strong character as well as his genius. The son of a Presbyterian minister, Barnard grew up in a religious environment that evidently induced him to contemplate life and the universe so deeply as to inspire him and his work. As a young student in France he cared little for the more frivolous aspects of life in the Latin Quarter or for modern French art. Acquiring as much knowledge and skill as he possibly could under Pierre Jules Cavelier's direction, he exhibited several of his sculptures in the Salon of 1894, notably *Two Natures*, a title borrowed from Victor Hugo's *Je sens deux hommes en moi*. The French reaction answered his prayers beyond all expectations. Suddenly French artists and critics proclaimed him a great master—bold, creative, and possessing an astonishing breadth and depth of conception. In *Two Natures* he had succeeded in bringing out the dualism in man and life. In other works, too, philosophical in conception and fresh, warm, and resourceful in execution, Barnard demonstrated how much he had learned from Michelangelo and the moderns. His massive group at the entrance of the Pennsylvania State Capital at Harrisburg, *The Burden of Life* and *Work and Fraternity*, evoked enthusiastic recognition from eminent French

30. See Huneker, *Promenades of an Impressionist*, 52–80; and *Musical Courier*, July 1, 1896, p. 19. The opening in 1929 of the Rodin Museum in Philadelphia attested to the high regard in which Americans held this renowned sculptor.

sculptors, including Rodin, who took a keen interest in American artists.[31]

To cite only one more of the many gifted American sculptors, Paul Wayland Bartlett (1865–1925) belonged to both the United States, the country of his birth, and to France, where he lived from the age of nine. His father, a sculptor and teacher, wanted to give his son the best education an artist could have, not only at the Ecole des Beaux-Arts where, at fourteen, he learned to draw and to model in Pierre Jules Cavelier's classes, but in the exciting and competitive artistic atmosphere of Paris. Attracted to animal sculpture, then in fashion,[32] he was privileged to enjoy the benefit of Emmanuel Frémiet's guidance at the Jardin des Plantes. Devoting himself in his quiet and concentrated way to his art, he produced many pieces of lively animal sculptures of which *The Bear Tamer* is probably most widely known.[33] His mastery of human anatomy and his skill in modeling animals won him the recognition which by 1895 placed him *hors concours* and made him a chevalier in the Legion of Honor. By 1908, he and Saint-Gaudens were the only Americans to be officers of the Legion. His statues *Michelangelo* and *Columbus* attested to more than the possession of technical skill; their dynamism and power of expression confirmed the depth of his artistry. He won, of course, the heart of Frenchmen with his equestrian statue of the *Marquis de Lafayette,* for which American youngsters had contributed their pennies in grateful acknowledgment for the Statue of Liberty France had given to the United States.[34]

It is evident that in the nineteenth century American progress in sculpture was phenomenal. Most of it was the work of innate

31. Alexander Blair Thaw, "George Grey Barnard, Sculptor," *World's Work,* V (1902), 2837–53; Craven, *Sculpture in America,* 442–50.

32. Americans admired and collected particularly the animal sculptures of Antoine Louis Barye; Bing, *La Culture artistique en Amérique,* 28–30.

33. Ellen Strong Bartlett, "Paul Bartlett: An American Sculptor," *New England Magazine,* XXXIII (1905), 369–82; Frances Keyzer, "Some American Artists in Paris," *The Studio,* XIII (London, 1898), 247.

34. Chester L. Barrows, *William M. Evarts: Lawyer, Diplomat, Statesman* (Chapel Hill, 1941), 469–70.

genius buttressed by disciplined devotion and an education and inspiration to which French sculptors made major contributions. In a speech Paul W. Bartlett delivered in Paris in 1913, he acknowledged the debt Americans owed to French art. And yet, besides the rock of commercial influence "which threatens shipwreck to the rational development of sculpture in America," he also very candidly alluded to the dangers of "the subversive tendencies of the newer art movements in France." Young American artists returned from France after several years, he said, "without knowing the first word of the real lesson of art, and with an epileptic mentality. They have been lured into circles where, under different forms, mental aberration is deliberately cultivated: where intellectual impotence passes for genius, and theories take the place of talent. It is learned that they have frequented studios in which drawing is done with closed eyes, in order to give better expression to the soul; where painting is but discordant daubing and where lumps and deformities pass for sculpture."[35] In sculpture, as in painting, the feeling grew in early twentieth-century America that the golden age of French art had come to an end.

35. For excerpts from Paul W. Bartlett's address, "What American Sculptors Owe to French Art," see New York *Times*, February 9, 1913, Magazine Section, p. 13.

CHAPTER XI

Architecture

Historically, English and French influence shaped American architecture up to the end of the nineteenth century. American colonial style had been modeled as much after English architecture as the Greek and Gothic revivals in America in the early and later nineteenth century respectively. Another major influence in this century can be traced to the changing styles of the French.[1] Following the decline in artistic taste and originality in the eighteenth century it was not until the late Restoration period that even the Ecole des Beaux-Arts in Paris abandoned the "teaching of pompous platitudes" regarding the forms and details of architecture. About that time three young students at this school, Joseph-Louis Duc, Felix-Louis-Jacques Duban, and Labrouste, were so inspired by Greek designs that before long they spearheaded a neo-Greek movement in architecture.[2] This new trend, displacing the ancient Roman and Empire styles preceding it, exercised a pervasive influence in

---

1. Montgomery Schuyler, *American Architecture and Other Writings* (2 vols.; Cambridge, Mass., 1961), II, 575; Henry Russell Hitchcock, *Architecture: Nineteenth and Twentieth Centuries* (Baltimore, 1958), 166–67, 170; Stanley D. Adshead, "A Comparison of Modern American Architecture with That of European Cities," *AR*, XXIX (1911), 113–26. In the years following the American Revolution, Major Charles Pierre L'Enfant played an important role in the architectural development of New York and Washington.

2. A. D. F. Hamlin, "Modern French Architecture," *AR*, X (1900), 150–53.

France and in the United States through Richard Morris Hunt, the first American student at the Ecole des Beaux-Arts. Thomas Jefferson's emphasis on classical architecture as a symbol of freedom greatly facilitated the ready acceptance of the neo-Greek style in America. By the middle of the nineteenth century, however, a reaction had set in, liberating France from overzealous devotion to the classicism that had stifled artistic creativity and spontaneity. For the next generation the French Renaissance style and the English Gothic revival affected American architects[3] whose flourishing enterprises were slowed down only by the Civil War and the economic depressions of 1857 and 1873. And in the final decades of the century, though still strongly dependent upon French and English practices, Americans strove to develop styles in tune with contemporary American tastes and landscapes, as well as methods most applicable to American needs.

The influence of the Ecole des Beaux-Arts on architectural training was more extensive in the United States than in Europe. Starting with 10 American students in the 1860s, there were 33 in the 1870s, 29 in the 1880s, and 152 in the 1890s.[4] Americans flocked to Paris for professional training not available elsewhere. High standards in draftsmanship and exposure to imaginative planning and composition benefited American students, whatever individual designs they developed after leaving the Beaux-Arts. The French school taught them to think of a building as an artistic unit, even though utility and cost affected the ultimate shape, particularly of public buildings. Simplicity, they learned, pleased the eye as well as the purse.[5] The artistic atmosphere of Paris and its ar-

3. James Early, "Romantic Thought and Architecture in the United States" (Ph.D. dissertation, Harvard University, 1953), 81, 148; see also Thomas E. Tallmadge, *The Story of Architecture in America* (New York, 1936), 144.

4. For the breakdown of these statistics, see James Philip Noffsinger, "The Influence of the Ecole des Beaux-Arts on the Architecture of the United States" (Ph.D. dissertation, Catholic University of America, 1955), 106–109. Usually graduates of American professional schools, American students at the Beaux-Arts performed so admirably that beginning French students felt disadvantaged; *ibid.,* 55. See also Charles Moore, *The Life and Times of Charles Follen McKim* (New York, 1970) 25–27.

5. As an American critic has pointed out, the overloaded Paris Opera building ran counter to this view. Benjamin, *Contemporary Art in Europe,* 106ff.

chitectural masterpieces, quite aside from exposure to constructive criticism, provided the kind of stimulation that students usually missed in the United States.[6] Some older American architects, who were either guided by designs of antiquity or their own imaginations, deprecated the "Frenchifying" of American architecture, but those trained in France passed the methods and principles acquired there on to many young compatriots who could not afford to attend the school in Paris.[7] Many American alumni of the Ecole des Beaux-Arts were appointed to the faculties of one or the other of nine architectural schools that came into existence in the United States between 1870 and 1895. In some instances experienced French architects filled teaching positions in these schools. Eugène Letang, a graduate of the Beaux-Arts, for instance, taught design at the Massachusetts Institute of Technology for eighteen years, to be succeeded in 1892 by the equally brilliant French designer Désiré Despradelle. Most of the late nineteenth-century American colleges of architecture also modeled their curriculums after that of the Ecole des Beaux-Arts.[8]

At least two other factors contributed to the considerable French impact on American architecture in the second half of the nineteenth century. The first involved the embellishment of Paris during the Second Empire. Napoleon III and Baron Georges Eugène Haussmann demonstrated that bold planners could beautify a big city, maintaining harmony in the overall design of individual buildings and a proper relationship between groups of buildings.[9] That American cities could not very well be made

6. A. D. F. Hamlin, "The Influence of the Ecole des Beaux-Arts on Our Architectural Education," *AR*, XXIII (1908), 242–44.

7. Ernest Flagg, "American Architecture as Opposed to Architecture in America," *AR*, X (1900), 178–80. As a tangible expression of their gratitude to France, some American architects established in the late 1880s the Prix Américain for outstanding French students of architecture. Ernest Flagg, "The Influence of French School on Architecture in the United States," *AR*, IV (1894), 223.

8. Noffsinger, "The Influence of the Beaux-Arts," 23–24; Thomas Hastings, "The Influence of the Ecole des Beaux-Arts upon American Architecture," *AR*, X (1901), 70; and Philadelphia Art Alliance, *Philadelphia Architecture in the Nineteenth Century* (Philadelphia, 1953), 15–16.

9. See Pinkney, *Napoleon III and the Rebuilding of Paris*, 4, 220. For the sake of architectural improvements benefiting the economy of Paris, they did not hesitate

over in the image of Paris did not seem to matter at first. The artistic superiority of Paris, for instance, was based on the fact that it was "an ordered and planned municipality," whereas New York was "a mere agglomeration, constructed according to the caprices of individual builders." The impressive architectural attainments of Paris during the Second Empire indeed underscored the suggestion that it had been "built by the State rather than its citizens."[10] And the second factor governing French influence on American architecture was related to the growth of American cities in the post–Civil War period and the appearance of wealthy citizens who loved the outward symbols of wealth displayed by the sumptuous mansions of the European upper classes. The chic and impressive facades that graced some of the avenues and streets of New York by the turn of the twentieth century attested to the lasting influence of the Beaux-Arts.[11] By the same token, the spirit of the time saw in the kind of monumental civic architecture of the Second Empire a symbolic expression of progress and civic pride, even though in America outward lavishness conflicted with traditional democratic notions of simplicity. Perhaps less impressive but as characteristic of French influence was the widespread adoption of the mansard roof, adding space and height to many houses.

Some contemporary evidence also revealed American criticism of the dominance of this French school; the criticism ranged from reservations to outright opposition. When Charles F. Mc-Kim, for example, was studying at the Beaux-Arts in 1869, his father, a pastor, advised him to spend six months in an architect's office in London because English architects were the ones who succeeded in New York. French and German architects, he cau-

---

to tear down entire blocks of old structures. Charles Moore, *Daniel H. Burnham: Architect of Cities* (2 vols.; Boston, 1921), II, 225.

10. Schuyler, *American Architecture*, II, 504, 577.

11. Claude Bragdon, "'Made in France' Architecture," *AR*, XVI (1904), 561–68; David F. Bowers (ed.), *Foreign Influences in American Life: Essays and Critical Bibliographies* (Princeton, N.J., 1944), 112–14; and Rosalie Thorne McKenna, "James Renwick, Jr., and the Second Empire Style in the United States," *American Magazine of Art*, XLIV (1951), 97–101.

tioned, were employed as draftsmen, receiving salaries from their English and American employers.[12] During the post–Civil War period demands for a national architecture were echoed widely. Why should Americans copy Doric or Gothic models? Critics argued that the excellent training at the Beaux-Arts applied to conditions prevalent in France and could not automatically be applied to the more modern requirements of the United States. The use of rough walls, high towers, and grotesque figures in American constructions seemed to be without reason. On balance, though, experience showed that American architects trained in France behaved in a fashion similar to that of American painters who had studied under the supervision of French masters. They were primarily interested in the acquisition of basic technical skills; but once at work at home, they reasserted their independence and were guided by their personal predilections and the needs and aesthetic development of their own country. The firms for which they worked upon their return from Paris taught them very quickly that "French ways are not our ways" and that practical financial considerations profoundly affected final plans.[13] The translations between 1875 and 1881 of Eugène Viollet-Le-Duc's *Discourses on Architecture*, furthermore, inspired American architects to develop a modern architecture based on the extensive use of metal and stone and designed to serve the modest needs of a democratic society rather than to ape the luxurious pretensions typical of the class-conscious high society of Europe.[14]

In search of appropriate forms for buildings in a rapidly growing and industrializing society, American architects were finally given trail-blazing direction by what came to be known as the "Chicago School." Louis Henri Sullivan of Chicago, admit-

12. James M. McKim to his son Charles, May 19, 1869, in Charles Follen McKim Correspondence, carton 7, LC. He had previously advised his son to study "the improved style of modern architecture in and near London. McKim, Sr., to his son Charles, February 23, 1869, Box 33, in Charles Follen McKim Papers, NYPL.

13. Flagg, "The Influence of French School," 211, 218; Herbert Croly, "The New World and the New Art," *AR*, XII (1902), 149; Early, "Romantic Thought and Architecture," 239–45.

14. Schuyler, *American Architecture, I,* 11, 33–34; Hitchcock, *Architecture* 197.

tedly indebted to the Beaux-Arts for his professional foundation, led the way with his guiding principle: "Form follows function." His sense of functionalism tried to meet the practical realities of life without ignoring deeply rooted social factors. Sullivan and Baron William Jenney, an engineer trained at the Ecole Polytechnique in Paris, pioneered in the 1880s with high-rise buildings using iron frames. Taking advantage of technological advances, the two men introduced in Chicago steel structures designed from a functional point of view and unencumbered by unnecessary decorations. Under their leadership, the schism that had traditionally existed between construction and architecture gave way to meaningful cooperation. Thereafter architects and engineers worked together closely designing and constructing office buildings, apartment houses, and public edifices. In the process, American engineers finally caught up with the longstanding artistic superiority of their French colleagues.[15] The high-rise commercial architecture of Chicago prompted a well-known French observer to react enthusiastically: "The simple force of need is such a principle of beauty. . . . The sketch appears here of a new kind of art, an art of democracy, made by the crowd and for the crowd, an art of science in which the certainty of natural laws gives to the most unbridled daring the tranquillity of geometrical figures."[16]

As far as some of the leading American architects who had been educated in France were concerned, Richard Morris Hunt (1827–1895) occupied a distinguished place. The first American admitted to the Ecole des Beaux-Arts in 1846, this nineteen-year-old youth, who enjoyed the reputation of being the most handsome American in Paris, studied under the direction of Hector

15. Hugh Morrison, *Louis Sullivan: Prophet of Modern Architecture* (New York, 1952), 253–57; W. Francklyn Paris, *The Hall of American Artists* (New York, 1952), 67–74; Carl W. Condit, *American Building Art: The Nineteenth Century* (New York, 1960), 232. The Union Centrale des Arts Décoratifs was so impressed with the originality and conception of the transportation building at the Chicago World Fair that it bestowed upon Sullivan gold, silver, and bronze medals.

16. Paul Bourget, *Outre-Mer: Impressions of America* (2 vols.; New York, 1895), I, 161.

Martin Lefuel. This connection opened doors to him that normally were closed to foreigners in France. Lefuel had been appointed as the architect for the new works on the Louvre. Thinking very highly of his American pupil, a Beaux-Arts graduate with distinction, Lefuel secured Hunt a position as inspector in charge of the design and working plans of the Pavillon de la Bibliothèque of the Louvre.[17] It was an extraordinary twist that a Yankee from Vermont was entrusted with the supervision of the construction of an imperial building in the Tuileries. Lefuel was so pleased with his American assistant that he did not want to let him return home in 1855. But Hunt rejected the notion that he should stay in France because America offered no gratifying opportunities in the fine arts. On the contrary, he optimistically envisioned a challenging artistic future in the United States, where he and the students trained by him could apply the lessons learned in France during a period of great architectural advances. Lefuel, after all, was only one of the masters who shaped Hunt's professional competence. He had the good fortune to watch the erection of Henri Labrouste's *Bibliothèque Sainte-Geneviève,* "the first attempt to use cast- and wrought-iron construction in an important public building from the foundations to the roof."[18] Upon his return home, Hunt's first designs particularly reflected his preference for the modern French Renaissance and its keenly developed sense for symmetry and elegance. The colorful and massive châteaux of the Loire country, built by expert craftsmen paying attention to minute detail in design and execution, had fascinated him from the time of his early travels through France.[19] The first townhouse he designed in New York, the Rossiter house on West 38th Street, betrayed his association

17. Montgomery Schuyler, "The Works of the Late Richard M. Hunt," *AR,* V (1895), 97–180; Allan Burnham, "The New York Architecture of Richard M. Hunt," *Journal of the Society of Architectural Historians,* XI (1952), 9–14; Henry Van Brunt, "Richard Morris Hunt," memorial address delivered at the American Institute of Architects, St. Louis, October 16, 1895.
18. Noffsinger, "The Influence of the Beaux-Arts," 11–13.
19. Paris, *The Hall of American Artists,* 41.

with the Beaux-Arts and Lefuel's work on the Louvre. The grandiose Victoria Hotel transplanted a Parisian sight to New York; and the Vanderbilt Hotel on Fifth Avenue created such a sensation that many new-rich Americans desired to add to the display of French fashions and furniture the illusion of a French château in the New World. The reasonably priced houses he designed for the sea resort at Newport, usually characterized by mansard roofs and economic space utilization, demonstrated his ability to adapt himself to American scenery.[20]

Although Henry Hobson Richardson (1838–1886) never graduated from the Ecole des Beaux-Arts, at which he had spent five years, from the time he returned to the United States in 1865 until his death in 1886 the "Richardson Romanesque" design dominated the architectural scene in the United States. Having failed to be admitted to the Beaux-Arts in 1859, he passed the entrance examinations the following year, ranking eighteenth among the sixty students who were accepted. Primarily interested in monumental architecture, in which the Beaux-Arts offered excellent instruction, Richardson threw himself into his studies in the same vigorous and mature manner that came to be so typical of his productive years. His preparation at the University of Louisiana and Harvard had helped to lay a solid educational foundation before he went to Paris to spend several years in the atelier of Jules Louis André whose knowledge and taste he respected and admired.[21] Eager to have as broad an experience as he could possibly obtain, Richardson also worked as a draftsman in the office of Henri Labrouste, the leading exponent of French rationalism and architect of the Bibliothèque Nationale.[22] Jacques Ignace Hittorff, the designer of the most modern railroad stations, introduced Richardson to the latest and most effective techniques

20. Schuyler, *American Architecture*, II, 76, 507.
21. Henry Russell Hitchcock, *The Architecture of H. H. Richardson and His Times* (Hamden, Conn., 1961), 24–50; Mrs. Schuyler Van Rensselaer, *Henri Hobson Richardson and His Works* (New York, 1888), 6–21.
22. Lewis Mumford, "The Regionalism of H. H. Richardson," in his *The South in Architecture* (New York, 1941), 82–88.

in this rapidly expanding field of architectural specialization.[23] And to round out his training he also studied painting for a time.

The versatile technical preparation he completed in France and the emphasis there on overall planning and composition aided him as much in his later work as did the habit he had acquired in France of carefully sketching his plans and compositions. Using this technique, he could leave it to draftsmen to complete the work under his supervision. As far as style went, he drew inspiration from the Romanesque architecture of the South of France. Unlike most of his contemporaries, he admired the artistic creations of the twelfth-century French masters; but he was also capable of innovations and he gave expression to robust personal tastes. The many monumental buildings which carry his imprint— among them the Buffalo State Hospital, Trinity Church in Boston, the Howard-Tilton Memorial Library in New Orleans, the Law School at Harvard, railroad stations, bridges, fountains, and apartment and commercial houses—secured him a prominent place in architectural history.[24] Though he was criticized for monotonous facades and too rugged and decorative constructions, contemporaries appreciated the personal energy and talents that his massive and powerful contributions evidenced. Just as Paris itself held no particular charm for him during his student years, he never developed any nostalgia for it. It remained simply the place that had started him off in the profession he really loved. When he returned to Paris later in life, with the reputation of a fabulously successful architect, he visited a few of his former fellow students at the Beaux-Arts, some of whom were now well-established government architects. It was very enlightening to him to learn from these French colleagues that they were thoroughly dissatisfied with the bureaucratic restrictions imposed upon them, compelling them to operate within the framework

23. Noffsinger, "The Influence of the Beaux-Arts," 16.

24. Ben Earl Looney, "Historical Sketch of Art in Louisiana," *LHQ*, XVIII (1935), 386–87; Jacques Gréber, *L'Architecture aux Etats-Unis* (2 vols.; Paris, 1920), I, 31; and Louis Gillet, "L'Architecture aux Etats-Unis et l'influence française," in E. Boutroux *et al.*, *Les Etats-Unis et la France* (Paris, 1914), 53–72.

of official styles, whether appropriate or not. They envied Richardson the degree of individualistic freedom he enjoyed in the exercise of his profession.[25]

In the three decades following the Civil War American architecture was as much in search of a workable equilibrium as the rest of society. Once the determination to reconstruct American society in a forward-looking fashion asserted itself, the ingenuity of American architects responded with a variety of architectural approaches. The resulting diversity of methods and styles reflected not only the individualistic professional freedom, but also the favorable conditions created for use of this freedom by the Civil War destruction, the great Chicago fire, and the World's Fair in 1893. The massive influx of immigrants and the phenomenal industrial expansion also added to the variety of styles employed. Naturally, these extraordinary conditions, changing the face of America within the short span of a generation, called for unusual resourcefulness. By and large, the architectural evolution of these decades embraced the fairly romantic phase headed by Richardson, the social functionalism advocated by Sullivan, and the modernized classical style preferred by such prominent architects as McKim, Mead & White, and many others.[26]

Richardson had laid too solid a foundation for Sullivan and McKim and their associates to ignore him; but they set in motion an identifiable reaction against Richardsonian style. Of the two challengers, Louis Sullivan (1856–1924), an American of French and Irish descent, subscribed unequivocally to Viollet-Le-Duc's view denying "the propriety of imposing on our age any reproduction of antique or medieval forms." A utilitarian, to whom architecture was as much a social function as an art, Sullivan emphasized in his high-rise steel structures in Chicago and St. Louis the realistic use of space by a modern mass society, without overlooking the desirability of artistic appearances.[27] Eventually,

25. Schuyler, *American Architecture*, I, 104–105.
26. Lewis Mumford, *The Brown Decades: A Study of the Arts in America,* 1865–1895 (New York, 1931), 165.
27. Fiske Kimball, *American Architecture* (New York, 1928), 150–59.

architects abroad adopted the protective terra-cotta casing in American steel structures, so effectively illustrated by Sullivan's Wainwright Building in St. Louis.

A third approach that gained considerable support in the last two decades of the century was led by McKim and his associates. Although Charles Follen McKim (1847–1909), an assistant in Richardson's office in the early 1870s, had been trained in Pierre Daumet's atelier at the Ecole des Beaux-Arts, his architectural tastes inclined more toward Rome than Paris.[28] His friend Stanford White (1853–1906), who had also been exposed to Beaux-Arts and Richardsonian experiences, joined McKim and Mead in the revival of abstract architectural forms. Impressed by Norman Shaw's return to a modernized version of neoclassicism in England, McKim led the movement in America that assigned simple architectural form and order a place of priority over functionalism and ornamentation.[29] Though intended to be contemporary and indigenous, their style amounted really to a combination of different styles adapted to modern times—classical, neocolonial, Shavian, Roman, and, sometimes, sixteenth and mid-nineteenth-century French. In 1909 the New York *Times*[30] asked: "Is not the Boston Library McKim's true monument?" A challenging contrast to Richardson's high Victorian Gothic Trinity Church, the Italianate Boston Public Library differed in material, shape, and color, and was at least in part inspired by the Bibliothèque Sainte-Geneviève in Paris.[31] Nevertheless, its design was McKim's, and the simplicity of its quadrangular structure, its impressive row of arches facing Copley Square, its staircases and murals made it a much-admired artistic attraction. Though the architects who designed the plans for the World's Fair in Chicago leaned generally toward McKim's concepts, the ephemer-

28. Thomas C. Richards, "The Career of an American Architect," Boston *Evening Transcript*, January 4, 1930.

29. Hitchcock, *Architecture*, 226–29; Kimball, *American Architecture*, 161–63.

30. New York *Times*, September 16, 1909.

31. Hoyt Granger, *Charles Follen McKim: A Study of His Life and Work* (Boston, 1913), 23–24.

al nature of architectural styles manifested itself paradoxically at the same time. Contemporary commercial architecture in America, with its emphasis on high steel structures and functional design, first advocated by Sullivan and after the late 1880s even more masterfully executed by Frank Lloyd Wright, ultimately prevailed over its neoclassical competitor.[32] As French influence on American architecture was gradually declining, modern American architecture was coming into its own, eventually to influence the forms and techniques of European architects.

32. Hitchcock, *Architecture*, 230–32.

CHAPTER XII

Cooperation in the
Natural Sciences

The flourishing of the sciences in France before, during, and after the Great Revolution owed as much to certain favorable conditions as the slow progress of science in the young American republic can be attributed to conditions that were not very conducive to their rapid advancement. Nineteenth-century French scientists could build on the momentum that modern science had gained in Europe, and their thorough training in the mathematical sciences provided them with an additional asset. The traditional emphasis on abstract thinking came naturally to an aristocratic society in which, according to Tocqueville, "science is more particularly called upon to furnish gratification to the mind." More concretely, in 1794, Joseph Lakanal, a member of the Committee of Public Instruction, urged the cultivation of the mathematical sciences because "they give the habit of accuracy: without them astronomy and navigation have no guide; architecture, both civil and naval, has no rule; the sciences of artillery and of fortification have no foundation."[1]

So strong were these sentiments that even the political storms of the revolutionary era did not uproot them. Since scientific ex-

1. Tocqueville, *Democracy in America,* II, 46; John T. Merz, *A History of European Thought in the Nineteenth Century* (4 vols.; London, 1903–1914), I, 111; G. de Bertier de Sauvigny, *The Bourbon Restoration,* trans. Lynn M. Case (Philadelphia, 1966), 332.

ploration necessitates the right of free and unrestricted inquiry, any curtailment of this freedom not only impedes the work of the explorer but also reflects on the political system of his country. That Paris was in the first half of the century looked upon as the metropolis of science evidently substantiated the freedom and financial support of its scientific community. The gradual loss of this preeminent place in the second half of the century reflected, therefore, the stifling consequences of insufficient backing and understanding.

On the whole, scientists in America labored under quite different conditions through most of the century. Their socially and politically pioneering country was much too preoccupied with furnishing the needs of the body to be overly concerned with pure mathematics and other abstractions. During the Restoration period French observers noted, moreover, that in their eagerness to become in every respect independent of Europe, American scientists lost valuable time in the development of the sciences by "trying to prove what had already been proved in Europe."[2] Even after Americans recognized the interdependence of the international science community, they continued to honor their scientists much less than was the practice in Europe. As Joseph Henry (1797–1878), one of the illustrious American scientists of the last century has pointed out: "In other countries, scientific discovery is stimulated by pensions, by titles of honor, and by various social and official distinctions." But instead of awarding those, he continued, "who enlarge the field of human thought and human power," Americans have heretofore recognized "but three principal means of distinction . . . : the acquisition of wealth, the possession of political power, and successful military achievement."[3]

2. Anne Wharton Smith, "Criticism of American Life and Letters," 82–83; Richard H. Shryock, "American Indifference to Basic Science During the Nineteenth Century," *Archives Internationales d'Histoire des Sciences* (October, 1948), 50–65.

3. Quoted in Bernard Jaffe, *Men of Science in America* (New York, 1958), 204–205.

To be a scientist in nineteenth-century America, one had to be a person wanting, in James Russell Lowell's words:

> To feel mysterious Nature ever new,
> To touch, if not to grasp, her endless clew,
> And learn by each discovery how to wait;
> To widen knowledge and escape the praise;
> Wisely to teach, because more wise to learn;
> To toil for Science, not to draw men's gaze.

Though the number of such American scientists was comparatively small, gifted and self-denying pioneers labored assiduously in every field of scientific endeavor. In a detailed and perceptive letter written in 1847, Louis Agassiz, the distinguished European naturalist who had come to reside in the United States, called the roll of Americans who had already made a name for themselves in the various sciences. If the aggregate picture of science in mid-century America looked respectable to him, his outlook for its future was very optimistic. What American scientists needed, he suggested to Henri Milne-Edwards (1800–1885), the prominent French zoologist, was confidence in themselves. Although prestige should be a gratifying by-product rather than the objective of accomplishments, human nature, Agassiz philosophized, was such that the seekers of prestige might well be induced to step up their efforts in order to merit recognition. He recommended therefore that as a mark of distinction the Société Philomatique de Paris award diplomas to some of the most outstanding American scientists. This recommendation was promptly implemented by honoring in this fashion James Dwight Dana, and others, including Agassiz, in subsequent years.[4]

Agassiz's confidence in the advancement of the sciences in America was not based merely upon his faith in the dedication and resourcefulness of its scientists, but on the most generous public support of their work as well. When he asked the public to underwrite a work on the natural history of the United States,

4. Louis Agassiz to Henri Milne-Edwards, May 31, 1847, HCL b MS Am 1419 (69).

in a matter of days laymen interested in science had subscribed $100,000.[5] To the amazement of Europeans, American citizens contributed funds to scientific institutions, museums, and observatories in amounts that in the Old World only governments provided. Motivated by civic and national pride, as well as by the realistic notion that the application of science to industry and society would promote the general welfare, these private investors were ultimately more concerned with the benefits of science to society than with the individuals who were making the benefits possible.

It is amazing how closely French and American scientists worked together, to further their own interests, to be sure, but also to advance science itself. In every area of scientific investigation they maintained contact with each other or at least endeavored to keep abreast of the latest progress. Naturally, they gradually moved from elementary to more complex matters of common interest, with Americans consciously trying to accelerate the pace that would enable them to reach a level of equality. To accomplish this goal lines of communication were established not only with French scientists, but with many others as well.

France extended financial support to its naturalists who embarked upon the exploration of the natural resources of the United States, hoping to discern the practical exploitation of these resources, as well as to gratify the scientists' thirst for knowledge. The success of French fur traders in North America in the past encouraged nineteenth-century French officials to underwrite scientific expeditions to America. At the beginning of the Restoration government, two able and artistically gifted French naturalists, Jacques Gérard Milbert and Charles Alexandre Lesueur, embarked for America; Milbert concentrated on the Northeast and his friend Lesueur principally on the Ohio and Mississippi Valley regions. Despite their backing by the ad-

5. See Auguste Laugel, "Revue des Sciences," *Le Temps,* May 28, 1861; Louis Agassiz to A. de Valenciennes, unsigned draft, probably 1856, HCL b MS Am 1419 (130); and Jules Violle, "L'Exposition de Chicago et la science américaine," *RDDM,* CXXIII (June, 1894), 604–10.

ministrators of the Musée d'Histoire Naturelle and the cooperation of Hyde de Neuville, the king's minister to the United States, the two were evidently making great personal sacrifices, enduring hardships and primitive conditions, as well as financial difficulties. According to Milbert's correspondence, the king's ministers did not keep their promises of support; he was compelled to protest: "I cannot live on 6,000 francs ($1,200) in a country where everything is much more expensive than in France, make acquisitions for the Museum, and provide for my family in Paris."[6]

While in America, Milbert received from the professors at the Natural History Museum in Paris requests for reptiles, certain great falcons, warblers, and every type of fish, above all molluscs without shell.[7] By the time Milbert finished his expedition, he had shipped many cargoes of dead and living animals of every category. Despite the careful handling of live animals sent across the ocean, some of them perished on the way to France. In view of the efforts and expenses involved in these shipments, the condition in which the animals arrived in Paris assumed vital importance. When Milbert, for instance, sent two great American rays to Paris he wanted to know whether the shipping arrangements had been satisfactory enough to be duplicated in the future. And when he was about to send a huge buffalo to Paris, he made the special request that official orders be given to disembark this animal very carefully, to put it for several days on a pasture to recover from the voyage, and to take it to the royal garden by boat so as not to expose it to curious multitudes.[8]

The customary letters of introduction to scientists at Harvard and Yale resulted in the kind of friendly reception Milbert had

6. Jacques G. Milbert to the administrators of the Jardin du Roi, New York, n.d., read at the meeting of January 15, 1822, MS. in Milbert Papers, ANF; Jean G. Hyde de Neuville to Georges Cuvier, December 29, 1819, *ibid.*
7. The administrators of the Musée d'Histoire Naturelle to Jacques G. Milbert, May 21, 1819, *ibid.*.
8. Jacques G. Milbert to the administrators of the Musée, June 21, and July 26, 1819, *ibid.*

hoped for. He was particularly pleased with Professor Benjamin Silliman's genuine desire for future exchanges between French and American naturalists.[9] Following their meeting, Silliman sent to Alexandre Brongniart, the eminent geologist, a box of marine fossils from the Catskill region.

American zoology and paleontology were also greatly furthered by Lesueur and his friend William Maclure who excelled in describing several species of fish in the rivers of the United States, fish largely unknown to European naturalists. Lesueur's explorations took him as far south as New Orleans and as far west as the Wabash, where he discovered several new types of chelonians. He even arranged for Europeans to be able to see such unknown curiosities as a live skunk and a wild turkey he had managed to catch in the woods of New Harmony. During his long stay in America, Lesueur maintained contact with the leading naturalists in Paris and with many members of scientific societies in New York and Philadelphia, besides contributing to the journal of the Natural Science Academy of Philadelphia, of which he became a member. To expedite the dissemination of the materials he found on his excursions, Lesueur made his own drawings and engravings, a precious legacy in the history of early nineteenth-century American science.[10]

It has been said that the systematic treatment of American zoology started with the publication of Alexander Wilson's *American Ornithology* (1808–1814), a work about which Baron Georges Cuvier commented: "He has treated American birds better than those of Europe have yet been treated." Besides Charles Lucien Bonaparte's early contributions to American ornithology, John James Audubon's work *Birds of America* (1827–1839) has become a classic, beautiful in the execution of its drawings, though not always scientifically accurate. As hopeful and anxious as Audubon was that his personal appeals in France

9. James Pierce to Alexandre Brongniart, November 25, 1822, in Musée d'Histoire Naturelle.

10. Ernest Théodore Hamy, "Les Voyages du naturaliste Charles-Alexandre Lesueur dans l'Amérique du Nord (1815–1837)," *Journal de la Société des Américanistes,* V (1904), 1–103; Adrien Loir, *Charles Alexandre Lesueur: Artiste et savant français en Amérique de* 1816 à 1839 (Le Havre, 1920).

would help him secure needed subscriptions for his expensive project, he left France in 1828 a very disappointed man. Even Cuvier's favorable review of Audubon's first volume did not result in more than thirteen subscriptions within two months. As experience also taught Louis Agassiz some time later, France was not as encouraging a market for the sale of scientific books as were England and Germany.[11]

That French naturalists wanted to play an active role in the comprehensive survey of the animal, vegetable, and mineral worlds of America was perhaps less remarkable than was the professional assistance the Frenchmen could count on from qualified American scientists. Soon after he had received his M.D. degree from the University of Pennsylvania, John Edwards Holbrook (1794–1871) visited Paris where he became friendly with several eminent French naturalists, particularly the herpetologist André-Marie-Constant Duméril and Achille Valenciennes who encouraged him to cultivate the science of herpetology in the United States. A generation later Holbrook returned to France as the highly praised author of the multivolume work *Herpetology of the United States* (1841); and French naturalists paid him the great compliment of asking him to determine or verify the identification of North American reptiles in the Musée d'Histoire Naturelle and the Jardin des Plantes.[12]

Indicative of the progress America had made in the sciences was a letter Henri Milne-Edwards wrote in 1843 to James Dwight Dana: "Although I had not yet the pleasure of corresponding

11. See A. S. Packard, Jr., "A Century's Progress in American Zoology," *American Naturalist,* X (1876), 591–98; David Starr Jordan (ed.), *Leading American Men of Science* (New York, 1910), 69; Alexandre B. Adams, *John James Audubon: A Biography* (New York, 1966), 345–52; Francis H. Herrick, *Audubon the Naturalist: A History of His Life and Time* (2 vols.; New York, 1917), I, 329–31; and Elmer Charles Herber (ed.), *Correspondence Between Spencer Fullerton Baird and Louis Agassiz: Two Pioneer Naturalists* (Washington, D.C., 1963), 86.

12. Theodore Gill, "Biographical Memoir of John Edwards Holbrook, 1794–1871," U.S. National Academy of Sciences, *Biographical Memoirs,* V (1905), 46–77. For the contributions of the French-American scholar Dr. Charles Girard to the herpetology and ichthyology of North America, see G. Brown Goode, "Bibliographies of American Naturalists: The Published Writings of Dr. Charles Girard," U.S. National Museum, *Bulletin,* No. 41 (Washington, D.C., 1891), v–vi.

with you I had long considered you as an old acquaintance, for a sort of fraternity exists between men who cultivate the same science, and the perusal of your valuable papers on siphonostoma had shown me that carcinology may now expect to reap as much benefit from the labor of American naturalists as from the observations of an European observer."[13] In a letter written three years later, Milne-Edwards expressed satisfaction that Dana's views with respect to polyps did not essentially differ from his own, and he found Dana's table of classification of different polyps so helpful that he promptly included it in an issue of the *Annales des Sciences Naturelles*. And on September 20, 1847, the distinguished French zoologist had the pleasure of notifying Dana that the Société Philomatique, having seen his important work on *Zoophytes*, had voted to make Dana one of its corresponding members. This encouraging recognition was couched in terms that not only honored an individual American scientist, but acknowledged that "the natural sciences are nowadays cultivated with equal success on both sides of the Atlantic."[14]

The selfless devotion to exacting scholarship which underlay the rapid progress of American science was also illustrated by Joseph Leidy (1823–1891). In 1848 this young medical doctor and curator at the Philadelphia Academy of Natural Sciences visited Europe, establishing personal contacts with British and French scientists and acquiring an idea about the comparative quality of collections in the British Museum and the Jardin des Plantes.[15] Like so many of his contemporary colleagues, Leidy was no narrow specialist. Distinguished as a comparative anatomist, his chief distinction as a scientist rested on his work as a pioneering vertebrate paleontologist. Early in his scientific work, he realized that the unfamiliarity of French paleontologists with the western United States made them unreliable as resources in his investigations of American fossils. In the course of his own

13. Daniel C. Gilman, *The Life of James Dwight Dana* (New York, 1899), 348–49.
14. *Ibid.*, 351.
15. Joseph Leidy, Diary, June 22, 1848, ANSP. On Leidy, consult Henry F. Osborn, *Impressions of Great Naturalists* (New York, 1928).

studies, he helped refine techniques for the preservation of damaged as well as whole specimens. But his most important paleontological contributions were contained in his monographs, *Mammalian Remains of Nebraska* (1853) and *Extinct Mammalian Fauna of Dakota and Nebraska* (1869) in which he established links between faunas in Europe and North America. His research in parasitology alerted him to the observation that certain parasitic forms transmitted from animals to man might be "one of the previously unrecognized causes of pernicious anaemia." French scientists recognized his genuine promise early in his career by making him, in 1851, a corresponding member of the Société de Biologie. In recognition of his brilliant accomplishments he received, thirty years later, the Cuvier medal from the Institute of France.

The developmental momentum of natural history in the United States was accelerated in 1846 with the arrival of Louis Agassiz (1807–1873), a Swiss naturalist with a strong base in Paris. An extraordinary combination of circumstances brought young Agassiz in contact with such eminent naturalists as Charles von Martius of Munich and Georges Cuvier of Paris who fostered his study of living and fossil fish. By the time Agassiz came to the United States to deliver some lectures and to study its natural history, his solid reputation rested on his geological and paleontological research. Indeed, the diversity of his scientific interests widened the circle of his social and professional contacts in the United States so quickly that in 1848 he was prevailed upon to accept a professorship in zoology at Harvard University. He demonstrated inexhaustible energy, both as a teacher who inspired his students to study the open book of nature and as a researcher who explored the zoological past and present of the country from which even the emperor's offer of the chair of paleontology in the Musée d'Histoire Naturelle could not lure him away.[16] He so cherished

16. Elizabeth Cary Agassiz (ed.), *Louis Agassiz: His Life and Correspondence* (2 vols.; Boston, 1885), II, 550–52; Catherine Owens Peare, *A Scientist of Two Worlds: Louis Agassiz* (Philadelphia, 1958), 34–35, 42–43; Arnold Guyot, *Louis Agassiz: A Biographical Memoir* (Princeton, N.J., 1883), 18–19; and Louis Agassiz to Benjamin Silliman, February 1, 1846, HCL MS Am 1419.

the opportunities and independence he found in the United States, not to mention the escape from the enervating in-fighting among professional cliques in Paris, that he confided to Martius that he would reject even an offer of absolute power to reorganize the Jardin des Plantes with a budget of fifty million francs.[17]

In 1856, after a deliberate lapse of ten years, he resumed his European correspondence, exchanging scientific data with such old French friends as Milne-Edwards, Elie de Beaumont, and Brongniart; and he always tried to support the exchange of animals from global regions not well represented in French and American collections.[18] His searching mind did not limit itself to simple identification and classification of the world of nature. His curiosity induced him to investigate larger relationships of plants and animals of different geographic regions and spanning long periods of time. He pondered, for instance, why the forests of America, though located in about the same latitude as those of Europe, were so different and generally resembled forests of the Molasses age.[19] Probably his most ambitious speculation was embodied in his *Studies About Glaciers* (1840). Once his friend Jean de Carpentier had aroused his curiosity about how the huge boulders in the Swiss mountains, differing from the formations over which they were located, got there, he defied the risks and gathered the evidence that ultimately confirmed his friend's theory. According to this theory, glaciers had been the vehicle that moved the giant rocks over long distances. In Agassiz's judgment, "great sheets of ice once covered vast European

17. Louis Agassiz to Charles Martius, November 3, 1858, HCL MS Am 1419 (140).

18. Henri Milne-Edwards to Louis Agassiz, November 22, 1863, HCL MS Am 1419 (495) ; Alphonse Milne-Edwards to Louis Agassiz, July 6, 1865, HCL MS Am 765.

19. Louis Agassiz to Henri Milne-Edwards, May 31, 1847, HCL MS Am 1419 (69). A generation later, in 1878, the American zoologist Edward D. Cope was amazed to find at Reims a collection that "combined the faunae of two or three formations of our western regions which are separate with us, and especially includes the beasts of the upper Missouri region which I discovered in 1865, which have never before been found in Europe. All are from Reims!" Persifor Frazer, "The Life and Letters of Edward Drinker Cope," *American Geologist,* XXVI (1900), 102.

spaces." European scientists considered this work so important that in 1864 Milne-Edwards expressed the hope that it would be extended to glaciers in America.[20] Agassiz's glacier theory tended to support Georges Cuvier's (1769–1832) cataclysmic theory. According to this eminent authority on comparative anatomy, there had been a succession of species on earth. But when these species, originally created by divine power, were extinguished by repeated natural catastrophes, new species, modeled on the previous types, appeared on the scene. This theory of evolution left so many questions unanswered that, at best, it stimulated thought, research, and controversy among scientists in several countries.

In the United States, differences of opinion with respect to evolutionary theories led to an alienation between Agassiz and some of his fellow scientists. In France, Georges Louis Buffon, from 1739 until 1788 director of the Royal Gardens in Paris, had cautiously suggested that the environment modified the structure of plants and animals which, in turn, adapted themselves to it. Others, including Geoffroy Saint-Hilaire (1772–1844) , were searching for meaningful explanations for the change in species. Eventually, Jeanne Baptiste Lamarck (1744–1829) published his *Philosophie Zoologique* (1809) in which he elaborated upon his laws of organic evolution and transmutation, contending that variations in species could be traced to direct and indirect actions of the environment and that the changes were inherited by the offspring. Lamarck's hypotheses were bitterly challenged by Cuvier whose authoritative reputation was at stake in this controversy.

Constantine Samuel Rafinesque (1783–1840) , the brilliant European-born naturalist who, despite great hardships, never tired of exploring the United States, had been in communication with Cuvier and other European scientists. His all-absorbing search for new species in America and his observations over a long period

20. Henri Milne-Edwards to Louis Agassiz, December 15, 1864, HCL MS Am 1419 (496) ; A. Hunter Dupree, *Asa Gray,* 1810–1888 (Cambridge, Mass., 1959), 226–27. On December 26, 1864, Agassiz sent an important communication to Milne-Edwards with reference to the metamorphoses of fish; see *Annales des Sciences Naturelles, Zoologie,* 5th ser., III (1865) , 55–58.

of time induced Rafinesque to develop views that foreshadowed Darwin's evolutionary theory. In 1833, he summed up his findings in his *Herbarium Rafinesquianum*: "Species and perhaps genera also are forming in organized beings by gradual deviation of shapes, forms, and organs, taking place in the lapse of time. There is a tendency to deviations and mutations through plants and animals by gradual steps at remote, irregular periods. This is part of the great universal law of *perpetual mutability* in every thing. . . . Every variety is a deviation which becomes a Species as soon as it is permanent by reproduction."[21]

If scientists disagreed on the question of evolution then and thereafter on scientific grounds, religious and personal considerations also continued to make it an explosive and divisive issue. The appearance of Charles Darwin's (1809–1882) *The Origin of Species* (1859) added so much fuel to this controversy that it caused a worldwide storm of protest. Reaction to Darwin was as critical in France as in the United States. Three years passed before a French edition of Darwin's work was published. Particularly religious antagonists who looked upon Darwin's principles of natural selection and the survival of the fittest as a new atheistic attack and a blasphemous repudiation of the Book of Genesis left no doubt about the extent of their dissent. That a scientist of Benjamin Silliman's prominence sided with Cuvier on the ground that geological evidence substantiated the theory of catastrophism made contemporary scientists and laymen pause. In retrospect, however, it was perhaps even more significant that Silliman was very much concerned with keeping the Bible's explanation of Creation intact.

21. Bernard Jaffe, *Men of Science in America*, 116–26; see also, Edward D. Cope, *On the Hypothesis of Evolution: Physical and Metaphysical* (New Haven, 1871), 4; B. C. Gruenberg, *The Story of Evolutions Facts and Theories on the Development of Life* (Garden City, N.Y., 1929), 281–83; Gertrude Himmelfarb, *Darwin and the Darwinian Revolution* (Garden City, N.Y., 1959), 206, 289–90; B. Glass, O. Tomkin, W. L. Strauss (eds.), *Forerunners of Darwin, 1745–1859* (Baltimore, 1959), 357–58; Helen Dean King, "Edward Drinker Cope," *American Geologist*, XXIII (1899), 1–41; Edward D. Cope, "On Archaesthetism," *American Naturalist*, XVI (1882), 454–59; and the scientific columns of *Le Temps*, July 23, 1861, and January 25, 1870.

Asa Gray, on the other hand, whom Darwin had taken into his confidence, refuted the charge of atheism and, in his own fashion, defended the hypothesis that man had evolved from lower species. This defense brought him into conflict with Agassiz who, as a supporter of Cuvier's views, felt compelled to part company with many of his colleagues. But despite the fact that certain scientists charged Agassiz's stand in the question of evolution with delaying the development of biology by half a century, his paleontological and zoological contributions were too solid to deprive him of a distinguished place in history. The recipient of the Prix Cuvier (1851) enjoyed a stature that helped to advance American science substantially.

Later in the century, the famous American zoologist Edward Drinker Cope (1840–1897) took exception to Darwin on the ground that natural selection per se could not produce variations. As a neo-Lamarckist, he explained the changes in terms of the theory that "use [or disuse] modifies structure in the animal kingdom." He asserted, moreover, that animals could actively influence their lives and that they passed newly acquired characteristics on to their descendants. In the history of science, the controversy over evolution constituted a major milestone. The fact that American scientists like Leidy and Cope had conducted research that led them to support the theories of Cuvier and Lamarck respectively, as well as Asa Gray's association with Darwin, demonstrated that Americans had begun to become part of the mainstream of science. And it augured well for the future of scientific inquiry in the United States that the defenders of Darwin did not permit themselves to be intimidated.

Having taken the initiative in the search for scientific explanations of the origin and evolution of species, European scientists continued to lead these discussions. Americans, however, were not satisfied with following the lead of Europeans in other scientific areas. In 1845 a member of the Entomological Society of Pennsylvania, John Lawrence LeConte, made a stirring appeal to American entomologists to become so professional that insects would no longer have to be sent to Europe for identification. "Are we to be bound by the mere dictum of some European entomologist, of equal indolence with ourselves," he asked, "who chooses to name the insects which we have discovered?"[22] Within the next decades two French and European entomological societies acknowledged the great strides made by their American friends. Indeed, for his work on insects and their control, Townend Glover (1813–1883), professor of natural sciences in the Maryland Agricultural College, received in 1865 the grand gold medal of Napoleon III. The jury of the entomological convention in Paris found his work "original in its style and character and deserving to be copied by the entomologists of France."[23] Glover studied the effects of insects on crops, originally as a staff member of the United States Bureau of Agriculture and later as entomologist in the new Department of Agriculture. His important research and his familiarity with the work of European entomologists put him in the forefront of his profession. French naturalists also appreciated the research of Dr. Asa Fitch who specialized in insects harmful to plants and animals and recommended remedies to control or eradicate them.[24] Pierre Joseph Michel Lorquin, a French lawyer and naturalist lured to California by the discovery of gold, supplied his friend Jean A. Boisduval, the famous French lepidopterist, with butterflies and moths he had caught in various parts of California. Such direct and indirect contacts continued to keep scientists on both sides of the Atlantic abreast of developments in their specialties.

From a strictly scientific point of view, Edward Swift Balch, an American naturalist, was fascinated by a visit to Armand Viré's catacombs in the Jardin des Plantes. Guided by a lighted

22. Harry B. Weiss, *The Pioneer Century of American Entomology* (New Brunswick, N.J., 1936), 155–59, 173, 185–86, 307-308. Such noted French entomologists as Etienne Mulssant and Jean Alphonse Boisduval had named many American insects.

23. Charles Richard Dodge, "The Life and Entomological Work of the Late Townend Glover," U.S. Department of Agriculture, Division of Entomology, *Bulletin*, No. 18 (Washington, D.C., 1888), 13–21.

24. See *Annales des Sciences Naturelles, Zoologie*, VII (1857), 265; and Asa Fitch, *First and Second Report on the Noxious, Beneficial and Other Insects of the State of New York* (Albany, N.Y., 1856, 1865, 1867).

candle, Viré and Balch descended the more than thirty winding stone steps to look at insects from caves. Though scientists had previously observed insects from the outside adapt themselves "to the requirements of living in total darkness, and to assume some of the characteristics and to move towards the forms of the cave dwellers," and vice versa, they had heretofore not known "how quickly these biological changes take place."[25]

French-American scientific contacts were not always limited to scientists. In some instances, the two governments developed science-related interests of mutual concern. Late in the nineteenth century, for instance, the French government sought information from America about "the means employed to preserve streams from depopulation or for encouraging their restocking."[26] French and American naturalists also worked closely with their governments in international attempts to prevent the extermination of seals and migratory birds subjected to indiscriminate killing.[27]

Early Franco-American cooperation in botany was even more extensive than in zoology. In the fall of 1785 self-interest and scientific curiosity brought three Frenchmen to the shores of the United States—André Michaux, his son François André, and the practical gardener Paul Saulnier. They set out to cultivate huge tree nurseries in Bergen, New Jersey, and Charleston, South Carolina, with the intent of providing France with lumber resources far superior to those obtainable on its own soil. Within a few years they shipped some sixty thousand trees to the Rambouillet nurseries, expecting to lay the foundation for a tree plantation of truly impressive scope. To their frustrated amazement, they discovered in 1790 that the queen had practically nullified their objective, because she had used the American trees as gifts for her imperial father in Austria and the private estates of some members of the French nobility. In the first decade of

25. Edward Swift Balch, Journal, Paris, June 2, 1899, II, 237–40, MS in UV.
26. French Legation to Thomas F. Bayard, June 25, 1886, FNTDS.
27. See enclosures in Henry Vignaud to James G. Blaine, Paris, April 28, 1892, DDFDS.

the nineteenth century François Michaux spent two more periods in the United States to salvage, with Napoleon's backing, the mission with which his father had originally been entrusted. To make doubly sure Eleuthère Irénée du Pont pleaded with Madame Josephine Bonaparte to help increase the national wealth of France by lending her support to the tree-planting enterprise. The seeds François shipped to France were reported to have ultimately produced nearly a quarter of a million trees.[28]

André Michaux's travels in America also resulted in the valuable publication of three monumental volumes entitled *Histoire des arbres forestiers de l'Amérique du Nord* and his *Flora Boreali-Americana*, a work that in time was replaced only by the comprehensive surveys of John Torrey and his associate Asa Gray.[29] By way of gratitude for the cooperation the Michauxs had received from American officials and the American Philosophical Society during their mission in the United States, François André Michaux provided in his will for a fund that later in the century helped finance scientific forestry in the United States. Even during the turbulent era of the French Revolution, Frenchmen continued to explore the botanical resources of America, patiently describing, identifying, classifying, and sometimes naming thousands of varieties of flowers, trees, plants, fruits, and vegetables. Although many of their shipments and descriptive documents were lost because of fire, theft, or shipping hazards, enough reached France to enrich the knowledge of botanists everywhere.[30]

28. Rodney H. True, "François André Michaux, the Botanist and Explorer," APS, *Proceedings,* LXXVIII (1938), 313–27; see also François Michaux's note, written in 1831, in Boston Public Library, Fr. 112; and du Pont, *Life of Eleuthère Irénée du Pont,* V, 347–52.

29. John H. Barnhart, "European Influences in American Botany," *Journal of the New York Botanical Garden,* XXVI (May, 1925), 102–11,; Susan Delano McKelvey, *Botanical Exploration of the Trans-Mississippi West,* 1790–1850 (Jamaica Plain, Mass., 1955), 65.

30. See J. Ewan, "L'Activité des premiers explorateurs français dans le S. E. des Etats-Unis," in *Les Botanistes français en Amérique du Nord avant 1850* (Paris, 1957), 17–32; William J. Robbins, "Les Botanistes français et la flore du Nord-Est des Etats-Unis: J. G. Milbert et Elias Durand," *ibid.,* 41–50; J. R. Schramm, "Influence, passée et présente, de François Michaux sur la foresterie et la recherche forestière en Amérique," *ibid.,* 287–300; and Ph. Guinier, "Ce que les jardins et les forêts de France doivent aux forêts américaines," *ibid.,* 329–37.

Among the many French naturalists who temporarily resided in the United States, Jacques Gérard Milbert left a rich scientific legacy. During eight years, from 1815 to 1823, he sent to the Museum of Natural History in Paris nearly eight thousand botanical, zoological, and geological specimens, including six hundred living trees and a great variety of animals. In his artistically illustrated *Itinéraire pittoresque du fleuve Hudson et des parties latérales de l'Amérique du Nord*, Milbert unveiled the fabulously beautiful and diverse world of nature in America. He also sounded the alarm of a conservation-oriented naturalist. Like the Michauxs, Milbert deplored the American tendency to cut down trees without regard to the consequences of deforestation on soil and natural windbreaks—devastating consequences, as the experience of France had demonstrated in the past.[31] As Gifford Pinchot, a graduate of Yale who in 1889 studied at the forestry school at Nancy, reminded his contemporary countrymen, the advice of the Michauxs and Milbert to utilize American forests in a more rational manner was as sound as ever.

Once nineteenth-century French scientists recognized the high caliber performance of their American colleagues, they cooperated with them splendidly.[32] Such American giants of the botanical world as John Torrey (1796–1873) and Asa Gray (1810–1888) were in close touch with Adolphe-Théodore Brongniart (1801–1876), of the Musée d'Histoire Naturelle, Joseph Decaisne (1807–1882), of the Jardin des Plantes, and such other eminent French botanists as Adrien Jussieu (1797–1853) and Jules Paul Benjamin Delessert (1773–1847). Both Torrey and Gray had met these and other botanists on their visits to Paris. And when they did not correspond with each other or keep themselves informed through the exchange of professional journals and books, they sent each

31. Constance D. Sherman, "A French Artist Portrays the Natural Bridge," *VMHB*, LXVIII (1960), 166–70.
32. For a time, "impudent pretenders to science (mostly foreigners)," seem to have given Europeans wrong impressions about American scientists. Amos Eaton to Adolphe Brongniart, October 2, 1833, in Musée d'Historie Naturelle; see also G. W. Featherstonhaugh to David Bailie Warden, November 2, 1831, in D. B. Warden Papers, Vol. VII, LC.

other packages with seeds, well-packed roots, or dried flowers and plants, in accordance with Gray's observation: "Botanical presents are like gifts among Indians. They always presuppose a return."[33] Even though such exchanges had been going on for a long time, Ernest-Saint-Charles Cosson (1819–1889), the president of the Botanical Society of France, was puzzled by the presence of so many European botanical species right next to the quite different local types in the California mountains.[34]

During a month in Paris, Torrey compared the large collection of plants which he had brought along with the specimens in Michaux's herbarium.[35] When Gray went to Europe in 1839, he visited Paris, but he also familiarized himself with the botanical collections in southern France, Italy, and Austria. He clearly intended to assume scientific leadership in questions involving American plant life and to establish his *Flora of North America* as the authoritative reference source Europeans would have to use.[36] At first a little handicapped by the language barrier, he wrote to Mrs. Torrey: "You would laugh most heartily to see me . . . in the Jardin des Plantes, endeavoring to carry on a conversation with . . . Decaisne."[37] But he managed, in part at least because everybody tried to help him. Decaisne and Gray together examined all the species they could find in the Jardin des Plantes, and they exchanged notes and papers, some of which had not yet been published. Delessert made it possible for Gray to study several marvelous private collections of plants in Paris. And Charles F. B. Mirbel, the distinguished specialist in vegetable

33. Quoted in Dupree, *Asa Gray*, 90–91; see also John Torrey to Asa Gray, May 2, 1834, and May 21, 1844, in Gray Herbarium, Cambridge; and Adrien Jussieu to John Torrey, July 26, 1844, in Bronx Botanical Garden. It is noteworthy that when in 1847 the Museum of Natural History sent Auguste Adolphe Lucien Trécul on a scientific mission to North America, the French Minister of Agriculture and Commerce charged him to gather information also about the farinaceous plants Western Indians used for their meals. McKelvey, *Botanical Exploration*, 1048–54.

34. Ernest Cosson to Asa Gray, August 22, 1864, in Gray Herbarium, Cambridge.

35. Andrew Denny Rodgers, *John Torrey: A Story of North American Botany* (Princeton, N.J., 1942), 107–109, 203.

36. Dupree, *Asa Gray*, 196, 235–36.

37. Jane Loring Gray (ed.), *Letters of Asa Gray* (2 vols.; Boston, 1893), I, 161–62, 191.

anatomy, willingly enlightened him about plant physiology.[38] Their consultations and mutual offers of practical assistance continued in the future, Gray being particularly happy with plants that Brongniart and Cosson had sent him from the Sandwich Islands and Algeria. In 1859, Brongniart in turn appreciated Gray's shipment of hundreds of dried plants from the newly opened western regions of the United States and about eleven hundred plants from the North Pacific, specifically from Hong Kong, Loo Choo, Bonin, and Japan.[39] Most generously, Professor Jean François Camille Montagne turned over to the Museum of Natural History in Paris the beautifully executed and rare pictures of living specimens of mushrooms which William Sullivant, of Columbus, Ohio, had dispatched to him.[40] To keep a promise made to the director of agriculture at Chapel Hill, North Carolina, the Society of Horticulture of the Gironde presented him with "a complete collection of beans . . . cultivated in France."[41] And to cite one final example of cooperation in the botanical field: When in the late 1860s the North American collection in the herbarium of the Jardin des Plantes disappointed Elias Durand, he generously donated to it some twelve thousand species, later known as the *Herbier Durand*.[42]

French and American botanists did not hesitate to make specific requests of each other. In 1878, for instance, Decaisne inquired about the possibility of securing Palmetto tree seeds, a tree unknown in Europe and likely to flourish in southern France.[43] Similarly, Brongniart asked George Engelmann, of St.

38. *Ibid.*, I, 23–24.
39. Asa Gray to Adolphe Brongniart, July 24, 1857, December 31, 1858, July 13, 1859, Musée d'Histoire Naturelle. See also Ernest Cosson to Asa Gray, February 24, 1864, March 14, 1865, and March 5, 1879, in Gray Herbarium, Cambridge.
40. William Sullivant to Professor Montagne, October, 1849, in Musée d'Histoire Naturelle.
41. B. Gerrich to John Hay, March 10, 1880, *Consular Dispatches,* Bordeaux, AMAE.
42. William J. Robbins, "French Botanists and the Flora of the Northwestern United States: J. G. Milbert and Elias Durand," APS, *Proceedings,* CI (1957), 367.
43. Joseph Decaisne to Asa Gray, March 9, 1878, in Gray Herbarium, Cambridge.

Louis, to make some of his new cacti available to him.[44] In 1881, a horticulturist from Marseilles showed a special interest in assembling as complete a collection of orchids as Americans would help him procure; and, in the same year, a horticultural society in Marseilles requested vegetable seeds that could be commercially exploited.[45] Always of mutual interest was information about plant and fruit diseases and how to cope with them. When Florida orange groves, for instance, were ravaged by an insect, the United States turned to the Agricultural Society of France for advice because a similar insect had once threatened the groves of southern France. And the United States was in a position to recommend remedies for potato diseases and to demonstrate the commercially significant fact that scales are not found alive on evaporated or sun-dried fruits.[46]

An important field in which Frenchmen and Americans developed both botanical and commercial interests was viticulture. Upon the collapse of Napoleon's empire, many French immigrants took advantage of generous terms the Congress of the United States granted them for the acquisition of land in the Alabama wilderness. There they set out to grow grapes and olives, believing that the climate would benefit their quite ambitious venture. Nature, however, taught them the sad lesson that neither the climate nor the soil favored them. To further complicate their dilemma, the settlers in the region provided a less than inviting atmosphere for these immigrants. Other experiments with the cultivation of grapes in Ohio, Kentucky, and Tennessee also turned out to be bitterly disappointing.[47] But these failures did not discourage the French immigrants forever, particularly when it was demonstrated that with proper care viticulture could flourish in favorable natural environments.

44. George Engelmann to Adolphe Brongniart, November 26, 1861, in Musée d'Histoire Naturelle.

45. See Lewis R. Gibbes Papers, Vol. XII, October 10, 1861, LC.

46. See John Hay to Horace Porter, January 13, 1899, FIDS; and Académie des Sciences, *Comptes Rendus,* LXXX (1875), 165–67.

47. Hammer Cobbs, "Geography of the Vine and Olive Colony," *Alabama Review,* XIV (April, 1961), 83–97; see also S. B. Buckley, "The Grapes of North America," *Senate Executive Documents,* 37th Cong., 2nd Sess., No. 39, pp. 478–86.

Another catastrophe, the Franco-Prussian War of 1870–1871, brought to the shores of the United States some highly experienced horticulturists who took a particular interest in grapes. The chief gardener of the Botanical Garden at Cambridge, Massachusetts, had been trained at the Botanical Garden in Paris; and his assistant was a French horticulturist whose establishment had been destroyed by the siege of Paris. In 1873, the French scientist Jules E. Planchon went to the United States to study American vines and their future in Europe,[48] especially their resistance to the phylloxera insect that caused French vine growers damages running into the hundreds of millions of dollars. In the same year, Emile Karst, the Alsatian-born banker and composer, assumed his post as French consul in St. Louis, rendering in that capacity invaluable service by sending millions of American grape cuttings for grafts on French vines.[49] It was clearly established that certain varieties of American grapes resisted the phylloxera as successfully in France as in the United States. Planchon worked closely with Charles V. Riley, the entomologist of the state of Missouri and one of the European-trained experts on the various issues related to the phylloxera.[50] Planchon had every reason to be pleased with the cooperation he received in America. Riley introduced him to his friend Andrew S. Fuller, of Ridgewood, New Jersey, an outstanding authority on vines. In Philadelphia, the botanist Thomas Meehan, in charge of the rich collections of the herbarium of the Academy of Natural Sciences, made all facilities available to him. As to the phylloxera, Planchon concluded that the characteristics of the American variety were identical with those of the European. Of the most far-reaching practical significance was the discovery that it was possible to graft the excellent vines of France on the trunks of American vines and thus help preserve them.[51] Careful tests also established

48. Jules E. Planchon, *Les Vignes américaines: Leur culture, leur résistance au Phylloxera et leur avenir en Europe* (Montpellier, 1875), 18–22, 76–77, 95–97.
49. Emile Karst, "Genealogy," MS in MoHS.
50. *Bulletin des Sciences de la Société Entomologique de France,* No. 55, meeting of July 14, 1875, pp. 151–53.
51. Charles V. Riley, "Vine Cultivation and Wine Making," *House Executive Documents,* 51st Cong., 1st Sess., No. 410.

that the soil and climatic conditions of French or American vines transplanted from one country to the other needed for their survival an environment similar to the one in which they had grown originally. Since the wine industry constituted a major source of income for many Frenchmen, they studied the diseases of vines and their treatment with intense concern.

As in horticulture and sericulture, so in viticulture, the French were the great teachers of Americans. To develop the distinctive qualities of French wines in America, American wine-makers even copied French methods of processing and storing wine. In the spring of 1856, Harry Hammond, the son of a South Carolina senator made a tour through the wine-producing regions of France. His excellent letters of introduction opened the doors of many French houses, enabling him to acquire a detailed knowledge of the many varieties of French wines and their treatment from the vineyards to their consumption in all parts of the world.[52] In view of the potential competition French wine producers faced from the United States, their cooperation in the Hammond tour seemed remarkably generous. Elias Durand, a French immigrant intimately familiar with the predilections of Americans, interpreted this cooperation differently. Prophetically, he ventured the opinion that "so long as the palate of Americans is not favorable to the wines of France, this country will not really become emphatically a wine-growing country and, of course, a rival of France in that branch of commerce."[53] By the same token, Planchon observed firsthand that French families in Louisiana and Canada continued to prefer French wines.

Since ancient times searching minds have speculated about natural phenomena and their possible interactions, about the origin and evolution of the earth and its relation to the universe. In the early nineteenth century the opposing theories of the French naturalists Lamarck and Cuvier were widely debated, Lamarck believing in the organic origin of the earth and life on it and Cuvier defend-

52. Manigault, "Autobiography," 242.
53. Elias Durand to Asa Gray, April 13, 1864, in Gray Herbarium, Cambridge.

ing his theory of repeated catastrophies that shaped its structure. Gradually, under British leadership, scientists of various lands moved from broad speculations to specific study of geological evidence. In these endeavors Americans cooperated closely with their colleagues abroad, claiming from 1840 on to be "at least equal to [their] intellectual rivals, and at certain times their leader."[54] An abundant number of geologists, including numerous state geologists and mineralogists, lent some tangible support to this confident claim. In 1832 the *American Journal of Science* carried an article under the title "Report on the Geology of Massachusetts, examined under the direction of the Government of that State, during the years 1830 and 1831," containing a geological map of the state and a discussion of its economic geology. The *Revue encyclopédique* promptly responded by deploring the fact "that there is so very small a part of the French territory, whose geological constitution is as well known to the public as is now the State of Massachusetts." Despite a capable corps of mining engineers, France, the *Revue* charged, was "being distanced in this race by America."[55] While it was true at this time that Americans were busily engaged in establishing detailed geological surveys of their land, theoretically they continued to be outdistanced by Frenchmen. Elie de Beaumont's paleogeographic map of Europe (1833) aroused their interest in the geographical history of ancient geological periods. The publication in 1833 of Beaumont's theory of the origin of mountains proved very stimulating. According to this theory, the cooling globe was condensing, compelling its already cool crust to suffer compression. In Europe, he contended, "the collapse of the crust occurred violently and rapidly at widely spaced intervals of time." This hypothesis suggested to him "mountain folding by horizontal compressive forces." About a decade later, two American geologists, the brothers Henri Darwin and William Barton Rogers,

54. Joseph Barrell, "The Growth of Knowledge of Earth Structure," in Edward S. Dana (ed.), *A Century of Science in America: With Special Reference to the American Journal of Science,* 1818–1918 (New Haven, 1918), 191–92.
55. Dana (ed.), *A Century of Science,* 163.

who had surveyed the great Appalachian mountain chains, were the first to refer to the folded structure of the Appalachians.[56] In his speculative paper "On the Origin of Continents," James Dwight Dana also explained the origin of some mountains as the result of the "wrinkling of the earth's surface" following the contraction of cooling hot earth.

Dana, who taught at Yale, was thoroughly familiar with the works of his European colleagues. His classic study, *System of Mineralogy* (1837), followed in 1862 by his *Manual of Geology*, established his solid standing in the scientific community.[57] While blazing his own trails, he preferred the French system of classifying minerals according to their chemical composition over the primarily descriptive method of the Germans. In his more specialized studies of crystallography he proceeded, following the famous discoveries embodied in René Just Haüy's (1743–1822) *Traité de minéralogie,* to develop by 1850 the most accurate classification of crystals.

Throughout the century French and American naturalists were in close touch. William Maclure, "the father of American geology," published in 1809 a geological map of America and facilitated the work of Charles A. Lesueur, the noted French painter-naturalist. Lesueur, who from 1816 to 1825 played an active role in the scientific community of Philadelphia, also supplied Cuvier with scientific data about America.[58]

Of the other relatively few French scientists who came to America, Joseph Nicolas Nicollet was one who contributed in the 1830s a *Map of the Hydrographic Basin of the Upper Mississippi River* based on his own explorations.[59] The fact that Jules Marcou's not entirely correct geological map of the United

56. *Ibid.,* 173–76.
57. William E. Ford, "The Growth of Mineralogy from 1818 to 1918," *ibid.,* 273–74; Jaffe, *Men of Science in America,* 267–73.
58. R. W. G. Vail, "The American Sketchbooks of a French Naturalist, 1816–1837: A Description of the Charles Alexandre Lesueur Collection, with a Brief Account of the Artist," American Antiquarian Society, *Proceedings,* n.s., XLVIII (April 20, 1938), 50–55.
59. Consult the Papers of Joseph N. Nicollet, Correspondence, 1832–42, LC.

States and Canada was widely circulated in mid-century Europe made it and his accompanying generalizations the target of so much American criticism that he was evidently discouraged from undertaking further original studies in his adopted country.[60] The most distinguished French visitor, Edouard P. de Verneuil, president of the Geological Society of France, was particularly impressed with America's Paleozoic deposits. On his travels in America in the summer of 1846 he tried to correlate the geological formations of New York with those of Europe and to establish more direct contacts with American men of science. Verneuil's analysis of the Paleozoic fossils of Europe and America led him to "the conviction that identical species have lived at the same epoch in America and Europe, that they have had nearly the same duration, and that they succeeded each other in the same order."[61] When Benjamin Silliman, the elder statesman of American science, visited Europe in 1851, Verneuil accompanied him to the Geological Museum of the Jardin des Plantes and to the School of Mines where he met other French colleagues and marveled at their precious collections. Professor Henri de Sénarmont, the famous mineralogist at the School of Mines, unhesitatingly permitted Silliman to inspect some of the "curious results" of his remarkable investigation "on the artificial formation of crystallized and anhydrous minerals, from solution . . . in advance of their publication."[62]

The mutual exchange of written materials, as well as of minerals, metals, and vegetable fossils between French and American naturalists kept them in constant communication. Alexandre Brongniart, (1770–1847), the eminent mineralogist and geologist of the Musée d'Histoire Naturelle, and his son Adolphe-

60. George P. Merrill, *The First One Hundred Years of American Geology* (New Haven, 1924), 308–10; William Blake, "Review of a Portion of the Geological Map of the United States and British Provinces by Jules Marcou," *American Journal of Science and Arts*, 2nd ser., XXII (1856), 383–88.
61. Charles Schuchert, "A Century of Geology," in Dana (ed.), *A Century of Science*, 9.
62. Benjamin Silliman, *Visit to Europe in 1851* (2 vols.; New York, 1853), I, 159–62.

Théodore, the prominent botanist, corresponded extensively with their transatlantic colleagues.[63] During the Second Empire, the reports of the French Academy of Sciences abounded in references to the geological explorations Dr. Charles T. Jackson described to his good friend Elie de Beaumont whom he had known since his geological trips in France in the early 1830s.[64] Scientists on both sides of the Atlantic displayed a strong desire for receiving the latest scientific data from abroad and for seeing their own investigations reported in foreign journals. Thus, Dr. John Lawrence Smith, of Louisville, Kentucky, a research scholar in chemistry and mineralogy, followed customary procedure when, in 1850, he addressed to the Academy of Sciences in Paris a memoir on emery deposits of Asia Minor.[65] Considering his paper meritorious, the Academy lost little time publishing it.

In the final decades of the century such noted French geologists as Achille Ernest Delesse, Gabriel A. Daubrée, Alfred Des Cloizeaux, and Charles E. Barrois continued to keep transatlantic professional channels open. Delesse extended to James Dwight Dana (1813–1895) the courtesy of sending him two lithological maps, summarizing his soon-to-be-published *Lithologie des mers de France et des mers principales du globe* (1871) ; but Delesse also requested that Dana translate his summary and have it, if at all possible, inserted in the *American Journal of Science*.[66] Des

63. For Brongniart's American correspondence between 1820 and 1837, see Musée d'Histoire Naturelle and LC photostats, Vols. 1965, 1966, and 1967. See also Adolphe Brongniart to Professor Silliman, October 18, 1823, MS Ch. A. 3.23, in Boston Public Library; and Adolphe Brongniart to Samuel G. Morton, February 8, 1836, in Samuel George Morton Papers, APS.

64. Académie des Sciences, *Comptes Rendus,* XX (1845), 593; XXXVIII (1854), 838–39; XLIII (1856), 883–84; XLIX (1859), 46-47; LX (1865), 421-23; and LXIX (1869), 1082–83. Beaumont was also friendly with J. Dwight Whitney, a student in the 1840s in the Ecole des Mines. Whitney, director of the Geological Survey of California, discovered in the 1860s a human skull in the volcanic bed of the Sierra Nevada. He speculated that humans must have lived on the Pacific Coast prior to the Ice Age. Edwin T. Brewster, *Life and Letters of Josiah Dwight Whitney* (Boston, 1909), 61; see also *Le Temps,* October 27, 1869.

65. F. A. P. Barnard, "Scientific Progress: The Exact Sciences," *Harper's Magazine,* LII (1876), 222.

66. Achille Ernest Delesse to James Dwight Dana, June 15, 1869, Mineralogical Papers, Yale.

Cloizeaux was fascinated by the compositional analogy between the deposits of Maine and Massachusetts with those of Auvergne and those of Nevada and California with those of such distant places as Oran and the Amsterdam Islands.[67] Barrois congratulated Alpheus Hyatt of the Cambridge Museum of Comparative Anatomy for his work on the *Genesis of the Arietidae* (1889), "one of the best models of paleontological inquiry and scientific method."[68] And Daubrée, who followed Dana's findings closely and occasionally reported them to the Academy of Sciences, appreciated the memoir Dana addressed to him about volcanic actions.[69] Once again, it was noteworthy that professional ties among these scholars were so solid that they did not wait for the publication of their investigations before passing their findings on to selected colleagues.

The American oil industry had a rather slow start. From the 1850s the United States had participated in the transatlantic competition with respect to "coal oil" and "paraffin illuminating oil." In the 1860s various new techniques for drilling oil far below the surface, including diamond drilling, reached the United States via Paris.[70] Probably alerted by the power needs of the Industrial Revolution, American geologists concentrated rather late in the century on the microscopic study of the mineral and chemical composition of rocks, especially igneous rocks. In the evolution of petrology as a science, the work of the French petrologists Ferdinand André Fouqué and A. Michel Lévy assumed a very practical significance.[71] Their publication in 1882, *Synthèse des minéraux et des rochers,* was soon followed up by the research of the Carnegie Geophysical Laboratory in Washington. The fu-

67. A. Des Cloiseaux to James Dwight Dana, April 30, 1878, *ibid..*
68. Charles E. Barrois to A. Hyatt, March 22, 1890, in A. Hyatt Correspondence, Box 1, Princeton Library.
69. Académie des Sciences, *Comptes Rendus,* LXXX (1875), 231–32; see also Achille Ernest Delesse to James Dwight Dana, January 27, 1879; and Gabriel Daubrée to James Dwight Dana, March 24, 1887, both in Mineralogical Papers, Yale.
70. R. J. Forbes, "Petroleum," in Singer (ed.), *A History of Technology,* V, 102–23.
71. Louis V. Pirsson, "The Rise of Petrology as a Science," in Dana (ed.), *A Century of Science,* 248–67.

ture of petrology, so vital to modern society, was greatly furthered by this kind of successive research development.

By the early nineteenth century, European scientists had already laid a solid foundation in modern chemistry. In relatively quick succession the world learned of Joseph Priestley's discovery of oxygen, Henry Cavendish's discovery that the combustion of hydrogen and oxygen produced water, Antoine Laurent Lavoisier's oxygen theory that overthrew the long-dominant phlogiston theory, John Dalton's atomic theory, Joseph Louis Gay-Lussac's law of gas combination, and shortly thereafter Count Amedeo Avogrado's hypothesis that under the same conditions of temperature and pressure equal volumes of gases contain the same number of molecules. Americans followed these and other advances in chemistry very attentively, but they were as yet unable to make significant contributions themselves.[72]

Initially, American interest in chemistry was accelerated by American medical students in Paris who considered a thorough knowledge of it essential. They sought admission to the courses of such inspiring teachers as Louis Nicolas Vauquelin (1763–1829) and Joseph Louis Gay-Lussac (1778–1850).[73] The class sizes of these celebrated professors varied considerably. In 1801, Dr. John C. Warren referred to Vauquelin's "small class of about forty, composed of first-rate men of science and noblemen from all parts of Europe." Dr. Peter S. Townsend mentioned in 1828 that Gay-Lussac's class was attended by a crowd "amounting to about 1,500." The lecture he heard Gay-Lussac deliver, "with much facility of language and accompanied with ingenious experiments," dealt with "heat and its operation upon solids, liquids & gases

72. Alexander Findlay, *A Hundred Years of Chemistry* (London, 1948); Benjamin Silliman, "American Contributions to Chemistry," *American Chemist,* V (1874), 71–114, 195–209; and Dana (ed.), *A Century of Science,* 288-97.

73. One of their American students, David Bailie Warden, helped keep scientists in his adopted country abreast of the progress in chemistry by arranging, in 1807, the shipment of fifty-five volumes of the *Annales de Chimie* to Samuel L. Mitchill, professor of chemistry, natural history, and philosophy at Columbia College. Francis C. Haber, "David Bailie Warden: A Bibliographical Sketch of America's Cultural Ambassador in France, 1804–1845," *Bulletin,* Institut Français de Washington, n.s., No. 3 (December, 1953), 75–118.

& the laws which govern the cooling of bodies."[74] Famous for his many experiments and discoveries, Gay-Lussac did not neglect the advancement of science in, as he wrote to the American chemist John Griscom, your "happy hemisphere." One of his former students with whom he kept in touch, Dr. Julius T. Ducatel, taught chemistry at the University of Maryland and wrote a *Manual of Toxicology*.[75]

The magnificent tribute the French Academy of Science paid to Benjamin Silliman (1779–1864) on his mid-century visit to this august body reflected its great esteem for this immensely productive scientist who made it his business to diffuse scientific knowledge in America. The author of the reputable two-volume work, *Elements of Geology* (1830), Silliman was well known to European scientists for his enterprising direction of the *American Journal of Science,* which he had launched in 1818. On this occasion, the renowned Louis Cordier, famous for his measurements of the earth's internal heat, introduced Silliman to Professor Constant Provost of the Sorbonne, the geologist who challenged Elie de Beaumont's theory of the origin of mountain ranges.[76] Many other eminent French scientists also found it instructive to exchange ideas with their unusual American confrère.

Another broadly educated and productive scholar was John Lawrence Smith (1818–1883), professor of medical chemistry and toxicology.[77] He was no stranger to Parisians. In 1843 he had become professionally involved in a much-publicized criminal case. It so happened that as a medical student in Paris he chanced to write a paper on the means of detecting arsenic in the human body. This court case revolved around the question of the amount

74. Edward Warren, *The Life of John Collins Warren, M.D.* (2 vols.; Boston, 1860), I, 57; see also, "Diary of Peter Solomon Townsend, M.D.," Paris, February 2, 1828, V, 177–80, NYAM.

75. Louis Gay-Lussac to John Griscom, Paris, September 13, 1818, John Griscom Correspondence, NYPL; Silliman, "American Contributions to Chemistry," 45–46.

76. John Fulton and Elizabeth H. Thomson, *Benjamin Silliman, 1779–1864: Pathfinder in American Science* (New York, 1947), 117, 173, 228.

77. Silliman, "American Contributions to Chemistry," 92; see also Benjamin Silliman, "Memoir of John Lawrence Smith, 1818–83," U.S. National Academy of Science, *Biographical Memoirs, II* (1886), 220–23.

of arsenic in the human body and "of its presence in hydrated peroxide of iron used as an antidote." Interestingly, Smith did not hesitate in this case to contradict his professor, Mateo Orfila, a well-known authority on toxicology, who eventually admitted his errors. Another of Smith's papers, "The Composition and Products of Distillation of Spermaceti," published in 1842 in the *American Journal of Science* and reproduced in the *Annales de chimie et physique,* proved his great independence. In it he demonstrated the inaccuracy of Michel Eugène Chevreul's view that spermaceti was a fat, when in fact it was a cetyl alcohol. A scholar throughout his life, Smith was honored by the Academy of Sciences of the Institut de France, which in 1879 elected him to a corresponding membership.

As scientific researchers were preoccupied with basic principles and the discovery of universally applicable laws in chemistry, industrial chemists were constantly trying to find practical solutions for specific challenges.[78] With the mutual desire to extract the largest amount of sugar from either beets, cane, or sorghum, French and American sugar producers watched each other hoping to learn from each other. In one instance, an unusual set of circumstances brought about a remarkable interaction. Norbert Rillieux, the grandson of one of Lafayette's soldiers in the American Revolutionary War, possessed such promising technical aptitudes that in 1825 his father sent him to a school in Paris. There, the young Louisianian of mixed blood (his grandmother had been a Negro) was not only socially accepted without reservations, the scientific community quickly recognized the merits of his informative publications. They secured him an appointment as an instructor of applied mechanics at the Ecole Centrale de Paris. But in 1833 he returned to Louisiana as the chief engineer of a large plantation. His interest in sugar engineering reached its high point with his ingenious invention of a machine capable of evaporating considerably more sugar

78. The development of America's chemical industry was amazingly slow in the nineteenth century.

at greatly reduced cost than any process in the past.[79] Although this invention enormously enriched Louisiana and sugar manufacturers around the globe, Rillieux, being a quadroon, decided before the Civil War to return permanently to France where he was not exposed to discrimination. Despite Rillieux's contribution, French and American experts agreed in mid-century that they had not yet managed to extract more than two-thirds of 90 percent of the juice contained in the cane.[80] Ever on the lookout for improved sugar production, American chemists familiarized themselves thoroughly with the superior beet-sugar industry of France. It was hoped that this knowledge would also help to expedite the success of experiments designed to produce crystal sugar from the juice of sorghum.[81]

As far as Americans were concerned, industrial chemistry merited top priority. In 1874 John L. Smith told fellow chemists that in the future there would be no excuse for them not "to stand side by side" with European co-workers "in the development of industrial chemistry." To underline the potential importance of this field, he reminded them that "in France alone, the annual value of chemical products is over $250,000,000 of which $125,-000,000 represents the articles of sulphuric acid, soda, soap, India-rubber, and candles."[82] It was not surprising, therefore, that in 1878 Harvey Washington Riley, a chemist in the United States Department of Agriculture, appreciated the opportunity the chemical section of the French Association for the Advancement of Science afforded him to visit industrial plants of special usefulness to him. Since by then, however, the chemical industry of France had fallen behind that of Great Britain and Germany, American

79. Harnett T. Kane, *Deep Delta Country* (New York, 1944), 45–46; Norbert Rillieux, "Commémoration du centenaire de la mise en marche de la première installation d'évaporation dans le vide à triple effet à la Louisiane en 1834," pamphlet, LSU.

80. J. P. Benjamin, "Louisiana Sugar," *De Bow's Review*, II (1846), 331–33.

81. Harvey W. Wiley, *An Autobiography* (Indianapolis, 1930), 168–74.

82. John Lawrence Smith, "The Century's Progress in Industrial Chemistry," *American Chemistry*, V (1874), 61–70; John Lawrence Smith, *The Progress and Condition of Several Departments of Industrial Chemistry*, in U.S.–Paris Universal Exposition, *Reports* (Washington, D.C., 1869).

chemical technology relied most heavily on chemists trained in the superior laboratories of Germany.[83]

Natural phenomena obviously drew scientists from different continents together. Such prominent physicists, astronomers, and meteorologists as François Jean Arago, Urban Jean Joseph LeVerrier, Jules C. Janssen, and Charles Delaunay in France and A. Dallas Bache, William C. Bond, Joseph Henry, Simon Newcomb, and Edward C. Pickering in the United States were in frequent contact. The heads of the observatories in Paris, Washington, and at Harvard saw many mutual advantages in the prompt exchange of information. As Bond, of Harvard, advised LeVerrier in 1849: "It is at all times especially important to us that we should have early intelligence of what is doing in the astronomical world of Europe."[84] Joseph Henry, the dedicated and ingenious secretary of the Smithsonian Institution, initiated the use of the transatlantic telegraph both for the transmission of weather reports and astronomic discoveries, thus enabling the director of the Marseilles Observatory, for instance, promptly to seek and find a newly discovered small planet.[85] The daily transmission of telegraphic weather reports from a wide range of stations could, as LeVerrier demonstrated in 1854, trace and predict the course of storms.

Government officials of both countries lent assistance to their scientists planning observations abroad. When France sent the scientific mission of Alfred Angot and his friend C. André to the

83. Harvey W. Wiley, Diary, August 24, 1878, Box 212, LC; L. F. Haber, *The Chemical Industry During the Nineteenth Century* (Oxford, 1958), 42, 78, 109, 142–43.

84. William C. Bond to Urbain Jean Joseph LeVerrier, March 2, 1849, in LeVerrier Papers, MS 3710, Institut de France. Up to the middle of the nineteenth century, observatories in Europe possessed larger and more complex instruments than those in the United States. American dependency on Europe in scientific matters eventually lessened with the growing awareness that in these respects the republic should not take a back seat to European monarchies. David F. Musto, "The Development of American Astronomy During the Early Nineteenth Century," in *Actes du 10e Congrès International d'Histoire des Sciences* (Paris, 1964), II, 734–35.

85. Académie des Sciences, *Comptes Rendus*, LXXVI (1873), 1346; Joseph Henry, *Scientific Writings* (2 vols.; Washington, D.C., 1886), I, 101–104, II, 451–56.

United States to observe the transit of Mercury in May of 1878, the government of the United States assured these gentlemen that "the Collector of Customs at New York has been directed to admit the scientific instruments and apparatus . . . to entry free duty and without examination."[86] Before coming to America Angot and André consulted Simon Newcomb as to the best location for observation, both from the point of view of their own installation and the availability of additional local resources. When the French Academy of Sciences planned "expeditions . . . to observe from various points of the globe the transit of Venus . . . in 1882," it asked for the same kind of cooperation.[87] And by way of reciprocity, in 1898 American officials asked for the consent of the French government to establish at Martinique "a fully equipped meteorological observatory furnished with more reliable instruments, for observation of atmospheric conditions, than have ever before been" used. The American government pledged that the data obtained from various stations in the West Indies and Central and South America, "of inestimable value in the prediction of the movement of dangerous tropical storms," were to "be made available for the commerce of all nations."[88] Ocean meteorology was an area in which the common interest of nations had led to the early awareness for common actions. Taking the initiative in this field, the distinguished American hydrographer Matthew F. Maury had as far back as 1853 played a leading role in the establishment of a uniform system of meteorological observations.[89]

There was hardly a development about which the concerned scientists did not inform each other. The impending activation of observatories in Albany, New York, and Toulon, France, was

86. William M. Evarts to Edward F. Noyes, March 18, 1878, FIDS; see also Alfred Angot to Simon Newcomb, April 19, and November 15, 1877, in Simon Newcomb Papers, container 15, LC.

87. François Henri Louis de Geoffroy to James G. Blaine, May 28, 1881, FNTDS.

88. J. B. Moore to Horace Porter, June 30, 1898, FIDS.

89. Académie des Sciences, *Comptes Rendus*, XXXIV (1852), 213–14; see also Ralph M. Brown, "Bibliography of Commander Matthew Fontaine Maury," *Bulletin of the Virginia Polytechnic Institute*, XXIV (December, 1930), 11–14.

promptly communicated. Substantive notices, of course, held the central interest. The fall, discovery, and description of meteors and the discovery of new stars were immediately brought to the attention of colleagues abroad. In January, 1835, French meteorologists were made aware of the extraordinary cold in America while Europe at the time experienced moderate climate.[90] This phenomenon and the occasional appearance of very large sunspots led A. Gautier and, subsequently, Joseph Henry to speculate on the influence of sunspots on earthly temperatures. Through an ingeniously planned experiment, in which he used a thermoelectrical apparatus, made by Ruhmkorff of Paris, Professor Henry established that, contrary to Sir William Herschel's idea "that the appearance of solar spots was connected with a more copious emission of heat . . . the spot emitted less heat than the surrounding parts of the luminous disc."[91] Minute observations of eclipses and the transit of other planets, as well as studies about terrestrial magnetism and winds, and the important meteorological data collected by the superintendent of the United States Coast Survey helped to build up a useful treasure of knowledge in France and the United States.[92]

If the telegraph in time expedited the transmission of information, the photocamera presented an invaluable visual medium for further analysis of data. The French admired the first photographic picture of the moon which the director of the Harvard Observatory sent in 1851 to the Academy of Sciences in Paris.[93] The noted French astronomer Charles Delaunay acknowledged the receipt of nine "magnificent photographic pictures of the eclipse of the moon on August 7, 1869" and assured his American correspondent that the accompanying report with respect to these pictures would be published in the Academy's

90. Académie des Sciences, Comptes Rendus, I (1835), 113–15.

91. Joseph Henry, "Observations on the Relative Radiation of the Solar Spots," APS, Proceedings, IV (June 20, 1845), 173–76; Thomas Coulson, Joseph Henry: His Life and Work (Princeton, N.J., 1950), 166–67.

92. See A. Vernier, "Causerie scientifique," Le Temps, November 16, 1869; M. Babinet, "Astronomie," RDDM (February, 1854), 847; and Académie des Sciences, Comptes Rendus, LV (1862), 649–51.

93. Pierre Rousseau, Man's Conquest of the Stars (New York, 1961), 270–72.

Comptes Rendus.[94] The research activities of American scientists gradually attracted the attention of French newspapers. *Le Temps*[95] lauded the careful attempts in America at photometric measurements designed to determine the amount of light transmitted to the earth by Jupiter and the moon respectively and the relationship between the light of the sun and that of the full moon. In recognition of their extraordinary sophistication, the French invited several American scientists to participate in the work of the Astrophotographic Congress in Paris (1887).[96]

American astronomers and meteorologists regretted that their contacts with French colleagues were largely limited to correspondence, exchange of publications, and American visits to France. Few French scientists acquired firsthand knowledge of the United States. In his *Reminiscences,* Newcomb fondly recalled his delightful walks with Delaunay in the grounds of the Paris Observatory at the time of his visit in 1871. Discussing on this occasion "French science in all its aspects," he was deeply impressed by this kind and brilliant man whose extraordinary mathematical investigation of the moon's motion had solidified his professional standing.[97] Trying to stimulate such vital personal contacts, Newcomb went out of his way to make the stay of the few French scientists who did come to America as pleasant and worthwhile as possible.[98]

94. Charles Delaunay to Alfred M. Mayer, November 16, 1869, in Hyatt and Mayer Correspondence, Box 2, Princeton. In 1874 Professor Jules Janssen volunteered to send to Newcomb drawings of the apparatus he had designed to photograph the transit of Venus. Janssen to Newcomb, April 19, 1874, in Simon Newcomb Papers, container 28, LC.

95. *Le Temps,* May 28, 1861.

96. Simon Newcomb, one of the most famous astronomers of his time, and Edward C. Pickering of the Harvard Observatory declined their invitations. Pickering, though, did submit specific suggestions for the consideration of the assembled scientists. Consult Académie des Sciences, Congrès Astrophotographique (1887), 93–99, MS in Institut de France. This congress concluded that the mass of new data and processes warranted composing a completely revised map of the heavens. See also R. L. Waterfield, *A Hundred Years of Astronomy* (London, 1938).

97. Simon Newcomb, *The Reminiscences of an Astronomer* (Boston, 1903), 329.

98. Simon Newcomb to J. Janssen, March 18, 1878, Letterbooks, 1862–80, container 4; Simon Newcomb to Eleuthère Elie Mascart, October 11, 1893, Letterbooks, 1884–98, container 6, in Simon Newcomb Papers, LC.

Unfortunately, the desire for closer Franco-American co-operation in the sciences was often frustrated by the notorious slowness with which French instrument-makers filled orders from America. Despite "the unquestioned eminence and genius of the artist technicians of France," Americans who were pressed for time reluctantly turned to German firms instead.[99] At the end of the century, Albert A. Michelson actually brought a German mechanic to Paris because he wanted to be "absolutely sure" of prompt and efficient attendance to his instruments. In 1892, Stanford University used still another approach by offering Dr. Rudolph Koenig a permanent position provided he would bring his tonometer, "the world's standard of vibration," from Paris to California. "I see no reason," suggested the writer of this offer, "why the manufacture of your famous apparatus might not be carried on here to advantage." Koenig's polite, but evasive, answer was in this instance less significant than the thinking underlying the original inquiry.[100]

In no scientific field was Federalist America as unfamiliar with the achievements of French scholars as in mathematics. American dependence on British guidance in this field was so great that the contemporary leadership of French mathematicians was not fully grasped by early nineteenth-century Americans until the British, who had acknowledged it, made Americans aware of it. Even then, instead of adopting the rigorous methods introduced by Baron Augustin Louis Cauchy in his *Cours d'Analyse de l'Ecole Polytechnique* (1821) and his later works, American readers generally received French mathematical texts that were not as up-to-date as would have been desirable.[101]

99. See A. B. Gould to Urbain Jean Joseph LeVerrier, October 13, 1855, in LeVerrier Papers, MS 3711, Institut de France; Newcomb-Feil correspondence, January 12, and February 6, 1884, in Simon Newcomb Papers, container 6, LC; Rudolph Koenig to Alfred M. Mayer, October 10, 1893, in Hyatt and Mayer Correspondence, Box 3, Princeton; and John H. Wilson, Jr., *Albert A. Michelson: America's First Nobel Prize Physicist* (New York, 1958), 116.

100. See copy of letter from Professor Sanford to Dr. Koenig, Palo Alto, November 30, 1892, in Hyatt and Mayer Correspondence, Box 3, Princeton.

101. Florian Cajori, *The Teaching and History of Mathematics in the United States* (Washington, D.C., 1890), 98–103.

Professor John Farrar, of Harvard, took the lead in acquainting American students of mathematics with French mathematicians. Between 1818 and 1820 he brought out the translations of Lacroix's *Algebra* and *Trigonometry*. Before long, Americans were also introduced to Etienne Bézout's theory of equations and to Adrien Marie Legendre's *Geometry* (1794).[102] It took the publication of George A. Wentworth's *Elements of Plane Geometry* half a century later (1877) to represent the first major challenge to Legendre's predominance in American schools. This Frenchman's simple and elegant treatment of mathematics exercised a splendid influence in the United States. Since its establishment at the beginning of the century, the United States Military Academy at West Point had followed the lead of France in its instruction in the exact sciences. Professor Claude Crozet, who in 1816 had been brought to West Point to teach descriptive geometry, published a text on it in 1821. Francis H. Smith, at one time an instructor at West Point and subsequently a professor of mathematics at the Virginia Military Institute, translated in 1840 Jean Baptiste Biot's *Essai de géométrie analytique,* previously used by West Point in its original form. Smith also brought out in English Louis-Etienne Lefebure's *Elements de trigonométrie.* Pierre Louis Marie Bourdon's *Elements d'algèbre,* originally translated by Farrar in 1831, found another translator in Edward C. Ross, a graduate of West Point, whose improved version of Bourdon found much acclaim.

The study of higher mathematics in the United States received its greatest boost from Nathaniel Bowditch's translation, with a commentary, of Pierre Simon Laplace's monumental work, *Mécanique céleste.* The first edition of *Celestial Mechanics,* which appeared in Boston in 1829, moved Legendre to congratulate Bowditch on the facility with which he explained Laplace's difficult text. The very fact that he deemed it worthwhile to publish such a highly advanced mathematical treatise impressed Legendre

---

102. *Ibid.,* 114, 128–30, 189; see also David E. Smith and Jekuthiel Ginsburg, A *History of Mathematics in America Before* 1900 (Chicago, 1934), 69–80; and David E. Smith, "L'Enseignement des mathématiques aux Etats-Unis," *L'Enseignement Mathématique,* III (1901), 166–67.

as an indication of the remarkable progress of the sciences in America.[103] Benjamin Peirce (1809-1880), who for nearly half a century taught mathematics at Harvard, and William Chauvenet (1820-1870), professor of mathematics at Washington University in St. Louis, both encouraged scores of American students to master the works of French mathematicians. In time, their own publications in mathematics and astronomy found gratifying recognition in France.[104] The same could be said with respect to a few other American mathematicians who in mid-century had profited from the instruction of leading French mathematicians.

As valuable as such contacts were, only in a few instances did nineteenth-century American scientists gain internationally recognized stature. In mathematics and physics, three men stood out. The first, Joseph Henry (1797-1878), professor of natural philosophy at Princeton and indefatigable secretary of the Smithsonian Institution, earned his laurels as a physicist. Having studied André Marie Ampère's famous work, in which he established the relation between electricity and magnetism, Henry subsequently succeeded in solving problems in the science of electromagnetism that had previously proved to be stumbling blocks.[105] His discovery of electromagnetic induction, actually one year before Faraday, and his invention of the electromagnetic telegraph which he operated with an "intensity" magnet, set the stage for the race between space and time in the modern age. On a visit to Europe in 1837 he made the acquaintance of many leading scientists in England and France. Though he was warmly received

103. See letter from Adrien Marie Legendre to Nathaniel Bowditch, February 4, 1830, in Boston Public Library; and Pierre Simon Marquis de Laplace, *Celestial Mechanics,* trans. Nathaniel Bowditch (5 vols.; New York, 1966-69). Bowditch's translation had been completed in 1817. For additional comments by Legendre, see page 64 of the first volume. In time, Professor Benjamin Peirce revised and corrected Bowditch's translation.

104. Cajori, *The Teaching and History of Mathematics,* 133, 154-55, 239-44. Peirce's *Linear Associative Algebra* (Washington, D.C., 1870) constituted the first major American contribution to pure mathematics; Thomas S. Fiske, "Mathematical Progress in America," American Mathematical Society, *Bulletin,* XI (1905), 239.

105. Sarah R. Riedman, *Trailblazer of American Science: The Life of Joseph Henry* (Chicago, 1961), 59-64; Bernard Jaffe, *Men of Science in America,* 184-92.

wherever he went, those French scientists who divided their interests between science and politics or who at the meeting of the Institut de France read newspapers instead of listening to the papers being presented made Henry wonder about the future of science in France.[106]

By far the most outstanding mathematical scholar the United States produced in the nineteenth century, Josiah Willard Gibbs (1839–1903), decided after his graduation from Yale to increase his knowledge at the universities of Paris, Berlin, and Heidelberg. Essentially a mathematical physicist, he selected particularly those courses in Paris in which the leading authorities could advance his understanding of the most complex theoretical mathematics.[107] Gibbs eventually became well known for his papers on thermodynamics and his famous publication *On the Equilibrium of Heterogeneous Substances* (1876–1878). The energy needs of industry, originally limited to improvements in the steam engine, had led the French physicist Sadi Carnot to the formulation of the first law of thermodynamics (1824). In time, several scientists, Gibbs prominent among them, were searching for thermodynamic applications to the most complex chemical problems. Gibbs, "the founder of chemical energetics," belonged to that exceptional minority of nineteenth-century Americans who appreciated the essential value of abstract science to the "practical" world. European scientists expressed their admiration for this brilliant theoretician who set the most demanding standards for himself. Nevertheless, Henry LeChatelier, who in 1899 translated Gibbs' *On the Equilibrium of Heterogeneous Substances* into French, regretfully noted that the world of science had been very slow in realizing how much it was indebted to this all-too-modest Yale professor.[108]

And finally, America's first Nobel Prize physicist, Albert A.

106. Riedman, *Trailblazer,* 125–28, 138.
107. Lynde Phelps Wheeler, *Josiah Willard Gibbs* (New Haven, 1952), 40–41; Bernard Jaffe, *Men of Science in America,* 308–15.
108. "The Scientific Papers of J. Willard Gibbs," *Bulletin des Sciences Mathématiques,* 2nd ser., XXXI (1907), Pt. 1, pp. 181–211. See also Forest Ray Moulton and Justus J. Schifferes (eds.), *The Autobiography of Science* (Garden City, N.Y., 1945), 465–67.

Michelson (1852–1931), acknowledged that, while the Germans had taught him many scientific facts, the French had stimulated him to see these facts in larger perspectives. He had carefully studied Hippolyte Louis Fizeau's (1819–1896) work on the absolute velocity of light; and, on the recommendation of Simon Newcomb of the United States Naval Observatory, he repeated the experiment that established Jean Foucault's (1819–1868) reputation. Trying to improve the method Foucault had employed to measure the velocity of light, Michelson invented his interferometer, which enabled him to determine the effect of the earth's motion on the observed velocity of light and to measure distances, with precision, with the help of the length of light waves.[109] When on May 5, 1893, Michelson, then a professor of physics at the University of Chicago, reported his experiments to the Société de Physique in Paris, his "monumental research" was enthusiastically received.

The founding of the *American Journal of Mathematics* and of the American Mathematical Society in the final decades of the century, both developments that helped disseminate mathematical knowledge, reflected the giant steps with which the United States was catching up in this field. Significantly, still another shift had taken place in the late nineteenth century. Germany, rather than France or England, became the major European training ground for American students of science.[110] The word spread quickly in the United States that the encyclopedic knowledge of German professors, their thoroughness, and their excellent laboratory facilities provided an incomparable experience.

The professional curiosity of scientists in France and America would have been sufficient to put them in touch with each other in order to fill evident gaps of knowledge. Many practical con-

109. John H. Wilson, Jr., *Albert A. Michelson*, 86–88; Dana (ed.), *A Century of Science*, 363; Albert A. Michelson and E. W. Morley, "Influence of Motion of the Medium on the Velocity of Light," *American Journal of Science*, XXXI (1886), 377–86.

110. Smith and Ginsburg, *A History of Mathematics in America*, 102–106, 113–14.

siderations gave further impetus to their cooperation in the exploration and application of scientific data. For as much as science was expected to further the progress of civilization and a better understanding of the universe, its more tangible benefits were seen in its boon to medicine, agriculture, industry, commerce, and shipping. Understandably, the emphasis on useful exchanges took priority over mere theoretical aspects of science, without underrating the essential value of fundamentals. French interest in such American resources as lumber, vegetables, vines, fish, and in geological surveys was matched by American interest in French seeds, by heavy reliance on French mathematicians in the military and public schools of the United States, and by special attention to the relatively advanced development of industrial chemistry in France. The diversified uses of meteorological data were of course fully appreciated by meteorologists in both countries. Their hobby-like fascination with their profession merely added a personal touch to their close official relationships.

But if the scientific advancement of their respective fields induced French and American scientists to assist each other in a remarkably mature fashion, it must also be noted that their national pride prompted them to be guided by different motivations. Until about the first half of the century, French scientists looked upon their headstart and superiority as entitling them to a benign leadership which could not but make their grateful, but inferior, status-conscious American colleagues very determined to lift their level of independent respectability as fast as possible. Gradually, in the natural sciences too, cooperation became ever more a two-way affair, with the United States catching up with and in some areas getting ahead of its European teachers. Still, as I. Bernard Cohen has honestly "reflected," in the nineteenth century even the most outstanding American scientists were not yet in a class with the giants among their European colleagues.[111]

111. I. Bernard Cohen, "Some Reflections on the State of Science in America During the Nineteenth Century," National Academy of Sciences, *Proceedings, XLV* (1959), 666–77.

CHAPTER XIII

Cooperation in the Medical Sciences

In the study of history we can ever so often observe breaks with the past which appear to be rather sudden, when in fact they culminate fairly long evolutionary developments. When certain ideas and techniques, moveover, become dominant, they usually affect society on a practically global scale. Advances in medicine in one country, for instance, were eventually incorporated in the practice of medicine in other countries. With few exceptions, early nineteenth-century American medicine followed the work of French pioneers. The American and French revolutions were accompanied and followed by profound changes in the field of medicine. And like these political and social revolutions, the one in medicine was also intellectually preceded by a major philosophical change. It involved the rejection of a priori reasoning and emphasis on observation in medical research. Under the impact of the Enlightenment, superstitious and supernatural notions and the purely symptomatic classification of disease gave way to anatomical study and observation. As Jean Jacques Rousseau had stated it, "All science is in the facts or phenomena of nature and their relationships, and not in the mind of man which discovers and interprets them."

From the close of the eighteenth century, France took a decisive lead in the establishment of the modern school of medical science. The phenomenal appearance of so many brilliant French scientists around the turn of the nineteenth century made this development possible. In quick succession they advanced man's knowledge with respect to pathology, diagnosis, and therapeutics, as well as chemistry and mathematics. Reference to only some of their most outstanding earlier contributions would have to include Lavoisier's discovery of the true nature of respiration and of the sources of animal heat; Xavier Bichat's development of general and pathological anatomy; François Magendie's experimental physiology; the isolation of plant alkaloids by Pierre Joseph Pelletier and Joseph Bienaimé Caventou; François Broussais' *History of Chronic Inflammations*; Jean Nicolas Corvisart's diagnostic use of percussion and René Théophile Laennec's invention of the stethoscope; Jean Bouillaud's, Gabriel Andral's, and Pierre Charles Alexandre Louis' treatment of diseases of the heart and lung; Pierre François Olive Rayer's work on diseases of the kidneys; Alexis Jean Baptiste Parent-Dûchatelet's and Charles Louis Maxime Durand-Fardel's research on diseases of the brain; Augustin Grisolle's research on pneumonia and Louis' on typhoid fever.[1]

While this very incomplete list suggests the breadth of the French attempt to conquer diseases, the introduction of statistical approaches to this task became as significant as did the later emphasis on experimental research. Statistical medical investigations had been scientifically advanced by Pierre Laplace's *Théorie analytique des probabilités* (1812).[2] Following it, the study of probabilities in medical statistics reached a sufficiently meaningful level to be used by medical researchers. In addition to Pierre Charles Louis' numerical method of observation in the

1. Elisha Bartlett, *An Essay on the Philosophy of Science* (Philadelphia, 1844), 295–98; Erwin H. Ackerknecht, "Elisha Bartlett and the Philosophy of the Paris Clinical School," *BHM*, XXIV (1950), 50; William H. Welch, "Some of the Conditions Which Have Influenced the Development of American Medicine, Especially in the Last Century," *Bulletin of the Johns Hopkins Hospital*, XIX (1908), 33–40.

2. See George Rosen, "Problems in the Application of Statistical Analysis to Questions of Health: 1700–1880," *BHM*, XXIX (1955), 40–43; Richard H. Shryock, "The History of Quantification in Medical Science," *Isis*, LII (1961), 215–37.

diagnosis and treatment of diseases, the employment of statistics led to major medical findings of great social significance. Studying the mortality differentials of different social classes, Louis René Villermé and Louis François Benoiston de Châteauneuf discovered that the life expectancy of urban workers in poor neighborhoods was lower than that of people living in better environments. The availability of such statistical facts helped the doctor as much as the reformer in their endeavors for better individual and public health.

In this context, it seems relevant to mention another relationship between social conditions and public health. In a lecture Professor Nathaniel Chapman delivered at the University of Pennsylvania in 1832, he stated that Jean Nicolas Corvisart, an eminent French medical authority, affirmed "that during the French Revolution the diseases of the heart increased to an alarming extent." The turmoils of public life and private distress, he suspected, caused serious heart troubles. Similarly, Philippe Pinel attributed to the French Revolution a noticeable rise in the number of mental cases. Perceptively, Dr. Benjamin Rush had already suggested, in a paper he read before the American Philosophical Society in 1774, that political and economic conditions affected mental and social health.[3]

As awareness of the impact of political and nutritional factors on health was often enhanced by statistical observations, the history of medical chemistry in France points toward an even more essential requisite in the development of medical science. Once the superstitious veil surrounding the study of chemistry in France had been lifted in the late seventeenth century, in Montpellier and Paris scientists of a high caliber laid the groundwork for a body of knowledge that by the time of the Great Revolution could place France in a leading position. One of the

3. Nathaniel Chapman, "Lectures on the Practice of Medicine," November 21, 1832, p. 36 (MS in University of Pennsylvania Library); Columbus Academy of Medicine, Minute Book, 1879–83, January 2, 1880, p. 23, OSHS; and George Rosen, "Social Stress and Mental Disease from the Eighteenth Century to the Present," Millbank Memorial Fund Quarterly, XXXVII (1959), 8–11.

early noted French chemists who contributed much to the study of medical chemistry, Nicolas Lemery (1645–1715), published, among other works, such significant treatises as a universal pharmacopoeia and a dictionary of simple drugs.[4] His son Louis and many others built on this foundation. In quick succession between 1817 and 1821, Pierre Joseph Pelletier and Joseph Bienaimé Caventou succeeded in extracting plant alkaloids, including the vitally important quinine.

A fascinating third explanation for the brilliant medical leadership of France in the first half of the nineteenth century must be traced to Napoleon I. From his point of view, it was bad enough to lose soldiers in battle; it was even worse for disease to decimate them. Fortunately, on December 4, 1794, the National Convention had ordered the establishment of medical schools at Paris, Montpellier, and Strasbourg to service military and naval as well as general hospitals. Napoleon insisted on postmortem examinations, particularly in military hospitals, which helped to build up such an unprecedented body of knowledge of morbid anatomy and pathology that the faculties of medicine in France possessed information far superior to that of other countries. Most of the young clinicians, moreover, who from the time of the French Revolution had performed their services in the large Paris hospitals, were disposed toward scientifically conducted medical research. They abandoned ontological approaches and turned to physiological medicine. Their concentration on localized pathology encouraged them to undertake daring, but potentially promising, operations.[5]

The French school emphasizing pathological anatomy was originally headed by such luminaries as Jean Nicolas Corvisart, René Laennec, Xavier Bichat, and François Broussais. Conscientious American doctors made it a point to read the latest French texts. Bichat's *Anatomie générale* (1801) should be singled

4. "An Account of the Origin, Progress, and Present State of the Medical School of Paris," *American Journal of Medical Sciences*, VIII (1831), 123–24.

5. Richard H. Shryock, "Nineteenth Century Medicine: Scientific Aspects," *Cahiers d'Histoire Mondiale*, III (1957), 880–908; George Rosen, "The Philosophy of Ideology and the Emergence of Modern Medicine in France," *BHM*, XX (1946), 328–39.

out because, following the lead of Giovanni Battista Morgagni, it further strengthened the foundation of modern pathological anatomy. In this work Bichat identified the tissues as the place where diseases are located. His *Researches on Life and Death* (1799), furthermore, elevated biology into a science embracing morphology and physiology. Corvisart, Napoleon's physician, wrote the first significant study on the *Organic Lesions of the Heart and Great Vessels.* Laennec's invention of the stethoscope, permitting mediate auscultation, secured for him a lasting distinction. Broussais' emphasis on physiological medicine, particularly the physiological interdependence of the body's organs, and his orientation toward local lesions earned him a universal reputation, though it also made him a controversial figure. His dogmatism and sarcastic attacks against "les vaches en médicine," the pretenders who disagreed with him, detracted from his brilliance and in many quarters evoked unfavorable reactions. Nevertheless, at the height of his influence, Broussais' theories dominated the medical world. For a time, his reputation was more widely respected in America than in France.[6]

Aside from the accomplishments of French medical scientists, their amazing energy and total involvement in their profession inspired Dr. John Bassett of Alabama to comment that they made him "blush for shame. Old men daily may be seen mixing their white locks with boys and pursuing their profession with the ardour of youth. There is not a solitary man in France that is idle; for if he was, that moment he would be outstripped."

The medical profession in the United States had so long been dependent on the British, whose books they could read without the help of a dictionary, that, despite the progress in France, many American doctors continued to follow the British lead.

6. Consult Francis R. Packard's work *The Early History of Science and Learning in America* (Philadelphia, 1942), 91–102; Erwin H. Ackerknecht, "Broussais or a Forgotten Medical Revolution," *BHM*, XXVII (1953), 321; M. Laignel-Lavastine and M. Raymond Molinery, *Clio Medica: French Medicine* (New York, 1934), 104–19; Esmond R. Long, *A History of American Pathology* (Springfield, Ill., 1962), 35; and George Rosen, "An American Doctor in Paris in 1828," *JHMAS* (1951), 64–115, 209–52.

Others, however, did recognize the inadequacy of their training and turn to their European colleagues for guidance. Particularly after 1821, such American publications as *Chapman's Journal* and the *Journal of Foreign Medical Science* put a growing emphasis on the dissemination of French materials. In them, discussion of medical progress in France was not limited to bibliographical references. Also the *North American Medical and Surgical Journal* (1821–1831) and the *American Journal of Medical Sciences* (1828–1831) paid increasing attention to the work done in Paris. In the 1850s the *New Orleans Medical and Surgical Journal* translated French articles regularly; and in the 1860s the *New Orleans Journal of Medicine* published review articles of French medical literature. Among others, Professors Samuel D. Gross and Alfred Stillé and Drs. Morton Dowler, Edmond Souchon, and James Seagrove Morel translated many French medical books and articles into English. The American Medical Association also made every effort to keep its members abreast of professional developments in all parts of the world.[7]

A carefully established estimate places the number of American doctors who visited Paris between 1820 and 1861 at 677.[8] Quite a few of them went to Paris for one or two years of postgraduate training under the direction of the best-known medical authorities in France. As a result of their special efforts, these doctors gained not only personal prestige, but upon their return home they were equipped to introduce the new clinical-pathologic methods into the institutions in which they taught and practiced their specialized skills. Strangely, though, this was not as simple and obvious a task as one might have expected. The sizable number of American doctors who possessed neither the energy nor the motivation to bring themselves professionally up-to-date defended traditional

7. Edgar M. Blick, "French Influences on Early American Medicine and Surgery," Mount Sinai Hospital *Journal*, XXIV (1957), 499–509.

8. See Russell M. Jones's informative article, "American Doctors in Paris, 1820–1861: A Statistical Profile," *JHM*, XXV (April, 1970), 143–57. The author is indebted to Professor Jones for his revised estimate, according to which the number of American doctors in Paris reached 752: 105 for the decade from 1820 to 1829; 222 from 1830 to 1839; 128 from 1840 to 1849; and 297 from 1850 to 1859.

treatments and attacked the "inroads of pathological anatomy, positive diagnosis, and arithmetic."[9] Instead of admitting their inadequacies, they complacently deluded themselves and their patients by pretending to be experienced and up-to-date experts. In spite of many major accomplishments, it was not until the end of the nineteenth century that, generally speaking, medicine in America reached a level of genuine respectability.

The majority of American medical students in Paris came from the chief centers of American medicine, Boston, New York, Philadelphia, and New Orleans. They applied themselves seriously to their studies, usually from sunrise to sunset. Oliver Wendell Holmes mentioned in one of his letters from Paris (1833) that he "had attended a lecture of an hour and a half and gone through a tedious dissection . . . before breakfast."[10] Dr. Jonathan Mason Warren of Boston described a typical day during his postgraduate studies in Paris: "From 6 until 8 A.M. I attend Chomel at the *Hôtel Dieu*, who is very celebrated for his knowledge of diseases of the lungs. At 8, Dupuytren begins his visit, which lasts an hour; and he afterwards lectures, with operations and consultations, which occupy the time till 11. Then I breakfast, and attend Richerand on Surgery from 12 to 1. From 3 to 4 I go to either Marjolin on Surgical Pathology, or Andral on Medical Pathology."[11] And in his "spare time" he jotted down detailed descriptions of operations he had watched the most skillful surgeons perform. After such a busy and demanding day, the students spent their evenings in social and cultural gatherings, wining, dining, attending concerts and theaters, and occasionally cultivating the acquaintance of physicians and surgeons at meetings of the Academy of Medicine.[12] These contacts with French colleagues proved to be invaluable. Another beneficial by-product of the academic and social life of the American doctors

9. Richard H. Shryock, "Trends in American Medical Research During the Nineteenth Century," APS, *Proceedings*, XCI (1947), 58–63.
10. John T. Morse, Jr., *Life and Letters of Holmes,* I, 86.
11. Howard Payson Arnold, *Memoir of Jonathan Mason Warren, M.D.* (Boston, 1886), 79.
12. Warren, *Life of John Collins Warren, M.D.*, I, 322.

in Paris—many, by the way, sons of doctors from different American communities—was that it promoted lasting professional ties. These personal friendships helped to foster an esprit de corps in the medical profession at home and, equally important, they facilitated the exchange of ideas and experiences.

As instructive as lectures and hospital rounds with famous surgeons were, American students derived the greatest benefit from private classes. It became a common practice with them to form a class of four or five and "to engage an intern of some important ward to teach the class everything that was to be learned from the various patients in the different beds."[13] These interns of eminent professors usually charged twenty francs (four dollars) per student, and were glad to earn one hundred francs so conveniently. These private arrangements supplemented the free public instruction by renowned surgeons. The best seats in Velpeau's amphitheater, for instance, were often occupied by Americans. Realizing that American students had come three thousand miles to make themselves masters in their profession, many of the hospital surgeons went out of their way to be helpful and kind to them.[14] The advantages to be found in Paris included postmortem examinations and large hospitals that offered opportunities for a much broader scope of case studies than were available in the United States. Unlike the lower class of American women, moreover, who were reluctant to go to a hospital because they did not want to expose themselves to embarrassing medical examinations, Parisian women of all classes usually did not display this kind of sensibility. In French hospitals, sick people lost their sex; they were viewed as patients who displayed "all diseased parts of the body unhesitatingly . . . without a thought of indelicacy."[15]

Although knowledgeable American doctors placed French medical science of the 1830s half a century ahead of that of

13. Manigault, "Autobiography," 130–31.
14. A. K. Gardner, *Old Wine in New Bottles*, 160–64.
15. Augustus Kinsley Gardner, *The French Metropolis: Paris as Seen During the Spare Hours of a Medical Student* (New York, 1850), 64.

England, they also detected a major defect in it.[16] From a practical point of view, there was too much emphasis on science and not enough on therapy, too much on diagnosis and not enough on curative methods. If anything, contemporary English and American physicians were guilty of the reverse procedure; they concentrated on treatment without having mastered diagnosis. In the perspective of life and history, as wise and learned a man as Oliver Wendell Holmes reminded us that greatness is relative to its time. Looking back, he reminisced in a philosophical mood: "How strange it is to look down on one's venerated teachers [Louis] after climbing with the world's progress half a century above the level when we left them! The stethoscope was almost a novelty in those days. The microscope was never mentioned by any clinical instructor I listened to while a medical student."[17] And yet, with all their limitations, these men of the past made the future progress of science possible. Dr. James Jackson of the Massachusetts General Hospital defended this view in a preface to one of Louis' works: "For thirty years I have been satisfied," he wrote, "that the physicians of Paris were laying the firmest foundation for the science of therapeutics, by studying the natural history of diseases; and by thus giving us rules for diagnosis and prognosis."[18]

Even from a social vantage point, the temporary residence in Paris in the pre–Civil War period widened the vistas of American citizens. But aside from the diversity of Paris' brilliant cultural offerings, the human shortcomings of some of its professors and students of medicine taught a few lessons not worth copying. Although France honored medical men of distinction far more than the United States, the vanity of some of these distinguished men often made "their tongues more cutting than their scalpels." Since most of the American students in Paris possessed

16. John T. Morse, Jr., *Life and Letters of Holmes*, I, 94.
17. Oliver Wendell Holmes, "Our Hundred Days in Europe, 1887" (MS in LC).
18. See Jackson's preface to the translated edition of Pierre Louis, *Researches on the Effects of Bloodletting in Some Inflammatory Diseases* (Boston, 1836), xxv–xxvi.

a high degree of maturity and had been brought up in a fairly Puritan and comfortable setting, they found French students as a class rude and vulgar. The whole Latin Quarter appeared to be "a sort of Bohemian Babel, the chosen home of rampant eccentricity, despising law and order, and full of lavish extravagance of word and deed."[19] As one contemporary Frenchman summed it up ironically: "These students of the Quartier Latin wanted to withdraw themselves from the pernicious influence of civilization." How familiar these comments sound to people living in the 1970s!

In the pre–Civil War period, a large number of American doctors pursued postdoctoral studies in the French capital and several doctors from New Orleans and other parts of Louisiana had earned their medical degrees in Paris. Others, charged with the responsibility of developing medical programs in the United States, explored the system of medical education in France for guidance. They discovered that for the sake of high quality instruction and professional standards France kept the number of medical colleges authorized to confer degrees fairly low. Supplementing the government-supported institutions, quite a host of noted professors of medicine usually offered private lectures attended by hundreds of students. It took four to five years in most European medical faculties before candidates could pass the final M.D. examination.[20] In a lecture Dr. Stillé delivered in 1846 in Philadelphia, he deplored the fact that, contrary to the European practice, medical students in the United States were required to attend medical college for only eight months if they had previously acquired a liberal education. Even this short preparatory medical education constituted a big step forward in comparison with the earlier custom of merely serving an "ap-

19. Arnold, *Memoir of Warren*, 80–82.
20. See William M. Meredith to John Bell, January 26, 1826, in William M. Meredith Papers, PHS. In the nineteenth century, France offered two medical degrees; one known as "*officier de santé*," the other as "*docteur en médicine*." The *officier de santé* did not have to present and defend a thesis and was allowed to practice only in one province. Dr. C. H. Benns, August 15, 1877, in Dr. William Pepper Papers, University of Pennsylvania.

prenticeship" in a doctor's office before hanging out a doctor's shingle. As one contemporary French observer commented, "In the United States it is not even necessary to be a doctor, properly speaking, in order to practice medicine." It was precisely this state of affairs that responsible professionals were determined to remedy. Relatively few American medical students, after all, possessed the resources and other requisites to study in Europe.

As American medical schools were developed to meet the needs of the rapidly growing population,[21] it became vital to emulate the example of continental schools. The emphasis in France on clinical training during the final two years of studies merited as much attention by American doctors as did the high degree of specialization available to French students. Agrégés delivered courses on just about every medical subject, enabling medical students to perfect themselves in areas of special interest. "Is it probable," asked Dr. Stillé, the noted professor of medicine at the Medical College in Philadelphia,"that men who are obliged to learn so much . . . can be inferior to practitioners whose medical pupilage is limited to eight months?"[22] France encouraged its students to devote four or five years to their studies by making the schooling relatively inexpensive and by reducing the pressure in connection with degree examinations. Although obliged to pass five major examinations, French medical students could take them in every branch separately, spacing them successively, while in the final quarter of the century students in the United States had to take all examinations within a very limited time span, usually at the end of three years.

Unlike the medical faculty at Paris, which was authorized to take bodies for anatomical purposes from hospitals, prisons, and poorhouses, medical instruction in the United States was handicapped by the inability to make autopsies. Some American

---

21. Between 1840 and 1876, there were 47 new medical schools founded; between 1873 and 1890, there were 114 new ones. Henry E. Sigerist, *American Medicine* (New York, 1934), 133.
22. Alfred Stillé, *Medical Education in the United States* (Philadelphia, 1846), 15; George Rosen, *The Specialization of Medicine* (New York, 1972), 20–22.

states made bodies of executed prisoners available for dissection, but public opinion was strongly opposed to such medical practice. This widespread attitude prompted even some American doctors to sneer that "the French physician gives infinite labor and pains to his diagnosis, and then hurries his patient to the dead-house to confirm it." A staunch defender of the conscientious thoroughness and brilliance of the French medical profession, Dr. Stanford E. Chaillé of New Orleans, suggested that this sneering comment be changed to read: ". . . and after death hurries to the dead-house to confirm his diagnosis." Doing this, he added, "you will substitute a flattering truth for a scandalous falsehood."[23]

Prejudices against women in medicine were then as strong in France as in the United States. The difference was primarily semantic. In France, it was regarded as "dangerous" to admit women to medical school; in the United States, women were deemed "too delicate." Mary Corina Putnam had the courage, nevertheless, to defy these prejudices. After her graduation from the Medical College in Philadelphia, she went to France where special privileges were granted to her for study in the library of the Ecole de Médecine. When she passed her last examination in July, 1871, and became a *docteur en médecine de la faculté de Paris,* she dedicated her inaugural dissertation thus: "To the faculty of Paris, which in according the honor of a degree to women, has risen to the height of French liberality."[24]

Americans also observed certain paradoxical situations in France. Some of the most outstanding French professors were so dedicated to their work in the hospitals that they had practically no time for a lucrative private practice; consequently, they remained poor. In another respect, some of the most widely read French authorities turned out to be incredibly poor teachers. They possessed an extraordinary capacity for making "a muddy subject still muddier." Even though such observations could not be ignored by Americans in the process of developing medical colleges,

23. Stanford E. Chaillé, "On Medicine in France and Practical Chemistry," *NOMSJ* (1867), 696.
24. Putnam (ed.), *Life and Letters of Mary Putnam Jacobi,* 140–41, 286–91.

the American Medical Association still looked to France for guidance in drafting laws governing the practice of medicine. It became quite obvious that proper registration laws had to be devised for the protection of the profession and the public, for in France, as elsewhere, despite laws against quackery, quacks operated for a time with comparative impunity. While the American Medical Society in Paris, founded in the 1850s and supported predominantly by doctors from southern states, was primarily established to be of assistance to colleagues coming temporarily to Paris, its members also wished to contribute to medical education in the United States by cultivating "a scientific and social acquaintance with the medical men of the Old World."[25] At a time of growing national consciousness, the most enlightened among American doctors recognized the international nature of science and the element of interdependence in human existence.

As much as American students of medicine marveled at the skill and sang-froid of French surgeons, they were somewhat astonished to find certain unsatisfactory conditions in French hospitals. Considering that tens of thousands of patients were at any given time treated in the numerous private and public hospitals—no social stigma was attached to those who sought relief in public hospitals—some allowance for faulty administration had in all fairness to be made. The main criticisms were the lack of cleanliness, the absence of proper ventilation, the paucity of well-trained nurses, and, above all else, neglectful postoperative treatment and attention. The Hospital du Midi, always crowded to capacity with 450 male venereal disease cases, enjoyed the unflattering reputation of being "the dirtiest hospital in Paris." If, unlike American and British doctors, their French colleagues showed an extraordinary carelessness about ablution, in certain instances their mere wiping of "dirtied" hands on an apron amounted to outright negligence.

In a letter Dr. John C. Warren (1778–1856) sent on December 31, 1837, to the trustees of the Massachusetts General Hospital[26]

25. *Constitution of the American Medical Society in Paris* (Paris, 1857).
26. "A Sketch of the French Hospitals," *NYMJ*, XVIII (1873), 218–19.

he mentioned recent improvements in the public hospitals of Paris. Whereas the number of patients at the Hotel Dieu used to be as high as five or six thousand, by 1837 it did not exceed twelve hundred. "But, although everything appears to be fair," he reported, "the mortality in these wards, especially after surgical operations, is much greater than in private houses. . . . The patients in the Hôtel Dieu," he continued, "are nursed by *Religieuses*, as are those in most of the Paris hospitals. . . . They fulfill their tasks with wonderful fidelity; and being persons of education and principle (they are transferred from Seminaries and Convents), they are much more to be relied on than common nurses." He noted furthermore that the doctors were overburdened: "The number of physicians to this great institution is ten; the surgeons three; so that each practitioner has about eighty patients." When the well-known New York surgeon Dr. Valentine Mott (1785–1865) visited Paris in the late 1830s, he could not understand why the most dexterous and the best-educated surgeons failed to follow through with the kind of care that should have been taken for granted. "The miserable system of ventilation," inadequate attention to after-treatment, "especially an insufficiency of nutritious food and stimulants at a time when the system was exhausted by irritation and suppuration," in Dr. Mott's judgment, frequently accounted for the fatal end of the patient after successful operations. On the basis of his observations he regretted, moreover, that French hospitals pushed the practice of depletion to such an extreme point of exhaustion that it frequently brought about a state of critical debility.[27] What American doctors simply could not understand was the French habit, as late as mid-century, of stuffing wounds with lint, thus keeping them too warm, and of not properly cleaning them or the skin adjacent to discharging sores. And finally, Dr. George Suckley, a United States Army surgeon, felt in 1858 that even second-rate American surgeons

27. Valentine Mott, *Travels in Europe and the East, 1834–41* (New York, 1845), 42; Samuel D. Gross, *Memoir of Valentine Mott* (Philadelphia, 1868), 31. See also, George Suckley, "Notes on the Practice in the Hospitals of Paris," *NYJM*, IV (1858), 351; and J. M. Guardia, "Traitement et hygiène des blessés," *Le Temps*, December 2, 1870.

would blush if they set fractured bones as improperly as many of their French colleagues. On the positive side, it should be noted that, unlike many medical officers in American hospitals who occupied their positions because of helpful connections, in Parisian hospitals these officers filled their posts because of their professional qualifications.[28]

In the final decades of the century the secretary general of L'Association de la Presse Médicale took note of the fact that, in contrast to the highly centralized administration of hospitals in Paris and the resultant red tape, individual initiative in late nineteenth-century American hospitals facilitated innovations and improvements. Dr. Marcel Baudouin praised particularly the incomparable training of American nurses and the speed with which ambulances moved into action. Competent and instantaneous care, he suggested, were not the only aspects Frenchmen charged with public health services could profitably study in the United States. Secretary General Baudouin singled out America's special hospitals, the isolation of contagious cases, and homes for retarded children as examples worthy of imitation.[29]

Geographical shifts in medical leadership clearly affected American medicine during the early phases of its professional development. Eighteenth-century English traditions gave way in the first half of the nineteenth century to French dominance, only in turn to be displaced by German medical schools under the leadership of such pioneers as Robert Koch (1843–1910) and Rudolf Virchow (1821–1902). Once medical progress depended on interaction between the clinic and the laboratory, German ingenuity made its mark.[30] It did not take American students of the post–Civil War period long to recognize that the most up-to-

28. A. K. Gardner, *Old Wine in New Bottles*, 77.

29. M. Bauduin, *Quelques remarques sur les hôpitaux des Etats-Unis* (Paris, 1894), 87.

30. Abraham Flexner, *La Formation du médecin en Europe et aux Etats-Unis* (Paris, 1927), 24–25; Thomas N. Bonner, *American Doctors and German Universities: A Chapter in International Relations, 1870–1914* (Lincoln, Nebr., 1963). Deploring the lack of adequate financial support, Louis Pasteur foresaw in 1871: "Our laboratories are the graves of the scientists." Erwin H. Ackernknecht, *Medicine at the Paris Hospital, 1794–1848* (Baltimore, 1967), 123.

date medical research and development was being carried on in Germany. They admired its modern laboratories, clinical opportunities, and exacting professional standards. The academic freedom in German universities came as a welcome surprise to them; and they also appreciated, in contrast to the rigidity prevailing in French schools, the flexibility allowed students in choosing courses in German medical schools.

During the era of Louis Philippe, Dr. Pierre Charles Alexandre Louis (1787–1872) exercised the most profound influence on American medical students in Paris. This tall and rather pale man, "showing the marks of sagacity and deep reflection," had set out to ascertain with arithmetical precision all the phenomena in fever cases. Skeptical about traditional therapeutics, Louis devoted his time exclusively to the most methodical and meticulous research on phthisis, typhoid, yellow fever, and bloodletting. The wards of Hôtel Dieu, La Charité, and La Pitié were his laboratory. While autopsies reinforced his research, he relied on minutely recorded case studies to provide himself with all available evidence. Convinced that "the truth is in the facts and not in the mind which observes them," his method of observation and recording collected so many facts that he had to devise a workable system of analysis and synthesis to make them yield useful data. In private conversations with Dr. John C. Warren of the Massachusetts General Hospital, Louis explained his mode of drawing his inductions: "First, from the journals of disease, containing at least sixty cases, he made a table, at the head of which was placed all the principal symptoms of the disease in separate columns; on the left hand of the table, the list of patients. Then in each column was placed the character of each symptom in each patient. Second, from this first table another was then made, in which were brought together the symptoms of each of the columns showing the number of cases in which any particular symptom appeared."[31] Since these tables and inferences were

31. See Warren's letter of December 31, 1837, in MHS; Elisha Bartlett, *An Inquiry into the Degree of Certainty in Medicine and into the Nature and Extent of Its Power Over Disease* (Philadelphia, 1848), 30–33; and William Osler, *An Alabama Student and Other Biographical Essays* (New York, 1908), 189–210, 232–47.

based on the most accurate observations, Dr. Warren hoped that Louis' private volume of memoirs of the Medical Society of Observation would be translated and published in the United States so that all medical students might master this method. And this was what it was: a new method of studying medicine, rather than a new system of medicine.

Because the great French pathologist required a great deal of reading, something most French medical students were not in the habit of doing, and because he assumed acquaintance with any subject matter under investigation, Louis was not the right teacher for beginners. Many of his students were therefore English and American doctors who had already earned their medical degrees. Until he moved in 1837 to the Hôtel Dieu, where his visits to the wards were followed by many medical students, only a few followed him at La Pitié. The privilege of observing his autopsies and of meeting with him in seminar conferences was necessarily limited to a small number. Quite a few felt close to him; all respected him. He became, as Oliver Wendell Holmes remarked, "the object of our reverence." Generous, unselfish, and gentle, this man of science was "modest in the presence of nature, fearless in the face of authority, unwearying in the pursuit of truth." As a teacher, he was demanding and inspiring; though ill at ease as a lecturer, he talked freely and often brilliantly by the bedside of a patient. Henry Ingersoll Bowditch, a devoted follower of Louis, presented in the winter of 1833 a paper before the Société Médicale d'Observation de Paris,[32] of which Louis was the president. After having been subjected to severe criticism by various members, for which Bowditch was grateful, he listened to Louis say: "In omitting to mention one thing in one part of the paper, he lost it all, for without that the whole remark is worth nothing." Bowditch took this comment for what it was meant to be, a lesson. Indeed, at the next meeting Louis said to him: "Well, my dear, we cut you severely last time, did we not?" But, he added, "a paper well criticized always is a good one.

32. Dr. James Jackson of Boston had organized this French medical club.

A poor paper is beneath criticism."[33] Bowditch could never forget the personal interest this great teacher had shown him. "When I, a young American stranger, fell ill in Paris," he recalled in later years, "Louis immediately sought out my residence and attended me like a father during a severe rheumatic fever which lasted for weeks." Impressed by the concern and kindness of this busy man of science, Bowditch could not help but wonder: "How many of our American professors would do the same favor to a young Frenchman who should happen to attend their lectures?"[34]

Besides contributing to knowledge about phthisis and typhoid fever, Louis' careful and extensive research established that bloodletting in pneumonia did not produce the effect with which doctors had generally credited it.[35] Louis, to whom modern clinical medicine is immensely indebted, must also be remembered for his common-sense observation that nature often heals more effectively than doctors. Great teachers are often judged by the accomplishments of their students. In the case of Louis, some of the most famous names in the history of American medicine studied under his direction.[36] Most notable among them were the Bostonians Henry I. Bowditch, Oliver Wendell Holmes, James Jackson, Jr., George C. Shattuck, J. Collins Warren, and J. Mason Warren. From New York had come John T. Metcalf, Charles L. Mitchell, and Valentine Mott, Sr. Representative of Philadelphia were William W. Gerhard, Casper C. Pennock, William Pepper, Sr., and Alfred Stillé. Upon return to the United States, some of them became eminent teachers in medical colleges in

33. Vincent Y. Bowditch, *Life and Correspondence of Henry Ingersoll Bowditch,* II, 273–74.
34. Henry Ingersoll Bowditch, *Brief Memories of Louis and Some of His Contemporaries in the Parisian School of Medicine of Forty Years Ago* (Boston, 1872), 28–29.
35. Henry R. Viets, *A Brief History of Medicine in Massachusetts* (Boston, 1930), 138.
36. For more detailed information about these doctors, see Guy Hinsdale, "The American Medical Argonauts: Pupils of Pierre Charles Alexandre Louis," *Transactions and Studies of the College of Physicians of Philadelphia,* 4th ser., XIII (1945), 37–43.

the North and South. Louis had taught them more than facts and techniques; he had set a personal and professional example worthy of emulation. American pathological research, however, did not follow his lead entirely, since there was as much interest in cures for diseases as in their identification.

Known as the "Napoleon of Surgery," Guillaume Dupuytren (1777–1835) disdained theoretical themes and lessons.[37] Clinical cases in which he could apply his knowledge and skill to the development of new surgical techniques constituted the kind of challenge that fascinated him. His operations were followed by as many as forty students jostling in every direction to see him perform. Those who observed him commented time and again that he was an extraordinary diagnostician and ingenious and quick in execution. In operations he demonstrated his remarkable ability to modify clinical practices if a particular case called for it.

Nevertheless, it matters little whether vanity or an excessively competitive drive to sustain his reputation as a brilliant surgeon induced Dupuytren to violate elementary porfessional ethics in a case involving the eminent American professor of surgery, Dr. Valentine Mott. While on a visit to Pisa, Dr. Mott learned from a distinguished Italian surgeon that Dupuytren laid claim to originality in operations on the lower jaw. This information shocked the American surgeon so much that he "felt an imperious obligation" to explain that at Dupuytren's request a translation was made of the lower jaw operations Mott had performed and

37. For comments on Dupuytren, see Francis R. Packard, *History of Medicine in the United States* (2 vols.; New York, 1963), I, 442; J. Chalmers Da Costa, "The French School of Surgery in the Reign of Louis Philippe," *AMH*, IV (1922), 78; Ferdinand Campbell Stewart, *The Hospitals and Surgeons of Paris* (New York, 1843), 214–15; and Bulletin de la Société Archéologique et Historique du Limousin, *Le Centenaire de la mort de Dupuytren*, 1835–1935 (Limoges, 1936). Dupuytren proved that, contrary to previous assumptions, certain scirrhous tumors were independent of the nerves and could be readily extirpated. This prompted an American to ask Valentine Mott: "Is it not probable that some of the affections treated in our country as chronic rheumatism or neuralgia, might be found to arise from these small tumours and relieved by a simple surgical operation?" G. P. Cammann to Valentine Mott, February 27, 1829, in NYHS.

publicly described "at least a year or more anterior to Dupuytren's." And, protested Mott, when the French surgeon "gave a clinique on the subject before his class in the Hôtel-Dieu ... *with my cases in his hands,* [he] NEVER BREATHED MY NAME." Indeed, to substantiate his claim that he was the first to undertake such an operation, Dupuytren had antedated the time at which he had performed it.[38] This incident of course reflects more on his character than on his professional skill. Besides admiring him as a surgeon, students also raved about the clarity and eloquence of his lectures, in which he emphasized questions of the greatest practical value.

But the autocrat of the Hôtel Dieu who daringly demonstrated what a surgeon could accomplish also earned the reputation of having no equal in brutality. Dr. Jonathan Mason Warren wrote to his father in 1832 that "if his [Dupuytren's] orders are not immediately obeyed he makes nothing of striking his patient and abusing him harshly." Walking down the hospital wards in a long white butcher's apron and a red night cap with a tassel of blue silk, he scolded patients "if their answers were not as prompt and laconic as the question he put to them." Pupils not fully prepared for his operations would not dare ever to expose themselves again to his abusive outbursts.[39] It was one thing to operate with sang-froid; it was another, as many American doctors noted with respect to many contemporary French surgeons, to appear more interested in a beautiful operation testing the surgeon's diagnosis and prognosis than in saving the life of the patient.[40]

One notable exception in this respect was Philibert Joseph Roux (1780–1854), a senior surgeon at La Charité. According to Dr. Warren, Roux was one of the few who could not be charged with neglecting his patients after surgery. On the contrary, he

38. Mott, *Travels in Europe,* 103–104.
39. "State of Medicine in Paris," *BMSJ,* XVIII (1838), 74.
40. In one of his lectures Dupuytren explained that the deteriorated condition of patients at the time of the operation limited their chances of successful recovery from amputations and other surgery. "Surgical Sketches," *BMSJ,* VIII (1833), 316–19.

was "very careful about his dressings at the operation and afterwards." A visiting American professor of surgery, whom Roux had invited to go through the ward with him, was surprised to see the chief surgeon "dress, with his own hand, every wound, ulcer, and fractured limb, and apply every bandage with a neatness and dispatch almost incredible." Upon the visitor's inquiry, the French surgeon confirmed with great conviction that he always performed these chores, not only for the sake of his patients, but to train his students as well.[41] Unlike Dupuytren, he also tried to lift the morale of his patients by reassuring them in his good-humored and encouraging way. The extent of Roux's experience was brought out in a conversation he carried on after an operation with his good friend Dr. Valentine Mott. Having just witnessed him perform a lithotomy by the lateral section, Mott congratulated Roux on the artful skill with which he had executed it. Roux replied that he ought to be an expert in it, having previously performed it about six hundred times. For that matter, he had operated on the cataract more than six thousand times. The American physician who was the first on whom he performed a staphylorrhaphy, the operation uniting a cleft palate, gratefully exhibited the success of that operation to the Academy of Sciences once he had regained his full power of speech.[42] Roux's eminence as a dexterous surgeon drew crowds of students to his hospital visits and operations. The extremely tedious length of his lectures, on the other hand, proved disappointing. This was particularly annoying, as happened many times, when after a ninety-minute explanatory introduction to a major operation, which had attracted a large audience, he remarked: "Gentlemen, I have no time to say more, and will defer the remainder to another day. So much of the morning has been occupied that the operation must necessarily be postponed."[43] Roux was one of those professors who socialized with his students;

41. William Gibson, *Rambles in Europe in 1839: With Sketches of Prominent Surgeons, Physicians, Medical Schools, Hospitals, etc.* (Philadelphia, 1841), 76–77.
42. Mott, *Travels in Europe*, 34–37.
43. Gardner, *The French Metropolis*, 67.

after a strenuous day, he liked to engage them in a game of dominoes in a nearby cafe.

Another famous French teacher whom American students respected was Armand-Louis Velpeau (1795–1867), professor of clinical surgery and anatomy, surgeon-in-chief at La Charité and surgeon at La Pitié. Americans took an especially fond interest in him because he had worked his way up, in spite of his early poverty. Arriving in Paris in wooden shoes and not knowing where his daily bread would come from, Velpeau overcame all obstacles. His industry, intelligence, character, and determination helped him pursue his professional goals so successfully that he eventually earned an outstanding reputation.[44] Dr. Valentine Mott, himself a surgical giant in the United States, spoke of Velpeau as by far the most scientific and best read surgeon he knew. An excellent teacher, brilliant operator, and profound anatomist, Velpeau was also acclaimed for his book, *Operative Surgery*.[45] American doctors relied heavily on the translated edition of this work that appeared in the United States in the 1840s, with valuable observations by Mott. In a letter to Dr. Mott, Velpeau graciously acknowledged that "my feeble authority will be more than doubly enhanced by being sustained upon your high reputation."[46] At least as widely known and used in America was Velpeau's *An Elementary Treatise on Midwifery*. Dr. Charles D. Meigs of Philadelphia, who translated this treatise by "one of the most enlightened and recent of the French authorities," justified his efforts with the observation that many other admirable French works on this subject had not been available to American doctors in translation. Through these books Velpeau became one of the most influential teachers of America's doctors. Those students who had the privilege of attending his well-organized and clearly presented lectures long remembered the value of another lesson

44. Oliver Wendell Holmes, *Writings of Oliver Wendell Holmes* (13 vols.; Boston, 1891), IX, 429.
45. In this work Velpeau made references to operations performed by American doctors.
46. Alfred Velpeau, *New Elements of Operative Surgery* (3 vols.; New York, 1847), I, xii–xvi.

he taught them:"Even in a trifling case he lays down important rules and principles."[47] This ability to relate details to larger concepts marked Velpeau as a truly gifted teacher.

The depth and breadth of his knowledge and the pace of his work schedule utterly amazed Americans. After two or three operations in the morning, he visited his patients in the hospital, lectured for an hour, and after a brief break saw out-of-door patients. In the afternoon he attended to his private patients at his own residence and still had energy left to make visiting calls. Despite the fact that he kept up this routine without ever taking a vacation, he found time for study and a little social life.[48] In the course of his call on Dr. William Gibson, professor of surgery at the University of Pennsylvania, Velpeau conversed for half an hour in a spirited fashion, revealing that many American and other foreign pupils of his kept him in touch with the medical literature of their country, sending him either translated texts or, at least, essential excerpts. Thus, he confessed, his former students did the heavy reading for him. When Gibson returned the courtesy call the following day, Velpeau showed him the translation of a letter he had requested of Gibson, "detailing the results of certain operations in my own practice."[49] Totally dedicated to the study and practice of medicine, this French giant received similar reports from other American surgeons.[50]

Americans identified as the most popular teachers: Jean Civiale,[51] the gentle and modest lithotritist; Auguste François

47. Philip D. Jordan, "A Naval Surgeon in Paris, 1835–36," *AMH*, III (1941), 73.

48. "Medical Heads and Medical Life in Paris," *CMJ*, IX (1854), 476–83.

49. Gibson, *Rambles*, 67–72.

50. Deserved as Velpeau's reputation was, he nevertheless was "the most bitter in his attacks upon the use of the microscope, stating that he placed more reliance in the diagnosis of tumor based upon its general characters and appearance to the naked eye than in the pretended presence of the so-called characteristic cancer cell." See "Letter from Paris," *PMSJ*, III (1855), 294.

51. Civiale afforded his friend Dr. F. Campell Stewart of New York "every facility in the investigation of those diseases whose seat is in the genito-urinary organs." Samuel W. Francis, *Biographical Sketches of Distinguished Living New York Physicians* (New York, 1867), 106. Civiale also gave Dr. Gibson some of his instruments for illustration in his classes back home. Gibson, *Rambles*, 90–91.

Chomel,[52] the leading authority on diseases of the lungs; Philippe Ricord,[53] the American-born principal surgeon at the hospital for venereal diseases; and Gabriel Andral,[54] the renowned and unostentatious authority on pathological anatomy and a pioneer in chemical examination of the blood in disease. American students found their competence and approachability humbling and inspiring. Reminiscing about these leading men of medical science, Henry I. Bowditch, himself a distinguished doctor in Boston, described Andral's ability to hold the undivided interest and rapt attention of the vast audience that came to his lectures at the Ecole de Médecine: "His learning seemed illimitable, and he would gather all of it before us to illustrate his theme. . . . Andral's tendencies were centrifugal, as Louis' were centripetal. That is, Andral, while obeying a certain impulse to rest on facts, would with his learning and imagination bring data from the opposite extremes of medical experience, and bind them into one vast whole."

Occasionally, universities offered students the entertaining spectacle of a dramatic rivalry between eminent professors. In the early 1830s, for instance, the aging Broussais (1772–1838) still defended his old though by now challenged theories. By an unfortunate coincidence, Andral (1797–1876), Broussais' young rival, lectured in the large amphitheater of the medical school immediately following Broussais. To secure a seat in the amphitheater, the two or three thousand students who came to listen to Andral arrived as much as half an hour earlier and were thus exposed to Broussais' "violent denunciations . . . against all who did not accept the doctrines of the *Phlegmasies Chroniques.*" Seeing that the seats, most of which had been empty at the begin-

---

52. The translated edition of Auguste François Chomel's *Elements of General Pathology,* trans. F. E. Oliver and W. W. Morland, was published in Boston in 1848; Long, *American Pathology,* 78. Chomel disapproved of generalizations on medical questions; Ackerknecht, *Medicine at the Paris Hospital,* 9.

53. A. K. Gardner, *Old Wine in New Bottles,* 86; see also "Dr. Philippe Ricord," *BMSJ,* CXXI (1889), 570–71.

54. Laignel-Lavastine and Molinery, *Clio Medica,* 120–23.

ning of his lecture, were gradually filling to capacity toward its end made the old man frantically squeak and gesticulate. By contrast, the moment Andral commenced speaking in his quiet, yet eloquent way, recorded Bowditch, "there fell over the vast hall of the Ecole de Médecine an entire silence, which was preserved with the greatest decorum . . . to the very end of the lecture."[55]

Practically every advance in physiology could be traced to François Magendie (1783–1855), who "turned the tide of physiological investigations from futile speculations to the rigid examination of experimental actualities." Magendie, founder of the *Journal de physiologie expérimentale* (1821–1831) and author of learned studies on the physical phenomena of life and diseases of the nervous system, demonstrated the motor and sensory functions of the spinal roots. Scientists acknowledged his major contributions with the highest respect. But while the medical world followed his experiments on animals with intense curiosity, it was not surprising that many Americans, vociferously opposed to what they considered cruelty to animals, called him a monster and a wretch.[56]

Claude Bernard (1813–1878), the outstanding experimental physiologist who succeeded Magendie at the Collège de France, studied the functions of the pancreas gland, the juice of which he found to play a major role in the digestive process. Through his research on the glycogenic function of the liver and his quantitative determination of blood sugar, he shed significant light on diabetes. Among many other findings, Bernard's discovery of the vasomotor system, furthermore, helped to explain the influence of the sympathetic nerves on body temperature. Conceptu-

---

55. Henry Ingersoll Bowditch, *Brief Memories*, 22–26; Samuel Wigglesworth, "Three Letters from Paris," dated April 24, 1836, in NYAM. While such respectful decorum was the norm at the Paris Faculty of Medicine, "general dissatisfaction with things as they are" prompted a hideously noisy opening of the school in 1866. *NYMJ*, IV (1867), 319.

56. J. C. Dalton, "Magendie as Physiologist," *International Review* (February 1880), 120–25; James M. D. Olmsted, *François Magendie: Pioneer in Experimental Physiology and Scientific Medicine in Nineteenth Century France* (New York, 1944).

ally, he emphasized that all functional activities of the body are interrelated and subordinate to its physiological needs.[57]

His experiments fascinated American students. They liked his lucid lectures and demonstrations. In a letter one of them sent home in 1851 he observed: "It was curious to see walking about the amphitheater of the Collège de France dogs and rabbits, unconscious contributors to science, with five or six orifices in their bodies from which, at a moment's warning, there could be produced any secretion of the body, including that of several salivary glands, the stomach, the liver, and the pancreas."[58] Claude Bernard took a special interest in American doctors. One of them, Silas Weir Mitchell, a graduate of Jefferson Medical College in Philadelphia and a distinguished neurologist, recalled the unforgettable lesson that when he once told Bernard "such and such must be the case," the famous physiologist replied: "Why think when you can experiment? Exhaust experiment, and then think."[59] Evidently keeping up with what was going on in his profession, Bernard occasionally referred in his lectures to medical research pursued in America. In one of his lectures in 1860, for instance, he acknowledged Dr. Mitchell's research on rattlesnake poison.

Another example of this kind involved the research of the American physiologist Dr. William Beaumont, who was largely concerned with chemical analysis of the digestive system and the significance of gastric juice. When Nicolaus Blondlot published in 1843 his *Traité analytique de la digestion: Considéré particulièrement dans l'homme et dans les animaux vertèbres* he gave evidence of familiarity with Beaumont's investigations.[60]

57. James M. D. Olmsted and E. Harris, *Claude Bernard and the Experimental Method in Medicine* (New York, 1952) ; Charles Singer, *A Short History of Scientific Ideas* (Oxford, 1959), 492–93; see also Austin Flint letter, dated June 28, 1854, in *BMJ*, X (1854), 325–26.

58. Olmsted and Harris, *Claude Bernard*, 69.

59. *Ibid.*, 70.

60. George Rosen, *Die Aufnahme der Entdeckung William Beaumont's durch die europäische Medizin* (Berlin, 1935), 30–31.

Years later, Claude Bernard mentioned them in his *Leçons de physiologie expérimentale appliqué à la médecine* (1856). In fact, Bernard took a lasting interest in Beaumont's work. At Bernard's suggestion a Dr. Willis Green Edwards wrote to Beaumont from Paris in 1850:

The publication of your observation, exposing so clearly and analytically the physiology of the stomach, was the commencement of a new era in the study of this important organ and those associated with it. Your experiments are constantly imitated here upon animals by a large number of investigating physiologists, among whom M. Bernard probably stands first. . . . His observations have necessarily been limited to animals and in the absence of yours upon man would lose much of their value, since no other evidence exists of the identity of the process of digestion in man and the lower animals. . . . M. Bernard feels some interest in knowing the subsequent history of Martin [Alexis St. Martin], and requested me to write you, inquiring whether you had kept sight of him . . . if he is still living.[61]

When Bernard learned of the well-being of St. Martin, he made a passing reference to it in a lecture.

Among the many American doctors who directly benefited from Bernard's guidance was Dr. Joseph Leidy, the distinguished Philadelphia scientist. In his diary of a visit to Europe in 1848, Leidy recorded with evident satisfaction that after Professor Bernard had exposed the roots of the sciatic nerves of a cat, he permitted him "to repeat the tractions on the different extremities, and with the same results."[62] As much as another American, Dr. S. Pollak of St. Louis, marveled at the immense size and equipment of Bernard's laboratory, he fondly remembered the modest luncheon to which the famous physiologist had invited him in a private room adjacent to the laboratory. This type of informality, which learned Americans encountered quite

61. Quoted in Jesse Myer, *Life and Letters of Dr. William Beaumont* (St. Louis, 1939), 289. For Beaumont's major contribution, accomplished under very primitive conditions, see Moulton and Schifferes (eds.), *The Autobiography of Science*, 309–12.
62. Joseph Leidy Diary, June 20, 1848, in ANSP.

frequently in French scientific circles,[63] accelerated their determination to be worthy contributors to their chosen specialties. Since a teacher can reach more students through his publications than he can through individual contacts, Bernard's influence on the medical profession in the United States was greatly enhanced by the publication of his lecture notes in English translation.[64]

The tradition of this Franco-American exchange of medical knowledge in the field of physiology was perpetuated by Charles Edouard Brown-Séquard (1817–1894), another of those dedicated scientists who sometimes lived on dry bread and water and without heat in winter, before he had worked his way up to the top. Of mixed American and French descent and a graduate of the Medical College of Paris, at one time or another he taught medicine at the University of Virginia, Harvard, and the Collège de France. In recognition of his solid accomplishments this neurophysiologist was asked in 1878 to occupy Claude Bernard's chair as professor of experimental medicine. Though he found it difficult to settle down in either the United States or France, he contributed much to the medical knowledge of both countries. His lectures and numerous publications on experimental physiology found a receptive audience. In his early lectures, published by the *Philadelphia Medical Examiner*, he contended that "every tissue possesses its vital properties in consequence of its peculiar organization and that in a completely developed animal nutrition is the source of the vital properties, inasmuch as it is the cause of the maintenance of organization." Among his many contributions to the medical sciences Brown-Séquard established that the decussation of the sensory fibers of the spinal cord is in the

63. Pollak, *Autobiography*, 213. Austin Flint cherished Claude Bernard's memorable gift to him: the operating table Magendie had used in his physiological laboratory.

64. James M. D. Olmsted, "The Influence of Claude Bernard on Medicine in the United States and England," *California and Western Medicine*, XLII (1935), 111–13, 174–76; see also James M. D. Olmsted, "The Contemplative Works of Claude Bernard," Johns Hopkins University, *BIHM*, III (1935), 335–54; and W. Riese, "Claude Bernard in the Light of Modern Science," *BHM*, XIV (1943),281–94.

cord itself. "The only direct effect of the section of the cervical part of the sympathetic," he maintained, "is the paralysis and consequently the dilation of the bloodvessels." A man of two continents, Brown-Séquard was ideally equipped to strengthen Franco-American cultural and professional relations.[65]

As far as certain medical specialties were concerned, the first American dermatologists were trained at the St. Louis Hospital in Paris. Henry Daggett Bulkley (1804–1872), a student of Laurent Théodore Biett (1781–1840) and P. L. Alphe Cazenave (1795–1877), disseminated in the United States the dermatological thoughts of his French and Swiss teachers. In fact, in 1845 he translated Cazenave's work into English. This *Manual of Diseases of the Skin* was shortly thereafter supplemented by Noah Worcester's *A Synopsis of Symptoms, Diagnosis and Treatment of the More Common and Important Diseases of the Skin*. Having received their training at St. Louis, Worcester and Bulkley's son Duncan also followed the theories of their Parisian masters who believed in the internal origin of skin diseases. By the middle of the nineteenth century A. P. Ernest Bazin challenged the long-standing assumption that itch mites in scabietic cases were confined to the hands, wrists, and feet. Finding that they spread out all over the body, he no longer limited the application of sulphur ointment in the treatment of scabies to the hands and feet. This simple discovery worked so well that it greatly reduced hospital confinement in these cases. His recognition, furthermore, of the role played by vegetable parasites in certain contagious skin diseases prompted him to search for agents that would effectively destroy these parasites. Bazin and later on Louis Philippe Alfred Hardy, another noted teacher at the St. Louis School, gave American dermatologists a much-needed sense of direction.[66]

65. James M. D. Olmsted, *Charles Edouard Brown-Séquard: A Nineteenth Century Neurologist and Endocrinologist* (Baltimore, 1946), 53–62, 124–31; M. Berthelot, "The Life and Works of Brown-Sequard," Smithsonian Institution, *Annual Report, 1897–98* (Washington, D.C., 1898), 677–96.

66. Paul E. Bechet, "L'Hôpital Saint-Louis: A Brief Biographical Sketch of Its Early Teachers and Their Influences upon American Dermatology," *AMH*, n.s., X (1938), 405–12.

The French also took an early lead in orthopedic surgery. Through surgery and various mechanical devices they relieved, as Dr. Mott pointed out, "almost every description of human deformity originating in the muscular system." Mott's good friend Dr. Jules Guérin had opened an orthopedic establishment in the vicinity of Paris that surpassed any other then in existence. Acquiring as much knowledge in this new branch as he could, Dr. Mott returned to the United States with every instrument and apparatus employed by Guérin and promptly used them in the American Orthopedic Institution he founded in New York City.[67]

In obstetrics, too, one of the knowledgeable early nineteenth-century American specialists, Dr. W. P. Dewees, professor of midwifery at the University of Pennsylvania, readily acknowledged his indebtedness to such a French authority as Baudelocque. For a long time American doctors found Velpeau's translated treatise on midwifery a helpful guide. American students in Paris interested in obstetrics usually received private instructions from midwives.[68]

The French did not close their eyes to venereal diseases, a public health problem of major magnitude. The Hospital du Midi for males averaged in mid-century about 3,300 patients each year afflicted with this disease; and the female syphilitic Hospital Lourcine averaged about 2,000. Dr. Philippe Ricord, the head of du Midi, possessed a worldwide reputation in this field, based on his clinical experience, encyclopedic knowledge, and publications. In Ricord's wards, cases could be observed that in a general hospital or in private practice would have been identified only in a much more advanced stage. Fifty of the three hundred beds in the Lourcine were reserved for children. Although females of all age groups sought treatment in this hospital, most of them were young—indeed, as young as fifteen years.[69] Whereas the

67. Mott, *Travels in Europe*, 54–56.
68. Russell M. Jones, "American Doctors and the Parisian Medical World, 1830–1840," *BHM*, XLVII (1973), 60; Stephen W. Williams, *American Medical Biography* (Greenfield, Mass., 1845), 120–26.
69. See Austin Flint letter, dated May 18, 1854, in *BMJ*, X (1854), 107–14; and "Dr. Philippe Ricord," *BMSJ*, CXXI (1889), 570–71.

people of the United States were morally indignant about prostitution and treated it as a crime, the French system of legalized prostitution, providing for police surveillance and requiring periodical medical examination, according to Dr. Austin Flint, mitigated at least some of the frightful consequences of syphilis.

Although French schools and general hospitals began to teach ophthalmology as a special branch of medicine only in the 1880s, important work in this field had attracted American specialists to Paris by the 1830s. Usually, American ophthalmologists who went to Europe to perfect their knowledge sought it from leading authorities in Berlin, Vienna, London, and Paris. In Paris in the 1840s and 1850s, such pioneer specialists as Dr. Henry W. Williams (1821–1895) of Boston and Dr. Elkanah Williams (1822–1888) of Louisville, for example, profited greatly from instruction in large private clinics, most famous among them those of Louis Auguste Desmarres (1810–1882) and Jules Sichel (1802–1868). In later years, the original work of Louis de Wecker (1832–1904) and Edmond Landolt (1846–1926) attracted physicians and surgeons from all over the world. If the spectacular clinical work of these and other great foreign-born oculists in Paris earned them an international reputation, their publications helped to solidify it.[70] Many American ophthalmologists thought highly of de Wecker's *Manuel d'ophthalmologie* (1889), which illustrated the latest developments in microscopy of the living eye, and of Landolt's *The Refraction and Accommodation of the Eyes and Their Anomalies,* translated in 1886 by Dr. C. M. Culver of Albany. As the *Boston Medical and Surgical Journal* had in 1847 offered its readers translated extracts from Professor Desmarres' *Treatise on the Diseases of the Eyes,* in the final decades of the nineteenth century the *American Journal of Ophthalmology* kept its readers informed of progress in ophthalmology in all parts of the world.[71]

70. See Alvin A. Hubell, *The Development of Ophthalmology in America,* 1800 *to* 1870 (Chicago, 1908); Burton Chance, *Clio Medica: Ophthalmology* (New York, 1939), 83–86; and William Campbell Posey and Samuel Horton Brown, *The Wills Hospital of Philadelphia: The Influence of European and British Ophthalmology upon It* (Philadelphia, 1931).

71 Ernest Hart, "Ophthalmology in Paris," *American Journal of Ophthalmo-*

In a related area, Dr. S. Pollak, of St. Louis, who visited the famous School of the Blind in Paris, reported that the simplicity and practicability of the Braille point type impressed him so much that he was determined to introduce it in all American schools for the blind. Dr. Pollak was pleased to find that even before his arrival he had been no stranger to Joseph Gaudet, the chief of instruction at the Paris School of the Blind. These two gentlemen continued to maintain contact and indeed collaborated when Dr. Pollak prepared a useful report for Gaudet, summing up his observations in various European schools for the blind.[72]

Among the many medical fields in which Frenchmen made pioneering contributions was mental health. The credit for advancing our knowledge about this human affliction and its treatment goes to Philippe Pinel (1745-1826) and his pupil Etienne Dominique Esquirol (1772-1840).[73] As physician at the Bicètre in Paris, Pinel demonstrated in the final years of the eighteenth century that an enlightened approach in the treatment of the insane produced promising results. Kindness and understanding accomplished more in dealings with these unfortunate patients than did punishment and brutality. Pinel's work at La Salpêtrière, the Parisian asylum for incurable women, confirmed his earlier observations and led in 1801 to the publication of his trail-blazing and influential *Traité médico-philosophique sur l'aliénation mentale.* In the second quarter of the century, La Salpêtrière, with a capacity for ten thousand patients,[74] afforded Esquirol the extraordinary opportunity of studying a hard core of fifteen hundred lunatics, idiots, and other mental cases, an impressively broad base for his research on the insane. By separating this multitude

---

logy, VI (1889), 147–53; see also "French Ophthalmological Society," *ibid.,* XIII (1896), 245–52.

72. Pollak, *Autobiography,* 109–11, 201, 213–14.

73. George Rosen, *A History of Public Health* (New York, 1958), 146; Norman Dain, *Concepts of Insanity in the United States,* 1789–1865 (New Brunswick, N.J., 1964), 14–15, 21–27, 69-74; G. P., "State of Medicine in Paris," *BMSJ,* XVIII (1838), 69–70.

74. Dr. Pollak suggested that its "economical management . . . could be studied by us with profit to the taxpayers." Pollak, *Autobiography,* 215.

of patients according to their degree of illness, he improved the recovery chances, particularly of those patients whose condition held out the greatest hope.

Implementing their enlightened views, the French made the lives of those confined to La Salpêtrière as pleasant as possible. Conscious attempts were made to avoid crowding. The spacious outdoor facilities with their gravel walks, shrubberies, and flowers were used to produce an atmosphere as "normal" as life on the outside. A church on the grounds remained constantly open and enabled those who wished to pray the opportunity to do so whenever they wished. Prayer, it was believed, and the enjoyment of beautiful paintings and statues, would prove soothing to the soul. When in 1828 Dr. Peter Solomon Townsend visited the asylum for lunatics in Rouen he found there similar conditions.[75] In his diary he referred to "the soothing and conciliatory" methods the doctors at Rouen used in trying to avoid the kind of torments patients suffered in the past when "barbarous brutal measures of violence and coercion . . . were in vogue." Townsend was impressed with the pleasant environment and comfortable accommodations provided for the patients. Their classification according to their individual degree of insanity prevented undesirable associations between curable and incurable patients, an important element in their improved well-being.

Specializing in work with defective children, Edouard Séguin (1812-1880) supported the view that through patient treatment idiocy could in some cases be ameliorated if not entirely cured. When he decided in 1850 to settle down in the United States, a land with a freer political atmosphere than France tolerated under Louis Napoleon, he enjoyed the reputation of being an authority on idiocy.[76] Another, though not original, approach was advocated by François Broussais. He suggested in his study *On Irritation and Insanity* (1831) that insanity was a disease of the body rather

75. See letter to *BMJ*, XC (1854), 107-12; and Peter S. Townsend Diary (January 7, 1828), III, 21-27, in NYAM.
76. Ivor Kraft, "Edouard Seguin and Nineteenth Century Moral Treatment of Idiots," *BHM*, XXXV (1961), 393-418.

than an affliction of the mind or soul. This and other contemporary French literature on diseases of the brain excited the interest of at least a few American students in Paris.

The observation reported in 1866 to the Academy of Medicine in Paris that increased consumption of alcohol caused a serious rise in mental disease did not seem unrelated to an earlier observation that "in most cases of insanity a generous and sometimes even a rich course of nutriment was infinitely preferable to the system of starvation and depletion so dogmatically recommended by some" doctors.[77] If psychiatrists had any doubt about the effect of chemical and psychological factors on the mental health of their patients, history provided them with very persuasive data. The *New York Medical Journal* rendered a service to the profession by reproducing in 1871 excerpts from a fascinating letter Dr. Brierre de Boismont, the public health officer of Paris, had written to a colleague in London about the effect of the Siege of Paris on the insane.[78] Referring to observations he had made at the time of the revolutionary violence in 1848, Boismont pointed out dramatically the disastrous impact of war and revolution on the mentally sick. (We have previously noted the correlation between a sharp rise in heart attacks caused by the excitements of the Great Revolution.) The mid-nineteenth-century revolution sharply intensified the fears of patients who were terror-stricken by their imagined impending execution. The Siege of Paris in 1871, accompanied by defective nourishment and nightly bombardments that robbed the patients of their sleep, caused severe depressions. "My poor patients," wrote Dr. Boismont, "were very much tormented by it, and great cries issued from a dormitory where thirty or more were huddled together in a state of great mental terror." Death caused by starvation relieved many of their misery. Psychiatrists familiar with these conditions and the mental by-products of war and revolution hoped, as Dr.

---

77. "Alcohol and Insanity," *NYMJ*, IV (1866), 237.
78. "Miscellaneous and Scientific Notes," *NYMJ*, XIII (1871), 771–72. For the full text, see *The Lancet*, March 4, 1871; see also Boismont's earlier letter in *L'Union Médicale*, Paris, July 20, 1848.

Boismont did, that intelligence and humanity would teach man in the future to bring about changes through enlightened reforms.

As in many areas of general medicine, Americans in the field of dentistry owed much to eighteenth- and early nineteenth-century French pioneers. Pierre Fauchard (1678–1863), of course, laid the foundation of modern dentistry.[79] It is striking, however, that despite such French contributions to the practice of dentistry as "incorruptible teeth" and devices for the support of artificial sets of teeth, the progress of dentistry in France lagged far behind its strides in medicine and surgery generally. Far from being pursued as a specialized branch of medicine, dentistry in nineteenth-century France was by and large in a sorry state.

Significant French dental literature reached the United States regularly and was frequently made available in English translation. The *American Journal of Dental Science* became a major source for the publication of these treatises and articles.[80] Fauchard's *Le Chirurgien dentiste ou traité des dents* was widely known in the United States. And the works of J. R. Duval, P. F. Blandin, and E. Magitot were usually available in translation. In 1843, J. B. Xavier, a Baltimore dentist, translated and published an important French work, originally published by J. B. Gariot in 1805, under the telling title: *Treatise on Diseases of the Mouth: The History of Its Diseases, the Means of Preserving It in Beauty and Health, and Operations Appertaining to the Dental Art.*[81]

Many of the techniques of French dentists were brought to the United States, particularly to Philadelphia, by immigrants. Joseph Lemaire opened his successful practice in that community in 1784. And James Gardette a Frenchman who had studied medi-

79. Bernhard W. Weinberger, *Pierre Fauchard: Surgeon-Dentist* (Minneapolis, 1941); Chapin A. Harris, *The Dental Art: A Practical Treatise on Dental Surgery* (Baltimore, 1839), 18; W. F. Kelsey, "Dentistry in France," *Johnston's Dental Miscellany*, VI (1879), 1–3.
80. See AADS, *A History of Dental and Oral Science in America* (Philadelphia, 1876), 229–31.
81. See *NYDJ*, III (1860), 6.

cine in Paris, practiced in Philadelphia from 1784 until 1829. He invented a plate to which teeth were fastened with the help of metal stems, and he has been credited with having been the first dentist to use gold leaves to seal cavities. One of the major developments in dentistry was the process by which Nicholas Dubois de Chamant demonstrated in 1788 the feasibility of full dentures of baked porcelain. Subsequently, James Gardette succeeded, in 1800, in applying atmospheric pressure to help hold dentures fast.[82] Although porcelain or mineral teeth had been used in France at least since 1774, for some strange reason they were not imported into the United States until 1817 when Dr. A. A. Plantou brought some to Philadelphia. These teeth were so coarse and so badly shaped that they were usually referred to as "French beans."[83] The recommendation by a certain Monsieur Taveau, of Paris, to use "silver paste" for permanent fillings, actually a mixture of pure silver and mercury, constituted another step forward in the history of dentistry. And in 1841 an important study on orthodontics appeared, in which J. M. A. Schangé, a Frenchman, described the wire crib designed to serve as a base for springs and ligatures.

Because the medical profession in France had long failed to consider dentistry a vitally important and integral field of medicine the medical standards of dental practitioners, as well as their social prestige, had been lowered.[84] The existence of a few outstanding French pioneers in the field of dentistry did not lead

82. Arthur Ward Lufkin, *A History of Dentistry* (Philadelphia, 1948), 116–19, 258–59; J. A. Taylor, *History of Dentistry* (Philadelphia, 1922), 143; Ch. Godon and A. Ronnet, *L'Art dentaire aux Etats-Unis en* 1893 (Paris, 1894), 4.

83. M. D. K. Bremner, *The Story of Dentistry: From the Dawn of Civilization to the Present* (New York, 1946), 88; AADS, *History of Dental and Oral Science*, 20–21. A letter in the New York Historical Society, dated February 18, 1861, indicates that a certain Dr. E. Bollmann had brought some artificial teeth from France prior to that date. He described them as "vastly superior to dead natural teeth" and offered fifty to one hundred of them to another New York dentist at $2 a piece. Greenwood Family Papers, in NYHS.

84. A dentist called "to attend a patient was expected to enter the house by the back-stairs." Thomas Evans, *Memoirs of Dr. Thomas W. Evans: The Second French Empire* (New York, 1905), 15.

to its full development and recognition. Indeed, there were only 5 dentists in Paris in 1790, only 20 in 1814, and about 140 in 1828. For the larger part of the nineteenth century the dental profession in France lacked officially defined qualifications and restraints, with the result that many self-celebrated dentists formed "a perfect legion of dishonor."[85] It was bad enough that in mid-nineteenth-century France tooth extractions were performed by mountebanks at street corners and fakirs at fairs, "where the howls of victims were drowned by the beating of drums, the clash of cymbals and the laughter and applause of the . . . crowd." It was even worse that the poor people who could not afford the expensive services of the few professionally trained dentists were duped by unscrupulous hucksters who claimed to be able to preserve teeth by "the new American process": "The most decayed and painful teeth are so improved in condition as to be unrecognizable after two applications of the American process. This process embalms the tooth, even to the alveolus, in such a manner that nothing remains except to stop the cavity to prevent the food from entering, and the tooth is cured forever. In fine, no more extractions with the American process." Another French advertiser claimed that his artificial plates "are retained by their perfection of adjustment. Their elastic base permits their adaptation over the most sensitive roots; they strengthen loosened teeth and render them useful." For filling he used "a cement whose inalterable solidity only increases with time."[86]

To make matters worse, many small coteries and jealous rivalries prevented the regulation of the practice of dentistry in France. Medical doctors looking upon dentistry as a branch of surgery wanted to limit the right of practicing it to qualified doctors only. If they had had their way, practitioners without diplomas and foreigners would have been barred from practicing dentistry. Those practitioners, however, who had acquired great competence as

85. See "Dentistry in France," *AJDS*, IV (1854), 486–87; and *AJLDS*, II (1841), 192.
86. Kelsey, "Dentistry in France," 1–3.

dental technicians reasoned: "While the doctors were studying anatomy and surgery, we were toiling in the workroom and acquiring more practical knowledge of our profession, and we consider that we ought in no way to be eclipsed by our more scientific brethren."[87] Even more than these technicians, the swarm of profiteering dental charlatans opposed legislative reform of the existing state of affairs for a long time. Nevertheless, those who insisted that the dental art required highly specialized medical training prevailed. From 1880 on, when the Dental College of Paris was founded, dentistry in France was at last put on a scientific and professional level.[88] Some French doctors promptly began to think in terms of preventive dental care. The municipal council of Paris approved their proposal of gratuitous dental service in the primary schools of Paris, providing for "a semi-annual examination of the mouths of all children in these schools whose parents have signified their willingness" to accept this program.[89]

American dentists learned as much from the French as they had to offer, and conditions compelled them to learn much. The premature decay of teeth and the recession of the gums of many Americans presented a major challenge. A French visitor to the United States recorded at the very beginning of the nineteenth-century: "You will scarcely find, among ten persons under thirty, one whose teeth are entirely sound; and it is a cause of particular regret that young and beautiful women between fifteen and twenty have generally their teeth disfigured with black spots, and the greater part of them gone."[90] These conditions, usually attributed

87. M. Stevens, "The Dental Profession in France," *AJDS*, 3rd ser., IX (1875), 179–80.

88. See "Unqualified Dentists in France," *Dental Cosmos*, XIX (1877), 381; "The Dental Profession in France," *Dental Cosmos*, XXII (1880), 277; M. Levett, "Dental College of Paris," *Dental Cosmos*, XXV (1883), 446–47; and E. Brasseur, *Rapport annuel des travaux de la Société Syndicale Odontologique de France* (Paris, 1884), 4–8.

89. "Gratuitous Dentistry in the Schools of Paris," *Dental Cosmos*, XXIV (1882), 44–45.

90. Constantine de Volney, *A View of the Soil and Climate of the United States of America* (Philadelphia, 1804), 226–29.

to the excessive use of sugar, salted food, and hot tea, no doubt prompted interested and ingenious minds to search for solutions that would permanently improve the dental health of the nation. The emergence of special schools of dental surgery in the United States, long unique in the medical profession, proved to be most helpful in this respect. The College of Dentistry in Philadelphia, famous for its facilities, methods, and accomplishments became the Mecca of foreign dental students from all parts of the world. From the middle of the nineteenth century on Americans raised the art of dentistry to such a high level that the United States assumed international leadership in the profession.[91]

The high regard in which American dentistry came to be held abroad[92] facilitated the emigration of some American dentists. Beginning with the Second Empire, France welcomed skillful dental practitioners from the United States. The prospects of fabulous incomes and of living in a stimulating cosmopolitan environment made Paris a superbly attractive residence. Dr. C. Starr Brewster of Charleston, South Carolina, began to practice dentistry in Paris in 1835. Dr. C. S. Putnam of New York City, who published in Paris one of the few dental journals in Europe, *Odontotechnique,* aroused much interest in his vulcanite rubber base for artificial teeth. Another American dentist who distinguished himself in the French capital was a certain Dr. Norman W. Kingsley of New York. His beautiful porcelain carvings of full and partial sets of teeth mounted on gold earned him the highest medals at the Paris World's Fair in 1855. Dr. John Allen of Cincinnati, Ohio, was similarly honored in 1867 for his formula for continuous gum body and his techniques for refining porcelain work. Around 1880 American dentistry made another

91. Jules Violle, "L'Exposition de Chicago et la science américaine," *RDDM,* (June, 1894), 610–11.

92. Chapin A. Harris' *Principles and Practices of Dental Surgery* (Philadelphia, 1839), the leading textbook in this field, went through many editions and revisions after its original publication. In 1874, it was finally translated into French and, with supplementary comments on recent French dental works, it served as the most comprehensive guide for French dentists. See preface by Dr. Edmond Andrieu in Chapin A. Harris and Philip H. Austen, *Traité théorique et pratique de l'art du dentiste* (Paris, 1874).

big step forward when Dr. Foster-Flagg demonstrated that plastic substances accomplished in less time and at less cost the same results as gold fillings.[93] Perhaps the most celebrated American dentist in Paris was Dr. Brewster's assistant, Dr. Thomas W. Evans, of Philadelphia. His expertise at gold fillings and preparations of amalgam alloys, as well as his demonstration of the applicability of vulcanized rubber as a dental base plate, earned him a great reputation. Eventually he became the dentist to the imperial court and was much in demand by the high society of France. Among his other most significant contributions ranked his report to the French government concerning the treatment of head and face wounds of victims of the Crimean War and the Italian campaign in 1859. The medical reforms subsequently instituted by the French army rested to a large extent on Evans' findings and recommendations. The unqualified respect extended to this dental surgeon also helped to raise the social and professional standing of many of his French colleagues.[94]

In 1881 thirty American dentists in Paris attended to the dental health of the upper class of the population. The poorer classes could not have afforded to pay $150 for a set of teeth, the minimum fee these dentists charged for their expertise.[95] Occasionally, as at the International Dental Congress in Paris in 1889, delegates from New York, Philadelphia, and Chicago who had come to attend this meeting, shared the latest techniques known to American dentists with their colleagues from all parts of the world.[96]

93. Burton Lee Thorpe, *Biographies of Pioneer American Dentists and Their Successors*, in Charles Koch (ed.), *History of Dental Surgery* (3 vols.; Fort Wayne, Ind., 1910), III, 147, 171, 514, 542–45; "State of Dentistry in 1860," *NYDJ*, III (1860), 101–108.

94. Maurice L. Charenton, *Le Docteur Thomas W. Evans: Dentiste de Napoléon III et les dentistes de son époque* (Paris, 1936); Henry Rainey, *Dr. Thomas W. Evans: America's Dentist to European Royalty* (Philadelphia, 1956).

95. W. C. Barrett, "European and American Dentistry Compared," *MDJ*, XIII (1881), 481–87; "American Dentists in Europe," *AJDS*, XI (1878), 574; and "Dentists in Paris," *AJDS*, XV (1881), 85–87.

96. Congrès Dentaire International à Paris (1889), *Comptes Rendus* (Paris, 1891), 7–10, 257–59, 312ff. See also *IIIᵉ Congrès Dentaire International* (4 vols.; Paris, 1901–1903), I, 63–64, and III, 179–81. Seventy-five Americans attended this dental congress in Paris. For the dental section of the International Medical Congress in Washington, D.C., see the journal, *L'Art dentaire* (April, 1888), 725–30.

The elite of American dentists in Europe organized in 1872 the *American Dental Society of Europe,* in an effort to promote the diffusion of knowledge about dental surgery among all members of the dental profession.[97] To the extent to which they realized this objective, they became ideal cultural ambassadors.

As French dentists saw it at the end of the nineteenth century, American dentistry had been aided and advanced by several factors. High quality dental training and experimental research constituted the most essential requisites for growth and development. With a few exceptions, practicing American dentists were much too impatient to write or read books about progress in their profession. They communicated their experiences and experiments therefore through brief notices in their professional journals. And at all times, they did not wait for the state to take the initiative in bringing about improvements. Progress in American dentistry resulted primarily from the endeavors of dedicated individual dentists and the generosity of certain private citizens who took a keen interest in all institutions of learning.

American patients, too, deserved a certain credit for their assistance in the rather rapid advancement of dental science in the United States. French dentists marveled at the placid cooperation of American patients, even in long and painful dental operations. By comparison, their own nervous and often uncooperative patients complicated their task and exhausted their patience.[98] Americans went to their dentists for treatment regardless of pain and length of operation, but hypersensitive French patients regarded those dentists best who hurt the least and finished their work the most quickly. The result of this attitude, according to

97. "The American Dental Society in Europe," Paris *Continental Gazette,* September 12, 1878. As French dentistry improved in the final quarter of the century, the financial rewards of American dentists in Paris declined sharply. See A. W. Harlan, "Dentistry in Europe," *Dental Brief,* II (1898), 735–37; and O. B. Buttles to his brother Augustus, April 4, 1876, in O. B. Buttles Correspondence, State Historical Society of Wisconsin; and A. Preterre, "French and American Dentists," *MDJ,* V (1873), 171.

98. Paul Dubois, *L'Art dentaire aux Etats-Unis* (Paris, 1888), 12, 43; Godon and Ronnet, *L'Art dentaire,* 136–37.

a conscientious dental surgeon in Paris, was that dentists "here will exclude pain from their operations . . . at the expense of thoroughness." This difference in attitude was reflected even in advertisements. Whereas American dentists guaranteed that their gold fillings and plates would outlive their patients, their French confrères guaranteed "extraction, fillings, platework . . . without a particle of pain."[99] The extent to which French patients influenced the practices of their dentists was also evidenced by their unwillingness to have their front teeth filled with gold. Although they were very conscious of the relationship between their teeth and their appearance, they considered the "golden mouths" of Americans a rather amusing display of bad taste.[100]

So far ahead of other countries was the development of dental surgery in the United States that the head of the world-renowned Parisian firm of Luer, specializing in medical instruments, resided for a while in the United States to study its excellent instruments.[101] Almost until the end of the nineteenth century American doctors usually ordered from this famous instrument-maker in the rue de l'Ecole de Médecine specialized precision tools needed in their offices and operating rooms. Early in the century Americans had been accustomed to turn to France for all kinds of medical equipment. In 1826, for instance, a New Yorker who planned to offer a course in physiology inquired whether he could buy in Paris, "large-sized colored plates of the visual apparatus, the ear, the larynx, the heart, and the brain with their parts." A Bostonian doctor, who had heard that subjects for dissection had

99. William Hirschfeld, "Conscientiousness in Dental Operations," *Dental Clippings*, III (1901), 208–11.

100. Chapin A. Harris, *The Dental Art: A Practical Treatise on Dental Surgery* (Baltimore, 1839), 26–28; see also *Dental Review*, V (1891), 365–66. As far back as February, 18+7, Dr. Charles Thomas Jackson of Boston reported to L. Elie de Beaumont that he had discovered "a mode of preparing spongy gold suitable for plugging teeth." See Charles T. Jackson Papers, MHS.

101. Thomas W. Evans, *Instruments and Apparatus of Medicine, Surgery and Hygiene*, in U.S. Commission, Universal Exposition, Paris, 1867, *Reports* (5 vols.; Washington, D.C., 1868–70), V, 7–13.

been brought well-preserved from Paris to New York, expressed a strong interest in such shipments.[102] By the time of the Paris Exposition of 1878, however, Frenchmen admired the tremendous progress the United States had made in the quality and ingenious variety of surgical instruments. Here was a people that learned fast and moved even faster, too much so actually for the undisturbed comfort of some perceptive citizens of the Old World.

France also occupied a leading place in the history of modern pharmacy. As far back as 1777 it had established a college for the professional training of pharmacists. From the beginning, pharmacy was treated as an auxiliary to the medical profession which dominated it in a supervisory capacity.[103] The United States and the rest of the world were indebted to France for certain important developments in pharmaceutical chemistry. Commenting in general terms, Dr. Valentine Mott praised "the analytical genius and inventive powers of the French in chemical science. . . . The accuracy of their processes and the profound results of their experiments have placed within the hands of the physician all the most valuable medicaments that we possess, in beautiful and simple forms."[104] New drugs obtained from vegetable substances and the precision with which French chemists could handle metallic preparations accelerated the important role of pharmacy in medicine. The ability to standardize specific drug dosages constituted a major accomplishment. The isolation of morphine from opium and of quinine from cinchona bark, as well as the preparation of such other alkaloids as strychnine and veratrine, illustrated the great benefits mankind could derive from scientific experimentation. The experimental approach by French physiologists actually helped transform pharmacology into an experimental science. To make the most of it, however, François

102. James M. D. Olmsted, "A Letter from Felix Pascalis of New York to François Magendie in 1826," *AMH*, 3rd ser., II (1940), 371–74.
103. Edward Kremers and George Urdang, *History of Pharmacy: A Guide and Survey* (Philadelphia, 1951), 86.
104. Mott, *Travels in Europe*, 53.

Magendie admitted that in addition to progress in chemistry and medicine, he also had to overcome "the age-old prejudice that drugs and poisons acted differently in man and animal."[105]

Many nineteenth-century French pharmacists were not satisfied with merely merchandizing known remedies. Unlike their counterparts in the United States and Great Britain, their scientific proclivities tended to engage them in chemical research of a highly pragmatic nature. After the discovery of chlorine in 1774, early in the nineteenth century three French chemists succeeded in adding the other Halogens—iodine, bromine, and fluorine—to the known chemical elements. François Magendie's *Formulary for the Preparation of New Medicaments,* which between 1821 and 1836 went through nine editions and several translations, disseminated the possible applications of the latest remedies known to medical science; and his own demonstrations of the effects of strychnine and the emetic properties of the ipecac root were scientific accomplishments of value to medicine. By 1821, his collaborator, Pierre Joseph Pelletier, and the pharmacist Joseph-Bienaimé Caventou had isolated the alkaloids strychnine, brucine, veratrine, cinchonine, quinine, and caffeine. A generation later, Jean Baptiste-Alphonse Chevalier rendered an important service to civilization with his publication of the *Dictionnaire des altérations et falsifications des substances alimentaires et commerciales* (1850–1852), a work in which he intelligently applied chemistry to the problems of food and drug adulteration.[106] The great strides made by French medicine in the first half of the nineteenth century were clearly paralleled and aided by the ingenious work of French pharmacists and chemists. As medical chemistry began to flourish, the *Journal médicale, de pharmacie, de toxicologie et des nouvelles scientifiques,* founded in 1825,

105. John Bostock, *Sketch of the History of Medicine: From Its Origin to the Commencement of the Nineteenth Century* (London, 1835), 231; Ackerknecht, *Medicine at the Paris Hospital,* 136.
106. Richard H. Shryock, *Medicine and Society in America,* 1660–1860 (New York, 1960), 131. In a series of scholarly articles, Alex Berman has focused on the important interrelations between chemistry, pharmacy, and medicine in nineteenth-century France. For specific references, see bibliography.

offered a valuable forum for the articulation of the latest progress made in these scientific fields.

In an address Oliver Wendall Holmes (1809–1894) delivered in 1860 before the Massachusetts Medical Society he acknowledged that the French were ahead of the Anglo-American world "in the art of prescribing for the sick without hurting them. . . . Their varied ptisans and syrups," he suggested, "are as much preferable to the mineral regimen of bug-poison and rats-bane . . . as their art of preparing food for the table to the rude cookery . . . of the islanders."[107] When in 1833 Pierre François Guillaume Boullay and his son Félix Polydore perfected the heretofore crude "process of percolation for extracting the soluble principles of vegetable drugs," American pharmacists immediately realized its importance.[108] Altogether, they followed developments in their profession very closely. Even in 1830 the Massachusetts College of Pharmacy contained a remarkably large collection of French books on chemistry and English translations of works by Nicolas Lémery Pierre Joseph Macquer, Antoine François de Fourcroy, Claude Louis Berthollet, Jean Antoine Chaptal, and Lavoisier. The *Journal of the Philadelphia College of Pharmacy,* since 1835 known as the *American Journal of Pharmacy,* also relied heavily on translated excerpts from French and German publications to keep its readers well informed about the latest pharmaceutical developments. This practice by no means inhibited it from publishing an occasional criticism of unsatisfactory work presented by foreigners.[109]

The College of Pharmacy in Philadelphia was greatly aided by Elias Durand, formerly pharmacist of the Grand Army of Napoleon I, who opened an apothecary in 1825. This attractive store, in which Durand used marble counters, French glassware,

107. Holmes, *Writings of Oliver Wendell Holmes,* IX, 204.

108. Joseph W. England (ed.), *The First Century of the Philadelphia College of Pharmacy,* 1821–1921 (Philadelphia, 1922), 114–15.

109. Kremers and Urdang, *History of Pharmacy,* 248; see also Franklin Bache to Benjamin Silliman, February 4, 1833, in NYPL. The Louisiana State University Archives owns a copy of C.-L. Cadet de Gassicourt's *Formulaire magistral et mémorial pharmaceutique,* published in Paris in 1814.

neatly arranged porcelain jars, and mahogany cabinets, became a major center of pharmaceutical information. Durand, the inventor of an apparatus for the bottling of mineral water, made a name for himself not only in the United States but in France where his invention was adopted as well. To foster Franco-American cooperation in the sciences and as a personal gesture, he generously presented the museum of the Jardin des Plantes in 1860 "an herbarium of over 100,000 specimens, covering 12,000 species of plants." And his student, Augustine J. L. Duhamel, the Philadelphia-born son of French parents, tried his best to perpetuate French influence on the profession in the United States.[110]

French contributions to American pharmacy were particularly strong in Louisiana, both in regard to legislative controls of pharmacy and the licensing of pharmacists.[111] Pharmacists in New Orleans customarily advertised the arrival of French drugs and medicines as a means of attracting customers to their stores. For that matter, the New York Historical Society possesses a printed announcement a New York dentist received in 1821 from a local French firm pointing with evident pride to the credentials of one of its owners who "for six years has taken courses in pharmacy and chemistry in the medical colleges in Paris."[112] More than any other publication, the *New Orleans Medical and Surgical Journal* tried to keep the profession in America abreast of the changes and trends in France. Its references to the *Journal de pharmacie* were even more frequent than those in the *American Journal of Pharmacy*.

Assuming that those connected with American pharmacological education would be interested in the proposed pharmacological course of the faculty of medicine in Paris, the New Orleans

110. England, *Philadelphia College of Pharmacy*, 357–59, 373.
111. David L. Cowen, "Louisiana, Pioneer in the Regulation of Pharmacy," *LHQ*, XXVI (1943), 3–13.
112. Place & Souillard, Pharmaciens, to Isaac S. Greenwood, January 1, 1821, in Greenwood Family Papers, NYHS. See also David L. Cowen, "A Roster of the Licensed Apothecaries of Louisiana, 1816–1847," *Journal of New Orleans College of Pharmacy*, VIII (1943), 4.

journal reproduced in 1860 the French guidelines for it. It was to comprehend:

1. A general exposition of the processes for the preparation of medicaments;
2. The special study of medicinal substances, including their natural history, physical and chemical characters, pharmaceutical forms, and their adulterations;
3. The art of prescribing;
4. The history of mineral waters, both natural and artificial;
5. The history of pharmacy among the ancients, and also the principal notions of the present time.[113]

Altogether, the French government tended to stiffen the requirements for the degree in pharmacy and medicine and to protect the public against unscrupulous venders of "médecines." These pretenders could nevertheless be found in France as well as in Louisiana, because the laws and regulations always proved to contain some loopholes or to be inadequately implemented. With respect to France, one correspondent pointed out "that notwithstanding its laws against dispensing of medicines on any order except that of an M.D.P., there is really little difficulty in procuring any medicine anyone pleases. Strange to say, though the French law interposes all its authority against the vending of poisons by the dispensing apothecary, it does not interfere with the wholesale druggist who sells them in quantity, practically to suit the purchaser."[114]

France showed at the end of the century great concern about the commercial exploitation of drugs. The tendency of Parisian

113. Bennet Dowler, "Pharmacology in France," *NOMSJ*, XVII (1860), 448–50.
114. Stanford E. Chaillé, "On Medicine in France and Practical Chemistry," *NOMSJ*, XXIV (1867), 691–92. A French doctor was shocked that during the gold rush even grocers sold drugs in California; see P. Garnier, "Voyage médicale en Californie," with introduction by Gilbert Chinard, *French-American Review*, II (1949), 135–83.

physicians "to prescribe specified manufactures of drugs" benefiting the manufacturer and the possible commercial collusion
between doctors and pharmacists aroused the special attention
of the legislature. Concern for the public's welfare manifested
itself also by the charitable institution in Paris of a night pharmaceutical service, which provided prompt pharmaceutical assistance
to the victims of nighttime accidents and restored to individual
pharmacists restful nights.[115] Of even greater social significance
was the laboratory of the Académie des Sciences. In 1886 some
twenty inspectors visited taverns and groceries in Paris, testing
on the spot the quality of food and drinks sold. Simple analysis
to determine whether these goods were unadulterated was free
of charge. When necessary, the availability of twenty-five chemists
in the laboratory facilitated more elaborate tests for a small
fee.[116] This protection of the public's health and pocketbook constituted the kind of progressive measure in which France was far
ahead of the United States.

By mid-century, Americans demonstrated such ingenuity in
the pharmaceutical field that the journal *La France médicale
et pharmaceutique* publicized the experiments and experiences
of American doctors and pharmacists likely to be of interest to
their colleagues in France.[117] At the International Congress of
Pharmacists in Paris (1867), Americans participated prominently
in the discussions and supported the decision of the congress to
bring about a more universal system of codes and formulae for
the preparation of pharmaceuticals.[118] The pharmacists of both
countries continued to learn from each other. By the end of the
century, however, competition restricted their business relations.
With few exceptions, France prohibited in 1879 the import of

115. M. K., "Paris Notes," *Western Druggist*, VIII (1886), 424–25.
116. "Notes and News," *ibid.*, 362.
117. See the following issues of *La France médicale et pharmaceutique*: May
1, 1854, p. 43; September 15, 1854, p. 187; February 15, 1855, pp. 56–57; April 1,
1855, p. 106; May 24, 1856, p. 165.
118. Congrès International des Associations et Sociétés de Pharmaciens, *Compte
Rendu Sommaire* (Paris, 1867), 11–16.

foreign medicaments.[119] A French law of April 19, 1898, provided that "any foreigner, even though having a French diploma as a graduate in pharmacy, shall not practice pharmacy in France," unless reciprocity was practiced.[120] As in other economic respects, protectionist thinking governed policies also in this field. In educational and cultural respects France traditionally maintained a very liberal attitude; in political and economic respects, it was self-centered and restrictive.

In the pre–Civil War period New Orleans, the "Paris of America," represented a world of its own. As a unique Franco-American community, it reflected in microcosm the culture and civilization of both France and the United States. Many of the well-to-do Louisiana planters and merchants valued French culture so much that they sent their sons to France for a humanistic and classical education. Those inclined to take up medicine as a profession remained there to earn their medical degrees at the most reputable centers. Once they had accomplished their goal of becoming a "Docteur en Médecine Parisien," they established their practices back home, proudly identifying themselves as D.M.P., the credential of excellence. The Hutchinson Memorial Hospital in New Orleans still treasures the medical register of New Orleans for the period from April, 1816, to August, 1854. The *Registre du comité médical de la Nouvelle Orléans* contains the list of ninety-five medical doctors, one dentist, thirteen pharmacists, and nineteen midwives with official diplomas from medical institutions in Paris, Montpellier, Lille, and Strasbourg. These people were authorized to practice their professions in the state of Louisiana. For unspecified reasons, the Comité refused, however, to accept the diplomas of six additional doctors and three midwives.

Differences in background, training, and cultural outlooks between the French-speaking and Anglo-American doctors oc-

119. See enclosure in Edward F. Noyes to William M. Evarts, February 21, 1879, in DDFDS.
120. Eugène Thiébaut to John Hay, November 22, 1898, in FNTDS.

casionally caused serious tensions. The more intellectually inclined French physicians harbored a certain contempt for the English-speaking "medical technicians."[121] Such attitudes tended to aggravate different approaches to such medical problems as, for instance, epidemics. Even worse was racial discrimination. Though an isolated case, Dr. Alexandre Chaumette, the first Creole physician in New Orleans, was subjected to discrimination. A native of New Orleans, Dr. Chaumette received his general and medical education in Paris. In an effort to prevent him from practicing medicine in New Orleans, his colleagues forced him to undertake a humiliating examination in spite of the fact that his French diploma did not justify the imposition of such a formality. Ultimately, he was admitted and the vast experience he had gained in French hospitals earned him the respect and gratitude to which he was entitled. This precedent encouraged other Creoles to acquire a French education and to prepare themselves for the medical profession.[122] The prevalence of yellow fever in the hot and humid Louisiana summers led many local medical scientists to engage in research designed to find the causes of and possible remedies against this disease. Another medical speciality in which Louisiana doctors seem to have established a numerical record exceeding that of other states concerned the operation of gastrohysterotomy. The many successful Caesarean operations were generally attributed to "the skill of the French surgeons."[123] In every region of the United States French-trained doctors attended to the medical needs of the people. In the Midwest, particularly in St. Louis, and in California, their surgical skills helped to relieve the troubles of many sick people.

121. John Duffy (ed.), *The Rudolph Matas History of Medicine in Louisiana* (2 vols.; Baton Rouge, 1958–62), I, 271. See also Alcée Fortier, "The Physician in the History and Literature of Louisiana," *NOMSJ*, LVIII (1905), 8–9; A. E. Fossier, "The Early History of Medical Education in New Orleans," *NOMSJ*, LXXXVII (1935), 501–506.

122. Desdunes, *Nos hommes et notre histoire*, 106; Duffy, *History of Medicine in Louisiana*, II, 238–39.

123. See William Colby Rucker, "Chervin, A Pioneer Epidemiologist: An Early Study of the Contagiousness of Yellow Fever," *LHQ*, VIII (1925), 434–48; R. P. Harris, "The Caesarean Record of Louisiana," *NOMSJ*, VII (1880, 938–41.

In St. Louis, Dr. Antoine François Saugrain (1763–1820) , born in Versailles and educated in Paris, successfully applied Dr. Edward Jenner's vaccination method. His preventive inoculations, for which he had originally brought some vaccine from Europe, endeared him to the local population. Such doctors as Charles Alexander Pope, one of St. Louis' renowned mid-century surgeons; M. L. Linton, professor of medicine at St. Louis University; and S. Gratz Moses, Joseph Bonaparte's physician in Bordentown, New Jersey, who in 1841 settled in St. Louis, had all had the benefit of medical instruction in Paris. Doctors called their French training to the public's attention as a mark of distinction. One of them, for example, advertised in 1819: "Doctor Gebert (lately from France) having received a regular diploma from the faculty of medicine in Paris, has the honor to offer his services to the inhabitants of St. Louis and its vicinity as a physician and surgeon."[124]

The French hospital in San Francisco and French benevolent societies wherever Frenchmen had clustered together rendered a great social service by helping to take care of the sick and needy. Not only in San Francisco, but also in Marysville and Sonoma, French hospitals were in operation from the early 1850s; and from 1860 a French benevolent society in Los Angeles attended to the needs of French transients. Among the French doctors in California was the colorful and adventurous nephew of the outstanding surgeon Dupuytren, J. B. Pigne-Dupuytren, who, after a rather dull life in Marysville, began to practice medicine in San Francisco in 1856. As an officer of the French National League, founded in San Francisco in the days of despair following the War of 1870–1871, he supported the League's cultural endeavors and contributed to the fine reputation of the French hospital.

124. John Thomas Scharf, *History of Saint Louis City and County* (2 vols.; Philadelphia, 1883), II, 1520–38. Dr. Daniel Brainard, who had spent several postdoctoral years in Paris and who became known for his research on the treatment of poisoned wounds, was made an honorary member of the *Société de Chirurgie de Paris*; see James N. Hyde, *Early Medical History* (Chicago, 1879), 28–29.

The most learned and renowned French doctor who came to San Francisco was Narcisse Joseph Martinache (1833–1892). Arriving in 1871, he specialized in ophthalmology and otology; his devoted service to the public and the French benevolent society were much admired.[125]

There can be no doubt that in the theory and practice of medicine France taught Americans much. But even in the mid-nineteenth century quite a few American physicians and surgeons had also made noteworthy contributions to the advancement of medical science. Dr. W. W. Gerhard of Philadelphia, one of Louis' pupils, established the clear differentiation between typhoid and typhus fever. The first accurate clinical study of tuberculous meningitis has also been associated with his name.[126] Another of Louis' pupils, indeed his favorite one, Dr. James Jackson, Jr., of Harvard, announced in a paper he delivered in 1833 before the Société Médicale d'Observation de Paris his discovery of the prolonged expiratory sound in phthisis.[127] Charles Luzenberg, professor of surgery at the University of Louisiana, followed the footsteps of his great teacher Dupuytren. Among his outstanding surgical attainments was a delicate operation involving the extirpation of the parotid gland. The *Gazette médicale de Paris* called it to the attention of its readers in 1835; and the operation also brought Luzenberg the rare honor of being appointed a corresponding member of the Académie Royale de Médecine.[128] The same honor was in the 1830s bestowed upon Valentine Mott of New York and James Jackson and John C. Warren of Boston. Velpeau and other eminent French surgeons were astonished

125. Henry Harris, *California's Medical Story* (San Francisco, 1932), 377–81.

126. E. B. Krumbhaar, "The History of Pathology at the Philadelphia General Hospital," *Medical Life* (April, 1933), 167. For Professor Louis' acknowledgement of Dr. Gerhard's research accomplishments, see Louis' letter to Dr. James Jackson, October 1, 1840, in James Jackson Papers, MHS.

127. Packard, *History of Medicine*, II, 1002.

128. Edmond Souchon, "Original Contributions of Louisiana to Medical Sciences," *Louisiana Historical Society Publications*, VIII (1914–15), 69–71; Samuel D. Gross (ed.), *Lives of Eminent American Physicians and Surgeons of the Nineteenth Century* (Philadelphia, 1861) 555–56.

when they learned of the skill and boldness of American surgeons.[129] Independent of each other, early in the century, Dupuytren in Paris and Dr. Physick in Philadelphia had performed similar operations for the opening of an artificial anus.[130] And Dr. Jacob Bigelow of Boston actually improved on Civiale's famous operation involving the crushing of stone in the bladder.[131] To Dr. Horace Green of New York the profession was indebted for his methodical and systematic treatment of the larynx.[132] The French government made one of the most original contributors to medical science, Dr. Charles Jean Faget of New Orleans, a knight of the Legion of Honor. His discovery in 1858 of a pathognomonic sign of yellow fever facilitated the early diagnosis of this dreaded sickness.[133] In the treatment of fractures, the United States was several years ahead of France. The assistant surgeon of the United States Army reported in 1858 that he had procured from New York the "straight apparatus" to demonstrate its effectiveness and the method of extension by adhesive plaster bands, as professor Nélaton, the chief surgeon of the Hôpital de la Faculté, had requested. Nélaton readily admitted the practical value of this technique in fracture cases, and he was satisfied that it did not result in detrimental side effects.[134] Extending the research that Andral had undertaken to determine the changes blood disease produced in organic elements, Dr. Charles Frick of Baltimore was pleased to find on his visit to Paris in 1856 that French pathologists appreciated his studies of the inorganic changes.[135] As an intern at the Lourcine Hospital

129. Arnold, *Memoir of Jonathan Mason Warren*, 158.

130. Louis Peisse, *Sketches of the Characters and Writings of Eminent Living Surgeons and Physicians of Paris* (Boston, 1831), 8–9.

131. Da Costa, "The French School of Surgery," 79.

132. Joseph Hammond Bryan, "The History of Laryngology and Rhinology and the Influence of America in the Development of This Specialty," *AMH*, n.s. V (1933), 152–53, 169. For French acknowledgement of Dr. Green's contribution, see also *Bulletin de l'Académie Impériale de Médecine*, XXIII (1857), 724–28, and XXV (1858), 99–101.

133. Souchon, "Original Contributions," 74–76.

134. George Suckley, "On Matters of Novelty or General Interest as at Present Exhibited in the Practice of the Hospitals of Paris," *NYJM*, 3rd ser., V (1858), 26.

135. Gross, *Eminent Physicians*, 819.

in Paris in the late 1860s, Dr. Thomas B. Curtis won the Prix Civiale, a prize for which the interns in Parisian hospitals openly competed. Dr. Curtis presented in his outstanding thesis carefully established guidelines for operating upon urethral strictures.[136]

One of the great American discoveries, harmlessly applied anesthesia, not only alleviated human suffering, it also enabled dentists and surgeons throughout the world to operate under unprecedented favorable conditions. As late as 1839, Velpeau, chief surgeon at La Charité, had taken the position that it was absurd to search for a painless method of operation: "The notion of doing away with pain in surgery," he contended, "is a chimera." Several Americans, however, were determined to conquer pain. Prominent among them was William Thomas Green Morton (1819–1868), a Boston dentist who sought to spare his patients the excruciating pain they suffered during the removal of the roots of old teeth. Aware of the shortcomings of nitrous oxide, an anesthetic applied by his partner, Dr. Horace Wells (1815–1848), Morton experimented with ether, a pain-relieving agent which, though known for centuries, had not been fully explored. Dr. Morton successfully applied ether in the extraction of a tooth on September 30, 1846, and subsequently demonstrated its effectiveness in a painless surgical operation performed by Dr. John C. Warren at the Massachusetts General Hospital.

Advised of these important developments, the French Academy of Sciences was simultaneously apprised of the claims of Dr. Charles T. Jackson (1805–1880), a Boston scientist who in his chemical laboratory had established the anesthetic effects of inhaling sulphuric ether and who had offered to cooperate with Morton. The Academy tried to stay out of the ensuing controversy in America involving priority claims for this discovery. With Solomonic wisdom, it awarded Jackson a prize for his discovery of the anesthetic effects of ether, and it honored Morton for intro-

136. Edward D. Churchill (ed.), *To Work in the Vineyards of Surgery: The Reminiscences of John Collins Warren*, 1842–1927 (Cambridge, Mass., 1958), 119–20.

ducing anesthesia into practical surgery.[137] The Academy's careful examination of all aspects of etherization found its climax in the experimental findings of some of its distinguished members. Their initial disappointments with it, due largely to inexperience and improvised equipment, were quickly overcome. Early in 1847, Jobert de Lamballe and Joseph-François Malaigne, surgeons at the St. Louis Hospital, confirmed successful etherization in several operations. Soon thereafter, Velpeau changed his mind and acknowledged "the blessings of this magnificent discovery," which, he was sure, "will assume unforeseen dimensions." Before long, and particularly after French manufacturers perfected the production of inhalators, the use of ether became a common practice throughout France, despite warnings "in the name of ethics and public security" about possible abuses in its application.[138] As chloroform was found to be another effective anesthetic, Pierre Flourens (1794–1867), the eminent physiologist, issued a more ominous warning: "If sulphuric ether is a marvelous and terrible agent, chloroform is more marvelous and more dangerous." But these prudent reservations in no way diminished the magnitude of this revolutionary breakthrough in the history of medicine.

In the fall of 1860, Edmond Souchon, whose home was in the southern United States, began to pursue his medical studies at the old Charity Hospital in Paris under the guidance of the world-famous Velpeau. By chance, Souchon in 1861 ran into Dr. James Marion Sims (1813–1883) who had recently arrived in Paris from

137. See Académie des Sciences, *Comptes Rendus*, XXIV (1847), 74–79, 492–94; XXV (1847), 29, 626, 905; XXX (1850), 210, 243–44; and Claude Bernard, *Leçons sur les anesthésiques et sur l'asphyxie* (Paris, 1875), 41–42. The Paris Medical Society elected Dr. Horace Wells of Hartford as an honorary member and acknowledged that to him "is due all the honor of having first discovered and successfully applied the use of vapors or gases whereby surgical operations could be performed without pain." Thorpe, *Pioneer American Dentists*, 364. See also the correspondence between Charles Jackson and Elie de Beaumont, in Charles T. Jackson Papers, MHS.

138. Raymond Neven, "The Introduction of Surgical Anesthesia in France," *JHMAS*, I (1946), 607; F. Willis Fisher, "The Ether Inhalation in Paris," *BMSJ*, XXXV (March 10, 1847), 109–13. About the experiences regarding the use of chloroform and cocaine in French surgery, see J. P. Judkins, "Letter from Paris," *PMSJ*, II, (1854), 245–52; and A. Preterre, "L'Art dentaire en Amérique," *L'Art dentaire* (June, 1891), 446–47.

New York where he practiced medicine and had made a name for himself as a gynecologist. Sims, a doctor in the prime of his life, had developed a method for successful surgery on a vesico-vaginal fistula, and he hoped to be able to demonstrate his method in Paris. It was fortunate that Sims met Souchon with whom he shared not only a common interest in medicine, but also a southern background. Even more important, Souchon was a young man who could introduce Sims to such a medical authority as Velpeau. That Dr. Sims was unknown in Paris was a handicap; but that he intended to teach renowned French surgeons how to cure vesicovaginal fistula sounded ridiculous. If anyone in the world could perform such an operation, "as everybody knew," it might be Jobert de Lamballe, of the Hôtel Dieu in Paris; and even he actually cured such cases only occasionally.

Velpeau, of rural stock and at times rough in his manners, could also be kind. He had, after all, secured for Souchon a little position which kept him from starving when the Civil War in America cut off his support from home. Velpeau did not conceal his skepticism about Sims's claim. After Souchon introduced Sims, Velpeau asked: "Well, what does he want?" "I want a case to demonstrate my operation," replied Sims, "if the professor will be kind enough to procure one for me." Velpeau tartly agreed to do this and, as Souchon recorded, "without a handshake or a word more" he turned away from the American doctor. By the time a case turned up the curiosity of the medical world in Paris had been aroused. Could Sims be taken seriously or was he an American braggart? With the exception of Lamballe, the whole galaxy of professors of surgery, including Velpeau, Nélaton, and Ricord, and throngs of medical students came to see for themselves the operation Dr. Sims performed in the little operating theater in the old Charity Hospital. Before he began the operation, Dr. Sims demonstrated it graphically. He then proceeded to operate under the watchful eyes of his French witnesses. He performed the operation with skill, grace, and in a comparatively short time. When it was finished, "a salvo of applause broke out from the benches." Quite understandably, the professors reserved judgment until the day when the sutures were removed. From then on, the American doctor's reputation was unassailable.[139] Even Velpeau acknowledged: "The suture . . . is of such difficult application that but few practitioners have ventured to make trial of it. . . . But Sims, with his speculum which made perfectly clear the whole formerly invisible field of operation, had overcome, one by one, all of these difficulties."[140] Henceforth French surgeons adopted the "American method" as standard procedure.

Distinguished professors of medicine asked Sims time and again to demonstrate his remarkably successful method to large classes.[141] Numerous women from all over France sought to consult him. Whatever Napoleon III thought about Americans politically the emperor and his wife greatly respected American doctors. Dr. Thomas Evans, as we have seen, attended to the dental welfare of the imperial family. And when Empress Eugénie once fell ill with diphtheria, Marion Sims was called upon to take care of her at St. Cloud. One of the professors with whom Sims developed a particularly close relationship was the eminent surgeon Pierre Marie Edouard Chassaignac, of the Hôpital Lariboisère, inventor of the *écraseur*, an instrument that severs by the gradual tightening of a wire loop. Whenever possible, he liked to have Sims accompany him on his hospital tours. Chassaignac introduced Sims to the Société de Chirurgie and read before it translations of two papers Sims had prepared—one on amputations and the other on vaginismus. Sims was "utterly amazed at the ignorance of French surgeons on some subjects."[142] In amputation cases, for instance, most French patients died,

139. Edmond Souchon, "Reminiscences of Dr. Marion Sims in Paris," Southern Surgical and Gynecological Association, *Transactions*, VII (1894), 27–38. The French government acknowledged his outstanding contributions by making him a knight of the Legion of Honor. Another American surgeon, Dr. Robert Battey of Georgia, notified the Société de Chirurgie in January of 1860 of his successful method in the same type of operation; see Robert Battey Papers, Emory University.

140. Quoted in Seale Harris, *Woman's Surgeon: The Life Story of J. Marion Sims* (New York, 1950), 128–29.

141. Henri L. Stuart, "Biographical Sketch of J. Marion Sims, M.D.," *Virginia Medical Monthly*, III (1877), 735.

142. J. Marion Sims, *The Story of My Life* (New York, 1885), 313–27.

whereas American doctors had devised lifesaving techniques for such cases. Sims, of course, learned a great deal from the giants of medicine in France. He often preferred, for example, to use the *écraseur* rather than the knife, and he made use of Nélaton's method of resuscitation from chloroform narcosis.

He was lionized even socially. Although Frenchmen normally did not invite foreigners to their homes, Dr. Sims became a target for invitations. His friendship in Paris with Sir Joseph Olliffe, the physician to the British Embassy, and with W. E. Johnston, a medical doctor from Ohio who enjoyed being a correspondent of the New York *Times* in Paris, also helped to introduce him and his wife to French society. Dr. Sims, in turn, extended his gracious hospitality to people of all nationalities. During the Civil War, he extended a helping hand to southerners in France who were in dire need of funds. And during the Franco-Prussian War, the fifty-seven-year-old Sims headed the Anglo-American Ambulance, which rendered an essential humanitarian service to the wounded of both armies. When the staff of this service marched on August 28, 1870, to the Gare du Nord, "hundreds of thousands of the citizens of Paris thronged the boulevards through which they marched, cheering and manifesting every possible expression of enthusiasm and satisfaction." The shouts of Vive l'Amérique expressed the appreciative sentiments of Frenchmen toward the United States.[143] In a sense, they summed up the genuine recognition Frenchmen also wished to extend to Dr. Sims, the extraordinary American who brought much honor to his country and his profession.

One of the giants of modern science, Louis Pasteur (1822–1895), to whose imagination, determination, and tireless efforts the world owes an incalculable debt, demonstrated how the principles of physics and chemistry lay at the heart of biology and medical

143. Stuart, *J. Marion Sims*, 737–40. When Marshal McMahon was wounded on September 1, 1870, he was pleased that Dr. Sims was among the doctors attending him.

science. Until the 1860s scientists disagreed as to the precise role of microscopic organisms in the process of fermentation and putrefaction. Some traced them to "spontaneous generation"; others contended that they were reproduced by specimens of their own kind. Pasteur's experiments enabled him to state with certainty that fermentation was the result of minute organisms and that it did not develop in sealed sterile solutions. This finding and the recognition that lactic and alcoholic fermentations were accelerated by exposure to air led to the famous Pasteurization process. Among other findings, the scientific researches of this outstanding chemist succeeded in identifying the bacilli responsible for the diseases of silkworms and in conquering the fatal cattle scourge known as anthrax, a bacillus previously discovered by Koch. These scientific accomplishments protected farmers everywhere against enormous financial losses.[144]

When Pasteur published in the June, 1863, issue of the *Comptes rendus hebdomadaires* his finding that "putrefaction is caused by living ferments," he provided Joseph Lister, a British surgeon, with the information that enabled him to revolutionize surgery.[145] As Lister acknowledged in his letter to Pasteur, dated February 13, 1874, "Your brilliant researches . . . demonstrated to me the truth of the germ theory of putrefaction, and thus furnished me with the principle upon which alone the antiseptic system can be carried out." Pasteur "raised the veil which for centuries had covered infectious diseases" and led Lister to the discovery of his method for destroying bacteria without injuring the tissues of the patient. While, in a general way, surgeons had known of carbolic acid as an antiseptic agent, Lister had been totally unfamiliar with Jules Lemaire's work, *De l'Acide phénique* (1863), which recommended carbolic acid for a great variety of therapeutic purposes. For this reason alone, the contemporary charge that Lister had followed Lemaire's lead was erroneous;

144. Christian Archibald Herter, *The Influence of Pasteur on Medical Science* (New York, 1904), 72–73.

145. Rhoda Truax, *Joseph Lister: Father of Modern Surgery* (New York, 1944), 85–89, 246–48; Douglas Guthrie, *Lord Lister: His Life and Doctrine* (Baltimore, 1949), 58, 84–87.

but more important, unlike Lemaire's practically indiscriminate application of carbolic acid and its use as a dressing, Lister's antiseptic system called for its carefully prescribed employment "so as to prevent the occurrence of putrefaction." French and other European hospitals lost little time in adopting Lister's antiseptic method. Though lagging behind Europe, American doctors soon became convinced of the validity of Lister's 1876 message to the International Medical Congress in Philadelphia: "We may have good healing without antiseptic treatment, but we cannot secure the best results." Lister's antiseptic system improved conditions in hospitals and surgery wherever it was introduced. That the interaction of French and British research thus benefited people everywhere also attested to the importance of disseminating scientific information.

A man like Pasteur was too dedicated to science ever to rest on his laurels. Next, he engaged in experiments aiming at the treatment of hydrophobia in man and rabies in dogs. After first experimenting with animals, Pasteur finally mustered enough courage, on July 6, 1885, to inoculate a child who had been bitten by an infected dog with a virus that had been carefully controlled and that had produced promising results in animals.[146] The experiment was so extraordinarily successful that Pasteur was hailed throughout the world as one of the greatest benefactors of civilization.

Despite his fame and the honors bestowed upon him, a letter he sent to a friend in December, 1887, revealed that he was short of funds for equipment and laboratories. "Ah! if we were in America," he wrote, "the land of generous and big initiatives!"[147] Pasteur liked the willingness of Americans to experiment with new techniques and to acknowledge those proven by others. He was very pleased when he read in 1869 that he was as popular with California winegrowers as the President of the United States.

146. Pasteur Vallery-Radot (ed.), *Oeuvres de Pasteur* (7 vols.; Paris, 1922–39), VII, 405–407.

147. Pasteur Vallery-Radot (ed.), *Pasteur: Correspondance, 1840–1895* (4 vols.; Paris, 1940–51), IV, 229–30.

One of them had followed the instructions in Pasteur's *Etudes sur le vin* and with great satisfaction had verified for himself the effects of the French scientist's process of heating wine. "These Americans," reacted Pasteur, "advance with giant steps while we take timidly one step after another and are often disposed to disparage rather than appreciate services rendered."[148]

Among the many American visitors he kindly agreed to see— and sometimes took on a tour of his laboratory and, after 1888, the Pasteur Institute in Paris—was Oliver Wendell Holmes, the well-known physician and poet. Holmes's own vivid description of this visit expressed his feelings and thoughts in a memorable fashion:

> I presented myself at his [Pasteur's] headquarters and was admitted into a court-yard where a multitude of his patients were gathered. They were of different ages and of many different nationalities. . . . I sent my card in to Mr. Pasteur, who was busily engaged . . . and presently he came out and greeted me. I told him I was an American physician who wished to look in his face and take his hand, nothing more. I looked in his face which was that of a thoughtful, hard-worked student. I took his hand, which has performed some of the most delicate and daring experiments ever ventured upon, with results of almost incalculable benefit to human industries, and the promise of triumph in the treatment of human disease which prophecy would not have dared to anticipate. I dare not say that I have a full belief that hydrophobia—in some respects the most terrible of all diseases—is to be extirpated or rendered tractable by his method of treatment. But of his inventive originality, his unconquerable perseverance, his devotion to the good of mankind, there can be no question. I look upon him as one of the greatest experimenters that ever lived, one of the truest benefactors of his race . . . to whom the God of nature has entrusted some of her most precious secrets.[149]

As a scientist, Pasteur recognized the international significance of all scientific advances and the need for international cooperation. He had unhesitatingly admitted several foreign doctors to his laboratory and afforded them the opportunity of studying his methods so that they could in time apply them in

148. Vallery-Radot (ed.) *Oeuvres de Pasteur*, III, 259–60.
149. Holmes, "Our Hundred Days in Europe," 10–11.

the institutes of their native countries. In the case of the prophylactic method against hydrophobia, he even supplied them upon return to their homelands with the serum necessary for inoculations. Dr. Valentine Mott, Jr., of the Bellevue Hospital in New York, studied as a young doctor under Pasteur and developed a close friendship with him. When Dr. Mott returned home, "Pasteur permitted him to bring with him the first inoculated rabbit that the scientist had up to that time allowed to be taken out of his laboratory."[150] In 1887 only few of the Americans who had heard about Pasteur's treatment of hydrophobia and rabies really believed in its lifesaving results. But Pasteur's faith in his method was so strong that he confidently advised American skeptics to wait until all shadow of doubt had been removed from their minds.

As fate would have it, Dr. Paul Gibier, the son of a French railroad station master and originally the only doctor of medicine in Pasteur's laboratory, became the target in the United States of many physicians who either questioned the efficacy of Pasteur's methods or denied the existence of hydrophobia or rabies. A case of several boys from Newark, New Jersey, who had been bitten by a rabid dog and had to risk a long delay before reaching the Pasteur Institute in Paris for inoculations, convinced Dr. Gibier of the necessity of an American institute capable of administering immediate treatment in cases of this kind. Listening to this suggestion of his pupil and co-worker, Pasteur not only went along with it, but gladly authorized Gibier to give his name to such an institute in New York.

Thus conceived, the Pasteur Institute in New York opened its doors at 178 West 10th Street in February of 1890. Unlike its alma mater in Paris, the American institute was not supported by public funds. Gibier nevertheless soon felt the need for more space to carry on experimental work. He transferred the institute

---

150. "Valentine Mott, Jr." (Typescript in NYAM), 256. Dr. Pierre Roux of the Pasteur Institute took pride in the fact that the Institute always had "fifteen to twenty students from all parts of the world, including several Americans." See Ida M. Tarbell, "Pasteur at Home," *McClure's Magazine*, I (1893), 336.

to a six-story building on Central Park West and 97th Street; it was from here that the first antitoxic sera made in the New World were distributed throughout the country. In 1898, the institute moved to Suffern, New York, where it owned an experimental station and a farm. Of 1,367 persons from all parts of the United States who received treatment at the institute during its first decade of existence, only 19 died of hydrophobia, a mortality rate of 1.39 percent.[151] With the help of a few eminent doctors, Gibier also founded the New York Bacteriological Institute in 1890, the purpose of which was "to maintain a research laboratory for the study of contagious diseases, especially hydrophobia, tuberculosis, diphtheria, etc., and to provide funds for the gratuitous treatment of indigents applying to the Pasteur Institute."[152]

Under Dr. Gibier's direction the Pasteur Institute in New York gained an outstanding reputation as a scientific laboratory at which organotherapy and serotherapy were first investigated and by which glycerinized vaccine lymph was introduced. In its March, 1895, issue, the *New York Therapeutic Review*, edited by Gibier, described the treatment of diphtheria with antitoxine made at the Pasteur Institute in New York. In June of 1894 Gibier had gone to Paris to investigate this matter. "There," the *Review* detailed, "he obtained complete data as to the processes of manufacture, procured the necessary instruments, among them an incubator capable of containing from fifteen to twenty gallons of cultures, and ventilated by Dr. E. Roux's method. . . . The cultures employed were the same as those used by Dr. Roux." The knowledge and equipment secured in Paris enabled the institute to manufacture the antitoxine on a practical scale.

It should be noted that, in spite of its demonstrated usefulness, the validity of Pasteur's treatment of hydrophobia continued to be doubted and the Pasteur Institute in New York was attacked as useless. Among those who vigorously opposed Pasteur's germ doctrines was Rollin R. Gregg of Buffalo who held that bacteria

151. "The First Decennial Work of the New York Pasteur Institute," New York Pasteur Institute, *Bulletin*, VIII (March, 1900), 1.

152. George Gibier Rambaud, M.D., "Paul Gibier, A.M., M.D.," *ibid.*, VIII (September, 1900), 12.

were not independent living organisms.[153] And Henry Bergh, president of the New York Society for the Prevention of Cruelty to Animals (SPCA) objected strenuously to "the barbarities of Monsieur Pasteur. . . . In the outraged name of science," he wrote in 1884, "this merciless empiric is poisoning the flocks and herds of France, after the fashion of his predecessor, the notorious Jenner of England."[154] While critical attacks against Pasteur's ideas and methods might have been expected in view of their novelty, the stubborn self-assurance of his critics amounted to arrogance based on pretension. In historical perspective Pasteur's reputation assured the obscurity of his critics. It is still amusing, though, to note that when Pasteur was awarded the baccalaureate degree in science his diploma indicated the grade: "mediocre."

That members of the American medical profession gained increasing confidence in their ability to meet the competition of their European colleagues was indirectly demonstrated by their participation in international congresses. Many of these medical congresses in the final decades of the century met in Paris, offering opportunities for meeting colleagues from all over the world and exchanging experiences with them. At such international meetings of general practitioners, ophthalmologists, veterinarians, and specialists in mental disorders, for instance, Americans from all parts of the United States, often representing medical societies and institutions, participated by reading papers or contributing to lively discussions. At the Congress of Veterinarians (1889) special attention was paid to the modern inspection system in American slaughterhouses.[155] And at the

153. Benjamin H. Landing, "Rollin R. Gregg of Buffalo: A Nineteenth Century Opponent of Pasteur and the Germ Theory of Disease," *BHM*, XXXVI (1962), 524–28; see also "The New York Pasteur Institute," *Virginia Medical Monthly*, XVII (October, 1890), 671.

154. Zulma Steele, *Angel in Top Hat* (New York, 1942), 137.

155. Cinquième Congrès International de Médecine Vétérinaire, *Compte Rendu* (Paris, 1890). Americans had learned much at the Veterinary School at Alfort, about six miles from Paris. Its ventilated and comfortable stables and operating rooms served as an example in the belated development of American veterinary practices. F. Peyre Porcher, "Visit to the Veterinary School and Grounds of Alfort," *CMJ*, IX (1854), 140–44. See also Austin Flint, letter dated June 26, 1854, *BMJ*, X (1854), 321–32.

Congress of Mental Medicine (1889), to cite another example, Dr. T. D. Crothers, the director of the Walnut Lodge Asylum at Hartford, Connecticut, presented the very progressive viewpoint that alcoholics who committed crimes should be treated by doctors in special hospitals rather than be punished or imprisoned. Such enlightened views impressed Europeans as much as the unexpected experience of meeting cultured gentlemen from the United States, presumably merely a semi-civilized country.

Hundreds of American medical doctors in the pre–Civil War era perfected their professional skills under the direction of the most knowledgeable medical authorities in France. During this period of brilliant breakthroughs in pathology, physiology, and pharmacology French medical scientists and surgeons readily welcomed these foreign students who had come to study their findings and observe their techniques in every field of medical specialization. Their exposure to the world's leading physicians and surgeons and to the facilities and practices of huge hospitals helped American doctors strengthen the foundation of their profession back home. Obviously, not all they saw and learned in Paris found their approval. As much, for instance, as they admired the audacity and skill of many French surgeons, they took serious exception to the inadequate postoperative treatment of patients in badly ventilated hospitals. On the other hand, the thorough education medical students received in France and the growing emphasis on experimental medical research commended emulation in the United States.

The presence of so many American doctors in Paris resulted in noteworthy cultural by-products. Acquaintances in Paris often developed into lifelong personal friendships that sustained a salutary esprit de corps back home. In addition to the general cultural stimulation that distinguished Paris, the lasting friendships between some American doctors and their French teachers not only kept professional lines of communication alive, but proved mutually gratifying from a human point of view as well.

In medicine, as in every other field, Americans branched out in every direction with the goal of mastering it as well as the most eminent teachers at home and abroad could teach them to: in France, in the pre-Civil War period; in Germany and England, in the final decades of the nineteenth century. They studied abroad if they could afford it, and they followed the latest medical developments abroad in their professional journals. What was new, particularly after the 1830s, was the attention French professors of medicine began to pay to American contributions. Such giants as Louis, Velpeau, and Bernard, for instance, kept in touch with their former students. Occasionally, they referred in their public lectures to the handling of certain medical cases in the United States. Aware of the earnest dedication with which many American doctors devoted themselves to their profession, these and other French men of medical science kept informed about medical developments in the United States, often through translated summary reports their American friends and colleagues sent them. Nevertheless, while American dentistry had long enjoyed a superior professional reputation, with the exception of some surgical feats, the progress of American medicine in the nineteenth century was not yet spectacular. It moved, however, in a promising direction. And, as this chapter illustrates, the part French guidance played in it, particularly up to the end of the Second Empire, was monumental.

Conclusion

France regarded its civilizing mission throughout the nineteenth century as a responsibility entrusted to a leading world power. Its cultivated citizens and cultural institutions gave generously of themselves in the conviction that their liberality furthered the advance of Western civilization. Eager to learn from others, the relatively large number of culturally interested Americans followed the European road of professional leadership and artistic creativity, never losing sight, however, of their American identity. Their strong desire for individual and national independence in the professions and the arts was sustained by their conviction that the superior political institutions of their country were destined to shape the future course of civilization, a destiny of which they wished to be worthy in every respect.

Although the roots of American civilization have been deeply embedded in European soil, new generations of independent Americans and European immigrants turned their backs on class- and tradition-ridden Europe to pursue their happiness in an environment that held out the most optimistic hopes for life and liberty. Originally "foolish dreams of universal happiness" had excited French intellectuals in the late eighteenth century as much as the people across the ocean. But when American realities profoundly disappointed these social theoreticians, they turned their backs on the United States. Future generations of liberty-loving Frenchmen, however, again looked for inspiration to the republican institutions of the politically stable United States.

Actually, both societies had much in common. They were Christian, essentially middle class, and within the framework of their respective institutions, both endeavored to contribute to the elevation of humanity. Both were blessed with rich natural resources that made them lands of opportunity. The legendary Horatio Alger stories in the United States were duplicated in France, where scientists, artists, and merchants of humble background could become famous if not always rich. Whatever else they liked in life, both valued the accumulation of wealth: Frenchmen, for the good life and security; Americans, for the better life and adventurous enterprise. And while they reproached each other for being overly materialistic, they probably did so to assert their cultural superiority.

Despite their national and historical differences both societies developed along many parallel lines. In both countries the advent of a new generation was usually accompanied by demands for greater individual freedom and experimentation with new styles in the arts, literature, music, and the theater. Classicism, romanticism, naturalism, impressionism, and realism became, in succession, as familiar terms and schools in the United States as in France. And while the avant-garde of the one generation in time usually became the traditionalists of the following generation, the cultural breaks between generations were not as clear-cut as embattled advocates of change would have wanted them to be. Finally, in both countries, voices were raised against alien influences. Some Americans objected strenuously to the growing Europeanization of American life while some Frenchmen opposed the creeping Americanization of their lives. These critics did not advocate cultural isolation; but they objected to this potential transformation of their own civilization.

Discussing a whole century of Franco-American relations, we must keep in mind that the historical development of France and the United States between 1800 and 1900 brought about such profound social, political, and cultural changes in both countries that at different times we are for all practical purposes dealing with quite different entities. France, wielding enormous power and influence in 1800, looked back in 1900 to Waterloo, Sedan, and several revolutions that had reduced its relative position on the scale of international power, despite the fact that in the meantime it had acquired a sizable colonial empire and that the glitter of its bourgeois civilization gave the deceptive appearance of the return of old glory. And need one recall that the young American republic had in the course of the century conquered a continent and become an empire power? Proud of their country, 75 million Americans confidently continued to build on the foundation laid by a population that in 1800 amounted to only 5 million. Looking back in 1900, unlike the French whose population had remained stagnant, Americans could see how their political and economic independence was constantly gaining momentum, despite such temporary setbacks as the Civil War and cyclical economic depressions. Their ability to overcome these calamities and to emerge from them stronger than ever had advantages and disadvantages for other powers. As the leading foreign customer and a potential ally of France in its attempts to hold the power of the British Empire in check, the United States was as useful to France in the nineteenth century as France had been to America when the colonies declared their independence from Great Britain. The prospect, however, of this rapidly growing transatlantic giant overwhelming Europe by absorbing it economically and confronting it with the necessity of adopting an undesirable style of life haunted an ever-increasing number of Frenchmen.

Although France was concerned about this prospect, it did very little to counteract it. Its early perception of this possible trouble was as keen as its reaction to it was verbally strong and persistent; but its actions were not sufficient to stem the tide of history. France protested against the expansion of the United States and the Monroe Doctrine, and it pursued a most irritating course during the Civil War in America. But its halfhearted support of the South and its ill-fated intervention in Mexico proved to be entirely inadequate measures to stop the advance of the dynamic Protestant republic. As alarmed as officials of the Third Republic were in 1898 about America's cynical acquisition of the possessions of the Spanish Empire, in the end, they became resigned to it. In fact, in the nineteenth century neither the French nor the American government intervened decisively in each other's foreign affairs. Whatever opposition they registered to specific policies did not, in the last analysis, disturb the semblance of mutual tolerance in their working relationships. It appeared that the political leaders of each country deemed it best to regard the other as a friendly reserve in times of national emergency.

If France did not wish to tackle the haunting American problem power-politically, one would logically have expected it to cope with it in other ways. Economically, it could have made a determined effort to modernize its productive capacity at a pace enabling it to remain in a strong competitive position. Or, it could have invested heavily in American land and mineral resources, as Great Britain did, at least to blunt the American challenge effectively. But bourgeois France was not enterprising enough to do either. Nor did many of its leading citizens familiarize themselves with American society by acquiring firsthand knowledge of it. Only a handful of them cared to be well informed and up-to-date about the model republic. It seemed that those voices that increasingly complained about the creeping Americanization of European life in the second half of the century were more preoccupied with preserving their "ancient" civilization, whose ethical and esthetic refinement could in their judgment not be surpassed, than with "modern" America per se. They were Europeans with a traditional outlook toward Greek and Roman civilization; and they were at best willing to take a special interest in the ancient civilizations of the Orient, but not in the culturally underdeveloped new forces stirring in North America. If to Renan, who professed sympathy for American society, "Americanization" meant quite generally the vulgarization of life, we find in the *Goncourt Journals* a more specific articulation of the consequences of America's cultural invasion. Disgusted with the emphasis on technological progress at the

Universal Exhibition at Paris in 1867, the Goncourts protested against the new trend of "industry lording it over art, the steam thrasher displacing the painting—in brief, the Federation of Matter. . . . It will be the barbarians of civilization who will swallow up the Latin world just as the horde of uncivilized barbarians devoured it in a former age."[1]

This exaggerated fear of the future, based more on emotions and notions than on knowledge, evidently assumed the triumph of the barbarians over the civilized peoples as the final outcome of the clash between American and European civilization. Frenchmen did not have to take such a pessimistic view of the final outcome of this cultural conflict to be justifiably concerned about the direction in which the United States was moving ahead, believing that its modern way of life would actually be an improvement over that of the past. Undoubtedly, the divergence of views about the cultural quality of life caused a profound alienation between French and American people. Instinctively, Frenchmen sensed that the speed and fascination with which Americans applied technological and scientific advances to industrial production, without analyzing the human and social consequences of the new processes, could indeed result in the irreversible burial of their comfortable way of life. Great Britain, Germany, and the United States—the Protestant countries leading the world into industrialization—pursued their courses independently, without consultation or coordination with other countries; but the stake of humanity in this revolutionary transformation of society appeared to be too great for France to let it pass without at least an expression of concern. But the best concerned Frenchmen could hope for was to slow down the pace of mechanization and dehumanization. The rapid growth of the United States, of its territory, population, industry, and power, long viewed with apprehension from the point of view of balanced distribution of power in the world, threatened to bring with it a cultural tidal wave of uncontrollable dimension.

1. André Billy, *The Goncourt Brothers* (London, 1960), 189; Lewis Galantière, *The Goncourt Journals, 1851–1870* (New York, 1937), 234.

A certain pattern characterized French behavior with respect to this disturbing prospect and the historical developments that made it possible. Let us briefly trace its record. The government of Louis XVI concluded its alliance with the United States because the reduction of the British Empire expected to result from it served its immediate self-interest. In later years, even after the sale of the Louisiana Territory, French governments maintained only a vaguely defined political relationship with the United States; they concentrated instead on advancing their interests more vigorously in Europe, Asia, and Africa. Similarly, French political and social philosophers looked to the institutional and social experiment growing out of the American Revolution for justification of their enlightened notions about society and government, only to lose interest in America's development when it appeared that its pioneer and frontier society could hardly serve as a model for an abstractly conceived improvement over Western civilization. Apprehending, furthermore, that the steady territorial expansion of the United States might eventually constitute a threat to its security, France repeatedly went through the motions of organizing the protection of its self-interest, only to abstain from going through with it when it appeared that the immediate calculable risks of such a course outweighed the incalculable long-term risks involved in America's aggrandizement.

This pattern of intense interest followed by irresolute evasion can also be recognized in the French approach to the study of the United States. In order to meet the objectionable challenge Americanization posed, Frenchmen had first to acquire an intimate knowledge of America and its society. The American colony in Paris and many of the American tourists whom they observed only superficially, or the few French publicists who after a short stay in the United States published their unbalanced and inadequate observations, often confirming their preconceived notions about this odd society in the New World, were unreliable sources for this educational need. Alexis de Tocqueville, Michel Chevalier, and Edouard Laboulaye counted among the relatively few Frenchmen who made a serious effort to enlighten their compatriots about American society. But they addressed the French public in the days of Louis Philippe and Napoleon III. If French interest in American society waned in mid-century, the Second Empire certainly wished to avoid playing into the hands of the republican movement by advertising the accomplishments of the American system. And, beginning with Adolphe Thiers, the conscious efforts of the Third Republic to promote a better understanding of America did not really catch fire. The quick recovery of France in the 1870s and the resumption of its role as a brilliant cultural center restored the pride of Frenchmen so completely that the enjoyment of their own comforts and accomplishments preoccupied them. On the whole, they were therefore by the end of the nineteenth century even more ignorant about the United States than Americans were about France. While travel alone does not necessarily change attitudes, it usually opens up new vistas. At least thousands of Americans visited France each year, while only a few Frenchmen deemed it worthwhile to visit "God's own country." Pierre de Coubertin, the director of the *Chronique de France,* observed in 1898 that Europeans did not understand the true nature of American civilization, having only marginally involved themselves in it. Americans, he pointed out, did not love money for its own sake, but for the enjoyment of life and power with which it could invest them. Their history, moreover, convinced him that they "possessed the instinct of domination and the means to exercise it."[2] Consequently, he asked, was it not foolish to ignore them?

France and Frenchmen obviously did not ignore the United States; they just permitted the American problem to drift without resolutely addressing themselves to it. Private French citizens dealt directly with Americans in connection with their common interests in the professions, arts, literature, religion, and business.

2. Pierre de Coubertin, "La Philosophie de l'histoire des Etats-Unis," *Revue bleue* (June, 1898), 708–15; "La Conquête des Etats-Unis," *Chronique de France* (1902), 107–113.

They often worked closely together to advance themselves and their particular field of endeavor. They considered the overall American problem, or "danger," as some overly alarmed writers referred to it, beyond their capacity or responsibility. Their person-to-person encounters with Americans impressed them with the laudable dedication, motivation, and cooperation of these citizens from another continent who were as concerned with the well-being and progress of humanity as they were themselves. In a way, it was admirable to watch these Americans catch up with their cultural time lag in the arts and sciences, once they had taken care of elementary necessities. Abstract references to the "American danger" and personal observations based on direct contacts with individual Americans simply could not be reconciled. The "danger" seemed to be more imagined than real and, in any case, nothing prevented the two civilizations from existing side by side. Such ideological and religious competitors as French monarchism and Catholicism and American republicanism and Protestantism after all demonstrated that they could peacefully coexist.

This did not mean that they could not be discriminating and critical in their reactions to each other. In some respects Frenchmen could judge American society more objectively than defensive and boastful Americans could do themselves. We have already noted crucial differences with respect to the far-reaching consequences of an ever-accelerated mechanization of industrial production. While Yankees looked upon their ingenious technological and organizational aptitudes as instruments of social progress, many Frenchmen, though equally excited and excitable about new gadgets, nevertheless felt uncomfortable about what these innovations might do to the kind of life to which they had been accustomed for generations.

They also did not hold back their reservations about the political system of the United States. Not just fanatic monarchists looking for criticism of American life and institutions in support of their own beliefs, but even Frenchmen sympathetic toward the United States questioned the validity of the institutional image Americans liked to convey so enthusiastically to anyone willing to listen. If democracy existed in the United States, its critics contended, then the leveling effects of its equalitarian tenets held out little hope for brilliant individuals rising above the masses. And it was these individuals, not the masses, who had historically advanced the frontiers of civilization. The pressures to which individuals were liable, moreover, from religious and civic groups watching to see whether their neighbors met the moral and social standards of the community, could be oppressive and at times intolerable. A political democracy that did not also guarantee the social freedom of the individual made a mockery of democratic principles. Therefore, these French critics contended, the social equality to which they had been accustomed even under monarchical rule was preferable, from the individual's point of view, because political freedom without social freedom amounted to a farce. Similarly, in their judgment, subjective interpretation and application of the law, not to mention mob trials, contradicted the American insistence that theirs was "a government of law, and not of men." However, the greatest damage to the credibility of America's image, the world's vaunted champion of freedom, was caused by the tolerance of slavery and racial discrimination against nonwhites. Whatever excuses Americans offered for these conditions, they were unacceptable to Frenchmen, for they demonstrated the undeniable existence of hypocritical double standards in American society.

Evidence abounds to the effect that racial discrimination and degradation in the United States embarrassed American propagandists and evangelists who tried to persuade Frenchmen to follow the lead of American republicanism and Protestantism. France's brief historical exposures to republicanism had not exactly encouraged the French people to try it again. Their temperament and tradition clearly indicated a preference for strong leaders. And the republican model across the ocean left, even ideologically, a great deal to be desired; besides, it operated under exceptional conditions, not present in France.

Considering the ancient roots of Catholicism in France, even in an age in which the popular hold of the Church in France was declining, American evangelists had little chance of converting people whose spiritual needs and artistic tastes were appealingly satisfied by the Church. French attachment to the Church was probably more conditioned by the emotional satisfaction they derived from artistic edifices and their colorful interiors and church music than from the reassuring belief in the Trinity—a kind of satisfaction that the more spiritual services in unpretentious Protestant chapels did not evoke in them. To the devout and humble Catholic masses the splendor of their churches contrasted agreeably with the drabness of their daily environment. These psychological factors also explained the different attitudes of Protestant Americans and Catholic Frenchmen with regard to art. The latter found nothing objectionable in immodest paintings and sculptures, whereas Protestants guided by strict Puritan codes left no doubt about their disapproval of the public exhibition of such "indecent" works.

American criticism of the French also ranged far. For one thing, Americans found the frequent allusions to their country's alleged cultural inferiority infuriating. Qualified American critics contended that Frenchmen not only underrated American culture, they also overrated their own. They maintained that as outstanding as nineteenth century French contributions had been in science and medicine, with few exceptions, those in literature, music, art, and the theater did not merit the generous acclaim accorded them. Aside from contemporary changes and perfections of style, these critics observed, French art lacked the qualities associated with the great masterworks of the past centuries: depth and timelessness. The light and entertaining works of nineteenth-century French writers, artists, and composers, on the whole, seemed more to cater to prevailing popular sentiments than to promote higher cultural standards. Their restless search for novelty appeared to be more stimulated by studied imagination than by spontaneous brilliance, as well as by a desire to reflect progressively rapid changes in society. In the nineteenth century, after all, experimentation and subjective interpretations and impressions assumed an excitingly liberating character. Despite these critical reservations, however, the contemporary prestige of France as the cultural center of the world was so high that literally thousands of American students of art and music went there for training. Emphatically, they limited themselves to the acquisition of skills and inspirational exposure, determined on their return home to be independently creative artists rather than disciples of French masters.

In the final decades of the centruy, Americans looked upon their assertion of cultural independence from Europe as the fulfillment of their earlier desire for it. National pride had as much to do with it as a growing anti-European outlook. Americans still appreciated the beautiful scenery of Europe and the benefits they had derived from exposure to stimulating teachers and the works of its great masters of art. But, with specific reference to France, all its dazzling appearances could not conceal the feeling that, like its nineteenth-century literature, its life was generally provincial. Seen in conjunction with the political instability that characterized the precarious existence of the Third Republic, this estimate led Americans to the conclusion that their own dynamic society indeed offered the best hope for the future.

France had missed opportunities of historic proportions to become a great power, when it failed in the wake of the mid-century revolutions to assume leadership of the liberal movement in Europe and, again, when it failed to recognize in the era of the Industrial Revolution that its traditional concepts of the comfortable and civilized life were ill-suited to meet the challenges of the evolving industrial civilization. Despite its artificial splendor and prestigious scientific and artistic accomplishments in the late nineteenth century, France, American critics noted, failed to muster the vigor and will to keep up with the changes of modern times.

It is no coincidence that the chapters on art, literature, and theater contain frequent references to the question of morality. Throughout the century, the controversies over this major issue reflected a characteristic difference in the two cultures. No political, social, or economic changes or foreign influences made America's Protestant, middle-class society budge from its strict adherence to rigid morals, a fact already noted by Tocqueville. Pleading the cause of the Union in 1861, a French Protestant leader extolled the virtues of American morality, inviting his readers to "open the journals and novels of the United States [and] you will not find a corrupt page in them. You might leave them all on the drawing room table, without fearing to call a blush to the brow of a woman, or to sully the imagination of a child." In this regard, nineteenth-century American society was not prepared to make compromises; the moral code applied universally. This meant, of course, that art, literature, theater, fashions, and social relationships were expected to observe it. If its enforcement restricted the freedom of the individual, this seemed justified on the ground that the code was designed to protect society against harmful abuses leading to decadence. The social discipline and individual self-control it imposed upon people included silence about certain matters it was not proper to talk or write about.

French writers, painters, and sculptors—to whom art was one thing and morality another; who were concerned with beauty, truth, and real life; whose works displayed sensuous scenes and nudes or contained detailed discussions of adultery and prostitution—held this narrow Puritan interpretation of morality in such contempt that they paid no attention to American charges of immorality. As artists, cherishing their freedom and inspiration, they preferred being labeled immoral rather than untrue. They doubted, moreover, that in private life Americans were as virtuous as they posed to be. They were inclined to believe that American church and community leaders may have been successful in outwardly enforcing their codes, but that in reality Americans were either hiding or not talking about their vices, whereas Frenchmen did not hesitate to discuss them openly and certainly refused to masquerade some socially ugly situations as virtue.[3] In other

3. Max O'Rell, "French versus Anglo-Saxon Immorality," *NAR*, CLIX (1894), 545–50.

words, the French suspected that, by and large, Americans did not behave very differently from other human beings. The difference was likely to be only one of degree.

In this connection, a very important point calls for clarification. The Hollywood-type American image of France as a shamelessly immoral society has all along been based on erroneous evidence. Just because a few French novelists dared to entertain the public with spicy descriptions of socially abnormal situations, or just because Paris tolerated brothels, reputedly more frequented by foreign visitors than by adult Frenchmen, or just because Paris permitted such an "indecent" dance as the cancan to be publicly performed, France was not immoral.[4] For that matter, people of different cultural backgrounds might well differ about what is moral and what is not. Whatever loose morals were admittedly practiced by some members of the French upper classes, the overwhelming mass of bourgeois and working-class families in Paris and the provinces believed in marital fidelity. They might flirt, be coquettish, and display their feelings more openly and demonstratively than Anglo-Americans, but that did not justify hanging the label "immoral" on the French people. It did not help of course that some American Protestants, who identified Catholicism with impurity and as a religion appealing to the senses, helped to spread the fiction of Catholic France being immoral. The perpetuation of this false image poisoned the French-American atmosphere unnecessarily.

Both countries have been victims of false images that marred their political and cultural intercourse. As we have noted, in the minds of nineteenth-century Americans, France epitomized social immorality in all cultural respects. The way to avoid its corrupting influence, urged the staunch believers in puritanism, was to avoid exposure to its contaminated life. But judging by the thousands of Americans who read corrupting French novels or flocked to the paradise of alleged immorality, at least they understood that truly moral people do not become corrupted by exposure to im-

4. Charles Wagner, *My Impressions of America* (New York, 1906).

morality and that France was a society composed as much of saints as of sinners. Also the image of the French as an irreligious and areligious people was too broadly asserted to reflect the attitudes of the entire population. In this respect, too, France was a society composed of believers and nonbelievers, of devout Catholics, Protestants, agnostics, and atheists.

In a way, France had to blame itself if its periodical political upheavals conveyed to the outside world the impression that Frenchmen were incapable of governing themselves and leaned toward strong-arm rule. Not only did this oversimplified image ignore the complexity of the political development in France, very unjustly, it also failed to point out that, regardless of its political system at any time, France was throughout the nineteenth century a cultural republic *par excellence.*

Similarly, the French image of the United States as a cultural wasteland, widely and often contemptuously disseminated in the first half of the century, hurt the sensibilities of the American people. Although, with the encouragement and assistance of some French professionals, American strides in the arts and sciences eventually compelled a reappraisal, in the meantime, truly intimate French-American relations, in any case difficult between Anglo-Americans and Latin French, were put in jeopardy. As we have seen, in both countries the works of foreign authors were eventually reappraised and opinions about them changed, both upward and downward. But reappraisal of the work of an individual cannot be compared with reappraisal of the cultural accomplishments of a country. Not only are the stakes higher in the latter case, the damage done to political and economic interrelations as a result of cultural deprecations may be irreparable.

The other image that impaired the development of truly close ties between France and the United States was that of the colossus whose insatiable appetite for self-aggrandizement threatened to endanger the security and civilization of Europe, indeed of the Western hemisphere. America's concept of Manifest Destiny and the frightening momentum of its expansion did provide a factual basis for this image. But the internal growth and external expansion of the United States proceeded at such a rapid pace that a long period of consolidation would have been needed before the colossus could have invaded Europe. Actually, at no time did the United States plan to conquer Europe or was it militarily and psychologically prepared for such an undertaking. On the contrary, the United States needed European manpower, capital, and know-how, all of which were available to it without resort to force. As far as France was concerned, the "American problem" was real enough. But if the United States "endangered" France, it did so indirectly because of the impact of its rapid rise on the rest of the world, not because it deliberately set out to challenge France and change the world order. Certainly, using the image of the colossus as a means of alerting its people to an impending danger neither protected the interests of France nor furthered French-American relations.

Ironically, in the final decade of the century ultramontane French Catholics deemed it convenient to spread the image of the American Catholic Church being dominated by power-grabbing, heresy-courting prelates. The very thought of a liberal American pope—further enhancing the global power of the North American colossus—also made the future of Europe assume a disquieting outlook.

Images work positively as well as negatively. The Marquis de Lafayette, who in America was usually seen as a model of selfless courage and moral virtue, in turn tried to convey to his countrymen the image of America, his "adopted country," as a land whose ideal institutions held out the kind of promise that merited the admiration of the world. The image of Lafayette in America as a helpful friend in war and peace and the projected image of him in France as a greatly admired personality in the United States actually helped to sustain his political influence in France. James Fenimore Cooper, commenting on the deplorable political and journalistic trends of Jacksonian Democracy, attributed them to a "large party of 'doctrinaires' [who] fancy excellencies under other systems, much as the ultra-liberals of Europe fancy perfections under our own."[5]

In the nineteenth century, erroneous images significantly contributed to very damaging misunderstandings between the two nations. And yet, transcending them all was the American image of France as a friendly power without whose assistance independence might not have been won. This single, gratefully remembered, act at the birth of the American republic and the sale of the Louisiana Territory constituted the only truly essential contributions of France to the United States prior to the First World War. What otherwise mattered most in the nineteenth century was that France abstained at crucial moments in American history from intervening in a decisively unfriendly fashion. Neither their fairly satisfactory trade relations nor their instructive and stimulating cultural interrelations during this entire period decisively shaped the development of either country. This state of affairs changed in the twentieth century.

By comparison, the image Americans had of Great Britain was that of an unfriendly power, despite the fact that since the end of the War of 1812 the two Anglo-Saxon powers had settled all their disputes peacefully. Their cultural affinity had nothing artificial about it. Their common heritage in language, law, literature, religion, and customs, buttressed in the nineteenth century by heavy British investments in the United States and considerable trade and immigration, actually tended to solidify their ancient family relationship. Neither Germany nor France could really establish as close an understanding.

Taking an overall view, we may say that person-to-person contacts and interactions between Frenchmen and Americans worked out beautifully. People-to people attitudes were friendly,

---

5. Lee Randol Barker, "James Fenimore Cooper's Idea of the Corrupting Influence of Europe on America, 1831–35" (Honors Thesis in History, Harvard University, 1962), 49; Anne C. Loveland, *Emblem of Liberty: The Image of Lafayette in the American Mind* (Baton Rouge, 1971); Russell M. Jones, "The Flowering Legend: Lafayette and the Americans, 1825–1834," *French Historical Studies*, IV (1966), 384–410.

but critical. And government-to-government relations were usually more strained than relaxed. On the whole, individual citizens of the two nations cooperated more closely and got along much better than did their governments. Nevertheless, friendly French-American cultural relations were not sufficient to prevent the deterioration of diplomatic relations, but they softened them and served as a bridge for continuous contact. The culture of a people has many roots and owes its healthy growth to many influences. The cultural cross-fertilization between France and the United States in the nineteenth century enriched their citizens and professions. But the general direction of French and American civilization, as indeed that of the Western world, paradoxically, seemed to impoverish the quality of life while attempting to improve it.

Selected Bibliography

To gather material for this study I have searched in collections throughout the United States and in several French depositories. As comprehensive as my research has been, consultation of unpublished sources of many more individuals, perhaps less known, might have yielded additional evidence. In many instances, however, original manuscripts are either nonexistent or still in the possession of families who will not make them available for public use, even for purposes of scholarship.

In addition to a large number of unpublished papers, letters, journals, and diaries, I relied heavily on all types of contemporary publications, particularly periodical journals and *revues*. A great many pertinent memoirs, books, articles, and doctoral dissertations supplemented these sources and permitted the incorporation of more recent analyses and evaluations. Scholars wishing to engage in further research on special topics may find the following bibliographical references helpful.

GENERAL SOURCES

MANUSCRIPT COLLECTIONS

Agazziz, Louis. HCL.
Allston, Joseph Blyth. Collection. SCHS.
Andrews, Charles Wesley. Letters. Duke University Library, Durham, N.C.
L'Athénée Louisianais. Papers, 1876 and 1880. Tulane University, New Orleans.
Balch, Edward Swift. Journal. UV.
Bancroft, George. Diary, 1821. MHS.
Bartlett, Paul Wayland. Papers. LC.
Battey, Robert. Papers. Emory University, Atlanta.
Berlioz, Hector. Correspondence. Columbia University, New York.
Bowdoin, John Tucker. Diary, 1818. VHS.
Brawley, William H. "Journal of a Trip in England and France, 1864–65." UV.

Breda, J. P. Papers. LSU.

Brewer, William Henry. Collection. Yale University, New Haven, Conn.

Brongniart, Adolphe. Correspondence. Musée d'Histoire Naturelle, Paris.

Brown, Henry Armitt. "Journal in Europe, 1866–67." PHS.

Buttles, O. B. Correspondence. State Historical Society of Wisconsin, Madison.

Cassatt, Mary. Correspondence. AAA.

Chasles, Philarete. Letters. HCL.

Cole, Thomas. "Diary of Second European Journey, 1841." New York State Library, Albany.

Coquelin, Constant. Collection. Yale University, New Haven, Conn.

Cosson, Ernest. Letters. Gray Herbarium, Cambridge, Mass.

Courbet, Gustave. Papers. Bibliothèque Nationale, Paris.

Cousin, Victor. Correspondence. Sorbonne, Paris.

Cox, Kenyon. Collection. Columbia University, New York.

Cranch, Christopher P. Papers. MHS.

Dana, James Dwight. Correspondence. Yale University, New Haven, Conn.

Decaisne, Joseph. Letters. Gray Herbarium, Cambridge, Mass.

Deprét, Louis. Letters. HCL.

Dreyfus, Alfred. Papers. HCL.

Du Pont, Eleuthère Irénée. Family Papers. EMHL.

Durand, Asher B. Journal. NYPL.

Durand, Elie M. Correspondence. Gray Herbarium, Cambridge, Mass.

Durand, John. Papers. Letters to C. H. Hart, 1884–1907. NYPL.

Endicott, George. Diary. NYPL.

Everett, Edward. Papers. MHS.

Feuillerat, Albert Gabriel. Papers. Yale University, New Haven, Conn.

Fischer, J. Francis. "Journal of a European Visit, 1831–33." PHS.

Francis, John W. Papers. NYPL.

French, Daniel Chester. Diary and Correspondence. LC.

French History Manuscript Collection. Yale University, New Haven, Conn.

Gayarée, Charles E. A. LSU.

Gibbes, Lewis R. Papers. LC.

Gifford, Sanford Robinson. "European Letters, 1855–56." AAA.

Gray, Asa. Correspondence. Gray Herbarium, Cambridge, Mass., and Yale University, New Haven, Conn.

Griscom, John. Correspondence. NYPL.

Holmes, Oliver Wendell. "Our Hundred Days in Europe" (1887). LC.

Hugo, Victor. Letters. HCL.

Hyatt & Mayer Correspondence. Princeton University, Princeton, N.J.

Jackson, Charles T. Papers. MHS.

James, Henry. Correspondence. HCL.

James, William. Correspondence. HCL.

Jussieu, Adrien. Correspondence. Bronx Botanical Garden.

LeConte, John L. APSL.

Leidy, Joseph. "Diary, 1848." ANSP.

LeVerrier, Urbain Jean Joseph. Papers. Institut de France, Paris. MS 3710.

Lucas, George. Correspondence. Walters Art Gallery, Baltimore, and NYMMA.

Manigault, Gabriel. Papers. SCHS.

Manigault, Gabriel Edward. "Autobiography." UNC.

McClintock, John. Letters. Emory University, Atlanta.

McKim, Charles F. Correspondence. LC.

Milbert, J. Papers. ANF.

Milne-Edwards, Henri. Correspondence. HCL.

Mineralogical Papers. Yale University, New Haven, Conn.

Moore, Charles. Papers. LC.

Mott, Valentine. Correspondence, 1829. NYHS.

"Dr. Valentine Mott, Jr.," Transcript MS 256. NYAM.

Mount, William S. Papers. NYHS.

Newcomb, Simon. Papers. LC.

Nicollet, J. N. Papers. LC.

Niles, Nathaniel. Papers. LC.

Norris, George W. "Diary." PHS.

Olmsted, Frederick Law. Correspondence. LC.

Parke, Charles H. "Notes on Europe, 1856." Henry E. Huntington Library and
Art Gallery, San Marino, Calif.

Pepper, William. Papers. University of Pennsylvania, Philadelphia.

De Peyster, Elizabeth Van R. "Diary of a Trip to Europe." NYHS.

Plée, Auguste. Papers. Musée d'Histoire Naturelle, Paris.

Poe, Edgar Allan. Letters. HCL.

Puvis de Chavannes, Pierre. Papers. Boston Public Library.

"Questions culturelles et scientifiques, 1897–1907, Etats-Unis." AMAE.

Reynes, Joseph. Family Papers. LSU.

Rives, Judith Page. "Diary, 1829–1851." Duke University Library, Durham, N.C.

Saugrain-Michau Collection. MoHS.

Simonin, Amédée H. "Diary and Correspondence." LC.

Townsend, Peter Solomon. "Diary, 1828." NYAM.

Silliman, Benjamin. Papers. Yale University, New Haven, Conn.

Tanner, Henry Ossawa. Papers. AAA.

Twain, Mark. Papers. UC.

Twiggs, John D. "Diary in Europe, 1846." UNC.

Vanderlyn, John. Correspondence. NYHS.

Waldeck-Rousseau, Rene. Papers. Institut de France, Paris. MS XLVIII (4607).

Walthers, Ferdinand H. "Music Papers." MoHS.

Warden, David Bailie. Papers. LC.

Whistler, James McNeill. Correspondence. LC and NYMMA.

Wiley, Henry Washington. "Diary, 1876." LC.

Wigglesworth, Samuel. Letters. NYAM.

Williams, John W. M. "Diary of a European Trip, 1867." UNC.

Wood, Trist. Correspondence. UNC.

PRINTED

Anderson, Frank Maloy. *The Constitution and Other Select Documents Illustrative of the History of France,* 1789–1907. New York, 1967.

Buckley, S. B. "The Grapes of North America." *Senate Executive Documents,* 37th Cong., 2nd sess., 478–86.

Foote, Lucy B. *Bibliography of the Official Publications of Louisiana,* 1803–1934. Baton Rouge, 1942.

House Reports , 32nd Cong., 2nd sess., 1853. "Ether Discovery: A Consideration of the Claims Made by W. T. G. Morton, Horace Wells and C. T. Jackson."

Louisiana Legislative Council. *The Government of Louisiana.* Research Study No. 13. Baton Rouge, 1959.

Moniteur Universel: Journal Officiel de la République Française, 1848.

Smithsonian Institution. *Annual Reports,* 1870–1900.

SUBJECT SOURCES

DEMOGRAPHY, INSTITUTIONS, SOCIOECONOMICS

Acomb, Evelyn M. and Marvin L. Brown, Jr. *French Society and Culture Since the Old Regime.* New York, 1966.

Altenbernd, August Lynn. "The Influence of European Travel on the Political and Social Outlook of Henry Adams, William Dean Howells, and Mark Twain." Ph.D. dissertation, Ohio State University, 1954.

Ameisen, Arthur. "The Effect of Judgments of Courts-Martial in France and in America: A Comparative Study of the Dreyfus Case." *American Law Review,* XXXIII (1899), 75–83.

Anderson, Emmett H. "Appraisal of American Life by French Travellers, 1860–1914." Ph.D. dissertation, University of Virginia, 1953.

Avery, Elizabeth H. "The Influence of French Immigration on the Political History of the United States." Ph.D. dissertation, University of Minnesota, 1895.

Awtrey, Hugh. *La Presse anglo-américaine de Paris.* Paris, 1932.

Barneaud, Charles. *Origines et progrès de l'éducation en Amérique.* Paris, 1898.

Baroncelli-Javon, J. G. de. *Une Colonie française en Louisiane.* New Orleans, 1909.

Barrell, George, Jr. *The Pedestrian in France and Switzerland.* New York, 1853.

Beaujour, Felix de. *Aperçu des Etats-Unis depuis 1800 jusqu'en 1810.* Paris, 1814.

Beaumont, Gustave de and Alexis de Tocqueville. *On the Penitentiary System in the United States and Its Application in France.* Carbondale, Ill., 1964.

Belisle, Alexandre. *Histoire de la presse franco-américaine.* Worcester, Mass., 1911.

Bellegarrigue, A. *Les Femmes d'Amérique.* Paris, 1853.

Benedict, Erastus C. *A Run through Europe.* New York, 1871.

Berthold, Eugenie. *Glimpses of Creole Life in Old St. Louis.* St. Louis, 1933.

Bertier de Sauvigny, G. de. *The Bourbon Restoration.* Translated by Lynn M. Case. Philadelphia, 1966.

Bertin, Georges. *Joseph Bonaparte en Amérique, 1815–1832.* Paris, 1893.

Betham-Edwards, M. *French Men, Women and Books: A Series of Nineteenth Century Studies.* Chicago, 1911.

Boehmer, George H. *History of the Smithsonian Exchanges.* Washington, D.C., 1882.

Bonnaud, Félix. *Cabet et son oeuvre.* Paris, 1900.

Boucher, François. *American Footprints in Paris.* New York, 1921.

Bourget, Paul. *Outre-Mer: Impressions of America.* 2 vols. New York, 1895.

Boutmy, E. "La formation de la nationalité aux Etats-Unis." *Annales de l'Ecole Libre des Sciences Politiques,* VI (1891), 585–603.

Bowers, David F., ed. *Foreign Influences in American Life: Essays and Critical Bibliographies.* Princeton, N.J., 1944.

Brogan, Denis William. *The Development of Modern France* (1870–1939). London, 1953.

Brooks, John Graham. "A Century of Foreign Criticism on the United States: A Study of Progress." *Chautauquan,* XLIX (1908), 184–236.

Brown, Lawrence Guy. *Immigration: Cultural Conflicts and Social Adjustments.* New York, 1933.

Brownell, W. C. *French Traits: An Essay in Comparative Criticism.* New York, 1902.

Buffum, Edward Gould. *Sights and Sensations in France, Germany, and Switzerland.* New York, 1869.

Byrnes, Robert F. *Antisemitism in Modern France: The Prologue to the Dreyfus Affair.* New York, 1969.

Cambon, Jules Martin. *France and the United States: Essays and Addresses.* New York, 1903.

Carr, William H. A. *The Du Ponts of Delaware: A Fantastic Dynasty.* New York, 1964.

Chambers, Samuel T. "Observations and Opinions of French Travellers in the

United States, 1790–1835." M.A. thesis, Georgetown University, 1949.

Chambrun, Adolphe de. *Droits et libertés aux Etats-Unis: Leurs origines et leur progrès.* Paris, 1891.

Champceix, Léodile de. *The American Colony in Paris in 1867.* Boston, 1868.

Channing, Walter. *A Physician's Vacation: Or, A Summer in Europe.* Boston, 1856.

Chasles, Philarète. "Les Américains en Europe et les Européens aux Etats-Unis." *RDDM* (February 1, 1843), 446–76.

———. "Les Américains et l'avenir de l'Amérique." *RDDM* (May 15, 1850), 616–66.

Chaumont, Vincent leRay de. *Souvenirs des Etats-Unis.* Paris, 1859.

Chevalier, Michel. *Lettres sur l'Amerique du Nord.* 2 vols. Paris, 1836.

———. *La Liberté aux Etats-Unis.* Paris, 1849.

———. *Society, Manners and Politics in the United States.* Boston, 1839; New York, 1966.

Chevrillon, André. *Alexis de Tocqueville et les Etats-Unis.* Paris, 1936.

Childs, Frances S. *French Refugee Life in the United States: An American Chapter of the French Revolution, 1790–1800.* Baltimore, 1940.

Chinard, Gilbert. *Tocqueville: De la Démocratie en Amérique.* Princeton, N.J., 1943.

———. "When the French Came to California." *CHSQ,* XXII (December, 1943), No. 4, and XXIII (March, 1944), No. 1.

Clarke, T. Wood. *Emigrés in the Wilderness.* New York, 1941.

Collier, Price. *America and the Americans: From a French Point of View.* New York, 1897.

Comettant, Oscar. *L'Amérique telle qu'elle est.* Paris, 1864.

———. *Le Nouveau Monde: Trois ans aux Etats-Unis.* Paris, 1861.

Cons, Louis. *Les Etats-Unis de 1789 à 1912.* Paris, 1912.

Cook, Will Mercer. "French Travellers in the United States, 1840–1870." Ph.D. dissertation, Brown University, 1936.

Copans, Simon J. "French Opinion of American Democracy, 1852–1860." Ph.D. dissertation, Brown University, 1942.

———. "Tocqueville's Later Years: A Reaffirmation of Faith." *Romanic Review,* XXXVI (April, 1945), 113–21.

Coubertin, Pierre de. *Universités transatlantiques.* Paris, 1890.

Cubberley, Edward P. *The History of Education.* Cambridge, Mass., 1948.

Cucheval-Clarigny, M. "La Presse américaine depuis l'indépendance." *RDDM* (May 15, 1857), 271–320.

Curtis, Eugene Newton. *The French Assembly of 1848 and American Constitutional Doctrines.* New York, 1918.

Daumard, Adeline. *La Bourgeoisie parisienne de 1815 à 1848.* Paris, 1963.

Dolan, Anne Marie. "The Literary Salon in New York, 1830–1860." Ph.D. dissertation, Columbia University, 1957.

Dommanget, Maurice. *Victor Considerant: Sa vie, son oeuvre.* Paris, 1929.

Dugard, Marie. *La Société americaine.* Paris, 1896.

Dulles, Foster Rhea. *Americans Abroad: Two Centuries of European Travel.*

Ann Arbor, Mich., 1964.

Dunn, Marie S ."A Comparative Study: Louisiana's French and Anglo-Saxon Cultures." *Louisiana Studies,* X (1971), 131–69.

Durbin, John P. *Observations in Europe, Principally in France and Great Britain.* New York, 1844.

Dutton, William S. *Du Pont: One Hundred and Forty Years.* New York, 1942.

Duvergier de Hauranne, Ernest. *Les Etats-Unis pendant la guerre de sécession: Vu par un journaliste français.* Paris, 1966.

———. *Huit mois en Amérique.* 2 vols. Paris, 1866.

Eddy, Daniel C. *Europa: Or Scenes and Society in England, France, Italy, and Switzerland.* Boston, 1859.

Ernst, Robert. *Immigrant Life in New York City, 1825–1863.* New York, 1949.

Eustis, James B. "Dreyfus and the Jewish Question in France: French and American Democracy." *Conservative Review,* II (August, 1899), 7–21.

Fecteau, Edward. *French Contributions to America.* Methuen, Mass., 1945.

Feuillerat, Albert. *French Life and Ideals.* Translated by Vera Barbour. New Haven, 1925.

Fischer, Eric. *The Passing of the European Age: A Study of the Transfer of Western Civilization and Its Renewal in Other Continents.* Cambridge, Mass., 1948.

Floyd, M. *Travels in France and the British Islands.* Philadelphia, 1859.

Forbes, Robert J. *Man, the Maker: A History of Technology and Engineering.* New York, 1950.

Fortier, Alcée. *Louisiana Studies: Literature, Customs and Dialects, History and Education.* New Orleans, 1894.

Fossier, Albert A. *New Orleans: The Glamour Period, 1800–1840.* New Orleans, 1957.

Freund, Ernst. "The Law of the Administration in America." *PSQ,* IX (1894), 403–425.

Fulton, Charles Carroll. *Europe Viewed Through American Spectacles.* Philadelphia, 1874.

Gager, Lelaye. *French Comment on American Education.* New York, 1925.

Gaillard, Henry. "La Condition des femmes dans la législation des Etats-Unis." Ph.D. dissertation, Université de Paris, 1899.

Gaillardet, Fréderic. *L'Aristocratie en Amerique.* Paris, 1883.

Galantière, Lewis. *The Goncourt Journals, 1851–1870.* New York, 1937.

Gardner, Augustus Kinsley. *The French Metropolis: Paris as Seen During the Spare Hours of a Medical Student.* New York, 1850.

Gaullieur, Henri. *Etudes américaines.* Paris, 1891.

Giddings, Thomas H. "Yankee Journalists in Europe, 1830–1848." Ph.D. dissertation, Columbia University, 1956.

Goodrich, S. G. *Recollections of a Lifetime: Or, Men and Things I Have Seen.* 2 vols. New York, 1856.

Goulet, Alexandre. "Une Nouvelle France en Nouvelle Angleterre." Ph.D. dissertation, Université de Paris, 1934.

Grandpierre, J. H. *Parisian Pastor's Glance at America.* Boston, 1854.

Guérard, Albert L. *French Civilization in the Nineteenth Century: A Historical Introduction*. London, 1914.

Haber, Francis C. "David Bailie Warden: A Bibliographical Sketch of America's Cultural Ambassador in France, 1804–1845." *Institut Français de Washington, Bulletin,* New Series, No. 3 (December, 1953), 75–118.

Halpern, Rose. "The American Reaction to the Dreyfus Case." M.A. thesis, Columbia University, 1941.

Ham, Edward Billings. "French National Societies in New England." *NEQ,* XII (1939), 315–32.

Handlin, Oscar. *Boston's Immigrants: A Study in Acculturation*. Cambridge, Mass., 1959.

Harvard et la France. Paris, 1936.

d'Haussonville, Cléron. *A Travers les Etats-Unis: Notes et impressions*. Paris, 1883.

Hemmings, F. W. J. *Culture and Society in France, 1848–1898: Dissidents and Philistines*. New York, 1971.

Hinds, Will Alfred. *American Communities and Cooperative Colonies*. Chicago, 1908.

Hippeau, Célestin. *L'Instruction publique aux Etats-Unis*. Paris, 1878.

Howe, William Wirt. "Roman and Civil Law in America." *Harvard Law Review,* XVI (1903), 342–58.

Hubbard, Genevieve Gregg. "French Travellers in America, 1775–1840." Ph.D. dissertation, American University, 1936.

Huret, Jules. *En Amérique: De New York à la Nouvelle Orléans*. Paris, 1904.

Hyde de Neuville, Jean Guillaume. *Mémoires et souvenirs*. 2 vols. Paris, 1888.

Iles, George. *Leading American Inventors*. New York, 1912.

James, Alice. *The Diary of Alice James*. Cambridge, Mass., 1894.

Jannet, Claudio. *Les Etats-Unis contemporains ou les moeurs, les institutions et les idées depuis la guerre de sécession*. 2 vols. Paris, 1889.

Jarves, James Jackson. *Parisian Sights and French Principles Seen Through American Spectacles*. London, 1853.

Johnson, Douglas. *France and the Dreyfus Affair*. London, 1966.

———. *Guizot: Aspects of French History, 1787–1874*. London, 1963.

Jones, Howard Mumford. *America and French Culture, 1750–1848*. Chapel Hill, N.C., 1927.

Jones, Russell Mosley. "The French Image of America, 1830 to 1848." Ph.D. dissertation, University of Missouri, 1957.

Jonveaux, Emile. *L'Amérique actuelle*. Paris, 1870.

Joyaux, Georges Jules. "French Press in Michigan: A Bibliography." *Michigan History,* XXXVI (September, 1952), and XXXVII (June, 1953).

———. "French Thought in American Magazines: 1800–1848." Ph.D. dissertation, Michigan State College, 1951.

Kendall, John S. "The Foreign Language Press of New Orleans." *LHQ,* XII (July, 1929), 363–80.

Klein, Selma M. "Social Interaction of the Creoles and Anglo-Americans in New Orleans, 1803–1860." M.A. thesis, Tulane University, 1940.

Koht, Halvdan. *The American Spirit in Europe: A Survey of Transatlantic Influences.* Philadelphia, 1949.

Krebs, Albert. "L'Expérience américaine de Clemenceau." *Rapports France-Etats-Unis* (August, 1952), 52–60.

Laboulaye, Edouard. *Lettres politiques: Esquisse d'une constitution républicaine.* Paris, 1872.

——. *Paris in America.* New York, 1863.

Lacroix, Rena. "Dr. Alfred Mercier: The Man and His Works." M.A. thesis, Louisiana State University, 1929.

Landes, David S. "French Entrepreneurship and Industrial Growth in the Nineteenth Century." *Journal of Economic History,* IX (May, 1949), 45–61.

Lauvrière, Emile. "La France dans le développement des Etats-Unis." *La Grande revue* (August, 1935), 268–94.

——. 'Une Nouvelle France en Nouvelle Angleterre." *Revue de l'histoire des colonies françaises,* XXIII (1935), 89–106.

Leaman, Bertha Ruth. "A Frenchman Visits Philadelphia in 1851." *Pennsylvania History,* VIII (October, 1941).

Lelièvre, Félix. *De l'émigration en Amérique depuis 1815 jusqu'en 1843.* Nantes, 1843.

Leuba, Edmond. *La Californie et les états du Pacifique: Souvenirs et impressions.* Paris, 1882.

Levasseur, Emile. *The American Workman.* Translated by Thomas S. Adams. Baltimore, 1900.

Lévy, Daniel. *Les Français en Californie.* San Francisco, 1884.

Lévy, Raphaël Georges. "Les Etudiants américains en France." *Revue internationale de l'enseignement,* XXXIII (February, 1897) 106–116.

Lochemes, Sister Mary F. *Robert Walsh: His Story.* New York, 1941.

Loeb, Charles Gerson. *Legal Status of American Corporations in France.* Paris, 1921.

Lucas, Charles. *Du Système pénitentiaire en Europe et aux Etats-Unis.* 3 vols. Paris, 1828–30.

McBride, John deWitt, Jr. "America in the French Mind during the Bourbon Restoration." Ph.D. dissertation, Syracuse University, 1954.

McDermott, John Francis. *The French in the Mississippi Valley.* Urbana, Ill. 1965.

——. *A Glossary of Mississippi Valley French, 1673–1850.* St. Louis, 1941.

——. "Louis Richard Cortambert and the First French Newspapers in Saint-Louis, 1809–1854." *Bibliographical Society of America, Papers,* XXXIV (1940), 221–53.

McMurtrie, Douglas C. "The French Press of Louisiana." *LHQ,* XVIII (1935), 947–65.

Magruder, Harriet. *A History of Louisiana.* Boston, 1909.

Mahieu, Robert G. "Les Enquêteurs français aux Etats-Unis de 1830 à 1837: L'Influence américaine sur l'évolution démocratique en France." Ph.D. dissertation, Université de Paris, 1934.

Malone, Dumas, ed. *Correspondence Between Thomas Jefferson and Pierre Samuel du Pont de Nemours,* 1798–1817. Boston, 1930.

Mandell, R. D. "The Affair and the Fair: Some Observations on the Closing Stages of the Dreyfus Case." *JMH,* XXXIX (September, 1967), 253–65.

Marmier, X. *Lettres sur l'Amérique.* 2 vols. Paris, 1851.

Martin, Thomas W. *French Military Adventurers in Alabama,* 1818–1828. Princeton, N.J., 1937.

Mayer, J. P. *Political Thought: The European Tradition.* London, 1939.

———. *Prophet of the Mass Age: A Study of Alexis de Tocqueville.* London, 1939.

Monaghan, Frank. *French Travellers in the United States,* 1765–1932. New York, 1933.

Montégut, Emile. *Libres opinions: Morales et historiques.* Paris, 1888.

———. "Les Conflits des races aux Etats-Unis: Les Indiens, les Nègres, l'immigration chinoise." *RDDM* (June 15, 1876), 785–826.

Montuclard, Maurice. *Conscience religieuse et démocratie.* Paris, 1965.

Morineau, Auguste de. *Essai statistique et politique sur les Etats-Unis d'Amérique.* Paris, 1848.

Morrow, Dwight W., Jr. "The Impact of American Agricultural Machinery on France, 1851–1914: With Some Consideration of the General Agricultural Impact until 1880." Ph.D. dissertation, Harvard, 1957.

Morse, Samuel F. B. *His Letters and Journals.* Edited and supplemented by his son Edward Lind Morse. 2 vols. Boston, 1914.

Mosse, George L. *The Culture of Western Europe: The 19th and 20th Centuries.* Chicago, 1961.

Mott, Valentine. *Travels in Europe and the East* (1834–41). New York, 1845.

Murat, Achille. *America and the Americans.* Translated by Henry J. Bradfield. New York, 1849.

Nasatir, A. P. *French Activities in California: An Archival Calendar-Guide.* Stanford, Calif., 1945.

Nevers, Edmond de. *L'Ame américaine.* Paris, 1900.

Nevins, Allan, ed. *America Through British Eyes.* New York, 1948.

O'Rell, Max. *A Frenchman in America.* New York, 1891.

Owen, Mary S. "An Analysis of the Frontiersman Based upon Observations of Contemporary French Travellers." Ph.D. dissertation, Indiana University, 1956.

Parish, Lestrois. *Emerson's View of France and the French.* Franco-American Pamphlet Series, No. 5. New York, 1935.

Perez, L. M. "French Refugees to New Orleans in 1809." *Southern History Association, Publications,* IX (September, 1905), 293–310.

Philips, Edith. "Les Réfugiés bonapartistes en Amerique (1815–1830)." Ph.D. dissertation, Université de Paris, 1923.

Pierson, George Wilson. *Tocqueville and Beaumont in America.* New York, 1938.

Podea, Iris S. "Quebec to 'Little Canada': The Coming of the French Canadians to New England in the Nineteenth Century." *NEQ,* XXIII (1950), 365–80.

Portalis, Albert Edouard. *Les Etats-Unis: Le Self-government et le césarisme.* Paris, 1869.

Pound, Roscoe. "The Influence of French Law in America." *Illinois Law Review,* III (1909), 354–63.

Poussin, Guillaume Tell. *Chemins de fer américains: Historique de leur construction.* Paris, 1836.

Prudhommeaux, Jules. *Icarie et son fondateur: Etienne Cabet.* Paris, 1907.

Rahv, Philip. *Discovery of Europe: The Story of American Experience in the Old World.* Boston, 1947.

Read, William A. *Louisiana-French.* Baton Rouge, 1931.

Rémond, René. *Les Etats-Unis devant l'opinion française, 1815–1852.* 2 vols. Paris, 1962.

Rod, Edouard. *Reflets d'Amérique.* Paris, 1905.

Rodrigue, Elisabeth M. "Les Voyageurs français aux Etats-Unis pendant la première moitié du dix-neuvième siecle." Ph.D. dissertation, Radcliffe College, 1945.

Rosengarten, Joseph G. *French Colonists and Exiles in the United States.* Philadelphia, 1907.

Rousiers, Paul de. *La Vie américaine.* Paris, 1892.

Roz, Firmin. *L'Energie américaine.* Paris, 1910.

Saint-Victor, Jacques Benjamin. *Lettres sur les Etats-Unis d'Amérique: Ecrites en 1832 et 1833, et adressées à M. Le Comte O'Mahony.* 2 vols. Paris, 1835.

Sanderson, John. *Sketches of Paris: In Familiar Letters to His Friends by an American Gentleman.* Philadelphia, 1838.

Scharf, John Thomas. *History of Saint Louis, City and County.* 2 vols. Philadelphia, 1883.

Scharf, John Thomas, and Thompson Westcott. *History of Philadelphia, 1609–1884.* 3 vols. Philadelphia, 1884.

Scherer, Edmond. *La Démocratie et la France.* Paris, 1883.

Scott, Robert. "American Travellers in France, 1830–1860." Ph.D. dissertation, Yale University, 1940.

Sheridan, Peter. "The Immigrant in Philadelphia, 1827–1860." Ph.D. dissertation, Georgetown University, 1957.

Sherwood, M. E. W. *Here & There & Everywhere: Reminiscences.* Chicago, 1898.

Siegfried, André and Jules. "The American Workman and the French." *International Quarterly,* VI (1902–1903), 353–65.

Simonin, Louis Laurent. *Le Monde américain: Souvenirs de mes voyages aux Etats-Unis.* Paris, 1877.

Skard, Sigmund. *The American Myth and the European Mind: American Studies in Europe, 1776–1960.* Philadelphia, 1961.

———. *American Studies in Europe.* 2 vols. Philadelphia, 1958.

Smith, Anne Wharton. "Criticism of American Life and Letters in the *Revue Encyclopédique,* 1819–35." Ph.D. dissertation, Northwestern University, 1943.

Snyder, J. F. "The Old French Towns of Illinois in 1839: A Reminiscence." *Journal of the Illinois State Historical Society,* XXXVI (December, 1943), 345–67.

Soissons, S. C. de. *A Parisian in America.* Boston, 1896.

Soltau, Roger. *French Political Thought in the Nineteenth Century.* New Haven, 1931.

Stowe, Harriet Beecher. *Sunny Memories of Foreign Lands.* 2 vols. Boston, 1854.

Szajkowski, Z. "The *Alliance Israélite Universelle* in the United States, 1860–1949." *American Jewish Historical Society Publications,* XXXIX (June, 1950), 389–443.

Tappan, Henry P. *A Step from the New World to the Old and Back Again: With Thoughts on the Good and Evil in Both.* 2 vols. New York, 1902.

Taylor, Bayard. *Views A-Foot: Or Europe Seen with Knapsack and Staff.* New York, 1902.

Tétrault, Maximilienne. "Le Rôle de la presse dans l'évolution du peuple franco-américain de la Nouvelle Angleterre." Ph.D. dissertation, Université de Paris, 1935.

Thébaud, Augustus J. *Three Quarters of a Century (1807 to 1882), A Retrospect: Forty Years in the United States of America.* New York, 1904.

Ticknor, George. *Life, Letters and Journals of George Ticknor.* 2 vols. Boston, 1876.

Tinker, Edward Larocque. *Creole City: Its Past and Its People.* New York, 1953.

————. *Writings in the French Language in Louisiana in the 19th Century: Biographic and Bibliographic Essays.* Translated by T. Rossi. Paris, 1932.

Tisch, Joseph LeSage. *French in Louisiana: A Study of the Historical Development of the French Language in Louisiana.* New Orleans, 1959.

Tissandier, Albert. *Six mois aux Etats-Unis: Voyage d'un touriste dans l'Amérique du Nord.* Paris, 1886.

Tocqueville, Alexis de. *Democracy in America.* 2 vols. London, 1835–40; New York, 1900.

————. *Livre du centenaire,* 1859–1959. Paris, 1960.

Toutain, Paul. *Un Français en Amérique: Yankees, Indiens, Mormons.* Paris, 1876.

Trollope, Frances. *Paris and the Parisians in 1835.* New York, 1836.

Tuckerman, Henry T. *America and Her Commentators.* New York, 1864.

Tuckley, Henry. *In Sunny France: Present-Day Life in the French Republic.* Cincinnati, 1894.

Tyler, Alice Felt. *Freedom's Ferment: Phases of American Social History to 1860.* Minneapolis, 1944.

Vail, Eugene A. *De La Littérature et des hommes de lettres des Etats-Unis d'Amérique.* Paris, 1841.

Van Dyke, Henry. *The Spirit of America.* New York, 1910.

Varigny, Charles Victor Crosnier de. *La Femme aux Etats-Unis.* Paris, 1893.

Villard, Léonie. *La France et les Etats-Unis: Echanges et rencontres (1524–1800).* Lyon, 1952.

Weber, Adna Ferrin. *The Growth of Cities in the Nineteenth Century: A Study in Statistics.* Ithaca, N.Y., 1963.

Wegelin, Christof. *The Image of Europe in Henry James.* Dallas, 1958.

Weigle, Clifford F. "The Rise and Fall of the Havas News Agency." *Journalism Quarterly,* XIX (September, 1942), 277–86.

West, W. Reed. *Contemporary French Opinion on the American Civil War.* Baltimore, 1924.

Wharton, Edith. *French Ways and Their Meaning.* New York, 1927.

Whitfield, Irene Therese. *Acadian Folk Song.* Baton Rouge, 1955.

———. *Louisiana French Folk Songs.* Baton Rouge, 1939.

Wick, B. L. "The Icarian Community: Story of Etienne Cabet's Experiment in Communism." *Midland Monthly,* III (1895), 370–76.

Willard, Emma. *Journal and Letters from France and Great Britain.* Troy, N.Y., 1833.

Willson, Beckles. *America's Ambassadors to France, 1777–1927.* London, 1928.

Wilson Bruno. *L'Evolution de la race française en Amérique.* Montreal, 1921.

Wilson, Harold F. "The North American Phalanx: An Experiment in Communal Living." New Jersey Historical Society, *Proceedings,* LXX (1952), 188–209.

Wish, Harvey. "The French of Old Missouri (1804–1821)." *Mid-America,* New Series, XII (1941), 167–89.

———. *Society and Thought in Early America: A Social and Intellectual History of the American People through 1865.* New York, 1950.

Wittke, Carl. *We Who Built America.* New York, 1939.

Wright, Hezekiah H. *Desultory Reminiscences of a Tour through Germany, Switzerland, and France.* Boston, 1838.

Wright, Louis B. *The Cultural Life of the American Colonies.* New York, 1957.

Wuarin, Louis. "La Femme et le féminisme aux Etats-Unis." *Bibliothèque Universelle,* LXIV (1894), 64–93.

Wyllys, Rufus Kay. "The French of California and Sonora." *PHR,* I (September, 1932), 337–59.

Yiannopoulos, Athanassios N., ed. *Civil Law in the Modern World.* Baton Rouge, 1965.

RELIGION

Ames, Mary Lesley, ed. *Life and Letters of Peter and Susan Lesley.* 2 vols. New York, 1909.

Baird, Henry M. *The Life of the Reverend Robert Baird, D.D.* New York, 1866.

Baird, Robert. *De La Religion aux Etats-Unis.* 2 vols. Paris, 1844.

Baisnée, Jules A. "L'Influence religieuse française aux Etats-Unis." *Les Etudes Américaines,* V (1947), 21–31.

Bargy, Henry. *La Religion dans la société aux Etats-Unis.* Paris, 1902.

Bertier de Sauvigny, G. de. "Le Protestantisme français sous la monarchie constitutionelle vu par les voyageurs américains." Société de l'Histoire du Protestantisme Français, *Bulletin* (January–March, 1970), 85–101.

Bianquis, Jean. *Les Origines de la société des missions évangéliques de Paris, 1822–1830.* 3 vols. Paris, 1930–1935.

Biever, Albert H. *The Jesuits in New Orleans and the Mississippi Valley.* New Orleans, 1924.

Billington, Ray Allen. *The Protestant Crusade, 1800–1860.* New York, 1938.

Bodley, John E. C. *The Church in France.* London, 1906.

Brunetière, Ferdinand. "Le Catholicisme aux Etats-Unis." *RDDM* (November 1, 1898), 140–81.

Charlton, D. G. *Positivist Thought in France during the Second Empire.* Oxford, 1959.

Clamageran, J. J. *De L'Etat actuel du protestantisme en France.* Paris, 1857.

Cochran, Joseph Wilson. *Friendly Adventures: A Chronicle of the American Church in Paris. 1857–1931.* Paris, 1931.

Collins, Ross W. *Catholicism and the Second French Republic, 1848–1852.* New York, 1923.

Coquerel, Athanase. "Catholicism and Protestantism in France." *Christian Examiner,* XLV (November, 1848), 363–89.

Cordey, Henri. *Edmond de Pressensé et son temps, 1824–1891.* Lausanne, 1916.

Corrigan, Raymond. *The Church and the Nineteenth Century.* Milwaukee, 1948.

Crooks, George R. *Life and Letters of the Rev. John McClintock, D.D.* New York, 1876.

Dansette, Adrien. *Histoire religieuse de la France contemporaine.* Paris, 1965.

Darbon, Michel. *Le Conflit entre la droite et la gauche dans le catholicisme français, 1830–1953.* Toulouse, 1953.

Delassus, Henri. *L'Américanisme et la conjuration antichrétienne.* Lille, 1899.

Doen, O. *Histoire de la société biblique protestante de Paris, 1818 à 1868.* Paris, 1868.

Domenech, Emmanuel. *Souvenirs d'outre-mer: Mes missions au crépuscule de la vie.* Paris, 1884.

Duclos, R. P. *Histoire du protestantisme français au Canada et aux Etats-Unis.* 2 vols. Paris, 1913.

Duncan, Herman Cope. *The Diocese of Louisiana: Some of Its History, 1838–1888.* New Orleans, 1888.

Ellis, John T. *The Life of James Cardinal Gibbons, Archbishop of Baltimore, 1834–1921.* 2 vols. Milwaukee, 1953.

Félice, G. de. *History of the Protestants of France.* New York, 1851.

Fonsegrive, Georges. "Américanisme et Américains." *La Quinzaine,* XXVII (1899), 306–318.

Forbes, Allan, and Paul F. Cadman. *Boston and Some Noted Emigrés.* Boston, 1938.

French Protestant Church, Charleston, S.C. *The Huguenot Church.* Charleston, S.C., 1912.

Garraghan, Gilbert Joseph. *The Catholic Church in Chicago, 1673–1871.* Chicago, 1921.

Gibbons, James Cardinal. *A Retrospect of Fifty Years.* 2 vols. Baltimore, 1916.

Girard, Louis. *Le Catholicisme en Europe de 1814 à 1878.* Paris, 1862.

Goodrich, Chauncey W. *Historical Sermon at the 70th Anniversary of the American Church, 21 rue de Berri.* Paris, 1927.

Guillemin, Henri. *Histoire des catholiques français au XIXe siècle, 1815–1905.* Paris, 1947.

Hamon, André Jean Marie. *The Life of Cardinal Cheverus, Archbishop of Bordeaux and Formerly Bishop of Boston, in Massachusetts.* Boston, 1839.

Herbmann, Charles G. "The Sulpicians in the United States." U.S. Catholic Historical Society, *Records and Studies*, IX (1916), 9–100, and X (1917), 38–116.

Hickey, Edward John. "The Society of the Propagation of the Faith: Its Foundation, Organization and Success (1822–1922)." Ph.D. dissertation, Catholic University of America, 1922.

Holden, Vincent F. "A Myth in L'Américanisme." *CHR*, XXXI (1945), 154–70.

Houtin, Albert. *L'Américanisme*. Paris, 1904.

Jonveaux, Emile. "Les Catholiques du nouveau-monde jugés par les protestants." *Le Correspondant*, LXXVI (1868), 826–64.

Joré, L. " Les Pères de la congrégation des Sacres-Coeurs en Californie, 1832–1837, 1848–1856, 1909–1935." *French American Review*, III (1950), 34–57.

Latreille, André. *Les Forces religieuses et la vie politique: Le Catholicisme et le protestantisme*. Paris, 1951.

Leclerc, Max. *Choses d'Amérique: Les Crises économique et religieuse aux Etats-Unis en 1890*. Paris, 1891.

LeGay, C. E. "Work of the American Chapel: Poor Children in Paris." *Christian World*, XXXV (February, 1884), 48–51.

"Lettres des missionaires français en Amérique." *Annales de l'Association de la Propagation de la Foi*. 12 vols. Lyon, 1827–1850.

Louvet, Louis Eugene. *Les Missions catholiques au XIXᵉ siécle*. Paris, 1895.

McAvoy, Thomas T. "Americanism, Fact and Fiction." *CHR*, XXXI(1945), 133–53.

———. *The Catholic Church in Indiana, 1789–1834*. New York, 1940.

———. *The Great Crisis in American Catholic History, 1895–1900*. Chicago, 1957.

Magnan, Dennis M. A. *Histoire de la race française aux Etats-Unis*. Paris, 1913.

Maignen, Charles. *Le Père Hecker: Est-il un saint? Etudes sur l'Américanisme*. Paris, 1898.

Maurain, Jean. *La Politique ecclésiastique du Second Empire de 1852 à 1869*. Paris, 1930.

Maynard, Theodore. *The Story of American Catholicism*. New York, 1941.

Mears, David O. *Life of Edward Norris Kirk, D.D.* Boston, 1877.

Meaux, Marie Camille Alfred. "Le Congrès catholique et le parlement des religions à Chicago." *Le Correspondant*, CLXXIV (1894), 3–16.

———. *L'Eglise catholique et la liberté aux Etats-Unis*. Paris, 1893.

Mellor, Alec. *Histoire de l'anticléricalisme français*. Tours, 1966.

Meng, John J. "A Century of American Catholicism as Seen Through French Eyes." *CHR*, XXVII (1941), 39–68.

Mérimée, Prosper. *Etudes anglo-américaines*. Paris, 1930.

Miller, Charles J. "British and American Influences on the Religious Revival in French Europe, 1816–48." Ph.D. dissertation, Northwestern University, 1947.

Milling, Chapman J. "The Acadian and San Domingan French." *Transactions of the Huguenot Society of South Carolina*, No. 62. Charleston, S.C., 1957. Pp. 5–36.

Montuclard, Maurice. *Conscience religieuse et démocratie: La Deuxième démocratie chrétienne en France, 1891–1902.* Paris, 1965.

Moreau, C. N. *Les Prêtres français émigrés aux Etats-Unis.* Paris, 1856.

Moynihan, James H. *The Life of Archbishop John Ireland.* New York, 1953.

Paré, George. *The Catholic Church in Detroit, 1701–1888.* Detroit, 1951.

Péchenard, P. L. "The End of Americanism in France." *NAR,* CLXX (1900), 420–32.

Phillips, C. S. *The Church in France, 1848–1907.* London, 1936.

Poujol, Pierre. *Notes sur une histoire sociale du protestantisme dans la France moderne, 1870–1931.* Paris, 1960, 1961.

Puaux, N. A. F. *Histoire populaire du protestantisme français.* Paris, 1894.

Ruskowski, Leo F. "French Emigré Priests in the United States, 1791–1815." Ph.D. dissertation, Catholic University of America, 1940.

Shahan, Thomas J. "The Catholicism of France." *Conservative Review,* III (1900), 278–98.

Smith, James W., and A. L. Jamison, eds. *The Shaping of American Religion.* 4 vols. Princeton, N.J., 1961.

Spencer, Philip. *Politics of Belief in Nineteenth Century France.* London, 1954.

Sperry. Willard L. *Religion in America.* New York, 1946.

Stephan, Raoul. *Histoire du protestantisme français.* Paris, 1961.

Sweet, William W. *Religion in the Development of American Culture.* New York, 1952.

Tardivel, Jules. *La Situation religieuse aux Etats-Unis: Illusions et réalité.* Paris, 1900.

Thurber, Edward G. *Historical Sermon, Preached at the 50th Anniversary of the American Church, Paris.* Paris, 1907.

Véron, Eugène. "Des Progrès de la liberté dans la théologie protestante." *Revue nationale et étrangère* (September–October, 1861), 321–55.

Veuillot, Eugène. "Etudes sur les Etats-Unis." *Revue du monde catholique,* XVII (1867), 75–101.

Wade, Mason. "The French Parish and Survivance in Nineteenth Century New England." *CHR,* XXXVI (1950), 163–89.

Weill, Georges. "Le Protestantisme français au XIXᵉ siècle." *Revue de synthèse historique,* XXIII (1911), 210–39.

Will, Allen S. *Life of James Cardinal Gibbons.* Baltimore, 1911.

PHILOSOPHY

Allen, Gay Wilson. *William James: A Biography.* London, 1967.

Allen, J. H. "Comte's Positive Philosophy." *Christian Examiner,* L (1851), 174–202.

Anderson, Paul R., and Max H. Fisch. *Philosophy in America: From the Puritans to James.* New York, 1939.

Barthélemy-Saint Hilaire, J. *Victor Cousin: Sa vie et sa correspondance.* 3 vols. Paris, 1895.

Baym, Max I. *The French Education of Henry Adams.* New York, 1951.

Becelaere, L. Van. *La Philosophie en Amérique, depuis les origines jusqu'à nos jours* (1607–1900): *Essai historique.* New York, 1904.

Bergson, Henri. *The Creative Mind: A Study in Metaphysics.* New York, 1946.

Boas, George. *French Philosophies of the Romantic Period.* Baltimore, 1925.

Bourdeau, J. *Pragmatisme et modernisme.* Paris, 1909.

Brauer, Herman. "The Philosophy of Ernest Renan." Ph.D. dissertation, University of Wisconsin, 1902.

Brownson, Orestes A. "Cousin's Philosophy." *Christian Examiner,* XXI (1836), 33–64.

———. "Jouffroy's Contributions to Philosophy." *Christian Examiner,* XXII (1837), 181–217.

———. *The Works of Orestes A. Brownson.* 20 vols. New York, 1966.

"Orestes A. Brownson as a Philosopher: Victor Cousin and His Philosophy." *American Quarterly Church Review and Ecclesiastical Register,* XIX (January, 1868), 532–47.

Caird, Edward. *The Social Philosophy and Religion of Comte.* New York, 1968. Originally published in Glasgow, 1885.

Chaumieux, André. "William James." *RDDM* (October 15, 1910), 836–64.

Chinard, Gilbert. *Jefferson et les idéologues: D'Après sa correspondance inédite avec Destutt de Tracy, Cabanis, J.-B. Say et Auguste Comte.* Baltimore, 1925.

Comte, Auguste. *Lettres d'Auguste Comte à Henry Edger et à M. John Metcalf.* Paris, 1889.

"Comte's Religion of Humanity." *Christian Examiner,* LXIII (1857), 18–36.

"Comtean Atheism." *American Quarterly Church Review and Ecclesiastical Register,* XX (July, 1868), 169–83, and XX (October, 1868), 329–43.

Cousin, Victor. *Elements of Psychology.* Translated, with an introduction, by Caleb S. Henry. New York. 1842.

Delattre, Floris. "William James Bergsonien." *Revue anglo-américaine,* I (1923–24), 1–24, 135–44.

Dugard, Marie. *Ralph Waldo Emerson: Sa vie et son oeuvre.* Paris, 1907.

Dumas, Georges. "Saint-Simon, Père du Positivisme." *Revue philosophique,* LVII (1904), 136–57, 263–87.

Durkheim, Emile. "Saint-Simon, fondateur du positivisme et de la sociologie." *Revue philosophique,* XCIX (1925), 321–41.

Dwight, Timothy. *Travels in New England and New York.* 4 vols. London, 1823.

Echeverria, Durand. *Mirage in the West: A History of the French Image of American Society to 1815.* Princeton, N.J., 1957.

"Faith and Science: Comte's Positive Philosophy." *Methodist Review,* XXXIV (1825), 9–37, 169–98.

Fleming, Donald. *John William Draper and the Religion of Science.* Philadelphia, 1950.

Fletcher, Ronald. *Auguste Comte and the Making of Sociology.* London, 1966.

Fouillée, A. "The Philosophy of Taine and Renan." *International Quarterly,* VI (1902–1903), 260–80.

Frothingham, Octavius Brooks. *Transcendentalism in New England: A History.* New York, 1876, 1959.

Gabriel, Ralph Henry. *The Course of American Thought.* New York, 1940.

Girard, William. "Du Transcendentalisme considéré essentiellement dans sa définition et ses origines françaises." *University of California Publications in Modern Philology,* IV (1916), 351–498.

———. "Du Transcendentalisme considéré sous son aspect social." *University of California Publications in Modern Philology,* VIII (1918), 154–226.

Gohdes, Clarence L. F. *The Periodicals of American Transcendentalism.* Durham, N.C., 1931.

Green, Arnold W. *Henry Charles Carey: Nineteenth Century Sociologist.* Philadelphia, 1951.

Gunn, J. Alexander. "Ribot and His Contribution to Psychology." *Monist,* XXXIV (1924), 1–14.

Hawkins, Richard Laurin. *Auguste Comte and the United States, 1816–1853.* Cambridge, Mass., 1936.

———. *Positivism in the United States, 1853–1861.* Cambridge, Mass., 1938.

Jaffe, Adrian. "Letters of Henry P. Tappan to Victor Cousin." *Michigan History,* XXXVI (1952), 300–306.

James, William. *Collected Essays and Reviews.* London, 1920.

———. *The Letters of William James.* 2 vols. Boston, 1920.

———. *A Pluralistic Universe.* New York, 1909.

———. *The Principles of Psychology.* 2 vols. London, 1890.

Janet, Pierre. *Principles of Psychotherapy.* New York, 1924.

Kallen, Horace Meyer. *William James and Henri Bergson: A Study in Contrasting Theories of Life.* Chicago, 1914.

LeBreton, Maurice. *La Personnalité de William James.* Paris, 1929.

Leighton, Walter L. *French Philosophers and New England Transcendentalism.* New York, 1968.

Lenoir, Raymond. "The Psychology of Ribot and Contemporary Thought." *Monist,* XXX (1920), 365–94.

Leroux, Emmanuel. *Le Pragmatisme américain et anglais: Etude historique et critique.* Paris, 1923.

Lovejoy, Arthur O. "William James as Philosopher." *International Journal of Ethics,* XXI (1911), 125–53.

Mackay, Fred H., and Emile Legrand. "Jean Martin Charcot, 1825–1893." *Archives of Neurology and Psychiatry,* XXXIV (1935), 390–400.

Manuel, Frank E. *The World of Henri Saint-Simon.* Notre Dame, Indiana, 1963.

Mead, George H. *Movements of Thought in the Nineteenth Century.* Chicago, 1936.

Michaud, Régis. *Mystiques et réalistes anglo-saxons, d'Emerson à Bernard Shaw.* Paris, 1918.

Perry, Charles M. *Henry Philip Tappan: Philosopher and University President.* Ann Arbor, Mich., 1933.

Perry, Ralph Barton. *The Thought and Character of William James.* New York, 1954.

Pochmann, Henry A. *German Culture in America: Philosophical and Literary Influences,* 1600–1900. Madison, Wisc., 1957.

Rankin, Henry William. "Charles Woodruff Shields and the Unity of Science." *Princeton Theological Review,* XIII (1915), 49–91.

Riley, Isaac Woodbridge. *American Thought: From Puritanism to Pragmatism and Beyond.* New York, 1941.

———. *American Philosophy: The Early Schools.* New York, 1958.

———. "Continental Critics of Pragmatism: French Critics." *Journal of Philosophy, Psychology, and Scientific Methods,* VIII (1911), 225–32.

———. "La Philosophie française en Amérique." *Revue philosophique* LXXXIV (1917), 393–428, and LXXXVII (1919), 369–423.

Robertson, John M. *Ernest Renan.* London, 1924.

Rogers, Arthur Kenyon. *English and American Philosophy Since* 1800: *A Critical Survey.* New York, 1922.

Saisset, Emile. "La Philosophie positive." *RDDM* (July 15, 1846), 185–220.

Schneider, Herbert W. *A History of American Philosophy.* New York, 1947.

Shillan, David. *The Order of Mankind as Seen by Auguste Comte.* Richmond Hill, England, 1963.

Simon, W. M. *European Positivism in the Nineteenth Century: An Essay in Intellectual History.* Ithaca, N.Y., 1963.

Smith, James Ward. "Pragmatism, Realism and Positivism in the United States." *Mind,* New Series, LXI, No. 242 (April, 1952), 190–208.

Smith, Martha B. "The Story of Icaria." *Annals of Iowa* (1965), 36–64.

Thilly, Frank. "La Philosophie américaine contemporaine." *Revue de métaphysique et de morale,* XVI (1908), 607–634.

Tillett, A. S. "Some Saint-Simonian Criticism of the United States Before 1835." *Romanic Review,* LII (1961), 3–16.

Wahl, Jean. *Les Philosophes pluralistes, d'Angleterre et d'Amérique.* Paris, 1920.

Wallace, Horace Binney. *Art, Scenery and Philosophy in Europe.* Philadelphia, 1855.

Weinstein, Leo. *Hippolyte Taine.* New York, 1972.

LITERATURE

Aldridge, Alfred Owen. "The Debut of American Letters in France." *French American Review,* III (1950), 1–23.

Allen, Gay Wilson, ed. *Walt Whitman Abroad.* Syracuse, N.Y., 1955.

Arnavon, Cyrille. *Les Débuts du roman réaliste américain et l'influence française.* Paris, 1946.

———. *Histoire littéraire des Etats-Unis.* Paris, 1953.

———. *Les Lettres américaines devant la critique française,* 1887–1917. Paris, 1951.

Asselineau, Roger. *The Evolution of Walt Whitman.* 2 vols. Cambridge, Mass., 1960–62.

———. *The Literary Reputation of Mark Twain, from* 1910 *to* 1950: *A Critical Essay and a Bibliography.* Paris, 1954.

Baldensperger, Fernand. "Balzac and His Conquest of the United States." *American Society Legion of Honor Magazine,* XXI (1950).

——. *James Fenimore Cooper in France.* Franco-American Pamphlets, Second Series, No. 12. New York ,1940.

—— "Walt Whitman and France." *Columbia University Quarterly,* XXI (1919), 298–309.

Bandy, W. T. "New Light on Baudelaire and Poe." *Yale French Studies,* No. 10 (1952), 65–69.

Basch, Victor. "Individualistes modernes, Ralph Waldo Emerson." *La Grande revue* (April, 1903), 73–102.

Bazalgette, Léon. *Walt Whitman: The Man and His Work.* Garden City, N.Y., 1920.

Bentzon, Thérèse. "Un Poète américain: Walt Whitman." *RDDM,* XLII (1872), 565–82.

Biencourt, Marius. *Une Influence du naturalisme français en Amérique: Frank Norris.* Paris, 1933.

Blanc. Marie Thérèse. *Les Nouveaux romanciers américains.* Paris, 1885.

Blémont, Emile. "La Poésie en Angleterre et aux Etats-Unis: Walt Whitman." *La Renaissance littéraire et artistique* (June and July, 1872), 53–55, 86–87, 90–91.

Bosset, Georgette. *Fenimore Cooper et le roman d'adventure en France vers 1830.* Paris, 1928.

Bovet, Marie-Anne de. "Un écrivain cosmopolite, Henry James." *La Nouvelle revue* (February, 1891), 532–56.

Bowen, Ray P. "A Comparison of the Methods of Composition in Cooper and Balzac." *French American Review,* III (1950), 297–313.

Boyesen, Hjalmor Hjorth. *Literary and Social Silhouettes.* New York, 1894.

Brooks, Van Wyck. *Howells: His Life and World.* New York, 1959.

——. *New England: Indian Summer,* 1865–1915. New York, 1940.

Brown, H. Junius. "A Few French Celebrities." *HNMM,* XLVII (1873), 833–42.

Brown, Ralph H. "American Opinion on Ernest Renan, 1863–1892." M. A. thesis, Columbia University, 1938.

Brown, Ruth E. "A French Interpreter of New England's Literature, 1846–1865." *NEQ,* XIII (1940), 305–21.

Bunner, H. C. *"Made in France": French Tales Retold with a United States Twist.* New York, 1893.

Cabot, James E. *A Memoir of Ralph Waldo Emerson.* 2 vols. Boston, 1887.

Cady, Edwin H. *The Realist at War: The Mature Years,* 1885–1920, *of William Dean Howells.* Syracuse, N.Y., 1958.

——. *The Road to Realism: The Early Years,* 1837–1889, *of William Dean Howells.* Syracuse, N.Y., 1956.

Cairns, William B. *A History of American Literature.* New York, 1930.

Cambiaire, Célestin Pierre. *The Influence of Edgar Allan Poe in France.* New York, 1927.

Cardwell, Guy Adams, Jr. "Charleston Periodicals, 1795–1860: A Study in Literary Influences." Ph.D. dissertation, University of North Carolina, 1936.

Catel, Jean, *Walt Whitman: La Naissance du poète.* Paris, 1929.

Caufeild, Ruby Van Allen. *The French Literature of Louisiana.* New York, 1929.

Cestre, Charles. "American Literature Through French Eyes." *Yale Review,* X (1920), 85–98.

———. "Emerson et la France." In *Harvard et la France.* Paris, 1936.

———. "Le Lyrisme de Walt Whitman." *Anglo-French Review,* I (1919), 395–408.

———. "Poe et Baudelaire." *Revue anglo-américaine,* XI (1934), 322–29.

———. "Walt Whitman: L'Inadapté." *Revue anglo-américaine,* VII (1930), 385–408.

———. "Walt Whitman: Le Mystique, le lyrique." *Revue anglo-américaine,* VII (1930), 481–504.

———. "Walt Whitman, le poète." *Revue anglo-américaine,* VIII (1930), 19–41.

Chadbourne, Richard M. "The Essay World of Emile Montégut." *PMLA,* LXXVI (1961), 98–120.

Chasles, Philarète. *Etudes sur la littérature et les moeurs des Anglo-Américains au XIXᵉ siècle.* Paris, 1851.

Chinard, Gilbert. "Early Intellectual Intercourse Between the United States and France." *California University Chronicle,* XVII (1915), 370–80.

———. "La Littérature française dans le sud des Etats-Unis, d'après le *Southern Literary Messenger* (1834–1864)." *RDLC,* VIII (1928), 87–99.

Chrétien, Louis-Emile. "La Pensée morale de Nathaniel Hawthorne, 1804–1864, symboliste néo-puritain: Esquisse d'une interprétation." Ph.D. dissertation, Université de Paris, 1932.

Clavel, Marcel. *Fenimore Cooper and His Critics: American, British and French Criticism of the Novelist's Early Work.* Aix-en-Provence, 1938.

Cochin, Henri. "Un Poète américain: Walt Whitman." *Le Correspondant, CIX* (November 25, 1877), 634–60.

Cohen, Rubin. "Balzac in the United States During the Nineteenth Century: A Study in Franco-American Cultural Relations." Ph.D. dissertation ,Columbia University, 1950.

Dargan, E. P. "Balzac and Cooper: Les Chouans." *Modern Philology,* XIII (1915), 193–213.

Denny, Margaret and William H. Gilman, eds. *The American Writer and the European Tradition.* Minneapolis, 1950.

Dépret, Louis. "La Poésie en Amérique: Henry Wadsworth Longfellow." *Mémoires de la Société des Sciences de Lille,* Fourth Series, No. 2 (1876), 293–341.

Dhaleine, L. *N. Hawthorne: Sa Vie et son oeuvre.* Paris, 1905.

Doumic, René. "Nos Humoristes." *RDDM* (October 15, 1899), 924–35.

Dugard, Marie. *Ralph Waldo Emerson: Sa Vie, son oeuvre.* Paris, 1907.

Edel, Leon. *Henry James.* 5 vols. Philadelphia, 1962–72.

Edwards, Herbert. "Zola and the American Critics." *American Literature,* IV (1932), 114–29.

Emerson, Ralph Waldo. *Representative Men: Seven Lectures.* Boston, 1856.

Epuy, Michel. *Anthologie des humoristes anglais et américains du 17ᵉ siècle à nos jours*. Paris, 1910.

Estève, Edward. "Longfellow et la France." *Bowdoin College Bulletin*, No. 146 (October, 1925).

Faust, Camille. *Le Génie d'Edgar Poe*. Paris, 1925.

Fay, Eliot G. "Balzac and Henry James." *French Reveiw*, XXIV (1951), 325–30.

———. "Henry James as a Critic of French Literature." *French American Review*, II (1949), 184–93.

Field, Mary Lee. "Henry James's Criticism of French Literature." Ph.D. dissertation, Wayne State University, 1972.

Foerster, Norman, ed. *The Reinterpretation of American Literature*. New York, 1928.

Forgues, E. D. "Etudes sur le roman anglais et américain: Les Contes d'Edgar A. Poe." *RDDM* (October, 1846), 341–66.

Françon, Marcel. "Poe et Baudelaire." *PMLA*, (1945), 841–59.

Frierson, William C., and Herbert Edwards. "The Impact of French Naturalism on American Critical Opinion, 1877–1892." *PMLA*, LXIII (1948), 1007–16.

Frothingham, O. B. "The Morally Objectionable in Literature." *NAR*, CXXXV (1882), 323–38.

Garnier, Marie-Reine. *Henry James et la France*. Paris, 1927.

George, Albert J. "Early American Criticism of Victor Hugo." *French Review*, XI (1938), 287–93.

Gibb, Margaret M. *Le Roman de Bas-de Cuir: Etude sur Fenimore Cooper et son influence en France*. Paris, 1927.

Gilkey, Robert. "Mark Twain: Voyageur et son image de l'Europe." Ph.D. dissertation, Université de Paris, 1951.

Griffith, Benjamin. "Balzac aux Etats-Unis." Ph.D. dissertation, Université de Paris, 1931.

Grossman, James. *James Fenimore Cooper*. New York, 1949.

Harper, George McLean. *Masters of French Literature*. Freeport, N.Y., 1901. Reprinted, 1968.

———. "The Place of French Literature." *Atlantic Monthly*, LXXXV (1900), 360–70.

Harrison, Katharine. "A French Forecast of American Literature." *South Atlantic Quarterly*, XXV (1926), 350–60.

Hawthorne, Nathaniel. *Passages from the French and Italian Notebooks*. Boston, 1874.

Hazard, Paul. "Chateaubriand et la littérature des Etats-Unis." *RDLC*, VIII (1928), 46–61.

Hazeltine, Mayo W. *Chats About Books, Poets, and Novelists*. New York, 1883.

Hellman, George S. *Washington Irving, Esquire: Ambassador at Large from the New World to the Old*. New York, 1925.

Henry, Marjorie Louise. "La Contribution d'un américain au symbolisme français: Stuart Merrill." Ph.D. dissertation, Université de Paris, 1927.

Higginson, Thomas W. *Henry Wadsworth Longfellow*. Boston, 1902.

Hocking, Elton. *Ferdinand Brunetière: The Evolution of a Critic.* Wisconsin University Studies in Language and Literature, No. 36. Madison, 1936.

Hoole, William Stanley. "The Literary and Cultural Background of Charleston, 1830–1860." Ph.D. dissertation, Duke University, 1934.

Hornstein, Simon. *Mark Twain: La Faillite d'un idéal.* Paris, 1950.

Howard, Besse D. "The First French Estimate of Emerson." *NEQ,* X (1937), 447–63.

Howells, William Dean. "Emile Zola." *NAR,* CLXXV (1902), 587–96.

Huneker, James. *Egoists: A Book of Supermen.* New York, 1909.

Jackson, Ernest. *The Critical Reception of Gustave Flaubert in the United States, 1860–1960.* The Hague, 1966.

Jacoby, John E. "Le Mysticisme dans la pensée américaine." Ph.D. dissertation, Université de Paris, 1931.

James, Henry. "Emile Zola." *Atlantic Monthly,* XCII (1903), 193–210.

———. *French Poets and Novelists.* London, 1878. Reprinted, 1972.

———. *The Lesson of Balzac.* New York, 1905.

———. "The Minor French Novelists." *Galaxy,* XXI (1876), 219–33.

Jannet, Claudio. *Les Etats-Unis contemporains.* 2 vols. Paris, 1889.

Jensen, G. E. *The Life and Letters of Henry Cuyler Bunner.* Durham, N.C., 1939.

Jeune, Simon. *De F. T. Graindorge à A. O. Barnabooth: Les Types américains dans le roman et le théâtre français, 1861–1917.* Paris, 1963.

Johnson, Maurice O. *Walt Whitman as a Critic of Literature.* University of Nebraska Studies in Language, Literature, No. 16. Lincoln, Nebr., 1938.

Jones, Howard Mumford. "American Comments on George Sand, 1837–1848." *American Literature,* III (1932), 389–407.

———. *History and the Contemporary: Essays in Nineteenth Century Literature.* Madison, Wisc., 1964.

———. "The Influence of European Ideas in Nineteenth Century America." *American Literature,* VII (1935), 241–73.

———. *The Theory of American Literature.* Ithaca, N.Y., 1966.

Jones, Malcolm B. "French Literature and American Criticism, 1870–1900." Ph.D. dissertation, Harvard, 1935.

———. "Translations of Zola in the United States Prior to 1900." *Modern Language Notes,* LV (1940), 520–24.

Jones, P. M. "Whitman in France." *Modern Language Review,* X (1915), 1–27.

Jones, Virgil L. "Gustave Aimard." *Southern Review,* XV (1930), 452–68.

Kanes, Martin. "La Fortune de Walt Whitman." Ph.D. dissertation, Université de Paris, 1953.

Kaplan, Harold. *Democratic Humanism and American Literature.* Chicago, 1972.

Keller, Hans. "Emerson in Frankreich: Wirkungen und Parallelen." Ph.D. dissertation, Universität zu Giessen, 1932.

Knapp, Samuel L. *American Cultural History, 1607–1829.* With an introduction by Richard Beale Davis and Ben Harris McClary. Gainesville, Fla., 1961.

Krause, Sydney J. *Mark Twain as Critic.* Baltimore, 1967.

Lacretelle, Pierre de. *Vie politique de Victor Hugo.* Paris, 1928.

Lagarde, Marie Louise. "Charles Testut: Critic, Journalist and Literary Socialist." M.A. thesis, Tulane University ,1948.

Lanux, Pierre de. *Young France and New America.* New York, 1917.

Lauvrière, Emile. *Edgar Poe: Sa Vie et son oeuvre.* Paris, 1904.

———. *Le Génie morbide d'Edgar Poe: Poésies et contes.* Paris, 1935.

———. "La Morbidité en Hawthorne." *Revue germanique,* (January–February, 1906), 130–35.

———. *The Strange Life and Strange Loves of Edgar Allan Poe.* Translated by Edwin Gile Rich. Philadelphia, 1935.

LeBreton, André. "Origines du roman balzacien." *Revue de Paris,* V (1903), 781–826.

LeBreton, Maurice. "Un Centenaire: Mark Twain." *Revue anglo-américaine,* XII (1935), 401–19.

LeBreton-Savigny, Monique. *Victor Hugo et les Américains, 1825–1885.* Paris, 1971.

Lemonnier, Leon. *Edgar Poe et la critique française de 1845 à 1875. Paris,* 1928.

———. *Edgar Poe et les poètes français.* Paris, 1932.

———. "L'Influence d'Edgar Poe sur les conteurs français symbolistes et décadents." *RDLC,* XIII (1913), 102–33.

———. *Mark Twain.* Paris, 1946.

———. "Quelques vieux jugements français sur la littérature américaine." *La Revue Européenne,* New Series (July–December, 1927), 175–81.

Lewisohn, Ludwig. *The Story of American Literature.* New York, 1939.

Lucas, E. *La Littérature anti-esclavagiste au dix-neuvième siècle: Etude sur Madame Beecher Stowe et son influence en France.* Paris, 1930.

Lüdeke, Henry. "The Democracy of Henry Adams and Other Essays: Zola and the American Public." In *Schweizer anglistische Arbeiten.* Bern, 1950. Bd. 24, pp. 78–110.

MacClintock, Lander. "Sainte-Beuve's Critical Theory and Practice After 1849." Ph.D. dissertation, University of Chicago, 1920.

———. "Sainte Beuve and America." *PMLA,* LX (1945), 427–36.

McGee, Sidney Lauront. "La Littérature américaine dans la *Revue des deux mondes,* 1831–1900." Ph.D. dissertation, Université de Montpellier ,1927.

Mahieu, Robert G. *Sainte-Beuve aux Etats-Unis.* Princeton, 1945.

Mantz, Harold Elmer. *French Criticism of American Literature Before 1850.* New York, 1917.

Markow, George. "Henry James et la France, 1843–1876." Ph.D. dissertation, Université de Paris, 1952.

Matthew, John. "Poe's Indebtedness to French Literature." *French Review* (February, 1936), 217–23.

Matthews, J. Brander. *French Dramatists of the 19th Century.* New York, 1901.

———. *These Many Years: Recollections of a New Yorker.* New York, 1917.

Matthiessen, Francis O. *Theodore Dreiser.* New York, 1951.

Mauclair, Camille. *Le Génie d'Edgar Poe, la légende et la vérité: La Méthode, la pensée, l'influence en France.* Paris, 1925

Messac, Régis. "Fenimore Cooper et son influence en France." *PMLA,* XLIII (1928), 1,199–1,201.

———. *Influences françaises dans l'oeuvre d'Edgar Poe.* Paris, 1929.

Michaud, Régis. "L'Art de Henry James." *Revue germanique,* III (1911), 257–73.

———. "Emerson et Montaigne." *Revue germanique,* X (1914), 417–42.

———. *L'Esthétique d'Emerson: La Nature, l'art, l'histoire.* Pairs, 1931.

———. *Mystiques et réalistes anglo-saxons.* Paris, 1918.

"Modern French Romance." *New York Review,* IV (1839), 441–56.

Mönch, Walter. *Frankreichs Dichtung von der Renaissance zur Gegenwart im Spiegel geistesgeschichtlicher Probleme.* Berlin, 1933.

———. *Das Gastmahl. Begegnungen abendländischer Dichter und Philosophen.* Hamburg, 1947.

Montégut, Emile. "Nathaniel Hawthorne." *Moniteur Universel,* June 27, July 11, and August 27, 1864.

———. "Un Penseur et poète américain: Ralph Waldo Emerson." *RDDM,* New Series, XIX (August, 1847), 462–93.

Mordell, Albert, ed. *Literary Reviews and Essays by Henry James on American, English, and French Literature.* New York, 1957.

Morris, George D. *Fenimore Cooper et Edgar Poe d'après la critique française du 19e siècle.* Paris, 1912.

———. "French Criticism of Poe." *South Atlantic Quarterly* (October, 1915), 324–29.

———. "Washington Irving's Fiction in the Light of French Criticism." *Indiana University Studies,* III (1916), 5–26.

Muenier, Pierre-Alexis. *Emile Montégut: Etude biographique et critique d'après des documents inédits.* Paris, 1925.

Navarre, Charles. *Les Grands écrivains étrangers et leur influence sur la littérature française.* Paris, 1930.

Oakes, Frances Etherudge. "The Whitman Controversy in France." Ph.D. dissertation, Florida State University, 1955.

Oda, Wilbur H. *The Subject of Realism in the* Revue de Paris, *1829–1858.* Philadelphia, 1943.

O'Rell, Max. "French versus Anglo-Saxon Immorality." *NAR,* CLIX (1894), 545–50.

O'Sullivan, Vincent. "La Littérature américaine." *Mercure de France,* January 16, 1919, pp. 246–57.

Pacey, W. C. D. "Henry James and His French Contemporaries." *American Literature,* XIII (1941), 240–56.

Page, Curtis Hidden. "Poe in France." *Nation,* LXXXVIII (January 14, 1909), 32–34.

Parish, Olive Shade. "The French View of Emerson." M.A. thesis, Yale University, 1929.

Parish, Lestrois. *Emerson's View of France and the French.* Franco-American Pamphlet Series, No. 5. New York, 1935.

Parrington, Vernon Louis. *Main Currents in American Thought.* 3 vols. New York, 1930.

Partridge, Eric. "Fenimore Cooper's Influence on the French Romantics." *Modern Language Review*, XX (1925), 174–78.

Patterson, Arthur S. *L'Influence d'Edgar Poe sur Charles Baudelair.* Grenoble, 1903.

Peyre, Henri. "American Literature Through French Eyes." *Virginia Quarterly Review*, XXIII (1947), 421–38.

———. *Modern Literature: The Literature of France.* Englewood Cliffs, N.J., 1966.

Phillips, Eva Margaret. *Philarète Chasles.* Paris, 1933.

Powers, Lyall H. "Henry James and French Naturalism." Ph.D. dissertation, Indiana University, 1955.

———. *Henry James and the Naturalist Movement.* East Lansing, 1971.

Pucciani, Oreste F. "The Literary Reputation of Walt Whitman in France." Ph.D. dissertation, Harvard, 1943.

Quesnel, Leo. "La Littérature aux Etats-Unis." *La Nouvelle revue*, XVI (May 1, 1882), 131–54.

———. "La Littérature d'imagination aux Etats-Unis." *La Revue politique et littéraire*, XIII (February 14, 1874), 777–82.

———. "Poètes américains: Walt Whitman." *Revue politique et littéraire*, Series 3, XXXIII (1884), 212–17.

Quinn, Arthur Hobson. *Edgar Allan Poe: A Critical Biography.* New York, 1941.

———. *A History of the American Drama: From the Beginning to the Civil War.* New York, 1943.

Quinn, Patrick Francis. *The French Face of Edgar Poe.* Carbondale, Ill., 1957.

Rabinowitz, Albert L. "Criticism of French Novels in Boston Magazines, 1830–60." *NEQ*, XIV (1941), 488–504.

Recht, Jean-Jacques. *Mark Twain and Europe.* Paris, 1951.

Rhodes, S. A. "The Influence of Walt Whitman on André Gide." *Romanic Review*, XXXI (1940), 156–71.

Richepin, Jean. *L'Ame américaine à travers quelques-uns de ses interprètes.* Paris, 1920.

Riding, Laura. *Contemporaries and Snobs.* New York, 1928.

Rosselet, Jeanne. "A Contribution to the Study of Victor Hugo in the United States." Ph.D. dissertation, Radcliffe College, 1930.

Roz, Firmin. *L'Evolution des idées et des moeurs américaines.* Paris, 1931.

———. "L'Idéalisme américain: Ralph Waldo Emerson." *RDDM* (February, 1902), 651–75.

Salvan, Albert J. *Zola aux Etats-Unis.* Providence, R.I., 1943.

Sarrazin, Gabriel. "Poètes modernes de l'Amérique." *La Nouvelle revue,* LII (May 1, 1888), 164–84.

Schalck de la Faverie, A. "Henry Wadsworth Longfellow." *Revue britannique* (1901), 247–68.

———. *Les Premiers interprètes de la pensée américaine: Essai d'histoire et de littérature sur l'évolution du puritanisme aux Etats-Unis.* Paris, 1909.

———. "Washington Irving." *Revue britannique* (1901), 43–52.

Schinz, Albert. "Victor Hugo: Le Grand poète humanitaire; champion de la cause de la paix universelle; promoteur de l'idée des Etats-Unis d'Europe." *French Review* (November, 1935), 11–25.

Scott, Arthur Lincoln. "Mark Twain as a Critic of Europe." Ph.D. dissertation, University of Michigan, 1947.

———. *Mark Twain at Large*. Chicago, 1969.

Seylaz, Louis. *Edgar Poe et les premiers symbolistes français*. Lausanne, 1923.

Shepherd, James L. "L'Amérique du Nord dans la littérature française, 1830–1840." Ph.D. dissertation, Université de Paris, 1953.

Simon, Jean. "French Studies in American Literature and Civilization." *American Literature*, VI (1934), 176–90.

Smith, Francis Prescott. "Washington Irving and France." Ph.D. dissertation, Harvard, 1938.

Spiker, Claude C. "The *North American Review* and French Morals." West Virgina University, *Philological Studies* (September, 1943), 3–14.

Starkie, Enid. *Flaubert: The Making of the Master*. New York, 1967.

Stewart, Charles Oran. *Lowell and France*. Nashville, Tenn., 1951.

Symons, Arthur. "The Decadent Movement in Literature." *Harper's Magazine* (November, 1893), 858–67.

Syveton, Gabriel. "Le Père des humoristes: Mark Twain." *Revue bleue* (February 13, 1897), 207–12.

Taupin, René. "L'Influence du symbolisme français sur la poésie américaine de 1910 à 1920." *Bibliothèque de la Revue de Littérature Comparée*, LXII (1929).

Therriault, Marie-Carmel. *La Littérature française en Nouvelle-Angleterre*. Montreal, 1946.

Tieghem, Philippe Van. *Les Influences étrangères sur la littérature française 1550–1880*. Paris, 1961.

Tuckerman, H. T. "Balzac." *Southern Literary Messenger* (1859), 81–99.

Varigny, C. de. "La Littérature comique aux Etats-Unis." *Revue bleue* (April 16, 1887), 495–501.

Verne, Jules. "Edgar Poe et ses oeuvres." *Musée des Familles*, XXXI (1864), 193–208.

Villard, Léonie. *La Poésie américaine: Trois siècles de poésie lyrique et de poèmes narratifs*. Paris, 1945.

Virtanen, Reino. "Emile Montégut as a Critic of American Literature." *PLMA*, LXIII (1948), 1265–75.

———. "Tocqueville and William Ellery Channing." *American Literature*, XXII (1950), 21–28.

Wegelin, Christof. "The Concept of Europe in American Fiction from Irving to Hawthorne: A Study in the Literary Exploitation of the Changing Attitude Toward the Old World." Ph.D. dissertation, Johns Hopkins University, 1947.

———. *The Image of Europe in Henry James*. Dallas, 1958.

Weinberg, Bernard. *French Realism: The Critical Reaction, 1830–1870*. New York, 1937.

Wetherill, Peter M. *Charles Baudelaire et la poésie d'Edgar Allan Poe*. Paris, 1962.

Winters, Yvor. "Edgar Allan Poe: A Crisis in the History of American Obscurantism." *American Literature*, VIII (1937), 379–401.

Wittke, Carl. "The American Theme in Continental European Literatures." *MVHR*, XXVIII (1941), 3–26.

Wright, C. H. C. *The Background of Modern French Literature*. Boston, 1926.

Wright, Willard H. Flaubert: A Re-evaluation." *NAR*, CCVI (1917), 455–63.

"Writings of Victor Hugo. *NAR*, XLIII (1836), 133–63.

Wyzema, Théodor de. "Une Histoire de la littérature américaine." *RDDM*, CXLVII (1898), 936–45.

———. "Notes sur les littératures étrangères: Walt Whitman, 1819–1892. *Revue bleue*, XLIX (1892), 513–19.

Young, Charles Lowell. *Emerson's Montaigne*. New York, 1941.

THEATER

Antoine, André. *Memories of the Théâtre-libre*. Translated by Marvin A. Carlson. Coral Gables, Fla., 1964.

B——, Madame de. *Memoirs of Rachel*. New York, 1858.

Baroncelli, J. G. de. *Le Théâtre français à la Nouvelle Orléans*. New Orleans, 1906.

Beauvallet, Leon. *Rachel and the New World*. New York, 1856.

Bernhardt, Sarah. *Memories of My Life*. New York, 1968.

Cheney, Sheldon. *The Theatre: Three Thousand Years of Drama, Acting and Stagecraft*. New York, 1963.

Chevalley, Sylvie. "Histoire du théâtre français à New York, 1826–1856." Ph.D. dissertation, New York University, 1950.

Colombier, Marie. *Voyages de Sarah Bernhardt en Amérique*. Paris, 1881.

Curry, Wade Chester. "Steele Mackaye: Producer and Director." Ph.D. dissertation, University of Illinois, 1958.

Falk, Bernard. *Rachel the Immortal*. London, 1935.

Fellows, Otis. "Rachel and America: A Reappraisal." *Romanic Review*, XXX (December, 1939), 402–413.

Hapgood, Norman. *The Stage in America*, 1897–1900. New York, 1901.

Hewitt, Barnard. *Theatre U.S.A.*, 1665 to 1957. New York, 1959.

Hughes, Glenn. *A History of the American Theatre*, 1700–1950. New York, 1951.

James, Henry. "The Parisian Stage." *Nation*, XVI (January 9, 1873), 23–24.

Kendall, John Smith. "Sarah Bernhardt in New Orleans." *LHQ*, XXVI (July, 1943), 770–82.

Knepler, Henry. *The Gilded Stage: The Years of the Great International Actresses*. New York, 1968.

Lombard, C. M. "French Romanticism on the American Stage." *RDLC*, XLIII (April–June, 1969), 161–72.

Mackaye, Percy. *Epoch: The Life of Steele Mackaye, Genius of the Theatre, in Relation to His Times*. New York, 1927.

MacMinn, George R. *The Theater of the Golden Era in California*. Caldwell, Idaho. 1941.

Mason, Alexander Hamilton. *French Theatre in New York: A List of Plays,* 1899–1939. New York, 1940.

Matthews, J. Brander. *The Theatres of Paris.* London, 1880.

Mayorga, Margaret G. *A Short History of the American Drama: Commentaries on Plays Prior to 1920.* New York, 1932.

Miller, Anna Irene. *The Independent Theatre in Europe: 1887 to the Present.* New York, 1931.

Newton, Lewis William. "Creoles and Anglo-Americans in Old Louisiana: A Study in Cultural Conflicts," *SSSQ,* XIV (June, 1933), 31–48.

Odell, George C. D. *Annals of the New York Stage.* 15 vols. New York, 1927–49.

Pruner, Francis. *Les Luttes d'Antoine au théâtre libre.* 2 vols. Paris, 1964.

Scott, Leonora Cranch. *The Life and Letters of Christopher Pearse Cranch.* Boston, 1917.

Sedgwick, Charles. "Unpublished Letters of French Actresses, 1798–1861." Ph.D. dissertation, Harvard, 1950.

Villard, Léonie. *Le Théâtre américain.* Paris, 1929.

Ware, Ralph Hartman. *American Adaptations of French Plays on the New York and Philadelphia Stages from 1834 to the Civil War.* Philadelphia, 1930.

Waxman, S. M. *Antoine and the Théâtre-libre.* Paris, 1926.

MUSIC

Ackere, Jules Van. *L'Age d' or de la musique française,* 1870–1950. Bruxelles, 1966.

Arpin, P. *Biographie de L. M. Gottschalk: Pianiste américain.* New York, 1853.

Barzun, Jacques. *Berlioz and the Romantic Century.* 2 vols. New York, 1969.

———. *New Letters of Berlioz,* 1830–1868. New York, 1954.

Bauer, Harold. "The Paris Conservatoire: Some Reminiscences." *Musical Quarterly,* XXXIII (1947), 533–42.

Bender, Lorelle Causey. "The French Opera House of New Orleans, 1859–1890." M.A. thesis, Louisiana State University, 1940.

Berlioz, Hector. *Memoirs,* 1803–1865. New York, 1935.

Brook, Donald. *Five Great French Composers.* London, 1947.

Chantavoine, Jean, and Jean Gaudefroy-Demombynes. *Le Romantisme dans la musique européenne.* Paris, 1955.

Chase, Gilbert. *America's Music: From the Pilgrims to the Present.* New York, 1955.

Chateau, Earl. "Histoire du développement des orchestres symphoniques aux Etats-Unis." Ph.D. dissertation, Université de Strasbourg, 1933.

Coeuroy, André. *Wagner et l'esprit romantique: Wagner et la France.* Paris, 1965.

Cooper, Martin. *French Music: From the Death of Berlioz to the Death of Fauré.* London, 1951.

Crosten, William L. *French Grand Opera: An Art and a Business.* New York, 1948.

Curtis, John. "A Century of Grand Opera in Philadelphia." *PMHB,* XLIV (1920), 122–57.

Curtiss, Mina Stein. *Bizet and His World.* New York, 1958.

Dickinson, Edward. *The Study of the History of Music*. New York, 1923.

Eames, Emma. *Some Memories and Reflections*. New York, 1927.

Eberlein, Harold D., and Cortlandt Van Dyke Hubbard. "Music in the Early Federal Era." *PMHB*, LXIX (1945), 103–27.

Elson, Louis C. *American Music*. New York, 1904.

Gilman, Lawrence. *Edward MacDowell: A Study*. New York ,1938.

Gipson, Richard M. *The Life of Emma Thursby*. New York, 1940.

Gottschalk, Louis Moreau. *Notes of a Pianist*. Edited by Jeanne Behrend. New York ,1964.

Griggs, John Cornelius. *Studien über die Musik in Amerika*. Leipzig, 1894.

Hauk, Minnie. *Memories of a Singer*. London, 1925.

Henderson, W. J. *The Story of Music*. New York, 1921.

Hervey Arthur. *French Music in the Nineteenth Century*. London and New York, 1903.

Howard, John Tasker, and George Kent Bellows. *A Short History of Music in America*. New York, 1957.

Hughes, Rupert. *Contemporary American Composers*. Boston, 1900.

———. *Famous American Composers*. Boston, 1906.

d'Indy, Vincent. *César Franck*. Paris, 1919.

Jones, F. O. *A Handbook of American Music and Musicians*. Buffalo, N..Y, 1887.

Kendall, John Smith. "The Friend of Chopin, and Some Other New Orleans Musical Celebrities." *LHQ*, XXXI (1948), 856–76.

Kmen, Henry. *Music in New Orleans: The Formative Years, 1791–1841*. Baton Rouge, 1966.

Kowalski, Henri. *A Travers l'Amérique: Impressions d'un musicien*. Paris, 1872.

Krehbiel, Henry E. "Foreign Musical Influence in America." *Etude*, XXXII (November, 1914), 792.

Lahee, Henry C. *Famous Pianists of To-day and Yesterday*. Boston, 1929.

———. *Famous Violinists of Today and Yesterday*. Boston, 1916.

Lang, Paul Henry. *Music in Western Civilization*. New York, 1941.

———, ed. *One Hundred Years of Music in America*. New York, 1961.

Lowens, Irving. *Music and Musicians in Early America*. New York, 1964.

Mason, Lowell. *Musical Letters from Abroad*. New York, 1854.

Mason, William. *Memories of a Musical Life*. New York, 1901.

Mathews, W. S. B., ed. *A Hundred Years of Music in America*. 2 vols. Chicago, 1889.

Mattfeld, Julius. *Variety: Music Cavalcade, 1620–1950*. New York, 1952.

Mount, May W. *Artists of New Orleans and Their Work*. New Orleans, 1896.

Offenbach, Jacques. *Offenbach in America: Notes of a Travelling Musician*. New York, 1877.

Page, Elizabeth F. *Edward MacDowell: His Work and Ideals*. New York, 1910.

Pierre, Constant. *Le Conservatoire national de musique et de déclamation, Paris: Documents historiques et administratifs*. Paris, 1900.

Ritter, Frederic Louis. *Music in America*. New York, 1883.

Rourke, Constance. *The Roots of American Culture and Other Essays*. New York, 1942.

Scudo, P. *L'Année musicale*. Paris, 1861.

Stone, James H. "Mid-Nineteenth Century American Beliefs in the Social Values of Music." *Musical Quarterly*, XLIII (1957), 38–49.

Tajan-Rogé, M. D. *Les Beaux-Arts aux Etats-Unis d'Amérique.* Paris, 1857.

Thomas, Fannie Edgar. "American Interests in Paris: Musical Relations Between France and America." *Musical Courier*, XXXVII (July 4, and December 7, 1898), and XXXVIII (May 10, 17, 1899).

Upton, George P. *Musical Memoirs: My Recollections of Celebrities of the Half-Century,* 1850–1890. Chicago, 1908.

Upton, William Treat. *William Henry Fry: American Journalist and Composer Critic.* New York, 1954.

Yerbury, Grace H. "Concert Music in Early New Orleans." *LHQ*, XL (April, 1957), 95–109.

DANCE

Anet, Claude. "Loïe Fuller in French Sculpture," *AR*, XIII (1903), 271–78.

Denby, Edwin. *Looking at the Dance.* New York, 1968.

Duncan, Irma. *Isadora Duncan: Pioneer in the Art of Dance.* New York, 1958.

Duncan, Isadora. *Ecrits sur la danse.* Paris, 1927.

———. *My Life.* New York, 1933.

Fuller, Loïe. *Fifteen Years of a Dancer's Life: With Some Accounts of Her Distinguished Friends.* Boston, 1913.

Kinney, Troy and Margaret W. *The Dance: Its Place in Art and Life.* New York, 1935.

Martin, John. *Book of the Dance.* New York, 1963.

Maynard, Olga. *The American Ballet.* Philadelphia, 1959.

Moore, Lillian. "George Washington Smith." *Dance Index*, IV (June–August, 1945), 87–135.

———. "Mary Ann Lee: First American Giselle." *Dance Index,* II (May, 1943), 60–71.

———. "The Petipa Family in Europe and America." *Dance Index*, I (May, 1942), 71–84.

Morris, Virginia Elizabeth. "The Influence of Delsarte in America as Revealed Through the Lectures of Steele Mackaye." M.A. thesis, Louisiana State University, 1941.

Shawn, Ted. *Every Little Movement: A Book About François Delsarte.* Pittsfield, Mass., 1954.

Sorell, Walter. *The Dance Through the Ages.* New York, 1967.

PAINTING

Adams, Adeline. *Childe Hassam.* New York, 1938.

Baldry, A. L. "James McNeill Whistler: His Art and Influence." *International Studio,* XX (1903), 237–45.

Barker, Virgil. *American Painting: History and Interpretation.* New York, 1950.

Baur, John I. H. *American Painting in the Nineteenth Century: Main Trends and Movements.* New York, 1953.

———, ed. "The Autobiography of Worthington Whittredge, 1820–1910." *Brooklyn Museum Journal,* I (1942), 5–69.

————. *Theodore Robinson*. New York, 1946.

Becker, Eugene Matthew. "Whistler and the Aesthetic Movement." Ph.D. dissertation, Princeton University, 1959.

Benjamin, Samuel G. W. *Art in America: A Critical and Historical Sketch*. New York, 1880.

————. *Contemporary Art in Europe*. New York, 1877.

————. "Practice and Patronage of French Art." *Atlantic Monthly*, XXXVI (September, 1875), 257–69.

Bérence, Fred. *Grandeur spirituelle du XIXᵉ siècle français*. 2 vols. Paris, 1959.

Bigot, Charles. "Le Salon de 1883." *GDBA*, XXVIII (1883), 10–11.

Bigot, Marie Healy. *Life of George P. A. Healy*. Chicago, 1913.

Bing, S. *La Culture artistique en Amérique*. Paris, 1896.

Bizardel, Yvon. *American Painters in Paris*. Translated by Richard Howard. New York, 1960.

Boas, George, ed. *Courbet and the Naturalistic Movement*. Baltimore, 1938.

Born, Wolfgang. *American Landscape Painting: An Interpretation*. New Haven, 1948.

Boutroux, E., et al. *Les Etats-Unis et la France*. Paris, 1914.

Brimo, René. *L'Evolution du goût aux Etats-Unis*. Paris, 1938.

Caffin, Charles H. "Some New American Painters in Paris." *Harper's Magazine*, CXVIII (1909), 284–93.

————. *The Story of American Painting*. New York, 1907.

Carey, John Thomas. "The American Lithograph: From Its Inception to 1865." Ph.D. dissertation, Ohio State University, 1954.

Cartwright, Julia. *Jean François Millet: His Life and Letters*. London, 1896.

Cary, Elisabeth Luther. "French Influences in Whistler's Art." *The Scrip*, I (1906), 312–26.

Cline, Isaac M. *Art and Artists in New Orleans During the Last Century*. New Orleans, 1922.

Cole, Helen. "American Artists in Paris." *Brush and Pencil*, IV (1899), 199–202.

Constable, W. G. *Art Collecting in the United States of America*. London, 1964.

Conway, John J. *Footprints of Famous Americans in Paris*. New York, 1912.

Cortissoz, Royal. *American Artists*. New York, 1923.

————. *John La Farge: A Memoir and A Study*. Boston, 1911.

Cox, Kenyon. *Artist and Public: And Other Essays on Art Subjects*. New York, 1914.

————. *Old Masters and New: Essays in Art Criticism*. New York, 1905.

Delécluze, E. J. *Les Beaux-Arts dans les deux mondes en 1855*. Paris, 1856.

Dezarrois, André. "Une Exposition d'art américain: Winslow Homer, John Sargent, Paul Manship." *Revue de l'art*, XLIV (1923), 142–55.

Downes, William Howe. *John S. Sargent: His Life and Work*. Boston, 1925.

————. *The Life and Works of Winslow Homer*. Boston, 1911.

————. *Twelve Great Artists*. Boston, 1900.

Drouet, Paul L. M. *Les Institutions artistiques et les beaux-arts en général aux Etats-Unis, au Canada et à l'Exposition de Chicago en 1893*. Caen, 1896.

DuCamp, Maxime. *Les Beaux-Arts à l'Exposition Universelle de* 1855. Paris, 1855.

Durand, John. *The Life and Times of Asher B. Durand.* New York, 1894.

Durand-Gréville, E. "Correspondance d'Amérique: L'Art aux Etats-Unis." *GDBA,* XXVIII (1886), 255–64.

———. "La Peinture aux Etats-Unis: Les Galeries priveés." *GDBA,* XXIX (1887), 65–75, 250–55.

Duret, Theodore. *Whistler.* Philadelphia, 1917.

Dussieux, L. *Les Artistes français à l'étranger.* Paris, 1876.

Earle, Helen L. *Biographical Sketches of American Artists.* Lansing, Mich., 1924.

Etex, Antoine. "De L'Etat des beaux-arts aux Etats-Unis d'Amérique en 1855." *RDBA,* VIII (1857), 61–63, 81–84, 125–27.

———. *Les Souvenirs d'un artiste.* Paris, 1877.

Ewers, John C. *Artists of the Old West.* New York, 1965.

Faust, Camille. *The French Impressionists,* 1860–1900. London, 1911.

Fink, Lois Marie. "The Role of France in American Art, 1850–1870." Ph.D. dissertation, University of Chicago, 1970.

French, H. W. *Art and Artists in Connecticut.* Boston, 1879.

Gardner, Albert Ten Eyck. *Winslow Homer, American Artist: His World and His Work.* New York, 1961.

Goodrich, Lloyd. *Thomas Eakins: His Life and His Work.* New York, 1933.

———. *Winslow Homer.* New York, 1944.

Gréard, Vallery C. O. *Meissonier: His Life and His Art.* New York, 1897.

Gregory, Horace. *The World of James McNeill Whistler.* Freeport, N.Y., 1969.

Grigaut, Paul L. *The French in America,* 1520–1880. Detroit, 1951.

Hamel, Maurice, "L'Exposition Universelle: Les Ecoles étrangères, Etats-Unis." *GDBA,* XXXI (1889), 382–84.

Hamerton, Philip Gilbert. *Art Essays: Modern Schools of Art—American and European.* New York, 1880.

Hamilton, George H. *Manet and His Critics.* New Haven, 1954.

Hanson, Lawrence. *Renoir: The Man, the Painter, and His World.* New York, 1968.

Harris, Neil. *The Artist in American Society: The Formative Years,* 1790–1860. New York, 1966.

Hartmann, Sadakichi. *A History of American Art.* 2 vols. Boston, 1932.

Healy, George P. A. *The Reminiscences of a Portrait Painter.* Chicago, 1894.

———. "Thomas Couture." *Century Magazine,* XLIV (1892), 4–13.

Hermant, Jacques. "L'Art à l'Exposition de Chicago." *GDBA,* X (1893), 237–53, 416–25, 441–61.

Huneker, James Gibbons. *Promenades of an Impressionist.* New York, 1910.

Hunt, William Morris. *Talks on Art.* Compiled by Helen M. Knowlton. Boston, 1898.

Inness, George, Jr. *Life, Art, and Letters of George Inness.* New York, 1917.

Isham, Samuel. *The History of American Painting.* New York, 1905.

Jarves, James Jackson. *Art Thoughts: The Experiences and Observations of an American Amateur in Europe.* New York, 1869.

Keyzer, Frances. "Some American Artists in Paris." *Studio*, XIII (1898), 246–52.

Knowlton, Helen Mary. *Art-Life of William Morris Hunt*. Boston, 1899.

Krebs, Albert. "Degas à la Nouvelle Orléans." *Rapports France–Etats-Unis*, No. 65 (August, 1952), 63–72.

La Farge, John. "The Barbizon School." *McClure's Magazine*, XXI (1903), 115–29, 586–99.

———. *The Higher Life in Art*. New York, 1908.

LaFollette, Suzanne. *Art in America*. New York, 1929.

Lattimore, Anne. "Winslow Homer, 1836–1910." *American Chronicle* (January, 1972), 39–42.

Laver, James. *French Painting and the Nineteenth Century*. London, 1937.

———. *Whistler*. New York, 1930.

Leeper, John Palmer. "Mary Cassatt and Her Parisian Friends." *Bulletin of the Pasadena Art Institute* (October, 1951), 3–10.

Looney, Ben Earl. "Historical Sketch of Art in Lousiana." *LHQ*, VIII (1935), 382–96.

Low, Will H. *A Chronicle of Friendships, 1873–1900*. New York, 1908.

———. *A Painter's Progress*. New York, 1910.

Mabee, Carleton. *The American Leonardo: A Life of Samuel F. B. Morse*. New York, 1943.

McIntyre, Robert G. *Martin Johnson Heade, 1819–1904*. New York, 1948.

McSpadden, Joseph W. *Famous Painters in America*. New York, 1923.

Mare, Marie de. *G. P. A. Healy, American Artist: An Intimate Chronicle of the 19th Century*. New York, 1954.

Mather, Frank Jewett, Jr. *Homer Martin: Poet in Landscape*. New York, 1912.

Mellquist, Jerome. *The Emergence of an American Art*. New York, 1942.

Morgan, John Hill. "The Work of M. Fevret de Saint-Mémin." *Brooklyn Museum Quarterly*, V (1918), 15–26.

Moskowitz, Ira. *French Impressionists*. New York, 1962.

Mount, Charles Merrill. *John Singer Sargent: A Biography*. New York, 1955.

Mount, May W. *Some Notables of New Orleans: Biographical and Descriptive Sketches of the Artists of New Orleans and Their Work*. New Orleans, 1896.

Mumford, Lewis. *The Brown Decades: A Study of the Arts in America, 1865–1895*. New York, 1955.

Neal, John. *Observations on American Art, 1793–1876*. Edited with notes by Harold Edward Dickson. State College, Pa., 1943.

Nélaton, Etienne Moreau. *Millet raconté par lui-même*. 2 vols. Paris, 1921.

Neuhaus, Eugene. *The History and Ideals of American Art*. Palo Alto, Calif., 1931.

Noble, Louis Legrand. *The Life and Works of Thomas Cole*. Edited by Elliot S. Vesell. Cambridge, Mass., 1964.

Norflett, Fillmore. *Saint-Mémin in Virginia: Portraits and Biographies*. Richmond, Va., 1942.

Novak, Barbara. *American Painting in the Nineteenth Century: Realism, Idealism, and the American Experience*. New York, 1969.

Pennell, E. R. and J. *The Life of James McNeill Whistler*. 2 vols. London, 1908.

Potonniée, Georges. *Cent ans de photographie,* 1839–1939. Paris, 1940.

Réau, Louis. *L'Art français aux Etats-Unis.* Paris, 1926.

Renoir, Jean. *Renoir: My Father.* Translated by Randolph and Dorothy Weaver. Boston, 1962.

Rewald, John. *The History of Impressionism.* New York, 1961.

Richardson, Edgar Preston. *Painting in America: The Story of 450 Years.* New York, 1956.

———. *A Short History of Painting in America: The Story of 450 Years.* New York, 1963.

———. *Washington Allston: A Study of the Romantic Artist in America.* Chicago, 1948.

Robinson, Theodore. "Claude Monet." *Century Magazine,* XLIV (September, 1892), 696–701.

Rutledge, Anna Wells. "Artists in the Life of Charleston: Through Colony and State, from Restoration to Reconstruction." *APS, Transactions,* New Series, XXXIX (1949), 101–260.

Saint-Gaudens, Homer. *The American Artist and His Times.* New York, 1941.

Salam, Cara Lu. "French Portraitists Who Worked in New Orleans During the Period 1830–1860." M.A. thesis, Louisiana State University, 1967.

Schwab, Arnold T. *James Gibbons Huneker: Critic of the Arts.* Stanford, Calif., 1963.

Segard, Achille. *Un Peintre des enfants des mères: Mary Cassatt.* Paris, 1913.

Seligman, Germain. *Merchants of Art, 1880–1960: Eighty Years of Professional Collecting.* New York, 1961.

Sensier, Alfred. *Souvenirs sur Th. Rousseau.* Paris, 1881.

———. *La Vie et l'oeuvre de J. F. Millet.* Paris, 1881.

Shattuck, Roger. *The Banquet Years: The Origins of the Avant-Garde in France, 1865 to World War I.* New York, 1968.

Sheldon, G. W. *American Painters.* New York, 1881.

———. *Hours with Art and Artists.* New York, 1882.

———. *Ideals of Life in France.* (With essays on art in France.) New York, 1890.

———. *Recent Ideals of American Art.* 2 vols. New York, 1890.

Sherard, Robert H. "American Artists in Paris." *Magazine of Art,* XVIII (1895), 224–29.

Sloane, Joseph C. *French Painting Between the Past and the Present: Artists, Critics and Traditions, from 1848 to 1870.* Princeton, 1951.

Smith, Albert Delmont. *European Influence on American Painting of the 19th Century.* New York, 1947.

Soissons, Emmanuel de Savoie Carignan. *Boston Artists.* Boston, 1894.

Stillman, William James. *The Autobiography of a Journalist.* 2 vols. Boston, 1901.

Stranahan, C. H. *A History of French Painting.* London, 1889.

Sweet, Frederick A. *The Hudson River School and the Early American Landscape Tradition.* Chicago, 1945.

———. *Miss Mary Cassatt: Impressionist from Pennsylvania.* Norman, Okla., 1966.

Tanner, H. O. "The Story of an Artist's Life." *World's Work*, XVIII (June and July, 1909), 11661–66, 11769–75.

Taylor, E. A. "The American Colony of Artists in Paris." *Studio,* LII (1911), 263–80, LIII (1911), 103–15, LV (1912), 280–90.

Thomson, David Croal. *The Barbizon School of Painters: Corot, Rousseau, Diaz, Millet, Daubigny, etc.* London, 1890.

Vail, Eugene A. *Réponse à quelques implications contre les Etats-Unis.* Paris, 1837.

Valerio, Edith. *Mary Cassatt.* Paris, 1930.

Van Dyke, John C., ed. *Modern French Masters: A Series of Biographical and Critical Reviews by American Artists.* New York, 1896.

Waern, Cecilia. *John LaFarge: Artist and Writer.* London, 1896.

Wheelwright, Edward. "Personal Recollections of Jean François Millet." *Atlantic Monthly,* XXXVIII (September, 1876), 257–76.

Wiesendanger, Martin and Margaret. *Nineteenth Century Louisiana Painters and Paintings from the Collection of W. E. Groves.* Gretna, La., 1971.

Wormser, Simone Olivier. "Whistler: Peintre protée." Ph.D. dissertation, Université de Paris, 1955.

Wuerfel, Edmund Henry. *American Art Association of Paris.* Philadelphia, 1894.

Young, Dorothy Weir. *The Life and Letters of J. Alden Weir.* Edited with an introduction by Lawrence W. Chisolm. New Haven, 1960.

SCULPTURE

Adams, Adeline. *Daniel Chester French: Sculptor.* Boston and New York, 1932.

———. *John Quincy Adams Ward: An Appreciation.* New York, 1912.

Bartlett, Ellen Strong. "Paul Bartlett: An American Sculptor." *New England Magazine,* XXXIII (December, 1905), 369–82.

Bartlett, Paul W. "What American Sculptors Owe to French Art." *NYT*, February 9, 1913, Magazine Section, p. 13.

Bell, Hamilton. "Un Sculpteur américain de descendance française: Auguste Saint-Gaudens (1848–1907)." *GDBA*, Fifth Series, I (1920), 367–82.

Brownell, William C. "French Sculptors." *Century Magazine,* XXXIII (1886–87), 194–99, 331–38, 718–23.

———. "The Sculpture of Olin Warner." *Scribner's Magazine,* XX (1896), 429–41.

Caffin, Charles H. *American Masters of Sculpture.* New York, 1903.

Chambrun, A. de. "Un Sculpteur américain né français: Saint-Gaudens." *RDDM* (February, 1932), 664–74.

Chase, George Henry, and Chandler R. Post. *A History of Sculpture.* New York, 1925.

Chinard, Gilbert, ed. *Houdon in America.* Baltimore, 1930.

Clark, William C., Jr., *Great American Sculptures.* Philadelphia, 1878.

Cortissoz, Royal. *Augustus Saint-Gaudens.* Boston, 1907.

Craven, W. *Sculpture in America.* New York, 1968.

Cresson, Margaret French. *The Life of Daniel Chester French: Journey into Fame.* Cambridge, Mass., 1947.

Dussieux, L. *Les Artistes français à l'étranger.* Paris, 1876.

Greenough, Frances Boot. *Letters of Horatio Greenough to His Brother, Henry Greenough.* Boston, 1887.

Greer, H. H. "Frederick MacMonnies, Sculptor." *Brush and Pencil,* X (April, 1902), 1–15.

McSpadden, J. Walker. *Famous Sculptors of America.* New York, 1927.

Migeon, Gaston. "Le Sculpteur Augustin Saint-Gaudens." *Art et Décoration,* V (1899), 43–49.

Nichols, Rose Standish, ed. "Familiar Letters of Augustus Saint-Gaudens." *McClure's Magazine,* XXXII (November, 1908), 1–16.

Post, Charles R. *A History of European and American Sculpture.* 2 vols. Cambridge, Mass., 1921.

Quélin, René de. "Early Days with MacMonnies in St. Gaudens' Studio." *Arts and Decoration,* XVI (1922), 424–25, 479.

Saint-Gaudens, Homer, ed. "Intimate Letters of Stanford White." *AR,* XXX (1911), 107–16, 283–98, 399–406.

———. *The Reminiscences of August Saint-Gaudens.* 2 vols. New York, 1913.

Strother, French. "Frederick MacMonnies, Sculptor." *World's Work,* XI (December, 1905), 6965–82.

Taft, Lorado. *The History of American Sculpture.* New York, 1925.

Tharp, Louise Hall. *Saint-Gaudens and the Gilded Era.* Boston, 1969.

Thaw, Alexander Blair. "George Grey Barnard, Sculptor." *World's Work,* V (1902), 2837–53.

Van Rensselaer, M. G. "Frederick Arthur Bridgman." *American Art and American Art Collections* (1889), 179–92.

Wallace, David H. *John Rogers: The People's Sculptor.* Middletown, Conn., 1967.

ARCHITECTURE

Adshead, Stanley D. "A Comparison of Modern American Architecture with That of European Cities." *AR,* XXIX (1911), 113–26.

Barney, J. Stewart. "The Ecole des Beaux-Arts: Its Influence on Our Architecture." *AR,* XXII (1907), 333–42.

Bragdon, Claude. "'Made in France' Architecture." *AR,* XVI (1904), 561–68.

Burnham, A. "The New York Architecture of Richard M. Hunt." *Journal of the Society of Architectural Historians,* XI (1952), 9–14.

Condit, Carl W. *American Building Art: The Nineteenth Century.* New York, 1960.

Cram, Ralph Adams. *My Life in Architecture.* Boston, 1936.

Croly, Herbert. "The New World and the New Art." *AR,* XII (1902), 135–53.

Early, James. "Romantic Thought and Architecture in the United States." Ph.D. dissertation, Harvard, 1953.

Flagg, Ernest. "American Architecture as Opposed to Architecture in America." *AR,* X (1900), 178–80.

———. "Influence of French School on Architecture in the United States." *AR,* IV (1894), 211–28.

Gillet, Louis. "L'Architecture aux Etats-Unis et l'influence française." In E. Boutroux, *et al. Les Etats-Unis et la France*. Paris, 1914.

Granger, Alfred Hoyt. *Charles Follen McKim: A Study of His Life and Work.* Boston, 1913.

Gréber, Jacques. *L'Architecture aux Etats-Unis.* 2 vols. Paris, 1920.

Hamilton, George H. "Realism and Idealism in Late Nineteenth Century American Art: Augustus Saint-Gaudens and Thomas Eakins." In *Akten des 21sten Internationalen Kongresses für Kunstgeschichte, Bonn, 1964.* Berlin, 1967.

Hamlin, A.D.F. "The Influence of the Ecole des Beaux-Arts on Our Architectural Education." *AR*, XXIII. (1908), 241–47.

———. "Modern French Architecture." *AR*, X (1900), 150–77.

Hastings, Thomas. "The Influence of the Ecole des Beaux-Arts Upon American Architecture." *AR*, X (1901), 65–90.

Hitchcock, Henry Russell. *Architecture: Nineteenth and Twentieth Centuries.* Baltimore, 1958.

———. *The Architecture of H. H. Richardson and His Times.* Hamden, Conn., 1961.

Kimball, Fiske. *American Architecture.* New York, 1928.

McKenna, Rosalie T. "James Renwick, Jr., and the Second Empire Style in the United States." *American Magazine of Art*, XLI V(1951), 97–101.

Moore, Charles. *Daniel Burnham: Architect Planner of Cities.* 2 vols. Boston, 1911.

———. *The Life and Times of Charles Follen McKim.* Boston, 1929.

Morrison, Hugh. *Louis Sullivan: Prophet of Modern Architecture.* New York, 1952.

Mumford, Lewis. *Roots of Contemporary American Architecture.* New York, 1952.

———. *The South in Architecture.* New York, 1941.

Noffsinger, James Philip. "The Influence of the Ecole des Beaux-Arts on the Architecture of the United States." Ph.D. dissertation, Catholic University of America, 1955.

Paris, W. Francklyn. *The Hall of American Artists.* New York, 1952.

Pinkney, David H. *Napoleon III and the Rebuilding of Paris.* Princeton, N.J., 1958.

Ponente, N. *Les Structures du monde monderne, 1850–1900.* Geneva, 1965.

Rensselaer, Mrs. Schuyler Van. *Henri Hobson Richardson and His Work.* New York, 1888.

Schuyler, Montgomery. *American Architecture and Other Writings.* 2 vols. Cambridge, Mass., 1961.

———. "The Works of the Late Richard M. Hunt." *AR*, V (1895), 97–180.

Viollet-le-Duc, E. E. *Discourses on Architecture.* 2 vols. Boston, 1881.

Walker, C. Howard. "William Robert Ware: 1832–1915." *Harvard Graduates' Magazine*, XXIV (September, 1915), 38–40.

Ware, W. R. *An Outline of a Course of Architectural Instruction.* Boston, 1866.

White, Theo B. *Philadelphia Architecture in the Nineteenth Century.* Philadelphia, 1953.

Wight, Peter B. "Daniel Hudson Burnham." *AR*, XXXVIII (1915), 1–12.

NATURAL SCIENCES

Adams, Alexander B. *John James Audubon: A Biography.* New York, 1966.

Agassiz, Elizabeth Cary. *Louis Agassiz: His Life and Correspondence.* 2 vols. Boston, 1885.

American Philosophical Society. *The Early History of Science and Learning in America . . . During the 18th and 19th Centuries.* Philadelphia, 1942.

Archibald, Raymond Clare. "Outline of the History of Mathematics." *American Mathematical Monthly,* LVI (January, 1949), No. 1.

Barnhart, John Hendley. "European Influences in American Botany." *Journal of the New York Botanical Garden,* XXVI (May, 1925), 102–11.

Benjamin, J. P. "Louisiana Sugar." *De Bow's Review,* II (1846), 322–45.

Cajori, Florian. *The Teaching and History of Mathematics in the United States.* Washington, D.C., 1890.

Caskie, Jaquelin Ambler. *Life and Letters of Matthew Fontaine Maury.* Richmond, Va., 1928.

Chinard, Gilbert. "André and François-André Michaux and Their Predecessors: An Essay on Early Botanical Exchanges Between America and France." In *American Philosophical Society, Proceedings,* CI (1957), 344–61.

Cohen, Ernest. "Semi-Century of Willard Gibbs' Phase Law, 1876–1926." *Science,* New Series, LXIV (1926), 621.

Cohen, I. Bernard. "Some Reflections on the State of Science in America During the Nineteenth Century." National Academy of Sciences, *Proceedings,* XLV (1959), 666–77.

Colloques Internationaux du Centre National de la Recherche Scientifique, Paris, September, 1956. *Les Botanistes français en Amérique de Nord avant 1850.* Paris, 1957.

Comptes Rendus et Analyses. "The Scientific Papers of J. Willard Gibbs." *Bulletin des sciences mathématiques,* 2nd Series, XXXI (1907), 181–211.

Cope, Edward Drinker. "On Archaesthetism." *American Naturalist,* XVI (1882), 454–69.

———. *On the Hypothesis of Evolution: Physical and Metaphysical.* New Haven, 1871.

———. *The Origin of the Fittest: Essays on Evolution.* New York, 1887.

Coulson, Thomas. *Joseph Henry: His Life and Work.* Princeton, N.J., 1950.

Couper, William. "Colonel Claudius Crozet." *West Virginia History Quarterly Magazine,* I (July, 1940), 255–69.

Dana, Edward S., et al. *A Century of Science in America.* New Haven, 1918.

Dana, James A. *Memoir of Arnold Guyot, 1807–1884.* Washington, D.C., 1886.

Dodge, Charles R. "The Life and Entomological Work of the Late Townend Glover." In *U.S. Department of Agriculture, Division of Entomology, Bulletin,* No. 18. Washington, D.C., 1888.

Dupree, A. Hunter. "Asa Gray: The Development of a Statesman of Science, 1810–1848." Ph.D. dissertation, Harvard, 1951.

———. *Asa Gray, 1810–1888.* Cambridge, Mass., 1959.

Essig, E. O. *A History of Entomology.* New York, 1931.

Findlay, Alexander. *A Hundred Years of Chemistry.* London, 1948.

Fisher, George P. *Life of Benjamin Silliman, M.D., L.L.D.* 2 vols. Philadelphia, 1866.

Frazer, Persifor. "The Life and Letters of Edward Drinker Cope." *American Geologist,* XXVI (August, 1900), 67–128.

Fulton, John F., and Elizabeth H. Thomson. *Benjamin Silliman,* 1779–1864: *Pathfinder in American Science.* New York, 1947.

Gifford, George E., Jr., ed. "An American in Paris, 1841–1842: Four Letters from Jeffries Wyman." *JHM,* XXII (1967), 274–85.

Gilman, Daniel C. *The Life of James Dwight Dana.* New York, 1899.

Goldschmid, Edgar. "Contribution des Etats-Unis à l'anatomie pathologique au début du dix-neuvième siècle." *Archives Internationales d'Histoire des Sciences,* I (April, 1948), 479–89.

Goode, G. Brown. "Bibliographies of American Naturalists: The Published Writings of Dr. Charles Girard." In *U.S. National Museum, Bulletin,* No. 41. Washington, D. C., 1891.

Gray, Asa. *Scientific Papers.* 2 vols. Boston, 1889.

Gray, Jane Loring, ed. *Letters of Asa Gray.* 2 vols. Boston, 1893.

Gruenberg, Benjamin C. *The Story of Evolution: Facts and Theories on the Development of Life.* Garden City, N.Y., 1929.

Guyot, Arnold. *Louis Agassiz: A Biographical Memoir.* Princeton, N..J, 1883.

Hamy, Ernest Théodore. *Les Voyages du naturaliste Ch. Alex. Lesueur dans l'Amérique du Nord,* 1815–1837. Paris, 1904.

Henry, Joseph. *Scientific Writings.* 2 vols. Washington, D.C., 1886.

Herber, Elmer Charles, ed. *Correspondence Between Spencer Fullerton Baird and Louis Agassiz: Two Pioneer American Naturalists.* Washington, D.C., 1963.

Herrick, Francis Hobart. *Audubon the Naturalist: A History of His Life and Time.* 2 vols. New York, 1917.

Hilgard, Eugene W. "Biographical Memoir of Joseph LeConte, 1823–1901." *National Academy of Sciences, Biographical Memoirs,* VI (1909), 147–218.

Himmelfarb, Gertrude. *Darwin and the Darwinian Revolution.* Garden City, N.Y., 1959.

Jaffe Bernard. *Men of Science in America.* New York, 1944, 1958.

Johnson, Thomas Cary, Jr. *Scientific Interests in the Old South.* New York, 1936.

Jones, Bessie Zaban, ed. *The Golden Age of Science: Thirty Portraits of the Giants of Nineteenth Century Science by Their Scientific Contemporaries.* New York, 1966.

Jordan, David Starr, ed. *Leading American Men of Science.* New York, 1910.

Kane, Harnett T. *Deep Delta Country.* New York, 1944.

Kay, James E. de. "Report About the Progress of the Natural Sciences in the United States During 1826." *Revue américaine,* II (1826–27), 244–56, 356–75.

Laplace, Pierre Simon. *Celestial Mechanics.* Translated, with a commentary, by Nathaniel Bowditch. 5 vols. New York, 1966–69.

Loir, Adrien. *Charles Alexandre Lesueur: Artiste et savant français en Amérique de 1816 à 1839.* Le Havre, 1920.

Lurie, Edward. *Louis Agassiz: A Life in Science.* Chicago, 1960.

McKelvey, Susan D. *Botanical Exploration of the Trans-Mississippi West, 1790–1850.* Jamaica Plain, Mass., 1955.

Merrill, George P. *The First One Hundred Years of American Geology.* New Haven, 1924.

Musto, David F. "The Development of American Astronomy During the Early Nineteenth Century." In *Actes du dixième Congrès International d'Histoire des Sciences,* II, 733–36. Paris, 1964.

Newcomb, Simon. *The Reminiscences of an Astronomer.* Boston, 1903.

Odgers, Merle M. *Alexander Dallas Bache: Scientist and Educator, 1806–1867.* Philadelphia, 1947.

Osborn, Henry F. *Cope, Master Naturalist: The Life and Letters of Edward Drinker Cope.* Princeton, N.J., 1931.

————. *Impressions of Great Naturalists.* New York, 1928.

Packard, A. S., Jr. "A Century's Progress in American Zoology." *American Naturalist,* X (1876), 591–98.

Peare, Catherine Owens. *A Scientist of Two Worlds: Louis Agassiz.* Philadelphia, 1958.

Planchon, Jules E. *Les Vignes américaines: Leur culture, leur résistance au Phylloxera et leur avenir en Amérique.* Montpellier and Paris, 1875.

Riedman, Sarah R. *Trailblazer of American Science: The Life of Joseph Henry.* Chicago, 1961.

Riley, Charles V. *Vine Cultivation and Wine Making.* Washington, D.C., 1891.

Rillieux, Norbert. *Commémoration du centenaire de la mise en marche de la première installation d'évaporation dans le vide à triple effet à la Louisiane en 1834.* Amsterdam, 1934.

Rodgers, Andrew Denny. *John Torrey: A Story of North American Botany.* Princeton, N.J., 1942.

Rodgers, Andrew Denny III. *American Botany, 1873–1892: Decades of Transition.* New York, 1968.

Rousseau, Pierre. *Man's Conquest of the Stars.* New York, 1961.

Shryock, Richard Harrison. "American Indifference to Basic Science During the Nineteenth Century." *Archives Internationales d'Histoire des Sciences* (October, 1948), 50–65.

Silliman, Benjamin. "American Contributions to Chemistry." *American Chemist,* V (1874), 71–114, 195–209.

————. *A Visit to Europe in 1851.* 2 vols. New York, 1853.

Simons, L. G. "The Influence of French Mathematics at the End of the Eighteenth Century Upon the Teaching of Mathematics in American Colleges." *Isis,* XV (1931), 104–23.

Singer, Charles. *A Short History of Scientific Ideas to 1900.* Oxford, 1959.

Smith, David Eugene, and Jekuthiel Ginsburg. *A History of Mathematics in America before 1900.* Chicago, 1934.

Smith, J. Lawrence. "The Century's Progress in Industrial Chemistry." *American Chemist,* V (1874), 61–70.

———. *The Progress and Condition of Several Departments of Industrial Chemistry.* Washington, D.C., 1869.

True, Rodney H. "François André Michaux: The Botanist and Explorer." American Philosophical Society, *Proceedings,* LXXVIII (1938), 313–27.

Vail, R .W. G. "The American Sketchbooks of a French Naturalist, 1816–1837: A Description of the Charles Alexander Lesueur Collection." American Antiquarian Society, *Proceedings,* XLVIII (1938), 49–155.

Waterfield, R. L. *A Hundred Years of Astronomy.* London, 1938.

Weiss, Harry B. *The Pioneer Century of American Entomology.* New Brunswick, N.J., 1936.

Wheeler, Lynde Phelps. *Josiah Willard Gibbs.* New Haven, 1952.

———. *Josiah Willard Gibbs: The History of a Great Mind.* New Haven, 1970.

Wiley, Harvey W. *An Autobiography.* Indianapolis, 1930.

Wilkinson, Norman B. *E. I. du Pont, Botaniste: The Beginning of a Tradition.* Charlottesville, Va., 1972.

Williams, Kenneth P. "A Comparison of the Solar Theories of Newcomb and LeVerrier, With Conversion Tables for the Nineteenth Century." *Indiana University Publications, Science Series,* No. 14. Bloomington, 1945.

Wilson, John H., Jr. *Albert A. Michelson: America's First Nobel Prize Physicist.* New York, 1958.

Woodward, R. S. "The Century's Progress in Applied Mathematics." *American Mathematical Society, Bulletin,* VI (1900), 133–63.

MEDICAL SCIENCES

Ackerknecht, Erwin H. "Broussais: Or a Forgotten Medical Revolution." *BHM,* XXVII (1953), 320–43.

———. "Elisha Bartlett and the Philosophy of the Paris Clinical School." *BHM,* XXIV (1950), 43–60.

———. *Medicine at the Paris Hospital,* 1794–1848. Baltimore, 1967.

———. *A Short History of Psychiatry.* New York, 1968.

"An Account of the Origin, Progress, and Present State of the Medical School of Paris." *AJMS,* VIII (1831), 109–24, 401–18.

Arnold, Howard Payson. *Memoir of Jonathan Mason Warren, M.D.* Boston, 1886.

Barrett, W. C. "European and American Dentistry Compared." *MDJ,* XIII (November, 1881), 481–87.

Bartlett, Elisha. *An Essay on the Philosophy of Medical Science.* Philadelphia, 1844.

———. *An Inquiry Into the Degree of Certainty in Medicine and Into the Nature and Extent of Its Power Over Disease.* Philadelphia, 1848.

Baudouin, Marcel. *Quelques remarques sur les hôpitaux des Etats-Unis.* Paris, 1894.

Bechet, Paul E. "L'Hôpital Saint-Louis: A Brief Biographical Sketch of Its Early Teachers, and Their Influence Upon American Dermatology." *AMH,* New Series, X (September, 1938), 405–12.

Berman, Alex. "The Cadet Circle: Representatives of an Era in French Pharmacy." *BHM,* XL (1966), 101–11.

———. "Conflict and Anomaly in the Scientific Orientation of French Pharmacy, 1800–1873." *BHM*, XXXVII (1963), 440–62.

———. "The Pharmaceutical Component of Nineteenth Century French Public Health and Hygiene." *Pharmacy in History,* XI (1969), 5–10.

———. "The Problem of Science in Nineteenth Century French Pharmaceutical Historiography." *Ithaca* (1962), 891–94.

———. "Romantic Hygeia: J. J. Virey (1775–1846), Pharmacist and Philosopher of Nature." *BHM*, XXXIX (1965), 134–42.

Berthelot, M. "The Life and Works of Brown-Sequard." Smithsonian Institution, *Annual Report,* 1897–98. Pp. 677–96. Washington, D.C., 1899.

Bick, Edgar M. "French Influences On Early American Medicine and Surgery." *Journal of the Mount Sinai Hospital, New York,* XXIV (July–August, 1957), 499–509.

Biggs, H. M. "The Etiology of Rabies and the Method of M. Pasteur for Its Prevention." *BMSJ,* CXIV (April 1, 1886), 298–302.

Blanton, Wyndham B. *Medicine in Virginia in the Nineteenth Century.* Richmond, Va., 1933.

Bowditch, Henry Ingersoll. *Brief Memories of Louis and Some of His Contemporaries in the Parisian School of Medicine of Forty Years Ago.* Boston, 1872.

———. *Remarks Related to Dr. Paine's Commentaries Upon the Writings of M. Louis.* Boston, 1840.

Bowditch, Vincent Y. *Life and Correspondence of Henry Ingersoll Bowditch.* 2 vols. Boston, 1902.

Brasseur, E. *Rapport annuel des traveaux de la Société Syndicale Odontologique de France.* Paris, 1884.

Bremner, M. D. K. *The Story of Dentistry: From the Dawn of Civilization to the Present.* New York, 1946.

Broussais, François Joseph Victor. *On Irritation and Insanity.* Translated by Thomas Cooper. Columbia, S.C., 1831.

Bulletin de la Société Archéologique et Historique du Limousin. *Dupuytren.* Limoges, 1935.

———. *Le Centenaire de la mort de Dupuytren,* 1835–1935. Limoges, 1936.

Chaillé, Stanford E. "On Medicine in France and Practical Chemistry." *NOMSJ* (1867), 691–706.

Chance, Burton. *Clio Medica: Ophthalmology.* New York, 1939.

Charenton, Maurice-L. *Le Docteur Thomas W. Evans: Dentiste de Napoléon III et les dentistes de son époque.* Paris, 1936.

Churchill, Edward D., ed. *To Work in the Vineyard of Surgery: The Reminiscences of John Collins Warren* (1842–1927). Cambridge, Mass., 1958.

Cowen, David L. "America's First Pharmacy Laws." *Journal of the American Pharmaceutical Association* (1942), 162–69, 214–21.

———. "Louisiana: Pioneer in the Regulation of Pharmacy." *LHQ,* XXVI (April, 1943), 3–13.

———. "A Roster of the Licensed Apothecaries of Louisiana, 1816–1847." *Journal of the New Orleans College of Pharmacy,* VIII (1943), 3–4.

Da Costa, J. Chalmers. "The French School of Surgery in the Reign of Louis Philippe." *AMH*, (1922), 77–79.

Dain, Norman. *Concepts of Insanity in the United States,* 1789–1865. New Brunswick, N.J., 1964.

Dalton, J. C. "Magendie as a Physiologist." *International Review* (February, 1880), 120–25.

Dexter, G. E., ed. *A History of Dental and Oral Science in America.* Philadelphia, 1876.

Dowler, B. "Pharmacology in France." *NOMSJ,* XVII (1860), 448–50.

Dubois, Paul. *L'Art dentaire aux Etats-Unis.* Paris, 1888.

Duffy, John, ed. *The Rudolph Matas History of Medicine in Louisiana.* 2 vols. Baton Rouge, La., 1958–62.

Eaton, Leonard K. *New England Hospitals,* 1790–1833. Ann Arbor, Mich., 1957.

Evans, Thomas W. *Instruments and Apparatus of Medicine, Surgery and Hygiene.* Washington, D.C., 1868–70.

———. *Memoirs of Dr. Thomas W. Evans: The Second French Empire.* Edited by Edward A. Crane. New York, 1905.

Fisher, F. Willis. "The Ether Inhalation in Paris." *BMSJ,* XXXV (1847), 109–13, 172–74.

Flexner, Abraham. *La Formation du médecin en Europe et aux Etats-Unis.* Paris, 1927.

Francis, Samuel W. *Biographical Sketches of Distinguished Living New York Physicians.* New York, 1867.

Gardner, Augustus Kinsley. *Old Wine in New Bottles: Or, Spare Hours of a Student in Paris.* New York and Boston, 1848.

Garrison, F. H. *An Introduction to the History of Medicine.* Philadelphia, 1929, 1960.

Gibson, William. *Rambles in Europe in* 1839: *With Sketches of Prominent Surgeons, Physicians, Medical Schools, Hospitals, etc.* Philadelphia, 1841.

Garnier, P. "Voyage médical en Californie." With an introduction by Gilbert Chinard. *French American Review,* II (1949), 135–83.

Godon, Ch. and A. Ronnet. *L'Art dentaire aux Etats-Unis en* 1893: *Une Mission en Amérique.* Paris, 1894.

Gross, Samuel D., ed. *Lives of Eminent American Physicians and Surgeons of the Nineteenth Century.* Philadelphia, 1861.

———. *Memoir of Valentine Mott.* Philadelphia, 1868.

Guthrie, Douglas. *Lord Lister: His Life and Doctrine.* Baltimore, 1949.

Hamilton, John B. *International Medical Congress, Transactions, Washington, September* 5–10, 1887. 3 vols. Washington, D.C., 1887.

Harris, Chapin A. *The Dental Art: A Practical Treatise on Dental Surgery.* Baltimore, 1839.

Harris, Chapin A., and Philip H. Austen. *Traité théorique et practique de l'art du dentiste.* Paris, 1874.

Harris, Henry. *California's Medical Story.* San Francisco, 1932.

Harris, Seale. *Woman's Surgeon: The Life Story of J. Marion Sims.* New York, 1950.

Herter, Christian A. *The Influence of Pasteur on Medical Science.* New York, 1904.

Hinsdale, Guy. "The American Medical Argonauts: Pupils of Pierre Charles Alexandre Louis." *Transactions and Studies of the College of Physicians of Philadelphia,* Fourth Series, XIII (April, 1945), 37–43.

———. "Our Medical Debt to France." *AMH,* Series 3, IV (1942), 154–66.

Hirschfeld, William. "Conscientiousness in Dental Operations." *Dental Clippings,* III (August, 1901), 206–14.

Holmes, Oliver Wendell. *Writings of Oliver Wendell Holmes.* 13 vols. Cambridge, Mass., 1891.

Hyde, James Nevins. *Early Medical Chicago.* Chicago, 1879.

Jackson, James. *Memoir of James Jackson, Jr., M.D.: With Extracts from His Letters and Reminiscences of Him by a Fellow Student.* Boston, 1836.

Jacobi, Mary Putnam. *A Pathfinder in Medicine.* New York, 1925.

Jones, Russell M. "American Doctors and the Parisian Medical World, 1830–1840." *BHM,* XLVII (1973), 40–65, 177–204.

———. "American Doctors in Paris, 1820–1861: A Statistical Profile." *JHM,* XXV (April, 1970), 143–57.

——— ."An American Medical Student in Paris, 1831–1833." *Harvard Library Bulletin,* XV (1967), 59–81.

Kelsey, W. F. "Dentistry in France." *Johnston's Dental Miscellany,* VI (January, 1879), 1–4.

Kraft, Ivor. "Edouard Séguin and Nineteenth Century Moral Treatment of Idiots." *BHM,* XXXV (1961), 393–418.

Kremers, Edward, and George Urdang. *History of Pharmacy.* Philadelphia, 1940, 1951.

Laignel-Lavastine, M., and Raymond Molinery. *Clio Medica: French Medicine.* Translated by E. B. Krumbhaar. New York, 1934.

Landing, Benjamin H. "Rollin R. Gregg of Buffalo: A Nineteenth Century Opponent of Pasteur and the Germ Theory of Disease." *BHM,* XXXVI (1962), 524–28.

La Roche, René. "Account of the Origin, Progress, and Present Stage of the Medical School of Paris." *American Journal of the Medical Sciences,* VIII (1831), 109–24, 401–18; IX (1831), 351–88.

Long, Esmond R. *A History of American Pathology.* Springfield, Ill., 1962.

Louis, Pierre Charles. *Research on the Effects of Bloodletting in Some Inflammatory Diseases.* Translated by C. G. Putnam, with Preface and Appendix by James Jackson. Boston, 1836.

Lufkin, Arthur Ward. *A History of Dentistry.* Philadelphia, 1948.

Medical Heritage Society. *The Medallic History of Pharmacy.* Chicago, 1972.

Miner, Leroy Mathew Simpson. *The New Dentistry: A Phase of Preventive Medicine.* Cambridge, Mass., 1933.

Morse, John T., Jr. *Life and Letters of Oliver Wendell Holmes.* 2 vols. Boston and New York, 1896.

Myer, Jesse S. *Life and Letters of Dr. William Beaumont.* St. Louis, 1939.

Neveu, Raymond. "The Introduction of Surgical Anesthesia in France." *JHMAS*, I (1946), 607–10.

Olmsted, James. *Charles-Edouard Brown-Séquard: A Nineteenth Century Neurologist and Endocrinologist.* Baltimore, 1946.

————. *Claude Bernard: Physiologist.* New York, 1938.

————. "The Contemplative Works of Claude Bernard." *BIHM,* III (1935), 335–54.

————. *François Magendie: Pioneer in Experimental Physiology and Scientific Medicine in Nineteenth Century France.* New York, 1944.

————. "The Influence of Claude Bernard on Medicine in the United States and England." *California and Western Medicine,* XLII (1935), 111–13, 174–76.

————. "A Letter from Felix Pascalis of New York to François Magendie in 1826." *AMH,* Series 3, II (1940), 371–74.

Olmsted, James, and E. Harris. *Claude Bernard and the Experimental Method in Medicine.* New York, 1952.

Osler, William. *An Alabama Student and Other Biographical Essays.* New York, 1908.

Packard, Francis R. *History of Medicine in the United States.* 2 vols. New York, 1963.

Peisse, Louis. *Sketches of the Characters and Writings of Eminent Living Surgeons and Physicians of Paris.* Translated by Elisha Bartlett. Boston, 1831.

Pollak, S. *The Autobiography and Reminiscences of S. Pollak, M.D., St. Louis, Mo.* St. Louis, 1904.

Putnam, Ruth, ed. *Life and Letters of Mary Putnam Jacobi.* New York, 1925.

Rainey, Henry. *Dr. Thomas Evans: America's Dentist to European Royalty.* Philadelphia, 1956.

Riese, W. "Claude Bernard in the Light of Modern Science." *BHM,* XIV (1943), 281–94.

Rosen, George. "An American Doctor in Paris in 1828. Selections from the Diary of Peter Solomon Townsend, M.D." *JHMAS* (1951), 64–115, 209–52.

————. "Die Aufnahme der Entdeckung William Beaumont's durch die europäische Medizin: Ein Beitrag zur Geschichte der Physiologie im neunzehnten Jahrhundert." *Abhandlungen zur Geschichte der Medizin und der Naturwissenschaften,* Heft 8. Berlin, 1935.

————. *A History of Public Health.* New York, 1958.

————. *Madness in Society: Chapters in the Historical Sociology of Mental Illness.* Chicago, 1968.

————. "The Philosophy of Ideology and the Emergence of Modern Medicine in France." *BHM,* XX (July, 1946), 328–39.

————. "Political Order and Human Health in Jeffersonian Thought." *BHM,* XXVI (1952), 32–44.

———. "Problems in the Application of Statistical Analysis to Questions of Health: 1700–1880." *BHM*, XXIX (1955), 27–45.

———. "Social Stress and Mental Disease from the Eighteenth Century to the Present: Some Origins of Social Psychiatry." *Millbank Memorial Fund Quarterly*, XXXVII (1959), 5–32.

———. *The Specialization of Medicine, with Particular Reference to Ophthalmology*. New York, 1944, 1972.

Shafer, Henry B. *The American Medical Profession, 1783 to 1850*. New York, 1936.

Shryock, Richard Harrison. "The Advent of Modern Medicine in Philadelphia, 1800–1850." *Yale Journal of Biology and Medicine*, XIII (July, 1941), 715–38.

———. "A Century of Medical Progress in Philadelphia, 1750–1850." *Pennsylvania History*, VIII (1941), 7–28.

———. *The Development of Modern Medicine*. Philadelphia, 1936.

———. *Empiricism versus Rationalism in American Medicine, 1650–1950*. Worcester, Mass., 1969.

———. "The History of Quantification in Medical Science." *Isis*, LII (1961), 215–37.

———. *Medicine and Society in America, 1660–1860*. New York, 1960.

———. "Nineteenth Century Medicine: Scientific Aspects." *Cahiers d'histoire mondiale*, III (1957), 880–908.

———. "Trends in American Medical Research During the Nineteenth Century." American Philosophical Society, *Proceedings*, XCI (1947), 58–63.

Sigerist, Henry E. *American Medicine*. New York, 1934.

Sims, J. Marion. *The Story of My Life*. New York, 1885.

Souchon, Edmond. "Original Contributions of Louisiana to Medical Sciences." *LHS, Publications*, VIII (1914–15), 66–88.

———. "Reminiscences of Dr. Marion Sims in Paris." *Southern Surgical and Gynecological Association, Transactions*, VII (1894), 27–38.

Steiner, Walter R. "Dr. Pierre-Charles-Alexander Louis: A Distinguished Parisian Teacher of American Medical Students." *AMH*, Series 3, II (1940), 451–60.

———. "Some Distinguished American Medical Students of Pierre-Charles-Alexander Louis of Paris." *BHM*, VII (1939), 783–93.

Stevens, Mordaunt. "The Dental Profession in France." *AJDS*, Series 3, IX (1875), 179–81.

Stewart, Ferdinand Campbell. *The Hospitals and Surgeons of Paris*. New York, 1843.

Suckley, George. "Notes on the Practice in the Hospitals of Paris: The 'Ecraseur,' 'Electric Cautery,' etc." *NYJM*, IV (1858), 341–55.

———. "On Matters of Novelty or General Interest as at Present Exhibited in the Practice of the Hospitals of Paris." *NYJM*, Series 3, V (1858), 21–32.

Taylor, J. A. *History of Dentistry*. Philadelphia, 1922.

Thorpe, Burton Lee. *Biographies of Pioneer American Dentists and Their Successors*. Fort Wayne, Ind., 1910.

Truax, Rhoda. *Joseph Lister: Father of Modern Surgery*. New York, 1944.
Vallery-Radot, Pasteur, ed. *Oeuvres de Pasteur*. 7 vols. Paris, 1939.
————. *Pasteur: Correspondance, 1840–1895*. 4 vols. Paris, 1951.
Velpeau, Alfred. *An Elementary Treatise on Midwifery: Or, Principles of Tokology and Embryology*. Translated by Charles D. Meigs. Philadelphia, 1831.
————. *New Elements of Operative Surgery*. 3 vols. New York, 1847.
Viets, Henry R. *A Brief History of Medicine in Massachusetts*. Boston, 1930.
Warren, Edward. *The Life of John Collins Warren, M.D.* 2 vols. Boston, 1860.
Weinberger, Bernhard W. *Pierre Fauchard: Surgeon-Dentist*. Minneapolis, Minn., 1941.
Wiriot, Mireille. *L'Enseignement clinique dans les hôpitaux de Paris entre 1794 et 1848*. Paris, 1970.
Woodward, Grace Steele. *The Man Who Conquered Pain: A Biography of William Thomas Green Morton*. Boston, 1962.
Yandell, D. W. *Notes on Medical Matters and Medical Men in London and Paris*. Louisville, 1848.

Index

4